P9-AFN-423

# ANNUAL REVIEW OF SOCIOLOGY

# ANNUAL REVIEW OF SOCIOLOGY

VOLUME 23, 1997

JOHN HAGAN, *Editor*
University of Toronto

KAREN S. COOK, *Associate Editor*
Duke University

http://annurev.org science@annurev.org 415-493-4400

ANNUAL REVIEWS INC. 4139 EL CAMINO WAY P.O. BOX 10139 PALO ALTO, CALIFORNIA 94303-0139

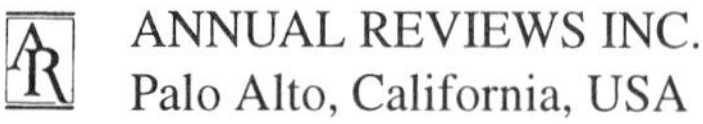

ANNUAL REVIEWS INC.
Palo Alto, California, USA



*International Standard Serial Number: 0360-0572*
*International Standard Book Number: 0-8243-2223-1*
*Library of Congress Catalog Card Number: 75-648500*



∞ The paper used in this publication meets the minimum requirements of American National Standard for Information Sciences—Permanence of Paper for Printed Library Materials, ANSI Z39.48-1984.



TYPESET BY TECHBOOKS, FAIRFAX, VA
PRINTED AND BOUND IN THE UNITED STATES OF AMERICA

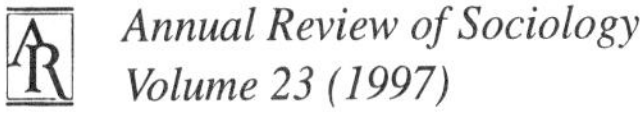

*Annual Review of Sociology*
*Volume 23 (1997)*

# CONTENTS



(*continued*) 

## RELATED ARTICLES FROM OTHER *ANNUAL REVIEWS*

From the *Annual Review of Anthropology*, Volume 26, 1997:

*Linguistic Relativity*, J. A. Lucy

*Marx and Anthropology*, W. Roseberry

*Trafficking in Men: The Anthropology of Masculinity*, M. C. Gutmann

*Doing Good? The Politics and Antipolitics of NGO Practices*, W. F. Fisher

*Europeanization*, J. Borneman and N. Fowler

*The Anthropology of Colonialism: Culture, History, and the Emergence of Western Governmentality*, P. Pels

*Politics of Identity in Latin America*, C. R. Hale

From the *Annual Review of Psychology*, Volume 48, 1997:

*Gender, Racial, Ethnic, Sexual, and Class Identities*, D. E. S. Frable

*The Effects of Stressful Life Events on Depression*, R. C. Kessler

*Key Issues in the Development of Aggression and Violence from Childhood to Early Adulthood*, R. Loeber and D. Hay

*Health Psychology: What Is an Unhealthy Environment and How Does It Get Under the Skin?*, S. E. Taylor, R. L. Repetti, T. Seeman

*Organizational Behavior in the New Organizational Era*, D. M. Rousseau

ANNUAL REVIEWS INC. is a nonprofit scientific publisher established to promote the advancement of the sciences. Beginning in 1932 with the *Annual Review of Biochemistry*, the Company has pursued as its principal function the publication of high-quality, reasonably priced *Annual Review* volumes. The volumes are organized by Editors and Editorial Committees who invite qualified authors to contribute critical articles reviewing significant developments within each major discipline. The Editor-in-Chief invites those interested in serving as future Editorial Committee members to communicate directly with him. Annual Reviews Inc. is administered by a Board of Directors, whose members serve without compensation.



ANNUAL REVIEWS OF

Anthropology
Astronomy and Astrophysics
Biochemistry
Biophysics and Biomolecular Structure
Cell and Developmental Biology
Computer Science
Earth and Planetary Sciences
Ecology and Systematics
Energy and the Environment
Entomology
Fluid Mechanics
Genetics
Immunology
Materials Science
Medicine
Microbiology
Neuroscience
Nuclear and Particle Science
Nutrition
Pharmacology and Toxicology
Physical Chemistry
Physiology
Phytopathology
Plant Physiology and Plant Molecular Biology
Psychology
Public Health
Sociology

SPECIAL PUBLICATIONS

Excitement and Fascination of Science, Vols. 1, 2, 3, and 4
Intelligence and Affectivity, by Jean Piaget

For the convenience of readers, a detachable order form/envelope is bound into the back of this volume.

*Annu. Rev. Sociol. 1997. 23:1–18*


# ON THE VIRTUES OF THE OLD INSTITUTIONALISM

*Arthur L. Stinchcombe*

Visiting Fellow, American Bar Foundation, and Part-time Professor, Department of Sociology, Northwestern University, Evanston, Illinois 60201

KEY WORDS: formal organization, competition, performance, contracts

ABSTRACT

Institutions are staffed and are created to do the job of regulating organizations. This staffing, and all the creative work that is involved in financing, governing, training, and motivating institutional actions by that staff in organizations, has been lost in recent institutional theorizing. This staffing was central to the old institutionalism, which is why it looked so different. The argument is exemplified by applying the insights of classical institutionalists to the legitimacy of court decisions as determined by the law of evidence, to the legitimacy of competition and the destruction of other organizations by competition, to the noncontractual basis of contract in commitments to maintain competence to do the performances required in contracts, and to the failure of institutions of capitalist competition and the substitution of mafia-like enforcement of contracts in postcommunist Russia. The institutions of the new institutionalism do not have enough causal substance and enough variance of characteristics to explain such various phenomena.

## *Introduction*

I was recruited into sociology by the institutional economists, especially by Thorstein Veblen; sociologists at Central Michigan College of Education read Veblen, while economists there did not. I started with *The Theory of the Leisure Class* (1934 [1899]), and then whatever of the Veblen corpus was in the CMCE library. I went on before graduate school to Karl Marx, Joseph Alois Schumpeter, and Max Weber, then in graduate school to John Maurice Clark, Clark Kerr, John R Commons, and many historians of law (because most economic institutions eventually make their way into the courts). I became a



0360-0572/97/0815-0001$08.00

sociologist in order to make a living as an institutional economist, since it was clear that I would make a poor living at that among economists.

My first intellectual identity, then, was shaped by the old institutionalists. They left behind a legacy of problems, more problems perhaps than solutions. The generative aspect of the old institutionalism, its openness to the macrosociological background structure behind firms, household consumption, and markets, gave me things to work on.

This made Berkeley the place to go for graduate school, because *TVA and the Grass Roots* (Selznick 1949) was about one way to institutionalize electricity and fertilizer production, as well as public versus private land tenure; *Union Democracy* (Lipset et al 1956) was about a form of appropriation of skill monopolies; *Work and Authority in Industry* (Bendix 1956) about one way to develop institutions of small-firm manufacturing of textiles. Selznick, Lipset, and Bendix were, whatever else they also were, institutional economists.

Institutions, I learned then, shaped the creation and functions of units in market and the relations between them. But unlike the institutions of modern institutionalism, people ran these institutions by organizing activities on their behalf. Institutions were, in the first instance, created by purposive people in legislatures and international unions, and in pamphlets of business ideologists in Northern England. Modern institutionalism, to create a caricature, is Durkheimian in the sense that collective representations manufacture themselves by opaque processes, are implemented by diffusion, are exterior and constraining without exterior people doing the creation or the constraining.

The purpose of this essay then is to take some selected problems of modern economic sociology, and some theoretical generative principles of the old institutionalism, and to show there is life in the old bones yet. In the background of the essay is a contrast between the old institutionalism in which people built and ran institutions, and the new Durkheimian institutionalism in which collective representations operate on their own. My primary purpose is generative rather than critical, so the picture I draw of the new institutionalism is contentious. But I hope that caricature is a stylized version of the central thrust of the newness of the new institutionalism, and particularly of the newness of its faults.

This is then a review by contrast of new institutionalist economic sociology. Its main purpose is to revive some central mechanisms from the old institutionalism, and to use that revivification to throw light on the broad contours of our present difficulties.

In the first part of the analysis, I treat particularly John Henry Wigmore, who studied the relation between the institutions of evidence law and the functioning of American and British courts as organizations. It is a peculiarity of such courts that they produce legitimate decisions, and so legitimacy is absolutely central to their survival, and that in order to produce legitimate decisions they have to use legitimate means, especially legitimate evidence. Producing such legitimate evidence is the product of adversary court organizations that involve judges, contending counsel, juries, and a flow of evidence from the outside from witnesses and documents, actions with legal consequences such as delivery of signed documents, arrests on probable cause, and the like, all of which have to be organized and legitimated (or delegitimated) by the court.

Because legitimacy is the intended product of these institutions, operating through court organizations, the whole enterprise is central to institutional theory. Much of the legitimacy of courts, as analyzed by Wigmore, has to do with effective means to achieve justice by intelligent processing of the substance of evidence. Compared to Wigmore's, modern institutionalism has an impoverished notion of legitimacy and of how the legitimacy of rituals depends on substantive good sense applied to questions of value.[1]

The second and third parts of this chapter treat the moral commitment aspect of contracts for transactions as central to the possibility of the existence of organizations in the market. The central old institutionalists treated are RH Coase, especially his "The Nature of the Firm" (1937), John R Commons, especially his *Legal Foundations of Capitalism* (1974 [1924]), Joseph A Schumpeter, especially his *Business Cycles* (Schumpeter 1964 [1939], pp. 46–83, 105–50; also see a more popular version of the argument in 1942), and Philip Selznick, especially in his *Leadership in Administration* (1957). The basic intuition here is Durkheim's observation that there is a noncontractual basis of contract.

In particular, the set of contracts that constitute a firm has a particular kind of noncontractual basis, outlined with great depth and perception by Commons. The function of that special basis for contracts that create firms is best outlined by Coase's classic paper on the nature of firm boundaries as activity sets within

[1]Wigmore was a lawyers' law historian. He tried to reformulate the history of the cases and statutes of the law of evidence so that it would make sense to judges and lawyers deciding evidence questions. That is, his institutional purpose was to influence courts (including contending counsel) to decide evidence questions so as to achieve justice, on average. Wigmore therefore tended to make more sense of history than probably was originally there and to ignore cases that did not make sense from his point of view. He also was not an ethnographer trying to reflect accurately the informal aspects of the use of evidence law in practice; his purpose was to be authoritative rather than ethnographic. Wigmore believed in institutions and in scholarship as a way to improve them. My own view is that he succeeded, but his purpose is different from my purpose here of showing that he was right about how the courts worked as institutions serving justice. Because I do not know the cases and history as well as he did, I am not in a position to criticize his analysis from within (Twining 1990 has some relevant material). Sociologists think of the law of evidence mainly in connection with constitutional cases on criminal law, especially for capital crimes against persons. Wigmore was well aware that most law practice is law on economic claims deriving from contract and property and that it has more to do with the contract clause in the Constitution than with the Bill of Rights, and most crime is against property. So for my purposes here, he is analyzing an economically relevant institution, court procedure on evidence questions.

which other elements of the firm have a competitive advantage over outside firms providing the same services or goods in the market, because of lesser "transaction costs." Schumpeter is the classic source on the relation to the larger competitive structure of capitalism of that monopoly advantage that comes from a firm's having superior productivity. All three writers are interested in the form of institutions that makes the competitive structure of capitalism possible, given what that structure is, namely the competition of firms that can do something better than anyone else.

The impoverished view of modern institutional theorists (especially in the "organizational ecology branch") reduces the conception of competition to that of the relations among organizations[2] that have the "legitimate" organizational form for that "population." This conception leaves out many aspects of what the traditional institutional theorists actually thought about competition. The transaction costs literature (e.g. Williamson 1975) preserves more of this content, except that it does not study legitimacy of the market itself, and so it has a vacuous description of what firms (as hierarchies) are contrasted to. The conceptions of Commons and Schumpeter of how competitive markets came to be legitimate are not vacuous.

The second part of this chapter concentrates on how contracts in the market come to be legitimate by the way they are constituted, by the mutual belief of the contracting parties that each is committed to the line of action promised in the contracts. We emphasize especially the commitment of a firm to be competent in the future to carry out the activities specified in the contracts. Contracts are what markets centrally consist of, so their legitimacy is central to the legitimacy of markets—a fact well known to institutional economists in the past. Coase then analyzes what it is about the firm that is the noncontractual basis of contracts, namely its special competencies. Commons analyzes these as they are embedded in working rules, while Schumpeter treats them as innovations that have specific kinds of effects on the capital market and therefore on business cycles. Selznick treats the processes by which commitment to competencies are built into organizations.

The third section treats the problem of the legitimacy in the law of market competition as a system, and its relation to the legitimacy of being able to do things better than competitors as a moral and legal claim on the profits of such competence.

The fourth section is an analysis of a classic formulation of the failure of institutions by Edward Banfield, especially in his *The Moral Basis of a Backward Society* (1967 [1958]). Banfield's basic argument is that institutions, and commitment to institutions, are essential to the creation of public goods. In turn,

[2]The firms are assumed to be identical, each firm counting as one, in most applications.

economic progress involved the production of public goods, including obvious ones such as roads or civil order, and not so obvious ones such as the willingness to discuss what we should do next in a spirit of honesty and compromise. When the institutional means to create public goods are not available, welfare seems to people to depend on looking out for themselves and their immediate kin, rather than on trying to create greater welfare for all. Banfield applied this analysis to Southern Italy. Diego Gambetta (1993) has a compatible analysis about why the Mafia as a business supplying guarantees for contracts in a distrustful environment does not constitute a good basis for economic development.

I apply this line of argument to explain why capitalism in Russia is not as successful as it has been in the West—perhaps not even as successful as socialism was—because the socialist institutions that enable people to create public goods have been destroyed but not replaced by institutions appropriate to capitalism. In particular, I argue that, under socialism, contracts between firms and the corporatist industrial authorities in central planning agencies were used to create many of the requisite public goods. The destruction of the capacity of those authorities to reward firms for public-oriented behavior has left the enforcement of contracts to Mafia-like organizations, as in Southern Italy when Banfield was there.

Older institutionalists did not assume that institutions were always there and always worked. Consequently the causes of variation in the effectiveness of institutions were part of Banfield's research program. The creation of public goods is particularly problematic in a war of each against all. Institutions can (but need not) reduce the impediments of the free rider problem, that people can benefit from public goods without contributing to their creation. The level of success in creating roads, or law and order, or bargaining in good faith are all sensitive indicators of institutional effectiveness. The "amoral familism" that Banfield found among Southern Italian villagers has its analog in the "amoral firmism" of postsocialist Russia, and in the mafias, a good deal like the southern Italian Mafia, that enforce contracts.

These are four rather different arguments. The first studies a clear case in which legitimacy of rituals in courtrooms varies with how well they substantively achieve justice in the use of evidence in the law and so produce legitimate decisions. My argument is that unless the rules of evidence are guided by considerations of justice, they do not produce legitimacy. The second studies why firms are willing to enter into contracts that require the counterparty to maintain into the future the competence to do the services contracted for. The argument is that only if firms are committed in several ways, including morally, will that promise to maintain competence be believed. The third outlines why it ever becomes legitimate for competitors to do damage to each other, and how civil law has had to be arranged so that that competitive conflict gives rise not to claims in court, but instead to "legitimate" competition. Schumpeter makes strong arguments that economic development depends on innovators, firms that do not imitate other firms but are nevertheless legitimately able to do damage to entrenched business interests. And he and Commons both argue that this legitimacy of competition has always been precarious, and that only a few kinds of institutions can successfully institute it. Finally we study institutions that sometimes do not work, and Hobbes's outcome of the war of each against all reigns. Banfield argues that when institutions do not work to create public goods, the incentives to morality and cooperation that otherwise flow from successful creation of public goods (e.g. higher income from economic development) fail to operate. Then only mafias, with the kind of consent they elicit, create even a primitive social order, a noncontractual game theoretical basis of contract that does not work as well as business ethics and effective civil law.

The overall argument of these four subarguments is that the blank places in writings of modern institutionalism come especially from lack of detailed theory and research about how particular institutions work. Much of the narrowness in modern institutionalism in organizational theory is explained by lack of detail in the conceptions of institutions. A narrow conception is easier to mathematize. This in turn is due to ignoring the work of people who put the detail into institutions and who constrain people and organizations to conform to institution's exteriority. But if the guts of the causal process of institutional influence are left out of the model, then we successfully mathematize abstract empiricism, an empiricism without the complexity of real life. Wigmore, Commons, Schumpeter, and Banfield knew a lot about variance in how, and how well, institutions work; it behooves us to imitate them.

## *Ritual Means of Survival vs. Institutionalized Values*

It is the duty of United States appellate courts to behave exactly as specified in institutional theory, namely to take as their principle of decision and of writing opinions the institutionalized standards specified by the Supreme Court. These and other institutionalized standards are embedded in the legitimate decisions at common law and statute law, defined as those that other courts, including the Supreme Court, would recognize as valid. Thus according to the new institutionalist principles announced in Meyer & Rowan (1977), the court organizations with their contending counsel, judges, juries, and flows of witnesses are engaging in the formalities of evidence law as a ritual to legitimate what they are doing. If there were no deeper principles behind this activity, there would be no sense in their writing opinions about why they decided the way they did, no reason for either of the contending parties to appeal, and so no reason to pay for appellate courts at all; it would be sufficient for them to say that the Supreme Court would probably favor the plaintiff (or the defense).

Thus it is only because we imagine that justice will be served that we set up the whole apparatus of appeals—of judges guessing what each other will say—to demand that they obey the legitimizing formal procedures that Meyer & Rowan specify and *Wigmore on Evidence* (1983 [1940]) describes. In short, the acceptance of the idea that the appellate court was a ritual would destroy its legitimacy. And it is clear that the written opinions of appellate courts are central to the allegation that it is not just a ritual, which could as well have been dispensed with by allowing the court of original jurisdiction to specify what was legitimate under the Constitution and to make its own guess about the Supreme Court; and the Supreme Court could in its turn merely send back a yes or no, without majority and minority and concurring opinions.

Similarly in scientific papers, the formal rituals of citation of scientists other than the author show that the author is oriented to contributing to a body of knowledge recognized by others; there is no obvious ritual reason for the results section that actually makes that contribution. We could enormously simplify the formal organization of journals if we did not have to have referee comment on the results section. There is the same trouble in explaining the actual algebra in an algebra textbook adopted by the California or Texas state textbook certification organizations, the actual fertilizer that backed up the coopted farmers on the Tennessee Valley Authority boards (Selznick 1949), the actual "cleaving only unto" that is the putative organizational consequence of the wedding vows, the actual dollars that back up the annual report of a corporation.

What we have to explain, then, is why it is so essential to organizations that their formal rituals not seem to be a shuck, and why they lose legitimacy as soon as it appears they are only interested in the letter of the law, the words in the vows, the places on the TVA boards, the right number of pages in the algebra books. Why did I, for example, get indignant when my son in the preschool learned the correct answer that it is hotter in summer because then the Northern Hemisphere is closer to the sun, and he favorably impressed the educational authority but not his father by "getting it right"? I was dissatisfied with the preschool book because its answer was substantively wrong, not because it was not officially authorized.

We do find formal ritual criteria of whether an appellate opinion is serious organizational substance; for example, what court an opinion comes from matters for its ritual status. But why is it that intermediate appellate courts take producing opinions with those ritual marks so seriously, as opposed to saying they guess the Supreme Court might decide yes (or no) and leaving it at that? Why would we be dismayed if an appellate court opinion had all the citations of cases but missed the point—more dismayed than if it missed citing a crucial case and so had to invent the principle of justice over again? Why would we be less dismayed if a school taught analytic geometry before Euclidean geometry, outside the canonical order, than if students never learned to treat geometrical problems with algebra?

In short, why is formality never enough for legitimacy, without some conviction that the formality is just a more abstract form of the substance? Why is it, for example, that a principle of legitimacy of a contract is "(d) The court shall determine whether the writing was intended by the parties as a final expression of their agreement with respect to such terms as are included therein" [California Code of Civil Procedure (as amended in 1978), as quoted in Wigmore (1983 [1940]) p. 75n]? The institutional rule here relies on a substantive determination about the wills of the parties, rather than just a formal reading of the content of the writing.

I believe we have recently underestimated the degree to which people accept institutions because they think the institutions have the right answer, because institutions embody a value that the people also accept. When Selznick (1949) showed that a major consequence of "grass roots" administration in the TVA was the cooptation of leading potential farmer opponents of TVA into the defense of government power generation in the Valley, we all thought this made TVA's claim to be democratic more suspect. Formal democracy was not good enough for us. Why would we expect that it would be good enough for other students of public administration or for citizens? We, too, did not want the TVA to go through the democratic motions, because we hold democracy as a value, not as a legitimator. Its legitimating capacity follows from its being a value.

We could investigate this by looking at which social movements succeed against formally institutionalized practices. For example, Jeremy Bentham undertook to argue that the formality of the rules of evidence in his time undermined the use of reason and good sense in legal inference (Twining 1990, pp. 38–41). The old institutionalist theory of Selznick and others is that reason and good sense are values, and formality a means to reason and good sense. Selznick's theory would predict Bentham's success. The view that justice matters to the legitimacy of the formality would predict that the law of evidence after Bentham would come to put a good deal more faith in the discretion of the judge, a good deal less faith in formal versions of the precedent in evidence law.

And that is what the modern textbooks on the codified statutory law of evidence say (Rothstein 1981, pp. 10–12). In part the new institutionalism would predict that Bentham should have lost out, particularly among lawyers who are dependent on predicting what the other lawyers that run the courts will decide. The profession of law depends on isomorphism, that the arguments they make will be the same as the arguments the courts will accept. It seems rather that lawyers wanted instead for judges to use reason and good sense, and not be bound by institutionalized rules except those that specified when and on what grounds the judge could intervene to use his/her good judgment. That is, in the long pull, lawyers favored rules that used the reason and good sense of judges, rather than formal rituals of correctness.

For example, one observes in the law of evidence that the criteria of evidence are applied much more strictly when a hearing deals with substantive rights than with the formalities of the course of an issue through the court system, so that hearings on a change of venue have very informal rules of evidence. Further, the law is more painstaking when the rights at stake are more serious, as in criminal cases compared to civil cases (e.g. exclusions of evidence because it was illegally obtained are much more common in criminal cases), in criminal trials as opposed to grand jury indictment hearings (e.g. the grand jury rather than the defendant decides what evidence the defendant can offer), in habeus corpus hearings than bail bond hearings, in cases of child custody rather than child support levels, in search and seizure of evidence rather than discovery hearings [*Wigmore on Evidence* (1983 [1940]) vol. 1A, pp. 25–332 gives a summary of variations in the law of evidence according to jurisdictions].[3] The more justice matters, in short, the greater the formality of the application of the law of evidence.

This point is crucial to our differences with the new institutionalism. We want to predict when the *institution* will demand more formality, not when the *organization* will more enthusiastically adopt the institution's standards, as Meyer & Rowan (1977) do. It is precisely because the behavior of institutional authorities in enforcing standards varies that it is important to notice that institutions are staffed, rather than being merely collective representations.

Similarly, votes in academic departments are counted much more carefully, and the votes are more likely to be by secret ballot and kept confidential (the doctrine being that one gets honest opinions only with immunity of the voter), when the issue is a crucial matter such as a tenure case. Another academic example: Graduate students are sent ritually out of the room when their dissertation defense is being debated and voted on, but not in a seminar where their contribution to discussion is to be debated. The criteria and procedure for examinations and their grading are often discussed in the syllabus and in faculty handbooks, whereas when the professor will actually appear for his office hours, as opposed to what is announced, is more informally discussed by angry students outside his or her door. In short, the more a judgment of academic

[3]When substantive rights are dealt with in administrative hearings (e.g. hearings on welfare rights) or by agreed arbitration, more informal laws of evidence apply. Here we would predict that the more important the substantive right, the more formal the rules of evidence compared to other administrative hearings or arbitration proceedings. Similarly Jerome Skolnick argues (1975 [1966], pp. 155–161) that the bigger the case, the more careful police are to follow the dictates of the law of evidence as well as other determinants of the quality of evidence (e.g. policemen make better witnesses than drug dealers), because they know evidence will be evaluated more strictly.

merit matters, the more formalized and institutionalized we find it to be. It is hard to imagine that this is all a matter of impression management, that no one really cares whether students and junior faculty are evaluated by what they have accomplished, rather than by formally correct procedures. But in particular, institutional authorities demand more conformity with institutional values the more important the decision is.

My argument then is that variations in the bindingness of institutional rituals are to be explained by beliefs about what the institution is for. The more important the issues at stake, the more important will be those rituals that are carefully justified as serving the value. As a criminal case passes from questioning on the street, to arrest, to indictment, to conviction, the degree of bindingness of the rules that make evidence legitimate increases. As the career consequences of an academic judgment increase in importance, the greater the formality of the specification of what is to be judged, the more likely committee rather than individual judgment, the larger the number of stages, and the more the rights of appeal. As a negotiation of a contract proceeds, so increases the degree of formality of judgment about what has been agreed to, whether the agreement is final, and whether the terms have been made clear either during the process of negotiation or by reference to the practice in a trade.

Formality and ritualization, then, increase with the substantive importance of the issue, because in general the reason for having things institutionalized and ritualized is that they matter. Or to put it the other way around, when the value system informing an institution ranks something as of high priority, it is more likely that the keepers of the institution will formalize conformity with the institution in a ritual designed to monitor, enforce, and enact the value of that something. The higher the priority, the higher the formality and ritual. The more ritualized a thing is in an institution, the less it is merely a ritual, because the more substantively important it is. Or to return to our example of evidence law, the more justice depends on a bit of evidence, the more formal evidence law there is about the introduction of that evidence.

## *Transaction Costs vs Moral Commitment*

The contracts that constitute a market are ordinarily agreements about future performances. It is that fact that makes the noncontractual part of contracts central, since the parties' predictions of each other's future behavior depend on predictions about each other's future morality. But in particular, one routinely contracts for another firm's services when that firm can do something better than one can do it oneself. Consequently, it is in particular the sort of morality that will guarantee the other firm's future competence that is central to the creation of most markets. If in the future the other firm is not going to be more competent at their business than you are, why make a contract with it?

To relate the old institutionalism to the institutionalism of transaction cost analysis, it is best to start with old transaction cost analysis, in Coase (1937). Coase defined the maximizing boundary of a firm as the division between the set of things it could do better or cheaper than it could hire or buy. An airplane developer and manufacturer can make planes better than an airline can. But it can only borrow the money to develop a passenger plane if airlines sign contracts in advance to buy (Newhouse 1982). Airlines will buy them for the future only if they believe manufacturers will seriously and competently use the money to develop and make a better airplane. Airlines will make commitments only if the airlines in their turn believe they themselves will still be able to compete in selling traveling and express shipping services.

In particular, airlines will have to sell airline services better than Boeing, Lockheed, or McDonnell-Douglas, for if the manufacturers were better at running airlines as well as at building airplanes, the airlines would merely be financing their competition. Bankers only believe the futures contracts between airlines and airframe manufacturers if they think the manufacturer can and will build a better airplane, and the airlines will still be there to buy it when the contract comes due. It is an immediate derivation of Coase's theory that part, at least, of the noncontractual element of contract has to be mutual belief in each other's future superior competence. Much of one's transaction cost has to do with trying to guarantee by contractual means the future competence of the counterparties, without giving over to them the rent of one's own superior future competence in one's own business. The nature of this system of mutual belief in each other's competence becomes particularly clear when a great deal of money, now and in the future, has to pass between three different kinds of firms, each relying on the success of the relation between the other two.

The expected return of all the transaction costs of these development, manufacturing, and loan contracts ultimately depends on the faith of all three parties that the manufacturer will show devotion to building better, cheaper, and safer airplanes. Unless there is competence and will behind that transaction-cost boundary, unless Boeing or Lockheed or McDonnell-Douglas can really do some things better than they (or anyone else) can buy on the market, the whole web of contracts comes crashing down. Likewise unless the airlines behind their firm's equilibrium boundary can do their job, there will be no money to pay for the better plane, so in turn no money for the manufacturer to pay the banker. The same, changing the changeable parts, holds for the banker pricing risks responsibly for the capital market, and using banking equity to back other contracts that split up the risks for appropriate parts of the capital market.

Transaction costs are worth paying, then, only when there are two (or in this case at least three) firms believably trying to be and do what it takes to be best at their own business. Only if a firm can be believed will any other firm prefer it to internal activities, thus creating the boundary between the two firms and the necessity of a contract.

Similarly, a university contracts out its janitoring and waste removal tasks, but keeps its research and teaching in-house, because it has a believable commitment to scholarship, and no noticeable commitment to clean buildings. It is the university's commitment to research and teaching that ultimately makes the waste management firm believe it will be paid for its contract, for the university's overhead costs will be paid only if students and grant-givers believe the university can and will do its job. Similarly the hospital buys a CATSCAN machine rather than build one itself, with the income or credit derived from its credibility to a client who thinks he may have had a stroke. If the client chooses the wrong hospital, that does not know enough to buy a CATSCAN machine, he might not get a second choice. And the CATSCAN manufacturer that sells to a hospital that cannot attract stroke patients will not be paid for the machine.

The "hierarchy" (Williamson 1975) that lies outside the market, protected by transaction costs barriers, has to be a thing that produces reliably on into the future, so that its predicted future competence justifies paying transaction costs now. The transaction cost (a cost of risk) of going into the emergency room of a hospital when one is perhaps having a stroke will only be paid if one thinks the medical workers care enough to be competent and to stay competent, to work even through their daughter's seventh birthday party if necessary, to triage mainly on the degree of urgency, to buy a CATSCAN machine before one has even had the stroke, and so on.

Of course, the degree to which organizations create their distinctive competencies by moral commitments is a variable. And the exact definition of what we would mean by that variable is difficult—presumably managerial commitment is more important than the commitment of hewers of wood and drawers of water, for example. But I imagine that we will define that variable more exactly by extracting indicators of it from Selznick's *Leadership in Administration* (1957) than by abstracting them from Oliver Williamson (1975), because Selznick was primarily developing a theory of the "distinctive competence" of an organization, its ability to realize values in a way no other organization could.

## *Birth and Death vs Institutions of Creative Destruction*

Schumpeter thought that many economic institutions that facilitated capitalism as we know it depended on values other than capitalism. Imperialism and mercantilism were driven by the value of power as much as by profit. Labor discipline could probably be achieved more easily by socialism than by a capitalism now shorn of its feudal governing classes. Values of democracy empirically associated with capitalism depended in their turn on competing political elites who wanted to govern first, profit from government afterwards. Schumpeter perhaps fits uncomfortably with Selznick as a comember of an old institutional school. But one of the positions he holds in common with the old institutionalists is that the form of competition among organizations is historically variable, depending a good deal on the values of the governing classes and their challengers.

In Schumpeter's argument the ruling institutions affected organizational ecology, and in particular what he called "creative destruction" (Schumpeter (1964 [1939]), 1942). In the long run, the big competitors of an earlier population of organizations are new; later, populations of organizations of a different sort that reshape the niches on which earlier organizational populations depend. If it is true that the oxygen atmosphere of earth was created by the first chlorophyll-using anaerobic populations, causing the long-run shift to oxygen-breathing animals and "creatively destroying" most anaerobic strains, then biological evolution has powerful analogies to Schumpeter's reasoning. Thus to analyze the within-species or within–"organizational population" competition is to miss the big story of evolution and of economic development: interspecies competition.

Thus Schumpeter was primarily interested in the institutions that allowed the peaceful[4] destruction of whole populations of organizations. To put it another way, he wanted to know how modern society created such precarious legitimacy for a given type of organization that the jobs, profits, or community-sustaining contributions of whole industries could be destroyed. If someone else built a better mousetrap, all the accumulated legitimacy that accounted for the first part of the climb of the old population of cat breeders up the Gompertz curve was not apparently enough. Schumpeter regarded this precariousness of the legitimacy of old populations of organizations as remarkable, and he therefore regarded the institutions that allowed such destruction of people's livelihood as precarious. He argued that it was such creative destruction that caused depressions (Schumpeter 1964 [1939]), and he was political scientist enough to know that governments and the economy were confronted with challenges to their legitimacy when they allowed such destruction and its accompanying depressions. He thought the remarkable institutions facilitating competition between species of organizations were extraordinarily precarious.

But I think the definitive analysis of what these institutions were is John R Commons's (1974 [1924]), especially his careful definition of the legal protection of competition (1974, pp. 83–134). Commons starts his analysis of what legitimate competition means for capitalism by distinguishing the legal defense

[4]At least Schumpeter preferred peaceful destruction—he knew that organizations and institutions were often created and destroyed by conquest, but he thought that was bad for economic development. As does Gambetta (1993).

of "working rules" of firms in competition[5] that are distinctive to a given corporation. These are defended legally in the sense that only the Board of Directors of a corporation can allocate the property of the corporation or permit access on the shop floor, and even stockholders cannot take away a lathe or four days of a firm electrician to satisfy their property interest. Interference with working rules invades the legally defended autonomy of a competitive corporation, the autonomy to have distinctive rules that allow them to do something innovative that can routinely give a monopolistic advantage in a niche in a market. When this is combined with an opportunity in the market (Commons 1974 [1924], pp. 153–157), it produces a "going concern value," and the institutional protection of economic opportunities distinctive to capitalism is the protection of that going concern value (Commons 1974:172–213).

What Commons (especially when combined with Schumpeter) managed to do, then, was to jump over the institutionalism of organizational ecology of one population (developed especially by Adam Smith for firms, and theorized differently by Hannan & Freeman 1977, 1989 recently) directly to the establishment of an evolutionary ecology of multiple competing species (defined by their working rules and by the opportunities—or niches—those exploit). Commons was an institutionalist and thought these were defended in the legal institutions of capitalism. When hooked together they explain also why Tobin's $q$-ratio of the market value of corporations to the replacement value of their assets is ordinarily greater than 1 in economic booms (Tobin & Brainard 1977), why there are business depressions in which that ratio goes down in populations being eliminated, and why both boom and, more surprisingly, bust are defended by institutions. There is no place for institutions to abolish organizations on a large scale in modern organizational ecology—they only legitimate them.

Darwinian evolution does not need institutions defending competition either within or between species. Humans defend themselves socially from competition by tariff barriers, racial prejudice, conspiracies in restraint of trade, guild regulations, patent offices, professional societies and licenses to practice, trade unions, zoning regulations, protection rackets, immigration and naturalization services, conquest of competitors, and the genocide of indigenous peoples.

In human history, competition has not ordinarily been legitimate. It is a wonder that modern organizational ecologists have not noticed this. Most institutional conditions restrict competition. Institutions that allow people's livelihoods and capital to be destroyed by competition are rare. Schumpeter and Commons knew that and considered the legitimacy of "exposure" to other people's "liberties" the main thing to be explained. Capitalism, particularly its legitimate competition and creative destruction part, is not at all natural but is

[5] See also essentially the same concept in "routines" in Nelson & Winter 1982.

instead an institutional creation. To use legitimacy to explain only the upswing of organizational growth rates, and to forget that the legitimacy of intensified competition by firms with innovations that destroys large legitimate populations, would have seemed a peculiar blindness in the days of Commons and Schumpeter, when Smoot-Hawley tariffs and immigration quotas were in the land. The precarious legitimacy of maquiladoras over the border in Mexico might teach us again that competition itself is still not very legitimate.

### *That Socialist Institutions Do Not Work Does Not Mean Capitalist Ones Do*

In many East European countries the populations have decided that they have tried capitalism and it does not work, so they are voting their old communist leaders back in. In the old institutionalism, the failure of capitalism to work in southern Italy was also argued by Edward Banfield, in *The Moral Basis of a Backward Society* (1967 [1958]). The basic idea of that book was that some sorts of institutions undermine capitalist organizations, and that they do so by failing to provide integrity in the achievement of public goods (law and order—especially civil law, city organization, roads, or economic development offices facilitating factory and firm foundation).

Banfield's basic notion was that if the nuclear family was so set up that its solidarity and interests invariably overrode those of other institutions, then those other institutions could not do their job. Institutions that depend on generosity of spirit and attention to collective welfare are especially vulnerable. Part of institutions' job was legitimating the fulfillment of occupational and leadership obligations in firms and in economically significant government operations. Large-scale corruption then in arenas requiring integrity in the pursuit of public goods is an outcome of a particular way of institutionalizing families. The Mafia and Cosa Nostra are in a certain sense not institutions because they are in the business of corrupting whatever institutions get in the way of short-run maximization of nuclear family interests (on the Sicilian Mafia, see especially Gambetta 1993).

The basic point can be illustrated if we consider the role of accreditation associations in education, the field where Meyer & Rowan (1977, pp. 354–356, citing their 1975 paper) first observed the powerful role of institutions. Accreditation societies do not have many formal powers, nor resources to distribute; they have only moral powers. One of the consequences is that they very generally ask for volunteers from several educational organizations to go inspect another one. Now imagine a South Italian or Sicilian social organization as described by Banfield sending out unpaid volunteers and making them hold to educational standards of the sort Meyer wants to explain, but without making an offer they can't refuse. Paying off the accreditors would surely make the formal report into even more cant and ritual than Meyer observes. A phrase from Teamsters' leader Jimmy Hoffa in a trade union debate over political action occurs to me: "There are two kinds of political action. You can make speeches, or you can give money. We give money." If schools gave money for accreditation, would the rituals of formal organization be convincing?

The extension of Banfield's institutional argument to capitalism can most easily be seen by calling on a really old fashioned institutionalist, Emile Durkheim (1933 [1893]). Durkheim held that the division of labor rested on the noncontractual elements of contract, the commitment to values of commercial honesty, nonstrategic use of bankruptcy, advertising with some information value, competence in one's occupation, and the like. Banfield's argument then might be read as asserting that both the contracts between firms, and between governments and firms, are not institutionalized under "amoral familism."

Now back to the attempt to introduce capitalism in Eastern Europe. The language describing Sicily is often used to describe the economic arrangements in capitalist Russia; the "mafia" in Russia does not have to be imported from Southern Italy. The legitimation of institutional relations under socialism was by way of the purposes of government, as manifested in government measures of outcome, government subsidies of production that was considered a public good, and the like. The contract between a firm and the government was hardly deeply theologically grounded, but it had noncontractual elements in the sense that other parts of the government would back up the corporatist industry *glavk* and help enforce conformity on the factory manager.

This central planning legitimation system for supply, quality control, measurement of productivity, labor relations regulation, pricing and payment for delivery of finished or semifinished goods, and so on, no longer legitimates. Calvinism giving supernatural sanctions for commercial integrity seems to be thin on the ground. The capacity of the population to create public goods, such as industry standards-setting, credit extension and its credit-rating system, honest brokerage in stock and bond markets, is crippled because that capacity used to be all embedded in the central planning system. The lack of intermediate corporate bodies with legitimacy of their own based on the expectation they will live up to their own moral system then produces a condition like that Banfield called amoral familism. And that is not good for capitalism in Russia or other East European countries, any more than it was good for capitalism in Southern Italy.

## *Ring Out the New, Ring In the Old*

The basic postulate here is that organizations that work well do so by paying people to serve values, to try to be competent, to conduct their business with integrity. It is easy to exaggerate the incentive effect of the payment, and to treat it as if it were only a game-theoretical token. But payment is an institutional tool as well, for we pay for things we believe in. I would argue that paying for things we believe in is the core of what an institution is. We accept tokens of credit rather than money incentives in algebra classes, and pay people to teach them, because we believe in algebra; the teacher does not get to cash in the A's he or she does not give out as in game theory, and the student does not get to cash them in at the store. Their only value is that everyone believes that there was some real mathematics behind them. Even new institutionalists at Stanford believe in algebra and are willing to pay for it, and they do not want to give that money to a school that does not believe in algebra. Nor do people want to give money to insurance companies that won't pay when they die, nor do they want to buy portable hard disk drives from a company that doesn't answer its technical help line,[6] nor to trust most of the capital markets in Eastern Europe. The combination of resources and believable commitment can only be created, so the old institutionalists argued, if people believe that the institutional enforcers themselves believe the values.

Only with that assumption, for example, can we explain why capitalism can first legitimate the horse-and-buggy industry and then legitimate the automobile industry that destroys it, without changing the basic institutions of capitalism. And it takes the failure of the assumption that enforcers of commercial contracts believe in honest dealing to see why the Russians and Ukrainians know so well that capitalism does not work: the institutional enforcers do not believe that commercial honesty is possible, so they do not bother to create it. The assumption of transaction cost analysis is that one can go out on the market, pay all the transaction costs, and (sometimes) get better performance than one could produce oneself. It is only the contrast of that market contract with what the firm can do better itself that makes the boundary around the firm or hierarchy an equilibrium in Coase's sense. But one cannot explain why there is any there there unless one is willing to believe that transaction partners will deliver the goods, will maintain the competence and responsiveness that makes the supplier's work superior to what the firm can do itself, at least until the contract is fulfilled. One pays the transaction costs by contracting with a supplier with competence superior to one's own. Otherwise the equilibrium firm size is the whole economy, perhaps as in the old USSR.

In short, the trouble with the new institutionalism is that it does not have the guts of institutions in it. The guts of institutions is that somebody somewhere really cares to hold an organization to the standards and is often paid to do that. Sometimes that somebody is inside the organization, maintaining its

[6]My advice is to call the technical support number before buying—Iomega has a wonderful computerized phone system for giving a client in trouble the runaround.

competence. Sometimes it is in an accrediting body, sending out volunteers to see if there is really any algebra in the algebra course. And sometimes that somebody, or his or her commitment, is lacking, in which case the center cannot hold, and mere anarchy is loosed upon the world.

ACKNOWLEDGMENTS

Brian Gran and Stephen Barley made detailed comments on a previous draft, Carol Heimer disciplined my tendency to precious writing, and Richard Lempert made detailed comments on the next-to-the-last draft.



*Literature Cited*

Banfield EC. 1967. (1958). *The Moral Basis of a Backward Society.* New York: Free Press

Bendix R. 1956. *Work and Authority in Industry: Ideologies of Management in the Course of Industrialization.* New York: Wiley/Berkeley: Univ. Calif. Press

Coase RH. 1937. The nature of the firm. *Economica* 4:386–405

Commons JR. 1974. (1924). *Legal Foundations of Capitalism.* Reprinted by Univ. Wisc. Press and Arno Press; originally published by Macmillan

Durkheim E. 1933. (1893). *On the Division of Labor in Society.* Transl./ed. G Simpson. New York: Macmillan

Gambetta D. 1993. *The Sicilian Mafia: The Business of Private Protection.* Cambridge, MA: Harvard Univ. Press

Hannan MT, Freeman M. 1989. *Organizational Ecology.* Cambridge, MA: Harvard Univ. Press

Hannan MT, Freeman M. 1977. The population ecology of organizations. *Am. J. Sociol.* 82:929–64

Lipset SM, Trow MA, Coleman JS. 1956. *Union Democracy.* Glencoe, IL: Free Press

Meyer JW, Rowan B. 1977. Institutionalized organizations: formal structure as myth and ceremony. *Am. J. Sociol.* 83(2):340–63

Meyer JW, Rowan B. 1975. *Notes on the structure of educational organizations.* Presented at Meet. Am. Sociol. Assoc., San Francisco

Nelson RR, Winter SG. 1982. *An Evolutionary Theory of Economic Change.* Cambridge, MA: Belknap-Harvard Univ. Press

Newhouse J. 1982. *The Sporty Game.* New York: Knopf

Rothstein PF. 1981. *Evidence in a Nutshell: State and Federal Rules.* St. Paul: West. 2nd ed.

Schumpeter JA. 1964. (1939). *Business Cycles: A Theoretical, Historical, and Statistical Analysis of the Capitalist Process.* [Abridged by Rindigs Fels]. New York: McGraw-Hill

Schumpeter JA. 1942. *Capitalism, Socialism, and Democracy.* New York: Harper Torch Books

Selznick P. 1949. *TVA and the Grass Roots.* Berkeley: Univ. Calif. Press

Selznick P. 1984. (1957). *Leadership in Administration: A Sociological Interpretation.* Berkeley: Univ. Calif. Press

Skolnick J. 1975. (1966). *Justice without Trial: Law Enforcement in Democratic Society.* New York: John Wiley. 2nd ed.

Tobin J, Brainard WC. 1977. Asset markets and the cost of capital. In *Economic Progress: Private Values and Public Policy: Essays in Honor of W. Fellner*, ed. R Nelson, B Balassa, pp. 235–62. Amsterdam: North Holland

Twining W. 1990. *Rethinking Evidence: Exploratory Essays.* Evanston: Northwestern Univ. Press

Veblen T. 1934. (1899). *The Theory of the Leisure Class.* New York: Modern Library

Wigmore JH. 1983. (1940). *Wigmore on Evidence: [Peter] Tiller's Revision.* 10 vols. Boston: Little Brown

Williamson O. 1975. *Markets and Hierarchies.* New York: Free Press/London: Collier Macmillan

*Annu. Rev. Sociol. 1997. 23:19–38*


# THE SAVINGS AND LOAN DEBACLE, FINANCIAL CRIME, AND THE STATE

*K. Calavita*
Department of Criminology, Law and Society, University of California, Irvine, California 92697

*R. Tillman*
Department of Sociology, St. John's University, Jamaica, New York 11439

*H. N. Pontell*
Department of Criminology, Law and Society, University of California, Irvine, California 92697

KEY WORDS: savings and loans, financial crime, white-collar crime, state, regulation

ABSTRACT

The savings and loan crisis of the 1980s was one of the worst financial disasters of the twentieth century. We argue here that much financial fraud of the sort that contributed to this debacle constitutes "collective embezzlement," and that this collective embezzlement may be the prototypical corporate crime of the late twentieth century. We further argue that the state may have a different relationship to this kind of financial fraud than to manufacturing crime perpetrated on behalf of corporate profits. In the conclusion, we suggest that an understanding of the relationship between financial fraud and state interests may open up new regulatory space for the control of these costly crimes. Our data come from a wide variety of sources, including government documents, primary statistical data on prosecutions, and interviews with regulators.

## INTRODUCTION

The savings and loan (S&L) crisis of the 1980s was one of the worst financial disasters of the twentieth century. Experts gauge its cost to US taxpayers over 30 years to be approximately $500 billion, including interest payments on the government bonds sold to finance the industry's bailout (US General Accounting Office, cited in Johnston 1990:1; National Commission on Financial Institution Reform, Recovery and Enforcement [NCFIRRE] 1993:4). Reliable estimates



0360-0572/97/0815-0019$08.00

of the percentage of losses due to criminal wrongdoing range from 10% to 44% (Office of Thrift Supervision 1990, Resolution Trust Corporation 1992, Akerloff & Romer 1993, NCFIRRE 1993).

The savings and loan scandal was by no means an isolated phenomenon in the high-flying 1980s. Insurance fraud, junk bond manipulation, insider trading, and securities fraud took their place alongside the thrift debacle in the headlines and on the nightly news. By the end of the decade, Charles Keating, Michael Milken, and Ivan Boesky had become household words, their names synonymous with corporate wrongdoing. Besides this ill-gotten notoriety, and the vast wealth accruing from their legitimate and illegitimate activities, these offenders had something else in common. Unlike much of the corporate crime of earlier decades addressed by so much of the scholarly literature—for example, the electrical company conspiracy, the Pinto scandal, unsafe practices in the pharmaceutical industry, and occupational safety and health violations (Geis 1967, Cullen et al 1987, Braithwaite 1984, Carson 1981)—their crimes had nothing to do with production or manufacturing but instead entailed the manipulation of money.

In this case study of the savings and loan disaster, we argue 1. that much financial fraud of this sort constitutes a specific form of corporate crime, what we call "collective embezzlement;" 2. that this collective embezzlement may be the prototypical corporate crime of the late twentieth century in the United States, in that it corresponds to the shift away from manufacturing or industrial capitalism to finance capitalism; 3. that the state may have a different relationship to collective embezzlement than to manufacturing crime perpetrated on behalf of corporate profits; and, 4. that by examining this change in the nature of corporate crime, and exploring the state's reaction to these offenses, we may be able to delineate with more precision the relationship between the state and economic activity and more generally to advance state theory. In the conclusion, we suggest that an understanding of the relationship between financial fraud and state interests may open up new regulatory space for the control of these costly crimes.

The data for this paper come from a wide variety of sources. In addition to secondary data such as government documents, regulators' reports, and other published accounts of the S&L crisis, we have gathered two kinds of primary data. The first consists of interviews with 105 government officials who were involved in policymaking, regulation, prosecution, and/or enforcement, in Washington, DC, and in field offices in California, Texas, and Florida, where the bulk of thrift[1] fraud took place. These unstructured, open-ended

[1]We use "savings and loans"and "thrifts" interchangeably here to refer to federally insured savings institutions that have as their primary historical function the provision of home mortgage loans. See Calavita & Pontell (1990, 1991, 1993) for a discussion of the regulatory changes in the early 1980s that freed these institutions to make direct investments, that effectively altered their function as home-mortgage lenders, and that provided extensive opportunities for fraud.

interviews provide substantial background information on techniques of fraud and the state response. Second, we have assembled several statistical data sets on the nature of thrift crime and the government's prosecution effort. These data were compiled from the statistics provided us by three federal agencies: the Resolution Trust Corporation (RTC, the federal agency created to manage and sell assets from seized thrifts); the Office of Thrift Supervision (OTS, which after 1989 took over from the old Federal Home Loan Bank Board the task of examination and enforcement); and the Executive Office of the US Attorneys (which made prosecutorial decisions). These statistical data provide detailed information on criminal referrals, indictments, convictions, and sentencing.

Of course the picture is far from complete and our data are necessarily imperfect. For one thing, we can never be sure how much crime goes undetected, nor whether the crimes that do come to light are representative of thrift crime in general. While this is a concern in all criminological research, it is particularly acute in the area of white-collar crime where fraud is often disguised within ordinary business transactions (Katz 1979), proving fraudulent intent is problematic, and potentially criminal wrongdoing consequently is not prosecuted. Using the "criminal referral" as our indicator of fraud goes partway in addressing this "front end" problem in white-collar crime research.

Criminal referrals, usually filed by examiners or regulators or by whistleblowers at the institution itself, describe suspected crimes, name individuals who may have committed crimes, and estimate dollar losses. These referrals are sent through the regulatory field office to the FBI and the US Attorney's Office for investigation, where in a relatively few cases they result in indictments. The accuracy of these referrals as a measure of thrift crime—like the accuracy of statistics on "crimes known to the police" as an indicator of street crime—is limited by the existence of a "dark figure of crime," that is, the significant number of crimes that are never detected or reported. We use criminal referrals here to gain some sense of the incidence and patterns of thrift crime, with the understanding that they do not cover the entire population of fraud.[2]

The following section draws on these data to describe the basic forms of thrift fraud. As we will see, despite their apparent complexity, many of these

[2]There may be some cases in which referrals were filed in the absence of actual criminal misconduct. However, our conversations with regulators, investigators, and prosecutors, and our perusal of the detailed referrals to which we gained access, suggest that these forms were by no means filed frivolously. Because of the amount of information required on these forms, and because the reputation of the agency that filed a referral was at stake, they were likely to be limited to the most egregious cases of suspected misconduct, particularly as caseloads bogged down in the late 1980s. See Calavita et al (1997) for a description of the triage-like prosecutorial decisions that resulted in indictments in only one case out of every seven criminal referrals in Texas, and one in four in California.

frauds were variations on a fixed number of themes. As one of our informants put it, "It was as if someone had found a cookie cutter" (personal interview).

## TYPES OF S&L FRAUD: HOT DEALS, LOOTING, AND COVERING UP

Corporate crimes of the sort involved in the savings and loan scandal are among the most complex white-collar offenses ever committed, leading one journalist to complain that when "regular people" tried to figure it out, they got "hopelessly bored and confused, as though they'd fallen a month behind in their high-school algebra class" (O'Rourke 1989:43). The concerned layperson is helped considerably by the fact that there are a limited number of basic formulas for abusing thrifts. Before describing these basic formulas, we need to note that our discussion is focused on insider abuse, by which we mean those frauds in which thrift owners and/or managers were central players, either alone or in collaboration with outsiders.

While some have implied that the industry's problems in the 1980s were brought on by outsiders who victimized thrifts (Lewis 1989, Lowy 1991), the schemes at the heart of the scandal required the participation of insiders. Our RTC data,[3] which allow us to identify the organizational positions of those cited in criminal referrals, confirm that high-level insiders were participants in the majority of these frauds. Of the 2265 criminal referrals in this data set, insiders were listed as suspects in 1294 or 63%. Far from a case of naive insiders being victimized by slick con artists, most thrift fraud at these institutions was self-inflicted.

At the most general level, we can decipher three types of insider abuse, called here hot deals, looting, and covering up. All involved one or more violations of federal bank fraud statutes, including prohibitions against "kickbacks and bribes" (18 USC Section 215); "theft, embezzlement, or misapplication of funds" (18 USC Sections 656,961c); "schemes or artifices to defraud federally insured institutions" (18 USC Section 1344); "knowingly or willfully falsifying or concealing material facts or making false statements" (18 USC Section 1001); "false entries in bank documents with intent to injure or defraud bank regulators, examiners . . . " (18 USC Section 1005); and/or "aiding and abetting and conspiracy" (18 USC Sections 2, 371). The following sections describe

[3]As part of its mandate to manage the assets of seized thrifts, the RTC collected data on criminal referrals through its Thrift Information Management System (TIMS). This system recorded and tracked criminal referrals at all RTC institutions (that is, those institutions that had been declared insolvent and taken over by the RTC). The TIMS data referred to here summarize the contents of "Category 1" (suspected thrift fraud of $100,000 or more) criminal referrals filed by the RTC or other federal agencies through May, 1992.

hot deals, looting, and covering up, and outline their contribution to the thrift debacle.

## Hot Deals

These investment frauds were the sine qua non of insider abuse, providing both the cash flow from which to siphon off funds and the transactional medium within which to disguise it. Four kinds of transactions were central in these deals. As Senate Banking Committee staff members Alt & Siglin (1990:3–5) explain, these transactions include such schemes as land flips, nominee loans, reciprocal lending, and linked financing. Land flips involve selling a property back and forth among two or more partners, inflating the price each time and refinancing the property with each sale until the value has increased many times over. Alt & Siglin (1990:4) use the following example:

> A sells a parcel of real estate to B for $1 million, its approximate market value. B finances the sale with a bank loan . . .. B sells the property back to A for $2 million. A finances the sale with a bank loan, with the bank relying on a fraudulent appraisal. B repays his original loan and takes $1 million in 'profit' off the table, which he shares with A. A defaults on the loan, leaving the bank with a $1 million loss.

While the flip technically could be achieved without the lending institution's participation, thrift insiders were often collaborators. For one thing, insiders were sometimes business associates of the corrupt borrowers, who at a future date would exchange the favor. In addition, while the lending institution was left with an overpriced property on its hands, in the short-term, it made upfront points and fees from the huge loans, from which executive bonuses could be drawn.

It was not unusual in the mid-1980s for partners to sit down and in one afternoon flip a property until its price was double or triple its original market value, refinancing with each flip. The playful jargon for this was "cash-for-trash," and the loans were "drag-away loans," because the intention from the beginning was to default, dragging away the proceeds. Don Dixon at Vernon Savings and Loan in Texas (nicknamed by regulators "Vermin") reportedly "flipped land deals [like] pancakes" (O'Shea 1991:76). He and associates like (fast Eddie) McBirney at Sunbelt Savings and Loan in Dallas (nicknamed by regulators "Gunbelt"), and Texas developer Danny Faulkner used land flips among other schemes to develop hundreds of miles of condominiums on I-30 northeast of Dallas. Officers at nearby Empire Savings and Loan financed the land flips to inflate the value of the land and provide the rationale for making the condo development loans despite an already glutted Dallas real estate market (personal interviews). Faulkner and his partners hosted weekend brunches at Wise's Circle Grill in the I-30 corridor. Invited guests included officials from Empire Savings and Loan, investors, appraisers, and increasingly, politicians who drew huge campaign contributions from the events. Over breakfast, properties quickly changed hands and millions of dollars of phony profits were made in a few hours (O'Shea 1991:32; personal interviews).

Nominee loans were often used in conjunction with land flips. Nominee lending used a straw borrower to circumvent loan-to-one-borrower regulations or restrictions on insider borrowing. One costly nominee loan partnership involved former dentist Duayne Christensen and real estate broker Janet McKinzie in Santa Ana, California. Christensen opened North American Savings and Loan in 1983. In partnership with McKinzie, Christensen used the thrift to make loans to his own real estate projects and to participate in multiple land flips, through a company owned and controlled by McKinzie. In one typical scheme, straw borrower David Morgan purchased property brokered by McKinzie's real estate company and financed by North American. He then resold the property at an inflated value to his own holding company. Fees and commissions poured into McKinzie's real estate brokerage. North American made upfront points and fees but apparently never saw the proceeds from the resale of any of the properties (US Congress, House Committee on Government Operations, Subcommittee on Commerce, Consumer, and Monetary Affairs 1987a:304-9). The thrift was closed in 1988, at a loss of $209 million.

Reciprocal lending was another way of circumventing restrictions against insider borrowing. Instead of making a loan directly to oneself, which would have sounded the alarm among regulators, two or more insiders at different thrifts made loans to each other. Making loans to each other is not in itself illegal, but making loans contingent on a reciprocal loan is fraud (Alt & Siglin 1990:5). These "daisy chains" often involved multiple participants, and unraveling them sometimes took investigators far afield of the original institution and exposed the complex conspiratorial quality of thrift fraud. One investigation in Wyoming in 1987 revealed a single daisy chain of reciprocal loans among four thrifts that by itself resulted in a $26 million loss to taxpayers (US Congress, House Committee on Government Operations, Subcommittee on Commerce, Consumer, and Monetary Affairs 1987b:79-80, 129-130). A Texas network included at least 74 daisy chain participants and involved all the insolvent thrifts in the state (US Congress, House Committee on Banking, Finance and Urban Affairs 1990:799-872).

Similar in logic to reciprocal lending arrangements, linked financing involves depositing money in a thrift, with the understanding that the depositor will receive a loan in return. Loan broker Mario Renda specialized in setting up linked financing deals, even advertising in the *Wall Street Journal*, the *New York Times*, and the *Los Angeles Times*: "MONEY FOR RENT: BORROWING OBSTACLES NEUTRALIZED BY HAVING US DEPOSIT FUNDS WITH YOUR LOCAL BANK: NEW TURNSTYLE APPROACH TO FINANCING" (quoted in Pizzo et al 1991:127).

Renda placed large brokered deposits in thrifts, for which he received a finder's fee, in return for which borrowers with credit "obstacles" received a generous loan from the thrift. Response to Renda's ads was overwhelming; according to his own court testimony, Renda brokered the deposits for hundreds of linked financing schemes.

Investigators and regulators report finding variations of land flips, nominee loans, linked financing, and reciprocal lending arrangements over and over in their autopsies of seized thrifts. Many hot deals combined elements of all four transaction frauds. So-called "ADC" (acquisition, development and construction) lending is a good example. ADC lending was a form of direct investment by thrifts in the 1980s, in which thrifts provided up to 100% of the financing for a speculative development project, reaping proceeds (and collecting on the loan) only if the development turned a profit. Points, fees, and several years of interest payments were often included in the loan, so that it appeared on paper to be in good standing, and the thrift recorded income from the self-funded points and fees. Fraudulent ADC lending was at the core of the S&L debacle in Texas and helps explain continued investment in Texas commercial real estate when the market was already glutted. As the National Commission on Financial Institution Reform, Recovery and Enforcement (1993:48) explains, "ADC loans were an attractive vehicle for abuse. They bound up in one instrument many of the opportunities available." A land flip might provide inflated collateral for a generous ADC loan; the loan then might be to a straw borrower who shared the proceeds with thrift insiders (nominee lending); thrift managers might make the loan contingent on a deposit or other investment (linked financing); and/or, thrift insiders might exchange loans to finance development projects with each other (reciprocal lending arrangements). As Texas S&Ls were pumped up with these huge development loans, they reported unprecedented paper profits from which thrift insiders extracted generous bonuses and dividends—one major form of "looting."

### *Looting*

Looting refers to the siphoning off of funds by thrift insiders and is thus more like traditional forms of crime than are the business transactions involved in hot deals. Because thrift management was doing the looting, it took different forms from a typical bank robbery or embezzlement by a lower-level employee. The most straightforward, but probably least common, way to loot was simply to remove deposits from the thrift and stash them away. Probably more common were shopping sprees with thrift funds, and excessive bonuses or other forms of compensation.

David Paul bought CenTrust Savings Bank in Miami in 1983 and quickly turned it into a megathrift with $9.8 billion in assets (Pizzo et al 1991:404–5;

Lowy 1991:152–53). Paul used over $40 million of CenTrust money for a yacht, a Rubens painting, a sailboat, Limoges china, and Baccarat crystal (Lowy 1991:152). In addition, he built the 47-floor Miami CenTrust skyscraper at a cost of $170 million (Mayer 1990:77; Pizzo et al 1991:405; Lowy 1991:152–53). When CenTrust collapsed, it was the largest S&L failure in the Southeast, costing taxpayers $1.7 billion. For his part in the insolvency, David Paul was convicted of 97 counts of racketeering and fraud and sentenced to eleven years in prison (*Los Angeles Times* 1994:D2).

Excessive compensation schemes were another way for insiders to loot their institutions. The US General Accounting Office (GAO)(1989:21) defines "compensation" as "salaries as well as bonuses, dividend payments, and perquisites for executives." A federal regulation limits permissible compensation for thrift personnel to that which is "reasonable and commensurate with their duties and responsibilities" (GAO:21). At the most expensive failures, executives typically paid themselves exorbitant bonuses and dividends, even as their thrifts were collapsing (GAO 1989:21). For example, Don Dixon and his top executives at Vernon took more than $15 million in bonuses between 1982 and 1986, at a time when the thrift was already deeply insolvent (O'Shea 1991:217–18). During the six years that David Paul was driving CenTrust into the ground, he paid himself $16 million in salary and bonuses, $5 million of it coming in 1988 and 1989 when the thrift was piling up losses from its junk bond investments (Pizzo et al 1991:406).

Of the 26 most costly failed thrifts studied by the US General Accounting Office (GAO)(1989:21), shopping sprees and excessive compensation had occurred in the vast majority. A large proportion of prosecutions have been for such looting, probably because of the relative ease of building a convincing body of evidence for these more straightforward frauds compared to the complex business transactions involved in hot deals (personal interviews). In any case, hot deals and insider looting went hand-in-hand: The deals provided the cash flow and reported income with which to finance shopping sprees and excessive compensation—indeed the ability to siphon off phony "profits" provided the incentive for hot deals and the rapid growth they fueled.

## *Covering Up*

As savings and loans teetered on the brink of insolvency, broken by hot deals and looting, their operators struggled to hide both the insolvency and the fraud. In some cases, the cover-up came in the form of deals whose primary purpose was to produce a misleading picture of the institution's state of health. US Attorney Anton R Valukas describes a number of such cover-up deals:

> In the prosecuted cases of Manning Savings and Loan, American Heritage Savings and Loan of Bloomingdale and First Suburban Bank of Maywood, when the [nominee] loans

> became non-performing the assets were taken back into the institution, again sold at inflated prices to straw purchasers, financed by the institution, in order to inflate the net worth of the bank or savings and loan. The clear purpose was to keep the federal regulatory agencies ... at bay by maintaining a net worth above the trigger point for forced reorganization or liquidation" (quoted in US Congress, House Committee on Government Operations, Subcommittee on Commerce, Consumer, and Monetary Affairs 1987b:99–100).

Insiders also could simply doctor their books to shield their thrift from regulatory action. At one S&L studied by the GAO (1989:41), three sets of books were kept—two on different computer systems and one manually. At another, $21 million of income was reported in the last few days of 1985 in transactions that were either fabricated or fraudulent, allowing the thrift to report a net worth of $9 million, rather than its actual negative $12 million (GAO 1989:44–45). McKinzie and Christensen at North America S&L prepared bogus documents when challenged by regulators. When the thrift was finally taken over, examiners found evidence of fake certificates of deposit, forged bank confirmation letters, and other cover-up materials (US Congress, House Committee on Government Operations, Subcommittee on Commerce, Consumer, and Monetary Affairs 1987a:308).

### *Relative Frequency of Hot Deals, Looting, and Covering Up: The Dallas OTS Files*

For a more detailed picture of the part these insider frauds played in the thrift crisis, we can look at a subsample of Category 1 criminal referrals in one state, Texas. Here we rely on data from files in the Dallas Office of Thrift Supervision (OTS). This OTS office maintained computer files on all criminal referrals for thrift fraud in Texas. We selected a 20% sample from this list of 1210 criminal referrals filed between January 1985 and March 1993, by choosing every fifth referral. We then examined the actual referral forms for each of the 241 cases in our sample, as well as the numerous supporting documents that accompanied these referrals. For each case, we coded the type of suspected violation, whether insiders were involved, and the estimated loss from the suspected crime.

Our main objective was to obtain a better sense of the crimes being reported at thrift institutions. Based on a careful perusal of these referral files, we developed 11 specific categories of insider fraud (including, for example, insider loans, land flips, kickbacks, falsification of documents, etc). While many of these categories overlapped in practice, since these frauds were usually complex and often contained several layers of deception, we made distinctions according to what the primary offense or central ingredient of the suspected misconduct was. We then sorted these offenses according to whether they constituted hot deals, looting, covering up, or some other broad category of fraud. For example, insider loans and land flips are hot deals, kickbacks are a form of looting, and falsification of documents is a method of cover-up.

Of the 241 cases of suspected misconduct, 193 involved insider fraud, as opposed to victimization by outsiders, which is consistent with the RTC data discussed above. More important here, all but three of the 193 insider fraud cases involved some form of hot deals, looting, or covering up. The most common form of fraud was hot deals, with various types of such deals comprising almost 68% of these suspected frauds and contributing by far the highest price tag—over $1.08 billion out of the total $1.6 billion in estimated losses.

## *Hot Deals and Looting as "Collective Embezzlement"*

In discussing different forms of white-collar crime, Sutherland (1983:231) described embezzlement: "The ordinary case of embezzlement is a crime by a single individual in a subordinate position against a strong corporation." Cressey, in *Other People's Money* (1953), focused on the lone white-collar embezzler, stealing from his or her employer. Traditionally, then, embezzlement has been thought of as an isolated act of an individual employee who steals from the corporation for personal gain.

Criminologists have typically drawn a sharp distinction between this "embezzlement" by individuals against the corporation and "corporate crime," in which fraud is perpetrated by the corporation on behalf of the corporation. For example, Wheeler & Rothman (1982:1405) speak of two distinct types of white-collar crime: "Either the individual gains at the organization's expense, as in embezzlement, or the organization profits regardless of individual advantage, as in price-fixing." Similarly, Coleman (1987:407) argues, "The distinction between organizational crimes committed with support from an organization that is, at least in part, furthering its own ends, and occupational crimes committed for the benefit of individual criminals without organizational support, provides an especially powerful way of classifying different kinds of white-collar crime."

Neglected in this dichotomy is the possibility of organizational crime in which the organization is a vehicle for perpetrating crime against itself, as in the hot deals and looting described here. This form of white-collar crime represents a hybrid between traditional corporate crime and embezzlement—crime by the corporation against the corporation—and might be thought of as "collective embezzlement." Unlike Sutherland's and Cressey's embezzlers, these "collective embezzlers" were not lone, lower-level employees but thrift owners and managers, acting in networks of coconspirators inside and outside the institution. Indeed, this embezzlement was often company policy. In some cases, it was the very purpose of the organization to provide a vehicle for fraud against itself. Wheeler & Rothman (1982:1406) have pointed to "the organization as weapon" in white-collar crime: "[T]he organization ... is for white-collar criminals what the gun or knife is for the common criminal—a tool to obtain money from victims." In the collective embezzlement of the thrift industry, the organization was both weapon and victim.

## COLLECTIVE EMBEZZLEMENT AND LATE TWENTIETH CENTURY CAPITALISM

As we approach the twenty-first century, the US economy—and those of other advanced capitalist countries—is compared to a "casino" (Bates 1989:D1, *Business Week* 1985:78–90). In this casino economy, the largest profits are made from placing a clever bet, not making a better mousetrap. Unlike in industrial capitalism where goods and services are produced to make a profit, in finance capitalism—where the "means of production" are currency trades, corporate takeovers, loan swaps, and futures trading—profits come from "fiddling with money" (Trillin 1989). Nobel Prize winner Maurice Allais underscores the magnitude of this shift from an economy based on the circulation of goods to one circulating money itself, pointing out that "more than $400 billion is exchanged every day on the foreign exchange markets, while the flow of commercial transactions is only about $12 billion" (quoted in Bates 1989:D1).

Beginning in 1980, the futures market, in which investors gamble on the future price of hogs, grain, tobacco, and other commodities, rapidly outpaced the production of the goods whose prices were being bet on. In 1983, US futures trading totaled $7 trillion, or $28 billion a day, and by 1985, futures trading was growing at a rate ten times the rate of industrial production (Harrison & Bluestone 1988:54). The US financial market was so active that in 1984, over $4 trillion in trades came through a single investment banking firm—First Boston Corp.—more than equaling the national GNP for that year (Plotkin & Scheuerman 1994:59).

As the management of money and financial speculation outstrip production as the greatest sources of profit, this finance capitalism spawns vast new opportunities for fraud such as the hot deals and looting discussed above. Further, there are relatively few constraints or risks associated with these lucrative opportunities. Unlike corporate criminals in the industrial sector who generally commit crime to advance corporate profits and are constrained by concern for their corporation's long-term survival, collective embezzlers in the casino economy have little to lose. With no long-term investment in the infrastructure of production, their main concern is to get in and out of the house with as much of the pot as possible. The effect of their crimes on the health of the casino, or even its long-term survival, are unimportant to these financial high-flyers. *Business Week* (1985:90) describes "all the games the casino society plays": "The object ... is to get rich today, come what may." Collective embezzlement, in which highly placed insiders loot their own institutions, may be the prototypical form of white-collar crime in this context, much as violations of fair labor standards or consumer protections are to the industrial production process.

## COLLECTIVE EMBEZZLEMENT AND THE STATE

Sociologists have long made a distinction between "social" regulations (such as occupational safety and health standards), which are aimed at controlling production processes, and "economic" regulations (such as insider trading restrictions), which regulate the market and stabilize the economy (Barnett 1981, Cranston 1982, Snider 1991, Yeager 1991). While the former protect workers and consumers against the excesses of capital—and tend to cut into profits—the latter regulate and stabilize the capital accumulation process and historically have been supported by affected industries.

This distinction is consistent with a structural approach to the state, which emphasizes the "objective relation" (Poulantzas 1969) between the state and capital (see also Althusser 1971, O'Connor 1973). This objective relation guarantees that the capitalist state will operate in the long-term interests of capitalists independent of their direct participation in the policymaking process or mobilization of resources. Central to this objective relation under capitalism, the state must promote capital accumulation because its own survival depends on tax revenues derived from successful profit-making activity, as well as the political stability that is contingent on economic growth. In addition, it must actively pursue "political integration" (Friedland et al 1977), "legitimation" (O'Connor 1973), or "the cohesion of the social formation" (Poulantzas 1969) in the interest of political survival and the economic growth upon which it depends.

In this structuralist rendition, the state enjoys relative autonomy in its efforts to realize these potentially contradictory functions. In direct contrast to the instrumentalist model espoused by Domhoff (1967, 1979) and others (Kolko 1963, 1965, Miliband 1969), structuralists argue that state managers are not captive to individual capitalists' interests and indeed are capable of violating those interests in order to pursue the broader and more long-term interests of capital accumulation and political legitimacy. Nonetheless, its autonomy is "relative." While the state may be free from the manipulation of individual capitalists or even of the business community as a whole, it is by no means autonomous from the structural requirements of the political economy within which it is embedded and which it must work to preserve (see Poulantzas 1969).

Regulation scholars who borrow from this perspective have generally focused on social—rather than economic—regulation. This literature addresses the lax enforcement of social regulations and ties that laxity to the capital accumulation function of the state and the perceived costs of interfering with profitable industry (Barnett 1981, Calavita 1983, Snider 1991, Yeager 1991). These scholars also note that the legitimation mandate of the state periodically requires that it respond to political demands to shore up worker safety, reduce environmental hazards, or enforce labor standards. The point, however, is that active enforcement of social regulation occurs primarily in response to public pressure and legitimation concerns, and it recedes once political attention has shifted elsewhere and state legitimacy is no longer threatened (Barnett 1981, Carson 1982, Walters 1985, Calavita 1983, Gunningham 1987, Yeager 1991).

In contrast, when the goal is economic regulation, the state tends to assume a more rigorous posture. Despite occasional protest from the individual capitalists at whom sanctions are directed, the state rather vigorously enforces regulations that stabilize the market and enhance economic viability. Unlike social regulations that are implemented primarily in response to on-again/off-again legitimation needs, economic regulations are integral to the capital accumulation process and are thus more consistently and urgently pursued (Barnett 1981, Snider 1991, Yeager 1991). While case studies are far fewer in this area, some excellent research has focused on the US Securities and Exchange Commission (SEC). As Yeager (1991) and Shapiro (1984) have shown, although the SEC is by no means omnipotent in the face of its powerful Wall Street charges, nonetheless it rather routinely seeks criminal sanctions and stiff monetary fines for elite offenders.

Extensive empirical research documents this enforcement discrepancy. Clinard et al's (1979) comprehensive analysis of enforcement actions against the 582 largest corporations in the United States during 1975 and 1976 found a strong relationship between level of enforcement and type of violation. While over 96% of "manufacturing violations" (involving social regulations concerning such things as product safety and food and drug standards) were handled entirely at the administrative level, only 41.5% of "trade violations" (involving economic regulations controlling bid-rigging and other unfair trade practices) were disposed of administratively. Further, while over 21% of trade violations were processed criminally, fewer than 1% of manufacturing violations were criminally processed, and no labor standard violations were prosecuted criminally. Clinard et al (1979:147) conclude, "Corporate actions that directly harm the economy were more likely to receive the greater penalties, while those affecting consumer product quality were responded to with the least severe sanctions. Although over 85 percent of all sanctions were administrative in nature, those harming the economy were most likely to receive criminal penalties" (see also Barnett 1981).

Based on these empirical findings and the structural theory with which they are consistent, the lenient treatment of corporate offenders documented by

Sutherland over 40 years ago and reaffirmed by subsequent white-collar crime scholars may be a function of the state's relationship to capital. It may be, however, that this documentation of leniency is related to the fact that the primary focus in this literature is on violations of *social* regulations that cut into profits.

*But, what of the collective embezzlement described above?* If the structural logic is valid, then the state should have an altogether different relationship to collective embezzlement in the thrift industry than to traditional corporate crimes in the manufacturing sector. For one thing, the structural model would predict—and the empirical literature reviewed above supports this prediction—that the state would take violations of economic regulations quite seriously. Further, we would expect that enforcing *banking* regulations, which lie at the very heart of the economic system, would be among the state's highest priorities and would thus be a showcase for enforcement.

In addition, remember that collective embezzlement is aimed not at enhancing corporate profits, but at personal profit-making at the expense of the institution. In the S&L context, this "crime by the organization against the organization" not only decimated individual institutions, but threatened the demise of the whole industry, and with it the financial stability of the US economy. As a senior staff member of the Senate Banking Committee put it, "This [thrift] industry is very close to the heart of the American economy. We teetered on the edge of a major, major problem here. Well ... we **got** a major problem, but we teetered on the edge of a major collapse .... All these financial industries could bring down the whole economy" (personal interview). For the state whose functions include capital accumulation and long-term economic stability, we would expect that containing this collective embezzlement would have been a top priority.

Instead, extensive evidence indicates that the state not only failed to avert the crisis but was complicitous in shielding thrift offenders from detection (Calavita & Pontell 1990, Calavita et al 1997, US Congress, House Committee on Standards of Official Conduct 1989, National Commission on Financial Institutions Reform, Recovery and Enforcement 1993). In the remainder of this paper, we argue that a close look at the evolution of the thrift crisis and the role of government in delaying its resolution suggests the need to go beyond the reductionism of current state theory, toward a more synthetic model of state activity.

## PUSHING THE LIMITS OF STATE THEORY

At first blush, the S&L debacle seems to reaffirm the instrumentalist notion of a state captured by monied interests in the form of campaign contributions and other less subtle forms of "honest graft" (Jackson 1988). Indeed, implicit or explicit collusion of government officials with thrift offenders seems to have played a significant role in thwarting regulation and thereby exacerbating the crisis. At the lowest level of field inspectors and examiners—those with front-line responsibility for detecting and reporting fraud—there were occasional instances of cooptation by fraudulent thrift operators. One strategy of thrift executives was to woo examiners and regulators with job offers at salaries several times higher than their modest government wages (Pizzo et al 1991, personal interviews).

More important than these relatively infrequent forms of outright collusion by regulators and examiners were close connections between thrift industry executives and elected officials. The powerful US League of Savings and Loans, the thrifts' major lobbying group in Washington and generous donor of campaign funds, was a significant force in deflecting regulatory scrutiny, underfunding regulatory agencies, and generally postponing the closure of insolvent and fraud-ridden thrifts.[4] While the "Keating Five"—the five Senators who challenged San Francisco regulators on behalf of Charles Keating—provide the most visible example of Congressional attempts to rein in regulators, they were not alone. Congressman Fernand St Germain, Chair of the House Banking Committee and cosponsor of the deregulatory legislation in the early 1980s that set the stage for the thrift crisis, was a frequent recipient of US League of Savings and Loans largesse. Having been observed regularly dining out in Washington on the US League's expense account, St Germain was investigated by the Department of Justice for conflict-of-interest violations. The Justice Department concluded that there was "substantial evidence of serious and sustained misconduct" by St Germain in his connections with the thrift industry. A House Ethics Committee investigation came to the same conclusion. No formal prosecution was initiated, and St Germain was voted out of office in 1988. He is currently a lobbyist for the thrift industry (Jackson 1988, Pizzo et al 1991).

House Speaker Jim Wright was particularly adept at intervening on behalf of his thrift benefactors and often called Federal Home Loan Bank Board (FHLBB) Chair Ed Gray to task for his attempts at aggressive thrift regulation. On several occasions, documented in the independent counsel's report to the House Committee investigating Wright's alleged conflicts of interest (US Congress. House Committee on Standards of Official Conduct 1989, see also the National Commission on Financial Institutions Reform, Recovery and Enforcement 1993), the Speaker of the House from Texas asked the chief regulator to back off of Texas thrifts and advocated on behalf of specific thrift owners who had contributed generously to his campaign fund.

This complicity of government officials is exactly what instrumentalists would predict, and it sharply contradicts the structuralist notions of relative

[4]For a detailed discussion of the role of government corruption in the S&L debacle, see Calavita & Pontell (1994) and Calavita et al (1997).

autonomy and the priority placed on economic regulation and long-term financial stability. The fact that state officials shielded the collective embezzlement of thrift operators at the expense of economic stability adds substantial credibility to the instrumentalist model of the impact of raw economic power and influence-peddling.

However, there is more to it than this. While it is true that the US League of Savings and Loans and its individual members exerted considerable influence in Congress, at the same time a vitriolic struggle between members of Congress and the FHLBB raged behind the scenes (Black 1994, Waldman 1990, US Congress. House Committee on Standards of Official Conduct 1989). By all accounts, Ed Gray and his staff at the FHLBB were stunned by the escalating thrift crisis in Texas and elsewhere, and they approached their assignment with urgency. Gray was said to have had his "Road to Damascus experience" (Black 1994:9) watching a homemade videotape of miles of abandoned condominiums east of Dallas financed by the insured deposits of Empire Savings and Loan. He spent the rest of his tenure at FHLBB attempting to reregulate thrifts and encountering resistance from the industry, the White House, and Congress. One investigative reporter described the attack on Gray and his dogged persistence: "If Gray's reign as the bank board's chairman had been a fight . . . they would have stopped it. . .. He stood in the middle of the ring . . . taking repeated blows. But he never fell to the canvas" (Binstein 1987:48).

This clash between regulators who were alarmed at the pending disaster and key members of Congress who shielded their thrift benefactors refutes not only the structural notions of uniform state purpose and relative autonomy, but instrumentalists' depiction of state actors as simply lackeys of monied interests. It suggests instead that relative autonomy may vary across the institutions that together comprise the state. Members of Congress, whose political careers depend on a steady influx of campaign funds, may be particularly susceptible to the demands of those with the resources to make large contributions. Civil servants in regulatory agencies, while certainly not immune to such political and financial pressures, may for structural reasons be less susceptible to them and periodically may take a more rigorous enforcement approach in the interests of economic stability.

This account of the evolution of the thrift crisis suggests the need for a synthetic model of state action. As we have seen from the literature cited above, the state is capable of concerted action and rigorous regulation in the interest of financial stability, consistent with structural theory. On the other hand, as we have seen in the savings and loan crisis, the real-life political actors who comprise the state have their own political and career interests and are susceptible to a variety of external influences. Thus, while the state has a structural interest in economic stability and therefore in containing collective embezzlement, instrumental influences on state actors can—and periodically do—neutralize that structural interest and derail the regulatory agenda.

## DISCUSSION

We have argued here that much of the insider fraud in the S&L industry in the 1980s constituted variations on "hot deals," "looting," and "covering up," and that some of these financial crimes can be thought of as collective embezzlement. Distinct from the corporate crime in the manufacturing sector first documented by Edwin Sutherland (1983), this collective embezzlement is motivated entirely by personal—not corporate—gain and erodes the institution's financial health.

We have also argued that the state's relationship to such collective embezzlement is quite different than to that of crimes perpetrated on behalf of the corporation. As a number of scholars have noted, the structurally based interest of the state in advancing corporate profits—or at least not interfering with them—helps explain the lenient treatment of corporate crime upon which the white-collar crime literature has generally focused. But to the extent that collective embezzlement undermines corporate profit-making and jeopardizes long-term economic stability, the structural restraints on enforcement do not apply; indeed, structural imperatives would dictate a quick and rigorous response.

However, as we have seen here, the US government response to the first signs of S&L fraud in the mid-1980s was conflicted and contributed to the crisis. Close examination of this response reveals that the savings and loan industry and its individual members were able to shield themselves temporarily through effective lobbying of key members of Congress and other officials. With regard to state theory, this pattern of government collusion in the crisis and intrastate struggle over regulation suggests the need for a more synthetic model, the beginnings of which we have sketched above.

This analysis, however, also has policy implications. First, in contrast to the regulatory catch-22 surrounding the enforcement of social regulations, the state has an unequivocal interest (both long-term and short-term) in containing collective embezzlement. The recognition of this new form of fraud for what it is, and the understanding of its objective relationship to the state and economic stability, might open up new regulatory space for deterrence and rigorous sanctions. After all, the looting described above—and its relationship to the state—is different from bank robbery only in its magnitude and its destabilizing effect on the whole economy. As the former Commissioner of the California Department of Savings and Loans told a Congressional committee, "The best way to rob a bank is to own one" (quoted in US Congress, House Committee on Government Operations 1988:34).

More broadly, this analysis suggests the need to revisit the role of monied interests in the political process, not just for the sake of political democracy but to shore up financial stability in this age of global economic transformation. For, while structural relations between the state and capital may allow—even dictate—a strict response to collective embezzlement, this response is subject to sabotage by those with the resources to woo policymakers with hefty campaign contributions. As one S&L regulator told us,

> "It was always the worst S&Ls in America that were able to get dramatically more political intervention.... If you know you are engaged in fraud, what better return is there than a political contribution" (personal interview).

In concluding, we urgently call for more research in this emerging area. While neither collective embezzlement nor its regulatory neglect are new, the epic proportions of these financial crimes and the increasing dominance of the finance capitalism on which they are based are unprecedented. Future research should build on the rich white-collar crime and state theory traditions to explore further the theoretical and policy implications of these important changes.

ACKNOWLEDGMENTS

The research reported here was supported under award 90-1J-CX-0059 from the National Institute of Justice. Points of view expressed in this document are the authors' and do not represent the official position of the US Department of Justice.



*Literature Cited*

Akerloff GA, Romer PM. 1993. Looting: the economic underworld of bankruptcy for profit. *Brookings Papers on Econ. Activity.* 2:1–73

Alt K, Siglin K. 1990. Unpublished Memorandum on Bank and Thrift Fraud to Senate Banking Committee Members and Staff. 25 July

Althusser L. 1971. *Lenin and Philosophy and Other Essays.* New York: Monthly Rev.

Barnett HC. 1981. Corporate capitalism, corporate crime. *Crime Delinquency* 27 (January): 4–23

Bates J. 1989. Columbia S&L Puts Its Loss at $226.3 Million. *Los Angeles Times.* 26 October 1989: D1-D2

Binstein M. 1987. In the belly of the beast: renegade vs. regulator. *Regardie's* 7 (July 11):45–55

Black WK. 1994. *Why (some) regulators don't think regulation works.* Paper for Annu. Conv. Allied Soc. Sci. Assoc. Boston

Braithwaite J. 1984. *Corporate Crime in the Pharmaceutical Industry.* London: Routledge & Kegan Paul

*Business Week.* 1985. The Casino Society. 16 September:78–90

Calavita KC. 1983. The demise of the Occupational Safety and Health Administration: a case study in symbolic action. *Soc. Probl.* 30:437–448

Calavita KC, Pontell HN. 1990. "Heads I win,

tails you lose:" deregulation, crime and crisis in the savings and loan industry. *Crime Delinquency* 36:309–341

Calavita KC, Pontell HN. 1991. "Other People's Money" revisited: collective embezzlement in the savings and loan and insurance industries. *Soc. Probl.* 38:94–112

Calavita KC, Pontell HN. 1993. Savings and loan fraud as organized crime: toward a conceptual typology of corporate illegality. *Criminology* 31:519–548

Calavita KC, Pontell HN. 1994. The state and white-collar crime: saving the savings and loans. *Law Soc. Rev.* 28(2):297–324

Calavita KC, Pontell HN, Tillman R. 1997. *Big Money Crime: Fraud and Politics in the S&L Crisis.* Berkeley, CA: Univ. Calif. Press. In press

Carson WG. 1981. *The Other Price of Britain's Oil: Safety and Control in the North Sea.* Oxford: Robertson

Carson WG. 1982. Legal control of safety on British offshore oil installations. In *White Collar and Economic Crime,* ed. P Wickham, T Dailey, pp. 173–96. Toronto: Lexington

Clinard MB, Yeager PC, Brissette J, Petrasek D, Harries E. 1979. *Illegal Corporate Behavior.* Washington, DC: US Govt. Printing Off. (USGPO)

Coleman JW. 1987. Toward an integrated theory of white-collar crime. *Am. J. Sociol.* 93:406–39

Cranston R. 1982. Regulation and deregulation: general issues. *Univ. South Wales Law J.* 5:1–29

Cressey D. 1953. *Other People's Money: A Study of the Social Psychology of Embezzlement.* Glencoe, IL: Free Press

Cullen FT, Maakstad WJ, Cavender G. 1987. *Corporate Crime Under Attack: The Ford Pinto Case and Beyond.* Cinncinnati, OH: Anderson

Domhoff GW. 1967. *Who Rules America?* Englewood Cliffs, NJ: Prentice Hall

Domhoff GW. 1979. *The Powers That Be.* New York: Random House

Friedland R, Piven FF, Alford R. 1977. Political conflict, urban structure, and the fiscal crisis. In *Comparative Public Policy: New Approaches and Methods,* ed. D Ashford. Beverly Hills, CA: Sage

Geis G. 1967. The heavy electrical equipment antitrust cases of 1961. In *Criminal Behavior Systems: A Typology,* ed. MB Clinard, R Quinney, pp.140–51. New York: Holt, Rinehart & Winston

Gunningham N. 1987. Negotiated non-compliance: a case study of regulatory failure. *Law & Policy* 9(1):69

Harrison B, Bluestone B. 1988. *The Great U-Turn: Corporate Restructuring and the Polarizing of America.* New York: Basic

Jackson B. 1988. *Honest Graft: Big Money and the American Political Process.* New York: Knopf

Johnston O. 1990. GAO Says S&L Cost Could Rise to $500 Billion. *Los Angeles Times.*7 April 1990: A1

Katz J. 1979. Legality and inequality: plea bargaining in the prosecution of white-collar and common crimes. *Law Soc. Rev.* 13:431–460

Kolko G. 1963. *The Triumph of Conservatism.* Glencoe, IL: Free Press

Kolko G. 1965. *Railroads and Regulations.* Princeton, NJ: Princeton Univ. Press

Lewis M. 1989. *Liar's Poker: Rising Through the Wreckage of Salomon Brothers.* New York: Norton

Los Angeles Times. 1994. CenTrust Chairman Sentenced to 11 Years. 2 December 1994: D2

Lowy M. 1991. *High Rollers: Inside the Savings and Loan Debacle.* New York: Praeger

Mayer M. 1990. *The Greatest Ever Bank Robbery: The Collapse of the Savings and Loan Industry.* New York: Scribners

Miliband R. 1969. *The State in Capitalist Society.* New York: Basic

National Commission on Financial Institution Reform, Recovery and Enforcement. 1993. *Origins and Causes of the S&L Debacle: A Blueprint for Reform. A Report to the President and Congress of the United States.* Washington, DC: USGPO

O'Connor J. 1973. *The Fiscal Crisis of the State.* New York: St. Martin's

Office of Thrift Supervision. 1990. Correlation between insider fraud and reported insolvency. Dallas District Office. Unpubl. rep.

O'Rourke PJ. 1989. Piggy banks. *Rolling Stones* 24(August 1989):43

O'Shea J. 1991. *Daisy Chain: How Borrowed Billions Sank a Texas S&L.* New York: Pocket

Pizzo S, Fricker M, Muolo P. 1991. *Inside Job: The Looting of America's Savings and Loans.* New York: Harper Collins

Plotkin S, Scheuerman WE. 1994. *Private Interest, Public Spending: Balanced-Budget Conservatism and the Fiscal Crisis.* Boston: South End

Poulantzas N. 1969. The problem of the capitalist state. *New Left Rev.* 58(November-December):67–87

Resolution Trust Corporation. 1992. *RTC Rev.* August, 1992. Washington, DC: USGPO

Shapiro S. 1984. *Wayward Capitalist: Target of the Securities and Exchange Commission.* New Haven, CT: Yale Univ. Press

Snider L. 1991. The regulatory dance: understanding reform processes in corporate crime. *Int. J. Sociol. Law* 19:209–36

Sutherland EH. 1983. *White Collar Crime: The Uncut Version.* New Haven: Yale Univ. Press

Trillin C. 1989. Zsa Zsa's Crowd Knows Why the Rich and Famous Deserve a Capital-Gains Cut. *Los Angeles Times.* 4 October 1989: B7

US Congress, House Committee on Banking, Finance and Urban Affairs. 1990. Effectiveness of Law Enforcement Against Financial Crime. Hearings before the Committee. Part 1. 101st Congress, 2nd Session

US Congress, House Committee on Government Operations, Subcommittee on Commerce, Consumer, and Monetary Affairs. 1987a. *Fraud and Abuse by Insiders, Borrowers, and Appraisers in the California Thrift Industry.* Hearings before the Subcommittee. June 13. 100th Congress, 1st Session

US Congress, House Committee on Government Operations, Subcommittee on Commerce, Consumer, and Monetary Affairs. 1987b. *Adequacy of Federal Efforts to Combat Fraud, Abuse, and Misconduct in Federally Insured Financial Institutions.* Hearings before the Subcommittee. November 19. 100th Congress, 1st Session

US Congress, House Committee on Government Operations. 1988. *Combating Fraud, Abuse, and Misconduct in the Nation's Financial Institutions: Current Federal Efforts are Inadequate. H. R. 100–1088*

US Congress, House Committee on Standards of Official Conduct. 1989. Report of the Special Outside Counsel in the Matter of Speaker James C. Wright (Phelan Report). February 21. 101st Congress, 1st Session

US General Accounting Office. 1989. *Thrift Failures. Costly Failures Resulted from Regulatory Violations and Unsafe Practices. Report to Congress. GAO/AFMD-89-62*

Waldman M. 1990. *Who Robbed America? A Citizen's Guide to the S&L Scandal.* New York: Random House

Walters V. 1985. The politics of occupational health and safety: interviews with workers' health and safety representatives and company doctors. *Can. Rev. Sociol. Anthropol.* 22:58–79

Wheeler S, Rothman ML. 1982. The organization as weapon in white collar crime. *Mich. Law Rev.* 80:1403–1426

Yeager PC. 1991. *The Limits of Law: The Public Regulation of Private Pollution.* Cambridge, UK: Cambridge Univ. Press

United States Code cited: 18 USC Section 2; 18 USC Section 215; 18 USC Section 371; 18 USC Sections 656, 961c; 18 USC Section 1001; 18 USC Section 1005; 18 USC Section 1344

*Annu. Rev. Sociol. 1997. 23:39–61*


# MODELING THE RELATIONSHIPS BETWEEN MACRO FORMS OF SOCIAL CONTROL

*Allen E Liska*
Department of Sociology, State University of New York, Albany, Albany, New York 12222; e-mail: AEL62@CNSIBM.albany.edu

KEY WORDS: social control, threat, conflict, welfare, mental-health

ABSTRACT

The last decade has witnessed a plethora of macro studies of various forms of social control ranging from lynching to hospitalization. Unfortunately, these specific areas of research tend to be isolated from each other and do not constitute a recognizable literature. This paper shifts the focus of study from substantive forms of social control to theoretical issues that cut across them. One such issue is the relationship between forms of social control. First, the paper explicates this issue. Second, the paper reviews and critiques three specific research literatures on the relationships between various forms of social control that are isolated from each other although they bear on the same theoretical questions. Third, the paper argues that bivariate relationships between forms of social control are not meaningful theoretically in that they are not clearly derived from general theories of social control. Fourth, the paper argues that we should focus on the causal processes and structures that underlie the relationships between forms of social control and explicate their implications for these relationships.

## INTRODUCTION

Although always an integral part of sociology, the study of social control has waxed and waned. Originally, the concept was defined broadly as any structure, process, relationship, or act that contributes to the social order; indeed, the concepts of social order and social control were indistinguishable (Meier 1982, Gibbs 1989). A consensus is now emerging that distinguishes social control from the social order it is meant to explain and that distinguishes among social



0360-0572/97/0815-0039$08.00

control processes. One basic distinction is between internal and external control processes. The former refers to a process whereby people adhere to social norms because they believe in them, feeling good, self-righteous, and proud when they do adhere to them and feeling bad, self-critical, and guilty when they do not. This process is sometimes termed "socialization." External control refers to a social process whereby people conform to norms or rules because they are rewarded with status, prestige, money, and freedom when they do adhere to them and are punished with the loss of them when they do not. This process is sometimes termed coercive, external, or just social control.

Only recently have researchers studied coercive social control as a dependent variable. These studies can be categorized as either micro or macro. Using individuals as the units of analysis, micro studies examine how various control activities such as arresting, prosecuting, and sentencing are affected by the legal, psychological, and social characteristics of people. These studies are reasonably well organized and synthesized, constituting a clearly defined body of literature. Using collectives, e.g. organizations and communities, as the units of analysis, macro studies examine how social control rates are affected by culture and social structure (Liska 1987, Horwitz 1990). Numerous studies examine the structure and functioning of the criminal justice system as the major social control bureaucracy, including studies of prison size and admission rates, prosecution rates, arrest rates, and police contact. Studies also examine the structure and functioning of the mental health system, focusing on factors that influence its size and social composition, as well as the structure and functioning of the social welfare system, focusing on factors that influence its size and scope, such as eligibility restrictions and payments. Additionally, studies examine various forms of collective action as social control, such as the historical emergence of the KKK, the historical pattern of lynchings, and the emergence of the Guardian Angels.

Most of these studies focus on only one organization, policy, or program of either the criminal justice, mental health, or welfare systems. They are organized or categorized by substantive forms of control (e.g. lynching, arrests, imprisonment, hospitalization, and welfare), rather than by theoretical propositions. For the most part these topical literatures are isolated from each other. Although they sometimes address similar issues, they do not build on each other or even cite each other. Researchers studying imprisonment are criminologists interested in prisons; researchers studying lynching are specialists in race relations or collective behavior; researchers studying mental hospital admissions are interested in mental health; and researchers studying welfare are experts in social services. Because macro social control research is balkanized into isolated pockets around diverse forms of control, theoretical issues that cut across these forms are blurred, and the boundaries that define the study of macro social control are diffuse and vague. Thus, although macro social control research has mushroomed, it has not contributed much to the development of macro social control theories over the last two decades.

In this paper I attempt to develop theoretical and empirical bridges between macro forms of social control as one strategy for overcoming the present diffusion or balkanization of the field. I first review three small and isolated literatures that examine the empirical relationships between macro forms of social control. I conclude that empirical generalities across and even within these literatures are difficult to uncover. Second, I examine the theoretical significance of relationships between forms of control, that is, the extent to which the magnitude and direction of such relationships can be derived from general theories of control. I conclude that relationships between forms of control are not easily derived from general theories of control, making empirical studies of these relationships theoretically marginal. Third, drawing on these three empirical literatures and on general theoretical perspectives of control, I model the underlying processes of control and then derive their implications for the magnitude and direction of the relationships between forms of control.

## RELATIONSHIPS BETWEEN FORMS OF CONTROL

I begin by examining the existing research literature on the relationships between forms of control. It is organized into three distinct bodies of research more or less isolated from each other: the relationship between the criminal justice system (CJS) and the mental health system (MHS), such as between prison and mental hospital populations; the relationship between the criminal justice system and the welfare system (WS), such as between prison admission rates and welfare eligibility restrictions; and the relationship between levels of formal and informal forms of lethal control, such as between legal executions and lynchings.

### *Criminal Justice And Mental Health Systems*

The relationship between the CJ and MH systems has been addressed through three research strategies: historical studies of the emergence of the two systems, social indicator studies of the covariation between the populations and admission rates of the two systems, and survey studies of the prevalence of mental illness among the prison population and the prevalence of criminality among the mental asylum population.

HISTORICAL STUDIES Social historians (Rothman 1971, Foucault 1965, 1978, Scull 1977, Ignatieff 1978, Garland 1985, Gillis 1989, Brown & Warner 1992) have examined the emergence of social control institutions in Europe and the United States during the seventeenth, eighteenth, and nineteenth centuries, a period that saw the rise of contemporary social control institutions such as asylums, prisons, reformatories, orphanages, and almshouses. While agreeing that these institutions were part of a general social reform movement, social historians disagree on the explanation. On one side of the debate, Rothman (1971) argues that as America shifted from an agricultural and a rural society to an industrial and an urban one, traditional forms of social control such as the family and religion ceased to be effective. In response, social reformers sought to build institutions that would instill the habits of discipline, obedience, and hard work of a bygone era. While these institutions may have achieved more control than reform, that was not the intention of the reformers. On the other side of the debate, Marxists (Ignatieff 1978, Scull 1977) embed the social reformers in the class structure of capitalism. Ignoring the reformer's proclaimed intentions, they explain the emergence of these control institutions as a concerted effort by elites to discipline the masses to the rhythms of capitalism.

Whatever their disagreements, social historians tend to agree that contemporary criminal justice and mental health systems emerged together as complementary responses by authorities and elites to the threat of urban disorder associated with the macro processes of urbanization, industrialization, and capitalism. Yet, other than hypothesizing that asylums and prisons emerged during similar periods in response to similar social conditions, these studies do not explore how these control bureaucracies function together to control threatening populations and actions. One exception is the recent work of Sutton (1990, 1991). Studying social control during the Progressive era, he argues that because of scarce resources, increases in some forms of control led to decreases in others. Specifically, increases in private institutions (more welfare oriented) for controlling youth led to decreases in public institutions (more coercive) for controlling them; decreases in almshouses led to increases in asylums; and increases in pensions led to decreases in asylums.

SOCIAL INDICATOR RESEARCH In the 1950s and 1960s considerable debate occurred on the medicalization of social problems, particularly crime. During the first half of the twentieth century, psychiatrists medicalized social problems, successfully arguing that the cause of many social problems, like crime, lies in the psychological malfunctioning of people and that the solution lies in the treatment of these people by medical specialists in treatment centers. Consequently, by the mid-1950s the US mental asylum population significantly increased to 500,000 (Morrissey 1982), compared to the US prison population of less than 200,000 (Bureau of Justice Statistics). However, from the mid-1960s these trends reversed. The asylum population significantly decreased and the prison population significantly increased, so that by the late 1970s the asylum population was down to 150,000 and the prison population was up to 300,000. The asylum population has continued to decrease slightly and the prison population has continued to rapidly expand, approaching 1,000,000 by the mid-1990s. These trend reversals in both populations have stimulated questions of the extent to which prisons and asylums are functional social control alternatives.

Using archival data, social indicators research addresses this question through an examination of the temporal and cross-sectional covariation between these two forms of control. Drawing on data from eighteen European and six non-European countries, Penrose (1939) originally suggested that social control systems evolve from physically controlling people (prisons) to medically treating them (asylums), thereby suggesting an inverse relationship between prison and asylum populations. In what is perhaps the first rigorous study of this question, Biles & Mulligan (1973) report a negative correlation (−78) between the 1968 US prison population and the number of hospital beds; but in a time series of the United States from 1930 to 1970, Grabosky (1980) reports a positive correlation (.42) between the size of the prison and mental hospital populations.

These studies have continued to yield inconsistent results, although they have become methodologically more sophisticated. Among the best are recent studies by Inverarity & Grattet (1989) and Sutton (1991). Using a time series from 1948 to 1985, Inverarity & Grattet report that the unemployment rate (taking the unemployed as a threatening population) affects the prison population and admission rates, the asylum population and admission rates, the welfare recipient rate, and the military personnel rate; but they report no evidence that these forms of control affect each other. On the other hand, using a pooled cross-section of states from 1880 to 1923, Sutton (1991) reports that a decrease in the adult almshouse population leads to an increase in the asylum population.

SURVEY RESEARCH Since the mid-1970s a third strategy has emerged for examining the relationship between the criminal justice and mental health systems. Stimulated by the recent deinstitutionalization of asylums, this strategy examines the mechanisms through which problematic populations move from one system to another (Steadman 1979, Arvanites 1992 1988, Cirincioe et al 1994). Because asylums today do not operate at full capacity, they provide space for overflows from other control bureaucracies, such as the criminal justice system. Various studies examine the extent to which threatening populations that in the past might have been admitted directly into asylums are now first processed into the criminal justice system. Rather than maintaining inmates with mental disabilities within an increasingly overcrowded criminal justice system, it seems likely that criminal justice authorities would be interested in transferring them to other control systems, such as the mental health system. Thus, the criminal justice experience of the mentally ill should have increased after deinstitutionalization.

One set of studies examines the criminal justice experience (such as being arrested, imprisoned, and jailed) of people admitted into asylums before and after deinstitutionalization, from the late 1960s to the late 1970s. Studies of arrest seem to support the above conclusion. In one of the first studies, Melick et al (1979) report that in New York, patients with prior arrests increased from 32% to 40% between 1968 and 1975. In a study of five states, Arvanites (1986) reports that patients with prior arrests increased from 29.8% to 46.6% between 1968 and 1978. The data for imprisonment are more inconclusive. In one of the best studies of this period, Steadman et al (1984) report that for six states between 1968 and 1978 prison inmates with prior mental hospitalization increased from 7.9% to 10.6%. However, reflecting the inconsistency in this literature, they also report that an increase occurred for only three of the states, but that it was large enough to outweigh the decrease for the other three states, yielding a net increase. If the mentally ill are over-arrested but not over-imprisoned, where are they going? Some researchers suggest that they are being warehoused in city and county jails. Studies suggest that approximately 5% to 20% of jail inmates are psychotic (Teplin 1990, Palermo et al 1992, Arvanites 1992). While the evidence is far from conclusive, researchers suggest that when the criteria for admission to mental asylums were strengthened, practically closing the front door of asylums, authorities managed the less seriously mentally ill within local jails and transferred the more serious into mental asylums through the side door via legal mechanisms, such as incompetency to stand trial.

In sum, over the years three bodies of research have emerged that address the relationships between the CJS and the MHS. Organized around disciplinary and research methods, these bodies of research coexist in splendid isolation from one another, although they address similar theoretical issues. Historical studies suggest that the criminal justice and mental health systems and many other forms of social control emerged together as complementary forms of control in response to conditions that threatened the seventeenth, eighteenth, and nineteenth century social order, particularly the position of ruling elites. Yet, over the years some forms have declined and others have expanded. Many scholars have come to study these forms, particularly the criminal justice and mental health systems, as functional alternatives. This work is organized by research methods: one examines the temporal and cross-sectional covariation between them, and the other examines the consequences of constricting one system (MHS) for the structure and functioning of the other (CJS).

In the interest of theoretical integration, it is important to conceptualize these three research areas as different strategies that address different aspects of the same theoretical issue. All three strategies implicitly, if not explicitly, assume a model where social threat to the social order affects the criminal justice and the mental health systems. Three causal processes are assumed.

One, an increase in social threat leads to an increase in both the criminal justice and mental health systems. This is the causal process assumed by the social historians in their studies of the emergence of social control institutions during the seventeenth, eighteenth, and nineteenth centuries. Two, an increase in either the criminal justice or mental health system leads to a decrease in social threat, which in turn leads to a decrease in other forms of social control. This is the process implicitly assumed by the social indicator researchers in their studies of functional alternatives. Three, tightening the restrictions for admittance into one system (MH) decreases the effect of social threat on that system; this in turn increases the effect of social threat on other control systems (CJ) and increases transfers from the constricted system (MH) to the other system (CJ), which then controls the problem populations of both systems. This is the process assumed by the survey researchers in their studies of the social composition of the criminal justice and mental health systems and in their studies of transfers from the criminal justice system to the mental health system before and after deinstitutionalization of the latter system.

### *Criminal Justice and Social Welfare Systems*

Welfare refers to those social arrangements that distribute benefits according to need. In modern societies the state is the major purveyor of these arrangements. There are at least three ways in which modern states distribute these benefits: occupational welfare, the redistribution of wealth through the nontaxation of occupational benefits, such as medical insurance; fiscal welfare, the redistribution of benefits through the taxation system; and public welfare, the direct redistribution of benefits. Discussion of welfare as social control is generally restricted to public welfare, particularly to those forms of public welfare (general assistance, aid to families with dependent children, and unemployment insurance) that appear to benefit the poor.

Up to the economic crisis of the 1970s, growth in social welfare was viewed as a by-product of industrialization, and variation in social welfare was viewed as the outcome of policies to balance unemployment and inflation. Since the crisis of the 1970s, during which high inflation and high unemployment coexisted, social welfare growth and variation have been viewed as more problematic. Viewing social welfare as primarily a governmental response to the social needy, one body of research examines the conditions by which the social needy influence governmental policy (unionization, labor political parties), and another body of research examines the structure of the state itself (centralized bureaucracy) as influencing government policy (Skocpal & Amenta 1985). Viewing social welfare as primarily a governmental response to control social disruption, particularly disruption detrimental to the interests of economic and political elites, another body of research (informed by conflict theory) examines the conditions (mobilization of workers, unemployment rates, urban riots) that threaten the positions and interests of economic and political elites; this research views welfare as an effort to "buy off" the disadvantaged, committing them to an unequal social order.

Piven & Cloward (1971) stimulated considerable controversy by arguing that the public welfare expansion, particularly of the AFDC program in the United States during the late 1960s and early 1970s, was a response to the urban riots during that period—an attempt to pacify an economically deprived and threatening population. Studies by Issac & Kelly (1981), Jennings (1983), Schram & Turbett (1983), and Chamlin (1989) provide various degrees of support for this thesis.

While conceiving of some forms of welfare as a form of social control, researchers have published very little on the relationship between welfare and other forms of social control. Various scholars (Box 1987, Box & Hale 1985) argue, however, that the relationship is negative. They point to cross-national comparisons that suggest that nations spending a lot on criminal justice spend very little on welfare and vice versa and to temporal trends that suggest that times of high criminal justice spending are times of low welfare spending and vice versa. For the most part these conclusions are based on only casual observations.

I have been able to locate just a few systematic studies. Using a US time series, Inverarity & Grattet (1989) report little direct effect of welfare benefits (AFDC payments) on prison admissions, controlling for unemployment, crime rates, age composition, and prison releases. They suggest that these social control bureaucracies may function independently of each other, affected more by their own internal dynamics than by the dynamics of other social control bureaucracies. Inverarity & McCarthy (1988) argue that the issue may be more complex. They report that prison admission is more sensitive to unemployment rates in the competitive than in the monopolistic sectors of an economy. In the latter sector the CJS is less important for social control, and the unemployed are less threatening because they are more likely to be unemployed temporarily rather than permanently and they are likely to be eligible for welfare benefits. Coercive control is reserved for the more marginal workers in the competitive sector. This research, thus, clearly suggests an inverse relationship between the CJS and WS. When economic activity is monopolistic, welfare becomes the predominate form of control; whereas when it is competitive, coercion becomes the predominate form of control.

Following up on this research, Colvin (1990) also suggests that certain forms of control may be more functional for certain modes of production and certain labor markets. The more monopolistic and primary the markets, the more likely welfare will be the form of control; the more competitive and secondary the markets, the more likely coercion (prison) will be the form of control. Using a cross-section of US counties, Colvin reports that increases in the degree to which markets are primary increases welfare rates and benefits and decreases imprisonment rates, but that the degree to which markets are monopolistic does not predictably affect either welfare or imprisonment rates (also see Lessan 1991, Schissel 1992). In sum, while there is considerable casual discussion of public welfare and imprisonment as alternative forms of social control, there has been very little systematic research. The research that has appeared provides no evidence that welfare and criminal justice systems directly or indirectly affect each other; instead, it suggests that the covariation between them depends on underlying causal conditions. If welfare rates are positively affected and imprisonment rates are negatively affected by the same conditions, then welfare and imprisonment rates should negatively covary, not because they are functional alternatives, but because they are affected in opposite directions by the same social conditions.

### *Legal Executions and Lynchings*

Recent years have witnessed a renewed research interest in lynching, particularly in the relationship between lynchings and legal state executions, in the South from the post–Civil War era to the Great Depression (Reed 1972). Two general hypotheses have been advanced. Some researchers hypothesize that legal executions and lynchings are functional alternatives or substitutable forms of social control that satisfy people's sense for justice and revenge. As executions increase, people's sense of justice and revenge is satisfied and lynchings decrease; as executions decrease, people's sense of justice and revenge is satisfied through various forms of self-help and vigilantism, including lynching (Phillips 1987). Other researchers argue that both executions and lynchings are attempts by ruling classes to manage the existing social order, and thus they hypothesize that legal executions and lynchings positively covary. As social threat, conflict, and tension increase, both lynchings and legal executions increase. While scholars have debated this issue for some time, researchers have recently addressed it empirically.

Using a North Carolina time series from 1889 to 1918, Phillips (1986, 1987) stimulated interest in this issue. He reports that lynchings and legal executions were positively related from 1889 to about 1903 and have been unrelated after that time. He argues that both were political responses of white authorities to racial threat and conflict during the Reconstruction era. When the conflict and threat were reduced through the political disenfranchisement of blacks around the turn of the century, both lynchings and executions ceased to perform a political function; thus, they decreased and ceased to covary.

Using an even more detailed and longer time series of both North Carolina and Georgia, Beck et al (1989) challenge these conclusions. For North Carolina they report no relationship between lynchings and executions either before or after disenfranchisement, and for Georgia they report a positive relationship between them only before disenfranchisement, providing some support for the conflict perspective. The racial threat hypothesis also suggests that after disenfranchisement, which decreased the black political threat, the total level of lethal violence against blacks should have decreased. For this hypothesis, they find no support for North Carolina and some support for Georgia. Beck et al (1989) conclude that there is some support for the threat hypothesis and little support for the functional hypothesis. Indeed, they argue that executions and lynchings were not substitute responses to the same social threat.

Massey & Myers (1989) examine the interrelationships between lynching, execution, and incarceration rates of black males in Georgia from 1882 to 1935. Upon controlling for drifts and trends in the three time series, they estimate cross-level correlations from 0 to 10 year lags between these three forms of social control, and they find just about no statistically significant correlations.

In the most recent research, Tolnay & Beck (1995) examine the covariation between legal executions and lynchings over time (1882–1930) and cross-sectionally for Southern states. While the time series suggests a negative effect of legal executions on lynchings, which is stronger in some periods than others, the overall effect is not statistically significant; while the cross-sectional analysis suggests a positive effect of executions on lynchings, which is stronger for some periods than others, the overall effect is not strong or statistically significant. (See related work by Soule 1992 and Olzak 1990.)

In sum, there is little evidence supporting the functional hypothesis that lynching and legal executions negatively covary. Only some mixed evidence supports the conflict perspective that they positively covary and that the strength of that covariation depends on level of social threat. Perhaps as Massey & Meyers (1989) conclude, it is time to rethink the traditional assumption that forms of repressive social control are interdependent.

## EMPIRICAL COMMONALITIES

I now briefly summarize the findings across the three substantive areas: criminal justice and mental health systems, criminal justice and welfare systems, and lynching and legal executions.

There is little to no empirical support that these forms of social control negatively covary. National time series analyses of the relationships between imprisonment and mental asylum admission rates and between imprisonment and welfare rates provide no support; state time series of the relationship between lynching and legal executions provide no support; and state cross-sectional analyses of the relationships between mental asylum and prison admission rates and between prison admission and welfare rates provide no support. While some research does document the flow of people between the mental health and criminal justice systems, the number of people involved is too small to produce a noticeable effect on the overall relationship between these two systems.

Some empirical evidence does however suggest that these forms of social control respond to the same causal conditions and thus positively covary. Historical research indicates that forms of today's criminal justice, mental health, and welfare systems emerged in about the same era in response to the same social conditions. Some time series research (Phillips 1986 & 1987, Beck et al 1989) suggests that lynchings and legal executions positively covary in response to the same social conditions (political threat and disenfranchisement); and a few time series and cross-sectional studies (Inverarity & Garattet 1989, Inverarity & McCarthy 1988, Colvin 1990) suggest that prison admission and welfare rates respond to similar causal conditions (unemployment in monopolistic industries and competitive markets). Thus they covary to the extent to which these causal conditions covary. Yet, even these studies show only a weak positive covariation.

If the relationships between forms of social control are weak, does this mean that these forms have little in common and might better be studied individually, and thus that the study of social control is nothing more than the aggregation of the study of specific forms of control? Indeed, Massey & Myers (1989) suggest that many forms of social control vary independently of each other, reflecting their internal organizational dynamics. Perhaps. Yet, we should not equate inconsistent and weak empirical relationships between forms of control with the lack of theoretical commonalities among them. Theoretically, commonalities among forms of social control should refer not to the strength or sign of the empirical relationships between them, but to the causal processes and structures underlying them. Focusing on these common processes highlights the theoretical commonalities among forms of control and, in principle, should allow us to theoretically derive the direction and magnitude of the relationships between them. Dependent on the complexity of such processes, positive or negative relationships and strong or weak relationships may be equally significant theoretically. I now turn to four major theoretical perspectives of macro social control for guidance on such common underlying social processes and their implications for the relationships between forms of social control.

## THEORETICAL PERSPECTIVES OF SOCIAL CONTROL

I first review the two classic macro perspectives of social control coming out of the 1950s, 1960s, and 1970s (functionalism and conflict theory) and then two emerging perspectives (social movement theories and the new structuralism) coming out of 1980s.

Conceiving of society as integrated and orderly, classic functionalism assumes that there is a general consensus on goals and values, that general needs for survival can be identified, that social structures function to maintain society's values-goals-needs, and that social structures can be explained by these functions (Durkheim 1938). While "modern or neo" functionalism may not make many of these assumptions (Alexander 1985), much contemporary social control theory and research is guided by them. Social control is thought to maintain society's values-goals-needs and indeed is thought to be explained by them. To the extent that the level and pattern of social control are effective—functional—they are assumed to persist and remain stable. These assumptions lead to hypotheses about social control and the relationship between forms of control. Assuming that social control remains stable at a level that is functional for a society, then as one form of control decreases for whatever reason, other forms will increase, or as one form satisfies society's needs for a specific level of control, other forms will decrease (the functional equivalence, tradeoff, or hydraulic hypothesis). While the direction of the relationship between forms of social control seems clear (negative), the process whereby an increase in one form leads to a decrease in another is not so clear. Traditional versions of the theory couched in the language and logic of system needs and functional equivalence are extremely ambiguous about causal processes; indeed, there is even some reluctance to talk in these terms. On the other hand, some versions of the perspective (Stinchcomb 1968) try to capture traditional notions of functionality in terms of causal feedback loops. In such a model (Figure 1, Model A), it is argued that an increase in one form of control (SC1) is functional to the extent to which it reduces social threat (ST), which in turn decreases other forms of social control (SC2), yielding a negative relationship between them.

Focusing on the fractures, conflicts, and competing interests within society, the conflict perspective assumes an uneven distribution of self interests in social control and of the power to implement them. It thus assumes that social control reflects the interests of the powerful (elites, authorities, and majorities) and that it is part of an overall strategy by them to manage the actions, events, and people that threaten their interests. Therefore, as the threat to their interest increases, the level and scope of social control increases (Blalock 1967, Turk 1969, Spitzer 1975, Quinney 1977, Hawkins 1987, 1994, Liska 1992, 1994).

Regarding the relationships between forms of social control, the conflict perspective is also ambiguous. Assuming that all forms of social control serve the interests of the powerful, on one hand it implies that all forms covary together; that is, an increase in the actions, events, and people that threaten the interests of the powerful leads to an increase in most, if not all, forms of social

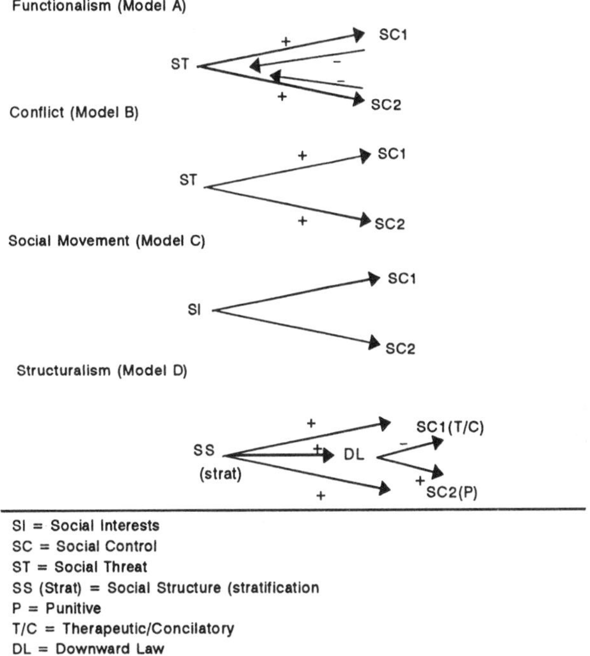


*Figure 1* Causal Models underlying theoretical perspectives.

control (Figure 1, Model B). On the other hand, it implies that if some forms of control are particularly successful at protecting the interests of the powerful, then other extant forms may decline and new forms may not emerge; that is, an increase in some forms of social control by decreasing threat may lead to a decrease in others, yielding a negative relationship between forms of social control, similar to the functional model (Figure 1, Model A).

Loosely drawing on both conflict, symbolic interaction, and social constructionist theories, the more recent social movements literature conceives of society as fluid and changing. It focuses on the social processes through which social interests and cultural identities emerge and galvanize into social movements and through which social movements both define and change social institutions and organizations. In contrast to more traditional conflict theories, the emphasis is less on threat to established interests than on the processes through which interests come to be defined, recognized, and mobilized. A vast body of studies examines the social processes through which social interests emerge to control drugs, alcohol, mental illness, and delinquency (Gusfield 1963, Platt 1969, Hagen & Leon 1977, Sutton 1988, Warner & Brown 1992), though which these interests galvanize into social movements, and through which these movements configure and reorganize the institutions and organizations of social control. A particular concern is the emergence of interests that galvanized into the Progressive movement and the processes by which these interests reconfigured the social control of juveniles and the mentally ill.

While this body of research examines various social movements that influence multiple forms of social control, the underlying theory remains sketchy. Research emphasizes uncovering the specific social and historical contexts of specific movements, rather than extrapolating generalities from these contexts and movements, such as the relationships between forms of social control. Some movements are very specific, such as the anti-alcohol movement (Garfield 1963), having few implications for other forms of control. Some are very general and far reaching, such as the Progressive movement, having implications for various control bureaucracies (e.g. delinquency, crime, mental health, and drugs) and thus for the relationships between them. With some exceptions (Sutton 1990, 1991), these relationships are not construed as problematic issues. Forms of social control are thought simply to emerge and covary to the extent to which emerging social interests find expression in them. Reflecting this focus, we substitute social interests (SI) for social threat in the model; reflecting the nature of the theory, we do not specify the signs of the causal paths from social interests to forms of social control (Figure 1, Model C).

The 1980s also witnessed a renewed interest in enduring structured social relations (e.g. Blau 1977). As exemplified in the work of Black (1976, 1984, 1993) and Horwitz (1990), structural theories embed the degree and form of social control in the structural characteristics of social relationships. Explanations of social control are couched in terms of these social relationships with minimal reference to human motives, values, and interests (or perceived threats to them). This perspective directs attention to different forms of control by explicitly developing typologies for classifying them. Black (1976), for example, describes four forms of social control: penal, compensory, conciliatory, and therapeutic; and Horwitz (1990) further develops these and others.

These forms of social control are embedded in general patterns of social relationships. Because many of these general patterns affect multiple forms of control, the perspective has implications for the relationships between them. As certain structural social relationships increase, some forms of social control increase and others decrease. For example, Black (1976) argues that as relational distance increases, remedial forms of social control (conciliatory and therapeutic) increase and accusational forms (penal and compensatory) decrease; as stratification increases, conciliatory forms decrease; as upward law (upper status victimizes lower status) increases, therapeutic and compensation forms increase and penal forms decrease; and as downward law (low status victimizes upper status) increases, therapeutic and compensation forms decrease and penal forms increase.

While selected bivariate propositions have clear implications for the direction of the relationships between forms of social control, the implications of the overall structure of the theory are not so clear (Greenberg 1983). For example, stratification increases penal, therapeutic, and compensative forms, implying a positive relationship between them; yet, stratification also increases vertical law (upward and downward law) relative to horizontal law (disputes among equals), which decreases therapeutic/compensative forms and increases punitive forms, thereby implying a negative relationship between them. In other words, the direct effect of stratification on penal and therapeutic/compensative forms implies a positive relationship between them, but the indirect effect of stratification on them through downward law implies a negative relationship between them (Figure 1, Model D). Because some bivariate propositions (e.g. the effects of stratification) imply a positive relationship between some forms of control and some bivariate positions (e.g. the effects of downward law) imply a negative relationship between these same forms, the implications of these bivariate propositions taken together are problematic. The strength and direction of the relationship between SC1 and SC2 in Figure 1, Model D, can only be derived by fomulating the problem in multivariate terms and then by specifying theoretically the strength and direction of the relevant causal parameters or by estimating them empirically.

In sum, each of the perspectives identifies commonalities in the casual processes that underlie macro forms of control. There is even some overlap and convergence among the perspectives as to the importance of social threat, although they differ on the sources and objects of that threat. Nonetheless, their assumptions and conceptualizations of the underlying processes (social threat or whatever) are ambiguous about its implications for the direction and magnitude of the relationships between forms of control.

The functionalist perspective, with its concern for functional alternatives, suggests a negative relationship between forms of social control but is unclear about the causal process by which an increase in one form leads to a decrease in others. Some versions of the conflict perspective seem to suggest a positive relationship, but others seem to suggest a negative relationship between forms of social control. The structural perspective, conceptualized as a series of bivariate propositions, suggests direct and indirect effects that sometimes imply inconsistent relationships between many forms of control. And the social movement perspective does not seem to formulate general hypotheses that specify the relationships between forms of social control. Grounding its work in specific historical contexts, it implies that the relationships between forms of control depend on specific historical contexts. It seems that the general theoretical perspectives of social control are much better at explaining specific forms of control than the relationships between them. This is one source of the balkanization problem.

## MODELING SOCIAL THREAT PROCESSES

The problem in deriving the implications of these perspectives is that they are indeed very general perspectives. While focusing attention on some underlying processes, sometimes multiple processes and sometimes inconsistent ones, they are more suggestive than deductive. Hence, the theoretical meaning of the direction and magnitude of a relationship between forms of control is not always clear. Drawing on these perspectives, I now try to more explicitly model specific social control processes and to extrapolate their implications for the relationships between forms of control. My goal is not to develop the model. Rather, it is to argue that by explicitly modeling underlying social processes, we can derive their implications for the relationships between forms of control; that these implications are not always simple but can be very sensitive to slight variations in these processes; and that by expressing these relationships in terms of underlying social processes, the relationships become theoretically meaningful.

I focus on social threat processes because they are central to most perspectives of social control. While disagreeing on the sources and consequences of threat, they agree on its significance. The conflict perspective and to some extent the social movement tradition focus on the conditions that are threatening to some social groups and not others, reflecting assumptions about tensions and conflicts in society; and the functional and structural perspectives focus on conditions that are threatening to most people and groups (e.g. violent crime and war), reflecting assumptions about social consensus.

At this point it is useful to distinguish and model the relationships between perceived social threat and its structural sources. Perhaps because perceived threat is so rarely measured in the macro literature, it is not distinguished from its structural sources. Both are used somewhat loosely and are interchangeable in the literature. Yet, there is no reason to assume that social conditions lead to social control unless they are perceived as threatening to economic and political elites, organizational authorities, or in some cases majorities. I thus explicate models in which perceived social threat (PST) mediates the effect of social structural sources of threat (SS) on forms of social control (SC) and in which the relationships between forms of control are expressed in terms of model processes.

In linking the relationships between forms of control to underlying social processes (social threat), I draw on the logic of causal modeling. I distinguish

Model A

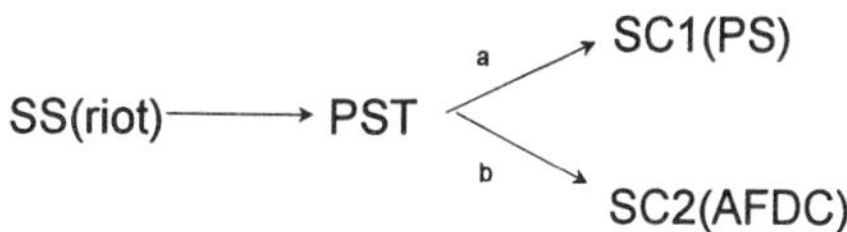


Model B

SS(CR) → PST
a → SC1(PS)
b ←
c → SC2(IR)

*Figure 2* Threat models. (SS, social structure; PST, perceived social control; PS, police size; AFDC, aid to families of dependent children; CR, crime rate; IR, imprisonment rate.

recursive from nonrecursive models. The former refers to models in which casuality is unidimensional. In terms of the models to follow, the sources of the covariation between forms of control are treated as exogenous variables: They affect forms of control but are not affected by them. Nonrecursive refers to models that include feedback loops. In terms of the models to follow, SS, PST, and forms of SC are treated as endogenous variables that are part of feedback loops.

## *Recursive Models*

In recursive models the implications of social processes for the variation among forms of control and for the covariation between them can be derived and expressed via the principles of path analysis. Thus if urban riots affect perceived social threat (PST), which in turn affects some agencies of the criminal justice system (police size) [as suggested by Jackson (1989)] and some programs of the social welfare system (AFDC) [as suggested by Pivan & Cloward (1971)], then we should expect these agencies and programs to be related. The exact magnitude and direction of the relationship can be derived from the principles of path analysis. For example, in Figure 2 Model A, the effect of SS (urban riots) on SC1 (police size) equals the effect of SS on PST times the effect of PST on SC1 (police size); the effect of SS on SC2 (AFDC) equals the effect of SS on PST times the effect of PST on SC2 (AFDC); and the correlation between SC1 (police size) and SC2 (AFDC) equals the effect of PST on SC1 times the effect of PST or SC2. If the effect of SS on PST equals .6, if the effect of PST on SC1 equals .5, and if the effect of PST on SC2 equals .4, then the effect of SS on SC1 equals .30 (.6 × .5), the effect of SS on SC2 equals .24 (.6 × .4), and the model derived correlation between SC1 (police size) and SC2 (AFDC) equals .20 (.5 × .4).

## *Nonrecursive Models*

To some degree, all of the theoretical perspectives assume, explicitly or implicitly, that some forms of social control affect perceived social threat either directly or indirectly by affecting structural sources of threat; yet, none of them elaborate the underlying causal processes or their implications for the relationships between forms of social control.

In doing so, it is important to distinguish clearly the structural sources of perceived threat from perceived threat itself. Some forms of social control may affect both, some may affect one but not the other, and some may affect neither. It is equally important to distinguish the direction of the effect. Some forms of control may reduce perceived social threat, and some may increase it. Consider the size of the police force (per capita). We generally assume that police size, via processes of deterrence, decreases many structural sources of perceived social threat (e.g. crime rates), thereby reducing perceived social threat. Police may also directly affect perceptions of social threat. By increasing police visibility and control activities (e.g. arrests), police size may reduce perception of social threat; but by symbolizing and reminding people of the crime problem, police numbers may increase perceptions of social threat. Observing police peacefully walking their beat may be comforting, but observing them in action—constantly in action—may be frightening. The net effect of police activity on perceptions of social threat may thus depend on the relative strengths and time lags of these processes.

The implications of such nonrecursive models for the relationships between forms of social control are very complex. I consider here just one relatively simple model. Model B in Figure 2 assumes just one structural source (crime rates) of perceived social threat (PST), which in turn positively affects two forms of control (police size and imprisonment rates), and one form (imprisonment rates) in turn affects it. If the feedback effect is negative (imprisonment rates decrease PST), then increments to the variables in the loop oscillate and dampen; if the feedback effect is positive (imprisonment rates increase PST), then increments to the variables in loop escalate. If the absolute value of the loop coefficients is less than one, which is generally the case when the coefficients are standardized, then the system equilibrates, allowing the calculation of the total effects of PST and SC1 (PS) on each other and of the covariance between SC1 (PS) and SC2 (IR) at equilibrium as well as at different stages in the equilibrium cycle.

Consider the following example using Figure 2 Model B. If the PST effect (coefficient *a*) on SC1 = .5 and the PST effect (coefficient *c*) on SC2 = .4, and if there is no feedback effect, then the implied correlation between SC1 and SC2 = .2 (.5 × .4). If there is a positive feedback (coefficient *b*), then the implied correlation between SC1 and SC2 is larger than .2. The direct effects of PST on SC1 and SC2 are enhanced by the positive feedback loop, which is reflected in the correlation between SC1 and SC2. (See Hayduk 1987 for an intuitive discussion of enhanced effects.) If the feedback effect is .2, .3, .4, or .5, the implied correlation between SC1 and SC2 is .24, .29, .34, or .39, respectively. On the other hand, if the feedback effect is negative, then the implied correlation is smaller than .2. The total effects of PST on SC1 and SC2 at equilibrium are less than the direct effects. If the feedback is −.2, −.3, −.4, or −.5, then the implied correlation between SC1 and SC2 is .09, .06, .03, or 0, respectively. Note that when the negative feedback effect (coefficient *b*) equals the positive threat effect (coefficient *a*), the implied correlations between PST and SC1 and between SC1 and SC2 are zero; and when the negative feedback effect (coefficient *b*) is larger than the threat effect (coefficient *a*), the implied correlation between SC1 and SC2 is negative.

This discussion is meant not to argue or demonstrate that any one of the models constitutes *the* model of the underlying causal process, but to illustrate that the relationships between forms of control are easily derivable when the underlying causal processes are explicitly modeled. The theoretical importance of these relationships lies not in their direction or magnitude, but in their derivability from a theoretical model of the underlying causal process. Depending on the model, the direction of the relationship may be either positive or negative, and its magnitude may be either small or large and be equally theoretically significant.

## SUMMARY

Studies of social control are theoretically dissipating. Rather than being organized around theoretical perspectives or even theoretical hypotheses, they are organized more and more around specific forms of control, such as prison admission rates; police size; mental hospital expenditures, release rates, and admissions rates; lynching rates; and AFDC growth rates. Researchers studying prison admissions are criminologists interested in prisons; researchers studying mental hospital admissions tend to be psychiatrists and psychologists interested in mental health; and researchers studying lynching tend to be sociologists and historicans interested in race relations. Hence, issues that cut across diverse forms of control are blurred, if not obscured. Studies of different forms of control that frame their work with similar theoretical hypotheses do not build on each other, do not cite each other, and frequently are not even aware of each other. While research has mushroomed, it has contributed little to the development of general social control theories.

One strategy to bridge the increasing balkanization of social control studies is to study the empirical relationships between forms of control. We have been able to locate three such mini literatures: the relationships between the criminal justice and mental health systems (generally prison and mental hospital admission and release rates), between the criminal justice and welfare systems (generally prison population and AFDC recipient rates), and between legal and illegal forms of control (generally state executions and lynch rates). Interestingly, while these literatures address similar issues, they, too, are isolated from each other, that is, they, too, do not build on each other or even cite each other.

Some empirical generalities, however, can be observed across these three literatures: Most prominently, the empirical relationship between these macro forms is rarely negative; it tends to be positive although it is weak and not always consistent across studies. What does this mean? Because the relationship is weak and mixed, it might be argued that specific forms of control follow their own internal dynamics, varying independently of each other form. Yet, weak empirical relationships between forms of control should not be equated with a lack of theoretical commonalities among them. Commonalities are found not in the empirical relationships between forms, but among the causal processes that underlie them. Dependent on the complexity of the casual process, the bivariate relationships between forms of control (the net outcome of these causal processes) can be positive or negative, weak or strong, and be equally theoretically significant.

For guidance on the nature of these causal processes and their implications for the relationships between forms of control, I review four general theoretical perspectives of social control. Ironically, while these perspectives inform and frame many studies of specific forms of control, they are very ambiguous about the relationships between forms of social control. The functionalist perspective, while explicit about the direction of these relationships, is very vague about the causal processes that underlie them. The conflict perspective is vague about even the direction of the relationships. The social movement perspective suggests that the direction depends on specific but unspecified social contexts. And the structural perspective frequently leads to inconsistent predictions about the strength and even the direction of these relationships.

Drawing on the three empirical literatures and the four theoretical perspectives, I formulate models of social threat processes that have implications for multiple forms of control and thus for the relationship between them. My concern is not to build the model of that process, but to develop plausible models and to explicate their implications for the relationships among forms of control. I distinguish between recursive and nonrecursive models because the principles (equations) for deriving their logical implications are different. The logical implications of recursive models are given by the principles of path analysis. While these models yield relatively clear and simple implications for the relationships between forms of control, even these implications can be more complicated when perceived threat is disaggregated into types, such as economic, political, and criminal, and when the effect of perceived social threat on specific forms of control depends on other variables such as the structure of markets. The implications of nonrecursive models can be quite complex. While the principles for deriving them have been developed, sociologists have rarely used them.

To reiterate, the theoretical significance of the relationships among forms of control lies not in their magnitude and direction but on being able to derive them from the causal processes that underlie them. Depending on the direction and magnitude of the underlying causal parameters, both recursive and nonrecursive models imply relationships among forms of control that can be either positive or negative and either weak or strong.

In conclusion, studies of social control are theoretically dissipating, organized more and more around specific forms of control. In an attempt to address this state of affairs, some research examines the relationship among forms of control. While this strategy is certainly useful, it is not always theoretically fruitful because the strength and even the direction of these relationships are not necessarily implied in more general theories of social control. Unless we are prepared to allow the study of social control to further dissipate, we need to shift the focus of study from specific forms of control to the social processes and structures that both define general theories of social control and underlie multiple forms of control. We must look for theoretical commonalities not in the bivariate relationships among forms of control, but in the social processes and structures that underlie them; and we must then express these bivariate relationships, whatever their direction and strength, in terms of these processes and structures.

ACKNOWLEDGMENTS

I wish to acknowledge the comments of Richard Felson, Steve Messner, Stewart Tolnay, and Larry Raffalovich.



*Literature Cited*

Alexander JC, ed. 1985. *Neo-functionalism.* Newberry Park, CA: Sage

Arvanites TM. 1988. The impact of state mental hospital deinstitutionalization on commitment for incompetency to stand trial. *Criminology* 26:307–20

Arvanites TM. 1992. The mental health and criminal justice systems: complementary forms of coercive control. In *Social Threat and Social Control,* ed. AE Liska, pp. 131–50. Albany: SUNY

Beck EM, Massey JL, Tolnay SE. 1989. The

gallows, the mob, the vote: lethal sanctioning of Blacks in North Carolina and Georgia, 1882 to 1930. *Law Soc. Rev.* 23:317–31

Biles D, Mulligan G. 1973. Mad or bad: the enduring dilemma. *Br. J. Criminol.* 13:275–79

Black D. 1976. *The Behavior of the Law*. New York: Academic

Black D. 1984. *Toward a General Theory of Social Control.* New York: Academic

Black D. 1993. *The Social Structure of Right and Wrong*. New York: Academic

Blalock HM Jr. 1967. *Toward a Theory of Minority Group Relations*. New York: Wiley

Blau PM. 1977. *Inequality and Heterogeneity.* New York: Free Press

Box S. 1987. *Recession, Crime and Punishment*. New York: Macmillan

Box S, Hale C. 1985. Unemployment, imprisonment and prison overcrowding. *Contemp. Crises* 9:209–28

Brown M, Warner BD. 1992. Immigrants, urban politics, and policing in 1980. *Am. J. Sociol.* 57:293–305

Bureau of Justice Statistics. 1986. *State and Federal Prisoners, 1925–85.* Washington, DC: Dept. Justice

Chamlin MB. 1989. A macro social analysis of change in police force size, 1972–1982. *Sociol. Q.* 30:615–24

Cirincione C, Steadman HJ, Robbins PC. 1994. Mental illness as a factor in criminality: a study of prisoners and mental patients. *Crim. Behav. Mental Health* 4:33–47

Colvin M. 1990. Labor markets, industrial monopolization, welfare, and imprisonment. *Sociol. Q.* 31:441–57

Durkheim E. 1938. *The Rules of Sociological Method.* Transl. SA Solovay, JH Mueller, ed. GEG Catlin. Glencoe, Ill: Free Press

Foucault M. 1965. *Madness and Civilization.*. New York: Vintage

Foucault M. 1978. *Discipline and Punishment.* Transl. A Sheridan. New York: Pantheon

Garland D. 1985. *Punishment and Welfare: A History of Penal Strategies*. Borkfield, VT: Gower

Gibbs JP. 1989. *Control: Sociology's Central Notion.* Urbana: Univ. Ill. Press

Gillis AR. 1989. Crime and state surveillance in Nineteenth-century France. *Am. J. Sociol.* 95:307–41

Grabosky PN. 1980. Rates of imprisonment and psychiatric hospitalization in the United States. *Soc. Indic. Res.* 7:63–70

Greenberg DF. 1983. Donald Black's *Sociology of Law*: a critique. *Law Soc. Rev.* 17:338–62

Gusfield J. 1963. *Symbolic Crusade.* Urbana: Univ. Ill. Press

Hagan J, Leon J. 1977. Rediscovering delinquency: social history political ideology and the sociology of law. *Am. J. Sociol.* 42:587–98

Hawkins DF. 1987. Beyond anomalies: rethinking the conflict perspective on race and criminal punishment. *Soc. Forces* 65:719–45

Hawkins DF. 1994. Ethnicity: the forgotten dimension of American social control. In *Inequality, Crime and Social Control,* ed. GS Bridges, MA Myers, pp. 99–116. San Francisco: Westview

Hayduk L. 1987. *Structural Equation Modeling With LISREL.* Baltimore: Johns Hopkins Univ. Press

Horwitz AV. 1990. *The Logic of Social Control.* New York: Plenum

Ignatieff M. 1978. *A Just Measure of Pain: The Penitentiary in the Industrial Revolution, 1850–1950.* New York: Pantheon

Inverarity J, Grattet R. 1989. Institutional responses to unemployment: a comparison of U.S. trends, 1948–1985. *Contemp. Crises* 13:351–70

Inverarity J, McCarthy D. 1988. Punishment and structure revised: unemployment and imprisonment in the U.S., 1948–1984. *Sociol. Q.* 29:263–79

Issac L, Kelly WR. 1981. Racial insurgency, the state, and welfare expansion: local and national level evidence from the postwar United States. *Am. J. Sociol.* 86:1348–86

Jackson PI. 1989. *Minority Group Threat, Crime, and Policing.* New York: Praeger

Jennings ET. 1983. Racial insurgency, the state and welfare expansion: a critical comment and reanalysis. *Am. J. Sociol.* 88:1220–36

Lessan GT. 1991. Macro-economic determinants of penal policy: estimating the unemployment and inflation influences on imprisonment rate changes in the United States, 1948–1985. *Crime, Law Soc. Change* 16:177–98

Liska AE, ed. 1992. *Social Threat and Social Control.* Albany: SUNY Press

Liska AE. 1994. Modeling the conflict perspective of social control. In *Inequality, Crime and Social Control,* ed. GS Bridges, MA Myers, pp. 58–71. San Francisco: Westview

Massey JL, Meyers M. 1989. Patterns of repressive social control in post-reconstruction Georgia, 1882–1935. *Soc. Forces* 68:458–88

Meier RF. 1982. Perspectives on the concept of social control. *Annu. Rev. Sociol.* 8:35–65

Melick ME, Steadman HJ, Cocozza JC. 1979. The medicalization of criminal behavior among mental patients. *J. Health Soc. Behav.* 20:228–37

Morrissey JP. 1982. Deinstitutionalizing the mentally ill: process, outcomes, and new directions. In *Deviance and Mental Illness,* ed. W Gove, pp. 147–76. Beverly Hills: Sage

Olzak S. 1990. The political context of competition: lynching and urban violence. *Soc. Forces* 69:395–422

Palermo GB, Gumz EJ, Liska FJ. 1992. Mental illness and criminal behavior revisited. *Int. J. Offender Theory Comp. Criminol.* 36:53–61

Penrose L. 1939. Mental disease and crime: outline of a comparative study of European statistics. *Br. J. Med. Psychol.* 28:1–15

Phillips CD. 1986. Social structure and social control: modeling the discriminatory execution of Blacks in Georgia and North Carolina, 1925–35. *Soc. Forces* 65:458–75

Phillips CD. 1987. Exploring relations among forms of social control: the lynching and execution of blacks in North Carolina, 1889–1918. *Law Soc. Rev.* 21:361–74

Piven FF, Cloward R. 1971. *Regulating the Poor: The Functions of Public Welfare.* New York: Vintage

Platt A. 1969. *The Child Savers.* Chicago: Univ. Chicago Press

Quinney R. 1977. *Class, State and Crime.* New York: McKay

Reed JS. 1972. Percent black and lynching: a test of Blalock's theory. *Soc. Forces* 50:356–60

Rothman DJ. 1971. *The Discovery of the Asylum.* Boston: Little, Brown

Rusche G, Kirchheimer O. 1939. *Punishment and Social Structure.* New York: Russell & Russell

Schissel B. 1992. The influence of economic factors and social control policy on crime rates changes in Canada. *Can. Sociol. Rev.* 17:405–28

Schram SF, Turbett JP. 1983. Civil disorder and welfare explosion: a two-step process. *Am. J. Sociol.* 48:408–14

Scull A. 1977a. Madness and segregative control in the rise of the insane asylum. *Soc. Probl.* 24:337–51

Scull A. 1977b. *Decarceration-Community Treatment and Deviant: A Radical View.* Englewood Cliffs, NJ: Prentice Hall

Skocpol T, Amenta E. 1985. Did capitalists shape social security? *Am. J. Sociol.* 50:572–85

Soule SA. 1992. Populism and black lynching in Georgia, 1890–1900. *Soc. Forces* 71:431–49

Spitzer S. 1975. Toward a marxian theory of deviance. *Soc. Probl.* 22:638–51

Steadman HJ, Monahan J, Duffee B, Hartsone E, Robbins PC. 1984. The impact of state mental deinstitutionalization of United States prison populations: 1968–1978. *J. Crim. Law Criminol.* 75(2):474–90

Steadman HJ. 1979. *Beating A Rap?* Chicago: Univ. Chicago Press

Stinchcombe AL. 1968. *Constructing Social Theories.* New York:Harcourt, Brace & World

Sutton JR. 1988. *Stubborn Children: Controlling Delinquency in the United States, 1640–1982.* Berkeley: Univ. Calif. Press

Sutton JR. 1990. Institutional responses to deviant children, 1890–1920. *Am. J. Sociol.* 95:1367–400

Sutton JR. 1991. The political economy of madness: the expansion of the asylum in progressive America. *Am. J. Sociol.* 56:665–78

Teplin LA. 1990. The prevalence of severe mental disorder among male urban jail detainees: comparisons with the epidemiologic catchment area program. *Am. J. Public Health* 80:663–69

Tolnay SE, Beck EM. 1995. *A Festival of Violence.* Urbana: Univ. Ill. Press

Turk A. 1969. *Criminality and Legal Order.* Chicago: Rand McNally

*Annu. Rev. Sociol. 1997. 23:63–95*


# GROWING UP AMERICAN: The Challenge Confronting Immigrant Children and Children of Immigrants

*Min Zhou*
Department of Sociology, University of California, Los Angeles, 264 Haines Hall, Box 951551, Los Angeles, California 90095-1551

KEY WORDS: the second generation, immigrant children, race/ethnicity, adaptation/assimilation, intergenerational relations

ABSTRACT

Since the 1980s, immigrant children and children of immigrant parentage have become the fastest growing and the most extraordinarily diverse segment of America's child population. Until the recent past, however, scholarly attention has focused on adult immigrants to the neglect of their offspring, creating a profound gap between the strategic importance of the new second generation and the knowledge about its socioeconomic circumstances. The purpose of this article is to pull together existing studies that bear directly or indirectly on children's immigrant experiences and adaptational outcomes and to place these studies into a general framework that can facilitate a better understanding of the new second generation. The article first describes the changing trends in the contexts of the reception the new second generation has encountered. The article then discusses the ways in which conventional theoretical perspectives about immigrant adaptation are being challenged and alternative frameworks are being developed. Thirdly, it examines empirical findings from recent research and evaluates their contribution to the sociology of immigration. Finally, it highlights the main conclusions from prior research and their theoretical and practical implications for future studies.

## INTRODUCTION

The phenomenal increase in contemporary immigration to the United States has given rise to a record number of children who, regardless of place of birth, are raised in immigrant families. Since the 1980s, a new generation of immigrant children and children of immigrants has become the fastest growing and the most



0360-0572/97/0815-0063$08.00

ethnically diverse segment of America's child population. The 1990 US Census has revealed that about 15% of all children in the United States are immigrant children or children of immigrant parentage, and that 59% of Latino-American children and 90% of Asian American children are members of the first or second generation, compared to 6% of non-Latino African-American children and 5% of non-Latino European-American children (Landale & Oropesa 1995).

Differing from their immigrant parents, immigrant children and children of immigrants lack meaningful connections to their "old" world. They are thus unlikely to consider a foreign country as a place to return to or as a point of reference. They instead are prone to evaluate themselves or to be evaluated by others by the standards of their new country (Gans 1992, Portes 1995). Given the fact that children of contemporary immigrants will represent a crucial component of future American society, how are we to understand these children's adaptation to their role as citizens and full participants in American society? How do migration processes, contexts of reception, and biculturalism impact the process of becoming American? Has assimilation continued to lead to upward social mobility? Has the younger generation of today's immigrants been able to assimilate into American society, following the path taken by the "old" second generation arriving at the turn of the century and advancing beyond their parents' generation?

Until the recent past, scholarly attention has focused on adult immigrants to the neglect of child immigrants and immigrant offspring, creating a profound gap between the strategic importance of these children and the knowledge about their conditions. The purpose of this article is to pull together existing studies that bear directly or indirectly on immigrant experiences and adaptational outcomes of the children of contemporary immigrants and to place these studies into a general framework that can facilitate a better understanding of these children's socioeconomic circumstances and life chances. In so doing, I first describe the changing trends in the contexts of the reception that the new second generation has encountered; I then discuss the ways in which conventional theoretical perspectives about immigrant adaptation are being challenged and alternative frameworks are being developed. Thirdly, I examine empirical findings from recent research and evaluate their contribution to the sociology of immigration. Finally, I highlight the main conclusions from prior research and their theoretical and practical implications for future studies.

## THE RISE OF THE NEW SECOND GENERATION

### *Who Makes Up the New Second Generation?*

The new second generation technically refers to the children of contemporary immigrants. The emerging literature on the new second generation, however, has discussed not only US-born children—the true second generation—but also contemporary immigrant children who have arrived in the United States before they reach adulthood (Gans 1992, Portes 1996). The latter group is also known as the "one-and-a-half generation," a term coined by Rubén Rumbaut to characterize the children who straddle the old and the new worlds but are fully part of neither (Pérez Firmat 1994, Rumbaut 1991). Usage of these generational terms has not been consistent (Oropesa & Landale, forthcoming). Depending on social and historical processes of immigration and particular nationality groups under study, the second generation is sometimes broadened to include foreign-born children arriving at pre-school age (0-4 years) because they share many linguistic, cultural, and developmental experiences similar to those of immigrant offspring (Zhou & Bankston, forthcoming). The one-and-a-half generation, on the other hand, is sometimes broken down into two distinct cohorts: children between 6 and 13 years of age as 1.5-generation children and those arriving as adolescents (aged 13 to 17) who are similar to first-generation children. Although scholars may vary in their ways of defining the new second generation, they have generally agreed that there are important differences between children of different cohorts of the one-and-a-half and second generation, particularly in their physical and psychological developmental stages, in their socialization processes in the family, the school, and the society at large, as well as in their orientation toward their homeland.

The main characteristics of the new second generation mirror those of contemporary immigrants, which are extraordinarily diverse in national origins, socioeconomic circumstances, and settlement patterns. Always the defining character of America, however, the composition and meaning of diversity today have changed significantly since the turn of the century. Most notably, contemporary immigrants have been predominantly non-Europeans. According to the Immigration and Nationalization Service, of the 7.3 million immigrants admitted to the United States during the 1980s (not counting undocumented immigrants), 87% came from Asia and the Americas, compared to the 8.8 million admitted during the 1910s who were predominantly from Europe. In the past decade, Mexico, the Philippines, China/Taiwan, South Korea, and Vietnam were the top five sending countries, followed by the Dominican Republic, India, El Salvador, and Jamaica. Immigrants from Mexico alone accounted for more than one fifth of total legal admissions as well as half of illegal immigrants.

The diversity in national origin has, accordingly, become a salient feature of the new second generation. The 1990 Census has shown that the foreign-born child population under 18 years of age is made up of 52% Latinos (53% of whom are Mexicans) and 27% Asians, and that the US-born cohort with at least one immigrant parent is made up of 48% Latinos and 24% Asians (Oropesa & Landale, forthcoming). More strikingly, about one out of three foreign-born children has at least one Mexican-born parent (Perlmann & Waldinger 1996).

Also different from the turn-of-the-century inflows, contemporary immigrants have come from diverse socioeconomic backgrounds. The 1990 Census has attested to the vast differences in levels of education, occupation, and income by national origins. For example, over 60% of immigrants (aged 25 years or older) from India and Taiwan report having attained college degrees, three times the proportion of average Americans, but less than 5% of those from Cambodia, Laos, El Salvador, and Mexico so report. Among the employed workers (aged 16 years or older), over 45% of immigrants from India and Taiwan have managerial or professional occupations, more than twice the proportion of average American workers, but less than 7% of those from El Salvador, Guatemala, and Mexico so report. Further, immigrants from India report a median household income of $53,000, compared to $30,000 for average American households; those from Cambodia, the Dominican Republic, El Salvador, Honduras, Laos, and Mexico report a median household income below $22,000.

The socioeconomic diversity suggests that the pathways to social mobility will not be a straight line nor unidirectional. While many immigrants continue to follow the traditional bottom-up route, significant numbers of new arrivals have bypassed the bottom starting line and moved directly into mainstream labor markets while dispersing into suburban middle-class communities. The implications for the new second generation are profound, since the current state and future prospects of immigrant children are related to the advantages or disadvantages that accrue to the socioeconomic status of their parents.

A third salient feature of contemporary immigrants is their geographic concentration. Unlike earlier European immigrants whose destinations were in the Northeast, contemporary immigrants have been disproportionately concentrated in the West. California accounted for over a third of the total arrivals of legal immigrants in the 1980s, while New York, the traditional largest receiving state, accounted for only 14% (Portes & Zhou 1995). The impact of geographic concentration is also felt in public schools in high immigration states. Again, California alone accounted for some 45% of the nation's immigrant student population, more than one out of ten school-aged children in the state were foreign born, and over a third of the state's school-aged children spoke a language other than English at home (Cornelius 1995).

## *The Changing Contexts of Reception*

Differences in national origins, socioeconomic backgrounds, and geographic patterns of settlement are important factors for immigrant adaptation. However, adaptational outcomes are also determined by structural conditions in the host society (Portes & Rumbaut 1996). The context of the reception that has greeted contemporary immigrants and their children has changed dramatically over the past three decades to create additional obstacles to "melt" the diverse body of immigrants and their offspring into a single mainstream.

Unlike earlier European immigrants, contemporary immigrants have been received in a peculiar circumstance: an emerging "hourglass" economy in which opportunities for social mobility shrink even among native-born Americans and a welfare state that is highly contested by the general public. Several major trends are especially unfavorable for the adaptation of the nation's newcomers and their children.

First, the gap between rich and poor, which progressively narrowed for most of the twentieth century, has been widening in recent years as it has been affected by globalization and economic restructuring. Only a portion of the American work force has seen its economic advantages steadily increase as information technology and management become more critical to the economy; most have experienced worsening conditions. During the 1980s, 80% of American workers saw their real hourly wages go down by an average of about 5% (Mishel & Bernstein 1992). Blue collar jobs, the kinds of jobs generally available to newly arrived immigrants, not only pay less than in previous years, but they are also disappearing at a particularly rapid rate, resulting in expanding classes of poor and rich and a shrinking middle class. In such an economic structure, even US-born Americans find their chances for economic mobility lessening. The situation for many immigrants is bleaker, except for the unusually fortunate, the highly educated, and the highly skilled (Waldinger 1996).

Contemporary economic hardships are different from the hardships of the Great Depression and hardships in many Third World countries. Although there is a growing class of poor Americans, there are relatively few deaths from starvation in the United States. Until the early 1990s, the welfare state had made access to public assistance relatively easy (Rumbaut 1994a, Tienda & Liang 1994). While opportunities for stable jobs with good incomes were rare for low-income individuals, food stamps and Aid to Families with Dependent Children were readily available. Public assistance did not provide a comfortable way of life, for welfare payments averaged less than half the amount defined as poverty level income (Sancton 1992:45); it did, nonetheless, provide a means of existence for the chronically poor, unemployed or underemployed. Yet, members of this expanding class of poor were not being offered chances for socioeconomic improvement; they were, for the most part, being fed and housed and maintained in their social and economic limbo. Such unfortunate circumstances were exacerbated just prior to the 1996 presidential election when President Bill Clinton signed a Republican welfare reform bill. The bill, which limits public assistance to two continuous years and mandates a five-year lifetime maximum, with neither public jobs nor childcare for recipients who exceed the limit and nothing for their children. This has changed the nature of the welfare state in new and significant ways: It cuts off the lifeline of the poor, especially children, driving them into deeper poverty; it also excludes legal immigrants from much access to basic forms of assistance, forcing poor immigrant families to swim or sink. Long-term effects of the welfare bill remain to be seen, but certainly millions of children will be thrown into poverty, and chances for the truly disadvantaged to get out of poverty will be even bleaker.

Second, poverty has been highly concentrated. The poor are not, of course, being housed evenly across the American landscape. Even before new information technologies and the globalization of production, the contraction of American manufacturing and the suburbanization first of the middle class population and later of middle class jobs have displaced the American working class. The disappearance of industrial jobs in urban areas where racial minorities concentrate has detached the middle class from the working poor, causing a high concentration of poverty in the most disadvantaged segments of the minority population in inner-city ghettos (Wilson 1987).

The problem of poverty concentration has worsened under large-scale economic restructuring, which has reduced the demand for low-skilled and semi-skilled immigrants and trapped them in unemployment and social isolation similar to that commonly facing native-born minorities in the most impoverished stratum of the society. The implication for members of younger generations is profound. Immigrant children from middle-class backgrounds benefit from financially secure families, good schools, safe neighborhoods, and other supportive formal and informal organizations, which ensure better life chances for them. Children with poorly educated and unskilled parents, in contrast, often find themselves growing up in underprivileged neighborhoods subject to poverty, poor schools, violence and drugs, and a generally disruptive social environment. Many immigrant children attend public schools in their neighborhood with a clear numerical majority of minority students. In Los Angeles County, for example, 57 unified school districts out of a total of 83 contain over half of nonwhite students, and 34 have more than three quarters of US-born minority and other immigrant students. In major immigrant-receiving cities such as Los Angeles, San Francisco, New York, and Miami, at least a third of the students in the entire school system speak a language other than English at home.

Third, there has been a drastic increase in the proportion of American children in one-parent families. Hernandez (1993) observed that between 1939 and 1988 the proportion of the officially poor children who lived in mother-only families increased from 10% to 57%, and that such an increase was counterbalanced by a virtually identical decline in the proportion living in two-parent families. The rise of single-parent families has aggravated the overall poverty trends for children. Relative to children living in intact families, the children living in one-parent or even blended families tend to be disadvantaged with regard to socioeconomic circumstances, psychological function, behavioral problems, education, and health and these conditions severely limit their life chances (Hernandez 1993).

Unfortunately, such disadvantages in family situations have worsened for poor immigrant families who have lived a longer time in the United States. Landale & Oropesa (1995) found significant increases of children living in single-parent families across generations of US residence and across many Asian and Latin American nationality groups. By the third generation, in particular, the prevalence of female headship among all nationality groups of Latin American children (ranging from 40% of Mexicans, 50% of Cubans, to 70% of Dominicans) and Filipino children (40%) constituted a serious disadvantage. This situation implies that even if the parental generation is able to work hard to achieve higher positions and higher incomes, their children's access to these gains may be seriously circumvented by family disruption (Landale & Oropesa 1995).

Fourth, there has been a growing "oppositional culture" among young Americans, especially among those who have felt oppressed and excluded from the American mainstream and who have been frustrated by the widening gap between a culture that highly values freedom and materialism and the reality of a dwindling economic future. Many of these American children have responded to their social isolation and their constrained opportunities with resentment toward middle-class America, rebellion against all forms of authority, and rejection of the goals of achievement and upward mobility. Because students in schools shape one another's attitudes and expectations, such an oppositional culture negatively affects educational outcomes. School achievement is seen as unlikely to lead to upward mobility, and high achievers are seen as sell-outs to oppressive authority. Matute-Bianchi (1986, 1991) found that the relationship between scholastic achievement and ethnicity did not hold for native-born Chicanos and Cholos, who had been uprooted from their Mexican heritage and were trapped in a caste-like minority status. They reacted to their exclusion and subordination with resentment, regarded efforts toward academic achievement as "acting white," and constructed an identity in resistance to the dominant majority white society. Suárez-Orozco (1991) reached similar conclusions about native-born Mexican Americans, who perceived the effect of the educational system as continued exploitation.

While there is a strong antiintellectual streak in American youth culture at all socioeconomic levels, the rejection of academic pursuits is especially intense among members of minority groups, who are more likely than members of the majority to identify school administrations with oppressive authority, to perceive their entry into the middle class as almost impossible, and to be in schools where learning is strongly discouraged by peers. It would be wise to avoid passing judgment on the children in these schools and to avoid blaming them for their responses to the world around them. Merton long ago (1938) described rebellion as an adaptive response to a gap between socially approved goals and available means of achieving those goals. Lowered chances for mobility create frustration and pessimism for all American young people, but these emotions are most strongly felt by those at the bottom. When those at the bottom are also members of historically oppressed minority groups, the frustration is mixed with the need to maintain self-esteem, so that rejection of middle class mores and opposition to authority become important strategies for psychological survival.

In underprivileged neighborhoods, in particular, immigrant children meet in their schools native-born peers with little hope for the future and are thus likely to be pressured by their peers to resist assimilation into the middle class as expected by their parents. These trends pose a challenge to all parents, but the challenge is especially daunting for immigrant parents with limited educational backgrounds, frequently limited English skills, and few resources.

## THEORETICAL DEVELOPMENTS IN RESEARCH ON IMMIGRANT ADAPTATION

### *The Assimilation Perspective Revisited*

In the literature on immigrant adaptation, the assimilation perspective has dominated much of the sociological thinking on the subject for the most part of this century. Central to this perspective is the assumption that there is a natural process by which diverse ethnic groups come to share a common culture and to gain equal access to the opportunity structure of society; that this process consists of gradually deserting old cultural and behavioral patterns in favor of new ones; and that, once set in motion, this process moves inevitably and irreversibly toward assimilation (Park 1928, Warner & Srole 1945, Wirth [1925] 1956).

While earlier assimilation theorists emphasized forces such as time, industrialization, and acculturation, Gordon (1964) conceptualized several types of assimilation: cultural or behavioral, structural, identificational, attitude-receptional, behavior-receptional, and civic assimilation. In Gordon's view, immigrants began their adaptation to the new country through cultural assimilation, or acculturation. Since cultural assimilation was for Gordon a necessary first step, it was considered the top priority on the agenda of immigrant adjustment. Gordon implied that acculturation would take place and continue indefinitely even when no other type of assimilation occurred (1964, p. 77).

But he argued that acculturation did not necessarily lead to other forms of integration into the host society (i.e. large-scale entrance into the institutions of the host society or intermarriage). Ethnic groups would remain distinguished from one another depending largely on the degree to which groups gained the acceptance of the dominant population (p. 159). Gordon anticipated, nevertheless, that ethnic minorities would eventually lose all their distinctive characteristics and cease to exist as ethnic groups as they pass through the stages of assimilation, eventually intermarrying with the majority population and entering its institutions on a primary-group level (pp. 70–71).

From the point of view of assimilation theorists, distinctive ethnic traits such as old cultural ways, native languages, or ethnic enclaves are sources of disadvantages that negatively affect assimilation (Child 1943, Warner & Srole 1945). Although complete acculturation to the dominant American culture may not ensure all immigrants full social participation in the host society, immigrants must free themselves from their old cultures in order to begin rising up from marginal positions. Between the 1920s and the 1950s, America seemed to have absorbed the great waves of immigrants, who arrived primarily from Europe. Sociological studies have indicated progressive trends of social mobility across generations of immigrants and increasing rates of intermarriages, as determined by educational attainment, job skills, length of stay since immigration, English proficiency, and levels of exposure to American cultures (Alba 1985, Chiswick 1977, Greeley 1976, Sandberg 1974, Wytrwal 1961).

### *Observed Anomalies*

Beginning in the 1960s, the conventional assimilation perspective with its application to the more recently arrived non-European immigrant groups has been met with challenges. Instead of eventual convergence in the outcomes of immigrant adaptation, several anomalies have been observed in recent research. The first anomaly concerns the persistent ethnic differences across generations. Studies on intergenerational mobility have found divergent rather than convergent outcomes, revealing that early and insignificant differentials in advantage result in substantial differences in educational and occupational mobility in later years (Becker 1963, Goffman 1963). In their study of educational attainment of 25 religio-ethnic groups in the United States, Hirschman & Falcon (1985) have found that neither generation nor length of US residence significantly influences educational outcomes. Specifically, children of highly educated immigrants consistently fare much better in school than do fourth- or fifth-generation descendants of poorly educated ancestors regardless of religio-ethnic backgrounds. In a study of the Irish, Italian, Jewish, and African Americans in Providence, Rhode Island, Perlmann (1988) found that, even with family background factors held constant, ethnic differences in levels of schooling and economic attainment persisted in the second and later generations and that schooling did not equally commensurate with occupational advancement for African Americans as for other European-Americans across generations.

Another anomaly is what Gans (1992) describes as the "the second generation decline." Gans notes three possible scenarios for today's new second generation: education-driven mobility, succession-driven mobility, and niche improvement. He observes that immigrant children from less fortunate socioeconomic backgrounds have a much harder time than other middle-class children to succeed in school, and that a significant number of the children of poor, especially dark-skinned, immigrants can be trapped in permanent poverty in the era of stagnant economic growth and in the process of Americanization because these immigrant children "will either not be asked, or will be reluctant, to work at immigrant wages and hours as their parents did but will lack job opportunities, skills and connections to do better" (pp. 173–74). Gans predicts that the prospects facing children of the less fortunate may be high rates of unemployment, crime, alcoholism, drug use, and other pathologies associated with poverty and the frustration of rising expectation (p. 183). Perlmann & Waldinger (1996) call this phenomenon "the second generation revolt." They argue that such revolt is not merely caused by exogenous factors, such as racial discrimination, declining economic opportunities, and the exposure to the adversarial outlooks of native-born youths, but also by endogenous factors inherent in the immigration process, including pre-immigration class standing and the size and the nature of immigrant inflows.

Still another anomaly is the peculiar outcomes of immigrant adaptation. Today, neither valedictorians nor delinquents are atypical among immigrant children regardless of timing and racial or socioeconomic backgrounds. For example, in the past 15 years, the list of top-ten award winners of the Westinghouse Science Talent Search, one of the country's most prestigious high school academic contests, has been dominated by the 1.5- or second-generation immigrants. Many of these immigrant children are "FOBs" (fresh off the boat) and from families of moderate socioeconomic backgrounds (Zhou 1997). While immigrant children are overrepresented on lists of award-winners or on academic fast tracks, many others are extremely vulnerable to multiple high-risk behaviors, school failure, street gangs, and youth crime. Even Asian Americans, the so-called "model minority," have seen a steady rise of youth gang memberships. Some of the Asian gang members are from suburban middle-class families, attend magnet schools, and are exceptionally good students. These anomalies immediately question the applicability of straight-line assimilation.

### *Alternative Theoretical Frameworks*

A major alternative framework is the pluralist perspective, which perceives American society as composed of a collection of ethnic and racial minority groups, as well as the dominant majority group of European Americans. It is concerned with a fundamental question of how the world would look different were the experiences of the excluded placed at the center of our thinking and with the ways in which immigrants actively shape their own lives rather than exist passively as beneficiaries or victims of "ineluctable modernizing and Americanizing forces" (Conzen 1991, p. 10). A central idea is that ethnicity can serve as an asset rather than a liability. This idea provides a means of understanding how ethnicity may be utilized as a distinct form of social capital (including such cultural endowments as obligations and expectations, information channels, and social norms) that contributes to adaptation (Glazer & Moynihan 1970, Handlin 1973).

From a pluralist point of view, preimmigration cultural attributes inherent to ethnicity are not necessarily absorbed by the core culture of the host society, but they constantly interact with it. Greeley contended that "ethnicity is not a way of looking back to the old world ... [but] rather a way of being American, a way of defining yourself into the pluralist culture which existed before you arrived" (1976, p. 32). Conzen and her associates conceptualized ethnicity as "a process of construction or invention which incorporates, adapts, and amplifies preexisting communal solidarities, cultural attributes, and historical memories," grounded in real-life context and social experience (Conzen et al 1992, pp. 4–5). According to these scholars, preimmigration cultural attributes cannot be equated with homeland cultures, because immigrants tend to select carefully not only what to pack in their trunks to bring to America, but also what to unpack once settled. Also, homeland cultural norms and values may not be entirely inconsistent with those of the host country. Just as some aspects of immigrant cultural patterns may continue in a state of uneasy coexistence with the requirements of the host country, other aspects of immigrant cultural patterns may "fit" the requirements of life there or may even be prerequisites for "making it in America" (Fukuyama 1993). Still others are modified, changed, adapted, transformed, reformed, and negotiated in the course of immigrant adjustments (Garcia 1996).

The pluralist perspective offers an alternative way of viewing the host society, treating members of ethnic minority groups as a part of the American population rather than as foreigners or outsiders and presenting ethnic or immigrant cultures as integral segments of American society. However, the questions of "second-generation decline" and "second-generation revolt" have been unanswered within this theoretical framework. While how people construct or invent their own ethnicity has been emphasized, how they also construct their own acculturation and assimilation has been understudied. Gans (1992) points out that pressures of both formal acculturation (through schooling) and informal acculturation (through American peers and the media) will impinge on the second generation. He reasons that immigrant children may be so overwhelmed by a youth culture and the freedoms (particularly personal choices in dress, dating, sexual practices) unavailable in their old country that, because of the sheer attractiveness of American culture, they may not be willing to accept immigrant parental work norms or to work in "un-American" conditions as many of their parents do, and that they may be unwilling to endure their parents' painstaking efforts toward upward social mobility. Perlmann & Waldinger (1996), however, caution that the deteriorating prospect in the new second generation is not simply a matter of exposure or Americanization but also a result of structural, group, or individual disadvantages associated with pre- and post-immigration experiences.

Moreover, the elusiveness of ethnic characteristics creates problems in the use of the pluralist framework as an explanatory tool. Each generation passes cultural patterns, often subtle patterns, to the next, but the mechanisms of this process are unclear, and many assumptions and attitudes of ethnic group members are hard to identify and measure (Archdeacon 1983). Also, the constituents of American diversity are not equal; maintaining a distinctive ethnicity can both help and hinder the social mobility of ethnic group members. For example, first-generation members of some immigrant minority groups, such as the Mexicans, have seldom been able to motivate their children to excel in school and move upward in the host society, while other groups, such as the Asians, have far more often succeeded in pushing younger people toward upward social mobility (Perlmann & Waldinger 1996).

Another major theoretical stance is the structural perspective, which offers a framework for understanding the differences in social adaptation of ethnic minority groups in terms of advantages and disadvantages inherent to social structures rather than in the process of acculturation or selective Americanization. This perspective presents American society as a stratified system of social inequality, in which different social categories—whether birth-ascribed or not—have unequal access to wealth, power, and privilege (Barth & Noel 1972). The ethnic hierarchy systematically limits access to social resources, such as opportunities for jobs, housing, and education, resulting in persistent racial/ethnic disparities in levels of income, educational attainment, and occupational achievement (Wilson 1987). Consequently, the benefits of "becoming American" depend largely on what stratum of American society absorbs the new immigrants.

Overall, the structural perspective raises skepticism about eventual assimilation and interethnic accommodation suggested by the assimilation perspective and implied by the pluralist perspective, because of inherent conflicts between the dominant and subordinate groups in the hierarchy. On the issue of immigrant adaptation, this perspective maintains that the process of becoming American may not lead uniformly to middle-class status, but rather to the occupation of different rungs on the ethnic hierarchy.

The segmented assimilation thesis provides another framework for examining the divergent outcomes of today's new second generation. Portes & Zhou (1993) observe that assimilation has continued to serve as a norm of immigrant adaptation, but that its outcomes have become segmented: Either confinement to permanent underclass memberships or rapid economic advancement with deliberate preservation of the immigrant community's values and solidarity is equally possible for the new second generation. This segmented assimilation thesis recognizes the fact that today's immigrants are received in various segments of American society ranging from affluent middle-class suburbs to impoverished inner-city ghettos. Such contextual differences mean that paths to social mobility may lead to upward as well as downward outcomes. In the case of those who start from the very bottom, of course, the outcome is not so much assimilating downward as staying where they are.

The question is what makes some immigrant groups susceptible to the downward path, or to the permanent trap, and what allows others to avoid it? Major determinants can include factors external to a particular immigrant group, such as racial stratification, economic opportunities, and spatial segregation, and factors intrinsic to the group, such as financial and human capital upon arrival, family structure, community organization, and cultural patterns of social relations. These two sets of factors affect the life chances of immigrant children not only additively but also interactively. Particular patterns of social relations in the family or the ethnic community may sometimes counter the trend of negative adaptation even in unfavorable situations. When immigrant children are under pressure to assimilate but are unsure which direction of assimilation is more desirable, the family or the ethnic community can make a difference if it is able to mobilize resources to prevent downward assimilation. The focus on the interaction between structural factors and sociocultural factors in recent research has shed new light on the understanding of the complex process of assimilation in the second generation.

## EMPIRICAL FINDINGS FROM CURRENT RESEARCH

Unlike adult immigrants whose levels of adaptation are often indicated by occupational attainment and income, levels of adaptation among young immigrants are generally measured by educational attainment—academic orientation, aspiration, and performance. Attending school—attaining knowledge and skills that may be capitalized upon in future labor markets—is a crucial first step toward successful adaptation to American society for immigrant children and children of immigrants. In the United States where public education is readily available to all children and where education is traditionally accepted as the main means of socioeconomic mobility, schooling often comes to occupy a central place in immigrant aspirations (Ogbu 1974). Studies on the new second generation have generally concerned a central question: How do various aspects of class, race/ethnicity, social capital derived from particular patterns of social relations within the immigrant family and the ethnic community, intergenerational relations, language skills, and ethnic identity affect the process of educational attainment of the children of contemporary immigrants? In this section, I review how these issues are addressed in recent research and show how new concepts are derived from empirical findings.

### *Class and Race/Ethnicity*

The socioeconomic circumstances of today's predominantly non-European-American second generation vary by race and ethnicity. Although many of them may have never experienced prejudice associated with a particular skin color or racial type in their homelands, immigrant children have confronted a reality in their host society where their ascribed physical features may become a handicap (Waters 1994, Portes 1995). Using the 1990 Census data, Oropesa & Landale (forthcoming) showed that poverty rates for immigrant children ranged from 21% among non-Latino European Americans, 24% for non-Latino African Americans, 27% for Asian Americans, and 41% for Latino-Americans. Among the second generation (US-born with at least one foreign-born parent), there was a substantial drop in poverty rates for all racial groups, but the magnitude of the decline varied by race: while poverty rates between the first- (or the 1.5-) and second generation dropped more than half among non-Latino European-American and Asian-American children, they dropped less than a third among non-Latino African-American and Latino-American children. The conditions for third-generation children (US-born children with US-born parents) were most disturbing: Except for Asian Americans, there was no appreciable socioeconomic improvement between second- and third-generation non-Latino European Americans and Latino Americans, but there was a significant deterioration among third-generation non-Latino African Americans whose poverty rate jumped up to 40%, a 26 percentage-point increase from that of their first-generation counterparts. These statistics reveal an obvious effect of race, implying a severe handicap associated with skin colors.

Why has the class status changed for the better among children of certain racial minority groups and for the worse among others with generation? Some researchers contend that the inequalities of class and race that plague American society are carried into the American educational system. Schools have thus become "arenas of injustice" (Keniston et al 1977) that provide unequal opportunities on the basis of class and race. Coleman and his associates (1966) found that social capital in the form of parental educational attainment and class status significantly affect academic performance of children in school and that children did better if they attended schools where classmates were predominantly from higher socioeconomic backgrounds. Davis (1993) found that poor African-American and Latino-American families who moved from inner-city neighborhoods did better in school and in labor markets than those left behind. The pattern generally held true for immigrant children who attended suburban schools.

Moreover, differences in outcomes of schooling have historically been linked to residential segregation on the basis of class and race. Minority children have suffered from unequal distribution of economic and educational resources that seriously curtail their chances in life and trap them in isolated ghettos. Ghettoization, in turn, produces a political atmosphere and a mentality that preserve class divisions along racial lines, leading to the greater alienation of minority children from American institutions and further diminishing their chances for upward mobility (Fainstein 1995).

But how would one account for the fact that immigrant children tend to do better than their US-born peers of similar socioeconomic background and attending public schools in the same neighborhood? Ogbu (1974) attributed different outcomes to a group's social status in the receiving society. He distinguished between immigrant/voluntary minorities and castelike/involuntary minorities. In his line of reasoning, either group members of racial minorities could accept an inferior caste status and a sense of basic inferiority as part of their collective self-definition, or they could create a positive view of their heritage on the basis of cultural and racial distinction, thereby establishing a sense of collective dignity (also see De Vos 1975).

While this was true for both immigrant minorities and caste-like minorities, the difference lay in the advantageous or disadvantageous aspects of racial or group identity. Ogbu (1989) showed from his research on Chinese-American students in Oakland, California, that in spite of cultural and language differences and relatively low economic status, these students had grade point averages that ranged from 3.0 to 4.0. He attributed their academic success to the integration of these students into the family and the community, which placed high values on education and held positive attitudes toward public schools.

The benefits of deliberate cultivation of ethnicity also appeared in the work of Gibson (1989), who found that the outstanding performance of Punjabi children in a relatively poor rural area of Northern California was a result of parental pressure put on children to adhere to their own immigrant families and to avoid excessive Americanization. Similarly, Caplan and his associates (1989) found that Indochinese refugee children (not including Cambodians and Hmongs) excelled in the American school system, despite the disadvantaged location of their schools and their parents' lack of education and facility with English. Caplan and his associates attributed academic achievement to cultural values and practices unique to Indochinese families. Even among Indochinese refugees, the ethnic effect was significant. Rumbaut & Ima (1988) found that Vietnamese high school students did much better in both GPAs and test scores than their Cambodian and Laotian peers, and that, overall, the strongest predictor of GPA was the measure of ethnic resilience.

More recently, Portes & Rumbaut reported findings from a large random sample of second-generation high school students in Florida and southern California, showing that parents' socioeconomic status, length of US residence, and homework hours significantly affected academic performance, but that controlling for these factors did not eliminate the effect of ethnicity (Portes & Rumbaut 1996, Rumbaut 1995, 1996). Kao & Tienda (1995) found, based on data from the National Education Longitudinal Studies (known as NELS), that parental nativity and children's birthplace had different effects on children's academic outcomes depending on race and ethnicity. Portes & MacLeod (1996), also using NELS, reported that the negative effect of disadvantaged group memberships among immigrant children was reinforced rather than reduced in suburban schools, but that the positive effect of advantaged group memberships remained significant even in inner-city schools.

In the most recent research on adolescent development, though originally not intending to focus on ethnic differences, Steinberg (1996) revealed a surprisingly prominent and strong role that ethnicity played in structuring adolescents' lives, both in and outside of school. He found that Asian-American students outperformed European-American students who, in turn, outperformed African-American and Latino-American students by significantly large margins, and that the ethnic differences remained marked and consistent across nine different high schools under study and after controlling for social class, family structure, and place of birth of parents. He also found that the ethnic effect persists in important explanatory variables of school success, such as the belief in the payoff of schooling, attributional styles, and peer groups. Steinberg concluded that ethnicity emerged as just as important a factor as social class and gender in defining and shaping the everyday lives of American children.

However, the advantage of ethnicity may be limited for caste-like minorities. If a socially defined racial minority group wishes to assimilate but finds that normal paths of integration are blocked on the basis of race, the group may be forced to take alternative survival strategies that enable them to cope psychologically with racial barriers but that do not necessarily encourage school success. Further, caste-like involuntary minorities may react to racial oppression by constructing resistance both as conformity—"unqualified acceptance of the ideological realm of the larger society"—and, more frequently, as avoidance—"willful rejection of whatever will validate the negative claims of the larger society" (Fordham 1996:39). As a consequence, it is the willful refusal to learn, not the failure to learn, that affects academic outcomes of the children of caste-like involuntary minorities (Kohl 1994, p. 2). The forced-choice dilemma confronting Chicano and Puerto Rican youth is a case in point. Gibson (1989) and Bourgois (1991) found that Chicano students and Puerto Rican students who did well in school were forcefully excluded by their coethnic peers as "turnovers" acting "white."

Nonetheless, not all immigrant groups can fit into the category of immigrant/voluntary minority. In the case of Dominican immigrants, Pessar (1987) noted that many first-generation members of the group were able to improve their living standards by pooling resources in their households and that they were mostly satisfied with what they had achieved, comparing their lives in America to their lives in the Dominican Republic. However, she cast doubt on whether the struggle of first-generation immigrants would steer the second generation to upholding their parent's aspirations and fulfilling their own expectations of socioeconomic mobility. She speculated that Dominican children were likely to be frustrated and disappointed if they found themselves trapped at the lower rungs of the occupational ladder, because of "blatant discrimination" and "lack of access to prestigious social networks" linking them to higher professions (1987, pp. 124–125). Portes & Stepick (1993) and Waters (1996) also noted such a trend among Haitian youth in Miami and West Indian youth in New York City toward rapid assimilation into ghetto youth subcultures, at the cost of giving up their immigrant parents' pride of culture and hopes for mobility on the basis of ethnic solidarity. This prospect of downward assimilation was also expected to disproportionately affect children of Mexican immigrants (Perlmann & Waldinger 1996).

Consequently, subordinate groups may react to their disadvantaged status with different strategies: Some may rely on social capital available in their own ethnic community to actively fight for acceptance by the larger society; others may consciously reject the ideology and norms of the larger society by reconstructing an ethnicity in resistance to the oppressing structure; still others may give up their struggle and remain trapped in the bottom of the society.

### *The Family, the Community, and Networks of Social Relations*

In the United States, the family is the most important institutional environment outside of school for socialization, adaptation, and the future social mobility of children. Success in school, one of the most important indications of adapting to society, depends not only on the cognitive ability and motivation of individual children, but also on the economic and social resources available to them through their families.

Socioeconomic status is certainly one of the most important characteristics of the family context because it influences where children live and where they go to school. While wealthier immigrant families are able to settle directly in suburban middle-class communities, most others are forced to settle in declining urban areas, starting their American life either in poverty or on welfare as in the case of refugees. The low socioeconomic status of those immigrant families just arriving subjects children directly to underprivileged segments of the host society and the associated disadvantages and pathologies.

However, socioeconomic status is not all that counts; just as important are family structures and their embedded family ties. Recent research has shown that immigrant children from intact (especially two-natural-parent) families or from families associated with tightly knit social networks consistently show better psychological conditions, higher levels of academic achievement, and stronger educational aspirations than those in single-parent or socially isolated families. Results from the survey of immigrant children in San Diego and Miami revealed that, regardless of race/ethnicity, immigrant students who retained strong cultural and family identity tended to outpace others in school, including their native-born European-American peers, because their immigrant families reinforced the values of hard work and educational achievement (Rumbaut 1994b, 1996, Portes 1995, Portes & Schauffler 1994). The case study on immigrant youth from troubled Central American countries showed that high-achievement motivation was significantly related to a strong sense of group affiliation, family loyalty, and obligation in helping their less fortunate relatives and folks still trapped in war and misery in their homeland (Suárez-Orozco 1989). The case study of Vietnamese youth in a poor neighborhood in New Orleans found that Vietnamese high school students who reported strong orientations toward traditional family values of obedience, industriousness, and helping others were more likely to do well in school than those who did not. However, the effects of independent thinking and concern with individual social prestige, which were most commonly associated with contemporary American society, were insignificant (Zhou & Bankston 1994). These consistent findings have highlighted the central role the family plays in the lives of immigrants and their children.

If the presence of both parents at home and well-connected family ties are considered sources of social capital, the loss, or truncation, of the family system can reduce the access to social resources available to children (Fernández-Kelly 1995, Rumbaut 1996). Most immigrant households in the United States are nuclear rather than extended families. While migration extends social and familial ties across national borders that facilitate further migratory flows (Landale 1996), it simultaneously disrupts the traditional family system upon arrival both in the immigrant family itself and in the social network to which the family is a part. In some cases, family disruption can cause serious problems for children's upbringing in the American context, when the family is separated by national borders and isolated from the ongoing networks of kinship relations in the homeland. The so-called "relayed migration" (Sung 1987) or "serial migration" (Waters 1996), a process under which members of an immigrant family arrive (both intentionally and involuntarily) at different times, can strain parent-child and sibling relationships. The truncation of family networks, a situation where routine interactions among kins and former neighbors or friends are broken, can weaken traditional mechanisms of control and support.

In other cases, however, immigrant families are able to mobilize ethnic resources to reconstruct systems of family ties in the United States by shifting and expanding the criteria for inclusion in the family circle. Many Vietnamese refugee families, for example, are broken down in fragments of nuclear or extended families as a common strategy of flight. These smaller units are sometimes further fragmented by leaving grandparents and younger children, or wives and younger children, behind in the hope of bringing them out after the fleeing family is resettled. As a result, some of the families may be extended to contain distantly related or even unrelated members, while other families may have closely related members left behind in Vietnam (Zhou & Bankston, forthcoming). Once resettled, however, families, friends, and distant relatives who were marginal members of the family circle in Vietnam may become part of the active circle of kin relations in the United States (Caplan et al 1989, Kibria 1993). This reconstructed family pattern has often given rise to a sense of collective strength in coping and to new mechanisms in reestablishing social ties and cooperative kin-based economic practices for immigrants to support one another in an alien environment (Kibria 1993, Perez 1994, Zhou & Bankston 1994). Studies on immigrant families of different ethnic groups have revealed similar patterns of family reconstruction (Booth et al 1996).

Even when immigrant families are maintained by two parents or extended kin and by a high level of conformity to traditional values, these families cannot function effectively in isolation, especially under unfavorable socioeconomic situations when the means of attaining family goals of "making it in America" is disrupted by the day-to-day struggle for survival and by the adversarial subcultures of the underprivileged segment of American society surrounding many immigrant families. How is it possible to ensure that immigrants and their offspring maintain their values and work habits and learn the skills for socioeconomic advancement? An answer to this question requires something more than a check-list of socioeconomic characteristics of individual families. The key is to examine the networks of social relations, namely how individual families are related to one another in the ethnic community and how immigrant children are involved in these networks.

The networks of social relations involve shared obligations, social supports, and social controls. When, for example, Korean Americans obtain from other Korean Americans low-interest loans requiring little collateral, or Chinese-American students receive encouragement and approval in after-school Chinese language classes for their general academic orientations, these are forms of social support inherent in particular patterns of social relations within the ethnic community. When, on the other hand, a group member experiences disapproval, or even ostracism, from co-ethnics for failing to attain a respected occupation, this is a form of social control. Zhou & Bankston (1994, forthcoming) proposed a model of ethnic social relations based on their study of Vietnamese adolescents in New Orleans. In the Vietnamese community in New Orleans, they observed that Vietnamese adolescents were constantly reminded of their duty to show respect for their elders, to take care of younger siblings, to work hard, and to make decisions upon approval of parents not simply within a particular family but in the community where other families practiced similar values. In this "watchful and ever-vigilant" community, young Vietnamese found little competition from other desiderata because the social world of their families was restricted to the closed and highly integrated circles of the ethnic group. Since what was considered good or bad was clearly specified and closely monitored by these networks, young people found it hard to "to get away with much." The researchers concluded that the conformity to traditional family values and behavioral standards required a high level of family integration into a community that reinforced these values and standards. The outcomes of adaptation, therefore, depend on how immigrant children fit in their own ethnic community, or in their local environment if such an ethnic community is absent, and how their ethnic community or the local environment fit in the larger American society. In the case of the Vietnamese, being part of a Vietnamese network appears to offer a better route to upward mobility than being Americanized into the underprivileged local environment, or for that matter, into the native-born mainstream youth subcultures.

While family ties function as an important source of support and control, recent research has found evidence to indicate that the cohesion of family ties tends to deteriorate with longer duration of US residence, as in the case of refugees from Central America (Gil & Vega 1996). Researchers have also cautioned that even strong cultural identities and social ties, which may be considered as sources of social capital, may sometimes be insufficient because of racial or class disadvantages. In a study of a ghetto African-American community, Stack (1974) showed that African-American families depended on patterns of co-residence, kinship-based exchange networks for survival. This means of survival, however, demanded the sacrifice of upward mobility and geographic movement, and it discouraged marriage, because of structural constraints such as the inexorable unemployment of African-American women and men. Welfare policies disrupted the support networks and conspired against the ability of the poor to build up equity. Similarly, Fernández-Kelly (1995) found, in a study of teenage pregnancies in a Baltimore ghetto, that kinship networks in ghettos were often graced with strong family and friendship bonds but that these networks lacked connections to other social networks that controlled access to larger sets of opportunities. Moreover, symbols of ethnic pride and cultural identity that developed in reaction to social isolation and racial domination (e.g. the sparkling mounds of braided hair of young African-American women) became signals that barred access to resources and employment in the larger society. Such truncated networks and reactive ethnicity could severely limit the ability of children to envision alternative paths out of the ghetto and to turn cultural capital into resourceful social capital (Fernández-Kelly 1995, Fordham 1996, Kohl 1994).

## *Intergenerational Relations*

The clash between two social worlds is the most commonly cited problem of intergenerational relations. In fact, intergenerational conflicts are not simply a unique immigrant phenomenon (Berrol 1995, Child 1943); they are also an American phenomenon rooted in the American tradition of a "moral rejection of authority" (Gorer 1963:53). In a recent study of Latino adolescents, Suárez-Orozco & Suárez-Orozco (1995) found that intergenerational conflicts are more common among European-American adolescents who are more ambivalent toward authority and schooling and are more peer-oriented than among Latino-American adolescents who are more respectful of authority and more family-oriented. They attribute this gap to the impact of changing American youth culture that glorifies contempt for authorities and a peer orientation, implying that assimilating into the American youth culture may cause more harm than good for immigrant adolescents.

In the United States, immigrant children often become Americanized so quickly that their parents cannot keep up with them. There is a fear in the older generation that their children will leave them, become like other American youth, and forget about their roots. This fear, however, has originated not from the process of acculturation but from the migration process itself. Migration disrupts normal parent-child relationships in a number of observable ways, shown in a number of case studies and surveys on immigrant children (Berrol 1995, Kibria 1993, Rumbaut 1994b, Sung 1987, Waters 1996, Zhou 1997). First, many immigrant families suffer lengthy separation from the father or mother or older siblings because of delayed reunification. When all the members are reunited, they have to make an effort to adapt to each other in a new situation. Second, working outside the home has become the norm and an economic necessity for women. This work role gives women some measures of independence but creates difficulty in child-rearing and weakens the status and authority of men. Also, face-to-face interaction between parents and children decreases as both parents are usually out working for long hours. Third, because parents lack proficiency in English, children often act as interpreters and translators for their parents. Such role reversal usually leads to greater dependence of parents on children and a loss of parental authority. Meanwhile members of the younger generation are anxious that they might never become "American" because of these intrinsic family ties.

Immigrant children and their parents tend to perceive their host society and their relationships with it from different angles. The younger generation tends to focus on current adjustment, paying attention to the external traits of what they have come to define as being "American." They struggle to fit in based on a frame of reference that they have acquired from their American peers and from television and other forms of mass media. They often find themselves confused by such questions as: How do I fit into American culture and my own ethnic culture at the same time? Which side should I stay loyal to, American or my own ethnic culture? Can I ever become American without leaving home? At times, they feel embarrassed by their parents' "old" ways.

Parents, on the other hand, are primarily concerned both with making the best of a new environment and with retaining traditional family life. These parental concerns tend to lead them to focus on the future and to emphasize discipline and scholastic achievement. When children respond to these emphases in an unexpected way, parents puzzle: Why are my children so disrespectful? How can I make my children understand that everything I am doing is for their own good? Can't they understand that I wouldn't have chosen a life here if it hadn't been for them? What should I do to keep my children from losing their cultural roots and from assimilating too much?

The frequent difficulties facing the new second generation arise from the struggles of individuals to balance the demands of American culture with those of tradition-minded parents (Dublin 1996). Portes & Rumbaut (1996, Chapter 7) conceptualize the acculturation gaps between immigrant parents and their children in a typology of "generational consonance versus dissonance." Generational consonance occurs when parents and children both remain unacculturated, or both acculturate at the same rate, or both agree on selective acculturation. Generational dissonance occurs when children neither correspond to levels of parental acculturation nor conform to parental guidance, leading to role reversal and intensified parent-child conflicts. According to Portes & Rumbaut, these acculturation patterns interact with contextual factors—racial discrimination, urban subcultures, and labor market prospects—to affect adaptational outcomes of children. When contextual factors are unfavorable, as is the case confronting the majority of today's second generation, consonant acculturation enables immigrant children to lean on material or moral resources available in the family and the immigrant community; it thus increases the probability of upward assimilation. On the contrary, dissonant acculturation severs ties between children and their adult social world, deprives children of family or community resources, and leads them farther and farther away from parental expectations. In this situation, immigrant children are likely to rebel against parental educational expectations and to assimilate into an adversarial academic orientation in response to discrimination, subcultural pressures, and blocked mobility, as exemplified by Haitian children in Miami and West Indian children in New York City (Portes & Stepick 1993, Waters 1994, 1996).

What determines intergenerational conflicts? Using a large random sample of over 5000 immigrant children in San Diego and Miami, Rumbaut (1994b) examined the possible effects of a number of objective and subjective predictors that measure children's demographic characteristics, family situations, language use, academic performance, and discrimination. He found that parent-child conflicts were significantly less likely to occur in families with both natural parents at home and with parents or siblings readily available to offer help with homework. But among females, conflicts were significantly more likely to occur in families where the mother was less educated and where economic well-being was perceived as having worsened, where children felt embarrassed by parents and had nobody to help with homework at home. Tensions were also likely to be exacerbated among children who preferred to speak English at home, who had low GPAs and educational aspirations, who spent much time watching television and too little time on homework, and who experienced discrimination or perceived themselves as being discriminated against.

Intergenerational conflicts, in turn, lead to dwindling parental authority and insufficient family communications and have significantly negative effects on children's self-esteem, psychosocial well-being, and academic aspirations (Gil & Vega 1996, Rumbaut 1996, Szapocznik & Hernandez 1988). However, whether the effects on children's adaptation are deleterious also depends on the specific context of exit from countries of origin and the context of reception upon arrival (Portes & Rumbaut 1996). Several studies on immigrant children have reported that intergenerational conflicts within families do not necessarily frustrate successful adaptation to a host society (Schulz 1983). The ethnic social structure can sometimes play an important role in mediating between individual families and the larger social setting. Immigrant children and parents often interact with one another in immigrant communities. If patterns of interaction are contained within a tightly knit ethnic community, these children and parents are likely to share their similar experiences with other children and parents. In this way, the community creates a buffer zone to ease the tension between individual self-fulfillment and family commitment. The community also serves to moderate original cultural patterns, to legitimize reestablished values and norms, and to enforce consistent standards. This situation resembles Sung's description of immigrant children in New York's Chinatown in the mid-1980s. Sung observed:

> For Chinese immigrant children who live in New York's Chinatown or in satellite Chinatowns, these [bi-cultural] conflicts are moderated to a large degree because there are other

> Chinese children around to mitigate the dilemmas that they encounter. When they are among their own, the Chinese ways are better known and better accepted. The Chinese customs and traditions are not denigrated to the degree that they would be if the immigrant child were the only one to face the conflict on his or her own (1987, p. 126).

Sung's finding suggests that frequent interactions with co-ethnics within an ethnic community could help young ethnic group members to develop a sense of identity that would ease bicultural conflicts. Similarly, in their case study of the Vietnamese in New Orleans, Zhou & Bankston (forthcoming) found that the bicultural tension did not produce rebellion; on the contrary, being both Vietnamese and American frequently caused children to achieve superior levels of performance. They reasoned that, first, parents did not just bring with them a desire to maintain traditional cultural patterns. The parents also, as a result of the process of migration and their own struggles for survival in a new land, developed a strong orientation toward upward mobility. Beliefs about parent-child relations were combined with this mobility orientation and modified by it. Second, parents were not alone in their efforts to control and guide their children. They maintained relations in closely knit ethnic networks that served to reinforce parental expectations and acted as bridges between Vietnamese family life and the surrounding American society.

Zhou & Bankston also analyzed in depth the pattern of gender role change to show how the immigrant orientation toward upward mobility could perpetuate and modify traditional cultural patterns. They found that in the case of the Vietnamese the older generation was willing to modify the original culture to adjust to life in the host society. Vietnamese Americans still believe that women should be subject to higher levels of social control and parental authority than men are. But the mobility orientation of Vietnamese Americans means that social control is no longer a matter of preventing women from acquiring education but rather it acts to push them toward educational excellence. Paradoxically, the young women who are more controlled by the family and the ethnic community show higher levels of adaptation to the American school environment (Forthcoming, Chapter 8).

These case studies of the Chinese in New York and the Vietnamese in New Orleans highlight the important role the ethnic community can play in channeling frustrations with cultural conflicts away from rebellion and instead turning cultural tensions into pressures for achievement. Whether results from these cases are generalizable across immigrant groups is inconclusive, however.

## *Patterns of Language Acquisition and Language Use*

Linguistic adaptation is another challenge for the new second generation. Proficiency in English has been regarded as the single most important prerequisite for assimilation into American society and as a strong social force binding the

American people together. Lack of English proficiency, aggravated by the problem of linguistic isolation and disadvantages associated with minority status, has been a severe handicap for new immigrants and their children. Geographically, some immigrant children are concentrated in linguistically distinctive neighborhoods where their native tongue is used more commonly than English by the people around them. This leaves immigrants in direct daily contact only with other immigrants or with members of native minorities rather than with members of the dominant majority, who have moved away from areas of immigrant concentration. At the school level, immigrant children often find themselves in classrooms with other immigrant children speaking a language other than English or with other native minority children with distinct inner-city accents. The Los Angeles Unified School District has recently identified 87% of the district's students as "minority" and 40% as having limited English proficiency (LEP) (Lopez 1996). Meanwhile, immigrant children constantly face the pressure to become proficient in English, from the pervasive pull of American popular culture and the media, from their school teachers, and from their often non-English speaking parents, who at the same time pressure them to preserve their ancestral tongues.

The issue of language, then, is one that must be addressed in any examination of the adaptation of immigrant children. Does the language problem confronting immigrant children hinder their assimilation into American society? Does the maintenance of parents' native tongues necessarily lead to unfavorable outcomes as these children adapt to school and grow into adulthood? The doctrine of "forcible assimilation" insists that English language skills compete with non-English language skills; that bilingualism causes academic failure, anxiety, and mental confusion of immigrant exposed to two languages; and that non-English skills should be wholeheartedly abandoned. Associated with this ideology has been a "sink or swim" linguistic policy in American public schools. Such a policy holds that children from non-English speaking homes should be placed in school environments where only English is tolerated.

In recent years, adherents of "forcible assimilation" have tended to advance a sociological, rather than a psychological, argument for monolingualism in schools. Advocates of the "English Only" movement maintain that bilingualism can inhibit social adaptation in a predominantly English-speaking society, creating a "new apartheid." This position, however, has been supported more often by rhetorical skills than by empirical evidence. One exception was a literature review of research on bilingualism from the US Department of Education (Baker & de Kanter 1981). This report reviewed past studies on bilingual education and evaluated the evidence on the advantages of bilingualism. It concluded that bilingually educated students score below average in both English skills and general academic achievement.

Unlike forcible assimilation, "reluctant bilingualism" is tolerant of bilingualism and supports its use in schools. However, the reluctant bilingualists endorse the use of non-English language only as a strategy for achieving the ultimate goal of linguistic assimilation. Reluctant bilingualists advocate programs of "transitional bilingual education." Transitional bilingualism is established as a stated policy of the US Government by the Bilingual Education Act of 1968. The goal is to help students keep up with reading, math, and other subjects in their native tongues while they are taught enough English to transfer to regular classrooms. The native language, from this view, is also treated as the source of a hindrance rather than as an asset.

The debate over the language issue has largely ignored the fact that language acquisition and language use are constrained by contextual factors as well as individual preferences. Lopez (1996) found that English monolingualism at home increased from one generation to the next, and that the shift was more rapid in the third generation than in the second generation. However, such a shift was more rapid among Asian-Americans than among Latino Americans across generations. Likewise, the shift from bilingualism (proficiency in both English and native language) to English monolingualism in the third generation was more substantial among Asian-Americans than among Latino Americans. He pointed out that the better maintenance of Spanish among Latino Americans, especially in the Southwest, is attributed to the proximity to Mexico, residential isolation from the dominant group, and ethnic concentration in the sense of sheer numbers.

How do language patterns shift and how does language use affect adaptational outcomes of immigrant children? The negative view of parental native languages has been challenged by studies on immigrant children since the 1960s (Portes & Rumbaut 1996, Chapter 6). A growing body of empirical evidence indicates that both cognitive abilities and scholastic achievement are actually positively associated with bilingualism. Tienda (1984) showed that the retention of Spanish proficiency did not hinder the socioeconomic achievement of Hispanic-American men, and that, at the minimum, bilingual education would not retard lifelong achievement. Fernández & Nielsen (1986) provided evidence from national logitudinal data that, among Hispanic- and European-American high school students, proficiency in both English and parental native languages was positively related to academic achievement. Matute-Bianchi (1986) found in an ethnographic study of Mexican-American children that advanced bilingual skills were related to a strong Mexican identity and that fully bilingual young Mexican-Americans tended to perform better in school than those who lacked proficient bilingual skills. She concluded that proficiency in the native language allows young people to gain greater access to the emotional and normative supports of the ethnic group. In a study of Chinese immigrant children in New York City's Chinatown, Sung (1987) found that bilingual students had higher student retention rates, more graduates, and higher self-esteem. She suggested that these positive outcomes were associated with the acceptance of distinctive ethnicity. Other researchers have found that language maintenance bilingual programs, as opposed to transitional bilingual programs, helped students learn the language of the dominant society effectively (Cazden & Snow 1990, Cummins 1980, 1981, Bhatnager 1980).

A recent two-period (1986–1987 and 1989–1990) study of the entire high school student cohorts in San Diego Unified School District (the nation's eighth largest) reported that, with the main exception of some Hispanic students who were generally of much lower socioeconomic status, all of the non-English immigrant minorities were outperforming their English-only co-ethnics as well as majority European-American students. This finding applied to both bilinguals (designated by the District as having fluent English proficiency—FEP) and semi-bilinguals (designated as having limited English proficiency—LEP), though FEP students did better than their LEP coethnics. In standardized tests, while English monolinguals tended to have the highest scores in reading comprehension, FEP students showed significantly higher scores in math than English monolinguals, for every nationality. The same study also reported that Vietnamese students, who are mostly members of the one-and-a-half generation, were among the ethnic groups with the highest GPAs, trailing only after Chinese, Koreans, and Japanese. In terms of dropout rates, however, the results were mixed. While FEP, or truly bilingual, students consistently showed much lower dropout rates than English monolingual students across all ethnic groups, LEP students were observed to be at the greatest risk of dropping out (Rumbaut 1995, Rumbaut & Ima 1988). Bankston & Zhou (1995) reported similar findings concerning the effect of literacy in the parental native language from their study of Vietnamese high school students in New Orleans.

Moreover, the ethnic language is intrinsic to ethnicity. Under certain conditions, it allows immigrant children to gain access to some kind of social capital generated from a distinctive ethnic identity, such as support and control from bilingual or non-English-speaking parents and ethnic communities. Bankston & Zhou (1995) found that literacy in the ethnic language was strongly associated with ethnic self-identification, which in turn, contributed to academic excellence. They concluded that advanced ethnic language abilities, such as literacy, were related to achievement because ethnic language skills tied immigrant children more closely to their traditions, their families, and their communities that enforce the values of academic achievement.

However, not all immigrant children can benefit from bilingualism because patterns of language use are affected by class, race/ethnicity, length of US residence, and other contextual factors. In an earlier study, Lopez (1976) found that the use of Spanish depressed occupational attainment indirectly by lowering educational achievement among Chicanos because Chicanos concentrated in areas and occupations that allow few returns to the knowledge of Spanish. Fernández and Nielsen (1986) also reported that the positive effect of bilingualism tended to diminish with longer duration of US residence, and that the frequent use of Spanish was negatively related to academic achievement after controlling for English and Spanish proficiency. They attributed the contradictory outcomes to a specific handicap associated with Hispanic membership.

The language issue, therefore, is not just an linguistic issue but has deep-rooted sociological implications. Of course, we cannot entirely discount the possibility that the effect of ethnic language on overall academic achievement may be due, in part, to a transference of cognitive development: Skills developed in learning to read the parental language may be transferred to other areas of intellectual endeavor, such as history, geography, or mathematics. Nevertheless, the acquisition of English and the maintenance of parental native languages do not function in isolation from social contexts (also see Bialystok & Hakuta 1994).

## CONCLUSION

For immigrant children and children of immigrants, growing up American can be a matter of smooth acceptance or of traumatic confrontation. Immigrant children are generally eager to embrace American culture and to acquire an American identity by becoming indistinguishable from their American peers. In some cases, however, they may be perceived as "unassimilated" even when they try hard to abandon their own ethnic identities. In other cases, they may be accepted as well-adjusted precisely because they retain strong ethnic identities. In the long journey to becoming American, the progress of today's one-and-a-half and second generation is largely contingent upon human and financial capital that their immigrant parents bring along, the social conditions from which their families exit as well as the context that receives them, and their cultural patterns, including values, family relations, and social ties, reconstructed in the process of adaptation. The host society offers uneven possibilities to different immigrant groups. These unequal possibilities may limit the opportunities of immigrant groups, but they do not necessarily constitute a complete denial of opportunity.

Immigrants are today being absorbed by different segments of American society, but becoming American may not always be an advantage for immigrant children and children of immigrants. When immigrants enter middle-class communities directly, or after a short transition, it may be advantageous for them to acculturate and assimilate. When they enter the bottom of the ethnic hierarchy of drastic social inequality, the forces of assimilation come mainly from the underprivileged segments of this structure, and this is likely to result in distinct disadvantages, viewed as maladjustment by both mainstream society and the ethnic community. In this case, young immigrants or children of immigrants may benefit by cultivating their ethnic ties in their ethnic communities to develop forms of behavior likely to break the cycle of disadvantage and to lead to upward mobility.

The interest in immigrant children and children of immigrants has recently been growing. However, there is still a big gap between the strategic importance of the new second generation and current knowledge about its conditions (Portes 1996). Data on which the existing body of research is based come mostly from regional survey research and ethnographic studies on selected immigrant groups. Census data sources have been, or are being, scrutinized by some researchers to describe the current state of immigrant children, their geographic distribution and demographic and socioeconomic characteristics, school attendance, fertility patterns, labor market opportunities facing entrants to the labor force, and the establishment of independent households (Hirschman 1994, Jensen & Chitose 1994, Mollenkopf et al 1995, Landale & Oropesa 1995, Zhou & Bankston, forthcoming). A major drawback of the census data (1980 and 1990) is that a critical variable—the birthplace of parents—has been dropped from the decennial census since 1980, making it impossible to identify directly the children of immigrants (Hirschman 1994). Researchers have to use the ancestry question as a proxy. This treatment of ethnic origin variable is problematic. Perlmann & Waldinger (1996) note that, because of high rates of intermarriages in the third generation, the respondent's choice of ethnic identity is selective, making it difficult to accurately predict the independent effect of ethnic origin on intergenerational mobility.

Moreover, the census data do not have any direct measures for contextual effects of the family, the school, the neighborhood, and the ethnic community, nor do they have detailed information on school performance. There are a few other national surveys that offer important data that the census lack, such as NELS and the National Longitudinal Study of Adolescent Health (known as "Add HEALTH"). These data sets have over-sampled some minority and immigrant groups and have detailed information about contextual influences of the family, the school, and the community on adolescent health, behavior, family life, peer relationships, goals, aspirations, academic performance, and related variables. However, they do not contain viable subsamples of the most recently arrived national-origin groups within broader regional categories to conduct comparative analyses.

For further theoretical inquiry, the following questions may offer some stimulus: Will members of a generation born or reared in the United States gradually be pulled away from a heritage vastly different from those of the Europeans who arrived over the course of this century? Will those who rebel against this heritage be the best-adjusted, socially and economically? Will racial barriers limit the participation of immigrant children in American life? How would being hyphenated Americans influence the ways in which immigrant children become assimilated, and why may some of these ways be more advantageous than others? Will immigrant families and ethnic communities persist in affecting the lives of children of the second generation? Will cultural distinctiveness of hyphenated Americans eventually melt down into a pot of Anglo-American homogeneity? If not, what will ethnic diversity mean for the offspring of today's new second generation? Each of these questions has theoretical as well as practical implications. Given the unique characteristics of and the scanty knowledge about the complex ways in which the second generation of new immigrants are "becoming American," future studies are both urgent and necessary.

ACKNOWLEDGMENTS

The research was supported by the Russell Sage Foundation and a UCLA Faculty Career Development Award. The author wishes to thank Rubén Rumbaut and an anonymous reviewer for their helpful suggestions, but she is exclusively responsible for the contents.



*Literature Cited*

Alba RD. 1985. *Italian Americans: Into the Twilight of Ethnicity.* Englewood Cliffs, NJ: Prentice-Hall

Archdeacon TJ. 1983. *Becoming American: An Ethnic History.* New York: Free Press

Baker K, de Kanter A. 1981. *Effectiveness of Bilingual Education: A Review of Literature.* Washington, DC: US Dep. Educ., Off. Plan. Budget & Eval.

Bankston CL III, Zhou M. 1995. Effects of minority-language literacy on the academic achievement of Vietnamese youth in New Orleans. *Sociol. Educ.* 68(Jan):1–17

Barth EA, Noel DL. 1972. Conceptual framework for the analysis of race relations: an evaluation. *Soc. Forc.* 50:333–48

Becker HS. 1963. *Outsiders: Studies in the Sociology of Deviance.* New York: Free Press

Berrol SC. 1995. *Growing up American: Immigrant Children in America, Then and Now.* New York: Twayne

Bhatnager JP. 1980. Linguistic behavior and adjustment of immigrant children in French and English schools in Montreal. *Int. J. Appl. Psychol.* 28:141–58

Bialystok E, Hakuta K. 1994. In *Other Worlds: The Science and Psychology of Second-Language Acquisition.* New York: Basic

Booth A, Crouter AC, Landale N, eds. 1996. *Immigration and the Family: Research and Policy on U.S. Immigrants.* New Jersey: Erlbaum Assoc.

Bourgois P. 1991. *In search of respect: the new service economy and the crack alternative in Spanish Harlem.* Paper presented Conf. on Poverty, Immigration, and Urban Marginality in Advanced Soc. Maison Suger, Paris, May 10–11

Caplan N, Choy MH, Whitmore JK. 1989. *The Boat People and Achievement in America: A Study of Family Life, Hard Work, and Cultural Values.* Ann Arbor: Univ. Mich. Press

Cazden C, Snow CE. 1990. English plus: issues in bilingual education. Preface. *Ann. Am. Acad. Polit. Soc. Sci.* 508:9–11

Child IL. 1943. *Italian or American? The Second Generation in Conflict.* New Haven: Yale Univ. Press

Chiswick BR. 1977. Sons of immigrants: Are they at an earnings disadvantage? *Am. Econ. Rev.* 67(February):376–80

Coleman JS, Cambell EQ, Hobson CJ, McPartland J, Mood AM, Weinfeld FD, York RL. 1966. *Equality of Educational Opportunity.* Washington DC: US Gov. Print Off.

Conzen KN. 1991. Mainstreams and side channels: the localization of immigrant cultures. *J. Am. Ethnic Hist.* 10(Fall):5–20

Conzen KN, Gerber DA, Morawska E, Pozzetta GE, Vecoli RJ. 1992. The invention of ethnicity: a perspective from the U.S.A. *J. Am. Ethnic His.* 11(Fall):3–41

Cornelius WA. 1995. Educating California's immigrant children: introduction and overview. In *California's Immigrant Children: Theory, Research, and Implications for Educational Policy,* ed. R. Rumbaut, WA Cornelius, pp. 1–16. La Jolla, CA: Cent. US-Mexican Stud., Univ. Calif., San Diego

Cummins J. 1980. The cross-lingual dimension of language proficiency: implications for bilingual education and the optimal age question. *Teach. Eng. Speakers Other Lang. Q.* 14:175–87

Cummins J. 1981. Four misconceptions about language proficiency in bilingual education. *Natl. Assoc. Bilingual Educ. J.* 5:31–45

Davis M. 1993. The Gautreaux assisted housing program. In *Housing Markets and Residential Mobility*, ed. GT Kingsley, MA Turner, pp. 243–54. Washington DC: Urban Inst. Press

De Vos GA. 1975. Ethnic pluralism: conflict and accommodation. In *Ethnic Identity: Cultural Continuities and Change*, ed. G De Vos, L Romanucci-Ross, pp. 5–41. Palo Alto, CA: Mayfield

Dublin T. 1996. *Becoming American, Becoming Ethnic: College Students Explore Their Roots.* Philadelphia, PA: Temple Univ. Press

Fainstein N. 1995. Race, segregation, and the state. In *The Bubbling Cauldron: Race, Ethnicity, and the Urban Crisis*, MP Smith, J Feagin. Minneapolis, MN: Univ. Minn. Press

Fernández-Kelly MP. 1995. Social and cultural capital in the urban ghetto: implications for the economic sociology and immigration. In *The Economic Sociology of Immigration: Essays on Networks, Ethnicity, and Entrepreneurship,* ed. A. Portes, pp. 213–47. New York: Russell Sage Found.

Fernández RM, Nielsen F. 1986. Bilingualism and Hispanic scholastic achievement: some baseline results. *Soc. Sci. Res.* 15:43–70

Fordham S. 1996. *Blacked Out: Dilemmas of Race, Identity, and Success at Capital High.* Chicago: Univ. Chicago Press

Fukuyama F. 1993. Immigrants and family values. *Commentary* 95(5):26–32

Gans HJ. 1992. Second-generation decline: scenarios for the economic and ethnic futures of the post-1965 American immigrants. *Ethnic Racial Stud.* 15(2):173–92

Garcia MC. 1996. *Havana USA: Cuban Exiles and Cuban Americans in South Florida, 1959–1994.* Berkeley: Univ. Calif. Press

Gibson MA. 1989. *Accommodation without Assimilation: Sikh Immigrants in an American High School.* Ithaca, NY: Cornell Univ. Press

Gil AG, Vega WA. 1996. Two different worlds: acculturation stress and adaptation among Cuban and Nicaraguan families. *J. Soc. Personal Relat.* 13(3):435–56

Glazer N, Moynihan DP. 1970. *Beyond the Melting Pot: The Negroes, Puerto Ricans, Jews, Italians, and Irish of New York City.* Cambridge, MA: MIT Press. 2nd ed.

Goffman E. 1963. *Stigma: Notes on the Management of Spoiled Identity.* Englewood Cliffs, NJ: Prentice-Hall

Gordon MM. 1964. *Assimilation in American Life: The Role of Race, Religion, and National Origins.* New York: Oxford Univ. Press

Gorer G. 1963. *The American People: A Study in National Character.* New York: Norton

Greeley AM. 1976. The ethnic miracle. *Public Interest* 45:20–36

Handlin O. 1973. *The Uprooted.* Boston, MA: Little, Brown. 2nd ed.

Hernandez DJ. 1993. *America's Children: Resources from Family, Government, and the Economy.* New York: Russell Sage Found.

Hirschman C. 1994. Problems and prospects of studying immigrant adaptation from the 1990 Population Census: from generation comparison to the process of 'becoming American'. *Int. Migrat. Rev.* 28(4):690–713

Hirschman C, Falcon L. 1985. The educational attainment of religio-ethnic groups in the United States. *Res. Sociol. Educ. Socialization* 5:83–120

Jensen L, Chitose Y. 1994. Today's second generation: evidence from the 1990 U.S. Census. *Int. Migrat. Rev.* 28(4):714–35

Kao G, Tienda M. 1995. Optimism and achievement: the educational performance of immigrant youth. *Soc. Sci. Q.* 76(1):1–19

Keniston K, Carnegie Council on Children. 1977. *All Our Children.* New York: Harcourt, Brace, Jovanavich

Kibria N. 1993. *Family Tightrope: The Changing Lives of Vietnamese Americans.* Princeton, NJ: Princeton Univ. Press

Kohl H. 1994. *"I Won't Learn from You" and Other Thoughts on Creative Maladjustment.* New York: New Press

Landale NS. 1996. Immigration and the family: an overview. In *Immigration and the Family: Research and Policy on U.S. Immigrants,* ed. A Booth, AC Crouter, N Landale, pp. 281–91. New Jersey: Lawrence Erlbaum

Landale RS, NS Oropesa. 1995. *Immigrant children and the children of immigrants: inter- and intra-group differences in the United States. Research pap. 95–02.* Popul. Res. Group, Mich. State Univ.

Lopez DE. 1976. The social consequences of Chicano home/school bilingualism. *Soc. Prob.* 24 (2):234–46

Lopez DE. 1996. Language: diversity and assimilation. In *Ethnic Los Angeles,* ed. R Waldinger, M Bozorgmehr, pp. 139–63. New York: Russell Sage Found.

Matute-Bianchi ME. 1986. Ethnic identities and patterns of school success and failure among Mexican-descent and Japanese-American students in a California high school: an ethnographic analysis. *Am. J. Educ.* 95:233–55

Matute-Bianchi ME. 1991. Situational ethnicity and patterns of school performance among immigrant and non-immigrant Mexican-descent students. In *Minority Status and Schooling: A Comparative Study of Immigrant and Voluntary Minorities,* ed. MA Gibson, JU Ogbu, pp. New York: Garland

Merton RK. 1938. Social structure and anomie. *Am. Sociol. Rev.* 3:672–82

Mishel L, Bernstein J. 1992. *The State of Working America: 1992–1993.* Washington, DC: Econ. Policy Inst.

Mollenkopf J, Kasinitz P, Waters M. 1995. *The immigrant second generation in metropolitan New York.* Res. proposal to the Russell Sage Found.

Ogbu JU. 1974. *The Next Generation: An Ethnography of Education in an Urban Neighborhood.* New York: Academic

Ogbu JU. 1989. *Cultural models and educational strategies of non-dominant peoples.* The 1989 Catherine Molony Memorial Lecture. New York: City Coll. Workshop Cent.

Oropesa RS, Landale NS. Forthcoming. Immigrant legacies: ethnicity, generation and children's family and economic lives. *Soc. Sci. Q.*

Park RE. 1928. Human migration and the marginal man. *Am. J. Sociol.* 33:881–93

Perez L. 1994. The household structure of second-generation children: an exploratory study of extended family arrangement. *Int. Migrat. Rev.* 28(4):736–47

Pérez Firmat GP. 1994. *Life on the Hyphen: The Cuban-American Way.* Austin, TX: Univ. Texas Press

Perlmann J. 1988. *Ethnic Differences: Schooling and Social Structure among the Irish, Jews, and Blacks in an American City, 1988–1935.* New York: Cambridge Univ. Press

Perlmann J, Waldinger R. 1996. *Second generation decline? Immigrant children past and present—a reconsideration.* Revised version of a paper presented in conference on Becoming American/America Becoming: International Migration to the United States. Com. on Int. Migrat. of the Soc. Sci. Res. Council, Sanibel Island, Fl., January 18–21

Pessar PR. 1987. The Dominicans: women in the household and the garment industry. In *New Immigrant in New York,* ed. N Foner, pp. 103–29. New York: Columbia Univ. Press

Portes A. 1995. Economic sociology and the sociology of immigration: a conceptual overview. In *The Economic Sociology of Immigration: Essays on Networks, Ethnicity, and Entrepreneurship,* ed. A Portes, pp. 1–41. New York: Russell Sage Found.

Portes A. 1996. Introduction: Immigration and its aftermath. In *The New Second Generation* ed. A Portes, pp. 1–7. New York: Russell Sage Found.

Portes A, MacLeod D. 1996. The educational progress of children of immigrants: the roles of class, ethnicity, and school context. *Sociol. Educ.* 69(4):255–75

Portes A, Rumbaut RG. 1996. *Immigrant America: A Portrait.* Berkeley: Univ. Calif. Press. 2nd ed.

Portes A, Schauffler R. 1994. Language and the second generation: bilingualism yesterday and today. *Int. Migrat. Rev.* 28 (4):640–61

Portes A, Stepick A. 1993. *City on the Edge: The Transformation of Miami.* Berkeley, Ca.: Univ. Calif. Press

Portes A, Zhou M. 1993. The new second generation: segmented assimilation and its variants among post-1965 immigrant youth. *Ann. Am. Acad. Polit. Soc. Sci.* 530:74–98

Portes A, Zhou M. 1995. Divergent destinies: immigration, poverty, and entrepreneurship in the United States. In *Poverty, Inequality, and the Future of Social Policy: Western States in the New World Order,* ed. K McFate, R Rawson, WJ Wilson, pp. 489–520. New York: Russell Sage Found.

Rumbaut RG. 1991. The agony of exile: a study of the migration and adaptation of Indochinese refugee adults and children. In *Refugee Children: Theory, Research, and Services,* ed. FL Ahearn, Jr, JL Athey, pp. 53–91. Baltimore: Johns Hopkins Univ. Press

Rumbaut RG. 1994a. Origins and destinies: immigration to the United States since World War II. *Sociol. For.* 9(4):583–621

Rumbaut RG. 1994b. The crucible within: ethnic identity, self-esteem, and segmented assimilation among children of immigrants. *Int. Migrat. Rev.* 28(4):748–94

Rumbaut RG. 1995. The new Californians: comparative research findings on the educational progress of immigrant children. In *California's Immigrant Children: Theory, Research, and Implications for Educational Policy,* ed. RG Rumbaut, WA Cornelius, pp. 17–69. La Jolla, Ca: Cent. US-Mexican Stud., Univ. Calif., San Diego

Rumbaut RG. 1996. Ties that bind: immigration and immigrant families in the United States. In *Immigration and the Family: Research and Policy on U.S. Immigrants,* ed. A Booth, AC Crouter, N Landale, pp. 3–45. New Jersey: Lawrence Erlbaum

Rumbaut RG, Ima K. 1988. *The Adaptation of Southeast Asian Refugee Youth: A Comparative Study.* Washington, DC: US Off. Refugee Resettlement

Sancton T. 1992. How to get America off the dole? *Time* (May 25):44–47

Sandberg NC. 1974. *Ethnic Identity and Assimilation: The Polish-American Community.* New York: Praeger

Schulz N. 1983. *Voyagers in the Land: A Report on Unaccompanied Southeast Asian Refugee Children, New York City 1983.* Washington, DC: US Catholic Conf., Migrat. Refugee Serv.

Stack CB. 1974. *All Our Kin: Strategies for Survival in a Black Community.* New York: Harper Colophon

Steinberg L. 1996. *Beyond the Classroom.* New York: Simon & Schuster

Suárez-Orozco MM. 1989. *Central American Refugees and U.S. High Schools: A Psychological Study of Motivation and Achievement.* Stanford, CA: Stanford Univ. Press

Suárez-Orozco MM. 1991. Immigrant adaptation to schooling: a Hispanic case. In *Minority Status and Schooling: A Comparative Study of Immigrant and Involuntary Minorities,* ed. MA Gibson, JU Ogbu, pp. 37–61. New York: Garland

Suárez-Orozco C, Suárez-Orozco MM. 1995. *Transformations: Migration, Family Life, and Achievement Motivation among Latino Adolescents.* Stanford, Ca.: Stanford Univ. Press

Sung BL. 1987. *The Adjustment Experience of Chinese Immigrant Children in New York City.* Staten Island, NY: Cent. Migrat. Stud.

Szapocznik J, Hernandez R. 1988. The Cuban American family. In *Ethnic Families in America,* ed. CH Mindle, RW Habenstein, R Wright SPAN. New York: Elsevier

Tienda M. 1984. Language, education, and the socioeconomic achievement of Hispanic origin men. *Soc. Sci. Q.* 65:519–36

Tienda M, Liang Z. 1994. Poverty and immigration. In *Confronting Poverty: Prescriptions for Change,* ed. SH Darzinger, GD Sandefur, DH Weinbers, pp. 330–64. Cambridge, MA: Harvard Univ. Press

Waldinger R. 1996. Ethnicity and opportunity in the plural city. In *Ethnic Los Angeles,* ed. R Waldinger, M Bozorgmehr, pp. 445–70. New York: Russell Sage Found.

Warner WL, Srole L. 1945. *The Social Systems of American Ethnic Groups.* New Haven: Yale Univ. Press

Waters M. 1994. Ethnic and racial identities of second-generation Black immigrants in New York City. *Int. Migrat. Rev.* 28(4):795–820

Waters M. 1996. Immigrant families at risk: factors that undermine chances of success. In *Immigration and the Family: Research and Policy on U.S. Immigrants,* ed. A Booth, AC Crouter, N Landale, pp. 79–87. New Jersey: Lawrence Erlbaum

Wilson WJ. 1987. *The Truly Disadvantaged: The Inner City, the Underclass, and Public Policy.* Chicago: Univ. Chicago Press

Wirth L. 1925/1956. *The Ghetto.* Chicago: Univ. Chicago Press

Wytrwal JA. 1961. *America's Polish Heritage: A Social History of Poles in America.* Detroit: Endurance

Zhou M. 1997. Social capital in Chinatown: the role of community-based organizations and families in the adaptation of the younger generation. In *Beyond Black and White: New Voices, New Faces in the United States Schools,* ed. L Weis, MS Seller, pp. 181–206. Albany, NY: State Univ. NY Press

Zhou M, Bankston CL III. 1994. Social capital and the adaptation of the second generation: the case of Vietnamese youth in New Orleans. *Int. Migrat. Rev.* 28(4):775–99

Zhou M, Bankston CL III. Forthcoming. *Growing Up American: The Adaptation of Vietnamese Adolescents in the United States.* New York: Russell Sage Found.

*Annu. Rev. Sociol. 1997. 23:97–120*


# FEMINIST THEORY AND SOCIOLOGY: Underutilized Contributions for Mainstream Theory

*Janet Saltzman Chafetz*
Department of Sociology, University of Houston, Houston, Texas 77204

KEY WORDS: varieties of feminist theories, feminist theory ghettoization, theory canon revision, ubiquity of gender, critiques of feminist theories

ABSTRACT

Feminist theories in sociology reflect the rich diversity of general theoretical orientations in our discipline; there is no one form of feminist theory. The development of these theories over the last 25 years has only recently begun to influence the mainstream theory canon, which has much to learn from their insights. This chapter demonstrates why feminist versions of the following theory types should be more fully integrated into mainstream sociological theory: neo-Marxist, macro-structural, exchange, rational choice, network, status expectations, symbolic interactionist, ethnomethodological, neo-Freudian, and social role. Feminist standpoint theory, an epistemological critique of mainstream sociology, is discussed at the beginning, and the chapter concludes with a brief account of the newly developing effort to theorize the intersection of race, class, and gender.

## INTRODUCTION

The term "feminist theory" is used to refer to a myriad of kinds of works, produced by movement activists and scholars in a variety of disciplines; these are not mutually exclusive and include: (*a*) normative discussions of how societies and relationships ought to be structured, their current inequities, and strategies to achieve equity; (*b*) critiques of androcentric classical theories, concepts, epistemologies, and assumptions; (*c*) epistemological discussions of what constitute appropriate forms, subject matters, and techniques of theorizing from a feminist perspective; and (*d*) explanatory theories of the relationship between gender and



0360-0572/97/0815-0097$08.00

various social, cultural, economic, psychological, and political structures and processes. Much of this work is explicitly interdisciplinary in inspiration and intended audience. To complicate matters further, there is no consensus on the exact meaning of the word "feminist," which makes it difficult to distinguish with precision between theoretical material that pertains to gender (e.g. Parsons 1949, 1955, which no one would label feminist) and gender-related theory that is specifically "feminist." Finally, there is little consensus among feminist sociologists about the basic theoretical questions that require an answer, resulting in the proliferation of theories at a low level of abstraction that explain specific phenomena (e.g. pay inequity), in addition to more abstract, general works.

To remain within the limits of one chapter, I confine this review in several ways, beginning by excluding feminist theory that has not been produced or used extensively by sociologists. While feminist theory is often defined as "women-centered" (e.g. Lengermann & Niebrugge 1996:436; Smith 1979, 1987; Alway 1995), I use a definition that focuses more broadly on gender, yet maintains the normative emphasis implied by all definitions of the term feminist, which thus enables one to distinguish feminist from other gender-relevant theory. Earlier (Chafetz 1988:5), I defined it in terms of four criteria, which guide my selection of theories to be reviewed in this chapter: (*a*) "gender comprises a central focus or subject matter of the theory"; (*b*) "gender relations are viewed as a problem .... [F]eminist theory seeks to understand how gender is related to social inequities, strains, and contradictions"; (*c*) "gender relations are not viewed as ... immutable"; and (*d*) feminist theory "can be used ... to challenge, counteract, or change a status quo that disadvantages or devalues women." I focus most of my attention on explanatory theories but eschew discussion of the numerous, more substantively narrow ones. Finally, I limit this review to writings produced since the broad-scale reemergence of feminist consciousness and activism in the late 1960s, which began to affect sociological discourse after about 1970. This limitation does not mean, however, that no works that could be considered feminist theory were produced by sociologists before this time (see Fitzpatrick 1990, Deegan 1988, Donovan 1985, Rosenberg 1982).

A decade ago, Stacey & Thorne (1985; also Laslett et al 1992, Alway 1995) bemoaned the failure of sociology in general, and sociological theory in particular, to incorporate feminist insights as central components of its work. During the last two decades, a significant amount of feminist sociological theory and epistemology has been produced, as reflected in two books that provide broad overviews (my undergraduate text, Chafetz 1988; a more sophisticated book edited by England 1993a), and one less comprehensive collection of theoretical papers (Wallace 1989). Several interdisciplinary feminist theory books, which incorporate some sociological theory, have also appeared (e.g. Tong 1989, Gergen 1988, Rhode 1990). Recent theory textbooks in sociology (e.g. Ritzer

1996, Etzkowitz & Glassman 1991, Waters 1994, Wallace & Wolf 1995) have begun to include some discussion of feminist theory, but they vary widely in the extent and nature of their coverage of the topic. These texts typically confine discussion of feminist theory to its own chapter or chapter section. This practice is problematic both because it allows scholars and students to easily skip the topic and because it makes the contributions of feminist theorists appear more narrow and homogeneous than they are. In addition, many texts still omit feminist theory altogether, and a number of important contemporary theorists (e.g., James Coleman, Jeffrey Alexander, Peter Berger, Anthony Giddens) have ignored both feminist theoretical insights and the very topic of gender in their "general" theories (Seidman 1994:304).

Some feminists focus on those contemporary theories and texts that ignore the contributions of feminist theories and the topic of gender and conclude that feminist contributions remain largely ghettoized within our discipline (e.g. Ward & Grant 1991, Alway 1995). My view is that, while progress has been made in integrating feminist concerns and insights into the discipline's theoretical discourse, much work remains to be done. This chapter demonstrates the abundance and variety of feminist theoretical insights that can and already have to some extent contributed to a more robust theoretical understanding of social life, one which reflects the centrality of gender in virtually all sociocultural contexts. It also demonstrates that feminist theories emanate from, critique, and revise the rich array of theoretical traditions that define our discipline. Space limitations preclude much discussion of precisely how feminist theories can be better integrated with mainstream ones. Rather, I focus attention primarily on reviewing the central insights of feminist theories in order to better inform those sociologists who may be unfamiliar with much of this body of work about the rich array of theoretical ideas that are at their disposal.

## EPISTEMOLOGICAL ISSUES

Much of the literature that is labeled "feminist theory" consists of epistemology and epistemological critiques of "malestream" sociology. Its foundations reflect several nonfeminist traditions, especially Marx's and Mannheim's discussions of ideology, Foucault's work on knowledge and power, and phenomenological and ethnomethodological approaches, the exact mix of influences varying by author. While this work makes important contributions to these traditions, for two reasons I believe that it is a misnomer to call this work feminist epistemology (or theory). First, the issues raised are not in any fundamental way different from those raised by many scholars who have worked in these traditions but have not been interested specifically in women or committed to feminism. Feminists extend their insights in important ways, but this does not constitute a uniquely feminist approach to sociology. Second, many women in sociology, whose scholarship they and others consider as well within the feminist tradition, do not agree with this perspective.

Feminist scholars in a number of disciplines critique what they define as mainstream, "masculinist," "objectivist," and "positivist" social science, and develop a "feminist" alternative called standpoint theory. In sociology, the two most widely cited are Dorothy Smith (especially 1987, 1990, also 1979, 1989) and Patricia Hill Collins (especially 1990, also 1986, 1989), whose basic ideas constitute the focus of this section (see also Harding 1986, 1991). Where Smith focuses on developing a "woman's standpoint," Collins' work is directed at an Afrocentric feminist standpoint epistemology. Smith explicitly locates the origins of her ideas in Marx, Foucault, and ethnomethodology, Collins primarily in Mannheim, several well-known contemporary feminist theorists in diverse disciplines (Chodorow 1974, 1978, Gilligan 1982, Harding 1986, Jaggar 1983, hooks 1981, Smith 1987, Harstock 1983, 1985), and a myriad of mostly female, African-American thinkers. The ideas expressed by these two scholars incorporate those of a large number of others (see Sprague & Zimmerman 1993 for a sympathetic yet critical discussion of standpoint theory, and Laslett et al 1992 for a review of Smith's work).

### *The Critique of Mainstream Sociology*

Smith and Collins (also Cook & Fonow 1986, Farganis 1986, Haraway 1988, in addition to those cited above) begin with the idea that all knowledge about the social world reflects the social position(s) of the knower and, therefore, at best can result in no more than a partial understanding of that world; there is no Archimedian perspective outside of one's socially constituted standpoint. Unlike some feminists who argue for the superiority of a woman's standpoint as disempowered "outsider," Smith and Collins explicitly recognize that a woman's or a feminist standpoint is no less situated and partial than those they critique. For Marx and Mannheim, the "standpoint" of a knower is defined in terms of social class. Smith adds gender and Collins adds race and gender to class in defining the chief dimensions of those standpoints. They begin their critique of accepted sociological knowledge on the basis that, until recently, the knowers had one common standpoint—that of white, middle class male; other standpoints have been effectively silenced as contributors of "credible" social scientific knowledge. Virtually all feminist scholars (and many others) agree that by diversifying the kinds of knowers in sociology, new questions are raised about social life, new data sought to answer them, and new interpretations of received wisdom are proffered. In short, different standpoints lead to differences in what scholars think about. However, for Collins and Smith this is merely the starting point in their critique of mainstream sociology.

Collins and Smith recognize the diversity of experiences, hence standpoints, among women. Nonetheless, their logics assume that each gender has a standpoint and that it results in profound differences between the ways women and men think, in addition to what they think about. Smith (1990) refers to "male-created discourse" and talks about male thinking as "objectifying" experience, thereby creating "lines of fault" between women's subjective experiences and the way women sociologists write about them (if they conform to the standards of the discipline), resulting in a "bifurcated consciousness." Women's everyday world is alienated and objectified by the very categories of analysis that, as sociologists, they are taught and expected to bring to their work, categories that reflect and support the "social relations of ruling" that oppress them. Collins (see also Dill 1979, 1983, King 1988) speaks of a "distinctive Afrocentric women's culture" of resistance (p. 11) which represents "the simultaneity of race, class and gender oppression" in a "matrix of domination." This leads them to reject white male "either/or" thinking, rather opting for a "both/and" orientation to intellectual (as well as practical) life. Collins describes "positivism" as "a Eurocentric masculinist epistemology" that is highly problematic for understanding African-American women's lives. She defines positivism as attempts to produce "objective generalizations" (p. 205): "[Scientists] aim to distance themselves from the values, vested interests, and emotions ... [and thus] decontextualize themselves [in order to become] detached observers and manipulators of nature." She criticizes this epistemology not only because it treats the subjects of research as objects (as does Smith), but also because of the absence of emotion, ethics, and values, and because of the preferred style of "adversarial debate" in establishing knowledge claims. Like Smith, Collins concludes that this mode of thinking by sociologists fosters a system that oppresses Black women.

To Smith and Collins, the taken-for-granted concepts, language and style of writing and of making truth claims in sociology are male-created, alien to women, and function to support patriarchy, specifically, "relations of ruling" (Smith) or "the matrix of domination" (Collins) more generally. It is here that other feminist sociologists (including this author) part company with standpoint theory, unconvinced that men's and women's ways of thinking categorically differ or that the dominant ways of doing sociology are inherently masculine and necessarily antithetical to feminists' concerns (see especially Coser 1989).

### *The Proposed Alternative*

Smith and Collins share a radical empiricism; feminist sociologists should eschew the standard, "masculinist" conceptual tools of the field and begin with immersion in women's experiences of everyday life. For Collins, an Afrocentric feminist epistemology uses the scholar's "own concrete experiences as situated knowers in order to express a Black women's standpoint" (p. 16). Smith recommends that we explore the world as "insiders" by making "the everyday world problematic" (1990, p. 26). In a tour-de-force examination of textual material, Smith (1990) demonstrates how the data used by sociologists are prepackaged by agencies and other professionals (e.g. physicians, police and courts, social workers) in ways that express and reinforce the relations of ruling and therefore must be eschewed in favor of examination of the direct experiences of the people whose lives we seek to understand.

Smith appears to assume that the process of thoroughly critiquing and deconstructing textual material created by sociologists and other agents of the ruling system, based on the female sociologist's own lived experience, will suffice to lead to new concepts and general (theoretical) understandings that reflect woman's standpoint. While she explicitly rejects a completely "subjectivist" sociology that avoids all abstraction, she does not explicate any method for moving from the realm of personal experience to a more abstract, systemic level of understanding, a level she presupposes by talking about patriarchy and capitalism.

Collins gives somewhat more concrete advice by outlining three specific components of an Afrocentric feminist epistemology, in addition to the emphasis on beginning with experience. First, knowledge claims should arise from dialogue and stress connectedness between and active participation of researchers and their subjects, not from adversarial relations between knowers and the objectification of research subjects. Second, "personal experience, emotions, and empathy are central to the knowledge validation process" (p. 215); emotion is not separate from intellect (a point seconded by Smith). Third, Collins calls for an ethic of personal accountability among sociologists; knowledge claims should be evaluated in terms of what one knows about the "character" (values and ethics) of the knower (p. 218). Nonetheless, it remains unclear in Collins' work exactly how the Afrocentric feminist sociologist should move from the descriptive level of women's everyday experience to the more abstract, theoretical level she presupposes by talking about African-American women's oppression within a system that is patriarchal, racist, and classist.

Ultimately, their rejection of abstraction as a masculine activity prevents Collins, and especially Smith, from proposing an epistemology that can inform feminist conceptual and theoretical development, beyond the prescription that it must be thoroughly inductive. This shortcoming they share with nonfeminist sociologists who share their critique of "positivism" in sociology and opt for thorough immersion in the world of everyday experience (e.g. most ethnomethodologists and some symbolic interactionists). However, wherever these "male" approaches are discussed in the sociological canon, Smith's and Collins's work deserve serious consideration as well. They add rich discussions of the importance of the previously silenced standpoints of (African-American) women for understanding the taken-for-granted aspects of everyday life. In addition, theoretical discussions of ideology and the sociology of knowledge need to include their works, inasmuch as they clearly demonstrate the necessity of broadening concern from focusing on class to including gender and race/ethnicity in understanding the social-rootedness of thought systems and the intellectual roots of social power.

### *The Issue of Essentialism*

Feminist standpoint theory, which is highly attuned to reification committed by mainstream sociologists, cannot avoid reifying the genders. While Smith and Collins explicitly recognize considerable variation among women (and presumably men) in their experiences and consciousness, their own logics, and many times wording, make it clear that they assume that there are overarching, gender-specific standpoints; they could not otherwise talk about a "masculine" form of discourse. In addition, Collins explicitly cites such feminist theorists as Gilligan (1982) and Chodorow (1978, also 1974), who argue that the genders are fundamentally different in their moral reasoning and capacities for/commitments to interpersonal relationships.

Positing dichotomous gender differences that are treated as transcultural and transhistorical is termed "essentialism," a view that has substantial currency among feminists in a variety of disciplines but is hotly contested in our own (e.g. Lorber et al 1981, Coser 1989, Epstein 1988). The empirical evidence for it is flawed, often based on small, nonrandom, American samples, and typically finds only modest differences, along with extensive overlap, between the sexes. Essentialist thinking converts differences of degree into differences of kind. The presumed but often unstated origin of essential differences includes psychodynamics rooted in the parental division of labor (Chodorow 1978) and biological sex (Rossi 1977, 1984). It has become common for feminist scholars to recognize within-gender categorical differences (e.g. race, class), but this awareness of difference has often failed to preclude essentialist thinking about basic personality and value orientations (e.g. the assumption that, regardless of other differences, women are nurturant and oriented toward personal relationships, while men are individuating and oriented toward abstract moral principles). Given that the evidence suggests modest between-sex and considerable within-sex differences on virtually all individual-level traits, a dichotomous gender variable is theoretically useless when speaking of individual-level phenomena. Explanations that begin by categorically attributing different characteristics to women and men—cognitive, emotional, relational, and/or behavioral—not only exaggerate differences in the distribution of such traits by gender, they also implicitly treat these variables as dichotomous rather than continuous. They reflect the "either/or" thinking explicitly rejected by Collins, yet implicit in her logic. One can legitimately talk about average differences between females and males on individual-level variables, but care must be taken to avoid reification by delineating the average differences in experiences/opportunities/constraints that account for them and by explicitly recognizing the range of within-gender variation and between-gender overlap. Moreover, a dichotomous conceptualization of gender can be a theoretically meaningful aspect of social structure, such as when one talks about the degree of male-female occupational segregation or the extent to which an ideology devalues females relative to males.

### *Conceptual Problems*

Treating differences of degree as differences of kind is also manifest in macro-level concepts employed by many feminist theorists, especially "patriarchy," "exploitation," and "oppression." One rarely reads statements that contain varying levels of these phenomena (e.g. society A is less patriarchal/oppressive/exploitative than B). They are usually treated as constants, and the emphasis is placed on understanding the particular form of patriarchy/oppression/exploitation in a given time, place, and/or within a specific socioeconomic structure (usually capitalism). Yet the empirical literature clearly demonstrates considerable cross-societal variation on those dimensions that can be taken as indicators of the level (not simply form) of gender inequality (e.g. Martin & Voorhies 1975, Sanday 1974, 1981, Blumberg 1978, 1984, Chafetz 1984).

These terms are infrequently defined, and when they are, their definitions are often too broad, thereby obscuring the dynamics of gender stratification systems. Patriarchy, for example, has been used to refer to some combination of the following: a type of family structure, an ideology (religious and/or secular), and one or more properties of the economy and/or polity. This kind of truth-asserting definition obscures questions of the extent to which and how these various phenomena are related to one another by assuming their empirical isomorphism. "Patriarchy" is often reified by the use of an active verb, as in "patriarchy causes/creates/requires . . . ." When this happens, the explanatory content evaporates completely. Regardless of conceptual problems, in the remainder of this chapter I use the vocabularies employed by the theorists whose works are being reviewed.

## NEO-MARXIST THEORIES

Marxist-inspired feminist theory, most of which today is called socialist-feminist, differs from orthodox Marxism (and orthodox Marxist feminism) by insisting that the nonwaged labor that maintains and reproduces workers, and is done overwhelmingly by women, is equally as important as waged labor, and that oppression for women results equally from patriarchy and from class structure, not simply as a by-product of class relationships. It differs from other feminist theories by insisting that, while not sufficient to bring about the demise of patriarchy, the abolition of capitalism is a necessary condition, inasmuch as capitalism derives numerous advantages, hence support from patriarchal institutions, ideology, and practices. While recognizing that patriarchy predated capitalism, and scarcely disappeared in twentieth century socialist nations, Marxist-inspired feminists argue that within capitalist systems, patriarchy assumes unique forms that are interwoven with capitalism in mutually supportive ways.

Within capitalist systems, the division of labor by gender makes women responsible for the unwaged maintenance and reproduction of the current and future labor force, variously termed domestic work, production of use value, or necessary labor. Women may also be involved in what is variously termed production of exchange value, social labor, or surplus value through waged work, as are men. The nonwaged work done by women is crucial and profitable for capitalists, who get its benefits for free, and, therefore, such labor is exploitative and oppressive for women. Although earlier in the history of capitalism most women were denied the opportunity to become "social adults" through waged labor (Sacks 1974), more recently they have been sought by capitalists as a source of cheap labor in a highly gender-segregated labor market (Eisenstein 1979). The gender inequities women experience in the labor market are linked both practically and ideologically to their responsibility for nonwaged domestic work (Eisenstein 1979, Vogel 1983, Shelton & Agger 1993). The dual exploitation of women within the household and in the labor market means that women produce far greater surplus value for capitalists than do men (Shelton & Agger 1993).

An ideology of patriarchy, or male supremacy, fostered by capitalists, undergirds and sustains both forms of female oppression. This ideology justifies women's nonwaged domestic responsibilities with reference to biologically rooted reproductive differences between men and women and justifies gender-based labor market inequities with reference to women's domestic obligations (Eisenstein 1979). In turn, working class men derive advantages both within the household (free domestic services and subservience from their wives, resulting from their economic dependence) and in the labor force (better paying jobs are reserved for men). No or low wages tie women to their better paid husbands in a subordinate position, and therefore to domestic labor, which in turn suppresses their wages (Hartmann 1984, Sacks 1974). Sacks (1974) argues that in this manner capitalists "compensate" men for their subordination to capitalist domination, which impedes the development of class consciousness among workers, reinforcing capitalist domination (also Shelton & Agger 1993, Sokoloff 1980). Wives' economic dependence also ties men more securely to wage-earning jobs, further serving the interests of capitalists by undermining potential rebellion against the system (Eisenstein 1979, Vogel 1983, Hartmann 1984).

Feminist scholars have extended Marxist-based world systems theory (and its cousin, dependency theory) by demonstrating how capitalist penetration by core nations of peripheral ones usually reduces the status of women, thereby exacerbating many problems (e.g. high fertility rates, poverty, and income inequality) in the peripheral nations (Ward 1984, 1990, 1993, Blumberg 1989). Ward (1993:48) criticizes world systems theory for assuming that women participate in the modern world economy only as members of households in which the male "head" is incorporated, thereby ignoring women's direct role in the global economy and their economic contributions in the informal labor market as well as in the household. A massive research literature on women and development demonstrates the usually widely disparate effects of socioeconomic development for men and women, to the detriment of women. These findings are largely ignored by world systems theorists, who assume that household members have unitary interests (see also Blumberg 1988, 1989). As a corrective, Ward (1993) emphasizes the need to fully incorporate the crucial contributions women make to the food supplies and general economies of poor nations (see also Mies 1986). Earlier, Ward (1984) proposed that the specific, local effects on women's work and status of Western capital penetration must be understood in terms of preexisting patterns of "patriarchal relations," including ideology and institutionalized patterns of male dominance. In addition, the gender-based presuppositions of Western (male) capitalists affect the distribution of new resources and opportunities between men and women in peripheral nations. Ward concluded that the level of foreign investment in peripheral nations and their trade dependency on core nations are positively related to the level of gender inequality.

By extending Marxist analysis to include nonwaged maintenance and reproductive labor, and broadening the Marxian concept of ideology to encompass patriarchal thought, Marxist-inspired feminists demonstrate that gender is as central a component as class in understanding exploitation/oppression within capitalist systems and in understanding how capitalist systems are maintained and strengthened. These contributions merit serious attention in any scholarly discussion of neo-Marxist thought.

## CULTURAL AND SOCIAL MACROSTRUCTURAL THEORIES

The macrostructural feminist theories that are not explicitly neo-Marxist divide mostly into two categories: those that emphasize the causal primacy of culture and ideology, and those that emphasize the centrality of socioeconomic factors (for a review of both see Dunn et al 1993). Recently, Collins et al (1993) attempted a grand synthesis of extant gender theories that emphasizes social structural constructs but includes elements from most other types of gender theory (see also Chafetz 1990, for a slightly less ambitious effort to do likewise). The social structural theories are sufficiently complex as to defy brief explication, beyond a listing of central constructs. What macrostructural theories have in common is their goal: to explain variation in the level of gender stratification across time/space, and/or to explain how a given level is maintained and changed (see Chafetz 1984:4–7 for a conceptual definition of "gender stratification").

Virtually all feminist scholars agree that ideologies and related symbols and rituals that devalue women and explain and justify different and unequal treatment by gender constitute an important component of gender stratification systems. A few anthropologists make a cultural construct central in their explanations (e.g. Rosaldo 1974, Ortner 1974, and especially Sanday 1981, also 1974). Ortner's (1974) and Rosaldo's (1974) arguments are relatively simple: Because of women's reproductive functions in birth and lactation, and the gendered division of labor within the household and broader society that are typically constructed based on them, women become more identified with "nature" and domesticity, men with "culture" and the public sphere. In turn, culture and the public sphere are more highly valued socially and, therefore, the more strongly differentiated and segregated the two spheres, the greater the level of gender inequality. In a more nuanced and fully developed theory, Sanday (1981) argues that each society has its own "sex-role plan" that delineates how relationships between men and women ought to be structured. These plans arise out of one of two overarching cultural orientations: an "inner," in which nature is sacred and the "female creative principle" is emphasized, and an "outer," in which nature is seen as dangerous, humans are seen as superior to nature, and men's activities (as hunters and warriors) are revered. These orientations are grounded in the level of environmental threat and embodied in creation myths, which emphasize male, female, or both sources of power in the universe. Enhanced threat leads to an outer orientation, the primacy of male deities, and male dominance. The degree of gender inequality is thus a direct function of the type of sex-role plan as it reflects the general cultural orientation.

Macrostructural social theories of gender stratification are typically systemic in nature, often include feedback loops, and emphasize as primary causal mechanisms one or more of the following: environmental, demographic, technological, economic, and political variables. Intervening constructs include the gender division of labor, ideology, and family structure. Lenski's (1966) societal typology, based on dominant technology and the resulting level of economic surplus, constitutes the starting point for several theories (e.g. Huber 1988, R Collins 1975, Chafetz 1984, Blumberg 1978). The extent to which the environment—physical and social—is dangerous or threatening constitutes another independent construct in some (e.g. Chafetz 1984, Sanday 1981, as discussed above, and especially Harris 1978, who emphasizes the role of warfare). Demographic variables that are considered important include sex ratio (especially by Guttentag & Secord 1983, also Chafetz 1984, 1990), population density (Harris 1978, Chafetz 1984, 1990), and fertility rates (Huber 1991). The size of the economic surplus, contingent upon technological base, is related to the level of gender stratification in a curvilinear fashion that peaks in agrarian/pastoral societies in the highest levels of inequality. The levels of fertility, population density, environmental harshness, warfare, and sex ratios are generally positively related to the level of gender inequality. One final independent construct concerns political structure, specifically, Collin's (1975, also 1972) thesis concerning the extent to which the political organization of the society (nation-state), rather than the household, monopolizes the legitimate use of force. He argues that (along with women's level of economic opportunity) the extent to which the political structure grants individual men the right to physically coerce wives constitutes the most important independent variable explaining the level of gender stratification. While many feminist scholars have explored the role of male violence against women in producing or maintaining gender inequality, Collins is alone in making male coercive power central to such a theory by linking it to a typology of political structure.

These independent constructs are typically linked to the level of gender inequality primarily through their impact on three intervening constructs. Like the Marxist-inspired feminists, virtually all macrostructural feminist theories focus on the key role of the gender division of labor—within the economy and between the economic and domestic realms. The more equal the access of women to economic roles in the nondomestic sphere (especially where they control the products of, and/or income derived from their work), the lower the level of gender inequality, and the more responsibility women have for the domestic sphere, the less equal their opportunities in the economic realm (especially Blumberg 1978, 1984, 1988, Collins et al 1993, Chafetz 1984, 1990). Besides the domestic division of labor, family structural variables of lineality and locality are also important intervening constructs (Martin & Voorhies 1975, Blumberg 1979, Chafetz 1984). Women fare worst where these two aspects of family structure favor the male side (patrilineage and patrilocality). Finally, like the Marxist-inspired feminists, but with less emphasis than that given by the cultural theorists, macrostructural social theories recognize the importance of religious and secular gender ideologies in buttressing systems of gender stratification (Blumberg 1978, 1984, 1988, Chafetz 1984, 1990).

Macrostructural feminist theories rarely attempt to demonstrate the impact of gender stratification on other aspects of social structure (except as feedback loops). However, they do demonstrate that virtually all aspects of sociocultural structure in all types of societies are implicated in the gender system. Theories concerning technology, work, ideology, family structure, political economy, demography, not to mention social inequality, that ignore the ubiquitous phenomenon of gender are radically incomplete, as are theories that attempt to explain social change and/or stability without reference to gender. Macrostructural feminist theories provide important insights concerning the linkages between gender stratification and other macrolevel structures and processes that should be incorporated into general structural theories.

## RATIONAL CHOICE AND EXCHANGE THEORIES

Rational choice theory has been a target of criticism by several feminist scholars, most notably England (1989, 1993b, England & Kilbourne 1990, also Zelizer 1994). Feminist critiques of it are rooted substantially in an essentialist logic, inasmuch as they accuse rational choice theory of assuming a selfish, separative, and non-emotional actor who is masculine, thereby ignoring the connective, altruistic, and emotional motivations, claimed to be characteristically feminine. This and related feminist criticisms of rational choice theory are discussed and rebutted by Friedman & Diem (1993). They also demonstrate the utility of this perspective for understanding gender inequality by examining the implicit rational choice analyses involved in several feminist studies. Their general point is that the studies they examine utilize "three mechanisms relied upon by rational-choice theorists to explain variation—institutional constraints, opportunity costs, and preferences . . ." (Friedman & Diem 1993:101). Rational choice thinking is also used in some recent discussions of family change in industrial nations, which focus on changes in women's roles and decision-making processes concerning number of children, age of first marriage and birth, divorce, and labor force participation (e.g. Chafetz & Hagan 1996). Not only is rational choice theory useful to analyses of gender issues, feminist critiques of it focus attention on weaknesses and gaps that require further attention. Specifically, the further development of this theory should include selfishness/altruism as a variable, consider the role of emotion, and explicitly include interpersonal preferences (Friedman & Diem 1993).

Social exchange theory, which reflects the same utilitarian tradition as rational choice theory, has not been the target of explicit feminist criticism (for an exception, see Harstock 1985), although the same criticisms apply to both. It has been employed by a few feminist theorists (e.g. Parker & Parker 1979, Bell & Newby 1976, Chafetz 1980, Curtis 1986) and is implicit in many feminist empirical studies of husband-wife relationships. The general theme of this perspective is that, given the traditionally greater resources available to men from sources outside the family, wives balance exchanges with their husbands by providing compliance and deference in return for financial support and access to other externally generated resources. Husbands also garner a considerable, self-reinforcing power advantage over their wives because of what Curtis (1986) defines as a contractual inequality based on the husband's provision of gifts and favors. These incur a debt for the wife which is unspecified, diffuse, and "can be infinite in effect" (p. 179.) However, as Parker & Parker (1979; also Chafetz 1980) note, as the gender division of labor outside the family changes, men's resource advantage and therefore the nature of spousal exchanges do as well. Unlike some uses of exchange theory, in the hands of feminist scholars the macro level environment, which shapes the distribution of resources and therefore the opportunities/constraints of exchange partners, is taken as the explicit starting point in understanding the nature of microlevel exchanges, which, in turn, are often analyzed in terms of their feedback impact on macrolevel phenomena. The use of exchange theory by feminists therefore exemplifies what Risman & Schwartz (1989) refer to as a microstructural approach to understanding gender inequality.

## NETWORK AND STATUS EXPECTATIONS THEORIES

Although representing very different theoretical traditions, feminist versions of status expectations and network theories both focus on how interactive relationships are shaped along structured gender lines and result in gender differentiation and inequality. Their logics are therefore similar to those discussed in the last section in that they also represent microstructural approaches to the study of gender inequality.

The feminist theory most carefully developed in tandem with a systematic research program deals with the relationship between gender, status expectations, and power/influence in goal-oriented groups (see review chapter by Ridgeway 1993, Ridgeway & Berger 1986, Meeker & Weitzel-O'Neill 1977, Lockheed 1985, Foschi 1989). The theory has implications for same-sex groups but is most fully developed and tested on mixed-sex groups (Ridgeway 1993). The central thesis is that, given the higher social status that accrues to males, both women and men typically enter mixed-sex groups with gender-based expectations that male members will be more competent than females in moving the group toward task achievement, i.e. "performance expectations" are higher for men. However, the salience of gender status is situationally induced and therefore context-specific (e.g. performance expectations may advantage women if the task is traditionally considered feminine). In the absence of a set of specified factors that reduce the salience of gender-based performance expectations, they become self-fulfilling prophecies that function to reduce women's self-confidence, prestige, power, and influence in group interactions. Moreover, because gender-based expectations are defined by group members as legitimate, individual women's attempts to counteract them will be rejected by other group members as inappropriate (Meeker & Weitzel-O'Neill 1977). The outcomes of mixed-sex groups will therefore usually reflect the preferences of its male members. Moreover, the process of group interaction will typically enhance the status and power of the male members, which is often "the basis on which many of the society's rewards of power, position, and respect are distributed" (Ridgeway 1993:193), that is, the basis of gender stratification.

Smith-Lovin & McPherson (1993:223) assert: "In one sense, it is impossible to have a network theory of gender" because the theory is concerned with the nature of relationships between actors, not actor characteristics. Nonetheless, in the only explicit theoretical discussion of gender differences and inequality from a network theory perspective, these authors convincingly argue that gender-related characteristics, usually viewed as essential differences developed through socialization, in fact result from the long-term impact of seemingly inconsequentially small differences in the network positions and structures in which boys and girls are typically located. Beginning with an analysis of single-sex childhood networks, they call upon a wealth of empirical literature to demonstrate how gender homophilous networks cumulate over the life course to create even greater gender differences in adult networks, which foster gender differences in aspirations, opportunities, and behaviors. Because they reflect ongoing network phenomena, these outcomes are amenable to change in response to changes in the nature of, and locations within, network structures for women and men, and therefore to public policy intervention. The authors also review some of the current inadequacies of the network literature for understanding gender segregation and inequality, weaknesses that, if addressed, would strengthen the general theory. These include: a focus on "small, unrepresentative populations" that are almost entirely single-sex; a focus on "elites" that are almost always male; a focus on "ego nets" that loses sight of the organizational context within which networks evolve; and a focus on one network in isolation from others in which actors are simultaneously involved (pp. 243–44).

Together, feminist versions of rational choice, exchange, status expectations, and network theories emphasize the importance of sociocultural structure for understanding the gendered nature of interaction and individual choice, and the patterned gender differences and inequalities that result from such interactions and choices. They thereby contribute important insights into the general theoretical issue of the nature of macro-micro linkages.

## SYMBOLIC INTERACTIONIST AND ETHNOMETHODOLOGICAL THEORIES

Feminist versions of symbolic interaction theory and ethnomethodology focus on gender as an ongoing accomplishment that emerges during interaction processes, both between and within the sexes. This perspective is succinctly captured in West & Zimmerman's term (1987) "doing gender," which refers to the work done during interactions in order to constantly recreate the partners' sense of their own and the other's gender (also West & Fenstermaker 1993, Fenstermaker et al 1991, Fenstermaker Berk 1985, Goffman 1977). Gender is an "emergent feature of social situations" (West & Fenstermaker 1993:151), not a static feature of structure or set of individual-level traits.

Gender is "omnirelevant" in that any action can be interpreted as exemplifying it (West & Fenstermaker 1993). Given the taken-for-granted view that there are two and only two sexes, and everyone belongs in (only) one of them, people characterize self and others by sex ("gender attribution") and then interpret and respond to virtually any kind of behavior according to its normative gender "appropriateness." The nature of masculinity and femininity varies, but the notion that men and women are fundamentally different does not. People are constantly creating the sense of gender difference and defining self and others through that lens (Kessler & McKenna 1978, Goffman 1977). West & Fenstermaker (1993: 157) assert: "persons engaged in virtually *any* activity can hold themselves accountable and be held accountable for their performance . . . *as women* or *as men* . . ." and will be legitimated or discredited accordingly. A major corollary is that, while the specific relevance of gender is always contingent upon the interaction context in which behavior occurs (Fenstermaker et al 1991), it is no less relevant to single-sex than to cross-sex interactions (Gerson 1985).

"Doing gender" not only (re)produces gender difference, it (re)produces gender inequality. One very important medium through which gender-construction work occurs is conversation. Numerous analyses of male-female conservation and language usage have been conducted (e.g. Fishman 1982, Mayo & Henley 1981, McConnell-Ginet 1978, West & Zimmerman 1977, Lakoff 1975). They conclude that conversation between men and women reinforces gender inequality, primarily because "the definition of what is appropriate conversation becomes men's choice. What part of the world [they] . . . maintain the reality of, is his choice . . ." (Fishman 1982:178). Men dominate conversations; women work hard to keep them going; women use verbal and body language in ways that weaken their ability to assert themselves and, therefore, reduce their power (McConnell-Ginet 1978, West & Zimmerman 1978, Lakoff 1975, Mayo & Henley 1981).

Another major mechanism by which gender inequality is reproduced through interaction is scripting (West & Fenstermaker 1993). The social scripts for many tasks are specifically associated with gender, and people "do gender" as part and parcel of doing them. Fenstermaker Berk (1985, also DeVault 1991) shows how the division of household labor, which numerous studies demonstrate is highly inequitable, provides the opportunity for both spouses to "do gender" and reinforce their own and their partner's gendered identities. Hochschild (1983) develops the concept of "emotional labor," which refers to the need to hide or fake one's feelings in order to please others, in discussing the gendered scripts associated with many traditionally female jobs. Kasper (1986) expands upon this concept, seeing it as integral to the scripts for female behavior in a variety of interaction contexts and as functioning to deny women an "integrated autonomous identity of their own" (p. 40). In turn, this impedes women's ability to achieve in the public sphere.

Schur (1984) uses an offshoot of symbolic interactionism, labeling theory, to demonstrate that femaleness constitutes a devalued and stigmatized master status that results in women being selectively perceived and reacted to primarily in terms of stereotypes about femaleness (p. 25). This leads to objectification of women, or their treatment as things rather than as persons, which allows others to treat them in degrading and exploitative ways. The result is a self-fulfilling prophecy, whereby women come to see themselves as inferior and to suffer from low self-esteem, passivity, in-group hostility, and identification with their (male) oppressors.

In an application of George Herbert Mead's concepts, Ferguson (1980) argues that men possess the power to define both specific situations and the generalized other. Women, therefore, "are defining themselves by reference to standards that brand them as inferior" (p. 155), thereby undermining their self-identity and producing self-blame for their problems. In addition, powerlessness forces women to become highly adept at taking the role of the (male) other, anticipating male wants in order to avoid negative sanctions; it prompts women to please, flatter, and acquiesce to men for the same reason (pp. 161–62). The result is that male power is buttressed.

Feminist versions of ethnomethodology and symbolic interactionism focus on the microlevel processes by which gender differences and inequality are constantly (re)created in everyday life. By demonstrating that both cross- and same-sex interactions normally entail "doing gender," they suggest that gender is a fundamental feature and outcome of all interaction, one that should comprise a central component of general interaction theories.

## NEO-FREUDIAN AND ROLE THEORIES

No thinkers were more thoroughly criticized by feminists during the 1960s and 1970s than Parsons and Freud. Nonetheless, the new specialty developed by feminist sociologists called itself by the Parsonian term, the sociology of sex roles; by the late 1970s, one of the most influential feminist theories in sociology was Chodorow's (1978, also 1974) neo-Freudian account of gender differentiation and inequality. The term "sex (gender) role" has since been abandoned by feminist scholars because it obscures power inequities, thereby depoliticizing gender (Stacey & Thorne 1985), and because it fails to articulate situational variation in role enactment (Lopata & Thorne 1978, West & Fenstermaker 1993:154–55). However, role analysis remains an important part of feminist theorizing because many specific social roles are entirely (e.g. wife/husband) or largely (e.g. numerous occupations) played by members of only one sex. Feminist Freudian theory continues to be developed (see reviews by Kurzweil 1989 and by Williams 1993; also Chodorow 1989).

The earlier sex/gender role perspective focused primarily on delineating the processes of childhood socialization (especially modeling, positive and negative sanctions) through which, beginning at birth, boys and girls are taught by parents, and later peers, schools, media, etc, "sex appropriate" gender identities (said to be all but immutable by about age 3) and gender normative behaviors (which are presumably trans-situational and therefore applicable in all interactions) (e.g. Cahill 1983, Lever 1976, Constantinople 1979, Lewis & Weinraub 1979, Coser 1986, 1975, Sattel 1976). This perspective is primarily rooted in cognitive development and symbolic interaction theories. Besides the problems mentioned above, the sex/gender role perspective also makes it all but impossible to explain gender-related changes at the individual or collective level. To the extent that childhood engenderment strongly shapes all subsequent behavior, it is difficult to explain how adults could change, and therefore, how new generations of children could be taught different gender conceptions. Katz (1979) introduces a life-cycle perspective to issues of gender socialization, an approach that can better accommodate change. This approach is elaborated by Lopata (1994), who examines specific social roles associated with women, rather than general sex/gender roles. She focuses on how the major social roles played by women (especially wife, mother, relative, homemaker, and employee) change over the life course and how and why they have changed with societal modernization, thereby reducing the hypothesized impact of early childhood learning. Likewise, Johnson (1989, 1993) revisits Parsons to show how one can revise his evolutionary theory and analysis of family roles usefully to account for recent changes in women's roles.

Like most socialization theories of engenderment, feminist neo-Freudian theory argues that, at a very early age, the two sexes develop gender identities and gender differentiated personalities that are highly stable over the life course. The two theory types differ in the processes by which this presumably occurs. The best known neo-Freudian feminist scholars are French, but the one who has most influenced feminist sociologists in the United States is Nancy Chodorow (especially 1978). Incorporating object relations theory into her revisions of Freudian thought, Chodorow argues that, because early childrearing is overwhelmingly a female task, children of both sexes have a woman as their primary love object. However, boys' and girls' Oedipal stage experiences and outcomes are vastly different because only girls share the sex of their primary love object. Because girls need not separate form their mothers to attain a gendered identity, they grow into women whose primary concern is with connection to other people. Given a different-sex primary love object, boys develop a gendered identity through separation, resulting in men who focus on individuation and a denial of affect. The gender-specific psychological orientations that result from the fact that women mother children of both sexes underpin male misogyny and dominance. Gilligan (1982) uses Chodorow's theory to refute Kohlberg's levels of moral reasoning. She argues that women's morality is different from (not at a lower level than) men's because it is based on personal relationships and obligations rather than abstract principles (which Kohlberg privileges). These two works are widely cited by feminist sociologists, despite extensive critique of their essentialist logic, psychological reductionism, and other problems (see Williams 1993 for a review of those critiques, and see Lorber et al 1981). Like socialization explanations, feminist neo-Freudian theory makes gender-related changes all but impossible to explain. A different kind of criticism of Chodorow's theory is developed by Johnson (1988), who concludes that it is fathers, not mothers, who reproduce gender differentiation in children and gender inequality among adults. Children of both sexes become "human" through interactions with their primary love object, a mother figure, who tends to minimize gender difference. Fathers differentiate their children much more on the basis of gender. In addition, children observe their mothers playing the wife role, which models gender inequality in relationship to their husbands.

## CONCLUSION

### *The Newest Trend in Feminist Theorizing*

The "hot topic" in the 1990s among feminist scholars is "the intersection of race, class and gender." Edited books (e.g. Anderson & Collins 1995a, Rothenberg 1992), special journal issues, program sessions, and a new section of ASA have been devoted to it. The central contention of this emerging focus is that the three forms of oppression are not separate and additive, but interactive and multiplicative in their effects. However, to date, very little theory has been produced on the topic; the growing literature remains overwhelmingly descriptive, and too often descriptive of a sample of women of only one race and class (or even specific occupation).

One exception is Collins (1990), who suggests several interesting ideas about how to theorize "one overarching structure of domination" that includes age, religion, and sexual orientation in addition to race, class, and gender (p. 222). She argues that people can simultaneously be oppressed and oppressor, privileged and penalized; that no one form of oppression is primary, although individuals and groups often define one as more fundamental and others as lesser; and that the matrix of domination has several layers (e.g. persons, group or community culture, social institutions), all of which are sites of potential resistance to domination. Moreover, different systems of oppression may rely on varying degrees of systemic versus interpersonal mechanisms of domination (pp. 226–27).

West & Fenstermaker (1995) reject the mathematical metaphor involved in Collins's (also Almquist 1989, Glenn 1985, Anderson & Collins 1995b) idea of intersecting systems of inequality. They point out that no one can experience gender without simultaneously experiencing their other statuses, so all outcomes are simultaneously "gendered," "raced," and "classed." Using an ethnomethodological approach, they argue that these are all ongoing accomplishments whose relevance cannot be determined apart from the context in which they are accomplished. Collins et al (1995) respond that West & Fenstermaker reduce oppression to difference and lose sight of the structural inequities that are fundamental to these statuses.

These efforts constitute the barest beginnings of theorizing about how various forms of inequality relate to one another. The recently developing queer theory (e.g. see Seidman et al 1994), which deals with the social construction of sexual identity and preference labels, especially those that are "marginal," is also interwoven with feminist theories. It is, however, beyond the scope of this chapter to discuss the theory. Both of these new issues reflect the perception by many feminists that prior theoretical efforts have been too middle class, white, and heterosexist, and that feminist theory must recognize diversity among women and therefore account for the multiplicity of forms of oppression, not just that experienced by otherwise privileged white women. Theoretical progress on the topic of how various systems of inequality interact could revolutionize the sociological understanding of social stratification, which, for too long, has theorized narrowly about inequality in terms of social class/status.

## *Feminist Theory and Mainstream Sociology*

Sociologists have always assumed that, as Lorber states (1994:36), "For humans, the social is the natural." However, until recently sociologists exempted gender from this assumption and largely ignored the topic. The most fundamental contributions of feminist theories have been to demonstrate the thoroughly sociocultural nature of all aspects of the gender system and the omnirelevance of gender to social life. This corpus of work demonstrates the daily "hard work," conducted at the micro- and macrolevels by individuals and social collectivities, that goes into (re)producing gender as a fundamental feature of social life, indeed, a more ubiquitous feature than social class.

Feminist theorists have used virtually all theoretical traditions in sociology as springboards to understand the gendered nature of social life. In the process, they have offered rich and important critiques of the inadequacies of traditional theories that have resulted from the masculine blinders their authors have worn. They have developed revisions of those traditions that broaden and deepen the discipline's understanding of social life. Gradually, albeit too slowly, these perspectives are becoming incorporated into the mainstream theory canon. It is my hope that this review may hasten that process.

ACKNOWLEDGMENTS

I am grateful to the following people for feedback on a draft of this chapter: my departmental colleagues Helen Rose Ebaugh, Joseph Kotarba, and David Klinger; also Dana Dunn, Paula England, Randall Collins, Ruth Wallace and an anonymous reviewer.



*Literature Cited*

Almquist E. 1989. The experiences of minority women in the United States: intersections of race, gender, and class. In *Women: A Feminist Perspective,* ed. J. Freeman, pp. 414–45. Mountain View, CA: Mayfield

Alway J. 1995. The trouble with gender: tales of the still-missing feminist revolution in sociological theory. *Soc. Theory* 13:209–28

Anderson M, Collins PH, eds. 1995a. *Race, Class and Gender: An Anthology.* Belmont, CA: Wadsworth

Anderson M, Collins PH. 1995b. See Anderson & Collins 1995a, Preface

Bell C, Newby H. 1976. Husbands and wives: the dynamics of the deferential dialective. In *Dependence and Exploitation in Work and Marriage,* ed. DL Baker, S Allen, pp. 152–68. London: Longman

Berger J, Zeldich M Jr., eds. 1985. *Status, Rewards and Influence.* San Francisco: Jossey-Bass

Blumberg RL. 1978. *Stratification: Socioeconomic and Sexual Inequality.* Dubuque, IA: Brown

Blumberg RL. 1979. A paradigm for predicting the position of women: policy implications and problems. In *Sex Roles and Social Policy,* ed. J Lipman-Blumen, J Bernard, pp. 113–42. Beverly Hills, CA: Sage

Blumberg RL. 1984. A general theory of gender stratification. In *Sociological Theory, 1984,* ed. R Collins, pp. 23–101. San Francisco: Jossey-Bass

Blumberg RL. 1988. Income under female versus male control: hypotheses from a theory of gender stratification and data from the Third World. *J. Fam. Iss.* 9:51–84

Blumberg RL. 1989. Toward a feminist theory of development. See Wallace 1989, pp. 161–99

Cahill S. 1983. Reexamining the acquisition of sex roles: a symbolic interactionist approach. *Sex Roles* 9:1–15

Chafetz JS. 1980. Conflict resolution in marriage: toward a theory of spousal strategies and marital dissolution rates. *J. Fam. Iss.* 1:397–421

Chafetz JS. 1984. *Sex and Advantage: A Comparative, Macro-Structural Theory of Sex Stratification.* Totowa, NJ: Rowman & Allanheld

Chafetz JS. 1988. *Feminist Sociology: An Overview of Contemporary Theories.* Itasca, IL: Peacock

Chafetz JS. 1990. *Gender Equity: A Theory of Stability and Change.* Newbury Park, CA: Sage

Chafetz JS, Hagan J. 1996. The gender division of labor and family change in industrial societies: a theoretical accounting. *J. Comp. Fam. Stud.* 27:187–219

Chodorow N. 1974. Family structure and feminine personality. See Rosaldo & Lamphere 1974, pp. 43–66

Chodorow N. 1978. *The Reproduction of Mothering: Psychoanalysis and the Sociology of Gender.* Berkeley, CA: Univ. Calif. Press

Chodorow N. 1989. *Feminism and Psychoanalytic Theory.* New Haven: Yale Univ. Press

Collins PH. 1986. Learning from the outside

within: the sociological significance of black feminist thought. *Soc. Probl.* 33:514–30
Collins PH. 1989. The social construction of black feminist thought. *Signs* 14:745–73
Collins PH. 1990. *Black Feminist Thought: Knowledge, Consciousness and the Politics of Empowerment.* Boston: Unwin Hyman
Collins PH, Maldonado LA, Takagi DY, Thorne B, Weber L, Winant H. 1995. Symposium on West and Fenstermaker's "Doing Difference." *Gender Soc.* 9:491–513
Collins R. 1972. A conflict theory of sexual stratification. In *Family, Marriage, and the Struggle of the Sexes,* ed. HP Dreitzel. New York: Macmillan
Collins R. 1975. *Conflict Sociology: Toward an Explanatory Science.* New York: Academic
Collins R, Chafetz JS, Blumberg RL, Coltrane S, Turner J. 1993. Toward an integrated theory of gender stratification. *Soc. Perspect.* 36:185–216
Constantinople A. 1979. Sex-role acquisition: in search of the elephant. *Sex Roles* 5:121–33
Cook JA, Fonow MM. 1986. Knowledge and women's interests: issues of epistemology and methodology in feminist sociological research. *Soc. Inquiry* 56:2–29
Coser RL. 1975. Stay home, little Sheba: on placement, displacement and social change. *Soc. Probl.* 22:470–80
Coser RL. 1986. Cognitive structure and the use of social space. *Soc. Forum* 1:1–26
Coser RL. 1989. Reflections on feminist theory. See Wallace 1989, pp. 200–7
Curtis R. 1986. Household and family in theory on inequality. *Am. Soc. Rev.* 51:168–83
Deegan MJ. 1988. *Jane Addams and the Men of the Chicago School, 1892–1918.* New Brunswick, NJ: Transaction Books
DeVault M. 1991. *Feeding the Family: The Social Construction of Caring as Gendered Work.* Chicago: Univ. Chicago Press
Dill BT. 1979. The dialectics of Black womanhood. *Signs* 5:545–55
Dill BT. 1983. Race, class, and gender: prospects for an all-inclusive sisterhood. *Fem. Stud.* 9:131–48
Donovan J. 1985. *Feminist Theory: The Intellectual Traditions of American Feminism.* New York: Ungar
Dunn D, Almquist E, Chafetz JS. 1993. Macrostructural perspectives on gender inequality. See England 1993a, pp. 69–90
Eisenstein Z. 1979. Introduction. In *Capitalist Patriarchy and the Case for Socialist Feminism,* ed. Z Eisenstein, pp. 5–55. New York: Monthly Rev.
England P. 1989. A feminist critique of rational-choice theories: implications for sociology. *Am. Sociol.* 20:14–20
England P, ed. 1993a. *Theory on Gender/Feminism on Theory.* New York: Aldine DeGrutyer
England P. 1993b. The separative self: androcentric bias in neoclassical assumptions. In *Beyond Economic Man: Feminist Theory and Economics,* ed. M Ferber, J Nelson, pp. 37–51. Chicago: Univ. Chicago Press
England P, Kilbourne BS. 1990. Feminist critique of the separative model of the self: implications for rational choice theory. *Ration. Soc.* 2:156–71
Epstein CF. 1988. *Deceptive Distinctions: Sex, Gender, and the Social Order.* New Haven: Yale Univ. Press
Etzkowitz H, Glassman R. 1991. *The Renascence of Sociological Theory: Classical and Contemporary.* Itasca, IL: Peacock
Farganis S. 1986. Social theory and feminist theory: the need for dialogue. *Soc. Inq.* 56:50–68
Fenstermaker Berk S. 1985. *The Gender Factory.* New York: Plenum
Fenstermaker S, West C, Zimmerman D. 1991. Gender inequality: new conceptual terrain. In *Gender, Family, and Economy: The Triple Overlap,* ed. RL Blumberg, pp. 289–307. Newbury Park, CA: Sage
Ferguson K. 1980. *Self, Society, and Womankind.* Westport, Conn: Greenwood
Fishman P. 1982. Interaction: the work women do. In *Women and Work: Problems and Perspectives,* ed. R Kahn-Hut, AK Daniels, R Colvard, pp. 170–80. New York: Oxford Univ. Press
Fitzpatrick E. 1990. *Endless Crusade: Women Social Scientists and Progressive Reform.* New York: Oxford Univ. Press
Foschi M. 1989. Status characteristics, standards, and attributions. In *Sociological Theories in Progress: New Formulations,* ed. J Berger, M Zelditch, B Anderson, pp. 58–72. Newbury Park, CA: Sage
Friedman D, Diem C. 1993. Feminism and the Pro(Rational) choice Movement; rational choice theory, feminist critiques, and gender inequality. See England 1993a, pp. 91–114
Gergen MM, ed. 1988. *Feminist Thought and the Structure of Knowledge.* New York: NY Univ. Press
Gerson JM. 1985. Boundaries, negotiation, consciousness: reconceptualizing gender relations. *Soc. Probl.* 32:317–31
Gilligan C. 1982. *In a Different Voice.* Cambridge, MA: Harvard Univ. Press
Glenn EN. 1985. Racial ethnic women's labor: the intersection of race, gender and class oppression. *Rev. Radic. Polit. Econ.* 17:86–108
Goffman I. 1977. The arrangment between the sexes. *Theory Soc.* 4:301–31
Guttentag M, Secord P. 1983. *Too Many*

*Women? The Sex Ratio Question.* Beverly Hills, CA: Sage

Haraway D. 1988. Situated knowledges: the science question in feminism and the privilege of partial perspective. *Fem. Stud.* 14:575–99

Harding S. 1986. *The Science Question in Feminism.* Ithaca, New York: Cornell Univ. Press

Harding S. 1991. *Whose Science? Whose Knowledge? Thinking from Women's Lives.* Ithaca, New York: Cornell Univ. Press

Harris M. 1978. *Cannibals and Kings: The Origins of Cultures.* London: Collins

Harstock N. 1983. The feminist standpoint: developing the ground for a specifically feminist historical materialism. In *Discovering Reality: Feminist Perspectives on Epistemology, Metaphysics, Methodology and Philosophy of Science,* ed. S Harding, MB Hintikka, pp. 283–310. Boston: Reidel

Harstock N. 1985. *Money, Sex and Power.* Boston: Northeastern Univ. Press

Hartmann H. 1984. The unhappy marriage of Marxism and feminism: towards a more progressive union. In *Feminist Frameworks: Alternative Theoretical Accounts of the Relations Between Women and Men,* ed. A Jaggar, P Rothenberg, pp. 172–89. New York: McGraw-Hill

Hochschild A. 1983. *The Managed Heart: Commercialization of Human Feeling.* Berkeley, CA: Univ. Calif. Press

hooks B. 1981. *Ain't I a Woman? Black Women and Feminism.* Boston: South End

Huber J. 1988. A theory of family, economy and gender. *J. Fam. Iss.* 9:9–26

Huber J. 1991. Macro-micro links in gender stratification. In *Macro-Micro Linkages in Sociology,* ed. J Huber, pp. 11–25. Newbury Park, CA: Sage

Jaggar AM. 1983. *Feminist Politics and Human Nature.* Totowa, NJ: Rowman & Allanheld

Johnson MM. 1988. *Strong Mothers, Weak Wives: The Search for Gender Equality.* Berkeley, CA: Univ. Calif. Press

Johnson MM. 1989. Feminism and the theories of Talcott Parsons. See Wallace 1989, pp. 101–18

Johnson MM. 1993. Functionalism and feminism: Is estrangement necessary? See England 1993a, pp. 115–30

Kasper A. 1986. Consciousness re-evaluated: interpretive theory and feminist scholarship. *Soc. Inq.* 56:30–49

Katz P. 1979. The development of female identity. *Sex Roles* 5:155–78

Kessler S, McKenna W. 1978. *Gender: An Ethnomethodological Approach.* New York: Wiley

King D. 1988. Multiple jeopardy, multiple consciousness: the context of black feminist ideology. *Signs* 14:42–72

Kurzweil E. 1989. Paychoanalytic feminism: Implications for Sociological theory. See Wallace 1989, pp. 82–97

Lakoff R. 1975. *Language and Woman's Place.* New York: Harper Colophon

Laslett B, Thorne B, Lemert C, Connell RW, Collins PH. 1992. Symposium on Dorothy E. Smith. *Soc. Theory* 10:60–87

Lengermann PM, Niebrugge J. 1996. Contemporary feminist theory. See Ritzer 1996, pp. 436–86

Lenski G. 1966. *Power and Privilege: A Theory of Social Stratification.* New York: McGraw-Hill

Lever J. 1976. Sex differences in the games children play. *Soc. Probl.* 23–24:478–87

Lewis M, Weinraub M. 1979. Origins of early sex-role development. *Sex Roles* 5:135–53

Lockheed M. 1985. Sex and social influence: a meta-analysis guided by theory. See Berger & Zeldich 1985, pp. 406–29

Lopata HZ. 1994. *Circles and Settings: Role Changes of American Women.* Albany, New York: SUNY Press

Lopata HZ, Thorne B. 1978. On the term "sex roles." *Signs* 3:718–21

Lorber J. 1994. *Paradoxes of Gender.* New Haven: Yale Univ. Press

Lorber J, Coser R, Rossi A, Chodorow N. 1981. On the reproduction of mothering: a methodological debate. *Signs* 6:482–514

Martin MK, Voorhies B. 1975. *Female of the Species.* New York: Columbia Univ. Press

Mayo C, Henley N. 1981. Nonverbal behaviour: barrier or agent for sex roles change? In *Gender and Nonverbal Behavior,* ed. C Mayo, N Henley, pp. 3–13. New York: Springer-Verlag

McConnell-Ginet S. 1978. Intonation in a man's world. *Signs* 3:541–59

Meeker B, Weitzel-O'Neill P. 1977. Sex roles and interpersonal behavior in task oriented groups. *Am. Sociol. Rev.* 42:92–105

Mies M. 1986. *Patriarchy and Accumulation on a World-Scale.* London: Zed

Ortner S. 1974. Is female to male as nature is to culture? See Rosaldo & Lamphere 1974

Parker S, Parker H. 1979. The myth of male superiority: rise and demise. *Am. Anthropol.* 81:289–309

Parsons T. 1949. The social structure of the family. In *The Family: Its Function and Destiny,* ed. RN Asher, pp. 173–201. New York: Harper

Parsons T. 1955. The American family: its relation to personality and to the social structure. In *Family, Socialization and Interaction Process,* ed. T Parsons, RF Bales, pp. 3–33. Glencoe, IL: Free Press

Rhode D, ed. 1990. *Theoretical Perspectives on Sexual Difference.* New Haven: Yale Univ. Press

Ridgeway C. 1993. Gender, status, and the social psychology of expectations. See England 1993a, pp. 175–97

Ridgeway C, Berger J. 1986. Expectations, legitimation, and dominance behavior in task groups. *Am. Sociol. Rev.* 51:603–17

Risman B, Schwartz P. 1989. Being gendered: a microstructural view of intimate relationships. In *Gender in Intimate Relationships,* ed. B Risman, P Schwartz, pp. 1–9. Belmont, CA: Wadsworth

Ritzer G. 1996. *Sociological Theory.* New York: McGraw-Hill

Rosaldo MZ. 1974. *Woman, Culture, and Society.* See Rosaldo & Lamphere 1974

Rosaldo MZ, Lamphere L, eds. 1974. *Women, Culture and Society.* Stanford, CA: Stanford Univ. Press

Rosenberg R. 1982. *Beyond Separate Spheres: Intellectual Roots of Modern Feminism.* New Haven: Yale Univ. Press

Rossi AS. 1977. A biosocial perspective on parenting. *Daedalus* 106:1–31

Rossi AS. 1984. Gender and parenthood. *Am. Sociol. Rev.* 49:1–19

Rothenberg PS, ed. 1992. *Race, Class and Gender in the United States.* New York: St. Martins

Sacks K. 1974. Engels revisited: women, the organization of production, and private property. See Rosaldo & Lamphere 1974, pp. 207–22

Sanday PR. 1974. Female status in the public domain. See Rosaldo & Lamphere 1974, pp. 189–206

Sanday PR. 1981. *Female Power and Male Dominance: On the Origins of Sexual Inequality.* Cambridge: Cambridge Univ. Press

Sattel J. 1976. The inexpressive male: tragedy or sexual politics? *Soc. Probl.* 23–24:469–77

Schur E. 1984. *Labeling Women Deviant: Gender, Stigma, and Social Control.* New York: Random House

Seidman S. 1994. *Contested Knowledge: Social Theory in the Postmodern Era.* Cambridge, MA: Blackwell

Seidman S, Stein A, Plummer K, Epstein S. 1994. Symposium: queer theory/sociology: a dialogue. *Soc. Theory* 12:166–248

Shelton BA, Agger B. 1993. Shotgun wedding, unhappy marriage no-fault divorce? rethinking the feminism-Marxism relationship. See England 1993a, pp. 25–41

Smith DE. 1979. A sociology for women. In *The Prism of Sex: Essays in the Sociology of Knowledge,* ed. JA Sherman, ET Black, pp. 135–87. Madison, WI: Univ. Wisc. Press

Smith DE. 1987. *The Everyday World as Problematic: A Feminist Sociology.* Boston: Northeastern Univ. Press

Smith DE. 1989. Sociological theory: methods of writing patriarchy. See Wallace 1989, pp. 34–64

Smith DE. 1990. *The Conceptual Practices of Power: A Feminist Sociology of Knowledge.* Boston: Northeastern Univ. Press

Smith-Lovin L, McPherson JM. 1993. You are who you know: A network approach to gender. See England 1993a, pp. 223–51

Sokoloff N. 1980. *Between Money and Love: The Dialectics of Women's Home and Market Work.* New York: Praeger

Sprague J, Zimmerman MK. 1993. Overcoming dualisms: a feminist agenda for Sociological methodology. See England 1993a, pp. 255–80

Stacey J, Thorne B. 1985. The missing feminist revolution in sociology. *Soc. Probl.* 32:301–16

Tong R. 1989. *Feminist Thought: A Comprehensive Introduction.* Boulder, CO: Westview

Vogel L. 1983. *Marxism and the Oppression of Women: Toward a Unitary Theory.* New Brunswick, NJ: Rutgers Univ. Press

Wallace R, ed. 1989. *Feminism and Sociological Theory.* Newbury Park, CA: Sage

Wallace R, Wolf A. 1995. *Contemporary Sociological Theory: Continuing the Classical Tradition.* Englewood Cliffs, NJ: Prentice Hall

Ward K. 1984. *Women in the World-System: Its Impact on Status and Fertility.* New York: Praeger

Ward K. 1990. *Women Workers and Global Restructuring.* Ithaca, New York: ILR

Ward K. 1993. Reconceptualizing world system theory to include women. See England 1993a, pp. 43–68

Ward K, Grant L. 1991. On a wavelength of their own? Women and sociological theory. *Curr. Perspect. Soc. Theory* 11:117–40

Waters M. 1994. *Modern Sociological Theory.* London: Sage

West C, Fenstermaker S. 1993. Power, inequality and the accomplishment of gender: an ethnomethodological view. See England 1993a, pp. 151–74

West C, Fenstermaker S. 1995. Doing difference. *Gender Soc.* 9:8–37

West C, Zimmerman D. 1977. Women's place in everyday talk: reflections on parent–child interaction. *Soc. Probl.* 24:521–29

West C, Zimmerman D. 1987. Doing gender. *Gender Soc.* 1:125–51

Williams CL. 1993. Psychoanalytic theory and the sociology of gender. See England 1993a, pp. 131–49

Zelizer VA. 1994. *The Social Meaning of Money.* New York: Basic Books

*Annu. Rev. Sociol. 1997. 23:121–45*


# POVERTY AND INEQUALITY AMONG CHILDREN

*Daniel T. Lichter*
Department of Sociology, 601 Oswald Tower, Pennsylvania State University, University Park, Pennsylvania 16802; e-mail: Lichter@pop.psu.edu

KEY WORDS: poverty, well-being, children, inequality, welfare

ABSTRACT

The deteriorating economic well-being of children portends less well-adjusted adults and a diminished economic future for America. A disproportionate share of today's poor children will become tomorrow's poor adults. This chapter discusses the concept, definition, and measurement of children's economic well-being and poverty. Children's current economic well-being is evaluated in comparative perspective—international, historical, and demographic. The chapter also evaluates the etiology of changes in children's absolute and relative economic well-being, focusing especially on the role of the changing family, parental employment, and levels of social provision for poor families. These "causes" are then evaluated in the context of recent public policy debates, including the devolution of federal welfare programs to the states.

## INTRODUCTION

A widespread and justified perception is that an increasing share of American children are "at risk," both materially and psychoemotionally. By current standards, children suffer disproportionately high rates of measured poverty, and they are often the innocent victims of rapid changes in our most fundamental institutions—the family, school, and government. The breakdown of the traditional nuclear family has meant that an increasing share of children live with an unmarried, typically poor mother (Bianchi 1990, Hernandez 1993). Or, if they live with two parents, they receive their primary child care from nonfamily members or formal providers because both parents must work, often at low wages, to ensure a living family income. The schools have been



0360-0572/97/0815-0121$08.00

unable to compensate for the social and economic deficits in the home (Booth & Dunn 1995). In fact, they are usually blamed for exacerbating the problems of poor children while promoting the intergenerational transmission of poverty (Corcoran 1995). Government often seems unable or unwilling to respond. For example, current debates about welfare reform—time limits and family caps—often come down to whether children in a rich society should bear the costs of current national and global macroeconomic shifts or whether they should suffer needlessly from the decisions of their parents regarding work and family life (Corbett 1993).

The purpose of this review is to place the changing economic circumstances of American children in proper perspective—a comparative one. The objective is to define and evaluate current absolute and relative definitions of children's changing economic deprivation and poverty. A comparative stance is necessary for accurately gauging the economic well-being of children across societies and for different subgroups of the population (e.g. racial and ethnic minority children). It is also required if we are to effectively monitor the changing well-being of children and measure the economic impact of public policy initiatives, including nascent state welfare reform legislation. This paper sets current policy debates within a broader historical or international perspective and identifies those factors or circumstances—such as the rise in female-headed families and declining real wages among less skilled young adults—that have contributed to the currently high levels of relative economic deprivation among children. Finally, this review stresses the increasingly important but often neglected topic of growing inequality in the economic circumstances of America's children.

To be sure, evidence of increasing poverty rates among children and for diverse segments of the population constitutes a strong basis for public concern. The short- and long-term deleterious consequences of poverty for children and for society are large and well documented (McLeod & Shanahan 1993, 1996, Hao 1995). Childhood poverty impairs physical growth, cognitive development (e.g. reading ability), and socioemotional functioning (e.g. behavioral problems, depression) (Hill & Sandfort 1995, Korenman et al 1995). Poor children are also more likely to be physically abused; indeed, effective parenting suffers in economically stressful environments (Conger & Elder 1994, McLanahan & Sandefur 1994, Kruttschnitt et al 1994). The incidence, duration, and chronicity of childhood poverty also have large negative effects on children's IQ, educational achievement, and later adult productivity (as measured by wage rates and hours worked), while increasing their adult welfare dependency (Zill 1993, Duncan et al 1994, McLanahan & Sandefur 1994). The implication is obvious: The effects of high rates of economic deprivation among today's children may only be fully realized by tomorrow's adults.

## MEASURING ECONOMIC WELL-BEING AND POVERTY

Most discussions of children's changing economic circumstances refer to the recent rise in children's poverty rates as officially measured by the US Census Bureau. Published in their Current Population Reports (P60 series), these rates are used by governmental agencies to establish eligibility criteria for various social insurance programs and public assistance. The official poverty income thresholds were set in the early 1960s at three times the income necessary to maintain an economy food plan devised by the US Department of Agriculture for families of various sizes (Orshansky 1965). With only slight subsequent modifications, the poverty income thresholds are adjusted each year for inflation using the Consumer Price Index (CPI). In 1994, a before-taxes income threshold of $15,029 was set for a family of four (US Bureau of the Census 1996).

Based on the Orshansky criteria, the trend in child poverty has been one of substantial reductions during the 1960s, which leveled off during the 1970s, and then increased in the 1980s and early 1990s (Figure 1). In 1994, 15.3 million or 21.8 percent of all American children lived in poor families. Although children comprised only 26.7 percent of the US population, they accounted for 40.1 percent of all poor persons (US Bureau of the Census 1996).

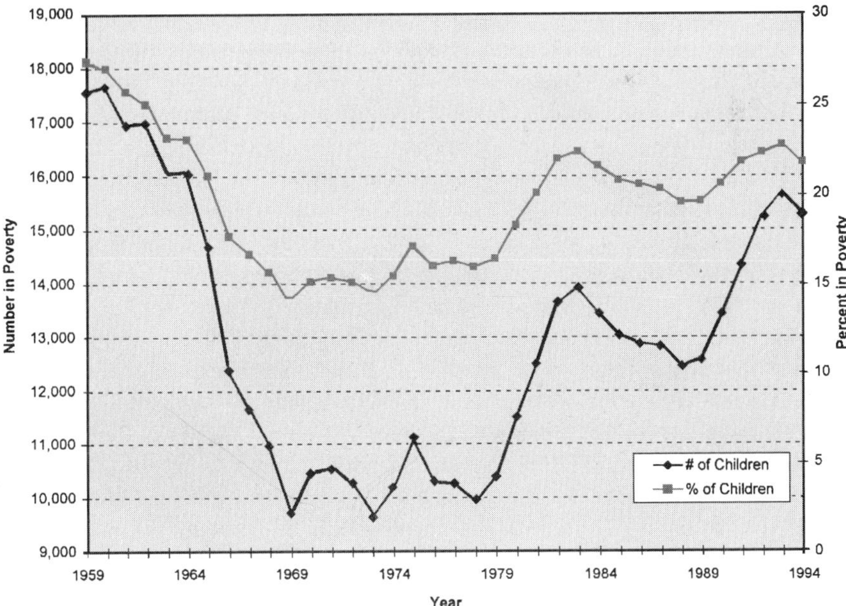


*Figure 1* Poverty status of children: 1959 to 1994.

This income-based measure of the prevalence of economic deprivation has many well-known limitations that confound policy discussions and have the potential to distort group comparisons in America's increasingly diverse population (Haveman et al 1988, Ruggles 1990, Citro & Michael 1995). The measure is adjusted for inflation each year, but not for the increases in real family income and consumption by children. It does not take into account near-income (e.g. food stamps) or in-kind public assistance (e.g. subsidized school lunches) for children. It does not correct for geographic differences in the costs of feeding, clothing, and sheltering children. It does not adjust for income that represents the costs of working (e.g. costs of childcare) or that is not available for the purchase of material goods or services (e.g. child support payments paid by the noncustodial parent at the expense of coresidential children), or that trades in the informal economy (e.g. bartering goods or services). Income is not adjusted for taxes, which have varied enormously across political units and over time. The various poverty thresholds do not adequately reflect economies of scale or measure "equivalent" poverty income for various family sizes and the adult-children composition. The measure also does not take into account the increasing share of children reared by single parents and their cohabiting partners, partners whose income often is excluded from calculations of official child poverty (Manning & Lichter 1996). Finally, despite rapid changes in the family, this measure still implicitly assumes that parental resources are invested in children—biological, step, noncustodial—in an equitable or altruistic way (i.e. equally or according to need).

With so many well-known limitations, how can we be certain that economic deprivation—as measured by the official poverty rate—has really increased by one third over the last two decades among America's children? Some researchers suggest that poverty should consider actual consumption levels rather than income alone (Mayer & Jencks 1995). Consumption-based measures typically show lower rates of poverty than do measures based on pre-tax income (Slesnick 1993, Lino 1996). The income generated in the household frequently is underreported in survey research (Edin 1995, Mergenbagen 1996), while household consumption is higher than expected on the basis of reported income. For 1988–1990, low-income families consumed goods and services worth more than twice their annual incomes (Mayer 1996).

Poor families and children also have more material possessions than they did a generation ago (Federman et al 1996). A smaller percentage than in the past live in substandard housing (i.e. without indoor plumbing or electricity). A larger percentage eat better (as measured by caloric intake)—a testimony perhaps to the food stamp program and the comparatively cheap food supply in this country. And they have greater access to material goods that were simply unavailable in the past (i.e. TV, air conditioners, etc). For example, 54.6% of persons in families receiving AFDC own a VCR (US Bureau of the Census 1995).

Such information, however, conveys little about the quality or adequacy of these material possessions or their relevance to children's well-being. Moreover, a recent study (Federman et al 1996) shows that 55.1% of poor families experienced at least one of the following deprivations during the past year (i.e. in 1992): evicted from home; utilities disconnected; telephone disconnected; housing with upkeep problems; crowded housing; no refrigerator; no stove; or no telephone. These same deprivations were experienced by only 13% of nonpoor families. The issue today arguably is less one of growing absolute material deprivation—that is still an empirical question depending on whether cash income or consumption is the relevant indicator—but rather whether child poverty or deprivation is morally defensible in an affluent society.

Growing relative economic deprivation is also a concern, as children in poor families have fallen behind other population segments. As described in the following section, child poverty in America is different from poverty in other rich countries. It is different from the recent and distant past on many dimensions (e.g. reliance on welfare income). And it is increasingly heterogeneous in magnitude, etiology, and consequences across different demographic segments (e.g. minority children, immigrants, children living with a single parent) of American society. Our preoccupation with absolute deprivation should not distract us from these relative dimensions of the family resources available to America's children (Duncan 1992, Lichter & Eggebeen 1993, Fischer et al 1996).

## AMERICAN CHILDREN IN COMPARATIVE PERSPECTIVE

### *Child Poverty Compared to Other Western Industrial Countries*

Whether child poverty rates in the United States are regarded as relatively high or low depends on one's standard of comparison. Rainwater (1995) compared poverty rates of families with children in the mid-1980s in the United States with seven other Western industrialized countries that spanned the range of social service provision. Using the Luxembourg Income Study database, he examined poverty in market-oriented economies like Canada and in social democratic welfare states like Sweden and the Netherlands. The United States by international standards had very high rates of child poverty (20.3% ), especially in comparison with Germany (4.9% ), Sweden (3.5% ), and the Netherlands (4%). The differences were even more striking among female-headed families with children. The rate for the United States was 57.9% compared with 19.7% in France, 16.5% in the United Kingdom, and 7.9% in the Netherlands.

These rates were calculated as one half the median family income (adjusted for age of the head and family size). But, because real family income is higher in the United States than elsewhere, these rates may not be strictly comparable. One half of the median family income may have more purchasing power in the United States than elsewhere. Other research, however, has calibrated "equivalent" income poverty thresholds in other countries to allow international comparisons. For example, Smeeding & Torrey (1988) converted the US income poverty line into the currencies of other countries. The official poverty threshold in the United States is roughly 42% of the median family income and is equivalent to slightly more than 50% of median family income in Sweden. Even with poverty comparisons based on equivalent currencies, however, US children compared unfavorably with children in most other Western industrialized societies considered.

There are many underlying reasons for the comparatively high poverty rates among American children. Rainwater (1995) argued, for example, that the difference resides primarily in the low ameliorative effects of public transfer income on poverty, especially for female-headed families with children. For these families, countries with both low earnings and low transfer incomes relative to the median equivalent income had the highest rates of child poverty. The United States ranked lowest when both factors were considered together, and in fact had the highest poverty rate among single-mother families with children.

Smeeding & Torrey (1988) showed that poor children in the United States received most of their transfer income from means-tested welfare programs, while European countries relied more heavily on universalist social insurance programs such as child allowances that all families with children received. Indeed, that pre-tax and pre-benefit poverty was actually higher on average in Europe than in the United States (Smeeding & Rainwater 1991, cited in Rodgers 1996). The limited safety net in the United States makes the adverse income effects of family disruption and unmarried childbearing especially large for women and coresidential children (Smock 1993, Casper et al 1994).

Others argue that the high rates of poverty among women (and their children) in the United States reflect its demographic heterogeneity, especially with regard to family structure (Casper et al 1994). But this explanation alone is incomplete. Using the Luxembourg Income Study, Smeeding et al (1988) showed that the percentage of poor children in a country was unrelated to the proportion of the families headed by a single parent. Sweden, for example, had a higher percentage of their children borne to unmarried women than in the United States. But the poverty rate of families headed by unmarried women in Sweden was only 6.5% . For single parent families without a wage earner, the poverty rates were 18.2 and 95.7%, respectively, in Sweden and the United States. These are extraordinarily large differences by any standard.

## *Child Poverty Compared to the Past*

Child poverty is different today from poverty in the past. To be sure, the recent rise in income-based poverty among children, despite the limitations of such measures, has been an important catalyst for legislative advocacy on behalf of children. But absolute increases in child poverty are arguably less important than several other relative dimensions of the current poverty problem. The rise in child poverty has occurred simultaneously with rising age inequality, real declines in income among poor children, a growing gap between rich and poor children, increasing dependence on welfare income, a changing family and spatial ecology of poverty, and the growing incidence of chronic or persistent poverty.

Children today are at once the poorest age segment in American society and the most vulnerable and innocent. Children have poverty rates that are nearly twice those of the elderly population, a situation without precedent in American history (Figure 2, see also Fuchs 1991). The rise in child poverty since 1980 occurred as poverty of the elderly declined substantially, largely

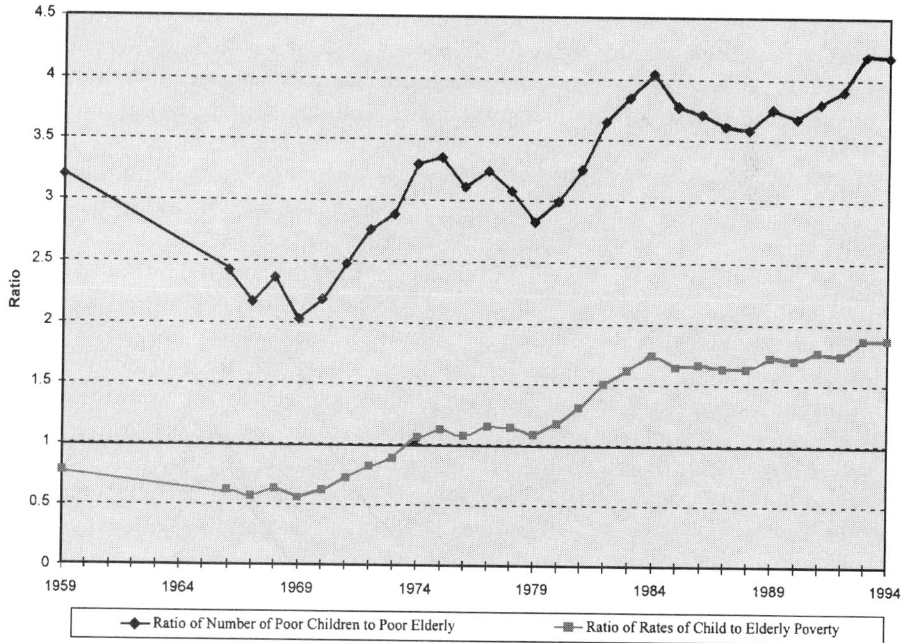


*Figure 2* Ratio of children in poverty to elderly in poverty: 1959–1994.

through government social insurance, including social security and Medicare (Preston 1984). Concerns today about child poverty cannot be separated from the issue of growing generational inequities and governmental investments that favor the elderly over children (Fuchs & Reklis 1992).

Poor children today are absolutely poorer than the poor children of a generation ago. Duncan (1992) showed that the median real income of the poorest families with children declined by 12% between 1970 and 1986 (see also Haveman et al 1988, Karoly 1994). Eggebeen & Lichter (1991) reported that the proportion of children in "deep poverty," i.e. below 50% of the poverty threshold, increased by one third between 1970 and 1988. Moreover, the median family income-to–poverty ratio among children in the bottom 20% of the family income distribution declined absolutely from .85 in 1969 to .68 in 1989 (Lichter & Eggebeen 1993). The poverty gap—the income required to lift poor children out of poverty—has grown substantially over the past decade.

Poor children today also are poorer in comparison to affluent children; i.e. the relative income gap between poor children and the "average" or "affluent" child increased sharply over the past decade or so. The percentage of children living in families below one half the median family income increased from 21.4% to 27.2% between 1970 and 1988 (Eggebeen & Lichter 1991). In 1969, the income-to–poverty ratio among the most affluent 20% of American children was 5.82 times greater than the figure for the poorest 20% . It was 8.72 times greater in 1989, because family income both declined among the poorest children and increased (by nearly 20%) among the richest children (Lichter & Eggebeen 1993).

The income mix of families of poor children today is different from two decades ago; they are now more likely to rely on welfare income and on other in-kind public assistance programs (Jensen et al 1993, Jensen & Eggebeen 1994). Nearly 10 million US children received AFDC in the early 1990s, a level without precedent, and over 13.5 million poor children lived in households receiving some form of means-tested assistance (US Bureau of the Census 1996). In 1989, 47.2% of poor children received cash assistance from government programs, compared with 24.6% in 1969. More important, the percentage of children's family income that is from welfare increased from 18.2% to 35.5% over 1969–1989 (Jensen et al 1993). One quarter of all poor children in 1988 were fully welfare-dependent (i.e. without any other source of income) compared with about 6% in 1959 (Hernandez 1993). This occurred at the same time when average welfare benefit levels for children declined and the antipoverty effectiveness of cash and near-cash transfers eroded (US Department of Health and Human Services 1996).

Poverty rates increased most dramatically among the children of working parents, rather than among the children of single parents (Annie Casey

Foundation 1996). The rising share of family income from welfare (noted above) is due primarily to significant declines in earnings from work among the poor. Indeed, a larger share of single mothers work today than in the past, and they have higher labor force participation rates than married mothers (Bianchi 1990, Hernandez 1993). The paradox is that work-based welfare solutions are now viewed as the panacea for poor children at the same time that the ameliorative effects of work have eroded, especially for women and the low skilled (Lichter et al 1994).

Poor children today are arguably more likely than in the past to be socially and spatially isolated from the nonpoor in schools, neighborhoods, and communities, in both urban and rural areas (Massey & Denton 1993, Garrett et al 1994, O'Hare 1995). In 1990, 54.6% of poor children lived in neighborhoods with rates of poverty exceeding 20% (Jargowski 1996). Moreover, for the 100 largest metropolitan areas, a larger proportion of America's poor children lived in poor census tracts (defined as 40% or more in poverty) in 1990 than in 1980 (Johnston 1997). A growing policy concern is whether the increasing geographic concentration of poverty in low-income urban neighborhoods or rural areas promotes maladaptive behavioral or cultural adjustments—juvenile delinquency, school dropout, and nonmarital childbearing—that perpetuate poverty into adulthood (Lichter 1993).

The family ecology of poor children is different today from that in the past. In the mid-1960s, about two thirds of all poor children lived with married-couple families or families with a male present (Rodgers 1996). Today, 8.5 million children (57% of poor children) live with a single parent. This a product of the acceleration of divorce rates during the 1970s and the continuing high rates of marital disruption today (Schoen & Weinick 1993). The poverty-producing effects of divorce are reinforced by out-of-wedlock childbearing, and nearly one third of all births today occur outside of marriage; thus about 50% of all children can expect to live some part of childhood in a single-parent family if current trends continue (Ventura et al 1995). The new freedom to make previously stigmatized choices about marriage and family life (e.g. divorce or cohabitation) may benefit adults but be harmful economically to their children (Bumpass 1990).

Poor children today are more likely than in the past to be chronically poor, i.e. suffer persistent bouts of poverty or recurrent poverty (Duncan & Rodgers 1989, Duncan & Rodgers 1991, Devine et al 1992). For 1992–1993, 8.3% of children were poor all 24 months, compared with 4.8% of all persons (US Bureau of the Census 1995). The average duration of poverty among female-headed families with children (during 1991–1993) was 3.9 months, compared with 6.9 months among married couple families with children (US Bureau of the Census, 1995). Long-term poverty implies policy solutions—training, remedial education, job growth—that differ from the short-term relief (e.g. food stamps) required at a time of need (Duncan 1992).

In sum, our current preoccupation with rising absolute poverty rates should not divert us from perhaps a more fundamental concern, i.e. that poverty for children is much different today than in the past along several dimensions. Today's poverty among children must be judged against the living conditions and consumption levels of society as a whole and other advantaged groups—current and past. It is with regard to this relative dimension of child poverty that the political rhetoric matches the reality. It also is this relative dimension that implies increasing social and cultural differentiation in the future as the current generation of poor children enters adulthood.

## *Child Poverty Compared Across Diverse Population Groups*

Poverty and prosperity are experienced differently across diverse segments of America society (see Table 1). Most evidence suggests that economic inequality has grown over time, both within and between the rich and poor, more educated and less educated, blacks and whites, married-couple families and single-parent families, native-borns and immigrants, city dwellers and suburbanites (Danziger & Gottschalk 1993, Levy 1995, Karoly 1994). We have at the same time become more heterogenous as a society along these same demographic dimensions. An important research question today is not whether differences exist—they surely do (Table 1)—but whether conventional poverty measures accurately portray group differences, and whether the underlying etiology of poverty for different

**Table 1** Poverty and prosperity among US children: 1994

| | Poverty | | Prosperity[b] | |
|---|---|---|---|---|
| | Number[a] | Rate | Number[a] | Rate |
| Total persons | 38,059 | 14.5 | 171,818 | 65.7 |
| Total elderly | 3,663 | 11.7 | 18,386 | 58.8 |
| Total children | 15,289 | 21.8 | 39,248 | 56.1 |
| Total white children | 9,346 | 16.9 | 33,949 | 61.5 |
| in married-couple families | 4,268 | 9.9 | 30,305 | 70.1 |
| in female-headed families | 4,099 | 45.7 | 2,517 | 28.1 |
| Total black children | 4,906 | 43.8 | 3,537 | 31.6 |
| in married-couple families | 617 | 14.6 | 2,468 | 58.2 |
| in female-headed families | 3,935 | 63.2 | 909 | 14.6 |
| Total Latino children | 4,075 | 41.5 | 2,746 | 28.0 |
| in married-couple families | 1,952 | 30.1 | 2,340 | 36.1 |
| in female-headed families | 1,804 | 68.3 | 270 | 10.2 |

(Source: Table 9, U.S. Bureau of the Census 1996).
[a]Number in 1000s.
[b]Above two times the poverty income threshold.

groups can be identified and appropriately addressed. The former is important for identifying groups most "at risk," while the latter question is important if reducing inequality is a social goal.

One criticism of the current official poverty measure is that it may not accurately reflect group differences in available family resources over time (Citro & Michael 1995). Perhaps the best example is the substantial and persistent heterogeneity in child poverty rates that exists across racial and ethnic groups in the United States (Hernandez 1993, Lichter & Landale 1995). In 1984, the official poverty rates of African American and Latino children were 43.8% and 41.5%, respectively, compared with a rate of 16.9% among white children (Table 1). But these differences in income poverty undoubtedly mask even greater differences in deep poverty, consumption and wealth, and long-term or chronic poverty.

For example, the child poverty rate in 1994 was 2.6 times greater among blacks than whites (Table 1), but 3.4 times greater using a measure of deep poverty (i.e. one half the poverty threshold) (US Bureau of the Census 1996). Moreover, nearly half of US blacks had a household net worth of less than $5000, compared to 22% among whites (US Bureau of the Census 1996). Black children also experience longer spells of poverty than whites (Duncan 1992). Period rates also ignore the greater incidence of recurrent poverty among black children (Duncan & Rodgers 1991). For 1991–1992, 15.1% of blacks were poor each month, compared with 3.1% of non-Latino whites (US Bureau of the Census 1995). This means, simply, that a higher proportion of poor black children at a given point in time will have been poor for a longer period of time or will have experienced more episodes of poverty. Cross-sectional studies that include poverty as a predictor at a single point in time are implicitly understating levels of economic inequality.

The conventional wisdom is that economic hardship is offset to some extent by institutionalized patterns of informal economic support and exchange among some groups, such as African Americans. But the empirical evidence is mixed. Quantitative studies suggest that poverty differentials are likely to be exacerbated as a result of ethnic-group differences in intergenerational economic support (e.g. money, food, housing) among elderly parents, their children, and grandchildren (Hogan et al 1993, McGarry & Schoeni 1995). The wealthiest children—a disproportionate share of whom are non-Latino whites—received the most income support from kin and friends. Moreover, household strategies to adapt to economic stress may mask or diminish economic deprivation among minority children. For example, families may adapt to economic hardship by "doubling up" with other families (Angel & Tienda 1982).

Children are an understudied segment among the immigrant population (Jensen & Chitose 1994). Over 15% of Latino children are first generation immigrants and another 44% are native-born children of foreign-born parents (Oropesa & Landale 1997). First and second generation Latino children experience disproportionately high rates of measured poverty—41% and 30% , respectively. The new welfare bill includes provisions to exclude legal immigrants (for up to 5 years), which means that future pretax/pretransfer comparisons in official income poverty will further distort true disparities in well-being across immigrant and native children.

At the same time, assessing relative racial and ethnic group differences—including new immigrants from Latin America and Asia—may be confounded by cultural differences in family formation processes. For example, child poverty among Puerto Rican children is exceptionally high in female-headed families relative to their counterparts in white families or in other racial and ethnic minority groups (Lichter & Landale 1995). The poverty rate among Puerto Rican children living with a single mother and her cohabiting partner, however, would be cut in half if all household income were included in its calculation (Manning & Lichter 1996).

To date, explanations for racial or ethnic differences (or other group differences) typically have focused less on the methodological artifacts described above and more on variations in job skills, work patterns, and family life. The parents of African-American and other minority children, for example, are typically less likely to be highly educated and to work at stable, high-paying jobs, and are more likely to be raising children alone (Hernandez 1993, Hogan & Lichter 1995). The earnings of college-educated, full-time employed men increased by 5.2% between 1979 and 1989 (Wetzel 1995), while men with a high school education experienced a real earnings decline of 6.5% . In the absence of educational equality between racial and ethnic groups, rising earnings returns to education in America will exacerbate interracial and interethnic differences in children's poverty and economic status.

Racial and ethnic differences in work patterns among women in single-parent and married-couple patterns also contribute to disparities in the economic status of children (Hernandez 1993, Lichter & Eggebeen 1994), but the effects of maternal employment vary widely across racial and ethnic groups. For black-white comparisons, employment differences account for virtually none of the black-white difference in child poverty among children in married couple households (Lichter & Eggebeen 1994), and only a small fraction of the racial difference among children living in single female households. On the other hand, over two thirds of the black-white difference in child poverty resided in the higher proportion of black children living in high-risk, female-headed families (Eggebeen & Lichter 1991). Racial inequality is further magnified by large differences in child support payments, a pattern reflecting racial differences in the income of noncustodial fathers and the higher nonmarital fertility rather than divorce (i.e. where child support and compliance are lower among African Americans than whites).

For other racial and ethnic groups, employment differences matter more. Lichter & Landale (1995) showed that a substantial percentage of the disproportionately high rates of child poverty among Mexican-Americans and Puerto Ricans was due to differences in work patterns. For example, the poverty gap between white and Puerto Rican children in single-parent families would be reduced by nearly 60% if Puerto Rican mothers had the same employment rates as Anglo mothers. Moreover, little of the high poverty rate among Puerto Rican children relative to other Latino groups (including Cuban-Americans and Mexican-Americans) can be attributed to the lack of local employment opportunities or to the concentration of Puerto Rican families in economically depressed racially or segregated cities (Landale & Lichter 1997).

In the final analysis, changing demographic composition—racial, immigrant, family, economic—and increasing child poverty are mutually reinforcing. Continuing socioeconomic and racial differentials in mortality and fertility, for example, contribute to a relatively higher proportion of minority children and lower proportion of minority elderly in the American population, which further exacerbates observed poverty differentials between the young and the old. Moreover, without significant reductions in racial inequality, recent and future compositional changes in America necessarily imply future increases in the proportions of children who are poor. Without the economic assimilation of new ethnic immigrants (or reduced immigration), America's demographic future necessarily implies increases in the child poverty rate. Without reductions in the inequality between men's and women's earnings, which gives rise in part to large economic disparities between children across family types, the "breakdown" in the family implies increases in poor children in America. Finally, without significant reductions in economic inequality across racial, ethnic, and gender groups, growing population heterogeneity implies increases in the population of poor children.

## THE ETIOLOGY OF CHANGING CHILD POVERTY AND INEQUALITY

Why has income poverty and economic inequality—the absolute and relative dimensions of poverty—increased among the families of children in the United States over the last two decades? The main reasons have been largely identified—changes in family structure, changing patterns of employment and earnings, and changes in public assistance. But much less agreement exists about the relative importance of these factors and, by extension, their possible solutions.

## *Changing Family Structure and Family Size*

Most discussions of child poverty begin with the transformation of the American family. On the one hand, a growing share of American children live with a single mother, while poverty rates for this group have remained high at nearly 50% for at least 30 years (Bane & Ellwood 1989). The simplicity of the argument contributes to its widespread appeal. If a greater share of children live in "high-risk" single-parent families today than in the past, then a greater proportion of children will be poor in the absence of any changes in single women's economic position. Indeed, Duncan (1992) showed that virtually all of the rise in poverty for families with children between 1970 and 1986 was due to the growth in single-parent families. Eggebeen & Lichter (1991) observed that roughly 50% of the post-1980 increase in poverty was attributable to changes in family composition. In a time series regression analysis, Rodgers (1996) explained 70% of the annual variation between 1966 and 1993 in the child poverty rate by the proportion of families with children headed by unmarried mothers.

To critics, such analyses appear to "blame the victim" or "blame women" for the rise in child poverty (Baca Zinn 1989, Hernandez 1993, Luker 1996). Such analyses also imply that children now living in female-headed families would have the same rates of poverty as children currently living in married couple families if only their mothers stayed married or became married. Increasing child poverty may not result from rising female headship, but rather rising economic hardship may be responsible for the breakdown in the family. In fact, Bane (1986) showed that 25% of white single mothers and 75% of black single mothers were poor before they became single mothers.

Few studies, however, have actually tracked children's economic trajectories over time (Duncan & Rodgers 1989, Duncan 1992), and fewer still have related changes in family income shifts to changes in children's family circumstances. Bianchi & McArthur (1991) examined, with data from the Survey of Income and Program Participation, children's economic circumstances before and after their parents divorced. Children in married couples that subsequently split up had an income-to-poverty ratio of 2.35 (before separation) compared with an income-to-poverty ratio of 2.87 among children with two parents always present. At the same time, the marital breakup resulted in a 12.6% decline in the income-to-poverty ratio among children, while the income-to-poverty ratio among children in intact families increased by 6.6% (between the first and eighth interviews). Duncan (1992) similarly showed that poverty among children of divorce increased from 12% to 27% during the period between one year prior to and one year after the divorce. After five years, the poverty rate dropped to 20%, but much of the improvement for children was due to remarriage. Bianchi & McArthur (1991) showed that the income-to-poverty ratio increased from 1.39 to 2.63—a 90% increase—among children whose mother remarried.

The Bianchi-McArthur study implies that marital disruption and low family income are mutually reinforcing. But the child poverty problem today also resides in the rise of nonmarital fertility among young mothers, a trend with no necessary economic cause. The rise in the ratio of nonmarital-to-marital fertility is inextricably tied to the rise in child poverty, in part because the poverty rates among children of unmarried mothers are substantially higher than among children of either married or divorced parents (Bianchi 1993). Compared with divorced mothers, unmarried mothers typically have less education and job-related skills, they are younger, they have younger children (which makes maternal employment difficult and childcare expensive), and they are much less likely to receive income assistance from the noncustodial father.

Finally, a paradox of current family processes is that the rise in child poverty rates has more to do with declining and low fertility among the nonpoor population than it does in the fertility behavior of the poor. Although family sizes have declined across all income groups, nearly 25% of the rise in child poverty between 1978 and 1987 resulted from increasing differentials in the mean number of children living in poor and nonpoor families (Eggebeen & Lichter 1991). At the same time, the decline in fertility in the United States overall, especially during the 1960s, was an important demographic factor responsible for rapid declines in child poverty during this period (Gottschalk & Danziger 1994). If fertility rates had remained unchanged, child poverty rates would have risen 7 and 3 percentage points for blacks and whites, respectively. Accordingly, a rise in fertility among the nonpoor would reduce measured poverty rates, but it would do little to help the 16 million children who are currently poor.

### *Changing Parental Work and Earnings*

This emphasis on family change is consistent with the empirical and historical record, although it should not divert attention from the fact that poverty and economic inequality among American children also are inextricably linked to the earning capacities of children's parents. Poverty among children living with two full-time working parents is virtually nonexistent (Hernandez 1993, Hogan & Lichter 1995). To be sure, this does not mean that simply moving all nonworking parents into the labor force will eliminate child poverty (Lichter & Eggebeen 1994, Lichter & Gardner 1996–97). Parents currently in the labor force are different (i.e. education and skills) from those not now working. Nor should changing employment rates per se be interpreted as the main engine of change in long-term trends in children's economic circumstances. For children living with two parents, the rise in maternal labor force participation rates, especially among young married mothers, means that more—not fewer—children today than in the past live with two parents contributing to family income (Hernandez 1993). For children living in female-headed families, a larger share of single women today than in the past (e.g. 1960) are employed. Indeed, 1% more children of unmarried mothers would be poor if unmarried mothers had the same employment rates as observed in 1960 (Eggebeen & Lichter 1991).

An obvious substantive implication is that the child poverty is less a problem of work than of finding work that pays a nonpoverty wage. Poverty rates among workers (using various definitions of worker) increased during the 1980s (Blank 1996), while an increasing share of the poor were working (Lichter et al 1994). This reflects macroeconomic shifts, especially the transformation of the economy from high-wage manufacturing jobs to low-wage service jobs, declining unionization, and global competition for cheap labor from abroad. Moreover, the minimum wage has also declined substantially in real terms since the early 1970s relative to the average wage of all workers. At the 1996 minimum wage of $4.25 hour, a full-time year-round worker would earn $8,500 annually. The income poverty threshold for a two-parent family with one child was $11,929 in 1994. Even when the new minimum wage of $5.15 goes into effect in 1997, the annual earnings of $10,300 is still $1,629 below the current poverty threshold.

More education is understandably viewed as the best solution to this problem. But it is worth noting that increases in child poverty occurred during the 1980s at the same time that educational levels generally increased and school dropout rates declined. In fact, educational levels actually increased during the 1980s more rapidly among the poor than the nonpoor (Shapiro 1989). This reflects the changing demographic composition of the poor; from an historical perspective, elderly persons, a group with lower levels of education, have experienced declines in poverty (for nonwork-related reasons) while young adults—those bearing and raising children—have experienced increases in poverty despite high levels of education. The implication is straightforward: The post-1980 rise in child poverty cannot be attributed to significant declines in human capital, job skills, or the work efforts of children's parents.

The changing demography of the poor population means that policies that stress macroeconomic growth may have only limited benefits for many poor people. Indeed, a "rising tide lifts all boats" is an inappropriate aphorism today, especially for children; local economic conditions are only modestly associated with children's poverty status (Friedman & Lichter 1997, Landale & Lichter 1997). Other factors also play a role. For example, the tendency for highly educated persons to marry each other has increased over time (Mare 1991), even if we adjust for the increasing demographic supply of highly educated women.

In addition, the rise in maternal employment was greater among women married to high-earning males (e.g. the top earnings decile) than among women married to low earners during the past decade or so (e.g. the bottom decile). Thus, educational marital homogamy and maternal employment have the potential to increase both family income inequality and the potential disparities between married couples with two workers and one worker (although the effects are small; see Cancian et al 1994). At the same time, growing income inequality was evident among all types of families with children, but especially among those headed by single mothers (Karoly 1994).

The rise in child poverty associated with increased childbearing among unmarried women also presumably has a work-related explanation. A common argument is that poor unmarried women lack access to "marriageable" or "economically attractive" men; thus, marriage is not an economically viable option for many poor women (South & Lloyd 1992, McLaughlin & Lichter 1996). In the absence of sufficient marital opportunities, the human need to love and be loved may be met through nonmarital childbearing and in single-parent families. Indeed, we have only a crude understanding of the social and economic conditions, cultural factors (including values and norms), and biological factors (i.e. changes in hormonal levels) that are responsible for increased sexual activity, pregnancy and abortion, and out-of-wedlock childbearing among unmarried women (see excellent discussion by Luker 1996). The recent emphasis on shortages of economically attractive males to marry necessarily implies that nonmarital fertility is "planned," i.e. women's fertility decisions are based on a rational calculus that takes into account marital opportunities, the economic attractiveness of potential marital partners, and other alternatives (including welfare). But most nonmarital births are in fact unintended (Ventura et al 1995), a fact that militates against strictly economic interpretations or arguments that attribute teen childbearing and rising poverty to shortages of "good men" to marry.

## *Changing Public Assistance and Government Policy*

Another common explanation for the rise in child poverty resides with the role of government policies. The new emphasis on behavioral poverty, i.e. poverty presumably caused by the bad decisions and bad values of parents, has been linked to explanations that stress the deleterious role of government, especially cash assistance programs like AFDC, in undermining the traditional family. Alternatively, others argue that government is not doing enough; indeed, the federal government has cut average cash assistance payments over the past decade and the new welfare bill will shift much of the responsibility for children's well-being to states. Is it too much government or too little government that has contributed to the relative decline in children's economic status?

For some analysts (Murray 1984), the decline in family values follows from the generosity of welfare programs that encourage nonmarital fertility and divorce, which indirectly harms children economically and emotionally. Most evidence indicates that such policies have played a modest role at best in family formation processes (Moffitt 1992). Garfinkel & McLanahan (1986) suggested that about 15% of the rise in female-headed families for 1960–1975 was due to rising welfare benefit levels. Another common argument is that welfare creates disincentives to work, especially among unmarried mothers, which reinforces the impoverished position of children living in female-headed families. Yet, Bane & Ellwood (1989) reported that the family income of children living with a single mother who worked full-time was $6817 (in 1986 dollars) compared with $6284 among children living with a nonworking single mother. Welfare is an option nearly as attractive as very low-wage work. The question remains whether it is high welfare or low earnings that is the more important disincentive to work.

The preceding discussion suggests that governmental policies, by undermining the traditional family, may have had an indirect negative effect on the well-being of American children. But the effects also may be more direct. For example, the average AFDC and food stamp benefit level for a mother with two children and no earnings declined from $10,169 to $7,471 between 1972 and 1991 in constant dollars (Haveman & Wolfe 1993). The ameliorative effects of welfare are, not surprisingly, both low and declining. In 1979, 42% of children were lifted out of poverty as a result of means- and nonmeans-tested cash and noncash transfers. This ameliorative effect declined to 32% by 1991. This compares unfavorably to the high and increasing effects observed among the elderly, from 77% to 81% over 1979–1991 (Ozawa 1995). Declining welfare benefit levels have contributed directly to the deteriorating economic well-being of poor children.

For working parents and their children not now dependent on welfare, reducing child poverty may require government intervention to help parents earn more (Plotnick 1989, Bianchi 1993). Raising the minimum wage potentially is one option that supports working families while presumably increasing the incentives to work. Another option is to expand the Earned Income Tax Credit for families with workers, especially those with previously weak attachments to the labor force (such as young adults). The availability of high-quality and subsidized childcare also will keep money in the hands of working parents, thus potentially benefiting children. Although it is unclear whether such efforts will slow the rise in income inequality (Danziger & Gottschalk 1994), they would most likely help those children at the bottom of the income distribution if work is available.

Enacting such legislation, however, will require a greater appreciation that children are a public good and that investments in children today are necessary for tomorrow's future (Fuchs & Reklis 1992, Bianchi 1993). To the dismay of some observers, recently signed welfare reform legislation will eliminate the largest cash assistance program that benefits poor children—AFDC. Public assistance programs will instead be administered through the mechanism of block grants to states for the purpose of tailoring programs to reflect local needs, resources, and values. Time limits on continuous participation (i.e. 2 years) and lifetime participation (i.e. 5 years) will be imposed, and new work requirements for recipients will be stipulated. One study estimates that an additional 1 million children will become poor as a result of the welfare legislation ("Personal Responsibility and Work Opportunity Reconciliation Act") passed by Congress and signed into law by President Clinton in August 1996 (The Urban Institute 1996).

The economic effects of new welfare policies on children are difficult to forecast; indeed, dire predictions typically are wrong because they stimulate new policies that avert the forecasted outcome. Any effects on children's economic well-being will ultimately depend on how states respond to their new charge and how responsive state and federal governments are to new exigencies or problems with the proposed system. Consequently, this is an especially propitious time for research on poor children. New workfare and time-limiting welfare programs, administered at the state level, will provide a natural laboratory for study of children. Presently, however, accurate predictions of the short- or long-term consequences for America's children simply lack a solid basis in data.

In sum, the literature on the role of government regarding child poverty is highly polarized and politicized. The emphasis on different causes implies different political agendas and different policy solutions. Behavioral explanations that emphasize the personal choices regarding work and family life are typically set against structural explanations that emphasize the role of labor market conditions and government. But the emphasis on family change is not incompatible with structural explanations focused on a declining economy for young and low-skilled parents. Monocausal explanations simply are incomplete and inadequate. It is equally important to keep in mind that the "causes" of poverty differ for different groups of children—whites and blacks, children in single-parent families and those living with two parents, and children of working and nonworking parents. Poverty rates will not be lowered among children without a multifaceted approach that builds strong families, promotes work and higher wages, and supports family and prowork public policies, including welfare policies.

## POVERTY TRANSITIONS AND INCOME STREAMS

The level of family income that defines children as poor or not poor is ultimately arbitrary. As a concept and measure, the prevalence of poverty per se is arguably less important than how the income and material resources available to children change over childhood, regardless of whether family income changes lead to poverty (as officially defined) or not. Divorce, for example, has potentially serious economic implications for children that do not always involve an episode of poverty but could impact children's home economic environment dramatically in the form of lower consumption levels (without the benefit of a governmental safety net). Economic deprivation is relative; in this case, it is defined in terms of the family's past levels of income and consumption.

The dynamic nature of the family income stream also raises important questions about the transitory or chronic nature of economic deprivation (however defined) and income inequality among children (Walker 1994). Income streams are linked in obvious ways to the entry into and exit out of welfare (Rank 1994, Harris 1996). Moreover, evidence of rising poverty among children and increasing polarization in the income distribution, although important, must not cause us to lose sight of the dynamic nature of shifts both upward and downward in the income distribution. We have only a very rudimentary understanding of the extent to which children are mired in poverty or in the lowest income quintile, and the extent to which poverty thresholds and income quintiles are permeable. A recent census study (Eller 1996) found that only 17.7% of poor children in 1992 exited poverty in 1993, and that a disproportionate share of children became newly poor in 1993 (4.0% vs 3.0% for all people). It remains an empirical question whether family transitions (including marriage and divorce), parental job mobility and employment dislocations, or governmental interventions matter most in transitions into and out of poverty.

The dynamic nature of income and other economic resources makes accurate measurement problematic, especially in light of the transitory nature of the new family living arrangements of children. For example, should cohabiting couples (including many divorced women with young children) be treated conceptually and analytically as quasi-married couple families, pooling the incomes of unmarried partners for the purpose of calculating child poverty rates? The conceptual problems are daunting (Eggebeen et al 1996, Manning & Lichter 1996). Cohabiting unions are highly unstable, and there is little evidence regarding the nature of intra vivos transfers of income or wealth (i.e. the extent to which a cohabiting partner contributes income for the benefit of children in the household). These are not small or esoteric issues. Nearly one half of all individuals will cohabit before marriage, nearly 30% of all nonmarital births occur to cohabiting couples, and rates of cohabitation among divorced women with children are very high (Bumpass & Sweet 1989, Manning 1993).

Finally, the transitory nature of family forms, the instability of most low-wage jobs, and the revolving door of welfare also contribute to a dynamic mix of income sources available to children. Is it absolutely low income (i.e. official poverty) or relatively low income that promotes deleterious socioemotional outcomes for children? Or, alternatively, is it the changing mix of income sources that affects children's short- and long-term well-being? The effects of poverty may be quite different depending on whether the family income available to children is from maternal work (i.e. where some income may be diverted to childcare) or from welfare (i.e. which may stigmatize persons, promote dependency, or reduce parental self-esteem). One recent study suggested that the relative mix of income from stepparents and biological parents has little effect on various children's outcomes, such as academic achievement and school problems (Hanson 1995). The income and involvement from the noncustodial father may likewise be a source of economic support that could have positive as well as negative effects on the lives of children (Blankenhorn 1994, King 1994, Seltzer 1994). The economic contribution, however sporadic, of noncustodial fathers may create obligations in female-headed families (i.e. visitation) that foster emotionally unhealthy, conflictual, or unwanted contacts between estranged parents or between noncustodial fathers and children. This is one argument for child support assurance programs in which the government acts as the intermediary between estranged partners with children.

## CONCLUSIONS

Since the "War on Poverty" in the 1960s, literally thousands of studies have been published on the topic of poverty (Sawhill 1988), including innumerable studies of poor children. Yet, there are roughly as many poor children today as before, the rate of child poverty now is at a 30-year high, and the income gap between rich and poor children is greater than at any time in recent memory (Lichter & Eggebeen 1993, Fischer et al 1996). Whether this apparent lack of progress reflects the inadequacies of the research, limitations in the efficacy of social policy, or the changing nature of poverty's causes is open to debate. It is clear, however, that previous research has not been translated into effective policy that benefits poor children, if measured by official trends in poverty and inequality.

No review can adequately convey the deep theoretical and empirical controversies and ideological differences that have marked previous research on the extent and etiology of poverty in America. Nor can it convey the tension that exists between dispassionate policy analysis and the passionate rhetoric often needed to initiative legislative action. This makes it difficult to separate the hyperbole about children's lives from the facts. At the same time, accurately measuring children's economic well-being and inequality, and accounting for trends so as to inform public policy, is more important than ever in light of current welfare reform and the new emphasis on behavioral poverty born of spatial and social isolation (Wilson 1987, Massey & Denton 1993). Indeed, increasing cultural differentiation—now and in the future—ultimately may depend more on relative differences in economic resources (i.e. inequality between and within groups) than on absolute poverty or low income per se.

As a field, we need to develop more sensitive measures of well-being that better reflect the relative and episodic nature of economic deprivation during childhood. We need to revisit previously ignored or discredited cultural arguments of welfare dependence and poverty. We need to identify the adaptive strategies of families (e.g. doubling-up or marriage) that surely will emerge as a result of welfare reform and that will either reinforce existing inequalities or, alternatively, cause families and their children to become economically self-sufficient (Lichter & Gardner 1996–97). We need to study the possible reciprocal relationships between poverty (especially during childhood) and biology (including physiology, cognitive traits, and temperament) that may perpetuate inequality from generation to generation. We need to better understand intergroup antagonisms and conflict, especially among racial and ethnic groups, and the growing class cleavages that make effective policy responses to poverty and welfare problematic. In short, conventional measures, traditional sociological and economic theories of poverty, and rigidly conservative or liberal ideologies can no longer be accepted uncritically or dismissed ad hominen if the future of America's poor children is to be anticipated with hope and promise.

## ACKNOWLEDGMENTS

I thank Alan Booth, Erica Gardner, Jeff Manza, Leif Jensen, Michael Shanahan, and the editor for helpful comments and assistance on various drafts of this paper.



*Literature Cited*

Angel R, Tienda M. 1982. Determinants of extended household structure: cultural patterns or economic need? *Am. J. Sociol.* 87:1360–83

Annie E. Casey Foundation 1996. *Kids Count Data Book.* Baltimore, MD: Annie E. Casey Found.

Baca Zinn M. 1989. Family, race, and poverty in the eighties. *Signs* 14:856–74

Bane MJ. 1986. Household composition and poverty. In *Fighting Poverty: What Works and What Doesn't,* ed. SH Danziger, DH Weinberg, pp. 209–31. Cambridge: Harvard Univ. Press

Bane MJ, Elwood D. 1989. One fifth of the nation's children: Why are they poor? *Science* 245:1047–53

Bianchi S. 1990. America's children: mixed prospects. *Popul. Bull.* 45:1–43

Bianchi S. 1993. Children in poverty: Why are they poor? In *Child Poverty and Public Policy,* ed. J Chafel, pp. 91–125. Washington, DC: Urban Inst.

Bianchi S, McArthur E. 1991. Family disruption and economic hardship: the short-run picture for children. *Curr. Popul. Rep., Ser. P-70, No. 23.* Washington, DC: US Gov. Print. Off.

Blank RM. 1996. *The New Economics of Poverty.* Princeton, NJ: Princeton Univ. Press

Blankenhorn D. 1995. *Fatherless America.* New York: Basic Books

Booth A, Dunn JF, eds. 1995. *Family-School Links: How Do They Affect Educational Outcomes?* Mahwah, NJ: Erlbaum

Bumpass LL. 1990. What's happening to the family? Interactions between demographic and institutional change. *Demography* 27:483–98

Bumpass LL, Sweet J. 1989. National estimates of cohabitation. *Demography* 26:615–25

Cancian M, Danziger S, Gottschalk P. 1994. Working wives and family income inequality among married couples. In *Uneven Tides,* ed. S Danziger, P Gottschalk, pp. 195–221. New York: Russell Sage Found.

Casper LM, McLanahan SS, Garfinkel I. 1994. The gender-poverty gap: what we can learn from other countries. *Am. Sociol. Rev.* 59:594–605

Citro C, Michael R. 1995. *Measuring Poverty: A New Approach.* Washington, DC: Natl. Acad.

Corbett T. 1993. Child poverty and welfare reform: progress or paralysis? *Focus* 15:1–17

Corcoran M. 1995. Rags to rags: poverty and mobility in the United States. *Annu. Rev. Sociol.* 21:237–67

Danziger S, Gottschalk P, eds. 1994. *Uneven Tides.* New York: Russell Sage Found.

Devine JA, Plunkett M, Wright JD. 1992. The chronicity of poverty: evidence from the PSID, 1968–1987. *Soc. Forces* 70:787–812

Duncan GJ. 1992. The economic environment of childhood. In *Children in Poverty: Child Development and Public Policy,* ed. A Huston, pp. 23–50. New York: Cambridge Univ. Press

Duncan GJ, Brooks-Gunn J, Klebanov PK. 1994. Economic deprivation and early childhood development. *Child Dev.* 65:296–318

Duncan GJ, Rogers WL. 1989. Longitudinal aspects of childhood poverty. *J. Marriage Fam.* 53:1007–21

Duncan GJ, Rogers WL. 1991. Has children's poverty become more persistent? *Am. Sociol. Rev.* 56:538–50

Edin KJ. 1995. The myths of dependence and self-sufficiency: women, welfare, and low-wage work. *Focus* 17:1–9

Eggebeen DJ, Lichter DT. 1991. Race, family structure, and changing poverty among American children. *Am. Sociol. Rev.* 56:801–17

Eggebeen DJ, Snyder AR, Manning WD. 1996. Children in single-father families in demographic perspective. *J. Fam. Issues* 17:441–65

Eller TJ. 1996. Dynamics of economic well-being: poverty, 1992–1993. Who stays poor? Who doesn't? *Curr. Popul. Rep. P70–55.* Washington, DC: US Gov. Print. Off.

Federman M, Garner TI, Short K, Cutter WB IV, Kiely J, et al. 1996. What does it mean to be poor in America? *Mon. Lab. Rev.* May:3–17

Fischer C, Hout M, Jankowski MS, Lucas SR, et al. 1996. *Inequality by Design.* Princeton, NJ: Princeton Univ. Press

Friedman S, Lichter DT. 1997. Spatial inequality and poverty among American children. *Popul. Res. Policy Rev.* 16: In press

Fuchs VR. 1991. Are Americans underinvesting in their children? *Society* 28:14–22

Fuchs VR, Reklis DM. 1992. America's children: economic perspectives and policy options. *Science* 255:41–44

Garfinkel I, McLanahan S. 1986. *Single Mothers and Their Children: A New American Dilemma.* Washington, DC: Urban Inst.

Garrett P, Ng'andu N, Ferron J. 1994. Is rural residency a risk factor for childhood poverty? *Rural Sociol.* 59:66–83

Gottschalk P, Danziger S. 1994. Family structure, family size, and family income: accounting for changing in the economic well-being of children, 1968–1986. In *Uneven Tides,* ed. S Danziger, P Gottschalk, pp. 165–93. New York: Russell Sage Found.

Hanson TL. 1995. *Income and child welfare: variations by gender and family structure. Off. Popul. Res. Work. Pap. 95–10*

Hao L. 1995. Poverty, public assistance, and children in intact and single-mother families. *J. Fam. Econ. Issues* 16:181–205

Harris KM. 1996. Life after welfare: women, work, and repeat dependency. *Am. Sociol. Rev.* 61:407–26

Haveman R, Wolfe BL. 1993. Children's prospects and children's policy. *J. Econ. Lit.* 7:153–74

Haveman R, Wolfe BL, Finnie RE, Wolff EN. 1988. Disparities in well-being among U.S. children over two decades: 1962–83. In *The Vulnerable,* ed. JL Palmer, T Smeeding, BB Torrey, pp. 149–70. Washington, DC: Urban Inst.

Hernandez D. 1993. *America's Children: Resources from Family, Government, and the Economy.* New York: Russell Sage Found.

Hill MS, Sandfort JR. 1995. Effects of childhood poverty on productivity later in life: implications for public policy. *Child. Youth Ser. Rev.* 17:91–126

Hogan DP, Eggebeen DJ, Clogg CC. 1993. The structure of intergenerational exchanges in American families. *Am. J. Sociol.* 98:1428–58

Hogan DP, Lichter DT. 1995. Children and youth: living arrangements and welfare. In *State of the Union: America in the 1990s,* ed. R Farley, 2:93–139. New York: Russell Sage Found.

Jargowski PA. 1996. Table PF. In *Trends in the Well-Being of America's Children and Youth: 1996,* ed. US Dep. Health Hum. Serv., p. 31. Washington, DC: Off. Assist. Secr. Plan. Eval.

Jensen L, Chitose Y. 1994. Today's second generation: evidence from the 1990 U.S. Census. *Int. Migr. Rev.* 28:714–35

Jensen L, Eggebeen DJ. 1994. Nonmetropolitan poor children and reliance on public assistance. *Rural Sociol.* 59:45–65

Jensen L, Eggebeen DJ, Lichter DT. 1993. Child poverty and the ameliorative effects of public assistance. *Soc. Sci. Q.* 74:542–59

Johnston G. 1997. *Neighborhoods and the changing spatial concentration of poverty.* PhD. diss. University Park: Penn. State Univ., Dep. Sociol. Unpublished

Karoly L. 1994. The trend in inequality among families, individuals, and workers in the United States: a twenty-five year perspective. In *Uneven Tides,* ed. S Danziger, P Gottschalk, pp. 19–97. New York: Russell Sage Found.

King V. 1994. Nonresidential father involvement and child well-being: Can dads make a difference? *J. Fam. Issues* 15:

Korenman S, Miller JE, Sjaastad JE. 1995. Long-term poverty and child development in the United States: results from the NLSY. *Child. Youth Ser. Rev.* 17:127–55

Kruttschnitt C, McLeod JD, Dornfeld M. 1994. The economic environment of child abuse. *Soc. Probl.* 41:299–315

Landale NS, Lichter DT. 1997. Geography and the etiology of poverty among Latino children. *Soc. Sci. Q.* 78:In press

Levy F. 1995. Incomes and income inequality. In *State of the Union,* ed. R Farley, 1:1–57. New York: Russell Sage Found.

Lichter DT. 1993. Migration, population redistribution, and the new spatial inequality. In *Demography of Rural Life,* ed. DL Brown, D Field, JJ Zuiches, pp. 19–46. University Park, PA: NE Reg. Cent. Rural Dev.

Lichter DT, Eggebeen DJ. 1993. Rich kids, poor kids: changing income inequality among American children. *Soc. Forces* 71:761–80

Lichter DT, Eggebeen DJ. 1994. The effect of parental employment on child poverty. *J. Marriage Fam.* 56:633–45

Lichter DT, Gardner E. 1996–97. Welfare reform and the poor children of working parents. *Focus* 18:(2):65–72

Lichter DT, Johnston GM, McLaughlin DK. 1994. Changing linkages between work and poverty in rural America. *Rural Sociol.* 59:395–415

Lichter DT, Landale NS. 1995. Parental employment, family structure, and poverty among Latino children. *J. Marriage Fam.* 57:346–61

Lino M. 1996. Income and spending of poor households with children. *Fam. Econ. Nutrit. Rev.* 9(1):2–13

Luker K. 1996. *Dubious Conceptions: The Politics of Teenage Pregnancy.* Cambridge, MA: Harvard Univ. Press

Manning WD. 1993. Marriage and cohabitation following premarital conception. *J. Marriage Fam.* 55:839–50

Manning WD, Lichter DT. 1996. Parental cohabitation and children's economic well-being. *J. Marriage Fam.* 58: In press

Mare RD. 1991. Five decades of educational assortative mating. *Am. Sociol. Rev.* 56:15–32

Massey DS, Denton NA. 1993. *American Apartheid: Segregation and the Making of the Underclass.* Cambridge, MA: Harvard Univ. Press

Mayer S. 1996. Trends in the economic well-being and life chances of America's children. In *Consequences of Growing Up Poor,* ed. Natl. Acad. Sci. Washington, DC: Natl. Acad. Press. In press

Mayer S, Jencks C. 1995. *Has poverty really increased among children since 1970? Work. Pap. 94–14.* Northwest. Univ. Cent. Urban Aff. Policy Res.

McGarry K, Schoeni RF. 1995. *Transfer behavior within the family: resutls from the asset and health dynamics survey. Natl. Bur. Econ. Res. Work. Pap. No. 5099*

McLanahan S, Sandefur G. 1994. *Growing Up with a Single Parent.* Cambridge, MA: Harvard Univ. Press

McLaughlin DK, Lichter DT. 1996. Poverty and the marital behavior of young women. *J. Marriage Fam.* 59: In press

McLeod JD, Shanahan MJ. 1993. Poverty, parenting, and children's mental health. *Am. Sociol. Rev.* 58:351–66

McLeod JD, Shanahan MJ. 1996. Trajectories of poverty and children's mental health. *J. Health Soc. Behav.* 37:207–20

Mergenbagen P. 1996. What can minimum wage buy? *Am. Demogr.* 18:32–36

Moffitt R. 1992. Incentive effects of the U.S. welfare system: a review. *J. Econ. Lit.* 30:1–61

Murray C. 1984. *Losing Ground: American Social Policy 1950–80.* New York: Basic Books

O'Hare WP. 1995. 3.9 million U.S. children in distressed neighborhoods. *Popul. Today* 22:4–5

Oropesa RS, Landale NS. 1997. Immigrant legacies: ethnicity, generation, and children's familial and economic lives. *Soc. Sci. Q.* In press

Orshansky M. 1965. Counting the poor; another

look at the poverty profile. *Soc. Sec. Bull.* 28:3–29

Ozawa MN. 1995. Antipoverty effects of public income transfers on children. *Child. Youth Serv. Rev.* 17:43–59

Preston S. 1984. Children and the elderly: divergent paths for America's dependents. *Demography* 21:435–57

Plotnick R. 1989. Directions for reducing child poverty. *Soc. Work* 34:523–30

Rainwater L. 1995. Poverty and the income packaging of working parents: the United States in comparative perspective. *Child. Youth Ser. Rev.* 17:11–41

Rank MR. 1994. *Living on the Edge*. New York: Columbia Univ. Press

Rodgers HR Jr. 1996. *Poor Women, Poor Children*. Armonk, NY: ME Sharpe. 3rd ed.

Ruggles P. 1990. *Drawing the Line*. Washington, DC: Urban Inst.

Sawhill IV. 1988. Poverty in the U.S.: Why is it so persistent? *J. Econ. Lit.* 31:1073–119

Schoen R, Weinick RM. 1993. The slowing metabolism of marriage; figures from 1988 US marital status life tables. *Demography* 30:737–46

Seltzer J. 1994. Consequences of marriage dissolution for children. *Annu. Rev. Sociol.* 20:235–66

Shapiro I. 1989. *Laboring for Less: Working but Poor in Rural America*. Washington, DC: Cent. Budget Policy Priorities

Slesnick DT. 1993. Gaining ground: poverty in the postwar United States. *J. Polit. Econ.* 1–38

Smeeding TM, Rainwater L. 1991. *Cross-national trends in income poverty and dependency: the evidence for young adults in the eighties*. Presented at the Joint Cent. Polit. Econ. Stud., Washington, DC

Smeeding TM, Torrey BB. 1988. Poor children in rich countries. *Science* 242:873–77

Smeeding T, Torrey BB, Rein M. 1988. Patterns of income and poverty: the economic status of children and the elderly in eight countries. In *The Vulnerable*, ed. JL Palmer, T Smeeding, BB Torrey, pp. 89–119. Washington, DC: Urban Inst.

Smock PJ. 1993. The economic costs of marital disruption for young women over the past two decades. *Demography* 30:353–71

South SJ, Lloyd KM. 1992. Marriage markets and nonmarital fertility in the United States. *Demography* 29:247–64

Urban Institute. 1996. http://www.urban.org. Washington, DC: Urban Inst.

US Bureau of the Census. 1995. *Beyond Poverty: Extended Measures of Well-Being: 1992. Curr. Popul. Rep., Ser. P-70, No. 50.* Washington, DC: US Gov. Print. Off.

US Bureau of the Census. 1996. *Income, Poverty, and Valuation of Noncash Benefits: 1994. Curr. Popul. Rep., P60–189.* Washington, DC: US Gov. Print. Off.

US Dep. Health and Human Services. 1996. *Trends in the Well-Being of America's Children and Youth: 1996.* Washington, DC: Off. Asst. Sec. for Planning and Eval.

Ventura SJ, Bachrach CA, Hill L, Kaye K, Holcomb P, et al. 1995. The demography of out-of-wedlock childbearing. In *Report to Congress on Out-of-Wedlock Childbearing*, ed. Dep. Health Hum. Service. Washington, DC: Natl. Cent. Health Stat.

Walker R. 1994. *Poverty Dynamics: Issues and Examples*. Aldershot: Avebury

Wetzel JR. 1995. Labor force, unemployment, and earnings. In *State of the Union*, ed. R Farley, 1:59–105. New York: Russell Sage Found.

Wilson WJ. 1987. *The Truly Disadvantaged*. Chicago: Univ. Chicago Press

Zill N. 1993. The changing realities of family life. *Aspen Q.* 5:27–51

*Annu. Rev. Sociol. 1997. 23:147–70*


# THE FIRST INJUSTICE: Socioeconomic Disparities, Health Services Technology, and Infant Mortality

*Steven L. Gortmaker*
Department of Health and Social Behavior, Harvard School of Public Health, Boston, Massachusetts 02115

*Paul H. Wise*
Department of Pediatrics, Boston Medical Center and Boston University School of Medicine, One Boston Medical Center Place, Boston, Massachusetts 02118

KEY WORDS: social and economic inequality, poverty, infant mortality, health services

ABSTRACT

Infant mortality has long been viewed as a synoptic indicator of the health and social condition of a population. In this article we examine critically the structure of this reflective capacity with a particular emphasis on how new health care technologies may have altered traditional pathways of social influence. The infant mortality rate is a composite of a series of component rates, each with its own relationship to social factors. Advances in health care have reduced dramatically the risk of mortality for the critically ill newborn, thereby elevating the importance of access to this care in shaping absolute and disparate infant mortality rates. These advances in health services technology have also had the effect of concentrating infant mortality among extremely premature and low birth-weight infants, a group tied directly to social factors operating through maternal influences and the general well-being of women.

In this manner, current patterns of infant mortality in the United States provide a useful illustration of the dynamic interaction of underlying social forces and technological innovation in determining trends in health outcomes. We review the implications of this perspective for sociological research into disparate infant mortality, including the social and economic structure of societies, access to health services, the potential for prenatal intervention, women's health status, and racial and ethnic disparities.



0360-0572/97/0815-0147$08.00

## DISPARITIES IN INFANT MORTALITY RATES: NO LONGER A SIMPLE SOCIAL MIRROR

High rates of death and disease among individuals of lower social and economic status have been extensively documented in industrialized countries throughout the past century. Indeed, in spite of substantial increases in economic indicators such as gross national product (GNP) and increases in dollars spent on medical care in the United States, socioeconomic disparities in mortality and morbidity persist to the present day (Marmot et al 1987, Hahn et al 1995, Pappas et al 1993). This documentation has been hailed as "one of sociology's most enduring contributions to the health field" (Williams & Collins 1995).

Infant mortality rates in particular have long been considered a sensitive indicator of the impact of socioeconomic disparities on the health of populations, due in large part to the special vulnerability of the newborn to poverty and substandard living conditions (Marx 1967). In this manner, infant mortality rates have typically been seen to represent a kind of "social mirror," reflecting broad inequalities in society and, because of the inherent innocence of young children, illuminating the machinery of social injustice (Wise & Pursley 1992). This reflective capacity has been circumstantially supported by the persistence of disparities in infant mortality rates throughout this century, mirroring the persistence of larger social and economic inequalities in the United States (Children's Bureau 1921, Gortmaker 1979a, Wise et al 1985).

A premise of the present review, however, is that mechanisms that traditionally defined infant mortality as a social mirror have been altered appreciably by rapid innovations in health services technology. Such technological change also creates new opportunities for socioeconomic differentiation as life-saving therapies or preventive interventions potentially are made available only to the economically advantaged. This, in fact, currently happens on an international scale, where many seriously ill newborns in developing countries die of conditions currently treatable by health services commonly available in the industrialized world.

The sociological literature has generally focused on the relationship between social and economic variables and the risk of infant mortality, but it has largely ignored the role of changing health care technology. In this review our aim is to illustrate the fact that there is now abundant evidence for the substantial impact of health services technology in reducing infant mortality rates, as well as for the powerful influence of social and economic inequalities independent of health services technology. We review the evidence for declining infant mortality rates in the United States and other industrialized countries, and we document the continuing disparities in rates by social and economic characteristics of the population. These different trends suggest that the interaction of social and technologic determinants has operated to decrease absolute rates while simultaneously maintaining broad disparities in these rates (Wise & Pursley 1992). In this empirical context, the perspective of Ogburn (Ogburn 1969) suggests that innovation in technology has resulted in a broad array of sociological consequences, only some of which have been examined.

We have accordingly structured this review to critically examine three issues:

1. The evolution of infant mortality patterns in the United States

2. The extent to which the long-documented mechanisms of socioeconomic influence on infant mortality have been altered by a technical revolution in modern health services for pregnant women and newborns

3. The impact of these altered causal pathways on the conceptual legitimacy of using infant mortality rates as a marker of social and economic inequalities

While our focus is on infant mortality, the empirical and theoretical work we cite can be directly applied to other arenas of disparate health outcomes as well. We focus on the United States experience, although similar issues arise in the other industrialized countries of the world.

## THE EVOLUTION OF INFANT MORTALITY PATTERNS IN THE UNITED STATES

One of the most enduring indictments of social and health policies in the United States is the consistently poor showing of the United States in international rankings of infant mortality. Although the United States is the wealthiest country in the world and expends more per capita on health and medical care than any other country, our infant mortality rates consistently rank below those of many other nations—twenty-second in 1990, below Italy, Spain, and Singapore (UNICEF 1992) (see Figure 1). While there are some reporting differences between the United States and other countries that contribute to these disparities (e.g. in some countries, an infant death during the first few hours after birth is not counted as a live birth), these can account for only a part of the differences observed (Hartford 1992). The clear message derived from these data is that the United States ranks lower than all the other industrialized countries in infant survival.

In addition to a relatively high overall rate of infant mortality, there are pronounced disparities within the United States among social, economic, racial, and ethnic groups and geographic areas. Some communities in the United States experience infant mortality rates resembling those of developing countries. The

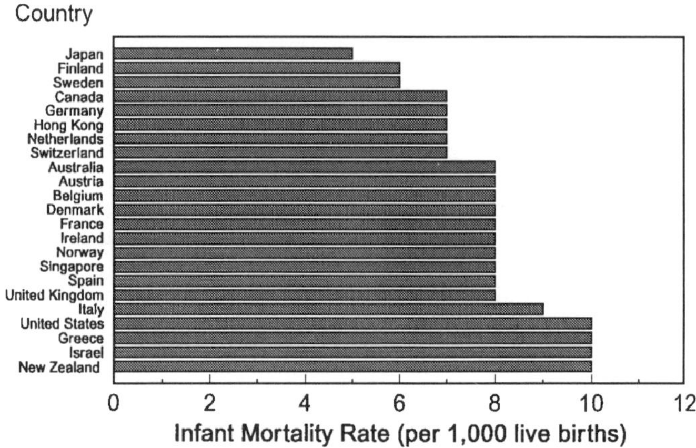


*Figure 1* #Infant mortality rates by country 1990.

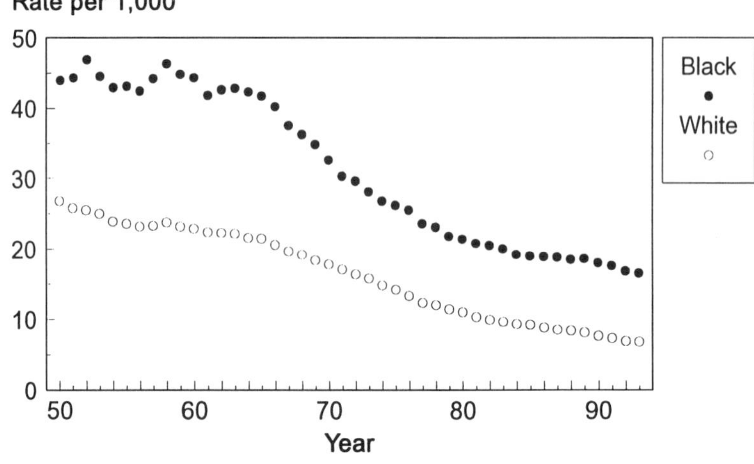


*Figure 2* Black and white infant mortality rates in the United States 1950–1993.

reasons for these disparities are complex but are generally thought to reflect the powerful effects of social and economic inequality.

One important indicator of continuing disparity is provided by trends in the infant mortality rates of black (African-American) and white infants in the United States during the period 1950–1993 (see Figure 2). These data document the persistently higher rate of infant mortality among African-American infants

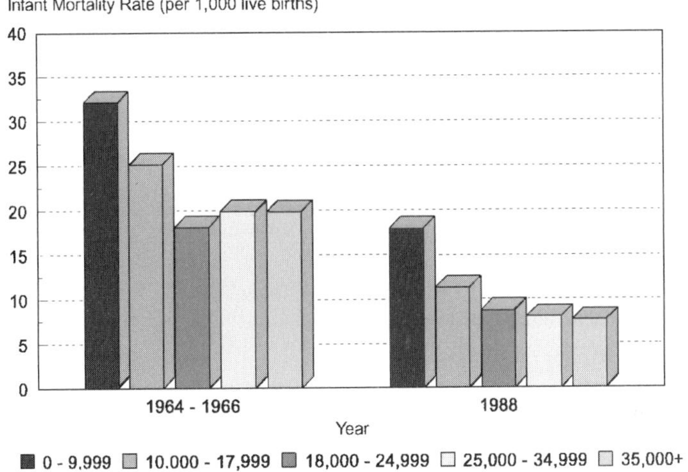


*Figure 3* Infant mortality rates by household yearly income in the United States 1964–1966 and 1988.

in the United States and describe a black/white disparity that has not been narrowing during the past three decades.

A striking recent confirmation of the persistence of economic disparities can be seen from tabulations of data from two national infant mortality studies in the United States, the 1964–1966 National Natality and Infant Mortality Followback Surveys (NNS and NIMS) (National Center for Health Statistics 1972) and the 1988 National Maternal and Infant Health Survey (Sanderson et al 1991) (Figure 3). These data provide the only national estimates of disparities in infant mortality by household income. The income categories are only approximately similar, because categories of income were used in the survey, adjusted for changes in the Consumer Price Index (United States Bureau of the Census 1989).

The 1964–1965 data precedes the implementation of Medicaid and thus provides important "baseline" information concerning economic disparities. The 1988 data comes after more than a decade of operation of this major health care financing program that includes poor families with children. Early evaluations of the implementation of Medicaid indicate that it helped to reduce disparities in the utilization of health services between poor and nonpoor families (Butler & Scotch 1978), while more recent studies have documented problems in access and declining physician participation in Medicaid (Yudkowsky et al 1990). The data displayed in Figure 3 indicate no attenuation in the relative risk of infant mortality experienced by women with lower, compared with higher, levels of household income during the past quarter of a century. These findings mirror those observed in Britain where, decades after the implementation of the National Health Service, social class disparities in infant mortality persist (Black et al 1982, Gray 1982).

The apparent lack of progress in improving the international ranking or reducing social disparities in infant mortality in the United States should not, however, be perceived as suggesting a lack of change in the overall rate or its underlying dynamics. Quite to the contrary, the past two decades have witnessed the most profound alterations ever recorded in the structure of infant mortality patterns in the United States. This dynamic character challenges the traditional social interpretation of the infant mortality rate and lies therefore at the heart of this discussion.

Although disparities persist, absolute rates of infant mortality for all groups in the United States have fallen dramatically over the past three decades. The infant mortality rate in 1990 was approximately 32% of the rate recorded in 1960. Similar dramatic reductions were seen for both black and white newborns, with the 1990 rates among whites being about 30% of the rate in 1960 and the 1990 rate among blacks being 37% of the earlier rate. Therefore, the persistence of social disparities in infant mortality has occurred in a setting of significant reductions in absolute rates, a consequence of the rapid improvements in health services technology surrounding childbirth.

## THE IMPACT OF HEALTH SERVICES TECHNOLOGY

In order to explore the determinants of these complex trends, it is useful first to recognize that the infant mortality rate is actually a composite of a number of component rates, each with its own set of relationships with social factors and health services technology. One broad categorization separates infant deaths into those occurring during the neonatal period (the first 28 days following birth) and those occurring during the postneonatal period (the rest of the first year of life). This distinction, based on age at death, serves as a traditional proxy for cause of death. Postneonatal deaths have historically been due to viral and bacterial processes such as gastroenteritis and pneumonia and to injuries, all of which have long been closely linked to socioeconomic factors like poverty-level income (Gortmaker 1979a). Neonatal mortality has been more deeply shaped by processes associated with birth, including congenital anomalies, prematurity and low birth weight, and obstetrical catastrophes associated with delivery. These causes, though generally associated with social variables, tend to operate more directly through maternal and pregnancy-related pathways. Although the divide between the causes of neonatal and postneonatal mortality has never been sharp, this stratification still holds some importance in that it attests to the heterogeneity of infant death and depicts an initial fork in potential pathways of social influence on infant mortality (Wise 1990).

In this context it is important to note that in 1990 approximately 63% of infant mortality in the United States occurred in the neonatal period, compared to 70% in 1950. This continuing concentration of death in the first 28 days has been due to a precipitous decline of both postneonatal and neonatal mortality during the 1960s, 1970s, and 1980s. While postneonatal mortality rates remain higher than those of many other industrialized countries, death in this age group from injuries and infectious processes has become relatively rare in the United States. The largest contributors to postneonatal mortality today include the consequences of prematurity and sudden infant death syndrome (SIDS), a diagnosis that probably captures a variety of pathologies but is broadly defined by the sudden, unexpected death of a previously healthy infant. Although SIDS is associated with an important social gradient, it is less profound than those related to more traditional postneonatal causes.

While postneonatal mortality has been altered significantly, neonatal mortality has been most substantially transformed. Because neonatal mortality is so deeply tied to the health of the newborn at birth, it is useful to stratify the neonatal mortality rate into two components based on birth weight, the most generally meaningful indicator of risk at birth. Birth weight operates in this manner because it reflects the adequacy of the intrauterine environment and serves as a general proxy for gestational age, which is difficult to assess accurately in large populations. Stratifying the neonatal mortality rate by birth weight results in defining two mechanisms by which differences in neonatal mortality can occur: differences in the distribution of birth weights [a larger portion of births falling into the very low birth weight (less than 1500 g) groups would generate a higher risk of neonatal death in the population] or differences in birth weight–specific mortality (higher mortality within each birth-weight group would generate higher overall neonatal mortality).

When neonatal mortality trends are examined in this manner, two major findings emerge. First, recent reductions in neonatal mortality in the United States have been due almost entirely to improvements in birth weight–specific survival; birth-weight distributions have remained relatively stable over the past 30 years. For example, national evidence indicates that during the period 1960–1980, 15% of the decline in white infant mortality risk can be attributed to improving birth-weight distribution, and 85% to improved birth weight–specific mortality. Among blacks, −3% of the change in infant mortality rates during this period can be attributed to a worsening birth-weight distribution, and 103% to declining birth weight–specific mortality (Buehler et al 1987).

Second, the primary determinant of the poor international standing of the United States and of social disparities in the infant mortality rate in the United

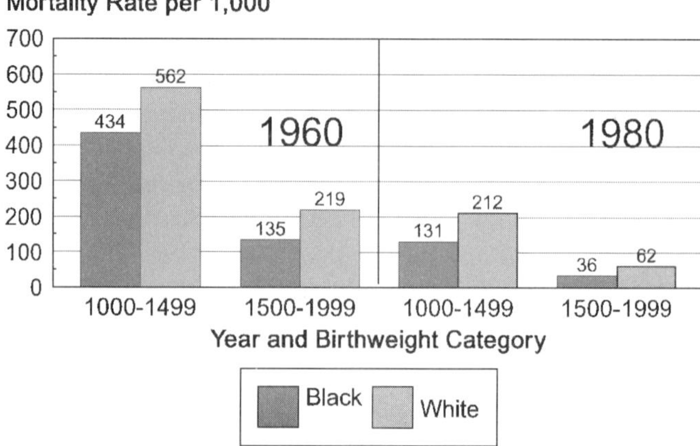


*Figure 4* Neonatal mortality rates by birth weight and race: United States, 1960 and 1980.

States is an elevated rate of extremely low birth-weight (i.e. less than 1000 g) infants; the survival rates of US newborns when birth weight is controlled are among the best in the world (Guyer et al 1982, Alberman et al 1992). Therefore, the substantial improvement in birth weight–specific survival in the United States has had the effect of concentrating mortality into the most premature and very low birth-weight categories, thereby making the United States infant mortality rate increasingly sensitive to factors associated with extreme prematurity. More than 50% of all neonatal deaths in the United States are currently due to newborns born at less than 25 weeks of gestation (the legal abortion limit is 24 weeks), and infants born weighing less than 1500 g make up 1.2% of all births but 64% of all neonatal deaths (Wise et al 1995).

What then is responsible for these major improvements in the survival rates of ill newborns? A series of studies have identified a revolution in medical management of high-risk deliveries and critically ill newborns as accounting for this improved survival. These dramatic reductions are graphically displayed in Figure 4, for both black and white infants weighing 1000–1999 g at birth during the period 1960–1980. During these two decades, the rate of neonatal death among black infants weighing 1500–1999 g at birth decreased 66%, and among whites this decrease was 67% (Buehler et al 1987).

The dramatic effectiveness of this technology, however, did not lead to an attenuation of social and economic disparities in infant mortality rates. The similar decline in rates among both black and white infants indicates similar access to this technology during this period. One study of a geographic region of the United States with virtual universal access to neonatal intensive care technology (Boston in the mid 1980s) reveals substantial social and economic differences in infant mortality rates, even though virtually all of these births occurred in Level III centers, meaning that all of the women and their infants had available the most sophisticated medical technology at birth (Wise et al 1988). These findings indicate that the causes of the decline in infant mortality rates—intensive care technology—are different from the effects of social and economic forces that still produce disparate outcomes. When effective medical technology is available to all in a geographic area, social and economic forces still emerge as visible factors.

In addition, this explanation also suggests that increases in infant mortality rates over coming decades could, paradoxically, be possible in areas that achieve an excellent system of access to neonatal intensive care and relatively low infant mortality rates. If restrictions in access to this neonatal intensive care occur, mortality rates could increase. As managed care systems increase in prominence in the United States in coming years, potential changes in access to services for high-risk infants need to be carefully evaluated (McCormick & Richardson 1995).

The remarkable success of neonatal intensive care has in many respects been overshadowed by questions of the appropriateness of intensive interventions for the most premature and seriously ill newborns. There are clear questions of cost although neonatal intensive care unit (NICU)-associated care is a minuscule component of overall health care spending, and studies have indicated NICU technology to be cost-effective as well as cost-beneficial for all but the very smallest infants (Office of Technology Assessment 1987, Boyle et al 1983). Moreover, the improved survival of ill newborns has produced little evidence of an aggregate increase in the prevalence of chronic childhood disorders, probably due to improvements in medical care (Shapiro et al 1983, Gortmaker & Sappenfield 1984, McCormick 1993). Although the exploration of the ethical and resource allocation issues involved in neonatal intensive care is, of course, important, and although the identification and elimination of iatrogenic health services must continue, such considerations should not obscure the documented effectiveness of neonatal intensive care in reducing mortality, nor the huge impact of these interventions in altering the nature of infant mortality in the United States.

We suggest that the structure of infant mortality in the United States has been altered forever by major technical advances in the clinical management of the high-risk pregnancy and the critically ill newborn. This contention, in turn, demands a reconsideration of the approaches used traditionally to examine the social determinants of infant survival as well as the practical strategies long advanced as being the most effective means of preventing infant death.

## SOCIAL INFLUENCE AND TECHNOLOGICAL INNOVATION

Perhaps the most striking characteristic of the vast literature concerned with the causal pathways of infant mortality is its profound dichotomization. One view focuses on the direct impact of social and economic environments on the risk of infant mortality, while the second focuses on the impact of variations in health services (Gortmaker 1979a). One example of the first approach to the infant mortality problem in the United States is provided by Marsden Wagner, in remarks to the National Commission to Prevent Infant Mortality:

> Infant mortality is not a health problem. Infant mortality is a social problem with health consequences. It is analogous to traffic accident mortality in children: the first priority for improving traffic accident mortality in children is not to build more and better medical facilities, but rather to change traffic laws and better educate drivers and children. In other words, the solution is not primarily medical, but environmental, social and educational. The same is true for infant mortality: the first priority is not more obstetricians or pediatricians or hospitals, nor even more prenatal clinics or well-baby clinics, but rather to provide more social, financial and educational support to families with pregnant women and infants (Wagner 1988).

This perspective focuses on the powerful role of social and economic forces in the production of disparities in infant mortality rates, and for many sociologists it is a signal illustration (in a world preoccupied with the drama of medical discovery) of the importance of social status in defining health. With deep historical roots, this elevation of social causation in defining an inherently tragic health outcome has held special currency as a stark counterargument to the claims of modern medicine. Steadily improving socioeconomic environments of families, including improvements in food supplies and in sanitation, have traditionally been credited with causing reductions in infant mortality and improvements in life expectancy. Only a very marginal part of this improvement in mortality has been attributed to improvements in the delivery of effective medical care. As Dubos noted in 1959:

> The control of childhood diseases . . . resulted more from better nutrition and sanitary practices than from the introduction of new drugs. It is remarkable, in contrast, that little practical progress has been made toward controlling the diseases that were not dealt with by the nineteenth-century reformers (Dubos 1959).

This elevation of social pathways as fundamental is, of course, well-supported by an extensive research base throughout this century, and it is precisely why the infant mortality rate is so widely embraced as a legitimate indicator of underlying social conditions. However, as we have discussed, recent decreases in infant mortality rates are due solely to improved health care technology. Social and economic disparities in infant mortality rates persist, but very little empirical data documents the mechanisms whereby inequalities are ultimately expressed in the biologic reality of infant death. Associations have been reported with infant mortality rates in multiple arenas where inequality is manifest, including the mother and household as discussed above, as well as the community and the larger society (LaVeist 1992, Kennedy et al 1996). Yet, one of the central tasks of any sociologic theory is to explain how inequality in these domains is ultimately transformed into infant death. This process, which might be termed "domain transformations" requires greater empirical inquiry. Do social and economic inequalities deprive people of the necessities of life such as nutrition, shelter, or social relations? Is social stress a major influence? Do these conditions increase the risk of infection or produce more risky health behaviors such as smoking (Gortmaker & Wise 1994)? Are multiple aspects of stratification involved, including characteristics of individual, household, and community? How do racism, sexism, and social class interact to impact infant health (Krieger et al 1993)? Is longer-term poverty a more fundamental cause than low income represented by the typical yearly income measure (Starfield et al 1991)?

One concern is that a tight focus on broad associations of infant mortality with social variables such as poverty, low educational attainment, or race and ethnicity can disrespect the power of technical interventions to alter both the intensity and nature of social and economic influence on infant survival. While it is important to document associations of inequality and infant mortality, it is even more important to understand underlying causal mechanisms, so that effective policies and programs can be developed. If a clinical or public health intervention is developed that is highly effective in preventing infant death from causes associated with poverty, then much, if not all, of a domain's established influence may fall away. Effective interventions, therefore, have the capability of uncoupling long recognized social influences such as poverty from specific outcomes such as infant death (Gortmaker & Wise 1994). Independent of such interventions, policies and programs can also focus on the often more difficult task of alleviating the underlying inequality as a social strategy.

Technical innovation can both modulate pathways of social influence and also create social influence for conditions traditionally insensitive to social factors. To illustrate this point, Jencks described the case of phenylketonuria (PKU), a genetically based disorder that can be controlled by a properly regulated diet (Jencks 1980). While PKU is a disorder that is completely genetic in origin, because there is a highly effective health intervention (diet in this case), any disparity in outcome can now be viewed as social in origin, particularly related to access to the intervention.

As noted above, new technology can also lead to increases in disparity. One newly emergent case that may fit this pattern is that of surfactant therapy for respiratory distress syndrome, a major cause of infant mortality due to prematurity.

After this therapy became available, neonatal mortality rates improved more for white than for black infants with similar very low birth weights (Hamvas et al 1996).

In this context, the impact of neonatal intensive care on recent trends in infant mortality in the United States provides an important arena for examining how technical innovation can alter traditional pathways of social influence. Such alterations are likely to be important for health conditions for which technical improvements in prevention or treatment are advancing rapidly.

The influence of social and economic forces on the prevalence of the HIV-1 (AIDS) virus is useful to explore from this perspective. The HIV-1 virus is not a major cause of infant mortality, but in some areas it has emerged as a substantial cause of early childhood death. A number of social factors have been associated with the risk of HIV-1 in infants and young children, in particular, maternal exposure to injection drug use (either her own or her sex partner's). Broader social forces are also at work: Housing destruction apparently led to the migration of a large IV drug-using population, with high rates of HIV-1 infection, throughout New York City (Wallace et al 1995). The development of new combination therapies for HIV-1–infected women and evidence for the effectiveness of the drug zidovudine (AZT) in preventing perinatal transmission (Connor et al 1994) (from infected mother to newborn child) have generated a new, powerful arena of social influence in determining relative access to an effective but often expensive intervention that can save infant lives.

Our intent in stressing the impact of technological innovation is not to diminish the fundamental importance of social forces in shaping patterns of infant mortality nor the relevance of sociology to their essential exploration. Rather, it is to call attention to the inherent volatility of this social influence and the importance of the sociology of health care in explaining this dynamic character. In this way, our objective in invoking the efficacy of clinical and public health intervention is not to limit the realm of sociology, but to plead for recognition among infant mortality specialists of an opportunity to expand their disciplinary embrace to include the social forces that shape both the dimensions of medical progress and differential access to the fruits of this technical struggle.

## FUTURE DIRECTIONS IN SOCIOLOGICAL RESEARCH

We point out the dynamic nature of the causes of infant mortality in order to highlight the importance of critical sociological research in illuminating how social and economic forces and health services technology will shape the risk of infant death in the United States in the years to come.

## *Societal Characteristics and the Generation of Disparities in Infant Mortality Rates*

A wide range of evidence indicates relationships between social and economic fortunes of societies and the risk of infant death. Some of the most dramatic historical evidence comes from studies of social structural change following World War II: Holland experienced very large increases in infant mortality as a consequence of starvation following the end of the war (Smith 1947, Susser & Stein 1994). Perhaps the most profound increase in infant mortality in an industrialized country to be observed during the past 30 years occurred in the USSR during the period 1971–1975—a 34% rise from 22.9 to 30.6 per 1000 (Davis & Feshbach 1980, Eberstadt 1981). The authorities in the USSR stopped publishing infant mortality rates soon thereafter, but the documented increases are unlike those seen anywhere in the industrialized world. More recent reports indicate a worsening of infant mortality rates in many Eastern European countries in the 1980s (Nanda et al 1993). Note that these recent increases occurred in the absence of modern neonatal intensive care capability.

Recent cross-sectional studies of countries and states indicate higher mortality rates in areas with greater income inequality (Waldman 1992, Kennedy et al 1996). Segregation indices are substantially correlated with rates of infant mortality among cities in the United States (Polednak 1991, LaVeist 1992). One study pointed out that countries with higher defense spending experience higher infant mortality rates (Woolhandler & Himmelstein 1985).

Others have examined yearly fluctuations in the economy. Brenner analyzed time-series data for the United States and other industrialized countries during the first half of the twentieth century and found evidence for an association between variations in rates of unemployment at the national level and rates of neonatal mortality (Brenner 1973, Brenner 1983). More recent evidence in support of this relationship has been reported, based on data from Los Angeles County, although the authors note very small effects (Catalano & Serxner 1992). One of the few individual level randomized studies based on the negative income tax experiment indicated that an income supplementation program can improve birth-weight outcomes (Kerher & Wohlin 1979).

Substantial limitations to these analyses of generally aggregate data exist: One fundamental problem is the difficulty of making causal inferences from geographically aggregated data (Susser 1994, Geronimus et al 1996). More importantly, these analyses generally do not provide insight into the pathways whereby social and economic conditions or the lack of effective health services may be producing disparities in infant mortality. During these times of enormous change in both the social and economic reconstruction of societies, including the current focus on "welfare reform" in the United States, and the reorganization of health services, it is crucial that different potential routes of influence are critically evaluated.

## *Access to Health Services*

One of the central consequences of the increasing efficacy of health services for the newborn is an increasing burden on society to provide these services equitably. In this sense, technical progress elevates the importance of access in the determination of disparities in mortality outcome.

Government-funded medical financing programs in the United States such as Medicaid have grown enormously in size and scope during recent decades. The Clinton administration attempted without success to considerably restructure the present health care system in the United States (The President's Health Security Plan 1993)—a system that can provide excellent quality of medical care, but that also leaves a substantial fraction of the population without financial coverage for health care (Blendon et al 1989). It is also a system that focuses most readily on treatment of illness, and less often and effectively on the prevention of illness. Research based on the National Health Insurance Experiment indicates that providing complete financial coverage for inpatient hospital care to children will not lead to mushrooming medical care costs. There is also no evidence to justify reimbursing acute ambulatory care at a higher rate than preventive services (Leibowitz et al 1985). However, the United States is still one of only two industrialized countries in the world (South Africa being the other) that do not provide financial coverage for health care for all pregnant women and children (Miller 1987).

It is not clear whether socioeconomic disparities in infant mortality could be eliminated by universal access to health services for children and women in the United States. We have already noted that disparities remain in Great Britain even though the National Health Service provides accessible care to the whole population. Universal coverage should help to reduce the number of areas reporting excess rates of infant death throughout the United States, now generally the poorest communities.

As neonatal intensive care technology has increased in effectiveness, access to this technology has become more crucial, and yet there are few studies of access to this care. Only a minority of hospitals can afford to staff neonatal intensive care units (NICUs), and this has lead to the regionalization of services (McCormick & Richardson 1995). One analysis of a metropolitan area in the 1970s found no social class disparities in neonatal mortality among very low birth-weight infants, indicating relatively uniform access to this emergency health service (Paneth et al 1982). A more recent analysis found a similar attenuation of the association of social factors and infant death among lower birth-weight infants (Eberstein et al 1990). Another study of four states in the early 1980s indicates substantial variation in access to NICU care, with sick rural infants most at risk of being born in a hospital without these capabilities (Gortmaker et al 1985). The most crucial changes, however, may now be appearing as managed care plans grow throughout the United States, and as pressures to limit costs may limit access to these services (McCormick & Richardson 1995). One recent analysis from California indicates substantially lower mortality and no greater costs among high risk births in hospitals with the best neonatal intensive care technology (Phibbs et al 1996), providing evidence that any limitations in access to this care in California could result in increased infant deaths. The rapid changes occurring in the organization of health services in the United States provide important opportunities to examine the sociology of access to these services—and corresponding health consequences—in the decades ahead.

### *Prenatal Risks and the Potential for Intervention*

Much of the public debate about infant mortality has focused on the potential for prevention via improved access to "prenatal care." While there are no definitive randomized controlled trials of the effectiveness of traditional prenatal medical care (for obvious ethical reasons), the preponderance of evidence supports the effectiveness of prenatal care in reducing the risk of low birth weight and in influencing the outcomes of pregnancy (Institute of Medicine 1985), particularly among high-risk populations (Gortmaker 1979b, Murray & Bernfield 1988). A wide variety of clinical circumstances make clear the benefits of prenatal medical care (Chalmers et al 1989). Careful monitoring during pregnancy means that high-risk deliveries and premature labor can be identified quickly and referred to the appropriate tertiary center for care, and this can lead to reduced mortality.

In spite of this evidence, the past few decades have demonstrated that improvements in prenatal health care have not substantially affected infant mortality rates. We have already noted that little of the decline in the infant mortality rate has been due to improved birth-weight distribution (the presumed outcome of improved of prenatal care) (Buehler 1987). It seems clear that expansion of access to the existing system of prenatal care will not solve the infant mortality problem, even though prenatal care can have greater impact as better outreach and delivery systems are devised (Institute of Medicine 1988). The development of more effective prenatal medical care, however, is for the most part contingent on a much better scientific understanding of the causes of preterm delivery, a phenomenon of largely unknown etiology (Paneth 1995).

In spite of these limitations, a variety of health-related behaviors of women increase the risks of infant mortality, including cigarette smoking, alcoholism, drug use including cocaine, poor weight gain during pregnancy, sexually transmitted diseases, and inadequate nutrition. These behaviors in turn are influenced by social and economic context, and hence intervention strategies focused on these risks can take many forms, ranging from clinical interventions (e.g. smoking cessation during the prenatal period) to state policy (e.g. cigarette taxation). Many of the interventions focused on these risks reside at least in part outside of the medical care system.

The evidence for the effects of cigarette smoking as a determinant of low birth weight (less than 2500 g) (Kramer 1987, Kleinman & Madans 1985) and on infant mortality (Kleinman et al 1988) is particularly striking and strong. Attributable risk estimates indicate that elimination of smoking among white married women could reduce rates of low birth weight by 19% (Kleinman et al 1985). Low-cost smoking cessation programs for pregnant women are effective (Windsor et al 1993) but not widely implemented. One barrier to this implementation is the fact that insurance carriers and Medicaid in general do not pay for these programs. An area of state policy with potentially substantial impact is increased excise taxes on tobacco, which can reduce cigarette consumption and discourage initiation of smoking among youth (Lewitt & Coate 1982, Manning et al 1991). Furthermore, bans on advertising and sales (Warner et al 1992), restriction of smoking in public places, and restricted sales of cigarettes to minors all significantly affect smoking rates in the United States.

Recent concern has focused upon the effects of cocaine and crack—a smokeable form of cocaine—in increasing the risk of premature labor. However, the estimated effects of cocaine and marijuana use upon fetal growth appear to be less than those estimated for the effects of cigarettes, even when valid measures of marijuana and cocaine use are applied (Zuckerman et al 1989). Given the lower prevalence of cocaine and marijuana use in the population, the attributable risks of poor birth outcomes associated with cigarettes appear much greater than those associated with cocaine.

Also operating outside the medical care system but producing higher birth weights is the Special Supplemental Nutrition Program for Women, Infants and Children (WIC). A series of studies from the United States indicate that participation in WIC produces higher birth weights (Kotelchuck et al 1984, Rush 1986). There is also evidence that FDA regulations concerning the nutritional content of food can improve birth outcomes: Supplementation of diet with folic acid, for example, can reduce the population risk of neural tube defects, which are major birth defects (Milunsky et al 1989).

Other prenatal risks and possible effective interventions have been identified. For example, studies of women's work have identified physically demanding work as contributing to prematurity and low birth weight (Naeye & Peters 1982, Homer et al 1990) as does environmental pollution (Mushak et al 1989) and toxic substances in worksites (Hemminiki et al 1983). Stress also increases risk of low birth-weight and preterm birth (McClean et al 1993), and social and psychological support produce positive effects during pregnancy (Elbourne et al 1989). One intriguing intervention study finds evidence for the effectiveness of nurse home visiting during pregnancy in improving birth outcomes among disadvantaged women (Olds et al 1986).

However, this evidence concerning risk and intervention does not necessarily help explain some of the more persistent disparities in infant mortality. For example, smoking behavior is not a likely explanation for observed racial disparities in birth-weight distribution because black women smoke cigarettes at rates roughly comparable to those of white women (Prager et al 1984). Studies controlling for smoking, alcohol use, and other social and economic characteristics fail to eliminate black/white differences in rates of low birth weight (Shiono et al 1986, Kramer 1995). This case illustrates the reality that an analysis of risks for infant mortality may not necessarily provide the best focus for an analysis of causes of disparity in infant mortality among population groups. This is the case with another often cited "cause" of high infant-mortality rates among black infants: high rates of teenage childbearing. Data clearly indicate that teenage pregnancy is associated with only a small minority of infant deaths, and so such data do little to help explain racial disparities in rates (Wise 1993).

These prenatal risks and interventions, therefore, remain an important arena of social and technical influence on infant outcome. However, prenatal effects, viewed in isolation, do not explain much of the differentiation in infant mortality rates over time or between different social groups. Rather, prenatal influences are perhaps best understood when viewed in a broader context that includes social and clinical mechanisms that operate over the continuum of a woman's reproductive life.

### *A Focus on Women's Health Status*

The impact of neonatal intensive care in concentrating infant mortality into the most premature group of newborns holds important implications for continued progress in reducing overall levels of, as well as disparate, infant mortality rates. Perhaps the most crucial need is to reconsider the current preoccupation with tightly focused efforts to intervene during the prenatal period. While our review has indicated evidence for effective strategies during the prenatal period, we have also noted that a large proportion of infant deaths occur to infants born before 25 weeks gestation. This is a very narrow window in which to concentrate prevention efforts. A more rational strategy would focus on linking improved parental care with broader initiatives to improve the health of women regardless of pregnancy status (Wise et al 1995).

Unfortunately, trends in the social, economic, and health status of women of childbearing age in the United States are not encouraging. The proportion of children living in poverty and of single-headed female households has increased over past decades. The proportion of children living in poverty in the United States declined during the 1960s and then increased during the 1970s and 1980s (Select Committee on Youth and Families 1989). Rates of children living in poverty in the United States are higher than those of the other industrialized countries (Smeeding & Torrey 1988).

A variety of health characteristics among women indicate a risk for poor pregnancy outcome, including elevated blood pressure, older age at childbirth (due mainly to improved fertility treatment—associated with increased risks of multiple births and prematurity), cigarette smoking, infections, sexually transmitted diseases, and alcohol and drug use. A review of trends in these factors over the past decades indicates no substantial evidence for improvement in women's health status (Gortmaker & Wise 1994). These issues may be particularly important for poor and minority women in the near future, in light of recent "welfare reform" legislation in the United States that will reduce future federal spending on poor households. One hypothesis concerning maternal health status is that optimal maternal health for childbearing may occur at different ages for African-American women, compared to non-Hispanic white women, in the United States, because health status declines with age among minority women due to the continuing impact of difficult socioeconomic environments (Geronimus 1992).

In light of these facts, reframing the infant mortality problem as an issue of women's health suggests that broader initiatives to address the health and well-being of women are essential. A focus on improving the health status of all women in the United States will require more than the provision of a right to health services. Changes include legal protection under the law, the right to choose abortion, support for work, maternity leave, and child care. Attention to the provision of cost-effective health promotion programs, including nutrition, smoking cessation, drug addiction treatment, and other services that typically fall outside the health care system.

While there is some evidence for intergenerational effects of deprivation (Emanuel 1986), the strongest evidence is that a woman's health prior to pregnancy is a substantial predictor of outcome and therefore should be the focus of research and intervention. In many ways the continuing focus on prenatal care as a preventive strategy epitomizes a strategy that comes too late to make a large impact on birth outcomes such as low and very low birth weight (Kempe et al 1992).

### *Race, Ethnicity, and Infant Mortality*

We have described the persistent racial and ethnic disparities in infant mortality rates in the United States. Despite much speculation, no evidence suggests that social, economic, or racial/ethnic disparities in the risk of death in infancy are caused by genetic differences. Any discussion of racial and ethnic differences in birth outcomes needs to acknowledge the limited extent to which social and economic variables—including racial discrimination—can be disentangled from crude proxies for biologically determined pathologic pathways (Krieger et al 1993, Herman 1996). The racial and ethnic categorizations used in most research on infant mortality in the United States should be seen as "proxies for specific historical experiences and a powerful marker for current social and economic conditions" (Williams & Collins 1995). Because of the unclear definition and measurement of "race" and "ethnicity" (Jones et al 1991) in virtually all large studies of infant outcomes and the confounding with a multitude of environmental differences, the potential causal role of "racial" and "ethnic" differences in the generation of disparate infant mortality rates is an issue that may be poorly served by current analytic approaches.

The pervasive effects of racist attitudes and beliefs and the legacy of slavery in the United States can often be difficult to measure, but the historical evidence is quite clear in documenting the profound influence of these forces upon the life chances of minorities (Krieger et al 1993, Williams 1996). It is important to remember that the racial differences noted for infant mortality are similar to differences documented for virtually all causes of mortality in the United States.

We have noted continuing black/white disparities in infant mortality in the United States. Other studies document the elevated rates of infant mortality among Native Americans (VanLandingham & Hogue 1994) and Hispanics (Bacerra et al 1991), and the important errors and inconsistencies in coding racial and ethnic categories that occur (Hahn et al 1992).

The roots of biologically determined explanations for disparities in infant mortality lie in both technical and political arenas. For example, technical arguments concerning black/white differences are based on evidence indicating that blacks experience a lower mean birth weight than do whites, while at the same time blacks experience lower birth weight–specific infant mortality among small infants (Buehler et al 1987). Some analysts have argued that a lower mean birth weight among blacks should require an adjustment when compared with white birth-weight distributions, thus reducing differences in low birth-weight rates (Wilcox & Russel 1983). This argument, while useful in some settings, has been widely misinterpreted as suggesting that the racial difference in mortality should similarly be adjusted and, thereby, technically reduced as well. This is flawed in two respects. First, the focus on mean birth weights ignores the fact that mean differences are not closely related to risk; rather, it is extreme birth weights (particularly extremely low birth weight) that are most closely related to the risk of infant death. Furthermore, black infant mortality is higher than white infant mortality because of the frequency of extremely low birth weight and associated prematurity (Rowley 1995). It is useful to remember here that the mean birth weight of blacks in the United States is similar to that for the Japanese, the population with the lowest infant mortality rate in the world; extreme low birth weight in Japan is relatively rare.

Second, this interpretation does not recognize that any adjustment in birth-weight distribution that reduces racial differences requires a compensatory adjustment in birth weight–specific mortality that increases racial differences. Adjustment for mean birth weight, therefore, can never reduce the actual excess mortality that occurs in blacks. The political utility of "biologically" determined racial disparities in infant mortality is derived from its potential exculpatory character in assessing the role of social and policy-based influences. To the extent that "biology" can be said to determine the scale of racial disparities in infant mortality, the role of social factors and health care provision is to that same extent removed from practical consideration. Together, the technical and political aspects of this issue have generated considerable confusion concerning how the social epidemiology of racial disparities in infant mortality has been understood in the deliberation of ameliorative public policies.

Because of a long-standing interest in the complexities of race, ethnicity, and social stratification in the United States, sociologists can contribute significantly to a more accurate understanding of racial and ethnic inequities in infant outcomes. The conceptual and daily dimensions of racial and ethnic differences, including discrimination and racism, their definition and measurement, and how risks and interventions can operate within different populations are all issues that demand greater study. The analysis of racism (Williams 1996), migration (Cabral et al 1990), and social and economic risks within populations (see e.g. Schoendorf et al 1992) and the outcomes of an expanding population of mixed racial and ethnic children (Collins & David 1993) constitute promising avenues of research.

## SUMMARY

Current patterns of infant mortality in the United States provide a useful illustration of the dynamic interaction of underlying social forces and technological progress in determining trends in health outcomes. Sociological research concerning infant mortality in the future needs to acknowledge the power of both social and economic forces and health care technology in the generation of disparities in infant mortality.

### ACKNOWLEDGMENTS

Preparation of this article was supported in part by grants from the Kaiser Family Foundation and the Initiative on Children of the American Academy of

Arts and Sciences, Cambridge, MA, 02138. We thank members of the Society and Health Working Group at the Harvard School of Public Health for their critical commentary and social support.

Visit the *Annual Reviews home page* at http://www.annurev.org.

*Literature Cited*

Alberman E, Schmidt E, Evans S. 1992. Survival of infants of very low birth weight. In *Proc. Int. Collaborative Effort on Perinatal and Infant Mortality,* Vol. III. Hyattsville, MD: US Dep. Health Hum. Serv.

Becerra JE, Hogue CJR, Atrash HK, Perez N. 1991. Infant mortality among Hispanics. A portrait of heterogeneity. *JAMA* 265:217–21

Black D, Morris JN, Smith C, Townsend P. 1982. *Inequalities in Health: The Black Report.* London: Penguin

Blendon RJ, Aiken LH, Freeman HE, Corey CR. 1989. Access to medical care for black and white Americans. *JAMA* 261:278–81

Boyle MH, Torrance GW, Sinclair JC, Horwood SP. 1983. Economic evaluation of neonatal intensive care of very-low-birth-weight infants. *N. Engl. J. Med.* 308:1330–37

Brenner MH. 1973. Fetal, infant, and maternal mortality during periods of economic stress. *Int. J. Health Serv.* 3:145–59

Brenner MH. 1983. Mortality and economic instability: detailed analyses for Britain and comparative analyses for selected industrialized countries. *Int. J. Health Serv.* 13:563–620

Buehler JW, Kleinman JC, Hogue CJR, Strauss LT, Smith JC. 1987. Birth weight-specific infant mortality, United States, 1960 and 1980. *Public Health Rep.* 102:151–61

Butler JA, Scotch RK. 1978. Medicaid and children: some recent lessons and reasonable next steps. *Public Policy* 26:3

Cabral H, Fried L, Levenson S, Amaro H, Zuckerman B. 1990. Foreign-born and US-born black women: differences in health behaviors and outcomes. *Am. J. Public Health* 80:70–72

Catalano R, Serxner S. 1992. Neonatal mortality and the economy revisited. *Int. J. Health Serv.* 22:275–86

Chalmers I, Enkin M, Keirse MJNC, eds. 1989. *Effective Care in Pregnancy and Childbirth.* Vol. I. *Pregnancy.* New York: Oxford Univ. Press

Children's Bureau. 1921. *Children's Bureau Publication No. 61. Rev.* Washington, DC: US Dep. Labor

Collins JW Jr, David RJ. 1993. Race and birth-weight in biracial infants. *Am. J. Public Health* 83;1125–29

Connor EM, Sperling RS, Gelber R, Kiselev P, Scott G, et al. 1994. Reduction of maternal-infant transmission of human immunodeficiency virus type 1 with zidovudine treatment. *N. Engl. J. Med.* 331:1173–60

Davis C, Feshbach M. 1980. Rising infant mortality in the U.S.S.R. in the 1970's. *US Bur. Census Ser. P-95. No. 74.* Washington, DC: USGPO

Dubos R. 1959. *Mirage of Health: Utopias, Progress and Biological Change.* New York: Harper & Row. (Quoted in 1980. *Readings in Medical Sociology,* ed. D Mechanic. New York: Free Press)

Eberstadt N. 1981. The Health Crisis in the U.S.S.R. *The New York Rev.* Feb. 19:23–31

Eberstein IW, Nam CB, Hummer RA. 1990. Infant mortality by cause of death: main and interaction effects. *Demography* 27:413–30

Elbourne D, Oakley A, Chalmers I. 1989. Social and psychological support during pregnancy. See Chalmers et al 1989, pp. 221–36

Emanuel I. 1986. Maternal health during childhood and later reproductive performance. *Ann. NY Acad. Sci.* 477:27–39

Geronimus A. 1992. The weathering hypothesis and the health of African-American women and infants: evidence and speculations. *Ethn. Dis.* 2:210–24

Geronimus A, Bound J, Niedert LJ. 1996. On the validity of using census geocode characteristics to proxy individual socioeconomic characteristics. *J. Am. Stat. Assoc.* 91:529–37

Gortmaker S, Sobol A, Clark C, Walker DK, Geronimus A. 1985. The survival of very low-birth weight infants by level of hospital of birth: a population study of perinatal systems in four states. *Am. J. Obstet. Gynecol.* 152:517–24

Gortmaker SL. 1979a. Poverty and infant mortality in the United States. *Am. Sociol. Rev.* 44:280–97

Gortmaker SL. 1979b. The effects of prenatal care upon the health of the newborn. *Am. J. Public Health* 269:653–60

Gortmaker SL, Sappenfield W. 1984. Chronic childhood disorders: prevalence and impact. *Pediatr. Clin. N. Am.* 31:3–18

Gortmaker SL, Wise PH. 1994. *The First Injustice: Socioeconomic Disparities in Infant Mortality in the United States: Theoretical and Policy Perspectives.* Soc. Health Work. Pap. Ser. No. 94–4, Nov. Boston, MA: Harvard Sch. Public Health

Gray AM. 1982. Inequalities in health. The Black Report: a summary and comment. *Int. J. Health Serv.* 12:349–80

Guyer B, Wallach LA, Rosen SL. 1982. Birthweight-standardized neonatal mortality rates and the prevention of low birth weight: How does Massachusetts compare with Sweden? *N. Engl. J. Med.* 306:1230–33

Hahn RA, Eaker E, Banker ND, Teutsch SM, Sasniak W, Krieger N. 1995. Poverty and death in the United States—1973 and 1991. *Epidemiology* 6:490–97

Hahn RA, Mulinare J, Teustch SM. 1992. Inconsistencies in coding of race and ethnicity between birth and death in US infants: a new look at infant mortality, 1983 through 1985. *JAMA* 267:259–63

Hamvas A, Wise PH, Yang RK, Wampler NS, Noguchi A, et al. 1996. The influence of the wider use of surfactant therapy on neonatal mortality among blacks and whites. *N. Engl. J. Med.* 334:1635–40

Hartford RB. 1992. Definitions, standards, data quality and comparability. In *Proc. Int. Collaborative Effort on Perinatal and Infant Mortality,* Vol. III. Hyattsville, MD: US Dep. Health Hum. Serv.

Hemminiki K, Kyyronen P, Niemi ML, Koskinen K, Sallmen M, Vainio H. 1983. Spontaneous abortions in an industrialized community in Finland. *Am. J. Public Health* 73:32–37

Herman A. 1996. Toward a conceptualization of race in epidemiologic research. *Ethn. Dis.* 6:7–20

Hogue CJ, Hargraves MA. 1993. Class, race, and infant mortality in the United States. *Am. J. Public Health* 83:9–12

Homer CJ, Beresford GA, James SA, Siegel E, Wilcox S. 1990. Work-related physical exertion and the risk of preterm, low birthweight delivery. *Paediatr. Perinat. Epidemiol.* 4:161–74

Institute of Medicine. 1985. *Committee to Study the Prevention of Low Birthweight. Preventing Low Birthweight.* Washington, DC: Natl. Acad. Press

Institute of Medicine. 1988. *Prenatal Care: Reaching Mothers, Reaching Infants.* Committee to Study Outreach for Prenatal Care, Div. Health Promotion and Diseases Prevention. Washington, DC: Natl. Acad. Press

Jencks C. 1980. Heredity, environment and public policy reconsidered. *Am. Sociol. Rev.* 45:723–36

Jones CP, LaVeist TA, Lillie-Blanton M. 1991. "Race" in the epidemiologic literature: an examination of the American Journal Epidemiology 1921–1990. *Am. J. Epidemiol.* 134:1079–84

Kehrer BH, Wolin C. 1979. Impact of income maintenance on low birthweight: evidence from the Gary experiment. *J. Hum. Resour.* 14:434–62

Kempe A, Wise P, Barkan SE, Sappenfield WM, Sachs B, et al. 1992. Clinical conditions associated with racial disparities in very low birth weight rates: a population-based study. *N. Engl. J. Med.* 327:969–73

Kennedy BP, Kawachi I, Prothrow-Stith D. 1996. Income distribution and mortality: cross-sectional ecological study of the Robin Hood index in the United States. *Br. Med. J.* 312:1004–7

Kleinman JC, Madans JH. 1985. The effects of maternal smoking, physical stature, and educational attainment on the incidence of low birth weight. *Am. J. Epidemiol.* 121:843–55

Kleinman JC, Pierre MB Jr, Madans JH, Land GH, Schramm WF. 1988. The effects of maternal smoking on fetal and infant mortality. *Am. J. Epidemiol.* 127:274–82

Kotelchuck M, Schwartz JB, Anderka MT, Finison KS. 1984. WIC participation and pregnancy outcomes: Massachusetts Statewide Evaluation Project. *Am. J. Public Health* 74:1086–92

Kramer JC. 1995. Racial and ethnic differences in birthweight: the role of income and financial assistance. *Demography* 32:231–47

Kramer MS. 1987. Intrauterine growth and gestational duration determinants. *Pediatrics* 80:502–11

Krieger N, Rowley DL, Herman AA, Avery B, Phillips MY. 1993. Racism, sexism, and social class: implications for studies of health, disease and well-being. *Am. J. Prev. Med.* 9:82–122 (Suppl.)

LaVeist TA. 1992. The political empowerment and health status of African-Americans: mapping a new territory. *Am. J. Sociol.* 97: 1080–95

Leibowitz A, Manning WG, Keeler EB, Duan N, Lohr KN, Newhouse JP. 1985. Effect of cost-sharing on the use of medical services by children: interim results from a randomized controlled trial. *Pediatrics* 75:942–51

Lewitt EM, Coate D. 1982. The potential for using excise taxes to reduce smoking. *J. Health Econ.* 1:121–45

Manning WG, Keeler EB, Newhouse JP, Sloss EM, Wasserman J. 1991. *The Costs of Poor*

*Health Habits*. Cambridge, MA: Harvard Univ. Press

Marmot MG, Kogevinas M, Elston MA. 1987. Social/economic status and disease. *Annu. Rev. Public Health* 8:111–35

Marx K. 1967. *Capital: a Critique of Political Economy.* Vol. I. *The Process of Capitalist Production,* ed. F Engels. Transl. S Moore, E Aveling. New York: Int. Publ.

McClean DE, Hatfield-Timajchy K, Wingo PA, Floyd RL. 1993. Psychosocial measurement: implications for the study of preterm delivery in Black women. *Am. J. Prev. Med.* 9:39–81(Suppl.)

McCormick MC. 1985. The contribution of low birthweight to infant mortality and childhood morbidity. *N. Engl. J. Med.* 312:82–90

McCormick MC. 1993. Has the prevalence of handicapped infants increased with improved survival of the very low birth weight infant? *Clin. Perinatol.* 20:263–77

McCormick MC, Richardson DK. 1995. Access to neonatal intensive care. *Future Child.* 4:162–75

Miller CA. 1987. A review of maternity care programs in Western Europe. *Fam. Plan. Perspect.* 15:207

Milunsky A, Jick H, Jick SS, Bruell CL, MacLaughlin DS, et al. 1989. Multivitamin/folic acid supplementation in early pregnancy reduces the prevalence of neural tube defects. *JAMA* 262:2847–52

Murray JL, Bernfield M. 1988. The differential effect of prenatal care on the incidence of low birth weight among blacks and whites in a prepaid health plan. *N. Engl. J. Med.* 319:1385–91

Mushak P, Davis JM, Crocetti AF, Grant FD. 1989. Prenatal and postnatal effects of low-level lead exposure: integrated summary of a report to the U.S. Congress on childhood lead poisoning. *Environ. Res.* 50:11–36

Naeye RL, Peters EC. 1982. Working during pregnancy: effects on the fetus. *Pediatrics* 69:724–27

National Center for Health Statistics. 1972. *Infant Mortality Rates: Socioeconomic Factors,* Ser. 22, No. 14. Washington, DC: USGPO

National Center for Health Statistics. 1986. *Health, United States. 1986.* DHHS Publ. No. (PHS) 87–1232. Public Health Serv. Washington, DC: USGPO

Office of Technology Assessment, US Congress. 1987. *Neonatal Intensive Care for Low Birthweight Infants: Costs and Effectiveness.* Health Technol. Case Study 38, OTA-HCS-38. Washington, DC: USGPO

Ogburn WF. 1973. The hypothesis of cultural lag. In *Sociological Theory: An Introduction,* ed. WW Williams, pp. 140–44. Chicago: Aldine. 1st ed. 1969

Olds DL, Henderson CR, Tatelbaum R, Chamberlin R. 1986. Improving the delivery of prenatal care and outcomes of pregnancy: a randomized trial of nurse home visitation. *Pediatrics* 77:16–28

Paneth N, Wallenstein S, Kiely JL, Susser M. 1982. Social class indicators and mortality in low birthweight infants. *Am. J. Epidemiol.* 116:364–75

Paneth NS. 1995. The problem of low birth weight. *Future Child.* 5:19–34

Pappas G, Queen S, Hadden W, Fisher G. 1993. The increasing disparity in mortality between socioeconomic groups in the United States, 1960 and 1986. *N. Engl. J. Med.* 329:103–9

Phibbs CS, Bronstein JM, Buxton E, Phibbs RH. 1996. The effects of patient volume and level of care at the hospital of birth on neonatal mortality. *JAMA* 276:1054–59

Polednak AP. 1991. Black-white differences in infant mortality in 38 standard metropolitan statistical areas. *Am. J. Public Health* 81:1480–82

Prager K, Malin H, Spiegler D, Van Natta P, Placek PJ. 1984. Smoking and drinking behavior before and during pregnancy of married mothers of live-born infants and stillborn infants. *Public Health Rep.* 99:117–27

The President's Health Security Plan. 1993. *The President's Health Security Plan.* New York: Random House

Rowley DL. 1995. Framing the debate: Can prenatal care help to reduce the black-white disparity in infant mortality. *J. Am. Women's Med. Assoc.* 50:187–93

Rush D. 1986. *Evaluation of the Special Supplemental Food Program for Women, Infants, and Children (WIC).* Vol. I. *Summary.* Off. Anal. Eval., Food Nutr. Serv., Dep. Agric. Washington, DC: USGPO

Sanderson M, Placek P, Keppel KG. 1991. The National Maternal and Infant Health Survey: design, content, and data availability. *Birth* 18:26–32

Schoendorf K, Hogue C, Kleinman J, Rowley D. 1992. Infant mortality in college-educated families: narrowing the racial gap. *N. Engl. J. Med.* 326:1522–26

Select Committee on Youth and Families, US House of Representatives. 1989. *US Children and their Families: Current Conditions and Recent Trends.* Washington, DC: USGPO

Shapiro S, McCormick MC, Starfield BH, Crawley B. 1983. Changes in infant morbidity associated with decreases in neonatal mortality. *Pediatrics* 72:408–15

Shiono PH, Klebanoff MA, Graubard BI, Berendes HW, Rhoads GG. 1986. Birth

weight among women of different ethnic groups. *JAMA* 255:48–52
Smeeding TM, Torrey BB. 1988. Poor children in rich countries. *Science* 242:873–77
Smith CA. 1947. The effect of wartime starvation in Holland upon pregnancy and its product. *Am. J. Obstet. Gynecol.* 53:599
Starfield B, Shapiro S, Weiss J, Liang KY, Ra K, et al. 1991. Race, family income, and low birth weight. *Am. J. Epidemiol.* 134:1167–74
Susser M. 1994. The logic in ecological: I. The logic of analysis. *Am. J. Public Health* 84:825–29
Susser M, Stein Z. 1994. Timing in prenatal nutrition: a reprise of the Dutch Famine Study. *Nutr. Rev.* 52:84–94
UNICEF. 1992. *State of the World's Children.* New York: United Nations
US Bureau of the Census. 1989. *Statistical Abstract of the United States.* Washington, DC: USGPO. 109th ed.
VanLandingham MJ, Hogue CJ. 1994. Birthweight-specific mortality risks for Native Americans and whites, United States, 1960 and 1984. *Soc. Biol.* 42:83–94
Wagner MG. 1988. Infant mortality in Europe: implications for the United States. Statement to the National Commission to Prevent Infant Mortality. *J. Public Health Policy* (Winter):473–84
Waldmann RJ. 1992. Income distribution and infant mortality. *Q.J. Econ.* 107:1283–1302
Wallace R, Wallace D, Andrews H, Fullilove R, Fullilove MT. 1995. The spatiotemporal dynamics of AIDS and TB in the New York Metropolitan region from a sociogeographic perspective. *Environ. Plann.* 27:1085–1109
Warner KE, Goldenhar LM, McLaughlin CG. 1992. Cigarette advertising and magazine coverage of the hazards of smoking. A statistical analysis. *N. Engl. J. Med.* 326:305–9
Wilcox AJ, Russel IT. 1983. Birthweight and perinatal mortality. II. On weight-specific mortality. *Int. J. Epidemiol.* 12:319–25
Williams DR. 1996. Racism and health: a research agenda. *Ethn. Dis.* 6:1–6
Williams DR, Collins C. 1995. Socioeconomic and racial differences in health: patterns and explanations. *Annu. Rev. Sociol.* 21:349–86
Windsor RA, Lowe JB, Perkins LL, Smith-Yoder D, Artz L, et al. 1993. Health education for pregnant smokers: its behavioral impact and cost benefit. *Am. J. Public Health* 83:201–6
Wise PH. 1990. Poverty, technology and recent trends in the United States infant mortality rate. *Paediatr. Perinat. Epidemiol.* 4:390–401
Wise PH. 1993. Confronting racial disparities in infant mortality: reconciling science and politics. *Am. J. Prev. Med.* (Suppl.) 9:7–16
Wise PH, First LR, Lamb GA, Kotelchuck M, Chen DW, et al. 1988. Infant mortality increase despite high access to tertiary care: an evolving relationship among infant mortality, health care, and socioeconomic change. *Pediatrics* 81:542–48
Wise PH, Kotelchuck M, Wilson ML, Mills M. 1985. Racial and socioeconomic disparities in childhood mortality in Boston. *N. Engl. J. Med.* 313:360–66
Wise PH, Pursley DM. 1992. Infant mortality as a social mirror. *N. Engl. J. Med.* 23:1558–60
Wise PH, Wampler N, Barfield W. 1995. The importance of extreme prematurity and low birthweight to US neonatal mortality patterns: implications for prenatal care and women's health. *J. Am. Med. Woman's Assoc.* 50:152–55
Woolhandler S, Himmelstein DU. 1985. Militarism and mortality. An international analysis of arms spending and infant death rates. *Lancet* 1:1375–78
Yudkowsky BK, Cartland JDC, Flint SS. 1990. Pediatrician participation in Medicaid: 1979 to 1989. *Pediatrics* 85:567–77
Zuckerman B, Frank DA, Hingson R, Amaro H, Levenson SM, et al. 1989. Effects of maternal marijuana and cocaine use on fetal growth. *N. Engl. J. Med.* 320:762–68

*Annu. Rev. Sociol. 1997. 23:171–89*


# SOCIOLOGICAL PERSPECTIVES ON MEDICAL ETHICS AND DECISION-MAKING

*Robert Zussman*
Department of Sociology, State University of New York—Stony Brook, Stony Brook, New York 11794

KEY WORDS: medical ethics, decision-making

ABSTRACT

Sociologists have not addressed directly the normative issues that constitute the core of medical ethics as an intellectual discipline. They have, however, contributed to a "realist" critique of medical ethics in practice. In regard to the institutionalization of "autonomy" around the principle of informed consent, they have noted widespread indifference on the part of patients, considerable variation among settings, and a persistent ability of physicians to deflect challenges to their authority. In regard to failed efforts to institutionalize "justice," sociologists have noted both the difficulty physicians experience moving from individual clinical decisions to a recognition of the collective consequences of those decisions and the social structures that shape allocation decisions along dimensions orthogonal to ethical concerns. Most importantly, however, medical ethics is an arena in which sociologists can revisit, in new form, old issues about the doctor-patient relationship, the relationship between medicine and gender, the meaning of death and dying, and the character of medical professionalism.

## INTRODUCTION

In the extended family of scholars that has formed over the last three decades around what has come to be known as medical ethics, sociology is a poor relative. Medical ethics is an intellectual discipline, but sociology has not assumed a prominent position in that discipline, and medical ethicists themselves have typically paid little attention to sociology. Medical ethics is also a set of institutionalized principles and procedures that have helped shape new modes of



0360-0572/97/0815-0171$08.00

medical practice. Sociologists have assumed a position as sympathetic critics of these new policies, but they are by no means their most important—let alone their only—critics. Nonetheless, medical ethics—both as an intellectual discipline and as a social movement—has provided sociologists an opportunity (or at least an excuse) to revitalize many of the long-standing preoccupations of medical sociology.

In this essay, I briefly review the relationship between sociology and medical ethics as an intellectual discipline. I then turn to the sociological critique of the institutionalization of medical ethics, concentrating primarily on the successful institutionalization of procedures meant to ensure "autonomy" and secondarily on less successful attempts to institutionalize "justice." In the final section of the review, I suggest that the most important contributions of the sociology of medical ethics are neither to medical ethics as an intellectual discipline nor even as a mostly sympathetic critique of the institutionalization of medical ethics, but to the development of a distinctively sociological understanding of medical practice.

## *Medical Ethics as an Intellectual Discipline*

No doubt, there have been self-conscious medical ethics at least since Hippocrates formulated the famous oath physicians still take on entering their profession. Even "modern" codes of medical ethics date from the eighteenth century in England and the middle of the nineteenth in the United States (Berlant 1975). This said, contemporary medical ethics, in the sense of sustained reflection on clinical decision-making based in systematic philosophy and theology, is probably no older than the 1954 publication of Joseph Fletcher's *Morals and Medicine*, and it reached intellectual maturity only in the 1960s and 1970s with the publication of many of the field's classic essays (Ramsey 1970, Veatch 1976).

Medical ethics is now a well-established discipline, with its own journals and institutes, although these are more often organized as centers with varying degrees of independence from conventional lines of university departments than as traditional academic units. Medical ethics has, however, been led far more by the parent disciplines of philosophy and theology than by sociology or any of the other social sciences. To some degree, sociologists and medical ethicists are competitors, fighting for often hotly contested space on the medical school curriculum, with medical ethics now displacing the social sciences. For the most part, however, sociology and medical ethics have treated each other with mutual indifference. Although a few medical ethicists have suggested that medical ethics would be revitalized by the inclusion of social science (Hoffmaster 1992, Crigger 1995, Peralman et al 1993), sociologists remain infrequent contributors to the leading journals of medical ethics. Even reviews of sociological books directly related to ethical issues are rare in those journals, and those reviews that are published are often critical. Neither, however, do sociological journals review even the most important works of medical ethics, and many sociologists, including those who formulate their work as related to ethical issues, rarely even attempt to treat philosophical or theological issues on their own terms.

The mutual indifference of medical ethicists and sociologists of medical ethics is, I would suggest, a matter of fundamental differences of purpose—of a contrast between medical ethics as a normative discipline and sociology as an empirical one. However, this claim needs qualification. Certainly medical ethics is more explicitly normative than sociology, and sociology, more explicitly empirical than medical ethics. Nonetheless, medical ethicists often incorporate empirical material into their analyses and recently have shown a growing inclination to do so. So too the sociology of medical ethics carries normative implications, often quite intentional, particularly (although not exclusively) in feminist discussions of medical practice (Ruzek 1979, Rothman 1989). At most then, the difference between medical ethics and the sociology of medical ethics is in the form of their normative statements: Sociology is almost always consequentialist; in contrast, medical ethics is given much more to "deontological" positions, evaluating acts as right or wrong even apart from consequences.

More important is the difference between medical ethics as an applied discipline and the sociology of medical ethics as an academic one. But this claim, too, requires qualification. Many textbooks and readers in medical ethics begin with discussions of general principles—utilitarianism, Kantian ethics, Rawlsian ethics—that require flights of abstraction unfamiliar to most sociologists (for example, Munson 1988). Conversely, sociologists of medical ethics seem prepared to grapple with the grubby details of hospitals, clinics, and patients' lives in a way matched by few ethicists. Nonetheless, medical ethics is fairly explicitly a branch of applied philosophy, and even its grandest abstractions are put to use in the service of formulating procedures and policies useful to "problems of therapeutic practice, health care delivery, and medical and biological research" (Beauchamp & Childress 1979, vi). In contrast, sociologists tend to use even grubby details as a route to more analytic observations. Ironically, then, it is the medical ethicists, trained in philosophy and theology and given to abstraction, who are often worldly, and it is the sociologists of medical ethics who are more often other-worldly (Gray & Phillips 1995). Both medical ethicists (Arras 1991, Kass 1990) and sociologists of medical ethics are prepared to analyze individual cases, but they do so for different purposes. For the sociologist, the case is typically exemplary. In contrast, for the medical ethicist, like the clinical physician and, to some extent, the lawyer, the case is often the end point. Put broadly, but with at least moderate accuracy, medical ethics may be thought of as the normative study of high principles for the purpose of guiding clinical decisions. In contrast, the sociology of medical ethics may be thought of as the empirical study of clinical decisions for the purpose of understanding the social structure of medicine. Clearly then, medical ethicists and sociologists of medical ethics travel much of the same terrain, but they do so traveling in different directions. If they do little more than wave as they pass, rarely stopping even for a chat, it is because they do not have a great deal to say to each other.

## *The Institutionalization of Medical Ethics: Informed Consent*

In a series of influential essays, Renee Fox (1989, 1990, Fox & Swazey 1984) has argued that the "ethos" of medical ethics has been dominated by an analytic individualism, organized around the value of "autonomy," that assigns prominence to "the notion of contract" while relegating "more socially-oriented values . . . to a secondary status" (1989, pp. 229–30). Fox's observations do not seem to me an accurate characterization of medical ethics as an intellectual discipline. Like many disciplines, medical ethics is far from consensual, and values of "beneficence" and "justice" have always competed, at least in more conceptual writings, with "autonomy" (National Commission 1978). Moreover, what Fox (1989) herself, writing in the 1980s, had the foresight to recognize as "incipient changes in the ethos of bioethics" have assumed even more prominence as ethicists have come increasingly to stress issues of distributive justice in response to a growing perception of a crisis in health care resources and costs (Callahan 1987, Childress 1990). Nonetheless, whatever qualifications one might introduce to Fox's characterization of medical ethics as an intellectual discipline, they represent a remarkably apt characterization of the ways in which medical ethics has been successfully institutionalized.

There has, of course, always been a practice of medical ethics, both in the sense that the actions of physicians and other health care personnel carry ethical implications and in the sense that medical training has long carried a significant element of moral education (Bosk 1979). However, the last 30 years in the history of medical practice are distinguished by the degree to which ethical considerations in medicine have been made explicit and subject to formal policies and procedures.

The bases of contemporary, institutionalized medical ethics can be found in the "Nuremberg Code," which, in response to the revelation of bizarre medical experiments in Nazi concentration camps, enunciated the principle of the "voluntary consent" of human subjects as essential to the ethical conduct of research. However, as the historian David Rothman (1991) has argued, the Nazi abuses were taken more as a cautionary tale about government interference with science than as an indication of any parallel problems in American medicine. The origin of contemporary medical ethics, then, is probably better dated to a series of well-publicized reports of abuses of the rights of dependent and vulnerable populations (poor, rural African-Americans, prisoners, soldiers, retarded children, and the debilitated aged) in the United States (Beecher 1966, Jones 1981). In responses to these revelations, particularly Beecher's 1966 *New England Journal of Medicine* report of 22 cases of ethical abuses in medical research, the US Public Health Service promulgated a set of rules providing protection for human subjects and requiring the establishment of Institutional Review Boards (IRBs) to provide peer review of ethical issues in all federally funded research.

Even had it been inclined to do so—which it was not—the Public Health Service could not have regulated clinical practice so easily as medical research. Nonetheless, consent also came to clinical practice, albeit more from the courts than from codes. To be sure, common law in the United States has long required the consent of patients to medical procedures. However, throughout most of the nineteenth century, this requirement was based primarily on the notion that the patient's consent was essential to the effectiveness of procedures (Pernick 1982). Only in the twentieth century, particularly since the 1914 Schloendorff case, was the requirement of obtaining consent made a matter of rights, and only since the 1957 California Salgo case has there been any requirement that consent must also be "informed." Since 1957, the doctrine of informed consent has been extended, both by courts and through legislation, to include an increasingly broad, "patient centered," set of standards of what constitutes adequate information. Although there is significant variation from state to state, not only does the legal doctrine of informed consent require physicians to disclose a wide range of information to patients—including the risks and benefits of procedures and alternatives to proposed treatments—but those requirements gain additional force from hospital policies that have routinized the process of obtaining consent (President's Commission 1982, Katz 1984, Faden & Beauchamp 1986).

Although based on similar principles, the development of policies bearing on termination of treatment has followed a more complex course, following somewhat different trajectories for newborns and for adults and involving not only both court cases and an ill-fated effort at federal regulation but also a long process in which hospitals themselves played a leading part in formulating procedures. It had long been an ill-kept secret in medicine that physicians did not always make maximal efforts to maintain the life of either disabled newborns or critically ill adults. But the issue became public only with the 1973 publication of an article on "Moral and Ethical Dilemmas in the Special Care Nursery" in which Duff & Campbell described the procedures he and his colleagues used to consult with patients in deciding to withhold potentially life-sustaining treatment in a newborn nursery. (Duff is perhaps better known to sociologists for his collaboration with August Hollingshead on their classic 1968 study, *Sickness and Society*.) Duff's article signaled the beginning of a controversy that continued through a series of so-called "Baby Doe" court cases, in which right-to-life advocates attempted to require surgery for a number of newborns against the wishes of both parents and physicians. These cases culminated in 1983, when the Reagan administration issued a set of regulations prohibiting discrimination against newborns on the basis of developmental disability. Although the Reagan rules were eventually overturned in court, the result has been the development of carefully constructed guidelines that allow parents and physicians to decide against treating newborns, but typically only with the oversight of newly formed neonatal ethics committees (President's Commission 1983).

The development of procedures for withholding treatment from critically ill adults developed along a more or less parallel course, although with significantly less federal involvement. In 1976, a New Jersey court ruled that Karen Quinlan, a young woman believed to have become permanently comatose, could be removed from a respirator. In the same year, in a special article in the *New England Journal of Medicine*, Rabkin and his colleagues described the procedures used at Beth Israel Hospital to guide "the process by which decisions not to resuscitate should be made." Since 1976, virtually every hospital in the country has followed Beth Israel's lead, establishing policies for "Do Not Resuscitate" or DNR orders that assign priority in decision-making to the wishes of the patient. And in the 1990 Cruzan case, although in a finding fraught with ambiguities, the United States Supreme Court confirmed that physicians could withdraw treatment from terminally ill patients so long as—given appropriate state-determined procedural safeguards—that decision is an accord with the patient's desires.

The process of institutionalization, then, has varied significantly in regard to experimentation with human subjects, the establishment of informed consent, withholding treatment from newborns, and withholding treatments from adults—with different forms of involvement by courts and the federal government, with varying degrees of leadership from hospitals, and with varying amounts of controversy. However, in each instance, the institutionalization of policies has taken shape around the principles of patient autonomy and self-determination. In effect, "informed consent," intended explicitly to increase the patient's ability to direct decisions bearing on his or her own treatment, has become the master solution to ethical issues. Thus, the solution to abuses in medical research has been a set of procedures designed to ensure that the participation of human subjects is voluntary; the solution to dilemmas in the treatment of handicapped newborns has been to ensure that parents receive priority in making decisions; and the solution to dilemmas in the treatment of adults has been an attempt to find procedures ensuring that the patient's own wishes take priority. To be sure, many of the applications of informed consent are remarkably complex. How, for example, can one ensure that a "substituted judgment" made on behalf of a comatose, no longer competent patient genuinely represents what that patient's wishes would have been in an unanticipated situation? How, for example, can one speak at all of the wishes of a newborn infant or a severely retarded adult who has never been competent? Yet, these complexities notwithstanding, the principle of informed consent and the underlying value of autonomy have themselves remained remarkably simple and straightforward.

Sociologists have generally expressed sympathy for informed consent. They have, however, also expressed considerable skepticism about its implementation. In summarizing a series of methodologically diverse studies, there is some danger of reporting greater consensus than, in fact, exists. Nonetheless, there does seem to be something of an emerging sociological critique of informed consent in practice. This critique, however, is not unique to sociology but is shared with a congeries of researchers so ill-defined as to lack even an agreed-upon name, but it includes physicians, nurses, and health policy scholars from a remarkably wide range of disciplinary backgrounds. Roughly epidemiological in style, these researchers have joined with sociologists to make a case that: 1. Although not matched in practice, there is a great deal of expressed support among physicians and other health care professionals for the principle of informed consent; 2. there is widespread indifference on the part of patients to the sort of participation envisioned by informed consent; 3. there are significant variations in practice among settings; and 4. physicians maintain significant authority over decisions, based primarily on claims to technical expertise.

1. At least at the level of principle, there is little resistance to informed consent among doctors, nurses, or other health care personnel. Perhaps the single most striking piece of evidence is a 1979 replication of a 1961 study of what physicians told cancer patients, showing a remarkable shift from near unanimity in not informing patients of a cancer diagnosis in 1961 to near unanimity in informing patients in 1979 (Oken 1961, Novack et al 1979). Similarly, both a Harris survey commissioned by the President's Commission on Biomedical Ethics (Louis Harris 1982) and a survey of matched samples of patients and physicians drawn from three Midwestern states (Haug & Lavin 1983) show widespread support among physicians for informing patients.

Practice, however, is a different matter. The failures of informed consent are probably best documented in regard to termination of treatment. There, a large body of literature based on surveys, chart review, and direct observation shows that patients themselves participate in probably somewhat less than one fifth of the decisions. Although surrogates, typically family members, participate more, those surrogates usually follow the lead of physicians who are ill-equipped to predict the preferences of patients and are less inclined toward aggressive treatment than either patients or family members (Jayes et al 1993, Smedira et al 1990, Hanson et al 1994, Bedell & Delbanco 1984, Wren & Brody 1992, Danis et al 1991). Similar failures of informed consent have been reported in research settings (Gray 1975), adult intensive care units (Zussman 1992), neonatal intensive care units (Guilleman & Holmstrom 1986, Anspach 1993), and in both general medicine and general surgery (Lidz et al 1982, 1983, 1984). As a result, the practice of informed consent becomes a "ritual" of patient care (Bosk 1980, Lidz et al 1983, Zussman 1992) rather than the intended occasion for substantive discussion between doctor and patient.

2. Despite the support for informed consent among physicians, there is widespread indifference on the part of patients. Read carefully, both the Harris and Haug surveys show that physicians are more inclined to inform patients than patients are to ask for information. More specifically, drawing on field research and patients' accounts of their own illnesses, both Lidz and his colleagues (1982, 1983, 1984) and Schneider (1997) have shown that patients may want physicians to keep them informed as a matter of courtesy or to enable them better to comply with physicians' recommendations. Only rarely are patients interested in full participation in decision-making processes.

At the same time, clinical ethics often ignores those issues—even those moral issues—that most concern patients. As Schneider & Conrad (1983), Charmaz (1991), Kleinman (1988) and Frank (1995) have all argued, not only is informed consent at the periphery of patients' experience but so, too, is patienthood more generally, especially for those with chronic illness in remission. As Frank (1995, p. 156) has suggested, "the ethical questions for members of the remission society are not adjudications of health care conflicts but how to live a good life while being ill." As a result, the kind of moral thinking that is embedded in the narratives of selfhood constructed by those with chronic illness is largely ignored in the institutionalization of medical ethics.

3. There is considerable variation in the effectiveness of informed consent across settings. Informed consent has probably been most effective with human subjects in a research setting, but even there variations are significant. The intense participation of patients and the close relationships between those patients and researchers, described by Fox (1959) in her pioneering study of an experimental ward prior to the institutionalization of informed consent, probably represents a relatively rare situation. Stressing the more typical situation in which medical scientists leading large research teams are unconstrained by intense patient contact, Barber et al (1973) reported that a significant minority of researchers, driven by competition for recognition and reward, were at least prepared to ignore the mandates of conventional ethical standards. Gray (Gray 1975, Gray et al 1978, Gray & Osterweis 1986) has also reported that in most

research settings informed consent is treated casually and that, in a research study of labor-inducing drugs, many women "mostly with low levels of education . . . did not even realize they had been entered into a research project, notwithstanding their having signed a consent form" (1986, 547).

If informed consent is unevenly effective in research settings, the failures are even greater in clinical settings. Lidz and his colleagues (1982, 1983, 1984), in particular, have argued that, as a legal doctrine, informed consent embodies a set of assumptions that are ill-suited to medical practice. Thus, the doctrine of informed consent assumes that "medical practice is discrete—that is, broken into distinct parts, or decision units—and that there can be consent by the patient to each of these individual parts" (Lidz et al 1982, p. 401). This assumption may make some sense in medical research, which may involve both explicit protocols and explicit points at which patients can decide whether to participate. In contrast, in clinical practice, especially in internal medicine, decision-making is far less explicit and is incremental. Only in surgery, where procedures have clear starting points and where there is an explicit chain of command, does the practice of informed consent even approach a model of physicians disclosing information before patients "decide" what course to follow.

4. The ability of physicians to claim authority based on their possession of specialized technical knowledge contributes to the ineffectiveness of informed consent. This claim is addressed both to physicians themselves, in a largely unself-conscious effort to reconcile expressed belief with practice, and to patients. In neonatal intensive care units, Anspach (1993), Guilleman & Holmstrom (1986), and Levin (1990) have all shown that physicians more often ask parents to "assent to a decision members of the nursery have already made" than they treat parents as "the principal participants in the life-and-death decisions" (Anspach 1993, p. 87). Anspach argues that the "decision-making process itself is structured to limit and constrain parental participation" (92). Staff typically meet among themselves before meeting parents and then present a "united front," do not expose parents to the full range of treatment options, and frequently slant the prognosis depending on the course of action they have independently decided to follow. Moreover, staff "employ a set of strategies to persuade the parents to accept the staff's point of view" (96). The most common of these is an appeal to expert authority which includes (*a*) reviewing test results (thereby appealing to the authority of technology); (*b*) noting that the baby has failed to improve; (*c*) assuring the parents that the nursery has done everything in its power to help the baby; [and] (*d*) letting the parents know that the baby is being kept alive by artificial means (97).

The potential tension between the expressed principle of involving parents in decision-making and the actual practices is diffused, in part, by structural factors that limit physicians' contact with patients and, in part, by discounting the views of "unsophisticated" parents. The result is that it is physicians, not parents, who are the leading decision makers.

Zussman's (1992) study of two adult intensive care units yielded similar results. As in neonatal units, physicians typically express a principled acceptance of patients' and families' priority in matters of "values" as they bear on the general direction of treatment. However, physicians, in effect, neutralized the patient's or family's preferences by narrowing the range of decisions. By formulating decisions as technical rather than value-relevant issues, physicians demarcate decisions as within the proper realm of medical expertise. While neither the study of adult intensive care units nor studies of neonatal units deny that the doctrine of informed consent has empowered patients and their families, all show quite clearly that the empowerment of patients falls far short of expressed intentions.

There is, then, a more or less standard sociological critique of informed consent. It is not, however, a philosophical critique of principles. Quite the reverse, there is an implicit sympathy for both informed consent and the underlying value of autonomy. Rather, it is a critique of the viability of informed consent, based in a structural analysis of the cultural authority of medicine and the social structures that prevent patients from participating in decisions bearing on their own care.

### *Failures of Institutionalization: The Allocation of Scarce Resources*

Medical ethicists have probably written as much about "justice" as "autonomy." To be sure, medical ethicists have tended—although with some recent signs of change—to treat broad questions of health care policy as beyond their scope, limiting themselves instead to questions of justice embedded in clinical decisions. But they developed no overarching, guiding principle equivalent to informed consent. The closest, perhaps, is a principle of medical utility (Knaus 1983), based loosely on the military metaphor of battlefield triage (Teres 1989). But even here there is significant dissent (Annas 1985). For decisions about the allocation of dialysis, organ transplants, or intensive care beds, there are no court cases of impact equivalent to Quinlan and Cruzan. And, because of their more transparent relationship to policy and to competing interests, proposals to institutionalize methods of allocating scarce resources have found a very different audience from proposals for ensuring informed consent. [In a study of the impact of various national commissions on medical ethics, Gray (1995) found that those reports organized around informed consent are cited more often in both medical journals and court cases than those reports addressed to questions of allocation.] However, the rapid growth of managed care, accompanied by the potential conflicts such care raises between the financial interests of physicians and the health interests of patients, has recently placed the allocation of resources high on the agenda of medical ethicists. On these matters, then, sociologists have assumed a very different stance than in regard to informed consent. Rather than showing the limited effect of new policies on how decisions are made, the task in regard to the allocation of scarce resources has been to show how decisions are made in the absence of explicit policies.

There is not a single history of clinical decisions about the allocation of scarce resources so much as a series of discrete histories, each organized around a particular set of issues. Organ transplantation has proceeded in fits and starts, marked by frequent successes, occasional failures (the artificial heart, animal-to-human transplants), spurts of activity and clinical moratoria, massive public interest, and both the celebration and demonization of pioneers in the field. Dialysis, a life-sustaining treatment for those with what would otherwise be terminal kidney disease, flared briefly as a public controversy in the 1960s before the passage of special legislation making treatment available to essentially all who need it. The allocation of beds in intensive care units, both neonatal and adult, has never become a public issue, but with the cost of intensive care accounting for one percent of the nation's GNP, it is perhaps the most pervasive site of allocation decisions.

Striking as the differences are among dialysis, organ transplants, and intensive care units, sociologists have demonstrated a remarkable similarity in the inability of either physicians or advisory boards to impose limits on treatments. These points have been made particularly powerfully by Fox & Swazey (1978, 1992) in a series of studies conducted over a span of more than a quarter century. In *Spare Parts* and, particularly, in *The Courage to Fail*, they show the difficulty both physicians and lay advisory boards experienced in maintaining consistent, let alone ethically rigorous, policies for denying either organ transplants or dialysis. In neonatal units, Guilleman & Holmstrom (1986), Anspach (1993), and Levin (1990) all report a strong bias in favor of aggressive treatment, even for high-risk infants, and to the neglect of what might be far more cost-effective prenatal care. Similarly, Zussman (1992) reports the difficulty physicians in adult intensive care units experience attempting to deny expensive treatment even to patients likely to be "tortured" by expensive treatments and who have little significant chance of surviving their hospital stay. Only a desire on the part of house staff to protect their colleagues from difficult admissions—a consideration driven by a sense of mutual obligation to fellow professionals rather than by any systematic criteria of "justice"—introduces any incentive to control the allocation of beds.

Some part of this tendency to overtreatment is probably explained by a general tendency to aggressive treatment, deeply rooted in the culture of American medicine (Payer 1988). But an at least equally compelling explanation points to the structural characteristics of American medicine: in particular, the sprawling character of the American health care system which, whether in organ transplants or intensive care units, allows a great number of actors to share in decisions without assigning clear responsibility to any particular actor (Fox & Swazey 1992). In contrast to the "closed system" of British medicine, which operates within fixed budgets, as the philosopher Norman Daniels (1986) has pointed out, American physicians operate within an "open system" in which they have no assurance that savings incurred on one patient will remain within the health care system at all. Accustomed to concerning themselves with that which they can control, physicians concentrate on the individual case while neglecting collective consequences.

As much as physicians ignore the collective consequences of their individual clinical decisions, those consequences are real. In some instances, this involves decisions that taken individually are made on universalistic criteria but in aggregate are highly particularistic. In intensive care units (Zussman 1992), to continue one example, house staff accept a notion of collective consequences and consistently weigh the needs of patients against each other in admission and discharge decisions; in contrast, private physicians consistently act as advocates, pressing to admit their own patients to the unit without regard to competing claims for beds. Although each group of physicians follows more or less rigorous ethical standards, the aggregate result is that wealthier patients with a private physician to act as an advocate are more likely to enter and remain in an intensive care unit than are poorer, ward patients represented by house staff. In other instances, the collective consequences become articulated in a political arena. Fox & Swazey (1978), to continue another example, argue that the 1972 amendment to the Social Security Act, making dialysis available on a virtually universal basis, was a humane response to a horror at the denial of life-prolonging treatment to identifiable individuals. But the consequence, they argue, as the cost of the dialysis program became evident, was to undermine the political viability of more extensive proposals for catastrophic health insurance.

In contrast to the almost haphazard way in which allocation decisions have been made in other settings, the rise of prospective payment systems and managed care represent attempts to introduce systematic incentives—if not always systematic standards—for physicians to introduce resource considerations into their decision-making processes. Prospective payment refers to the effort to control spending by the establishment of fixed reimbursements for hospitals on the basis of diagnostic-related groupings (DRGs) rather than on the basis of costs incurred. Managed care is a general term referring to a wide variety of plans and organizations—including health maintenance organizations and preferred provider organizations—that provide some sort of review of physicians' decisions and, in some cases, financial incentives for physicians to limit care. Prospective payment on the basis of DRGs applies to hospital reimbursement rather than to physician reimbursement. As a result, although prospective payment has received a great deal of attention from health policy analysts, it has excited much less attention among medical ethicists focused on developing appropriate criteria for clinical decisions. In effect, prospective payment puts the physician in the position of a defender of the patient against a hospital with new incentives to limit both length of stays and intensity of treatment. Managed care, however, is different. By introducing sometimes direct financial incentives for physicians to limit care, managed care threatens the "fiduciary ethic" (that is, the primary responsibility of the physician to their patient's well being), which is the longstanding basis of physicians' claims to trustworthiness (Gray 1993, Morreim 1991, Wolfe 1994, Rodwin 1993)

Although there is not yet a great deal of sociological research on either DRGs or managed care, what research there is suggests that the effects of financial incentives, while powerful, are indirect. Gray (1993), for example, did not find a great deal of difference in the behavior of for-profit and not-for-profit organizations. Similarly, Hillman and his colleagues (1989) found that financial incentives are more powerful in group model HMOs than in independent physician associations, while Notman and his colleagues (1987) found that physicians reduced lengths of stay in response to the introduction of DRGs despite both a hostility to financial considerations and a lack of detailed knowledge of DRGs. Put somewhat differently, these findings suggest that physicians respond to financial incentives within a collective context rather than as income-maximizing individuals, that their responses are mediated by the networks of physicians in which they are embedded and possibly by long-term career contingencies.

To summarize, three points, at least, have recurred across a wide range of issues: 1. a recognition of the difficulty physicians have moving beyond individual clinical decisions to an understanding of the collective consequences of those decisions; 2. a recognition, often omitted from the discourse of medical ethics, of the complex and powerful set of social relations that shape decisions when they are made; 3. an insistence that, despite the indifference of physicians, those consequences are both real and powerful, the collective consequences of their individual decisions.

## *The Sociological Uses of Medical Ethics*

The critique of the institutionalization of medical ethics—both its successes and its failures—is distinctively sociological. But it is not unique to sociology, and it is a critique that responds to an agenda set more by medical ethicists, hospitals, and health professionals than by sociologists themselves. There is, however, another agenda that emerges much more clearly from sociologists themselves. This is, in part, a matter of using ethical issues in medicine as the site for exploring general, theoretical issues in sociology. Chambliss (1996), for example, examines nurses' views of life and death decisions as an instance of the routinization of moral judgment, as an example of how organizations make the extraordinary seem ordinary. Similarly, Anspach (1987, 1993) examines physicians' and nurses' differing responses to critically ill newborns in a neonatal intensive care units as an instance of the "ecology of knowledge," of the ways in which differential locations within an organization produce selective views of the same "reality." Only slightly farther afield, Bosk (1980) looks at the management of medical mistakes as an instance of responses to deviance more generally. And running through virtually all of the sociology of medical ethics are reflections on the social structure of occupations and professions.

In invoking sociological theory, I do not mean, however, to invoke the tired distinction between sociology in medicine and sociology of medicine (Strauss 1957). To be sure, there are significant differences between a sociology that follows the agenda of medicine (or medical ethics) and one that follows the theoretical agenda of its own discipline. But there is an alternative to either of these approaches: a sociology that looks at substantive issues in medicine but that does so in its own terms, with its own preoccupations, rather than following the lead of other disciplines.

Most fundamentally, the rise of institutionalized medical ethics has transformed the doctor-patient relationship. To be sure, the effects of efforts to empower patients seem limited at best: the ability of physicians to neutralize the newly won rights of patients through appeals to technical expertise are simply a specific instance, under conditions of unusually explicit challenge, of the more general process by which physicians dominate medical encounters (Waitzkin 1982, Fisher 1986). At the same time, however, the self-conscious application of law and policy to what was once a more private encounter makes clear how difficult it is to understand that relationship in terms of an ahistorical functionalism (Parsons 1951, Szasz & Hollander 1956). More specifically, the entrance of medical ethics into the doctor-patient relationship seems to be accelerating a movement to a more contractual model in which doctor and patient meet with a more limited set of obligations than was once the case (Zussman 1992, Fox & Swazey 1993, Zerubavel 1980).

The ethical issues accompanying the development of new reproductive technologies have also become a critical point for redefining the relationship, both substantive and symbolic, between women and medicine. Despite their frequent appearance in highly publicized court cases and in the quieter efforts of hospitals to develop protocols for their use, it is still far from clear how American medicine will treat genetic counseling, in vitro fertilization, and surrogate motherhood (Bosk 1992, Kolker & Burke 1994, Rothman 1986)—or how American women will respond to that treatment. Nonetheless, it is clear that each will become an arena in which the meaning of motherhood and the value of children will be fought out. Moreover, all suggest a remedicalization of pregnancy at precisely the moment that other trends are pushing toward its demedicalization.

So, too, medical ethics is the site at which a transformation in the meaning of death seems to be in process. The development of explicit procedures for terminating treatment seems to have ended the type of blatant discrimination between rich and poor, African-American and European-American, once reported by Sudnow (1967) as a pervasive feature of emergency room medicine (Crane 1975). More generally, though, DNR protocols have become the site for a redefinition of death as a loss of consciousness rather than a loss of physiological functioning. And, more generally yet, although death is surely still far from an integral part of hospital life, the very establishment of protocols for terminating treatment makes death more visible and thus helps undermines the extensive efforts hospitals once made to hide death by isolating the dying patient both psychically and physically (Glaser & Strauss 1965, Aries 1981).

Not least, the institutionalization of medical ethics is helping to transform the relationship among practitioners. If, as Freidson (1975) could once report, collegial oversight in medicine was both rare and exercised lightly, this is no longer so clearly the case. Although the rise of managed care is almost surely the major factor accounting for the extension of collegial control, the institutionalization of medical ethics provides a language in which this control may be put and a series of forums in which to do so.

Nowhere, though, are the sociological uses of medical ethics more apparent than in the analysis of nursing as an occupation. The rise of medical ethics has probably contributed less to a renewed sociological interest in nurses than has a feminist interest in a predominantly female occupation and perhaps a general tropism in sociology toward those without power (Anspach 1993, Brannon 1994, Chambliss 1996, Fisher 1995, Marrone 1995, Wolfe 1988, Fox et al 1990, Melosh 1982). Moreover, because nurses lack authority, they are less relevant to ethical decisions than are the physicians in whose shadows they work. If the point is simply to evaluate the effectiveness of institutionalized ethics, nurses are, for the most part, beside the point. But this is not the point. Rather, nurses' responses to ethical issues are interesting to sociologists precisely because nurses represent a different orientation to medical care than do physicians. In particular, they represent not only a less technical orientation to medical care but also what might be called an "ethics of care." Where physicians rely heavily—and, at times, almost exclusively—on diagnostic technologies, nurses represent a prognostic mode that draws more on the patient's participation in the type of interaction that can be observed or intuited only in the context of an ongoing relationship. While physicians' communication with patients is often oriented toward transmitting information or making specific decisions, nurses represent a style of communication with patients that is oriented more toward encouraging understanding. Where physicians are preoccupied with the process of cure and often indifferent to the patient's experience during that process, nurses represent a concern for care, particularly with the management of pain, emotional as well as physical. In all these senses, nurses represent an alternative to the kind of contractual model implicit in contemporary medical ethics. To be sure, sociologists have demonstrated uncertainty as to the reality of this ethos and even considerable ambivalence as to its desirability. Nonetheless, they have consistently used the discussion of an ethos of care as a means of raising issues that are more or less systematically ignored in medical ethicists. They have, in short, used nurses as a means of reaching beyond a medical ethics that is limited to specific, delimited decisions and toward what might be thought of as a medical morality that permeates the everyday as well as the unusual.

The sociology of medical ethics is not the same as medical ethics: It is more empirical, less normative, and, most importantly, sets its scope beyond an examination of the clinical decisions that preoccupy conventional medical ethicists. Much of the sociology directed most explicitly to medical ethics has contributed to a sympathetic critique of institutionalized procedures and policies meant to ensure ethical standards in clinical decisions. But the sociology of medical ethics, I have suggested, is at its best when it goes beyond clinical decisions to an examination of the structure of American medicine. I would argue, then, that the sociology of medical ethics is not—and should not be—about medical ethics so much as about the social organization of medicine more generally. Sociologists have long noted a remarkable cultural authority as one of the distinguishing marks of the medical profession (Freidson 1970, Starr 1982, Larson 1977, Conrad & Schneider 1980). The rise of institutionalized medical ethics—no matter how limited in practice—is both a symptom and source of a waning of that authority. Medical ethics, then, is new arena in which to make sense of new developments in old issues. This is, in part, a matter of reclaiming issues that have been formulated in narrowly ethical terms for a broader sociological agenda. But it is also, in part, a matter of treating the institutionalization of medical ethics as a source for an ongoing social transformation of American medicine. If the task of the sociology of medicine is to make sense of the doctor-patient relationship, the relationship between medicine and gender, the meaning of death and dying, and the character of medical professionalism, it cannot do so without paying attention to medical ethics.

*Literature Cited*


Annas GJ. 1985. The prostitute, the playboy, and the poet: rationing schemes for organ transplantation. *Am. J. Public Health* 75:187–89

Anspach R. 1987. Prognostic conflict in life-and-death decisions: the organization as an ecology of knowledge. *J. Health Soc. Behav.* 28:215–31

Anspach R. 1993. *Deciding Who Lives: Fateful Choices in the Intensive-Care Nursery.* Berkeley: Univ. Calif. Press

Aries P. 1981. *The Hour of Our Death.* New York: Knopf

Arras JD. 1991. Getting down to cases: the revival of casuistry in bioethics. *J. Med. Philos.* 16:29–51

Barber B, Lally J, Makarushka JL, Sullivan D. 1973. *Research on Human Subjects: Problems of Social Control in Medical Experimentation.* New York: Russell Sage. 263 pp.

Beauchamp T, Childress JF. 1979. *Principles of Biomedical Ethics.* New York: Oxford Univ. Press

Bedel SE, Delbanco TL. 1984. Choices about cardiopulmonary resuscitation in the hospital: When do physicians talk with patients? *N. Engl. J. Med.* 310:1089–93

Beecher HK. 1966. Ethics and clinical research. *N. Engl. J. Med.* 174:1354–60

Berlant JL. 1975. *Professional Monopoly: A Study of Medicine in the United States and Great Britain.* Berkeley: Univ. Calif. Press

Bosk CL. 1979. *Forgive and Remember: Managing Medical Failure.* Chicago: Univ. Chicago Press

Bosk CL. 1980. Occupational rituals in patient management. *N. Engl. J. Med.* 303:71–76

Bosk CL. 1992. *All God's Mistakes: Genetic Counselling in a Pediatric Hospital.* Chicago: Univ. Chicago Press. 195 pp.

Brannon RL. 1994. *Intensifying Care: The Hospital Industry, Professionalization, and the Reorganization of the Nursing Labor Process.* Amityville, NY: Baywood. 185 pp.

Callahan D. 1987. *Setting Limits: Medical Goals in an Aging Society.* New York: Simon & Schuster. 256 pp.

Chambliss DF. 1996. *Beyond Caring: Hospitals, Nurses and the Social Organization of Ethics.* Chicago: Univ. Chicago Press

Charmaz K. 1991. *Good Days, Bad Days: The Self and Time in Chronic Illness.* New Brunswick, NJ: Rutgers Univ. Press. 311 pp.

Childress J. 1990. The place of autonomy in bioethics. *Hastings Cent. Rep.* 20:12–17

Conrad P, Schneider J. 1980. *Deviance and Medicalization.* St. Louis: Mosby

Crane D. 1975. *The Sanctity of Social Life.* New York: Russell Sage

Crigger BJ. 1995. Bioethnography: fieldwork in the lands of medical ethics. *Med. Anthropol. Q.* 9:400–17

Daniels N. 1986. Why saying no to patients in the United States is so hard. *N. Engl. J. Med.* 314:1380–83

Danis M, Southerland LI, Garrett J, Smith JL, Hielema F, et al. 1991. A prospective study of advance directives for life-sustaining care. *N. Engl. J. Med.* 324:882–88

Duff R, Hollingshead A. 1968. *Sickness and Society.* New York: Harper & Row

Duff RS, Campbell AGM. 1973. Moral and ethical dilemmas in the special care nursery. *N. Engl. J. Med.* 289:890–94

Faden RR, Beauchamp TL. 1986. *A History and Theory of Informed Consent.* New York: Oxford Univ. Press

Fisher S. 1986. *In The Patient's Best Interest: Women and the Politics of Medical Decisions.* New Brunswick, NJ: Rutgers Univ. Press. 214 pp.

Fisher S. 1995. *Nursing Wounds: Nurse Practitioners, Doctors, Women Patients and the Negotiation of Meaning.* New Brunswick, NJ: Rutgers Univ. Press. 259 pp.

Fletcher J. 1954. *Morals and Medicine.* Princeton, NJ: Princeton Univ. Press

Fox R. 1959. *Experiment Perilous.* Glencoe, IL: Free Press

Fox R. 1989. *The Sociology of Medicine.* Englewood Cliffs, NJ: Prentice Hall

Fox RC. 1990. The evolution of American bioethics: a sociological perspective. In *Social Science Perspectives on Medical Ethics,* ed. G Weiss, pp. 201–17. Dordrecht: Kluwer

Fox RC, Aiken LH, Messikomer CM. 1990. The culture of caring: AIDS and the nursing profession. *Milbank Q.* 68:226–56

Fox RC, Swazey JP. 1978. *The Courage to Fail.* Chicago: Univ. Chicago Press. 2nd ed.

Fox RC, Swazey JP. 1984. Medical morality is not bioethics—medical ethics in China and the United States. *Perspect. Biol. Med.* 27:336–60

Fox RC, Swazey JP. 1992. *Spare Parts: Organ Replacement in American Society.* New York: Oxford Univ. Press. 254 pp.

Frank AW. 1995. *The Wounded Storyteller: Body, Illness, and Ethics.* Chicago: Univ. Chicago Press. 213 pp.

Freidson E. 1970. *Profession of Medicine.* New York: Harper & Row

Freidson E. 1975. *Doctoring Together: A Study*

*of Professional Social Control.* Chicago: Univ. Chicago Press
Glaser B, Strauss A. 1965. *Awareness of Dying.* Chicago: Aldine
Gray BH. 1975. *Human Subjects in Medical Experimentation: A Sociological Study of the Conduct and Regulation of Clinical Research.* New York: Wiley Intersci.
Gray BH. 1993. *The Profit Motive and Patient Care: The Changing Accountability of Doctors and Hospitals.* Cambridge: Harvard Univ. Press
Gray BH. 1995. Bioethics commissions: What can we learn from past successes and failures? In *Society's Choices: Social and Ethical Decision Making in Medicine*, ed. RE Bulger, EM Bobby, HV Fineberg, pp. 261–305. Washington, DC: Natl. Acad. Press. Inst. Med.
Gray BH, Cooke RA, Tannenbaum AS. 1978. Research involving human subjects. *Science* 201:1094–101
Gray BH, Osterweis M. 1986. Ethical issues in a social context. In *Applications of Social Science to Clinical Medicine and Health Policy,* ed. LG Aiken, D Mechanic, pp. 543–64. New Brunswick, NJ: Rutgers Univ. Press
Gray BH, Phillips SR. 1995. Medical sociology and health policy: Where are the connections? *JHSB* (Extra Issue):170–82
Guilleman JH, Holmstrom LL. 1986. *Mixed Blessings: Intensive Care for Newborns.* New York: Oxford Univ. Press
Hanson LC, Danis M, Mutran E, Keenan N. 1994. Impact of patient incompetence on decisions to use or withhold life-sustaining treatment. *Am. J. Med.* 97:235–41
Harris L, & Associates. 1982. Views of informed consent and decisionmaking: parallel surveys of physicians and the public. In *President's Commission for the Study of Ethical Problems in Medicine and Biomedical and Behavioral Research, Making Health Care Decisions.* Vol. 2. *Appendices, Empirical Studies of Informed Consent,* pp. 17–314. Washington, DC: USGPO
Haug MR, Lavin B. 1983. *Consumerism in Medicine.* Beverly Hills, CA: Sage
Hillman AL, Pauly MV, Kerstein J. 1989. How do financial incentives affect physicians' clinical decisions and the financial performance of health maintenance organizations? *N. Engl. J. Med.* 321:86–92
Hoffmaster B. 1992. Can ethnography save the life of medical ethics? *Soc. Sci. Med.* 35:1421–31
Jayes RL, Zimmerman JE, Wagner DP, Draper EA, Knaus WA. 1993. Do-not-resuscitate orders in intensive care units: current practices and recent changes. *J. Am. Med. Assoc.* 270:2213–17
Jones JH. 1981. *Bad Blood: The Tuskegee Syphilis Experiment.* New York: Free Press. 272 pp.
Kass LR. 1990. Practicing ethics: Where's the action? *Hastings Cent. Rep.* 20:5–12
Katz J. 1984. *The Silent World of Doctor and Patient.* New York: Free Press
Kleinman A. 1988. *The Illness Narratives: Suffering, Healing, and the Human Condition.* New York: Basic Books
Knaus W, Draper E, Wagner D. 1983. The use of intensive care: new research initiatives and their implications for national health policy. *Milbank Mem. Fund Q.* 61:561–83
Kolker A, Burke BM. 1994. *Prenatal Testing: A Sociological Perspective.* Westport, CT: Bergin & Garvey. 221 pp.
Larson MS. 1977. *The Rise of Professionalism.* Berkeley: Univ. Calif. Press
Levin BW. 1990. International perspectives on treatment choice in neonatal nurseries. *Soc. Sci. Med.* 30:901–12
Lidz CW, Meisel A, Holden JL, Marx JH, Munetz M. 1982. Informed consent and the structure of medical care. In *President's Commission for the Study of Ethical Problems in Medicine and Biomedical and Behavioral Research, Making Health Care Decisions.* Vol. 2. *Appendices, Empirical Studies of Informed Consent,* pp. 317–410. Washington, DC: USGPO
Lidz CW, Meisel A, Osterweis M, Holden JL, Marx JH, Munetz M. 1983. Barriers to informed consent. *Ann. Intern. Med.* 99:539–43
Lidz CW, Meisel A, Zerubavel E, Carter M, Sestak M, Roth L. 1984. *Informed Consent.* New York: Guilford
Marrone C. 1995. *Home again: professional and patient responsibilities in home health care nursing.* PhD Diss., Dep. Sociol., State Univ. New York-Stony Brook. Unpublished
Melosh B. 1982. *The Physician's Hand.* Philadelphia: Temple Univ. Press
Morreim EH. 1991. *Balancing Act: The New Medical Ethics of Medicine's New Economics.* Boston: Kluwer Acad.
Munson R. 1988. *Intervention and Reflection: Basic Issues in Medical Ethics.* Belmont, CA: Wadsworth. 3rd ed. 602 pp.
National Commission for the Protection of Human Subjects of Biomedical and Behavioral Research. 1978. *The Belmont Report: Ethical Principles and Guidelines for the Protection of Human Subjects in Research.* Washington, DC: USGPO
Notman M, Howe KR, Rittenberg W, Bridgham R, Holmes MR, Rovner DR. 1987. Social policy and professional self-interest: physician responses to DRGs. *Soc. Sci. Med.* 25:1259–67

Novack DH, Plumer R, Smith RL, Ochitill H, Morrow GD, Bennett JM. 1979. Changes in physicians' attitudes toward telling the cancer patient. *JAMA* 241:897–900

Oken D. 1961. What to tell cancer patients. *JAMA* 175:1120–28

Parsons T. 1951. *The Social System.* Glencoe, IL: Free Press

Payer L. 1988. *Medicine and Culture.* New York: Penguin

Peralman RA, Miles SH, Arnold RM. 1993. Contributions of empirical research to medical ethics. *Theor. Med.* 14:197–210

Pernick MS. 1982. The patient's role in medical decisionmaking: a social history of informed consent in medical therapy. In *President's Commission for the Study of Ethical Problems in Medicine and Biomedical and Behavioral Research. 1982. Making Health Care Decisions.*Vol. 3. *Appendices, Studies on the Foundations of Informed Consent,* pp. 1–35. Washington, DC: USGPO

President's Commission for the Study of Ethical Problems in Medicine and Biomedical and Behavioral Research. 1982. *Making Health Care Decisions.* Vol. 1. *Report, The Ethical and Legal Implications of Informed Consent in the Patient-Practitioner Relationship.* Washington, DC: USGPO

President's Commission for the Study of Ethical Problems in Medicine and Biomedical and Behavioral Research. 1983. Seriously ill newborns. In *Deciding to Forego Life-Sustaining Treatment: Ethical, Medical and Legal Issues in Treatment Decisions,* pp. 197–230. Washington, DC: USGPO

Rabkin MT, Gillerman G, Rice NR. 1976. Orders not to resuscitate. *N. Engl. J. Med.* 295:364–66

Ramsey P. 1970. *The Patient as Person.* New Haven: Yale Univ. Press

Rodwin MA. 1993. *Medicine, Money, and Morals: Physicians' Conflicts of Interest.* New York: Oxford Univ. Press

Rothman BK. 1986. *The Tentative Pregnancy.* New York: Viking

Rothman BK. 1989. *Recreating Motherhood: Ideology and Technology in a Patriarchal Society.* New York: Norton

Rothman D. 1991. *Strangers at the Bedside.* New York: Basic Books

Ruzek SB. 1979. *The Women's Health Movement: Feminist Alternatives to Medical Control.* New York: Praeger. 350 pp.

Schneider CE. 1997. *Patients, Doctors, and Decisions: Rethinking Autonomy.* New York: Oxford Univ. Press. In press

Schneider JW, Conrad P. 1983. *Having Epilepsy: The Experience and Control of Illness.* Philadelphia: Temple Univ. Press. 280 pp.

Smedira NG, Evans BH, Grais LS, Cohen NH, Lo B, et al. 1990. Withholding and withdrawal of life support from the critically ill. *N. Engl. J. Med.* 322:309–15

Starr P. 1982. *The Social Transformation of American Medicine.* New York: Basic Books

Strauss R. 1957. The nature and status of medical sociology. *Am. Sociol. Rev.* 22:200–4

Sudnow D. 1967. *Passing On: The Social Organization of Dying.* Englewood Cliffs, NJ: Prentice-Hall

Szasz T, Hollander M. 1956. Thomas Szasz and Marc Hollander: basic models of the doctor-patient relationship. *Arch. Intern. Med.* 97:585–92

Teres D. 1989. Triage: an everyday occurrence in the intensive care unit. In *Rationing of Medical Care for the Critically Ill,* ed. MA Strosberg, IA Fein, JD Carroll, pp. 70–75. Washington, DC: Brookings Inst.

Veatch R. 1976. *Death, Dying and the Biological Revolution.* New Haven: Yale Univ. Press

Waitzkin H. 1987. *The Politics of Medical Encounters: How Patients and Doctors Deal with Social Problems.* New Haven: Yale Univ. Press. 311 pp.

Wolf ZR. 1988. *Nurse's Work, the Sacred and the Profane.* Philadelphia: Univ. Penn. Press

Wolfe SM. 1994. Health care reform and the future of physician ethics. *Hastings Cent. Rep.* 24:28–41

Wren K, Brody SL. 1992. The do-not-resuscitate order in the emergency department. *Am. J. Med.* 92:129–33

Zerubavel E. 1980. The bureaucratization of responsibility: the case of informed consent. *Bull. Am. Acad. Psychiatr. Law* 8:161–67

Zussman R. 1992. *Intensive Care: Medical Ethics and the Medical Profession.* Chicago: Univ. Chicago Press

*Annu. Rev. Sociol. 1997. 23:191–214*


# SOCIOLOGICAL RATIONAL CHOICE THEORY

*Michael Hechter*
Department of Sociology, University of Arizona, Tucson, Arizona 85721;
e-mail: hechter@u.arizona.edu

*Satoshi Kanazawa*
Department of Sociology, Uris Hall, Cornell University, Ithaca,
New York 14853-7601; e-mail: Satoshi.Kanazawa@cornell.edu

KEY WORDS: macrosociology, micro-macro link, general theory, empirical research

ABSTRACT

Although rational choice theory has made considerable advances in other social sciences, its progress in sociology has been limited. Some sociologists' reservations about rational choice arise from a misunderstanding of the theory. The first part of this essay therefore introduces rational choice as a general theoretical perspective, or family of theories, which explains social outcomes by constructing models of individual action and social context. "Thin" models of individual action are mute about actors' motivations, while "thick" models specify them ex ante. Other sociologists' reservations, however, stem from doubts about the empirical adequacy of rational choice explanations. To this end, the bulk of the essay reviews a sample of recent studies that provide empirical support for particular rational choice explanations in a broad spectrum of substantive areas in sociology. Particular attention is paid to studies on the family, gender, and religion, for these subareas often are considered least amenable to understanding in terms of rational choice logic.

## INTRODUCTION

In the last decade rational choice theory has gained influence and visibility in many of the social sciences and in related disciplines such as philosophy and law. To appreciate just how rapidly its influence has spread, consider political



0360-0572/97/0815-0191$08.00

science, a discipline in many respects similar to sociology. According to one estimate, the proportion of articles based on rational choice premises published in the *American Political Science Review* rose from zero in 1957 to nearly 40% in 1992 (Green & Shapiro 1994, p. 3). Job candidates specializing in rational choice now command a hefty premium in American political science departments.

Given its own disciplinary history, which is often characterized in relentlessly holistic terms, sociology would appear to be a most unpromising terrain for the spread of rational choice ideas and methods. Indeed, resistance to the approach has been notable (Baron & Hannan 1994, Petersen 1994). No American sociology department currently specializes in rational choice; only one even offers its graduate students a concentration in it. No jobs are listed for specialists in the area. This is in contrast to the situation in Western Europe, particularly in the Netherlands, Germany, and Sweden, where rational choice is considerably more institutionalized.

Yet many sociologists, like the character in Moliére's *Bourgeois Gentilhomme* who was startled to learn that he was speaking prose, unwittingly rely on rational choice mechanisms in their own research. Signs of the growing acceptance of sociological versions of rational choice can be found in the establishment of the journal *Rationality and Society*, and in the regular proceedings of lively sections devoted to the approach in both the American and the International Sociological Associations meetings.

Some of the skepticism about rational choice among sociologists arises from misunderstanding. One criticism of rational choice focuses on the lack of realism in its assumption that we calculate the expected consequences of our options and choose the best of them. A vast body of social research reveals that people often act impulsively, emotionally, or merely by force of habit. Think how agonizing decisions about jobs, spouses, and children can be. Were people the informed and calculating agents that rational choice theorists assume them to be, such decisions would not be particularly wrenching. Since these choices often take an emotional toll, it is easy to conclude that the theory is implausible.

This conclusion, however, rests on a common misconception about the nature of rational choice. The theory does not aim to explain what a rational person will do in a particular situation. That question lies firmly in the domain of decision theory. Genuine rational choice theories, by contrast, are concerned exclusively with social rather than individual outcomes. Given that each individual acts rationally, will the aggregate outcome therefore be "rational" or desirable? Not necessarily. Regarded as stable equilibria, in which agents have no incentive to deviate from their course of action, given others' behavior, social outcomes can be both unintended and undesirable. The overgrazing of the commons is a classic example of this dark side of Adam Smith's invisible hand.

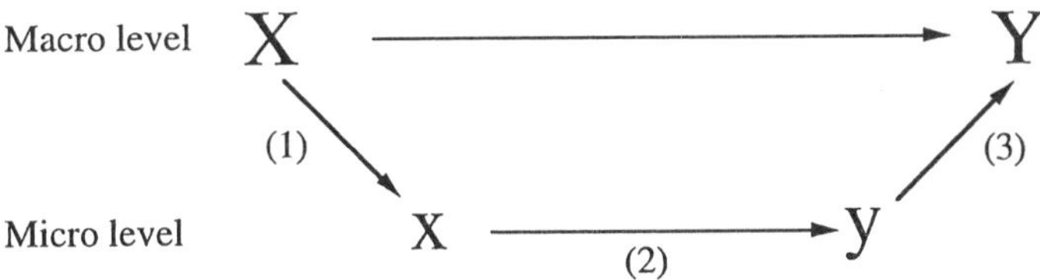


*Figure 1* The multilevel structure of rational choice explanations (after Coleman 1990, p. 8).

Unlike decision theory, rational choice theory is inherently a multilevel enterprise (Figure 1). At the lower level, its models contain assumptions about individual cognitive capacities and values, among other things. Relation (2), for example, describes how a person who is subject to a given social structure at $T_1$ will behave at $T_2$ on the basis of these assumptions. Whereas relation (2) is necessary, it is far from the whole story. At the higher level, rational choice models also contain specifications of social structures. These social structures serve both as the social and material context (X) for individual action, and as new structures (Y) resulting from the actions of individuals whose behavior is described by the lower level assumptions (Coleman 1990, pp. 1–23). Since norms and other kinds of institutions enter the models both as contexts for and as outcomes of action, rational choice theories do not rest on premises pertaining exclusively to individuals.

A second criticism of rational choice focuses on its motivational assumptions. Rational choice theorists regard both individual values and structural elements as equally important determinants of outcomes, but for methodological reasons their empirical applications typically place greater emphasis on social structural determinants. In consequence, rational choice explanations often are consistent with those of other general perspectives, such as structuralism and network analysis, that are usually regarded as lying well within the sociological mainstream (Goldthorpe 1996). One source of this methodological predilection lies in concerns about measurement. Values and other internal states are far more difficult to measure than structural constraints, which are external to individuals (Hechter 1992). Measuring values from the verbal responses to direct survey questions is problematic (Fischhoff 1991). Some progress in measuring values is being made, however. For example, matching models (Logan 1996a) offer one means of measuring individual values indirectly without relying on peoples' responses to questions about their own internal states.

The treatment of values in rational choice theory is due not only to methodological considerations; it is also a reaction to the complexity that is inherent in the multilevel nature of the theory. To reduce this complexity to more manageable limits, rational choice theorists assume some model of individual action, often one based on subjective-expected utility theory. They disagree about the most appropriate model, however. And so rational choice is more a rubric or a family of theories than a single all-encompassing one.

Perhaps the most important division separates "thin" and "thick" models of individual action (Ferejohn 1991; for a fuller discussion of the differences between rational choice theories, see Goldthorpe's unpublished paper "Rational Action Theory for Sociology"). Thin rational choice models are unconcerned with the particular values (or goals) which individuals pursue. These models are based on a small number of strong assumptions: for example, that whatever an individual's values may be, they must be stable and transitive (if someone prefers a to b, and b to c, they must prefer a to c). Rational choice theories based on thin models—such as those usually found in economics and social choice theory—are highly universalistic and to that extent resemble theories in physics and biology concerning the optimal behavior of atoms and organisms.

Thick models of individual action, advocated long ago by Max Weber, are substantively richer, for they countenance some aspects of intentionality. Since people have reasons for what they do, their behavior is predictable only if we know what motivates them. Thick models therefore specify the individual's existing values and beliefs. There are several means of doing so, but the most popular strategy has been to assume that individuals seek maximum quantities of exchangeable private goods such as wealth and, arguably, power or prestige. Wealth is commonly valued because it can be exchanged for a multitude of other goods in the marketplace. Thick models allow that individuals also value nonexchangeable goods—that some people live for the music of Mozart, and others for the thrill of horse racing. Indeed, the models assume that for any given individual, idiosyncratic values of this sort can outweigh the common one. Hence, without knowing each person's unique value hierarchy, individual behavior is unpredictable. As the size of groups increases, however, these idiosyncratic values tend to cancel each other out. In many circumstances the remaining common value permits quite accurate behavioral predictions at the collective level (Hechter 1994). Some rational choice theories specify other common values that individuals pursue, such as uncertainty reduction (Friedman, Hechter & Kanazawa 1994), local status (Frank 1985), and distributive justice (Jasso 1990, 1993). Other rational choice theories are beginning to model the processes that might be responsible for the formation of these common values (Becker 1996, Chai forthcoming).

Contrary to some perceptions (England & Kilbourne 1990, pp. 160–61), thick rational choice theories do not necessarily assume that individuals are selfish agents. These theories can postulate any individual values at all, not excluding complete altruism. What is required is merely that individuals are self-interested, not selfish (Friedman & Diem 1990).

Thin models are substantively empty. They can be made consistent after the event, therefore, with nearly any kind of behavior. Thick ones—such as those postulating wealth-maximization—often are just plain wrong. To the degree that the idiosyncratic values are not distributed randomly in a population, explanations based on the pursuit of exchangeable private goods such as wealth, power, and prestige will fail. Since outcomes may be partially a function of individual motivations, predictions made on the basis of thick models can be mutually inconsistent. Such inconsistencies can only be resolved on the basis of empirical evidence. That decision theorists can routinely invalidate subjective expected utility theory is also troubling, even if they have yet to formulate an alternative superior to it. All told, the mechanisms of individual action in rational choice theory are descriptively problematic. Is a theory of higher-level outcomes invalidated by the inaccuracy of its lower-level mechanisms? Rational-choice theorists deny that it is (see Hechter 1996).

Not all sociological reservations about rational choice derive from misunderstanding, however. Above all, rational choice is a theory-driven enterprise: Many authors seem to value formal proofs of theories more than the confirmation of these theories on the basis of rigorous empirical tests. Advocates often argue on its behalf, with not a little hauteur, by asserting that rational choice is the best available general theory in the social sciences. Since theories ultimately are judged by their capacity to account for empirical observations, the criticism (levelled by Green & Shapiro 1994, among others) that many rational choice theories are either false or remain untested cuts close to the bone.

The appeal of rational choice in sociology is unlikely to increase substantially until the approach provides demonstrable empirical payoffs in a wide variety of substantive areas. In what follows, we review a sample of empirical applications of rational choice in sociology published in English since 1988, when the last survey of the contributions of rational choice to macrosociology appeared (Friedman & Hechter 1988, pp. 204–11). Whereas most of these are explicitly derived from rational choice premises, we also discuss several theoretically unmotivated studies that report findings consistent with rational choice. Inclusion of this latter category of studies may be questioned. After all, if such studies can be carried out without reference to rational choice, then why is the theory necessary? One answer is that rational choice provides a heuristic framework that permits the diverse findings in all of these fields to be unified. Another is that it aids in making the logical links between different theories more explicit. Finally, readers should be aware that this essay is not a survey of sociological rational choice in its entirety, for it ignores the purely theoretical developments that continue to make up the bulk of research in this field (Coleman 1990 is the most important of these).

## RECENT EMPIRICAL APPLICATIONS OF SOCIOLOGICAL RATIONAL CHOICE

Many critics readily concede that rational choice may be appropriate for the analysis of voluntary exchanges in the Gesellschaft, which constitutes the traditional terrain of economics. However, they contend that it can shed little or no light on social relations in the Gemeinschaft—those involving the family, religion, and gender. For this reason, we begin our review with recent applications in these areas.

### *The Family and Demography*

The family was once thought to fall outside the purview of rational choice (Sen 1983) because this primordial institution (Coleman 1993) engenders hot motivations—love and hate—rather than cold benefit/cost calculations. In a number of influential writings, Becker (1974, 1981) questioned the wisdom of dividing social relations into separate domains, each requiring its own distinctive analysis (Abell 1991). Following his lead, rational choice now is routinely applied to individuals' family decisions.

Two recent programmatic statements in this subarea resonate strongly with rational choice. The concept of "family adaptive strategies" (Moen & Wethington 1992) captures the notion of choice under constraints (with the family as the unit of decision-making) in life course studies in sociology. Likewise, Smith (1989) calls for a multilevel analysis of fertility. Many of the findings in the empirical literature are entirely consistent with rational choice theories. For example, Lloyd & South (1996) show that, net of individual characteristics, men's transition to first marriage is strongly influenced by the structural constraints they face, in the form of the availability of prospective partners in the local marriage market. South & Lloyd (1995) demonstrate that the aggregate divorce rates fluctuate with the structural opportunities available to spouses; the quantity and quality of potential new marital partners in the local marriage market significantly increase the risk of marital dissolution. This substantiates Becker's (1974, pp. S21–S23) suspicion that men and women continue to search for mates even while they are married. Together, these studies indicate that marriage and divorce are subject to the same external opportunities and constraints as exchanges in the market.

Other research exemplifying how structural factors shape individual behavior and social outcomes (relations 1 and 2 in Figure 1) includes Brewster's (1994, Brewster et al 1993) study of community effects on adolescent sexual activities; Lee et al's (1994) analysis of the neighborhood effects on residential mobility; Hoem's (1991) demonstration of the impact of legal changes on marriage rates in Sweden; and Hoem's (1993) findings concerning the effects of legal incentives on childbearing.

In contrast to marriage and divorce, standard microeconomic explanations of parenthood in the postindustrial age have not fared so well empirically. Prior to industrialization and the implementation and enforcement of child labor laws, having children made ample economic sense to parents. But why do individuals in the postindustrial age continue to have children when their net economic benefit for doing so is negative? Friedman et al (1994) propose a theory of uncertainty reduction to account for parenthood in advanced industrial societies. They argue that children in the postindustrial age serve as a means to reduce uncertainty for women and couples, and they predict that those who face greater uncertainty in their lives and/or lack alternative means to reduce uncertainty are more likely to become parents. This theory has been largely supported in its first empirical test (Wu 1996).

Once people decide to have children, when do they stop? Yamaguchi & Ferguson (1995) explain rates of stopping and spacing childbearing by assuming that parents derive higher value from having children of both sexes than from having those of a single sex. Thus they predict that parents with two boys or two girls are more likely to have a third child than are parents of a boy and a girl, and the conclusions of their analysis of census data are consistent with this prediction.

In addition to its contributions to the study of fertility, rational choice has also been applied to migration. Jasso & Rosenzweig (1990) study immigration to the United States as a matching process. On the one hand, potential immigrants must decide to emigrate from their countries of origin and choose a country of destination. On the other, host countries evaluate potential immigrants on a set of criteria and decide whom to welcome (Jasso 1988). Successful legal immigration takes place only when there is a match between the self-selective immigration decisions of foreign-born persons and the eligibility-conferring decisions of the host nations (Jasso & Rosenzweig 1990, p. 7). Immigration therefore is a process of matching between two sets of actors, each attempting to achieve goals and operating under constraints created by the other.

Because migration should entail some loss of social capital (Coleman 1990), parental support ought to be crucial for the life prospects of children subsequent to family migration. Hagan et al (1996) analyze the mobility histories of Toronto families and find support for Coleman's expectation that the negative effects of migration are more significant in families with uninvolved fathers and unsupportive mothers. (See Farkas 1996 for a comprehensive study of the effects of social and cultural capital on individuals' achievements.)

### *Religion*

Religion is another subject once deemed unpromising for rational choice analysis. This has not prevented the development of a lively rational choice literature about it, however (Stark et al 1996; Warner 1993 is a comprehensive review).

The rational choice approach to religion draws a close analogy between religion and the market economy (Stark & Bainbridge 1985, 1987, Young 1997). It conceives of a religious economy consisting of religious firms and religious consumers. Religious firms compete against one another to offer religious products and services to consumers, who choose between the firms. Stark & Bainbridge (1987) extend this analogy and offer a large number of propositions concerning the religious economy.

They argue, for example, that the more pluralistic a religious economy is, the higher the level of religious mobilization. To the extent that there are many religious firms competing against each other, they will tend to specialize and cater to the particular needs of some segments of religious consumers. This specialization and catering in turn increase the number of religious consumers actively engaged in the religious economy. This proposition has been confirmed in a number of empirical studies. A positive correlation between pluralism and religious mobilization and commitment has been found in 17 Western nations (Iannaccone 1991), in 45 Catholic nations (finding an inverse relationship between Catholic monopoly and Catholic commitment) (Stark 1992), in 150 largest US cities in 1906 (Finke & Stark 1988), in 942 towns and cities in New York State from 1855 to 1865 (Finke et al 1996), and in 284 municipalities in Sweden (Hamberg & Pettersson 1994). Further, just as state regulation makes for inefficient business firms, state regulation of religion also makes for inefficient religious firms and dampens the mobilization of religious consumers (Chaves & Cann 1992).

It is well known that strict churches are strong and growing in the contemporary United States, whereas liberal ones are declining (Kelley 1972). For Iannaccone (1992, 1994) religious experience is a jointly produced collective good. Thus members of a church face a collective action problem. Strict churches, which often impose costly and esoteric requirements on their members, are able to solve this problem by weeding out potential free riders, since only the very committed would join the church in the face of such requirements. Finke & Stark (1992) use this theory to account for the winners and losers in the history of the religious economy of the United States. Consistent with the notion that religious experience is a collective good, Iannaccone et al (1995) show that churches that extract more resources from their members (in the form of time and money) tend to grow in membership.

### *Gender*

Although critics (Ferber & Nelson 1993, Risman & Ferree 1995) have claimed that rational choice is oblivious to gender distinctions, and therefore is unable to account for female behavior, here, too, there is disconfirming evidence

(Friedman & Diem 1990, 1993). Thus Brinton (1993) explains persistent gender inequalities in Japan partly as a function of parents' (mostly mothers') calculated decisions to invest more in their sons' education than in their daughters'. Due to the absence of a reliable social security system and the continued importance of a patrilineal family system, Japanese parents are financially dependent on their sons in their old age. This gives parents an interest in raising financially secure sons. By contrast, daughters will be incorporated into other families. Brinton (1989) also explains the disparity in educational attainment between Japanese men and women in rational choice terms. Japanese employers tend not to hire university-educated women because they have very few years left to work for the company before they invariably retire to get married at around age 25 (Brinton 1992). University-educated women thus represent poorer investment prospects for the company than women with high school or junior college education who leave school at an earlier age and also can be hired at lower wage rates. Given these constraints imposed by the employers, most Japanese women choose not to pursue a university education. In a study that addresses occupational specialization by gender, Cowen (1996), an economist, seeks to explain why so few women have become famous painters in history. His evidence shows women were discouraged from pursuing careers in the visual arts by the constraints of marriage and childbearing.

Supporting Hechter (1987), and later Friedman et al (1994, Hypothesis S-1), Treas (1993) demonstrates that a "collectivized" financial arrangement among married couples (joint bank accounts without separate ones for husbands and wives), which increases the financial dependence of the spouses on their marriage, is strongly associated with more stable unions. The general conclusion of Treas's study of married couples' financial organization is that principles of transaction cost economics accurately describe the choices of both husbands and wives. Treas & Giesen's (1996) analysis of a national probability sample from the National Health and Social Life Survey shows that, while men are more likely to have extramarital affairs than women, identical considerations of opportunities, costs, and benefits underlie both men's and women's decision to engage in illicit sex.

Mackie (1996) offers an intriguing explanation for the varying fates of two institutions affecting women in less developed societies. Whereas female genital mutilation persists in Africa despite modernization, public education, and legal prohibition, female footbinding lasted for a thousand years in China but ended in a single generation. Mackie argues that each institution is a self-enforcing convention maintained by interdependent expectations on the marriage market. Footbinding in China was overturned by the establishment of associations of parents who pledged not to footbind their daughters nor let their sons marry footbound women. Such pledge associations have not been established in Africa, however, and female genital mutilation persists there.

## *Organizations*

At least since Coase (1937), rational choice analyses of organizations have proliferated. Since most of the research on capitalist firms is conducted by economists, it is not reviewed here. However, some sociologists have also made contributions. Thus Petersen (1992) analyzes the earnings of 63,000 salespersons in 178 department stores and finds that those who work under output-related payment systems (and receive either straight commission or salary plus commission) earn considerably more than those who work under non-output-related payment systems (and receive straight salary alone). Workers in the former system earn more because they are individually rewarded for working harder, while those under the latter system do not because they have no incentive to work harder. (For another analysis of the capitalist firm, see Raub & Keren 1993.)

Hedström (1994) combines rational choice with network analysis to explain the spatial diffusion of labor unions in Sweden from 1890 to 1940. Individuals' decisions to form a labor union are influenced not only by their expectations of what others will do, but also by their knowledge of what others in their immediate network have done in the past. As anticipated, both spatial properties of the network and its density turn out to be important determinants of the speed and success of labor union formation. Brüderl et al (1993) explain career mobility in a large West German company in terms of the organizational structure and hierarchies, and Greve (1994) similarly explains job mobility in Norway in terms of organizational diversity.

Haveman (1995, Haveman & Cohen 1994) uses the characteristics of the industry and organizational ecology at the meso level to account for individual careers and job turnover at the micro level, which then aggregate to tenure distributions at the organizational level. Her work therefore exemplifies the multilevel causal structure (albeit meso-micro in this case) typical of rational choice theory. Abell (1988, 1990) studies industrial producer cooperatives in Tanzania, Sri Lanka, and Fiji and concludes that the key to their success lies in support organizations. While agricultural and commercial sectors have distinct capital advantages over the industrial sector in these developing nations, these established sectors have no compelling incentive to promote cooperatives. Abell & Mahoney (1988) examine similar cooperatives in India, Peru, and Senegal and note that one of the determinants of their success in these countries is the solidarity, whether exogenously or endogenously produced, of cooperative members.

Other rational choice sociologists focus on noncapitalist firms and on unconventional organizations like urban and criminal gangs. Walder's (1986) analysis of Chinese factories focuses on the attainment of compliance in a communist system. Although workers in capitalist firms usually are motivated both by firm-internal sanctions and by pressure from the labor market, the latter source of incentives was largely unavailable in China at the time of Walder's study. Instead, motivation was provided by much stronger dependence and monitoring mechanisms than those typically found in capitalist firms. Workers in China depended on factory leaders for the satisfaction of a broad range of social benefits that could not be satisfied elsewhere. Dependence was further increased by workers' inability to switch jobs. (Hechter & Kanazawa 1993 show that similar mechanisms are routinely employed in capitalist firms in Japan.) Nee (1992) accounts for the relative success of private firms over their state and collective counterparts in the transitional economy of China in terms of the former's transaction cost advantage over the latter. In contrast, Walder (1995) attributes China's rapid industrial growth under its transitional economy to the higher efficiency of public firms, especially those run by local governments, which face different financial incentives and constraints than the central government.

Two notable qualitative contributions to the literature on organizations are Gambetta's (1993) analysis of the Sicilian Mafia, and Jankowski's (1991) ethnographic study of urban street gangs in three American cities. For Gambetta, the Mafia is a firm offering private protection in a society where state protection often is unreliable. (Jankowski's gangs also offer protection for the residents of low-income neighborhoods who are not well-served by police.) Because the Mafia lacks legitimacy and cannot guarantee its products, it must first convince potential customers of their quality. Gambetta interprets seemingly bizarre aspects of the Mafia—its arcane rituals, obscure symbols, and blood ceremonies—as attempts to make credible commitments to customers and rivals alike.

### *Crime and Deviance*

Deterrence theory has long been identified as an application of rational choice (Gibbs 1975). With Cornish & Clarke (1986), rational choice theories of crime emerged to explain criminal behavior as a function of expected reward and punishment, weighted by the subjective probability of detection (Piliavin et al 1986). Jacobs' (1996) interviews with 40 active crack dealers show that their behavior and their interpersonal strategies are jointly determined by their desire to maximize profit from their sales and to minimize the possibility of arrest by undercover narcotics officers. The dealers, who mostly interact with anonymous clientele, employ a perceptual shorthand on unfamiliar clients; these are observational and testing techniques to detect deception on the part of the clients. Horney & Marshall's (1992) analysis of data collected from incarcerated adult offenders of major felonies confirms that the criminals' subjective perception of the risk of detection is realistically updated by their own experience in the particular crime; those who commit the crime often without getting caught lower their expectation of detection while those who are caught most of the time subsequently increase their perception of risk. Recently, rational choice perspectives on crime have converged with the routine activity approach (Clarke & Felson 1993). Both distinguish between criminality (the decision to become involved in a particular form of crime) and crime (an actual criminal event), and explain the latter in terms of opportunities—the simultaneous presence of criminal target and absence of risk of detection.

A distinctive thrust of rational choice theories of crime is their conception of criminality as a function of higher expected material returns from criminal activities relative to those from conventional pursuits. Williams (1989), Jankowski (1991), and MacLeod (1995) all provide ethnographic accounts to show that teenagers in low-income neighborhoods make deliberate decisions to pursue criminal activities because few legitimate alternative means to make as much money are available to them. Jankowski (1991, pp. 180–193) notes that, in some chronically poor neighborhoods, gang membership has become a family tradition, and many parents actively encourage their children to belong to the same gangs to which they themselves belonged when they were younger, much as parents with Ivy League educations encourage their children to attend their alma maters. Pezzin (1995) argues that economic incentives and opportunity costs exert a powerful influence on criminal career duration and desistance choice. Her analysis of the National Longitudinal Survey of Youth shows that future expected criminal earnings have a strong negative effect on the decision to terminate a criminal career among youths between the ages of 16 and 22. Since the effect of the availability of legal income-generating activities is just as strong as that of perceived cost of punishment, Pezzin argues that the carrot may work just as efficiently as the stick in shortening the length of criminal careers.

Pampel & Gartner (1995) provide a multilevel explanation for variations in homicide rates in 18 advanced industrial nations. Other researchers stress the need to include institutional factors in the explanations of crime. Hechter & Kanazawa (1993) use Hechter's (1987) theory of group solidarity to explain the low crime rates in contemporary Japan. They argue that the higher dependence of the Japanese on their groups and their higher visibility within the groups increase their conformity to social norms. They reject cultural explanations of low crime rates in Japan by showing that China and South Korea, which share many cultural characteristics with Japan, have higher crime rates, and that the same mechanisms of dependence and visibility work to induce conformity among American auto workers in Japanese transplants factories. Petee et al's (1994) finding that the deterrent effects of informal sanctions are the strongest among communities characterized by higher levels of integration is also consistent with Hechter's (1987) theory, which predicts that compliance to norms is a multiplicative function of the dependence and the efficiency of social control.

Finally, one of the most influential modern theories of crime and deviance, Hirschi's (1969) control theory, has a strong rational choice flavor (see Hirschi 1986, 1994). This theory explains juveniles' propensity to engage in delinquency in terms of preferences ("attachment," "belief"), opportunity cost ("commitment"), and resource scarcity ("involvement"). Nagin & Paternoster (1994), among others, provide empirical support for control theory.

### *Comparative-Historical Sociology*

Many have claimed that the scope of rational choice theory is limited to the capitalist era, for previous social formations were much less individualistic. However, rational choice historical sociologists have accounted for variation in state autonomy and policy implementation in absolutist societies on the basis of dependence and control mechanisms. Thus Kiser (1986–1987) suggests that the most autonomous early modern monarchs had independent resources and faced the weakest monitoring (legislative and judicial) institutions. Kiser et al (1995) show that in the case of war—a policy that rulers tended to favor more than their subjects—high ruler autonomy resulted in more frequent war initiation in early modern Western Europe.

Even the most autonomous rulers must delegate authority to agents if they are to implement policies, however. Hence, agency theory ought to cast light on the causes and consequences of tax administration. For instance, when the ruler's monitoring capacity is poor, tax farming should be a more efficient means of providing state revenue than bureaucratic administration because it gives agents stronger incentives to collect taxes and surrender them to rulers (Kiser 1994). Supportive evidence is found both in early modern Prussia (Kiser & Schneider 1994) and Imperial China (Kiser & Tong 1992). In a similar vein, Adams (1996) explains the failure of the Dutch East Indies Company, and contrasting success of the English East Indies Company, in terms of the problems that the European owners faced in controlling their agents in Asia. The Dutch company collapsed when colonial servants saw better alternative opportunities offered by the English company, and the Dutch owners were not able from afar to stop their servants' defection.

Explaining major institutional shifts is one of the great challenges of historical sociology. Both of the popular perspectives in historical sociology—structuralism and cultural analysis—would appear to face insuperable difficulties in accounting for institutional change endogenously. One such institutional change is the subject of Friedman's (1995) recent study. Until the late nineteenth century, in all Western societies the custody of children after their parents' divorce or separation was presumptively and routinely awarded to their fathers.

Then, between 1880 and 1920, in all of these countries presumptive custody shifted from the father to the mother. Due to rising divorce rates, these states faced the prospect of having to support a large number of divorced women on welfare. In order to avoid this expenditure, Friedman argues, they transferred the custody of children from fathers to mothers, making fathers responsible for the financial welfare of their children. Divorced fathers' child support payments also secondarily contributed to the economic welfare of their former spouses, the custodial mothers. By this means, all Western countries avoided supporting divorced women and took responsibility only for the education of children.

## *Political Sociology*

Although collective action is an abiding concern of rational choice research on politics, much of the effort has been theoretical and therefore falls outside of the purview of this review (for a comprehensive but acerbic review, see Udèhn 1995). There are notable exceptions, however. In an impressive study, Brustein (1996) seeks to explain the rise of the Nazi party in interwar Germany. Hitler's rise is often ascribed to his party's manipulation of emotional voters susceptible to *ressentiment*, but Brustein argues that the popularity of the National Socialists was due to their strategic adoption of policies that appealed to the pocketbook interests of a large and socially heterogeneous part of the electorate. One of his intriguing conclusions is that Hitler had to conceal his antisemitism in order to gain popularity among blue-collar workers. Brustein's theory is strongly supported by his analysis of data on more than 42,000 Nazi members who joined the party between 1925 and 1933.

Survey data collected and analyzed by Opp et al (1995) reveal how the macro outcome of the successful protest movement in East Germany in 1989 was an aggregate result of the values, incentives, and network ties of Germans at the micro level. These individuals' decisions to participate, in turn, were influenced by macrolevel political conditions. In contrast, Shlapentokh (1995) accounts for the absence of collective protests in Russia in the face of deteriorating social and economic conditions in 1992–1994 in terms of individuals' expectations that such collective action would not be successful.

## *Stratification and Mobility*

Human capital theory long has been the principal rational choice approach to stratification. A vast sociological literature on labor markets compares its merits to those of status attainment and structural perspectives. However, a new rational choice approach to stratification has been developed. Logan (1996b) employs a two-sided logit methodology to model employment outcomes (the matching of workers to jobs) as a function of explicitly rational choices made by workers and employers under structural constraints. The jobs that employers supply function as the constraints within which workers make their choices, given their preferences; the supply of workers functions as the constraint within which employers make their choices, given their preferences. Further, the preferences of the employers for certain types of workers create the constraints for the workers, and the preferences of the workers for certain types of jobs create the constraints for the employers. Logan's analysis of General Social Survey data showcases the utility of this new method.

Until 1967, secondary schools in Ireland charged their students tuition fees, and these costs were thought to be barriers to educational attainment for children from working-class families. However, when these tuition fees were eliminated by the educational reform of 1967, access to secondary education did not become more egalitarian. Raftery & Hout (1993) argue that, due to the high employment rate and high wages in the Irish economy in the late 1960s, the opportunity costs of continuing education (in the form of forgone wages) were high, relative to the cost of tuition fees, now eliminated. Thus, it did not make much economic sense for Irish children of working-class families to continue formal education and postpone full-time employment, even in the absence of tuition fees, and the educational reform failed to have the intended effect. Breen & Whelan's (1993) analysis concurs with Raftery & Hout (1993).

Walder (1992) provides a macro-meso explanation of stratification among organizations in a socialist economy, and he tests it with survey data gathered in a large Chinese industrial city. Budgetary resources of the local government and its dependence on a work organization jointly determine how much revenue the local government extracts from the organization. The level of revenue extraction by the government determines (at the meso level) the organization's abilities to provide benefits to its employees, which then aggregates (at the macro level) to inequalities among organizations. Walder's (1992) explanation of organizational stratification in China is therefore another example of the multilevel causal structure of rational choice theory.

### *Race and Ethnic Relations*

Most of the rational choice research in this area has been theoretical, with relatively few empirical applications. Clark (1991), however, finds empirical support for Schelling's (1971) theory that slight differences in residents' preference for the racial composition of their neighborhood quickly lead to extreme segregation. Nee et al (1994) contend that the structure of ethnic and ethnically mixed economies in Los Angeles is a function of the economic opportunities and constraints that Asian immigrants face as well as of their skills and qualifications. While most Asian immigrants prefer to work outside of their ethnic enclaves to take advantage of higher pay and better working conditions, many are unable to do so because of their lack of occupational and language skills.

One means of upward mobility available to immigrants of little occupational and language skills is entrepreneurship. Sanders & Nee (1996) demonstrate that the self-employment status among Asian and Hispanic immigrants is strongly facilitated by human capital (foreign-earned formal education) and financial and social capital available from their family members. Those with spouses and other family members who can contribute to their business are more likely to succeed as entrepreneurs than are single immigrants.

Split labor market theory can explain how ethnic and racial antagonism arises, but it cannot account for interracial solidarity. Brown & Boswell (1995) use Heckathorn's (1988, 1989, 1990) theory of group-mediated social control to address the possibility of interracial solidarity or strikebreaking under split labor market conditions. Their qualitative comparative analysis of the Great Steel Strike of 1919 largely supports their predictions.

Chai's (1996) theory of ethnogenesis seeks to explain the location of ethnic boundaries in developing societies. The theory proposes a link between cooperation and altruism in small, rural communities. Then it predicts how these altruistic preferences, in conjunction with structural factors and rational behavior, generate boundaries for larger-scale ethnic collective action. The theory is applied to the creation of new ethnic groups among the Pan-Igbo in Nigeria, the Luba-Kasai in Zaire, the Pan-Malays in Malayasia, and the Muhajir in Pakistan.

Group process researchers mostly concentrate on the dynamics of dyads and small groups. Research in this tradition began with Emerson's (1962) seminal analysis of exchange relations in dyads, which was later extended to exchange networks (Cook & Emerson 1978). Currently at least four theories compete in the field of network exchange: Bienenstock & Bonacich's core theory (1992, 1993; Bonacich & Bienenstock 1993, 1995); Cook & Yamagishi's power-dependence theory (1992; Yamagishi & Cook 1993); Friedkin's expected value theory (1986, 1992, 1993); and Willer et al's exchange resistance theory (Markovsky et al 1988, Markovsky et al 1993, Lovaglia et al 1995, Skvoretz & Lovaglia 1995). Since this field relies heavily on the experimental testing of key hypotheses (Skvoretz & Willer 1993), it resembles what Collins (1994) calls "high-consensus, rapid-discovery" science.

Currently there is a debate about the determinants of dyadic cohesion among self-interested rational actors. On the one hand, Kollock (1994) argues that when the outcome of an exchange is uncertain, individuals make commitments to particular exchange partners in order to reduce uncertainty (see also Yamagishi & Yamagishi 1994). On the other, Lawler & Yoon's (1993, 1996) theory of relational cohesion maintains that individuals experience positive affect from successfully negotiated and completed exchanges. Then self-interested actors develop affective commitment to particular exchange partners, even in the face of more attractive offers, in order to consume this positive affect from continued exchange with the same partner.

Sometimes research on group processes has clear macrolevel implications. Orbell & Dawes' (1991, 1993) "cognitive miser" theory explains social welfare, order, and efficiency at the macro level in terms of dyadic interactions at the micro level. Their theory argues that intending cooperators are more likely to play dyadic Prisoner's Dilemma games than intending defectors, when they have the option not to play. Then the outcomes of most completed games are mutual cooperation, whereby the players enjoy the fruit of cooperation, which aggregates to order and economic surplus at the macro level. Their laboratory experiment (Orbell & Dawes 1993) confirms the theory's crucial hypothesis that intending cooperators are more likely to choose to play than intending defectors.

The problem of cooperation and public goods provision is usually conceived of as an *n*-person Prisoner's Dilemma game. In contrast, Diekmann's (1985, 1986, 1993) "volunteer's dilemma" game captures the problem of cooperation in situations where there is a potential diffusion of responsibility (Darley & Latanè 1968, Latané & Darley 1970). The public good in the volunteer's dilemma is produced by a single volunteer (with the effect of additional volunteers completely superfluous), and there is no pure dominant strategy; players are better off defecting if there is at least one cooperator, but better off cooperating if there is none. The volunteer's dilemma points to the utility of sociological rational choice theory in that the use of a strictly game-theoretic solution—a mixed Nash equilibrium strategy—leads to highly inefficient outcomes. An optimal level of cooperation requires communication and coordination among actors, which is fostered by social norms (Diekmann 1985). The experimental evidence shows that subjects do not employ strictly game-theoretic solutions (Diekmann 1986, 1993).

### *Medical Sociology*

Whereas medicine has been an important site for the application of behavioral decision theory, rational choice is in its infancy in medical sociology. Thoits (1994), however, calls for more emphasis on human agency, and on the deliberate choices that individuals make, in the study of stress and depression. Her analysis of panel data shows that individuals are often able to solve potential problems in their lives (and thus are not affected by them), and that only those they fail to solve lead to psychological symptoms. Although Pescosolido's (1992) "social organization strategy" framework ostensibly is critical of rational choice, it is entirely consistent with the version of rational choice presented in the present essay. Her analysis of individuals seeking medical help specifically incorporates network structures and uses network ties and information gathered from past interactions as resources and social capital. (Knoke 1990 and Burt 1992 offer other examples of how network analysis can be integrated with rational choice.)

Broadhead & Heckathorn (1994, Broadhead et al 1995) conceive of AIDS prevention as a collective action problem. They use agency theory and Heckathorn's theory of group-mediated social control to argue that peer-driven intervention programs are more effective in combating AIDS. Extensive ethnographic data support their contention.

## CONCLUSION

Sociological rational choice is an inherently multilevel enterprise. It seeks to account for social outcomes on the basis of both social context and individual action. In this respect it often differs, at least in emphasis, from other (thin) versions of rational choice theory that are employed in much economic analysis and game theory. Sociological rational choice is beginning to make empirical contributions to a broad range of substantive topics in the discipline. While applications of rational choice in subfields like politics, labor markets, formal organizations, and criminology by now are traditional, the approach has also begun to make empirical advances in areas formerly regarded as inhospitable, such as the family, gender, and religion. At the same time, a growing number of theoretically uncommitted empirical researchers are testing rational choice theories—sometimes unwittingly—in their own domains. These studies will reveal much about the scope and limits of rational choice theory. Invariably, their findings will strengthen certain versions of rational choice theory at the expense of others.

Beyond the crucial task of subjecting existing rational choice theories to empirical tests, we discern three future directions for developing sociological rational choice theory. To better explain social outcomes arising from individual action, rational choice theorists must begin to understand the origin and the nature of values that motivate human behavior (Hechter et al 1993). Values—and the preferences derived from them—are one of two major categories of determinants of individual behavior in rational choice theory, the other being institutional constraints. Rational choice has been mute on the origin and nature of individual values. This silence has been justified under the dictum de gustibus non est disputandum. Due to the difficulty of arriving at valid and reliable measures of internal states (Hechter 1992), rational choice theorists usually impute values to actors by assumption. The typical value assumption has been wealth maximization because wealth is highly fungible. Thus actors who may hold various idiosyncratic values can be expected to pursue wealth as a means to achieve their divergent goals (Hechter 1994). Yet some research also has advanced atypical value assumptions, including uncertainty reduction (Friedman et al 1994), local status (Frank 1985), distributive justice (Jasso 1990, 1993), and regret-dissonance reduction (Chai, forthcoming).

Even if we know what values and preferences actors hold, their decision-making mechanisms are contested. Hence the study of decision algorithms is a second promising field of inquiry. Subjective expected utility maximization theory, the foundation of most macroscopic rational choice theories, posits that actors are forward-looking maximizers. Based on the available information and their best estimates of what the future holds, actors assign subjective probabilities to various future states of the world and make their decisions according to these subjective probabilities. However, critics have pointed out that this forward-looking process of decision-making is cognitively too demanding for most human actors (Petersen 1994). Others have proposed alternative decision algorithms. Macy (1993) argues that individuals are backward-looking adaptive learners who adjust their decisions on the basis of the past outcomes associated with their choices, and he provides experimental evidence (Macy 1995) supporting his contention. In contrast, Heckathorn (1996) argues that individuals sometimes are sideways-looking cultural imitators whose decisions emulate those made by their neighbors who are doing well. In his view, whether actors are forward-, backward-, or sideways-looking depends on the nature of available information about the future. If genuine and accurate information is available about the future, then actors will assess the subjective probabilities of various states of the world as predicted by the subjective expected utility maximization model. If the past is the best predictor of the future, then actors will be backward-looking. If the future is best known by observing who is doing well in the present, then actors will be sideways-looking imitators.

The ultimate challenge for sociological rational choice theory is explaining the emergence of institutions. Unlike values and preferences, institutions are intersubjective and therefore more easily measurable. So far this has not led to concerted research on institutional emergence, however. Still, a handful of forays have been made. Contributions to Hechter et al (1990) begin to tackle the emergence of a small handful of institutions, and Coleman (1990) provides one framework for understanding how norms emerge among actors with specific interests and resources. Logan's (1996a,b) two-sided logit model offers a promising new way to trace the origins of institutional constraints for actors to their exchange partners' preferences. And Chai & Hechter (1997) propose an elementary model for the emergence of the state and of social order. However, an endogenous theory of institutional emergence remains a distant goal at this time.

ACKNOWLEDGMENTS

Thanks to Mary Brinton, Sun-Ki Chai, Karen Cook, and Christine Horne for comments on an earlier draft of this review.

*Literature Cited*


Abell P. 1988. *Establishing Support Systems for Industrial Co-Operatives: Case Studies from the Third World.* Aldershot, Engl: Avebury

Abell P. 1990. Supporting industrial cooperatives in developing countries: some Tanzanian experiences. *Econ. Indust. Democracy* 11:483–504

Abell P. 1991. Homo sociologicus: Do we need him/her? *Sociol. Theory* 9:195–98

Abell P, Mahoney N. 1988. *Small-Scale Industrial Producer Co-Operatives in Developing Countries.* Delhi: Oxford Univ. Press

Adams J. 1996. Principals and agents, colonialists and company men: the decay of colonial control in the Dutch East Indies. *Am. Sociol. Rev.* 61:12–28

Baron JN, Hannan MT. 1994. The impact of economics on contemporary sociology. *J. Econ. Lit.* 22:1111–46

Becker GS. 1974. A theory of marriage: Part II. *J. Polit. Econ.* 82:S11–S26

Becker GS. 1976. *The Economic Approach to Human Behavior.* Chicago: Univ. Chicago Press

Becker GS. 1981. *A Treatise on the Family.* Cambridge: Harvard Univ. Press

Becker GS. 1996. *Accounting for Tastes.* Cambridge: Harvard Univ. Press

Bienenstock EJ, Bonacich P. 1992. The core as a solution to exclusionary networks. *Soc. Networks* 14:231–44

Bienenstock EJ, Bonacich P. 1993. Game-theory models for exchange networks: experimental results. *Sociol. Perspect.* 36:117–35

Bonacich P, Bienenstock EJ. 1993. Assignment games, chromatic number, and exchange theory. *J. Math Sociol.* 17:243–59

Bonacich P, Bienenstock EJ. 1995. When rationality fails: unstable exchange networks with empty cores. *Ration. Soc.* 7:293–320

Breen R, Whelan CT. 1993. From ascription to achievement?: origins, education and entry to the labour force in the Republic of Ireland during the twentieth century. *Acta Sociol.* 36:3–17

Brewster KL. 1994. Race differences in sexual activity among adolescent women: the role of neighborhood characteristics. *Am. Sociol. Rev.* 59:408–24

Brewster KL, Billy JOG, Grady WR. 1993. Social context and adolescent behavior: the impact of community on the transition to sexual activity. *Soc. Forces* 71:713–40

Brinton MC. 1989. Gender stratification in contemporary urban Japan. *Am. Sociol. Rev.* 54:549–64

Brinton MC. 1992. Christmas cakes and wedding cakes: the social organization of Japanese women's life course. In *Japanese Social Organization,* ed. TS Lebra, pp. 79–107. Honolulu: Univ. Hawaii Press

Brinton MC. 1993. *Women and the Economic Miracle: Gender and Work in Postwar Japan.* Berkeley: Univ. Calif. Press

Broadhead RS, Heckathorn DD. 1994. AIDS prevention outreach among injection drug users: agency problems and new approaches. *Soc. Probl.* 41:473–95

Broadhead RS, Heckathorn DD, Grund J-PC, Stern LS, Anthony DL. 1995. Drug users outreach workers in combating AIDS: preliminary results of a peer-driven intervention. *J. Drug Issues* 25:531–64

Brown C, Boswell T. 1995. Strikebreaking or solidarity in the great steel strike of 1919: a split labor market, game-theoretic, and QCA analysis. *Am. J. Sociol.* 100:1479–519

Brüderl J, Preisendörfer P, Ziegler R. 1993. Upward mobility in organizations: the effects of hierarchy and opportunity structure. *Eur. Sociol. Rev.* 9:173–88

Brustein W. 1996. *The Logic of Evil: The Social Origins of the Nazi Party, 1925 to 1933.* New Haven: Yale Univ. Press

Burt RS. 1992. *Structural Holes: The Social Structure of Competition.* Cambridge, MA: Harvard Univ. Press

Chai S-K. 1996. A theory of ethnic group boundaries. *Nations Nationalism* 2:281–307

Chai S-K. 1997. *Creating Identity from Rational Action: A General Theory of Preference and Belief Formation.* Ann Arbor: Univ. Mich. Press. In press

Chai S-K, Hechter M. 1997. A theory of the state and of social order. *J. Math. Soc.* In press

Chaves M, Cann DE. 1992. Regulation, pluralism, and religious market structure: explaining religion's vitality. *Ration. Soc.* 4:272–90

Clark WAV. 1991. Residential preferences and neighborhood racial segregation: a test of the Schelling segregation model. *Demography* 28:1–19

Clarke RV, Felson M. 1993. *Routine Activity and Rational Choice.* New Brunswick, NJ: Transaction

Coase RH. 1937. The nature of the firm. *Economica N.S.* 4:386–405

Coleman JS. 1990. *Foundations of Social Theory.* Cambridge: Harvard Univ. Press

Coleman JS. 1993. The rational reconstruction of society. *Am. Sociol. Rev.* 58:1–15

Collins R. 1994. Why the social sciences won't become high-consensus, rapid-discovery science. *Sociol. Forum* 9:155–77

Cook KS, Emerson RM. 1978. Power, equity and commitment in exchange networks. *Am. Sociol. Rev.* 43:721–39

Cook KS, Yamagishi T. 1992. Power in exchange networks: a power-dependence formulation. *Soc. Networks* 14:245–66

Cornish DB, Clarke RV, eds. 1986. *The Reasoning Criminal: Rational Choice Perspectives on Offending.* New York: Springer-Verlag

Cowen T. 1996. Why women succeed, and fail, in the arts. *J. Cult. Econ.* 20:93–113

Darley JM, Latané B. 1968. Bystander intervention in emergencies: diffusion of responsibility. *J. Pers. Soc. Psychol.* 8:377–83

Diekmann A. 1985. Volunteer's dilemma. *J. Confl. Resolut.* 29:605–10

Diekmann A. 1986. Volunteer's dilemma: a social trap without a dominant strategy and some experimental results. In *Paradoxical Effects of Social Behavior: Essays in Honor of Anatol Rapoport,* ed. A Diekmann, P Mitter. Heidelberg: Physica-Verlag

Diekmann A. 1993. Cooperation in an asymmetric volunteer's dilemma game: theory and experimental evidence. *Int. J. Game Theory* 22:75–85

Emerson RM. 1962. Power-dependence relations. *Am. Sociol. Rev.* 27:31–41

England P, Kilbourne BS. 1990. Feminist critiques of the separative model of self: implications for rational choice theory. *Ration. Soc.* 2:156–71

Farkas G. 1996. *Human Capital or Cultural Capital? Ethnicity and Poverty Groups in an Urban School District.* New York: Aldine

Ferber MA, Nelson JA, eds. 1993. *Beyond Economic Man: Feminist Theory and Economics.* Chicago: Univ. Chicago Press

Ferejohn JA. 1991. Rationality and interpretation: Parliamentary elections in early Stuart England. In *The Economic Approach to Politics: A Critical Reassessment of the Theory of Rational Action,* ed. KR Monroe, pp. 279–305. New York: HarperCollins

Finke R, Guest AM, Stark R. 1996. Mobilizing local religious markets: religious pluralism in the Empire State, 1855 to 1865. *Am. Sociol. Rev.* 61:203–18

Finke R, Stark R. 1988. Religious economies and sacred canopies: religions mobilization in American cities, 1906. *Am. Sociol. Rev.* 53:41–49

Finke R, Stark R. 1992. *The Churching of America 1776–1990: Winners and Losers in Our Religious Economy.* New Brunswick, NJ: Rutgers Univ. Press

Fischhoff B. 1991. Value elicitation: Is there anything in there? *Am. Psychol.* 46:835–47

Frank RH. 1985. *Choosing the Right Pond: Human Behavior and the Quest for Status.* New York: Oxford Univ. Press

Friedkin N. 1986. A formal theory of social power. *J. Math. Sociol.* 12:103–26

Friedkin N. 1992. An expected value model of social power: predictions for selected exchange networks. *Soc. Networks* 14:213–30

Friedkin N. 1993. An expected value model of social exchange outcomes. In *Advances in Group Processes,* ed. EJ Lawler, B Markovsky, K Heimer, J O'Brien, 10:163–93. Greenwich, CT: JAI

Friedman D. 1995. *Towards a Structure of Indifference: The Social Origins of Maternal Custody.* New York: Aldine de Gruyter

Friedman D, Diem C. 1990. Comments on England and Kilbourne. *Ration. Soc.* 2:517–21

Friedman D, Diem C. 1993. Feminism and the pro- (rational-) choice movement: rational-choice theory, feminist critiques, and gender inequality. In *Theory on Gender/Feminism on Theory,* ed. P England, pp. 91–114. New York: Aldine de Gruyter

Friedman D, Hechter M. 1988. The contribution of rational choice theory to macrosociological research. *Sociol. Theory* 6:201–18

Friedman D, Hechter M, Kanazawa S. 1994. A theory of the value of children. *Demography* 31:375–401

Gambetta D. 1993. *The Sicilian Mafia: The Business of Private Protection.* Cambridge: Harvard Univ. Press

Gibbs JP. 1975. *Crime, Punishment and Deterrence.* New York: Elsevier

Goldthorpe JH. 1996. The quantitative analysis of large-scale data-sets and rational action theory: for a sociological alliance. *Eur. Sociol. Rev.* 12:109–26

Green DP, Shapiro I. 1994. *Pathologies of Rational Choice Theory: A Critique of Applications in Political Science.* New Haven: Yale Univ. Press

Greve HR. 1994. Industry diversity effects on job mobility. *Acta Sociol.* 37:119–39

Hagan J, MacMillan R, Wheaton B. 1996. New kid in town: social capital and the life course effects of family migration on children. *Am. Sociol. Rev.* 61:368–85

Hamberg EM, Pettersson T. 1994. The religious market: denominational competition and religious participation in contemporary Sweden. *J. Sci. Study Relig.* 33:205–16

Haveman HA. 1995. The demographic metabolism of organizations: industry dynamics, turnover, and tenure distributions. *Admin. Sci. Q.* 40:586–618

Haveman HA, Cohen L. 1994. The ecological dynamics of careers: the impact of organizational founding, dissolution, and merger on job mobility. *Am. J. Sociol.* 100:104–52

Hechter M. 1987. *Principles of Group Solidarity.* Berkeley: Univ. Calif. Press

Hechter M. 1992. Should values be written out of the social scientist's lexicon? *Sociol. Theory* 10:214–30

Hechter M. 1994. The role of values in rational choice theory. *Ration. Soc.* 6:318–33

Hechter M. 1996. Through thick and thin: How far can theory predict behaviour? *Times Lit. Suppl.* March 29, p. 15

Hechter M, Kanazawa S. 1993. Group solidarity and social order in Japan. *J. Theor. Polit.* 5:455–93

Hechter M, Nadel L, Michod RE. 1993. *The Origin of Values.* New York: Aldine de Gruyter

Hechter M, Opp K-D, Wippler R. 1990. *Social Institutions: Their Emergence, Maintenance and Effects.* New York: Aldine de Gruyter

Heckathorn DD. 1988. Collective sanctions and the creation of prisoner's dilemma norms. *Am. J. Sociol.* 94:535–62

Heckathorn DD. 1989. Collective action and the second-order free-rider problem. *Ration. Soc.* 1:78–100

Heckathorn DD. 1990. Collective sanctions and compliance norms: a formal theory of group-mediated social control. *Am. Sociol. Rev.* 55:366–84

Heckathorn DD. 1996. The dynamics and dilemmas of collective action. *Am. Sociol. Rev.* 61:250–77

Hedström P. 1994. Contagious collectivities: on the spatial diffusion of Swedish trade unions, 1890–1940. *Am. J. Sociol.* 99:1157–79

Hirschi T. 1969. *Causes of Delinquency.* Berkeley: Univ. Calif. Press

Hirschi T. 1986. On the compatibility of rational choice and social control theories of crime. See Cornish & Clarke 1986, pp.105–18

Hirschi T. 1994. Preface to the Japanese Edition. *Causes of Delinquency.* Tokyo: Bunka Shobo

Hoem JM. 1991. To marry, just in case...: the Swedish widow's-pension reform and the peak in marriages in December 1989. *Acta Sociol.* 34:127–35

Hoem JM. 1993. Public policy as the fuel of fertility: effects of a policy reform on the pace of childbearing in Sweden in the 1980s. *Acta Sociol.* 36:19–31

Horney J, Marshall IH. 1992. Risk perceptions among serious offenders: the role of crime and punishment. *Criminology* 30:575–94

Iannaccone LR. 1991. The consequences of religious market structure: Adam Smith and the economics of religion. *Ration. Soc.* 3:156–77

Iannaccone LR. 1992. Sacrifice and stigma: reducing free-riding in cults, communes, and other collectivities. *J. Polit. Econ.* 100:271–91

Iannaccone LR. 1994. Why strict churches are strong. *Am. J. Sociol.* 99:1180–211

Iannaccone LR, Olson DVA, Stark R. 1995. Religious resources and church growth. *Soc. Forces* 74:705–31

Jacobs BA. 1996. Crack dealers and restrictive deterrence: identifying narcs. *Criminology* 34:409–31

Jankowski MS. 1991. *Islands in the Street: Gangs and American Urban Society.* Berkeley: Univ. Calif. Press

Jasso G. 1988. Whom shall we welcome?: elite judgments of the criteria for the selection of immigrants. *Am. Sociol. Rev.* 53:919–32

Jasso G. 1990. Methods for the theoretical and empirical analysis of comparison processes. *Sociological Methodology 1990,* ed. CC Clogg. Washington, DC: Am. Sociol. Assoc.

Jasso G. 1993. Choice and emotion in comparison theory. *Ration. Soc.* 5:231–74

Jasso G, Rosenzweig MR. 1990. *The New Chosen People: Immgrants in the United States.* New York: Russell Sage Found.

Kelley D. 1972. *Why Conservative Churches are Growing.* New York: Harper & Row

Kiser E. 1986–1987. The formation of state policy in western European absolutisms: a comparison of England and France. *Polit. Soc.* 15:259–96

Kiser E. 1994. Markets and hierarchies in early modern tax systems: a principal-agent analysis. *Polit. Soc.* 22:284–315

Kiser E, Drass KA, Brustein W. 1995. Ruler autonomy and war in early modern western Europe. *Int. Stud. Q.* 39:109–38

Kiser E, Schneider J. 1994. Bureaucracy and efficiency: an analysis of taxation in early modern Prussia. *Am. Sociol. Rev.* 59:187–204

Kiser E, Tong X. 1992. Determinants of the amount and type of corruption in state fiscal bureaucracies: an analysis of taxation in early modern Prussia. *Comp. Polit. Stud.* 25:300–31

Knoke D. 1990. *Political Networks: The Structural Perspective.* Cambridge: Cambridge Univ. Press

Kollock P. 1994. The emergence of exchange structures: an experimental study of uncertainty, commitment and trust. *Am. J. Sociol.* 100:315–45

Latané B, Darley JM. 1970. *The Unresponsive Bystander: Why Doesn't He Help?* New York: Appleton-Century-Crofts

Lawler EJ, Yoon J. 1993. Power and the emergence of commitment behavior in negotiated exchange. *Am. Sociol. Rev.* 58:465–81

Lawler EJ, Yoon J. 1996. Commitment in exchange relations: test of a theory of relational cohesion. *Am. Sociol. Rev.* 61:89–108

Lee BA, Oropesa RS, Kanan JW. 1994. Neighborhood context and residential mobility. *Demography* 31:249–70

Lloyd KM, South SJ. 1996. Contextual influences on young men's transition to first marriage. *Soc. Forces* 74:1097–1119

Logan JA. 1996a. Rational choice and the TSL model of occupational opportunity. *Ration. Soc.* 8:207–30

Logan JA. 1996b. Opportunity and choice in socially structured labor markets. *Am. J. Sociol.* 102:114–60

Lovaglia MJ, Skvoretz J, Willer D, Markovsky B. 1995. Negotiated exchanges in social networks. *Soc. Forces* 74:123–55

Mackie G. 1996. Ending footbinding and infibulation: a convention account. *Am. Sociol. Rev.* 61:999–1017

MacLeod J. 1995. *Ain't No Makin' It: Aspirations and Attainment in a Low-Income Neighborhood.* Boulder, CO: Westview

Macy MW. 1993. Social learning and the structure of collective action. In *Advances in Group Processes,* ed. EJ Lawler, B Markovsky, K Heimer, J O'Brien, pp. 1–35. Greenwich, CT: JAI

Macy MW. 1995. PAVLOV and the evolution of cooperation: an experimental test. *Soc. Psychol. Q.* 58:74–87

Markovsky B, Skvoretz J, Willer D, Lovaglia MJ, Erger J. 1993. The seeds of weak power: an extension of network exchange theory. *Am. Sociol. Rev.* 58:197–209

Markovsky B, Willer D, Patton T. 1988. Power relations in exchange networks. *Am. Sociol. Rev.* 53:220–36

Moen P, Wethington E. 1992. The concept of family adaptive strategies. *Annu. Rev. Sociol.* 18:233–51

Nagin DS, Paternoster R. 1994. Personal capital and social control: the deterrence implications of a theory of individual differences in criminal offending. *Criminology* 32:581–606

Nee V. 1992. Organizational dynamics of market transition: hybrid forms, property rights, and mixed economy in China. *Admin. Sci. Q.* 37:1–27

Nee V, Sanders JM, Sernau S. 1994. Job transitions in an immigrant metropolis: ethnic boundaries and the mixed economy. *Am. Sociol. Rev.* 59:849–72

Opp K-D, Voss P, Gern C. 1995. *Origins of a Spontaneous Revolution.* Ann Arbor: Univ. Mich. Press

Orbell J, Dawes RM. 1991. A cognitive miser theory of cooperators' advantage. *Am. Polit. Sci. Rev.* 85:515–28

Orbell JM, Dawes RM. 1993. Social welfare, cooperators' advantage, and the option of not playing the game. *Am. Sociol. Rev.* 58:787–800

Pampel FC, Gartner R. 1995. Age structure, socio-political institutions, and national homicide rates. *Eur. Sociol. Rev.* 11:243–60

Pescosolido BA. 1992. Beyond rational choice: the social dynamics of how people seek help. *Am. J. Sociol.* 97:1096–1138

Petee TA, Milner TF, Welch MR. 1994. Levels of social integration in group contexts and the effects of informal sanction threat on deviance. *Criminology* 32:85–106

Petersen T. 1992. Payment systems and the structure of inequality: conceptual issues and an analysis of salespersons in department stores. *Am. J. Sociol.* 98:67–104

Petersen T. 1994. On the promise of game-theory in sociology. *Contemp. Sociol.* 23:498–502

Pezzin LE. 1995. Earnings prospects, matching effects, and the decision to terminate a criminal career. *J. Quant. Criminol.* 11:29–50

Piliavin I, Thornton C, Gartner R, Matsueda RL. 1986. Crime, deterrence, and rational choice. *Am. Sociol. Rev.* 51:101–19

Raftery AE, Hout M. 1993. Maximally maintained inequality: expansion, reform, and opportunity in Irish education, 1921–1975. *Sociol. Educ.* 66:41–62

Raub W, Keren G. 1993. Hostages as a commitment device. *J. Econ. Behav. Organ.* 21:43–67

Risman BJ, Ferree MM. 1995. Making gender visible: comment on Coleman. *Am. Sociol. Rev.* 60:775–82

Sanders JM, Nee V. 1996. Immigrant self-employment: the family as social capital and the value of human capital. *Am. Sociol. Rev.* 61:231–49

Schelling T. 1971. Dynamic models of segregation. *J. Math Sociol.* 1:143–86

Sen A. 1983. Economics and the family. *Asian Dev. Rev.* 1(2):14–26

Shlapentokh V. 1995. Russian patience: a reasonable behavior and a social strategy. *Eur. J. Sociol.* 36:247–80

Skvoretz J, Lovaglia MJ. 1995. Who exchanges with whom: structural determinants of exchange frequency in negotiated exchange networks. *Soc. Psychol. Q.* 58:163–77

Skvoretz J, Willer D. 1993. Exclusion and power: a test of four theories of power in exchange networks. *Am. Sociol. Rev.* 58:801–18

Smith HL. 1989. Integrating theory and research on the institutional determinants of fertility. *Demography* 26:171–84

South SJ, Lloyd KM. 1995. Spousal alternatives and marital dissolution. *Am. Sociol. Rev.* 60:21–35

Stark R. 1992. Do Catholic societies really exist? *Ration. Soc.* 4:261–71

Stark R, Bainbridge WS. 1985. *The Future of Religion: Secularization, Revival, and Cult Formation.* Berkeley: Univ. Calif. Press

Stark R, Bainbridge WS. 1987. *A Theory of Religion.* New York: Peter Lang

Stark R, Iannaccone LR, Finke R. 1996. Religion, science, and rationality. *Am. Econ. Rev.* 86(2):433–37

Thoits PA. 1994. Stressors and problem-solving: the individual as psychological activist. *J. Health Soc. Behav.* 35:143–59

Treas J. 1993. Money in the bank: transaction costs and the economic organization of marriage. *Am. Sociol. Rev.* 58:723–34

Treas J, Giesen D. 1996. *Sex, gender, and rational choice: determinants of infidelity among married and cohabiting couples.* Presented at Annu. Meet. Am. Sociol. Assoc., Aug. 16–20, New York

Udéhn L. 1995. *The Limits of Public Choice.* London: Routledge

Walder AG. 1986. *Communist Neo-Traditionalism.* Berkeley: Univ. Calif. Press

Walder AG. 1992. Property rights and stratification in socialist redistributive economies. *Am. Sociol. Rev.* 57:524–39

Walder AG. 1995. Local governments as industrial firms: an organizational analysis of China's transitional economy. *Am. J. Sociol.* 101:263–301

Warner RS. 1993. Work in progress toward a new paradigm for the sociological study of religion in the United States. *Am. J. Sociol.* 98:1044–93

Williams T. 1989. *The Cocaine Kids: The Inside Story of a Teenage Drug Ring.* Reading, MA: Addison-Wesley

Wu Z. 1996. Childbearing in cohabitational relationships. *J. Marriage Fam.* 58:281–92

Yamagishi T, Cook KS. 1993. Generalized exchange and social dilemmas. *Soc. Psychol. Q.* 56:235–48

Yamagishi T, Yamagishi M. 1994. Trust and commitment in the United States and Japan. *Motiv. Emot.* 18:129–66

Yamaguchi K, Ferguson LR. 1995. The stopping and spacing of childbirths and their birth-history predictors: rational-choice theory and event-history analysis. *Am. Sociol. Rev.* 60:272–98

Young LA. 1997. *The Rational Choice Theory of Religion.* New York: Routledge

*Annu. Rev. Sociol. 1997. 23:215–31*


# THE CHANGING ORGANIZATIONAL CONTEXT OF PROFESSIONAL WORK

*Kevin T. Leicht*
Department of Sociology, 140W Seashore Hall, University of Iowa, Iowa City, Iowa 52242; e-mail: leicht@blue.weeg.uiowa.edu

*Mary L. Fennell*
Department of Sociology, Box 1916 Maxcy Hall, Brown University, Providence, Rhode Island 02912

KEY WORDS: professionals, formal organizations, careers, institutional theory, career mobility

ABSTRACT

Our paper represents an attempt to stimulate continued sociological interest in professional work. Our review suggests that understanding professional work is central to understanding larger workplace changes in the late twentieth century. Some researchers have documented the increasingly diverse arrangements for the delivery of professional services, even as others point to a convergence of professional control around accountability and cost containment issues. Claims of diverging interests across work settings are often confounded by greater racial, gender, and ethnic diversity among professionals. We suggest that the study of professional careers provides an avenue for studying the diversification of professionals and work settings. Future research should also follow changes in the prestige rankings of different organizational arrangements from the viewpoint of professionals, professional associations, and clients. Finally we warn researchers that managerial groups seeking control of professional work have professional agendas of their own which constrain the possibilities for sweeping change.

## INTRODUCTION

Sociologists' long-term interest in professional work can be traced to the founders of sociology in their discussions of authority (Durkheim 1933, Bendix 1956), bureaucracy (Weber 1947), and class conflict (Marx 1889). More recent



0360-0572/97/0815-0215$08.00

analyses of the nature of professional work and its implications have entered discussions of postindustrial class and political systems (Giddens 1994, Inglehart 1990, Manza et al 1995) and new social movements (Eder 1993, Jenkins & Leicht 1996). These larger sociological concerns have mirrored developments in the study of the professions themselves. Since Friedson last reviewed the changing nature of professional control (Friedson 1984), many developments have occurred in the study of professional work. Much of this work is motivated by the belief that the relationship between professions and complex organizations is changing rapidly.

Our review focuses on the changing nature of professional work and, specifically, the changing multifaceted relationship between professionals and employment settings for professionals. We draw primarily on literature from law, medicine, engineering, and science, though our arguments apply to other sectors as well. We avoid defining precisely what professional work is, in favor of examining the role that organizations play in facilitating and placing limits on traditional professional work (Friedson 1986). Our review emphasizes the important role that professional careers play in examining the changing nature of professional work. Professional careers are strongly institutionalized in that they are shaped through socialization processes and generally accepted professional norms defining what "typical" and "distinguished" professional careers look like. The actual shape of those careers, however, is increasingly conditioned by opportunities within organizations, and the organizations within which professional work is done are themselves undergoing dramatic changes in both control structures and accountability.

A focus on the institutionalization of professional careers serves to link the study of professional control to organizational theory. Employers of professionals must contend with institutional norms about professional careers when they tap into the labor market for professionals. Organizations under specific environmental pressures shape reactions to pre-existing, institutionalized professional norms. In addition to the usual responses to institutional pressure (isomorphism—see Scott 1993), organizations may also attempt to shape professional norms, directly confront professional norms, or engage in avoidance of professional norms (Baum & Oliver 1991, Oliver 1991).

The next section discusses the growing variation in settings where professional work takes place and the implications this diversity has for notions of professional careers. This is followed by a discussion of the possible convergence of institutional practices around a singular model of professional careers. We also examine diversification of interests among professionals, fragmentation of professional interests, and the fragmentation of work organizations more generally, with an emphasis on the growing professionalization of managerial work. Finally, we outline a future research program on professional careers that takes these new developments into account, and we briefly consider methodological issues pertinent to such research.

## THE INCREASING DIVERSITY OF PROFESSIONAL WORK SETTINGS

Over a decade ago in Volume 10 of this series, Friedson argued that the nature of professional control has changed from that of a fairly informal collegial relationship among peers to more formalized relationships that have segmented professionals within fields along a number of dimensions. Chief among them is the stratification of professionals into rank-and-file practitioners and supervisory elites. Although the exercise of bureaucratic controls by professionals over professionals has been well documented for many years across most of the traditional professions (Goode 1957, Scott 1982, Nelson 1988), we suspect that the locus of that control has begun to shift. Scott's three basic models (1982) for embedding professionals within organizational settings—autonomous, heteronomous, and conjoint—were still based on the assumption that professionals control professionals, even in bureaucratic settings.

Now, however, the range of organizational settings in which professionals work has far exceeded earlier models of the solo practice, the partnership, group practice, large law firm or the large modern hospital. Professionals are found as salaried employees of for-profit and nonprofit organizations, of government units of all sorts, of freestanding nongovernment organizations (NGOs), endowed research organizations, universities, foundations, and corporations (Derber & Schwartz 1991, Abbott 1988, 1991). In many if not all of these settings, the control of professional work is no longer necessarily vested in peers, or even in the administrative elite of the profession; hierarchical control over professional work is often vested in professional managers of the employing organization. Some argue that the control of professional work by nonprofessionals extends to decisions concerning compensation (as in corporate law firms, see Tolbert & Stern 1991), and even to the the evaluation of professional performance (as in the establishment of effectiveness research-based protocols in medicine for performance review by third-party payers; see Hafferty & Light 1995).

For example, one of the fastest growing segments of the legal labor market is that of in-house legal departments of large corporations (Curran 1986, Halliday 1987, Leicht & Fennell 1996). Little is known about the structure of in-house legal departments, other than that new female law school graduates are increasingly hired for such positions (Roach 1990) and that differential employment patterns exist for men and women lawyers in corporate legal departments. In medicine, a parallel expansion is underway in the rise of managed care organization (MCOs), which contractually link physicians to third-party payers as either employees (as in HMOs) or contracted providers (as in preferred provider organizations). In both types of MCOs, medical work and clinical decision-making are directly subject to control of the MCO (Dill 1995, Mechanic 1994). And both law and medicine exhibit trends toward incorporation of the worksite into large, multiorganizational firms, either regionally, nationally, or internationally dispersed (Fennell & Alexander 1993, Stevens 1989).

Given this expansion in the types of organizational settings in which professional work is done, a plethora of unanswered questions remains concerning the career mobility of professionals either within or between these various settings. Traditional notions of which professional work settings are the most valued, prestigious, or well compensated are no longer reliable. The hallowed settings of the university-based teaching hospital, the private law firm, or the tenured faculty position have slipped on dimensions of stability, security, and autonomy (compensation has always been problematic in academia). Within different professions, though, we have no firm handle on the extent to which the relative prestige ranking of various settings has changed or is changing (Halliday 1987, Fligstein 1990, Hagan 1990), or to what extent newly developed or profoundly changing practice settings fit into those rankings (Leicht et al 1995). Although physicians at first resisted participating in MCOs, it would appear that now even the most esoteric specialists have decided to join the trend, many assuming that "the age of managed care" is inescapable. Given policy and insurer emphasis on primary care physicians as gatekeepers in the managed care system, how will specialty rankings within medicine change as a result of the uneven distribution of referral power? Recent data suggest an increase in the number of medical students preferring primary care over specialization (Kassebaum et al 1995), which may lead to long-term changes in the specialty structure within medicine. In corporate law, the traditional long-standing relationship between corporate customer and law firm is now being jettisoned in favor of either more frequent "spot contracting" with multiple firms, or the development of internal legal departments (Tolbert & Stern 1991). Again, how have these changes affected status rankings within the legal profession? We also do not know to what extent significant mobility has occurred across diverse work settings, or whether mobility across settings is more valuable to the individual career (in terms of either earnings or prestige gains) than mobility within settings. We return to these issues in a later section of this paper.

## THE CONVERGENCE OF CONTROL STRUCTURES

Even as the settings of professional work have become more diverse, the structures and bases of control over professional work appear to be converging, both across and within professions and across work settings. This would be predicted by institutional theory as the expected result of isomorphic adaptation over time. Institutional isomorphism is a process whereby groups of organizations move toward similar organizational forms and practices over time as they compete for political power and institutional legitimacy. DiMaggio & Powell (1983) outlined three mechanisms through which isomorphic change occurs: coercive pressure from governing bodies or the state; mimetic pressure on organizations to copy existing forms when faced by conditions of great uncertainty; and the normative expectations of powerful professional groups within organizations. However, when the norms are themselves in flux, and the power of the profession becomes unstable, the balance may shift toward coercive and mimetic pressure, both of which may be more influential when uncertainty in a sector or organizational field is high (Fennell & Alexander 1987, Derber & Schwartz 1991). Friedson's work (1994) suggests another basis for the "new professionalism" is control through expertise that is blended with an openness to inspection/evaluation by both peers and external parties. We suspect such a model may be possible in the future, but at present indications are that control over professional work is slipping firmly into the realm of corporate and bureaucratic control, as Starr predicted for medicine some time ago (1982). Specifically, professional practice in many sectors is increasingly driven by pressure for revenue generation and accountability to the state and to avoid legal prosecution.

Examples can be found in many sectors. In medicine, the primary "norms" and emphases of the sector have shifted from access and quality issues to cost containment and service reduction (Alexander & D'Aunno 1990, Flood & Fennell 1995, Prechel & Gupman 1995). Clinical practice guidelines have been developed and used across subspecialties to standardize clinical practice and by managed care plans to deny reimbursement and shape cost-effective service delivery (Hafferty & Light 1995). Lawyers are pressed to build up stables of clients and maximize billable hours (Nelson 1988, Wallace 1995), while the decision-making of the judiciary is shaped by sentencing guidelines and tort law (Tonry 1993, Stolzenberg & D'Alessio 1994, Kramer & Ulmer 1996). Engineers are increasingly pressed to demonstrate the cost-effectiveness of their designs (Perrucci 1971, Whalley 1991), and scientists in both the private sector and within universities are expected to generate research grants as well as follow university and federal guidelines on the use of human subjects, data security, and reporting procedures (Long 1992, Long et al 1993, Gieryn 1983). Since the mid-1980s, university and college curricula have been modeled on guidelines issued by the American Association of Colleges, and quality assessment in higher education emerged from the curriculum reform movement (Ratcliff 1996, Banta & Associates 1993). In all of these examples, practice guidelines have both shaped the content of professional decision-making and provided a vehicle through which accountability for professional practice can be explicitly measured. Evaluation of professional performance in medicine, judicial sentencing, and academia have used compliance with practice guidelines as an important indicator of appropriate or high quality work.

In many ways, this change in control within professions reflects changes discussed by Friedson (1984) and Hafferty & McKinlay (1993) concerning the impact of external threats to professional autonomy. Those threats impinge on multiple levels of professional work, from the terms of work to the conditions and content of work. For example, within medicine the intrusion of managed care has interjected an additional layer of authority between the provider and the patient in such a way that the referral to a specialist is no longer simply the decision of the primary care physician, since the choice of specialist and the treatment by that specialist is often constrained by contract relationships and reimbursement policies. Thus, the terms and conditions of medical work have changed due to structural changes in health care organizations. The content of medical work is then constrained by the use of clinical practice guidelines by HMOs and MCOs to structure clinical decision-making. Guidelines have been incorporated within managed care settings as part of their adoption of "total" or "continuous quality improvement" (CQI) methods to assess quality and control costs (Burns et al 1992, AHCPR 1995). Physician practice profiles are routinely constructed from chart audits and compared to guideline recommended practice patterns. Physicians who have aberrant profiles (usually over-usage of costly tests or procedures) are then encouraged to adjust their practice behaviors to better comply with the organization's preferred profile. Thus we find direct incursions on medicine's control over its core technology (Hafferty & Light 1995).

The popularity of the CQI movement in health care is itself an interesting organizational phenomena, which suggests the importance of mimetic isomorphic processes of change. Very little evidence is available to justify claims of effectiveness of CQI in medical settings; nonetheless the Joint Commission on Accreditation of Healthcare Organizations (JCAHO) has rewritten its accreditation procedures on quality to promote and endorse the use of CQI in hospitals (JCAHO 1992). Hospitals and clinics have rushed to train their members in the language and methods of CQI, following the lead of both JCAHO and each other (mimetic isomorphism), in order to benchmark their organization's performance against the rest of the industry (Flood & Fennell 1995).

Medicine is not alone in its acquiescence to external pressures for accountability and cost containment. Universities are subject to severe financial pressures, as federal support for tuition grants and research funding has steadily declined. Rewards within the university are increasingly distributed on the basis of revenue generation. Promotions, prestigious chairs, and salary increases are given on the basis of a mix of criteria in which innovative scientific research that advances knowledge is still valued but is increasingly displaced by an emphasis on scientific research that is funded or that generates patents (Bok 1993, Long 1992, Long et al 1993). At the same time, many academic disciplines in both the sciences and the liberal arts are subject to increasingly difficult pressures to retain talented faculty in the face of limited and dwindling rewards. The private sector has expanded its search for top quality professionals and represents an increasingly valued alternative career track for academics (Abbott 1991).

## DIVERSIFICATION OF INTERESTS AMONG PROFESSIONALS

The diversification of the locations of professional work and the increasing pressure to generate revenue and control costs have led to questions about the diversification of interests among professionals and the overall state of the professions generally. The debates surrounding these changes are often couched in terms of professionalization, deprofessionalization, and (in some cases) proletarianization (Derber & Schwartz 1991). Debates about professionalization and deprofessionalization often fail to separate the content of professional work from the context where the work is performed (see Abbott 1991). Further, the relationship between diversification of professional interests and deprofessionalization is usually left unspecified.

Evidence for the diversification of professional interests is fragmentary. Researchers usually point to the growing racial, ethnic, and gender diversity of recent cohorts as a sign of the diversification of professional interests (see Menkel-Meadow 1989 and Epstein 1993 on law, Zuckerman et al 1991 on science, Chamberlain 1988 on academia, Morrison & Von Glinow 1990 on management, and Bonner 1992 on medicine). Other research points to well-publicized disputes within professional associations or challenges to their governance of professions (Hafferty & Light 1995, Halliday 1987). Relatively little research asks professionals from different social backgrounds working in different organizational contexts what they view as the nature of their professional role or (perhaps more importantly) how they view their professional roles as they are carried out by professionals in other organizational contexts. Evidence regarding the effects of cost containment on professional divisiveness is relatively fragmentary as well, with most of the evidence confined to medicine (Hafferty & McKinley 1993, Leicht et al 1995). In theory, uniform pressures for cost containment should produce relatively uniform responses that mitigate the effects of diversified professional interests on professional practice. However, there is still relatively little research that examines the effects of cost containment on the content and context of professional work (but see Clark & Estes 1992, Feder et al 1987, Flood et al 1994, Prechel & Gupman 1995).

Researchers' attempts to study the consequences of diversification and cost containment are often confounded by the diversification of professional work settings. In addition, it is often not clear which professional workers are affected and which workers were in fact the targets of systematic organizational changes (Leicht et al 1995). We suspect this is partly due to the fact that these changes have mostly affected individual practitioners and either (*a*) have not affected the content and context of work for other, more elite professionals at all, or (*b*) have enhanced the autonomy and responsibility of relatively elite professionals by placing them in control of cost containment initiatives. Further, almost no research has examined whether these social and organizational changes affect the content of professional practice or merely the context where professional work takes place (excepting Hoff & McCaffery 1996, Abbott 1988, 1991).

To date, extant research has been imprecise in isolating these differences in diversification effects and clarifying their relationship to different work settings. To what extent is interest-diversity the result of changes in the demographic composition of professional workers over time versus changes in organizational arrangements? To what extent do the two overlap? Has the growing demographic diversity of professionals led to different "strategies of resistance" for different professionals facing threats to professional prerogatives? Some evidence suggests that diversification in professional work settings should lead to diversification of professional interests (see Abbott 1991, Hoff & McCaffery 1996). But this effect could be confounded by a diversity of responses to the same organizational arrangements as well. In the last section we outline a research program to partially address these issues.

## CAREERS AND CAREER MOBILITY AMONG PROFESSIONALS

Professional careers provide one linchpin for studying professional diversification and the organizational context of professional work. It is through the professional career that the benefits of professional life (status and income) are accrued. Career paths trace the training outcomes (degrees and location) and job transitions of individuals over their work lives. The professional career path represents the observable history of how individuals have been socialized into appropriate professional roles (Kagan & Nelson 1985, Nelson 1988, Nelson et al 1992, Powell 1985, Rosen 1989). The typical professional career path is likely to change if diversity in organizational arrangements leads to diversity of interests and demographic diversity among professional workers (see Kunda 1992). Further, it is by changing career outcomes that the interests of professionals are likely to diverge. Current and future research should draw on the study of professional careers as an arena in which to examine professional diversification and fragmentation.

One question raised by research on diverse professional settings is whether the labor market for professionals is segmented by either gender or function (Hagan 1990, Wallace 1993, Long 1992). Gender segmentation has been most widely publicized in popular debates about the "mommy track" in the legal profession and the glass ceiling in management. Both are structural barriers that act to depress mobility among professional women. In addition, most professions have been conceptually dichotomized by function into elites and practitioners. Elites represent a small percentage of the knowledge producers for the profession and are usually housed in universities, whereas non-elite practitioners consume and apply the knowledge produced and disseminated by elites (Friedson 1994). This difference has not been a major cleavage in most professions because elite members were responsible for the training of practitioners, elites depended on strong demand for and the relatively high status of practitioners in the wider society to bolster their own social status, and elites were vastly outnumbered by practitioners and shared similar incomes and social statuses (Abel 1989, Stinchcombe 1990). However, the widening diversity of professional work settings suggests that this relatively stable conception of professional stratification will (and has begun to) change. With this change will come an array of new questions about professional careers and stratification that were not salient for most professions until as recently as ten years ago.

The first and most obvious question one could ask as organizational arrangements diversify is whether there are systematic differences in those recruited into professional roles in different settings. Governments and universities traditionally have been the major avenues for career advancement for women and minorities in diversifying labor markets. There is considerable pressure placed on these work settings to conform to equal employment opportunity laws (Powell & Dimaggio 1991, Bridges & Villemez 1994). Within law, the growing use of in-house counsel has opened a mobility alternative to private, independent legal practice in law firms (Spangler 1986, Epstein 1993). In medicine, the rise of HMOs, PPOs, and other group practice arrangements has made salaried work a rising proportion of medical practice (Hafferty & Light 1995). A key question to be addressed by future research is whether professionals with different characteristics are more likely to end up in some specific organizational contexts and not in others.

A second, related question is whether there is significant and typical career mobility across diverse work settings and (if so) what the consequences are for individual professionals who move between settings. This may be a highly significant indicator of fragmentation and segmentation in professional work.

If organizational contexts constitute segmented, separate labor markets that people enter into early in their careers and rarely (if ever) leave, this would signify that professional work was becoming fragmented. Alternatively, if the boundaries between organizational settings are relatively permeable and show no consistent pattern of career movements, this would suggest that professionals have been able to maintain a relatively coherent occupational labor market tied to generalist knowledge. We think a more likely pattern is one of path dependence, where there are systematic movements between work settings and where the prediction of the destination work setting depends critically on the immediately prior work setting.

A further extension of this question is whether mobility across organizational contexts is more valuable for a professional career than mobility within specific contexts. This question is complicated by the problem that many new organizational arrangements for professional work (for example, storefront legal service providers) do not have well-established professional and career stratification patterns, and the demographic and social backgrounds of professionals in both new and older established work settings are changing.

A related concern involves the relative prestige rankings of different organizational arrangements. Traditional research on the relative prestige rankings of professional settings assumes that independent, fee-for-service practice is the standard by which all organizational arrangements are judged. However, numerous professional groups (such as accountants and engineers) have never established clear norms concerning organizational arrangements for professional work. Many new arrangements do not have clear counterparts that predate their appearance in the 1970s and 1980s, and this makes overtime comparisons of status rankings difficult. Further, it is not clear that younger professionals are as committed to long-established professional practice norms, especially in law and medicine (Halliday 1987). These problems could be partially (but not completely) overcome by surveying professionals at different stages of their careers, including older professionals whose entry into professional life predates many of the new organizational arrangements. On a related issue that is critical for the overall evaluation of professional work, status, and privilege, we know little about the relative rankings of organizational contexts by clients of professionals, outside of public opinion surveys about HMOs (Strang 1995).

A second key to understanding the organizational context of professional work is to engage in systematic comparisons of the career mobility of professionals and others who work in the same organizational settings. In situations where organizations are setting the agenda for the context of professional work, there should be divergent mobility patterns in different organizational settings. However, this is only part of the comparison that is needed. Researchers should also answer the question of whether the career patterns of professionals are distinctive. If there is considerable isomorphic pressure from employing organizations, then professional career mobility will look like the career mobility of other white-collar employees. It also suggests that professional norms are not well established or have been subordinated (Kunda 1992). As Abbott (1988) has argued, the focus on isomorphic pressures from organizations as well as professions means that researchers should study multiple professional groups interacting with each other and with nonprofessional groups in the same organizational settings.

## A FUTURE RESEARCH PROGRAM ON THE DIVERSIFICATION OF PROFESSIONAL WORK

Our review of the existing literature on organizational contexts and professional work suggests that there are many exciting questions in need of research. Further, there is a wide array of documentary data sources on professionals that have yet to be fully exploited. Much of this documentary data comes from professional directories that provide historical information on individual professionals (the legal profession has the richest information sources in this instance). Researchers will want to engage in extensive interactions with professional associations in order to gain access to association documents, newspapers, media releases, and reactions to new organizational arrangements. Almost all of our future research suggestions draw on organizational theory and especially on institutional theory (see Scott 1995, Powell & DiMaggio 1991) and focus on the study of institutional arrangements, careers and mobility, and job content.

### *Changing Institutional Arrangements*

At the institutional level, work is needed on the rise and decline of organizational arrangements. In some professions, established organizational arrangements for delivering services have carried considerable institutional weight. In fact, the prestige of a profession is often dictated by the ability of professionals to determine the organizational form under which service will be delivered. If medicine represents one extreme where (traditionally) there are strong institutionalized norms dictating appropriate organizational forms for professional practice, engineering may be at the other extreme (compare Starr 1982 to Kunda 1992).

One fruitful avenue of future research at the institutional level would be to study the rise and decline of organizational arrangements using the theory and methods of organizational ecology (Hannan & Freeman 1989). Most new developments in the organization of professional work in the United States have occurred in the twentieth century, and the history of new professional organizational forms is usually well documented as competitors seek to legitimize new organizational arrangements through appeals to the state, consumers, and (ultimately) practitioners. Further, the interest groups that develop around new organizational arrangements often create support groups and professional associations of their own to monitor and support the growth of the new organizational form. These interest groups and professional associations could be a rich source of new data on the rise and decline of organizational forms.

In addition to examining the usual processes that organizational ecology draws attention to (legitimation and competition), researchers will want to pay particular attention to newer processes discussed in the interaction between organizational populations—competition, complementarity, and path dependence (see Carroll & Harrison 1994). Some organizational forms compete directly against each other for the same service niche. Other forms act in synergy with each other, aiding the legitimation and growth of each organizational form in itself. Further, the success of some organizational forms will depend critically on their start-up date relative to the existence and establishment of other organizational forms. To date, organizational ecology has been used to explain the rise and decline of HMOs (Strang 1995) and funeral directors (Torres 1991) but has not been applied to the development of other organizational forms in different professional settings (for a slightly different treatment of state bar associations, see Halliday et al 1993).

At the microlevel, researchers should address questions of professional, client, and professional association acceptance of new organizational forms. This aspect of future research could employ survey and field research methodologies along with comparative historical analysis.

Quantitative survey research methodology could be used to study the acceptance of new organizational arrangements by clients. In addition to its amenability to random sample survey research techniques, this research problem could be addressed with in-depth interviews of corporate clients on the verge of adopting new organizational arrangements for the purchase of professional services, or clients who have made divergent choices in the forms of professional services they consume. For example, we still have relatively little information about the decision-making processes leading to the corporate adoption of HMOs and employee reactions to them. The delivery of some professional services (accounting is the most obvious example) can be radically changed by the use of information technologies, yet the arrangements for delivering services in this way often violate the institutional expectations of clients (Fischer & Dirsmith 1995). Survey and field research on actual client decision-making is needed in addition to research on the general ranking of different organizational arrangements for professional work from clients' perspectives.

Researchers could also focus their attention in the field and in surveys on professional acceptance of organizational arrangements. As stated above, this type of research needs to be sensitive to likely cohort differences in evaluations and exposure to new organizational forms. Again, sample surveys providing general rankings of different organizational arrangements are needed in addition to field research on reactions to (and rationales for) specific organizational arrangements.

Finally, researchers could focus on professional associations (both dominant and dissident) and their reactions to changing organizational arrangements. Much of this work would involve comparative historical analyses of documents, newspapers, press releases, convention minutes, and other literature produced by professional associations. These projects should focus not only on the association's reaction to external developments, but also on the internal debates and reactions to conflict over new organizational arrangements and the constellations of interests involved.

## *New Research on Professional Careers and Mobility*

Another needed track within this research program should focus on professional careers, using institutional theory (Leicht et al 1995) or prior research on careers in other settings (Rosenbaum 1984, DiPrete 1989, Diprete & Grusky 1990). Many directories of professionals allow for the study of cohorts of professionals as they enter and leave the labor market (see for example the *Martindale-Hubbell Law Directory* or the *Law and Business Directory of Corporate Counsel*, various years). More systematic methodological work in conjunction with professional associations could help to gauge the accuracy and coverage embodied in these directories so that methodological corrections can be made (where appropriate). Initially, researchers will probably do well to collect more systematic career information on a single organizational arrangement, putting studies together for comparative analysis later on.

Ultimately we think that researchers should turn their attention toward systematic comparisons of multiple organizational settings for a single existing profession. Key questions that studies of this kind could address include: 1. Do organizational settings draw professionals from different backgrounds? 2. Do career mobility patterns within and across settings lead to the clustering of elite practitioners? 3. How do the career patterns of professionals differ across organizational settings? 4. Are there systematic patterns of mobility across organizational settings, and if so, what are the consequences of that mobility?

There are at least two other avenues for new research that need to be mentioned. The growing heterogeneity of the settings where professional practice takes place provides an ideal opportunity to compare the careers of different professionals to each other and to those of other white-collar workers, especially managers (see Abbott 1988 for an example). One could argue that the latest rounds of corporate downsizing represent an attempt by managers to assume professional status by substituting bureaucratic hierarchies with loosely coupled subcontracting and consulting arrangements (Boyett & Conn 1992). The study of professional careers must ultimately recognize that employment arrangements are changing rapidly for other white-collar workers as well.

Most prior work on changing organizational arrangements ultimately mentions (or at least implies) that the job content of professional work has changed. This is an area where many good field studies already exist (Abbott 1988, Kunda 1992, Thomas 1995). Future field research should track job content changes very carefully, noting the progression of changes in organizational arrangements and following technological innovations and their actual use (see Barley & Kunda 1992, Rule & Attewell 1989). In addition to exhaustive field work on the actual content of job tasks across settings, we need research that conducts systematic interviews with various professionals to assess their reaction to changes in job content.

### *The Professionalization of Everyone?*

In 1964, Wilensky asked the question whether virtually all occupations would or could become professionalized (Wilensky 1964). With corporate downsizing at the middle-management level and the rapid movement toward subcontracting arrangements, outsourcing, organizational work teams, and other nonbureaucratically oriented work arrangements, we would argue that the organizational form in which many white-collar services will be delivered will at least superficially resemble traditional professional practice.

Ultimately, the changing organization of professional work is complicated by other features of contemporary work organizations. Managers and those assigned the duties of administrative control in work organizations are also engaged in professional projects (Barley & Kunda 1992, Marglin 1974), and part of these projects involve the creation of workplace norms concerning autonomy and accountability that are similar to those enjoyed (or allegedly enjoyed) by professionals. The relationship between professional workers and employing organizations is complicated by the (real or alleged) decline of bureaucracy as an organizing principle of work organizations (see Boyett & Conn 1992). It is no longer true (if it ever was) that managers are oriented toward control of their employees. Instead, we argue that managers are oriented toward maximizing their own autonomy and that this explains their behavior more readily than control orientations, especially with regard to managing professional employees. At a minimum, researchers addressing the relationship between professionals and organizational arrangements need to be sensitive to broader changes in workplace organization that go beyond the traditional emphasis on professionals in bureaucracies.

Researchers interested in the changing organizational context of professional work face an exciting, new, and complicated empirical world for their research.

Our review has only touched the surface of the many issues with which researchers in this area are currently struggling. We hope that our review will stimulate new generations of researchers to enter an area of study that represents a unique interface between organizational theory, social stratification, and the historical analysis of institutional change in professional work.

## ACKNOWLEDGMENTS

This project was supported by the National Science Foundation (SBR#9310557).



*Literature Cited*

Abbott AD. 1988. *The System of Professions: An Essay on the Division of Expert Labor.* Chicago: Univ. Chicago Press. 435 pp.

Abbott AD. 1991. The future of professions: occupation and expertise in the age of organization. *Res. Sociol. Organ.* 8:17–42

Abel R. 1989. *American Lawyers.* New York: Oxford Univ. Press

Agency for Health Care Policy and Research. 1995. *Using Clinical Practice Guidelines to Evaluate Quality of Care. AHCPR Publ. No. 95–0045.* US Dep. Health Hum. Serv., Washington, DC

Alexander JA, D'Aunno T. 1990. Transformation of institutional environments: perspectives on the corporatization of U.S. health care. In *Innovations in Health Care Delivery,* ed. S Mick, pp. 53–85. San Francisco: Jossey-Bass. 281 pp.

Banta TW, & Associates, ed. 1993. *Making a Difference: Outcomes of a Decade of Assessment in Higher Education.* San Francisco: Jossey-Bass

Barley SR, Kunda G. 1992. Design and devotion: surges of rational and normative ideologies of control in managerial discourse. *Admin. Sci. Q.* 37:363–99

Baum JAC, Oliver C. 1991. Institutional linkages and organizational mortality. *Admin. Sci. Q.* 36:187–218

Bendix R. 1956. *Work and Authority in Industry: Ideologies of Management in the Course of Industrialization.* New York: Wiley. 466 pp.

Bok D. 1993. *The Cost of Talent: How Executives and Professionals Are Paid and How It Affects America.* New York: Free Press

Bonner TN. 1992. *To the Ends of the Earth: Women's Search for Education in Medicine.* Cambridge: Harvard Univ. Press. 232 pp.

Boyett JH, Conn HP. 1992. *Workplace 2000: The Revolution Reshaping American Business.* New York: Plume

Bridges W, Villemez W. 1994. *The Employment Relationship: Causes and Consequences of Modern Personnel Administration.* New York: Plenum

Burns LR, Denton M, Goldfein S, Warrick L, Morenz B, Sales B. 1992. The use of continuous quality improvement methods in the development and dissemination of medical practice guidelines. *Qual. Rev. Bull.* 18:434–39

Carroll GR, Harrison JR. 1994. On the historical efficacy of competition between organizational populations. *Am. J. Sociol.* 100:720–49

Chamberlain MK, ed. 1988. *Women in Academe: Progress and Prospects.* New York: Russell Sage. 415 pp.

Clark L, Estes CL. 1992. Sociological and economic theories of markets and nonprofits: evidence from home health organizations. *Am. J. Sociol.* 97:945–69

Curran BA. 1986. American lawyers in the 1980's: a profession in transition. *Law Soc. Rev.* 20:19

Derber C, Schwartz WA. 1991. New mandarins or new proletariat?: professional power at work. *Res. Sociol. Organ.* 8:71–96

Dill A. 1995. Case management as a cultural practice. *Adv. Med. Sociol.* 6:81–117

DiMaggio PJ, Powell WW. 1983. The iron cage revisited: institutional isomorphism and collective rationality in organizational fields. *Am. Sociol. Rev.* 48:147–60

DiPrete TA. 1989. *The Bureaucratic Labor Market: The Case of the Federal Civil Service.* New York: Plenum

DiPrete TA, Grusky DB. 1990. The multilevel analysis of trends with repeated cross-sectional data. *Sociol. Methodol.* 20:337–68

Durkheim E. 1933. *The Division of Labor in Society.* New York: Free Press

Eder K. 1993. *The New Politics of Class: Social Movements and Cultural Dynamics in Advanced Societies.* Newbury Park, CA: Sage

Epstein CF. 1993. *Women in Law.* New York: Basic Books. 491 pp. 2nd ed.

Feder J, Hadley J, Zuckerman S. 1987. How did Medicare's prospective payment system affect hospitals? *N. Engl. J. Med.* 317:867–73

Fennell ML, Alexander JA. 1987. Organizational boundary spanning in institutionalized environments. *Acad. Manage. J.* 30:456–76

Fennell ML, Alexander JA. 1993. Perspectives on organizational change in the US medical care sector. *Annu. Rev. Sociol.* 19:89–112

Fischer MJ, Dirsmith MW. 1995. Strategy, technology and social processes within professional cultures: a negotiated order, ethnographic perspective. *Symb. Interact.* 18:381–412

Fligstein N. 1990. *The Transformation of Corporate Control.* Cambridge: Harvard Univ. Press. 391 pp.

Flood AB, Fennell ML. 1995. Through the lenses of organizational sociology: the role of organizational theory and research in conceptualizing and examining our health care system. *J. Health Soc. Behav.* 36:154–69

Flood AB, Scott WR, Shortell SM. 1994. Organizational performance: managing for efficiency and effectiveness. In *Health Care Management: A Text in Organizational Theory,* ed. SM Shortell, A Kaluzny, pp. 316–51. Albany: Delmar. 3rd ed.

Friedson E. 1984. The changing nature of professional control. *Annu. Rev. Sociol.* 10:1–20

Friedson E. 1986. *Professional Powers: A Study of the Institutionalization of Formal Knowledge.* Chicago: Univ. Chicago Press. 241 pp.

Friedson E. 1994. *Professionalism Reborn: Theory, Prophecy and Policy.* Chicago: Univ. Chicago Press. 238 pp.

Giddens A. 1994. *Beyond Left and Right: The Future of Radical Politics.* Stanford: Stanford Univ. Press. 276 pp.

Gieryn TF. 1983. Boundary-work and the demarcation of science from non-science: strains and interests in professional ideologies of scientists. *Am. Sociol. Rev.* 48:781–94

Goode WJ. 1957. Community within a community: the professions: psychology, sociology and medicine. *Am. Sociol. Rev.* 25:902–14

Hafferty FW, Light DW. 1995. Professional dynamics and the changing nature of medical work. *J. Health Soc. Behav.* 36:132–53

Hafferty FW, McKinlay JB, eds. 1993. *The Changing Medical Profession: An International Perspective.* New York: Oxford Univ. Press. 261 pp.

Hagan J. 1990. The gender stratification of income inequality among lawyers. *Soc. Forces* 68:835–55

Halliday TC. 1987. *Beyond Monopoly: Lawyers, State Crises, and Professional Empowerment.* Chicago: Univ. Chicago Press

Halliday TC, Powell MJ, Granfors MW. 1993. After minimalism: transformations of state bar associations from market dependence to state reliance, 1918–1950. *Am. Sociol. Rev.* 58:515–35

Hannan MT, Freeman J. 1989. *Organizational Ecology.* Cambridge: Harvard Univ. Press

Hoff TJ, McCaffrey DP. 1996. Adapting, resisting and negotiating: how physicians cope with organizational and economic change. *Work Occup.* 23:165–89

Inglehart R. 1990. *Cultural Shift in Advanced Industrial Society.* Princeton, NJ: Princeton Univ. Press

Jenkins JC, Leicht KT. 1997. Class analysis and social movements: a critique and reformulation. In *Reworking Class,* ed. JR Hall, pp. 386–417. Ithaca, NY: Cornell Univ.

Joint Commission on Accreditation of Healthcare Organizations. 1992. *Cornerstones of Healthcare in the Nineties: Forging a Framework of Excellence.* Hot Springs, VA: Homestead

Kagan RA, Nelson RL. 1985. On the social significance of large law firm practice. *Stanford Law Rev.* 37:399–464

Kassebaum DG, Szenas PL, Ruffin AL, Masters DR. 1995. The research career interests of graduating medical students. *Acad. Med.* 70:848–52

Kramer JH, Ulmer JT. 1996. Sentencing disparity and departures from guidelines. *Justice Q.* 13:81–106

Kunda G. 1992. *Engineering Culture: Control and Commitment in a High-Tech Corporation.* Philadelphia: Temple Univ. Press. 297 pp.

Leicht KT, Fennell ML. 1996. *Gender representation in corporate law: normative and coercive effects on the structure of corporate legal departments.* Presented at Annu. Meet. Am. Sociol. Assoc., 91st, New York

Leicht KT, Fennell ML, Witkowski KM. 1995. The effects of hospital characteristics and radical organizational change on the relative standing of health care professions. *J. Health Soc. Behav.* 36:151–67

Long JS. 1992. Measures of sex differences in scientific productivity. *Soc. Forces* 71:159–78

Long JS, Allison PD, McGinnis R. 1993. Rank

advancement in academic careers: sex differences and the effects of productivity. *Am. Sociol. Rev.* 58:703–22

Manza J, Hout M, Brooks C. 1995. Class voting in capitalist democracies since WWII. *Annu. Rev. Sociol.* 21:137–63

Marglin SA. 1974. What do bosses do? The origins and functions of hierarchy in capitalist production. *Rev. Radic. Polit. Econ.* 6:33–60

Marx K. 1889. *Capital.* New York: Appleton

Mechanic D. 1994. Managed care: rhetoric and realities. *Inquiry* 31:124–28

Menkel-Meadow C. 1989. Feminization of the legal profession: the comparative sociology of women lawyers. In *Lawyers in Society: Comparative Theories,* ed. RL Abel, PSC Lewis, pp. 196–255. Berkeley: Univ. Calif. Press

Morrison AM, Von Glinow M. 1990. Women and minorities in management. *Am. Psychol.* 45:200–8

Nelson RL. 1988. *Partners with Power: The Social Transformation of the Large Law Firm.* Berkeley: Univ. Calif. Press. 376 pp.

Nelson RL, Trubek DM, Solomon RL. 1992. *Lawyers' Ideals/Lawyers' Practices: Transformations of the American Legal Profession.* Ithaca, NY: Cornell Univ. Press

Oliver C. 1991. Strategic responses to institutional processes. *Acad. Manage. Rev.* 16:145–79

Perrucci R. 1971. Engineers: professional servants of power. *Am. Behav. Sci.* 14:492–506

Powell MJ. 1985. Developments in the regulation of lawyers: competing segments and market, client and government controls. *Soc. Forces* 64:281–305

Powell WW, DiMaggio PJ. 1991. *The New Institutionalism in Organizational Analysis.* Chicago: Univ. Chicago Press. 478 pp.

Prechel H, Gupman A. 1995. Changing economic conditions and their effects on professional autonomy: an analysis of family practitioners and oncologists. *Sociol. Forum* 10:245–71

Ratcliff JL. 1996. *Discretion and constraint in faculty decision-making regarding the curriculum.* Presented at Annu. Meet. Am. Sociol. Assoc., 91st, New York

Roach SL. 1990. Men and women lawyers in in-house legal departments: recruitment and career patterns. *Gen. Soc.* 4:207–19

Rosen R. 1989. The inside counsel movement, professional judgment and organizational representation. *Ind. Law J.* 64:479–553

Rosenbaum JE. 1984. *Career Mobility in a Corporate Hierarchy.* Orlando: Academic. 328 pp.

Rule J, Attewell P. 1989. What do computers do? *Soc. Probl.* 36:225–41

Scott WR. 1995. *Institutions and Organizations.* Newbury Park, CA: Sage

Scott WR. 1982. Managing professional work: three models of control for health organizations. *Health Serv. Res.* 17:213–40

Scott WR. 1993. The organization of medical care services: towards an integrated theoretical model. *Med. Care Rev.* 50:271–302

Spangler E. 1986. *Lawyers for Hire: Salaried Professionals at Work.* New Haven, CT: Yale Univ. Press. 233 pp.

Starr P. 1982. *The Social Transformation of American Medicine.* New York: Basic Books. 514 pp.

Stevens R. 1989. *In Sickness and in Wealth: American Hospitals in the Twentieth Century.* New York: Basic Books

Stinchcombe A. 1990. *Information and Organizations.* Berkeley, CA: Univ. Calif. Press. 391 pp.

Stolzenberg L, D'Alessio SJ. 1994. Sentencing and unwarranted disparity: an empirical assessment of the long term impact of sentencing guidelines in Minnesota. *Criminology* 32:301–10

Strang D. 1995. Health maintenance organizations. In *Organizations in Industry,* ed. GR Carroll, MT Hannan, pp. 162–85. New York: Oxford Univ. Press

Thomas R. 1995. *What Machines Can't Do.* Cambridge MA: MIT Press

Tolbert PS, Stern RN. 1991. Organizations of professionals: governance structures in large law firms. *Res. Sociol. Organ.* 8:97–117

Tonry M, ed. 1993. *Crime and Justice: A Review of Research.* Chicago: Univ. Chicago Press. 195 pp.

Torres DL. 1991. What, if anything, is professionalism?: Institutions and the problem of change. *Res. Sociol. Organ.* 8:43–68

Wallace JE. 1993. Professional and organizational commitment: compatible or incompatible? *J. Voc. Behav.* 42:333–49

Wallace JE. 1995. Corporatist control and organizational commitment among professionals: the case of lawyers working in law firms. *Soc. Forces* 73:811–40

Weber M. 1947. *The Theory of Social and Economic Organization.* New York: Oxford Univ. Press. 436 pp.

Whalley P. 1991. Negotiating the boundaries of engineering: professionals, managers, and manual work. *Res. Sociol. Organ.* 8:191–215

Wilensky HL. 1964. The professionalization of everyone? *Am. J. Sociol.* 70:137–58

Zuckerman H, Cole JR, Bruer JT, eds. 1991. *The Outer Circle: Women in the Scientific Community.* New York: Norton. 351 pp.

*Annu. Rev. Sociol. 1997. 23:233–61*


# THE MEASUREMENT OF AGE, AGE STRUCTURING, AND THE LIFE COURSE

*Richard A. Settersten, Jr.*
Department of Sociology, Case Western Reserve University, Cleveland, Ohio 44106-7124; e-mail: ras2@po.cwru.edu

*Karl Ulrich Mayer*
Max Planck Institute for Human Development and Education, Lentzeallee 94, Berlin, Germany; e-mail: sekmayer@mpib-berlin.mpg.de

KEY WORDS: life events, life transitions, life review, life history, longitudinal

ABSTRACT

The measurement of age, age structuring, and the life course has become more problematic as the study of human lives has moved toward more detailed analyses and explanations. As we seek to better understand the course of human lives in contemporary and changing societies, the effective empirical measurement of its key concepts simultaneously becomes more pressing and more complicated. We first review the critical concepts of, and measurement strategies associated with, age and age structuring—including a discussion of different types of age, subjective age identification, age norms and age expectations, critical life events, life phases, and life review. We then discuss state-of-the-art methods for measuring the life course, especially through life history and event matrices, and we close the chapter with some comments on the organization, analysis, and modeling of data.

## INTRODUCTION

Within the social sciences, the measurement of age, age structuring, and the life course must be considered within the context of three very different debates and problem areas. First, it is related to the more general problem of how the lives of individuals are connected to the development and change of larger social



0360-0572/97/0815-0233$08.00

collectives, of societies as a whole, and to the course of history (Elder 1996, Mayer 1986). Second, it is related to the interaction of biological, psychological, and social aspects of individual development (Baltes et al 1996). And third, it is related to a lively debate on the social construction of time (Nowotny 1989). We must limit our discussion to a select number of issues within these three areas, guided primarily by decisions about the importance of certain concepts and measures for empirical research.

The measurement of age, age structuring, and the life course has become more problematic as the study of human lives has moved away from global images and theoretical categories toward more detailed analyses and explanations. Over the last century, everyday ideas about what constitutes the "normal biography" have become less clear. While we have little problem conjuring up images about the life of a Yorkshire coal miner or Iowa farmer, our images about the majority of lives in contemporary society seem to lack the same degree of clarity. Our scientific treatment of the life course must allow for the heterogeneity, discontinuity, and contingency that exists in present-day societies.

Earlier notions of the life cycle, life span, or life course were at least in principle based on holistic conceptions of human lives (O'Rand & Krecker 1990). The dominant theme was borrowed from biology: maturation and growth, followed by decline and regression. Only as a minor subtopic did the idea of lifelong development, whether actual or potential, surface (Baltes et al 1996). As the study of human lives became more elaborate, sociological treatments were differentiated from those of biology and psychology; and even sociological treatments were segmented into a number of specialties (e.g. sociology of youth, sociology of old age, educational and occupational sociology, demography, and family studies). The challenge now lies in moving away from this fragmentation to a truly integrative study of the life course.

Chronological *age*, a property of individuals, may stand as a proxy for biological maturation, psychological development, membership in larger social categories (e.g. cohort), or life stage or phase. *Age structuring* refers to the fact that every society uses age in important ways, and the experiences, roles, and statuses of individuals are often tied to age (Kertzer 1989). And the concept of the *life course* refers to the way in which social institutions shape and institutionalize individual lives in the interconnected domains of education, family, and work (Mayer & Tuma 1990). Thus, educational trajectories, employment histories and occupational careers, and family and residential histories in part compose the life course. The life course might be understood as an objective "biography," though the term biography has increasingly been used in a more narrow sense, and is usually understood to be the subjective interpretation and construction of the life course by individuals themselves (Bertaux & Kohli 1984).

While birth and death dates mark an individual's historical presence, the concept of *cohort* is reserved for an aggregate of individuals anchored together in historical time (normally defined on the basis of birth year). It is ultimately used as a basis for searching for common collective properties (or "cohort effects") brought about by the fact that historical events and conditions may impinge similarly on a cohort as they grow up, grow old, and die. In this chapter, unfortunately, we are unable to treat the problems associated with conceptualizing and measuring cohort. For a general introduction, interested readers might consult Ryder's (1965) classic paper on the concept of cohort, and Rosow's (1978) classic paper on the measurement of cohort.

So while the life course can be viewed as an event history of a single individual, it can also be viewed at aggregate level (e.g. as something shared by a cohort), as a property of cultures themselves, and as something that can be compared across historical periods or between nation-states.

We first review the critical concepts of, and measurement strategies associated with, age and age structuring—including a discussion of different types of age, subjective age identification, age norms and age expectations, critical life events, life phases, and life review. We then discuss state-of-the-art methods for measuring the life course, especially through life history and event matrices, and we close the chapter with some comments on the organization, analysis, and modeling of data.

## MEASURING AGE AND FORMS OF AGE STRUCTURING

Age is one of the most primary social and cultural categories. Age usually operates interdependently with sex, and both age and sex are universal categories (LaFontaine 1978, Linton 1942, Parsons 1942). Age and sex serve as important dimensions in both cognition and social structure. Cognitively, they function as convenient categories for the mapping of social and cultural expectations about life experiences and roles. The categories of age and sex are also of importance to the individual personality, particularly where self-identification and self-perceptions are concerned. In social structure, the categories of age and sex are common dimensions by which institutions are organized (e.g. aspects of our familial, educational, and occupational institutions are organized by age and sex).

As we mentioned earlier, age structuring refers to the fact that every society "has a distinctive way of dealing with age and, accordingly, that roles are in some ways age-linked" (Kertzer 1989, p. 5). Age structuring can be *formal*, at the level of social structure and social institutions, where key concepts have included "cohorts, roles, and age strata, and their relationship to political, economic, kinship, and other social systems and historical changes in these systems" (Kertzer 1989, p. 6). Age structuring can also be *informal*, where key concerns have been how individuals go about dividing the life course into meaningful segments, what kinds of behavior are considered appropriate for individuals of different ages, and what notions exist about the proper timing and sequencing of life events and transitions.

AGE STRUCTURING AND GENDER Most researchers have assumed that age structuring, whether formal or informal, may be quite different for men's and women's lives, given that "the very division by gender is in itself conditioned by age structuring, with the salience of gender distinctions dependent on age" (Kertzer 1989, p. 12). Similarly, Hagestad (1991) has noted that anthropological work on transitions has suggested that men and women may attach different social meanings to age, and that men and women may use different guidelines to measure the progress of their lives. For example, a long anthropological tradition focuses on *rites de passage*—rites that structure movement through lifetime by age and sex, and provide a means by which roles are assigned and resources are allocated (Benedict 1938, Glaser & Strauss 1974, van Gennup 1908). Given that men's and women's lives are often thought about and experienced differently, our measures must be sensitive to these differences.

AGE STRUCTURING ALONG OTHER SOCIAL DIMENSIONS Population-level behavioral patterns often show that the way the life course is actually experienced goes hand-in-hand with social location. The most prominent social dimensions in the literature on the demography of life-course events and transitions include sex (as discussed above), cohort/age, race/ethnicity, and social class (education, occupation, income, or some combination). While most scholars recognize that multiple definitions of the life course may emerge along various social dimensions, little empirical work has examined this variability, particularly at the level of subjective experience (Fry 1990). As a result, researchers should continue to describe and explain these multiple definitions and experiences, and our measures must allow for these complexities.

AGE STRUCTURING AND LIFE SPHERES In most Western societies, many institutions are formally organized by age to some degree. For example, primary and secondary educational institutions are heavily age-graded (Angus et al 1988). Similarly, work institutions often structure prospects for promotion by age and seniority (Lashbrook 1996, Lawrence 1996, Rosenbaum 1984), and retirement policies and benefits are often structured around age (Henretta 1994, Kohli 1994).

The degree of both formal and informal age structuring may vary by life sphere. For example, it has been argued that age is more salient in the economic and political spheres than it is in the family sphere (for further explication of this debate, see Settersten & Hagestad 1996b). Nonetheless, because lives are lived in multiple spheres, and because these spheres are often experienced in dramatically different ways, our measures must be sensitive to these differences.

AGE STRUCTURING ACROSS CULTURES Project A.G.E., a cross-cultural research project headed by anthropologists Fry and Keith, is devoted to studying the meaning of age and aging in a variety of cultures, including seven communities on four continents (Hong Kong; Swarthmore, Pennsylvania; Momence, Illinois; Blessington, Ireland; Clifden, Ireland; the pastoral Herero of Botswana, South Africa; and the !Kung Bushmen, of Botswana, North Africa). Project A.G.E. researchers have found that chronological age has the strongest salience in communities that are part of modern, industrialized societies. In the least industrialized communities, especially among the !Kung Bushmen and those in rural Clifden, Ireland, questions about age make little sense to respondents (Keith et al 1994).

This example speaks to the fact that researchers must be sensitive to cross-cultural differences in how the life course is conceptualized, the assumptions they make about (or even impose upon) a given culture and, in turn, the ways in which age and aspects of the life course are measured.

Similarly, there is a great deal of cross-national variation in the degree to which age rules and age preferences are embedded within laws and social policies, as well as in the organization of social institutions that are connected to the state (Cain 1976, Eglit 1985, Neugarten 1982). For example, in many countries rights and responsibilities are explicitly structured by chronological age. Examples of these rights and duties include age regulations around voting, driving, drinking, working (especially with regard to child labor), marrying, compulsory school, or seeking public offices. Eligibility for pensions, social services, or social insurance are also often dictated by age. Many of the discussions about legal ages center around questions of how soon in life individuals should be granted adult rights and obligations, or how late in life these rights and obligations should be retained (Cain 1976).

General references to age-related categories without clearly specified ages are also common in legislation (e.g. "minors," "the elderly") (Cain 1976). As Mayer & Schoepflin (1989, p. 200) have noted, "age groups are a favorite way of dividing up social problems," and larger age groups are often targeted for service bracketing.

These studies indicate that the state and many of its policies often rely on, and even create, conceptions of the life course. A critical examination of the state and its policies may provide further insights about the ways in which age, age structuring, and the life course are treated in a society.

AGE STRUCTURING AND NEW TIME BUDGETS FOR THE LIFE COURSE Researchers have begun to explore the ways in which the demography of an aging society, particularly increases in longevity, may have changed the nature of family and social life (Hagestad 1988, Riley 1986, Uhlenberg 1980). For example, roles have been prolonged, the sequencing of roles over lifetime has become more varied and complex, and family relationships have the potential to become more active and intense (Riley 1986). Similarly, Hagestad (1991, p. 25) and others have suggested that historical change along key demographic dimensions (life expectancy, mortality, fertility, nuptiality) has led to new "time budgets of adulthood," where the average number of years spent in various work and family roles has dramatically increased (Andersen 1985, Gee 1987, Watkins et al 1987). However, from an empirical standpoint, we still have much to learn about the ways in which family and social life have specifically been transformed by these new demographic parameters, and our measures of age, age structuring, and the life course must take these parameters into account.

## *Measuring Different Types of Age*

Research on aging and the life course hinges upon the effective measurement of age. As Bytheway (1990) notes, somewhere in the process of doing our research the questions "How old are you?" or "When where you born?" must be asked. But apart from error (e.g. difficulty remembering one's age or date of birth) or deception (e.g. intentionally misrepresenting one's age or birthdate) on the part of a respondent, the measurement of chronological age seems relatively straightforward. Chronological age can be measured in a number of ways, ranging in level of specificity—it can be expressed in days, months, or years. When the question is "How old are you?", the information gathered is normally expressed in "completed years." Of course, the same basic information is obtained with the question "What is the date of your birth?", but Bytheway (1990) reminds us that this question is quite different from the question "How old are you?" First, date of birth relates to a past event, while age is instead a current characteristic. Second, date of birth remains the same throughout life, while age is, of course, always changing. And third, complete birthdate (in month-day-year) is more precise. If only birthyear is asked, the calculation of age is likely to involve some rounding error. Some researchers have even asked both questions, but at separate points in the data-gathering process, as a consistency check. Jolicoeur and colleagues (1988) even make a distinction between postnatal age, measured from the day of birth, and total age, measured from the day of conception (obtained by correcting postnatal age with average duration of pregnancy, 0.75 years).

These examples serves as important reminders that we must ask ourselves why age is being measured and how it will be used; answers to these questions will dictate the best format for measuring age. Regardless of how it is operationalized, age is often the most powerful piece of information about an individual (Schroots & Birren 1988).

At the same time, we know that chronological age itself is an "empty" variable—we rarely assume that it is age itself that causes a behavior; instead, it is whatever age presumably indexes that is thought to be important. For example, age is often used as a predictor of an individual's physical and emotional maturity, of an individual's readiness to assume certain responsibilities, or even of the probability that an individual will experience various medical or social problems (Chudacoff 1989, Fry 1986). Still, researchers often give little thought to what exactly it is that age indexes, and they often do not spend enough time specifying the mechanisms through which age plays a role in the models they develop and test. In addition, researchers should think more critically about whether the things we hope to index by using age might instead be measured more directly, or about the conditions under which age is a relevant dimension to begin with (Ward 1984).

Similarly, tests of age differences are often tests of arbitrarily-defined age brackets, sometimes into very broad bands (e.g. 55–74, 85+), or into smaller 5- or 10-year bands. Ironically, all of the care taken to measure age accurately is lost when these brackets are constructed. Worse still, researchers habitually break down their data in this way without compelling rationale. Why are a particular set of age brackets meaningful? And why we should expect to find important differences along these divisions? We must also begin to think more critically about the circumstances under which we should "hold age constant" in our analyses, rather than routinely control for age without justification.

However, as people grow older, and as variability among similarly-aged individuals increases over the life course (Dannefer 1987), chronological age may become less useful as an index. As a result, Birren and colleagues (Birren & Cunningham 1985, Schroots & Birren 1988) suggest that alternative, and more specific, measures of age must be developed, measures that are more sensitive to individual differences. Birren & Cunningham (1985, p. 8), for example, discuss three distinct kinds of age: 1. *biological age*, which is defined by an individual's "present position with respect to his [or her] potential life span. Thus, an individual's biological age may be younger or older than his [or her] chronological age"; 2. *social age*, which is defined by an individual's "roles and habits with respect to other members of the society of which he is a part. An individual may be older or younger depending on the extent to which he shows the age-graded behavior expected of him by his particular society or culture";

and 3. *psychological age*, which is defined by the "behavioral capacities of individuals to adapt to changing demands."[1] Birren and his colleagues argue that while psychological age is clearly tied to biological and social ages, psychological age is a larger concept and includes the "use of adaptive capacities of memory, learning, intelligence, skills, feelings, motivations, and emotions for exercising behavioral control or self-regulation."

Birren suggests that these three types of age are highly independent from one another, except, perhaps, at their boundaries. While Birren's typology is useful for explicating the concept(s) of age, he and his colleagues offer little detailed advice on how these different types of age might be measured, except to say that the measurement of biological age would involve the "assessment of functional capacities of vial or life-limiting organ systems," while the measurement of social age would involve "such aspects as the individual's type of dress, language habits, and social deference to other persons in leadership positions" and the social institutions to which an individual belongs. (Some of what Birren describes as "social age" is discussed below in the section Measuring Age Norms and Age Expectations). To our knowledge, most of the discussion about biological, social, and psychological age has been conducted at a conceptual level, and few studies have attempted to measure and empirically validate these three types of age and their independence.

In an earlier discussion, Neugarten & Hagestad (1976, p. 36) also remind us that chronological age is often a poor indicator of biological, social, or psychological age. First, there are important individual differences in development. As such, age is only a "rough indicator" of an individual's status along biological, social, or psychological dimensions. Second, age is "only meaningful in relational terms, as in signifying that one is younger or older than someone else, closer or farther from birth or death, or in marking progress compared to other persons in one's reference group." Finally, chronological age is "meaningless unless there is knowledge of the particular culture and of the social meaning[s] attached to given chronological ages." Despite these problems, Neugarten & Hagestad (1976) argue that chronological age is "an indispensable index." Clearly, chronological age has convenient and practical uses as an administrative and normative gauge—it is an easily measured, objective, and universal attribute. As a result, it has become a prominent criterion for classifying and

[1]Schroots & Birren (1988) also review an additional type of age: *functional age*. Functional age is defined in terms of an individual's ability to adapt to his or her environment. Functional age may exist as a fourth type of age in its own right, and an individual's capacity for functioning in daily life could be understood through measures such as biological, psychological, and social age. Another conceptualization is that functional age may exist as a subdimension of each of the three types of age discussed earlier—leading to a specialized conception of biological, psychological, or social age defined in terms of functional criteria.

ordering society. Similarly, Birren & Cunningham (1985, p. 12) suggest that "because age is such a powerful index, it will probably always be used to classify data while we are en route to explanations using variables other than the mere ages of individuals."

### *Subjective Age Identification*

Research on subjective age identification examines how old a person feels, into which age group he or she categorizes him or herself, or how old one would like to be, regardless of one's actual age. This has been a lively tradition since the 1960s. As an earlier review by Cutler (1982) notes, subjective age is typically measured with a single item phrased something like: "Do you feel that you are: young, middle-aged, old, or very old?" (e.g. Markides & Boldt 1983). Across studies, of course, there are slight variations in the item stem or in the number and type of response categories. In many gerontological studies, subjective age identification is restricted to whether an individual defines himself or herself as "old" or "very old." Often, this type of age is referred to as *identity age*.

Along these lines, Barak & Stern (1986) further delineate four aspects of identity age based on Kastenbaum and associates' (1972) "Ages of Me" instrument: *Feel age* ("I feel as though I am in my . . . "), *look age* ("I look as though I am in my . . . "), *do age* "I do most things as though I were in my . . . "), and *interest age* ("My interests are mostly those of a person in his/her . . . "). For Barak & Stern's items, the response categories are decades of life, starting with the 1920s and ending with the 1980s; Goldsmith & Heiens (1992) have recommended that the 1910s and 1990s decades might also be added if appropriate for the sample. Together, these four dimensions are labeled *cognitive age* (Barak & Stern 1986).

Other popular measurements strategies move away from identification with a larger age group, and instead ask for a more specific age response. The original version of Kastenbaum and colleagues' (1972) "Ages of Me" instrument elicited specific ages. For example, another version of *feel age* is simply: "How old do you feel?" or "What age do you feel on the inside?" (Underhill & Cadwell 1983; also see Cremin 1992, Thompson 1992). Similarly, *desired age* is also easily asked: "What age would you most like to be?".

In studies of *comparative* or *relative age identification*, respondents are normally asked whether they feel older, the same, or younger than most other people their chronological age. Here, the comparison is between oneself and other similarly-aged people. In addition, few investigators have examined a version of comparative age that keeps the comparison internal; that is, whether an individual feels older, the same, or younger than his or her chronological age (e.g. Baum & Boxley 1983).

In most research studies, these various types of subjective age are often then compared to an individual's actual chronological age. In doing so, even more types of age may result (for examples, see Barak [1987], Barak & Gould [1985]). Besides chronological age, other correlates of subjective age have been considered, the most popular being physical health, emotional health, gender, race and ethnicity, marital status, social participation, socioeconomic status, and retirement status (see reviews by Barak & Stern 1986, Baum & Boxley 1983, Montepare 1991, Montepare & Lachman 1989).

All of the measures described above are *self-perceived ages*—they ultimately reference the subjective ages of an individual him- or herself. One might also consider *other-perceived age*, or the age status(es) of individuals as evaluated by others (e.g. Lawrence 1974). The important point here is that this body of research generally does not anchor age in simple chronological terms, but it instead attempts to ground age at a phenomenological, subjectively experienced, level.

### *Measuring Age Norms and Age Expectations*

Elementary, ascriptive categories often take on complex social meanings (e.g. influencing attitudes, behaviors, language), and age is no exception. For excellent reviews, see Hagestad (1990), Hagestad & Neugarten (1985), Keith et al (1994), and Neugarten & Hagestad (1976).

Age is one of the most salient social and cultural dimensions, and this salience may be reflected in informal age norms and expectations that govern behavior. In terms of sociological theory, (age) norms are prescriptions or proscriptions about behavior in the form of "should" and "should not"; they are supported by consensus; and they are enforced through various mechanisms of social control, particularly social sanctions—positive, to keep people "on track," and negative, to bring straying individuals "back into line" (Berger 1963, Blake & Davis 1964, Gibbs 1965).

Assumptions about the salience of age, and the power of age norms, underlies much research and writing on the life course. Yet a great deal of "conceptual ambiguity and theoretical uncertainty" surrounds the terms "age norm" and "age-normative" in the life-course literature (Hagestad 1990, p. 160). Common uses of these terms range from (*a*) *statistical age norms* (descriptions of statistical regularity in the timing of life events and transitions in the larger population or for subgroups of the population), to (*b*) *optimal age norms* (collective notions about the "best," "ideal," or "preferred" ages to experience various life transitions), to (*c*) *prescriptive* and *proscriptive age norms* (collective, shared expectations about when certain transitions "should" or "should not" occur, respectively).

While a handful of studies have intended to examine the presence of informal age "norms," their use and measurement of the concept "norm" has overlooked its core prescriptive or proscriptive essence. Most investigators have used the term "norm" either in the statistical or optimal senses described above, even though the prescriptive/proscriptive most fully-captures the essence of normative. Along these lines, Marini (1984) has criticized past research on age "norms," arguing that researchers have not actually measured social norms but have instead focused on the "ideal" and "preferred" domains. Researchers who have conducted their work at the "optimal" level have often assumed that notions about what is "best," "ideal," or "preferred" are synonymous with notions about what "should" or "ought to" be. Similarly, when demographers find regularity in life-course patterns at a population level, they often believe that the regularity reflects, and is driven by, cultural age prescriptions or proscriptions. Hogan (1985, p. 70), for example, has argued that "in the United States, the appropriate ages for events are [not well-specified], but the statistical regularities in the timing of events are suggestive of underlying [informal] norms." Marini (1984), however, has noted that behavior that is "statistically regular" may not be "normative," just as behavior that is "statistically irregular" may not be "non-normative."

The pioneering work of Neugarten and her colleagues at the University of Chicago during the late 1950s and early 1960s explored age "norms" and age "constraints." Two of the instruments that were used in their Kansas City Study of Adult Life are most relevant here: "Timetables for Men and Women" and the "Age Norm Checklist." The 11-item "Timetables for Men and Women" instrument generally asks respondents what they think the best age is for accomplishing a variety of transitions (e.g. "What do you think is the best age for a man to marry?" "What do you think is the best age for most people to leave home?"). For these timetable items, respondents give either a specific age or a small age band. Consensus was measured as the proportion who cite an age (or ages) within a short age span. Depending on the breadth of responses given for any particular item, the age span used for calculating consensus for that item ranged anywhere from 2 to 15 years; their approach was to select a band that "produced the most accurate reflection of the consensus that existed in the data."

The 48-item "Age Norm Checklist" asks whether respondents "approve of, feel favorable" or "disapprove of, feel unfavorable" about a variety of behaviors at different ages (e.g. "A woman who wears bikini on the beach—when she's 45; when she's 30; when she's 18" or "A man who buys himself a red sports car—when he's 60; when he's 45; when he's 25"). Responses are then scored to "reflect the degree of refinement with which the respondent makes age discriminations," with higher scores indicating greater age constraint.

One article in particular, Neugarten, Moore, & Lowe (1965), has become the single standard citation as the classic study of informal age norms. These investigators have been criticized, though, for posing most of their questions at the optimal level (asking about the "best" age to accomplish various transitions) rather than the prescriptive level (the age one "should" or "ought to" experience major life transitions), and for not actually examining whether social sanctions or other consequences are thought to exist for violating these optimal-age timetables (Marini 1984). However, they have examined whether respondents "approve" or "disapprove" of persons of different ages engaged in a variety of more micro-level, lifestyle-related behavior (as discussed above).

Later, Passuth & Maines (1981) essentially replicated Neugarten's approach, and their conference paper is often cited as a follow-up to Neugarten, Moore, & Lowe's (1965) classic study. The work of Fallo-Mitchell & Ryff (1982), Plath & Ikeda (1975), Zepelin et al (1987), Gee (1990), Peterson (1996), and Settersten & Hagestad (1996a 1996b) has also used Neugarten's items in some capacity, though these studies have improved upon some of the original items (e.g. creating items about work for women that parallel previous items asked only about men; or splitting single items that asked about "people" into two separate items about men and about women), added new items (e.g. returning home) and eliminated others, added follow-up questions, altered scoring strategies, or varied research and sampling designs.

For additional information on research instruments related to age norms and expectations, readers might also consult an earlier review by Hagestad (1982). Hagestad's review covers other seminal instruments, including Wood's (1972) "Age-Appropriate Behavior" (which asks 41 questions about the age at which a person is old enough to do various things, or the age at which a person is too old to do other things) and Bultena & Wood's (1969) "Normative Attitudes Toward the Aged Role" (which asks 8 questions about whether it is proper for older men, women, or couples to engage in a various activities).

Another body of research has examined the images associated with people of different ages, especially images about personality traits and characteristics. The most prominent of these instruments were part of Hagestad's (1982) compilation, including Hickey & Kalish's (1968) "Perceptions of Adults" (which prompts young respondents to give the ages that they associate with people who are "mean or unkind," "lonely," or "busy"; people who "like children and young people," or people they like to help), Neugarten & Peterson's (1957) "Age Association Items" (a 34-item index that asks for the age that respondents associate with a variety of feelings or behaviors, such as "a man who gets the most pleasure from his children," "when a woman gets most pleasure from sex," "the prime of life for a man"), and Cameron's (1972, 1976) "Comparison of Age Groups" (which asks respondents to compare young, middle-aged, and old adults on dimensions of masculinity and femininity, and on dimensions of fun and happiness).

Along these lines, the recent work of Heckhausen and her colleagues (Heckhausen et al 1989, Heckhausen & Baltes 1991) is also noteworthy. With the goal of examining perceptions of developmental gains and losses throughout adulthood, Heckhausen uses a checklist of 385 adjectives covering perceptions of the personality (e.g. "impulsive"), social (e.g. "friendly"), and intellectual (e.g. "ready-witted") characteristics of people of different ages.

## *Critical Life Events*

Within the larger field of research on life events and transitions, there is a smaller body of work that focuses on "critical" or "stressful" events. This tradition begins most notably with Holmes & Rahe (1967) and their Social Readjustment Rating Scale (also sometimes referred to as the Schedule of Recent Events). Holmes & Rahe asked respondents to indicate whether they had recently experienced any number of 43 different events, ranging from events as major as "death of a spouse" or "jail term," to events as minor as a "vacation" or "minor violations of the law."

Many later inventories have essentially sought to improve upon Holmes & Rahe's earlier measure, normally expanding the scope of items, rewording existing items that are ambiguous, or altering the scaling procedures. These include the Life Events Inventory (Cochrane & Robertson 1973), the PERI Life Events Scale (Dohrenwend et al 1978), the Paykel Scale (Paykel et al 1971), the Life Experiences Survey (Sarason et al 1978), and the Life Events Questionnaire (Chiriboga & Dean 1978, Chiriboga 1984). Other measures move away from major life events, and instead focus on everyday hassles (e.g. "concerns about owing money," "home maintenance") and uplifts (e.g. "daydreaming," "feeling healthy," "laughing") (Holahan et al 1984, Kanner et al 1981, Lewinsohn et al 1985, Wagner et al 1988). Many of these inventories have been used primarily with non-aged, and often clinical, populations.

To remedy the age bias of these inventories, several investigators have incorporated items that are more appropriate for elderly populations (e.g. "age discrimination," "trouble with Social Security"). These inventories include the Elders Life Stress Inventory (Aldwin 1992), the Geriatric Scale of Recent Life Events (Kahana et al 1982), the Geriatric Social Readjustment Rating Scale (Amster & Krauss 1974), the Louisville Older Persons Event Scale (Murrell & Norris 1984), the Small Life Events Scale (Zautra et al 1986), modified versions of the Schedule of Recent Events (Mensh 1983, Wilson 1985), and the Pleasant and Unpleasant Events Schedules (Teri & Lewinsohn 1982). However, many of the items in these inventories weigh heavily toward declining physical and mental health (e.g. "loss of hearing or vision," "difficulty walking," "painful arthritis," "move to home for the aged"). Some measures also include events that happen to children or grandchildren (e.g. "child married," "death of a grandchild").

There are several problems often associated with these inventories. First, a very select set of the larger universe of possible events is sampled (as one might expect), but events that are more common for young adults, men, whites, and the middle class are over-represented. In addition, negative and undesirable events are over-represented, and "non-events" (events that are expected to happen, but never occur) are omitted. Some people are, of course, also never "at risk" to experience certain events (e.g. one cannot experience the death of a child if one has not become a parent).

Second, not all events are equally important, and the procedures used for weighting events varies dramatically between studies. Some investigators have developed weights using independent raters; others asked the respondents themselves to weight events subjectively; and still others derived weights empirically—using group mean ratings or regression techniques. Many have abandoned the complexities associated with weighting, and have opted to use no weights at all.

Third, there are problems associated with the reliability of recall over long time periods. However, most of the measures intend to tap events that have occurred within a limited span of time, usually within the last year. For those interested in the life course, though, the issue of recall is more problematic, since the unit of time becomes lifetime (or at least lifetime to the present day).

Fourth, a number of problematic assumptions run through this literature: (*a*) That life events cause psycho-social disturbance (rather than the other way around). (*b*) That the direction of change is almost always negative (in part, this reflects the fact that most inventories focus on negative rather than positive events). (*c*) That effects are primarily additive in nature (the greater the number of events experienced, the greater the impact), and (4) that the impact of life events is usually direct and short-term. Future work might better explore whether psycho-social states instead predispose individuals to experience a certain set of events; whether and under what conditions positive change might result from negative experiences; whether relationships of other functional forms (especially nonlinear) might also be operating; and whether and how the effects of events may be delayed, dissipate, or grow over time.

Fifth, researchers might better classify events along multiple dimensions (e.g. major versus minor; anticipated versus unanticipated; controllable versus uncontrollable; typical versus atypical; desirable versus undesirable; acute versus chronic). In addition, researchers might begin to gather information about the resources to which people have (or had) access as a means for coping with various events, especially those events deemed as "stressful."

Two measurement instruments stand out as exemplars: The Standardized Life Events and Difficulties Interview (SL), developed by Kessler & Wethington (1992) at the University of Michigan in the United States; and its predecessor, the Life Events and Difficulties Schedule (LEDS), developed by Brown and colleagues (Brown & Harris 1978) at Bedford College in England. The LEDS has been used in England, Europe, Canada, and Africa. Both schedules provide a very comprehensive understanding of severe life events, ongoing stresses and difficulties, and life turning points. The LS is a more structured version of the open-ended, semi-structured LES, and is more in line with conventional survey techniques. Both schedules, however, require intensive training of interviewers. The pilot version of the LS instrument is monumental (exceeding 200 pages), and is currently being validated against the original LEDS. Unlike many of the inventories cited earlier, Kessler & Wethington, and Brown and his associates, do not seek to develop composite measures of events.

A related approach is to focus on the plausible links between one or more specific life events and a specific outcome, usually one related to well-being (e.g. George 1989, Krause 1991, McLanahan & Sørensen 1985, Palmore et al 1985).

For other discussions of the meaning and measurement of stressful life events, see Cohen (1988), Inglehart (1991), and Thoits (1983). For discussions on later life in particular, see Chiriboga (1989), Ensel (1991), and Murrell et al (1988).

### *Measuring Life Phases*

We now turn to a brief discussion of larger life phases—how individuals in a given society construct a "mental map of the life cycle" (Neugarten & Hagestad 1976), dividing the span of time from birth to death into distinct categories.

An earlier review by Hagestad (1982) reviewed a number of measurement strategies which, with slight modifications, remain the most dominant approaches. Neugarten & Peterson's (1957) "Phases of Adulthood" instrument from the Kansas City Study of Adult Life is representative of these measures, asking "What would you call the periods of life, the age periods most people go through? At what age does each begin, for most people? What are the important changes from one period to the next, for most people?" For strategies of this sort, respondents are asked to provide their own divisions and labels.

Another common strategy is to provide respondents with predetermined labels and ask them to generate the age parameters they associate with those labels. Cameron's (1969) "Age Parameters" questions are good examples of this: Cameron asks for the ages at which "young adult," "middle-aged," "old," and "aged" begin. Similarly, Drevenstedt's (1976) "Onset of Adult Phases" questions ask for age parameters, but also make distinctions between men's and women's lives—asking for the ages at which a male becomes a "young man," a "middle-aged man," and an "old man," and the ages at which a female becomes a "middle-aged woman" and an "old woman." Some of Neugarten & Peterson's (1957) "Age Association Items" are in this format as well.

The simplest strategy has been to provide respondents with the label for the life phase and a number of preset response categories. The National Council on

Aging's (1975) "Onset of Old Age" adopts this approach, asking "At what age do you think the average man becomes "old"? "Under 40 years, 40 to 44 years, 45 to 49 years, [etc, in 4-year brackets] 90 years or older." Respondents were also given the options of "Never," "It Depends," "When he stops working," "When his health fails," "Other," or "Unsure." A follow-up question asks respondents to give their reasons for choosing a particular age band. In addition, a similar series of questions were asked about women.

Anthropologists associated with Project A.G.E. developed an innovative strategy for examining perceptions of the life course (Keith et al 1994): the "Age Game." Respondents are given a deck of cards that contain descriptions of various personae (e.g. "A male, high school graduate, single, is working, living with parents" or "A female, working, married, two children both of whom have recently married" or "A male, widowed, retired, living with adult children"), and are asked to sort the deck based on guesses about the ages of the people described on the cards. After respondents have finished the sorting process, they are asked: "What name would you give to the age-bracket or the age-group of the people you have placed in this pile? Are there any other words you might use to describe this general age group? Roughly, what is the age or range of ages in terms of years of the people described in this pile?"

Theorists and researchers have also relied on life stages or developmental phases as a favorite way of conceptualizing human lives from birth to death (e.g. Eisenstadt 1956, Erikson 1980). The differentiation of life phases has been seen as an historically emergent property of modern societies, beginning with "childhood," "adulthood," "old age" (Borscheid 1992, Ehmer 1990). Childhood was eventually differentiated into "early childhood," "youth and adolescence," and "post-adolescence." Adulthood was also segmented into "early adulthood," "mid-life," and "old age." Old age was split into the "young-old" and the "old-old" (Neugarten 1974), or the "third and fourth ages" (Laslett 1991). Note, however, that Neugarten's original formulation of young-old and old-old was meant to distinguish that proportion of the elderly population who "are relatively healthy, relatively affluent, relatively free from traditional responsibilities of work and family, and who are increasingly well-educated and politically active" from those who are not—regardless of their ages (Neugarten 1974, p. 187). Over time, gerontological researchers have increasingly defined the young-old and old-old in purely chronological terms—with the young-old defined as those between 65 and 74, or between 65 and 84; and with the old-old defined as either those aged 75 or older, or aged 85 or older.

Another approach has been to divide the life course into a series of positions vis-à-vis the welfare state: as non-recipients and non-contributors (e.g. children, housewives), contributors (e.g. the economically active), and recipients (e.g. elderly, unemployed, disabled, maternity leave) (Mayer & Schoepflin 1989).

Researchers who have concentrated on the economic participation of males, and the functional requirements of capitalist societies, have described the "triangularization of life" (Smelser & Halpern 1978) and the "tripartition of the life course" (Kohli 1994). That is, the life course is composed of three distinct segments, an early part devoted to education and training, a middle part devoted to work, and a final part devoted to retirement.

As a result, education- and work-related activities may mark the transition from one life phase to another. "Old age," for example, is often defined by eligibility rules for the receipt of pensions or Social Security benefits, or by the legal or actual retirement ages. However, as a measure of "old age," age at retirement entails a number of obvious problems. First, many older persons remain employed in some capacity after retirement, while others do not have gainful work from which to retire. Second, the receipt of pension payments and social security benefits may not coincide with age at retirement. Third, age at retirement tells us little about an individual's level of physical and mental functioning, degree of autonomy or dependency, or level of social participation. The distinction between the "young-old" and the "old-old" (cited above) has been prompted by the facts that: (a) average age at retirement has fallen markedly during the last decade, and is now between the ages of 55 and 60 in most advanced countries (Kohli 1994), (b) the upper end of the life span has extended, and (c) there is an enormous degree of variability in the functional ability of older persons at any given age (Maddox 1987).

There are now several good examples of strategies for measuring the multidimensional process of aging using interview or survey methods (see Berkman et al 1993, from the MacArthur Foundation Research Network on Successful Aging; Baltes et al 1993, from the Berlin Aging Study). Nonetheless, we still do not have well-developed measures of the transition to dependency in old age. While measures related to Activities of Daily Living (ADL, IADL) capture declining abilities for self-care, these measures do not take support structures and social settings into account. In this area, measurement might be improved by adopting the logic of life course analysis (discussed later). For example, one might conceptualize the transition to dependency as a series of different states (e.g. first being unable to work, followed by the receipt of informal help, the receipt of formal help in the home, and institutionalization). The duration of time spent in these various states could then be used to better understand the course of this process.

## *Life Review and Life History*

The continuity of subjective biographical identity, and of personality characteristics and behavioral dispositions, provides a sense of integrity in life. While individuals may engage in reminiscence and life review activities throughout the life course, these activities seem especially salient during middle and old age, functioning to bridge earlier and later segments of life (Erikson 1980, Levinson 1986, Neugarten 1968, Staudinger 1989).[2] In addition to their research value, reminiscence and life review techniques are also popular therapeutic tools (e.g. Butler & Lewis 1982, Coleman 1986, deVries et al 1990, Haight 1991). Life review and reminiscence activities often help individuals achieve a sense of self-worth, coherence, and reconciliation with one's past; maintain perceptions of competence and continuity; and pass on one's cultural heritage and personal legacy (Wong & Watt 1991).

The most common approaches to life review and reminiscence involve unstructured or semi-structured interviews. Interviews are usually conducted with individuals, but family and group sessions may be conducted as well (e.g. Botella & Guillem 1993, Birren & Deutchman 1991, deVries et al 1990). Examples of key questions include "What do you see as important or significant in your life?" (Lewis 1971), "What family members have had a major impact in shaping your life? Why?" (deVries et al 1990), "Describe three memories that you've been thinking about lately" (David 1990), "What were the most important events? What were the most difficult decisions?" (Tismer 1971), "Tell something of your past that is most important to you—that is something that has had the most influence on your life" (Wong & Watt 1991). Others have had revealing discussions centered around cherished objects (e.g. photographs, jewelry, books, paintings) (Sherman 1991).

Other investigators have not examined the content of reminiscence, but have instead asked about their frequency or affective quality. For these purposes, Havighurst & Glasser's (1972) questions are commonly used: "Looking back over the last several weeks, would you say you have done a great deal, some, or very little reminiscing?" and "Would you most often characterize your reminiscence activities as most pleasant, pleasant, or unpleasant?"

Another interesting approach to life review is to ask a series of questions about life *revision*; that is, to ask respondents to identify what they would do differently if they had their lives to live over again. For example, DeGenova (1992) created a life revision index based on 35 questions with the stem "If you had your life to live over again, how much time would you spend ...", with the response categories being "much more, more, same, less, much less." The items in DeGenova's index cover 7 different life domains: family (e.g. "developing close relations with your children"), work (e.g. "worrying about your job"),

[2]Staudinger (1989) notes that while the terms "life review" and "reminiscence" are often used synonymously, they should be recognized as distinct. Reminiscence, Staudinger argues, is the simple recalling of life events, something that can be "triggered quite unwillingly by the reminiscer"; life review, on the other hand, involves the interpretation and evaluation of those events and often requires more "active engagement of the person who is reviewing his or her life" (p. 71). Life review, as Butler (1963, p. 67) reminds us, "is not synonymous with, but includes, reminiscence."

friendships (e.g. "keeping up with good friends"), health (e.g. "taking good physical care of your body"), education (e.g. "pursuing your education"), leisure (e.g. "traveling"), and religion (e.g. "developing your spirituality"). Of course, additional depth could be gained through a series of follow-up questions on what exactly respondents would do differently, and why they would allot their time in new ways.

A related approach is to ask subjects to graph their lives. For example, Runyan (1980) and several earlier studies (Clausen 1972, Pressey & Kuhlen 1957) gave respondents a graph with ages 5 through 40 calibrated on the horizontal axis, and personal morale (spanning from 0, or "rock bottom," to 9, "absolute tops") on the vertical axis. Respondents were asked to draw a curve indicating their degree of happiness in over those years, and were then asked to discuss the reasons for their ratings. Similarly, others have administered blank-grid life graphs with only 5-year age demarcations (from 0 through 80) on the horizontal axis, and have asked subjects the following question: "Can you visualize how your life could be put into a graph? That is, ups and downs, level periods, rises and declines, etc. Assuming that you live until at least 80 years of age, how do you think that a graph of your life will look?" (e.g. Back & Bourque 1970, Bourque & Back 1977, Back & Averett 1985). Depending on the age of the subject and the age span of the graph, some subjects respond in terms of how they think their lives will unfold (prospectively), others in terms of how their lives actually did unfold (retrospectively), and still others provide a mix of both. While these graphs may be used with any age group, this method may be especially useful in research with middle-aged and aged respondents, particularly as a way to structure life review discussions or to gather life history data.

Readers interested in other applications of reminiscence and life review methods might consult two recent edited volumes by Haight & Webster (1995) and Hendricks (1995). Life *history* methods, which are related to life review methods, are a primary means for collecting data on the life course. These methods are considered in detail in the next section.

## MEASURING THE LIFE COURSE

As discussed in the introduction, the *life course* refers to the "social processes extending over the individual life span or over significant portions of it, especially [with regard to] the family cycle, educational and training histories, and employment and occupational careers. The life course is shaped by, among other things, cultural beliefs about the individual biography, institutionalized sequences of roles and positions, legal age restrictions, and the decisions of individual actors" (Mayer & Tuma 1990, p. 3).

Life trajectories, transitions, and events are central concepts in the study of the life course (Elder 1985). The concept of the *life trajectory,* similar to that of a career, is long in scope, and refers to "a pathway defined by the aging process or by movement across the age structure" (Elder 1985, p. 31). The individual life course is composed of multiple, interdependent trajectories (for example, work, family, and educational trajectories).

Trajectories are punctuated by a sequence of successive life events and transitions. Events and transitions are brief in scope, and refer to changes in state. However, an *event* is usually conceptualized as a relatively abrupt change, while a *transition* is usually conceptualized as a more gradual change. Transitions and events are always placed within a larger trajectory, and the trajectory gives them "distinctive form and meaning" (Elder 1985, p. 31).

The concepts of timing, sequencing, duration, and spacing are often used to describe life events, transitions, and the characteristics of larger trajectories (Hagestad & Neugarten 1985). *Timing* refers to the age at which given transitions occur in the life course. *Sequencing* refers to the order in which transitions are experienced over the life course. *Duration* refers to the length of time spent in any give state. *Spacing* refers to the amount of time between two or more transitions, the pace at which multiple transitions are experienced.

In addition to these basic concepts, the researcher must identify the life domains and state spaces to be measured. A natural and convenient way to do this is to structure data collection on activities in the domains of family (e.g. parents, siblings, spouses or partners, children), education and training (e.g. schools, training places, credentials), employment (e.g. employment contracts, occupational activities, firm membership, sector location), and residence and household (e.g. places of residence, household composition).

While these dimensions describe the primary activities across life, a more complete picture of the life course must also include more marginal periods and events—such as brief periods of training, second or part-time jobs, periods of unemployment or sickness (for examples, see Mayer & Brückner 1989).

## *Calendars, Life History Matrices, and Event Histories*

Life history matrices plot life domains, and specific events and transitions within them, over time (Balan et al 1969, Freedman et al 1988, Frank & van der Burgh 1986; readers interested in working with archival data might consult a recent monograph by Elder et al 1994). In life history matrices, the first column calibrates time, and the remaining columns specify domains and events of interest. The date an event began is indicated in the appropriate row, and its duration is then charted vertically. The advantage of this type of instrument is that activities in multiple life domains are simultaneously mapped onto one frame, and the relationships between them are easily seen. In addition, inconsistencies are easily detected and can be double-checked immediately with the respondent.

Many of these instruments are also easily self-administered. The great disadvantage of these measures is that little information can be noted in matrix cells (e.g. it is difficult to note detailed information about occupational titles). As a result, only a very crude and, in most cases, insufficient picture of the life course can be constructed using life history matrices.

A more adequate means for collecting data on life histories is exemplified by the Life History Questionnaire applied in six surveys of the German Life History Study (Mayer & Brückner 1989), which built upon the Norwegian Life History Study (Rogoff-Ramsoy 1973). In developing this instrument, the goal was not only to extract monthly data for several life domains, but also to obtain a wide variety of contextual information on each state. For these purposes, complete event histories (from birth to the present) were collected in each life domain, beginning with the residential history. In the case of residential history, for example, data are gathered on every residential "state," including the month and year that mark the beginning and end points, the size and type of residence, geographic location, and the composition of household. The residential history is taken first because it provides a good anchor for the recollection of information on other trajectories. In a similar format, general schooling, occupational training, primary employment, secondary employment, and military service trajectories are charted and then reviewed for all periods that are unaccounted. Thus, the main content of these surveys becomes the life history itself (for theories, rationale, and applications, see Blossfeld et al 1991, Mayer & Tuma 1990).

In the German Life History Study, this technique was applied in both personal and computer-assisted telephone interviews with persons between the ages of 29 and 103 (Brückner 1994). It results in rich and accurate time-continuous data. Of course, there are high costs associated with interviewing time (in most cases, between 1.5 and 3 hours), the editing process (including return calls to respondents to clarify inconsistencies), and the training of interviewers and editing staff. When respondents agreed, their personal and telephone interviews were also audiotaped; those recordings were then used during the process of editing data. Shorter versions of this instrument are possible when either the number of life domains and/or the range of contextual variables are restricted.

## *Retrospective Versus Prospective Measurement Strategies*

Although retrospective methods are often used in cross-sectional studies, the data itself, at least in principle, may approach that obtained by a sufficiently long panel study (that is, respondents are interviewed only once, but information is gathered on the entire life course). One-time retrospective surveys offer an excellent alternative to longitudinal designs, especially for those interested in the life course as a whole (Featherman 1980). The most common problem associated with retrospective data concerns the accuracy and precision of recall

(Dex 1991). This criticism, however, applies to any kind of autobiographical data, regardless of research design.

When retrospective data are cross-checked against data from archival sources (e.g. registry, school, or firm records) some degree of inconsistency is likely to emerge. This incongruence is often taken as evidence that retrospective data are not completely reliable, even though archival data may be equally fallible. However, once common sources of error are known, these errors can be taken into account when research instruments are being designed; as a result, the amount of measurement error may be substantially reduced (Brückner 1990). An advantage of most life history instruments is that they address complete histories in a systematic fashion, embedding events and transitions in both diachronic and synchronic life contexts.

Data on the life course can also be collected prospectively (e.g. in panel studies with multiple measurement points). For example, the Panel Study of Income Dynamics (PSID) in the United States, the first major household panel, became the model for similar studies in Germany, the Netherlands, Great Britain and Sweden. However, even panel designs are not exempt from problems associated with retrospective measurement (Featherman 1980), since information is usually gathered on the period of time before the survey began, and on the period of time that elapses between measurement points. The major disadvantage of panel studies is, of course, that one must wait many years until a sufficient span of the life course can be described.

Readers interested in further discussion of issues related to data quality in longitudinal research might consult a recent edited volume by Magnusson & Bergman (1990).

## *Data Organization and Analyses*

Standardized, quantitative life histories from large samples have been collected since the late 1960s (Balan et al 1969, Blum et al 1969, Rogoff-Ramsoy 1973). But it was not until the mid-1970s and early 1980s that adequate methods for data organization, retrieval, and analysis became available (e.g. Allison 1984, Blossfeld et al 1989, Courgeau & Lelievre 1992, Flinn & Heckman 1982, Griffin 1993, Mayer & Tuma 1990, Singer & Willett 1991, Yamaguchi 1991).

The recent sociology of the life course has almost accomplished its mission to show that lives are differentiated, event-related, and episodic, and must be examined and analyzed in a step-by-step piecemeal fashion. Descriptive techniques for survival data and stochastic models for discrete events in continuous time (known as hazard rate or event history models) have been shown to be especially useful in analyzing life history data. A major charge of critics has been that these methods atomize lives into unrelated transitions and episodes. In contrast, these critics have called for methods to better represent total trajectories with typologies (Abbott 1983, Abbott & Forrest 1986, Abbott & Hrycak

1990, Chan 1995). One technique in particular—"optimal matching," which seeks to unravel sequence patterns—has been proposed, but it remains to be seen whether it holds its promise.

In response, proponents of event-history methods have insisted that the position of their critics is doubly misleading: They argue that both trajectories and the richness of individual biographies can, in fact, be modeled well with event-history procedures. In addition, they suggest that typological approaches, especially those that seek to represent sequences, make inadequate use of the temporal character of the data, and are insufficient for covering the entire range of possible pathways in most empirical applications (Mayer 1986, Mayer & Tuma 1990).

Readers interested in learning more about various techniques for analyzing longitudinal data, including the analysis of sequences, might consult a recent casebook of applications edited by Magnusson and colleagues (1991).

## CLOSING STATEMENT

We have argued that the measurement of age, age structuring, and the life course have become more problematic as the study of human lives has moved toward more detailed analyses and explanations. Our scientific treatment of the life course must allow for the heterogeneity, discontinuity, and contingency that exists in present-day societies. Earlier notions of the life cycle, life span, or life course, were at least in principle based on holistic conceptions of human lives. However, as the scientific treatment of human lives became more elaborate, our approaches became increasingly fragmented not only across academic disciplines, but also within them. Yet life-course research must address many different analytic levels if it is to be comprehensive. The challenge now lies in moving away from this fragmentation to a truly integrative study of the life course. Herein lies our paradox: As we seek to better understand the course of human lives in contemporary and ever-changing societies, the effective empirical measurement of its key concepts simultaneously becomes more pressing and more complicated.



*Literature Cited*

Abbott A. 1983. Sequences of social events. *Hist. Meth.* 16(4):129–47

Abbott A, Forrest J. 1986. Optimal matching for historical sequences. *J. Interdisciplin. Hist.* 16:471–94

Abbott A, Hrycak A. 1990. Measuring resemblance in sequence data: an optimal matching analysis of musicians' careers. *Am. J. Sociol.* 96(1):144–85

Aldwin CM. 1992. The Elders Life Stress

Inventory: Egocentric and nonegocentric stress. In *Stress and Coping in Later-Life Families,* ed. MA Stephens, JH Crowther, SE Hobfoll, DL Tennenbaum, pp. 49–69. Hemisphere

Allison P. 1984. *Event History Analysis.* Beverly Hills, CA: Sage

Amster LE, Krauss HH. 1974. The relationship between life crises and mental deterioration in old age. *Int. J. Aging Hum. Dev.* 5(1):51–55

Andersen M. 1985. The emergence of the modern life cycle in Britain. *Soc. Hist.* 10(1):69–87

Angus D, Mirel J, Vinovskis MA. 1988. Historical development of age-stratification in schooling. *Teacher's Coll. Record* 90:33–58

Back K, Averett C. 1985. Stability and change in life graph types. In *Normal Aging III: Reports from the Duke Longitudinal Studies, 1975–1984,* ed. E Palmore, W Busse, G Maddox, J Nowlin, I Siegler, 3:290–305. Durham, NC: Duke Univ. Press

Back K, Bourque LB. 1970. Life graphs: aging and cohort effect. *J. Gerontol.* 25(3):249–55

Balan J, Browning HL, Jelin E, Litzler L. 1969. A computerized approach to the processing and analysis of life histories obtained in sample surveys. *Behav. Sci.* 14:105–20

Baltes PB, Lindenberger U, Staudinger U. 1996. Life-span theory in developmental psychology. In *Theoretical Models of Human Development,* ed. R Lerner, Vol. 1, *Handbook of Child Psychology,* ed. W Damon. New York: Wiley

Baltes PB, Mayer KU, Helmchen H, Steinhagen-Thiessen E. 1993. The Berlin Aging Study (BASE): Overview and design. *Ageing Soc.* 13(4):483–515

Barak B. 1987. Cognitive age: a new multidimensional approach to measuring age identity. *Int. J. Aging Hum. Dev.* 25(2):109–28

Barak B, Gould S. 1985. Alternative age measures: a research agenda. In *Advances in Consumer Research,* ed. EC Hirschman, MB Holbrook, 12:53–58. Provo, UT: Assoc. Consumer Res.

Barak B, Stern B. 1986. Subjective age correlates: a research note. *Gerontologist* 26(5):571–78

Baum SK, Boxley RL. 1983. Age identification in the elderly. *Gerontologist* 23:532–37

Benedict R. 1938. Continuities and discontinuities in cultural conditioning. *Psychiatry* 1:161–67

Berger P. 1963. *Invitation to Sociology: A Humanistic Perspective.* Garden City, NY: Doubleday

Berkman LF, Seeman TE, Albert M, Blazer D, Kahn R, et al. 1993. Successful, usual, and impaired functioning in community-dwelling elderly: findings from the MacArthur Foundation Network on Successful Aging. *J. Clin. Epidemiol.* 46:1129–40

Bertaux D, Kohli M. 1984. The life-story approach. *Annu. Rev. Sociol.* 10:215–37

Birren JE, Cunningham WR. 1985. Research on the psychology of aging: principles, concepts and theory. In *Handbook of Aging and Psychology,* ed. JE Birren, KW Schaie, pp. 3–34. New York: Van Nostrand Reinhold

Birren JE, Deutchman DE. 1991. *Guiding the Autobiography Group for Older Adults: Exploring the Fabric of Life.* Baltimore: Johns Hopkins Univ. Press

Blake J, Davis K. 1964. Norms, values, and sanctions. In *Handbook of Modern Sociology,* ed. RE Faris, pp. 456–84. Chicago, IL: Rand McNally

Blossfeld HP, Hamerle A, Mayer KU. 1989. *Event History Analysis: Statistical Theory and Application in the Social Sciences.* Hillsdale, NJ: Lawrence Erlbaum

Blum Z, Karweit N, Sørensen AB. 1969. *A Method for the Collection and Analysis of Retrospective Life Histories.* Baltimore, MD: Johns Hopkins Univ. Press

Borscheid P. 1992. Der alte Mensch in der Vergangenheit. In *Zukunft des Alterns und gesellschaftliche Entwicklung,* ed. PB Baltes, J Mittelstrass, pp. 35–61. Berlin/New York: Walter de Gruyter

Botella L, Guillem F. 1993. The autobiographical group: a tool for the reconstruction of past life experience with the aged. *Int. J. Aging Hum. Dev.* 36(4):303–19

Bourque LB, Back K. 1977. Life graphs and life events. *J. Gerontol.* 32:669–74

Brown G, Harris T. 1978. *The Social Origins of Depression.* New York: Free Press

Brückner E. 1990. Die retrospective Erhebung von Lebensverlaeufen. In *Lebensverlaeufe und sozialer Wandel,* ed. KU Mayer, pp. 374–403. Opladen: Westdautscher Verlag

Brückner E. 1994. *Lebensverlaeufe und gesellschaftlicher Wandel. Konzept, Design and Methodik der Erhebung von Lebensverlaeufen der Gerburtsjahrgaenge 1919–1921.* Berlin: Max Planck Institute fü Bildungsforschung

Bultena G, Wood V. 1969. Normative attitudes toward the aged role among migrant and nonmigrant retirees. *Gerontologist* 9(3):204–8

Butler RN. 1963. The life review: an interpretation of reminiscence in the aged. *Psychiatry* 26:65–76

Butler RN, Lewis M. 1982. *Aging and Mental Health: Positive Psychosocial and Biomedical Approaches.* St. Louis: Mosby

Bytheway B. 1990. Age. In *Researching Social Gerontology: Concepts, Methods, and Issues,* ed. SM Peace, pp. 9–18. Newbury Park, CA: Sage

Cain LD. 1976. Aging and the law. In *Handbook of Aging and the Social Sciences,* ed. RH Binstock, E Shanas, pp. 342–68. New York, NY: Van Nostrand Reinhold

Cameron P. 1969. Age parameters of young adult, middle aged, old, and aged. *J. Gerontol.* 24(2):201–2

Cameron P. 1972. Stereotypes about generational fun and happiness versus self-appraised fun and happiness. *Gerontologist* 12(2):120–23

Cameron P. 1976. Masculinity/femininity of the generations: as self-reported and as stereotypically appraised. *Int. J. Aging Hum. Dev.* 7:143–51

Chan TW. 1995. Optimal matching analysis. *Work Occup.* 22(4):467–90

Chiriboga DA, Dean H. 1978. Dimensions of stress: perspectives from a longitudinal study. *J. Psychosomatic Res.* 22:47–55

Chiriboga DA. 1984. Social stressors as antecedents of change. *J. Gerontol.* 39(4):468–77

Chiriboga DA. 1989. The measurement of stress exposure in later life. In *Aging, Stress and Health,* ed. KS Markides, CL Cooper, pp. 13–41. New York: Wiley

Chudacoff HP. 1989. *How Old Are You? Age Consciousness in American Culture.* Princeton, NJ: Princeton Univ. Press

Clausen JA. 1972. The life course of individuals. In *Aging and Society: A Sociology of Age Stratification,* Vol. 3, ed. M Riley, M Johnson, A Foner, New York: Russell Sage Found.

Cochrane R, Robertson A. 1973. The life events inventory: a measure of the relative severity of psycho-social stressors. *J. Psychosomatic Res.* 17:135–39

Cohen L. 1988. *Life Events and Psychological Functioning: Theoretical and Methodological Issues.* Newbury Park, CA: Sage

Coleman P. 1986. Issues in the therapeutic use of reminiscence with elderly people. In *Psychological Therapies for the Elderly,* ed. I Hanley, M Gilhooly. London: Crome Hall

Courgeau D, Lelievre E. 1992. *Event History Analysis in Demography.* Oxford: Clarendon

Cremin MC. 1992. Feeling old versus being old: views of troubled aging. *Soc. Sci. Med.* 12:1305–15

Cutler S. 1982. Subjective age identification. In *Research Instruments in Social Gerontology,* ed. D Mangen, W Peterson, pp. 437–62. Minneapolis, MN: Univ. Minn. Press

Dannefer D. 1987. Aging as intracohort deferentiation: accentuation, the Matthew effect, and the life course. *Sociol. For.* 2:211–36

David D. 1990. Reminiscence, adaptation, and social context in old age. *Int. J. Aging Hum. Dev.* 30(3):175–88

DeGenova MK. 1992. If you had your life to do over again: What would you do differently?. *Int. J. Aging Hum. Dev.* 34(2):135–43

deVries B, Birren JE, Deutchman DE. 1990. Adult development through guided autobiography: the family context. *Fam. Relat.* 39:3–7

Dex S. 1991. The reliability of recall data: a literature review. *Working papers of the ESRC Research Center on Micro-social change (Paper 11).* Colchester: Univ. Essex

Dohrenwend BS, Krasnoff L, Askenasy AR, Dohrenwend BP. 1978. Exemplification of a method for scaling life events: the PERI life events scale. *J. Health Soc. Behav.* 19:205–29

Drevenstedt J. 1976. Perceptions of onsets of young adulthood, middle age, and old age. *Soc. Sci. Med.* 31(1):53–57

Eglit H. 1985. Age and the law. In *Handbook of Aging and the Social Sciences,* ed. RH Binstock, E Shanas, pp. 528–53. New York: Van Nostrand Reinhold. 2nd ed.

Ehmer J. 1990. *Sozialgeschichte des Alters.* Frankfurt/Main: Suhrkamp

Eisenstadt SN. 1956. *From Generation to Generation: Age Groups and Social Structure.* Glencoe, IL: Free Press

Elder GH Jr. 1985. Perspectives on the life course. In *Life Course Dynamics: Trajectories and Transitions, 1968–1980,* ed. GH Elder, pp. 23–49. Ithaca, NY: Cornell Univ. Press

Elder GH Jr. 1996. The life course paradigm. In *Examining Lives in Context: Perspectives on the Ecology of Human Development,* ed. P Moen, GH Elder, K Luescher, pp. 101–39. New York: Am. Psychol. Assoc.

Elder GH Jr, Pavalko E, Clipp E. 1994. *Working with Archival Data.* Newbury Park, CA: Sage

Ensel WM. 1991. Important life events and depression among older adults. *J. Aging Health* 3:546–66

Erikson E. 1980. *Identity and the Life Cycle.* New York: Norton

Fallo-Mitchell L, Ryff CD. 1982. Preferred timing of female life events: cohort differences. *Res. Aging* 4:249–67

Featherman D. 1980. Retrospective longitudinal research: methodological consideration. *J. Econ. Business* 32:152–69

Flinn CJ, Heckman JJ. 1982. New methods for analyzing individual event histories. In *Sociological Methodology,* ed. S Leinhardt, pp. 99–140. San Francisco, CA: Jossey-Bass

Frank G, van der Burgh RM. 1986. Cross-cultural use of life history methods in gerontology. In *New Methods for Old-Age Research: Strategies for Studying Diversity,* ed. CL Fry, J Keith, pp. 185–207. Boston, MA: Bergin & Garvey

Freedman D, Thornton A, Camburn D, Alwin D, Young-DeMarco L. 1988. The life history

calendar: a technique for collecting retrospective data. In *Sociological Methodology*, ed. C Clogg, pp. 37–68. Washington, DC: Am. Sociol. Assoc.
Fry CL. 1986. Emics and age: age differentiation and cognitive anthropological strategies. In *New Methods for Old Age Research: Strategies for Studying Diversity*, ed. CL Fry, J Keith, pp. 105–31. South Hadley, MA: Bergin & Garvey
Fry CL. 1990. Changing age structures and the mediating effects of culture. In *Opportunities and Challenges in an Ageing Society*, ed. WJA van den Heuval, R Illsley, A Jamieson, K Knipscheer, pp. 29–43. Amsterdam: Elsevier
Gee EM. 1987. Historical change in the family life course of Canadian men and women. In *Aging in Canada*, ed. V Marshall, pp. 265–87. Markharn, Ontario: Fitzhenry & Whiteside. 2nd ed.
Gee EM. 1990. Preferred timing of women's life events: a Canadian study. *Int. J. Aging Hum. Dev.* 31(4):279–94
George LK. 1989. Stress, social support, and depression over the life course. In *Aging, Stress and Health*, ed. KS Markides, CL Cooper, pp. 241–67. New York: Wiley
Gibbs J. 1965. Norms: the problem of definition and classification. *Am. J. Sociol.* 70:586–94
Glaser B, Strauss A. 1974. *Status Passage*. New York: Aldine
Goldsmith RE, Heiens RA. 1992. Subjective age: a test of five hypotheses. *Gerontologist* 32:312–17
Griffin LJ. 1993. Narrative, event-structure analysis, and causal interpretation in historical sociology. *Am. J. Sociol.* 98(5):1094–1133
Hagestad GO. 1982. Life-phase analysis. In *Research Instruments in Social Gerontology*, ed. D Mangen, W Peterson, pp. 463–532. Minneapolis, MN: Univ. Minn. Press
Hagestad GO. 1988. Demographic change and the life course: some emerging trends in the family realm. *Fam. Relat.* 37:405–10
Hagestad GO. 1990. Social perspectives on the life course. In *Handbook of Aging and the Social Sciences*, ed. R Binstock, L George, pp. 151–68. New York: Academic. 3rd ed.
Hagestad GO. 1991. Trends and dilemmas in life course research: an international perspective. In *Theoretical Advances in Life Course Research*, ed. WR Heinz, pp. 23–57. Deutscher Studien Verlag Weinheim
Hagestad GO, Neugarten BL. 1985. Age and the life course. In *Handbook of Aging and the Social Sciences*, ed. R Binstock, E Shanas, pp. 36–61. New York: Van Nostrand & Reinhold. 2nd ed.
Haight B. 1991. Reminiscing: the state of the art as a basis for practice. *Int. J. Aging Hum. Dev.* 33(1):1–32
Haight B, Webster J, eds. 1995. *The Art and Science of Reminiscing: Theory, Research, Methods, and Applications*. Washington, DC: Taylor & Francis
Havighurst R, Glasser R. 1972. And exploratory study of reminiscence, *J. Gerontol.* 27:243–53
Heckhausen J, Dixon R, Baltes PB. 1989. Gains and losses in development throughout adulthood as perceived by different age groups. *Dev. Psychol.* 25(1):109–21
Heckhausen J, Baltes PB. 1991. Perceived controllability of expected psychological change across adulthood and old age. *J. Gerontol.* 46(4):P165–73
Hendricks J, ed. 1995. *The Meaning of Reminiscence and Life Review*. Amityville, NY: Baywood
Henretta J. 1994. Social structure and age-based careers. In *Age and Structural Lag*, ed. MW Riley, RL Kahn, A Foner, pp. 57–79. New York, NY: Wiley
Hickey T, Kalish R. 1968. Young people's perceptions of adults. *J. Gerontol.* 23(2):215–19
Hogan DP. 1985. The demography of life span transitions: temporal and gender comparisons. In *Gender and the Life Course*, ed. A Rossi, pp. 65–78. New York: Aldine
Holahan CK, Holahan CJ, Belk SS. 1984. Adjustment in aging: the roles of life stress, hassles, and self-efficacy. *Health Psychol.* 3:315–28
Holmes TH, Rahe RH. 1967. The social readjustment rating scale. *J. Psychosomatic Res.* 11:213–18
Inglehart MR. 1991. *Reactions to Critical Life Events: A Social Psychological Analysis*. New York: Praeger
Jolicoeur P, Pontier J, Pernin MO, Sempe M. 1988. A lifetime asymptotic growth curve for human height. *Biometrics* 44:995–1003
Kahana E, Fairchild T, Kahana B. 1982. Adaptation. In *Research Instruments in Social Gerontology*, ed. D Mangen, W Peterson, pp. 145–90. Minneapolis, MN: Univ. Minn. Press
Kanner AD, Coyne JC, Schaefer C, Lazarus RS. 1981. Comparison of two modes of stress measurement: daily hassles and uplifts versus major life events. *J. Behav. Med.* 4(1):1–39
Kastenbaum R, Derbin V, Sabatini P, Arrt S. 1972. "The ages of me": toward personal and interpersonal definitions of functional aging. *Aging Hum. Dev.* 3:197–211
Keith J, Fry CL, Glascock AP, Ikels C, Dickerson-Putman J, et al. 1994. *The Aging Experience: Diversity and Commonality Across Cultures*. Newbury Park, CA: Sage

Kertzer DI. 1989. Age structuring in comparative and historical perspective. In *Age Structuring in Comparative and Historical Perspective,* ed. DI Kertzer, K Warner Schaie, pp. 3–21. Hillsdale, NJ: Lawrence Erlbaum

Kessler R, Wethington E. 1992. *Interview schedule for the Life Experiences Study.* Inst. Soc. Res., Surv. Res. Ctr., Univ. Michigan, 1992–1993, Ann Arbor

Kohli M. 1994. Work and retirement: a comparative perspective. In *Age and Structural Lag,* ed. MW Riley, RL Kahn, A Foner, pp. 80–106. New York, NY: Wiley

Krause NF. 1991. Stressful events and life satisfaction among elderly men and women. *Journals Gerontol.: Soc. Sci.* 46:S84–92

LaFontaine JS. 1978. *Sex and Age as Principles of Social Differentiation.* New York: Academic

Lashbrook J. 1996. Promotional timetables: an exploratory investigation of age norms for promotional expectations and their association with job well-being. *Gerontologist* 36(2):189–98

Laslett P. 1991. *A Fresh Map of Life. The Emergence of the Third Age.* Cambridge, MA: Harvard Univ. Press

Lawrence B. 1996. Organizational age norms: Why is it so hard to know one when you see one? *Gerontologist* 36(2):209–20

Lawrence J. 1974. The effects of perceived age on initial impressions and normative role expectations. *Int. J. Aging Hum. Dev.* 5:369–91

Levinson DJ. 1986. A conception of adult development. *Am. Psychol.* 1:3–13

Lewinsohn PM, Mermelstein RM, Alexander C, MacPhillamy DJ. 1985. The Unpleasant Events Schedule: A scale for the measurement of aversive events. *J. Clin. Psychol.* 41(4):483–98

Lewis CN. 1971. Reminiscing and self-concept in old age. *J. Gerontol.* 26:240–43

Linton RA. 1942. Age and sex categories. *Am. Sociol. Rev.* 7:589–603

Maddox G. 1987. Aging differently. *Gerontologist* 27:557–64

Magnusson D, Bergman LR. 1990. *Data Quality in Longitudinal Research.* New York, NY: Cambridge Univ. Press

Magnusson D, Bergman LR, Rudinger G, Törestad B. 1991. *Problems and Methods in Longitudinal Research: Stability and Change.* New York, NY: Cambridge Univ. Press

Marini MM. 1984. Age and sequencing norms in the transition to adulthood. *Soc. Forces* 63:229–44

Markides KS, Boldt JS. 1983. Change in subjective age among the elderly: a longitudinal analysis. *Gerontologist* 23:422–27

Mayer KU. 1986. Structural constraints in the life course. *Hum. Dev.* 29:163–70

Mayer KU, Brueckner E. 1989. *Lebensverlaeufe und Wohlfahrtsentwicklung. Konzeption, Design and Methodik der Erhebung von Lebensverlaeufen der Geburtsjahrgaenge 1929–1931, 1939–1941, 1949–1951.* Berlin: Max Planck Inst. Bildungsforschung

Mayer KU, Schoepflin U. 1989. The state and the life course. *Annu. Rev. Sociol.* 15:187–209

Mayer KU, Tuma NB. 1990. Life course research and event history analysis: An overview. In *Event History Analysis in Life Course Research,* ed. KU Mayer, NB Tuma, pp. 3–20. Madison, WI: Univ. Wisc. Press

McLanahan SS, Sørensen AB. 1985. Life events and psychological well-being. In *Life Course Dynamics,* ed. G Elder, pp. 217–38. Ithaca, NY: Cornell Univ. Press

Mensh IN. 1983. A study of a stress questionnaire: the later years. *Int. J. Aging Hum. Dev.* 16(3):201–07

Montepare JM. 1991. Characteristics and psychological correlates of young adult men's and women's subjective age. *Sex Roles* 24:323–33

Montepare JM, Lachman ME. 1989. "You're only as old as you feel": self-perceptions of age, fears of aging , and life satisfaction from adolescence to old age. *Psychol. Aging* 4:73–78

Murrell SA, Norris FH. 1984. Resources, life events, and changes in positive effect and depression in older adults. *Am. J. Community Psychol.* 12(4):445–64

Murrell SA, Norris FH, Grote C. 1988. Life events in older adults. See Cohen 1988, pp. 96–122

National Council on Aging. (1975). *The Myth and Reality of Aging in America.* Washington, DC: Natl. Council on Aging

Neugarten BL. 1968. Adult personality. In *Middle Age and Aging,* ed. BL Neugarten, pp. 137–47. Chicago, IL: Univ. Chicago Press

Neugarten BL. 1974. Age groups in American society and the rise of the young-old. *Ann. Am. Acad. Polit. Soc. Sci.* 187:187–98

Neugarten BL. 1982. *Age or Need? Public Policies for Older People.* Beverly Hills, CA: Sage

Neugarten BL, Hagestad GO. 1976. Age and the life course. In *Handbook of Aging and the Social Sciences,* ed. R Binstock, E Shanas, pp. 35–55. New York: Van Nostrand Reinhold

Neugarten BL, Moore JW, Lowe JC. 1965. Age norms, age constraints, and adult socialization. *Am. J. Sociol.* 70:710–17

Neugarten BL, Peterson WA. 1957. A study of

the American age-grade system. *Proc. 4th Congr. Int. Assoc. Gerontol.* 3:497–502

Nowotny H. 1989. *Eigenzeit–Entstehung und Strukturierung eines Zeithefuehls.* Frankfurt am Main: Suhrkamp Verlag

O'Rand M, Krecker L. 1990. Concepts of the life cycle: their history, meanings and issues in the social sciences. *Annu. Rev. Sociol.* 16:241–62

Palmore EB, Cleveland WP, Nowlin J, Ramm D, Siegler IC. 1985. Stress and adaptation in later life. In *Normal Aging III: Reports from the Duke Longitudinal Studies, 1975–1984,* ed. E Palmore, W Busse, G Maddox, J Nowlin, I Siegler, pp. 341–56. Durham, NC: Duke Univ. Press

Parsons T. 1942. Age and sex in the social structure of the United States. *Am. Sociol. Rev.* 7:604–16

Passuth PM, Maines DR. 1981. *Transformations in age norms and age constraints: evidence bearing on the age-irrelevancy hypothesis.* Pap. pres. World Congress Gerontol., Hamburg

Paykel ES, Prusoff BA, Uhlenhuth EH. 1971. Scaling of life events. *Arch. of Gen. Psychiatry* 25:340–47

Peterson C. 1996. The ticking of the social clock: Adults' beliefs about the timing of transition events. *Int. J. Aging Hum. Dev.* 42(3):189–203

Plath DW, Ikeda K. 1975. After coming of age: adult awareness of age norms. In *Socialization and Communication in Primary Groups,* ed. TR Williams. The Hague: Mouton

Pressey S, Kuhlen R. 1957. *Psychological Development through the Life Span.* New York: Harper & Row

Riley MW. 1986. Men, women, and the lengthening of the life course. In *Gender and the Life Course,* ed. A Rossi, pp. 333–47. New York: Aldine

Rogoff-Ramsoy N. 1973. *The Norwegian Occupational Life History Study: Design, purpose, and a few preliminary results.* Unpublished ms. Oslo, Norway: Inst. Appl. Soc. Res.

Rosenbaum JE. 1984. *Career Mobility in a Corporate Hierarchy.* New York: Academic

Rosow I. 1978. What is a cohort and why? *Hum. Dev.* 21:65–75

Runyan WM. 1980. The life satisfaction chart: perceptions of the course of subjective experience. *Int. J. Aging Hum. Dev.* 11(1):45–64

Ryder N. 1965. The cohort as a concept in the study of social change. *Am. Sociol. Rev.* 30:843–61

Sarason IG, Johnson JH, Siegel JM. 1978. Assessing the impact of life changes: development of the Life Experiences Survey. *J. Consult. Clin. Psychol.* 46:932–46

Schroots JF, Birren JE. 1988. The nature of time: implications for research on aging. *Contemp. Gerontol.* 2:1–29

Settersten RA, Hagestad GO. 1996a. What's the latest? Cultural age deadlines for family transitions. *Gerontologist* 36(2):178–188.

Settersten RA, Hagestad GO. 1996b. What's the latest? II. Cultural age deadlines for educational and work transitions. *Gerontologist* 36(5):602–13

Sherman E. 1991. *Reminiscence and the Self in Old Age.* New York: Springer

Singer JD, Willett JB. 1991. Modeling the days of our lives: using survival analysis when designing and analyzing longitudinal studies of duration and the timing of events. *Psychol. Bull.* 110(2):268–90

Smesler NJ, Halpern S. 1978. Historical triangulation of family, economy, and education. *Am. J. Sociol.* 84:288–315

Staudinger UM. 1989. *The Study of Life Review: An Approach to the Investigation of Intellectual Development Across the Life Span.* Berlin, Germany: Max Planck Inst. Hum. Dev. Educ.

Teri L, Lewinsohn P. 1982. Modification of the Pleasant and Unpleasant Events Schedules for use with the elderly. *J. Consulting Clin. Psychol.* 50(3):444–45

Thoits PA. 1983. Dimensions of life events that influence psychological distress: An evaluation and synthesis of the literature. In *Psychosocial Stress,* ed. HB Kaplan, pp. 33–103. Orlando, FL: Academic

Thompson P. 1992. "I don't feel old": subjective ageing and the search for meaning in later life. *Aging & Soc.* 12:23–47

Tismer KG. 1971. Vergangenheitsbezug im hoeheren Alter. *Zeitschrift fur Entwicklungspsychologie und Paedagogische Psychologische Psychologie* 3:14–24

Uhlenberg P. 1980. Death and the family. *J. Fam. Hist.* 5:313–20

Underhill L, Cadwell F. 1983. "What age do you feel" age perception study. *J. Consumer Marketing* 1:18–27

van Gennep A. 1960, originally 1908. *The Rites of Passage.* Chicago, IL: Univ. Chicago Press

Wagner BM, Compas BE, Howell DC. 1988. Daily and major life events: a test of an integrative model of psychosocial stress. *Am. J. Community Psychol.* 16(2):189–205

Ward RA. 1984. The marginality and salience of being old: When is age relevant? *Gerontologist* 24:227–32

Watkins SC, Bongarts J, Menken JA. 1987. Demographic foundations of family change. *Am. Sociol. Rev.* 52:346–58

Wilson RW. 1985. Assessing the impact of life change events. In *Normal Aging III: Reports from the Duke Longitudinal Studies,*

*1975–1984,* ed. EB Palmore, EW Busse, GL Maddox, JB Nowlin, IC Siegler, pp. 356–72. Durham, NC: Duke Univ. Press

Wong PTP, Watt LM. 1991. What types of reminiscence are associated with successful aging? *Psychol. Aging* 6:272–79

Wood V. 1972. *Role allocation as a function of age.* Presented at Annu. Meet. Gerontol. Soc. Am., 26th, Miami Beach

Yamaguchi K. 1991. *Event History Analysis.* Newbury Park, CA: Sage

Zautra AJ, Guarnaccia CA, Dohrenwend BP. 1986. The measurement of small life events. *Am. J. Community Psychol.* 14:629–55

Zepelin H, Sills R, Heath M. 1987. Is age becoming irrelevant? An exploratory study of perceived age norms. *Int. J. Aging Hum. Dev.* 24(4):241–55

*Annu. Rev. Sociol. 1997. 23:263–87*


# CULTURE AND COGNITION

*Paul DiMaggio*
Department of Sociology, 2-N-2 Green Hall, Princeton University, Princeton, New Jersey 08544; e-mail: dimaggio@phoenix.princeton.edu

KEY WORDS: sociology of culture, social classification, social cognition, schemata

ABSTRACT

Recent work in cognitive psychology and social cognition bears heavily on concerns of sociologists of culture. Cognitive research confirms views of culture as fragmented; clarifies the roles of institutions and agency; and illuminates supra-individual aspects of culture. Individuals experience culture as disparate bits of information and as schematic structures that organize that information. Culture carried by institutions, networks, and social movements diffuses, activates, and selects among available schemata. Implications for the study of identity, collective memory, social classification, and logics of action are developed.

## INTRODUCTION

The study of culture in everyday life remains a virtuoso affair. Interpretive studies offer great insight but fail to build on one another. Cultural theory has become highly sophisticated but not fully operational. These riches ready the field for takeoff, like the study of social stratification in Sorokin's day (1957 [1927]). But before the study of lived culture can become a cumulative enterprise, scholars must clarify the cognitive presuppositions behind their theories of what culture does and what people do with it, and the fundamental concepts and units of analysis (Jepperson & Swidler 1994, Wuthnow 1987).

Recent work in cognitive psychology and social cognition provides resources for both tasks. After describing recent convergence between cultural sociology and psychology, this chapter considers lessons of recent work on cognition for presuppositions about the nature of culture; develops implications of these lessons for sociological work on identity, collective memory, social classification, logics of action, and framing; and points to key problems that remain unsolved.



0360-0572/97/0815-0263$08.00

Rather than offer an exhaustive review of cognitive sociology per se (see Zerubavel 1997) or work in psychology relevant to culture (see D'Andrade 1995), I emphasize tensions and affinities between recent cognitive research and work in the sociology of culture with the aim of bringing the former into the service of the latter. I focus on how people use culture, rather than the production of culture, ideology, or culture embedded in the physical environment. The point is not to psychologize the study of culture, but to lay a foundation for a view of culture as working through the interaction of shared cognitive structures and supra-individual cultural phenomena (material culture, media messages, or conversation, for example) that activate those structures to varying degrees.

## SOCIOLOGY AND PSYCHOLOGY: POINTS OF CONVERGENCE

A handful of sociologists have appreciated the potential of cognitive science to inform sociological work on culture (Carley 1989, Cicourel 1973, Schwartz 1981, White 1992), and some social constructionists have anticipated important results of cognitive research (Berger & Luckman 1967, Garfinkel 1987 [1967], Zerubavel 1991). For the most part, however, sociologists of culture have ignored relevant work by cognitive psychologists, social psychologists, and public-opinion researchers. This omission reflects a mismatch between the modal intellectual styles of humanistic, interpretively oriented cultural sociologists and experimentally oriented positivistic psychologists, as well as the disappointing legacy of Parsons' efforts at disciplinary fusion, which psychologized culture, reducing it to shared values, norms, and attitudes.

### *Sociology: More Complex Views of Culture*

In recent years, however, common ground between sociology of culture and psychology has grown. The major development within sociology has been a shift to a more complex understanding of culture. Thirty years ago, most sociologists viewed culture as a "seamless web" (Swidler 1997), unitary and internally coherent across groups and situations. In effect, culture was portrayed as a latent variable influencing in common such manifestations as media images, responses to attitude questionnaires, and the values embodied in everyday practices. Individuals were presumed to acquire culture in the course of socialization and, in the popular oversocialized view (Wrong 1961), to enact it unproblematically. It followed from this perspective that there was little reason to worry about constructs used to study culture, for any kind of "cultural stuff" could serve as an indicator of the underlying latent variable.

By contrast, recent work depicts culture as fragmented across groups and inconsistent across its manifestations (Martin 1992). The view of culture as values that suffuse other aspects of belief, intention, and collective life has succumbed to one of culture as complex rule-like structures that constitute resources that can be put to strategic use (Bourdieu 1990, Sewell 1992, Swidler 1986).

This shift makes studying culture much more complicated. Once we acknowledge that culture is inconsistent—that people's norms may deviate from what the media represent as normal, or that our preconscious images and discursive accounts of a phenomenon may differ—it becomes crucial to identify units of cultural analysis and to focus attention upon the relations among them. In effect, our measures stop being indicators of a latent variable (culture), and their relationship to culture becomes analogous to that of education, income, and place of residence to social stratification: separate phenomena, analytically related to a common theoretical construct, the relations among them a matter for empirical investigation (D'Andrade 1995 notes similar trends in anthropology).

Similarly, once we acknowledge that people behave as if they use culture strategically, it follows that the cultures into which people are socialized leave much opportunity for choice and variation. Thus our attention turns to ways in which differing cultural frames or understandings may be situationally cued. Addressing such issues requires more elaborate and contestable psychological presuppositions than did the culture-as-latent-variable view.

## *Psychology: More Complex Views of Cognition*

Such questions make it sensible for sociologists of culture to turn to psychology for insight into the mechanisms through which shared culture enters into cognition. Yet nothing guarantees that psychologists, who have their own research agendas, can help us. Thirty years ago, behaviorism made psychology essentially irrelevant to the study of culture. Twenty years ago, psychologists casting off the yoke of behaviorism focused primarily on the acquisition of skills and capacities of little interest to most sociologists of culture. Even a dozen years ago, the implications for cultural sociology of many of the ideas and research traditions that are most useful today were still unclear.

What has happened to make psychology useful to sociologists of culture? First, psychologists have rejected behaviorism, accepted and demonstrated the existence of mental structures used to perceive, process, and retrieve information, and found ways to make inferences about such structures. Second, just as sociological research has demonstrated culture's complexity and fragmentation, psychological research has demonstrated the complexity of memory and provided glimpses of the partitioning of mental structures by domain. Third, recent foci of psychological research (schemata, categories, mental models, and so on) are much richer in cultural content than the formal operations or intellectual capacities that once preoccupied cognitivists and developmentalists

(Rogoff & Chavajay 1995). Fourth, some psychologists have taken notice of such sociological topics as cross-cultural differences in cognition (Shweder & Bourne 1991, Markus & Kitayama 1991), elite/popular interaction in cultural change (Moscovici 1984), and "distributed cognition" (i.e. the social division of cognitive labor) (Resnick et al 1991, Salomon 1993).

In addition to expanding the grounds of shared interest between the two disciplines, such developments have also softened two important epistemological differences. Whereas most sociologists of culture have been steadfastly antireductionist, resisting efforts to portray culture as the aggregate of individual subjectivities, psychology has focused upon the individual. Increasingly, however, as I shall argue, psychological research bolsters and clarifies the view of culture as supra-individual, and even addresses supra-individual aspects of cognition directly [as in work on pluralistic ignorance (Miller & Prentice 1994)].

Second, some sociologists of culture rejected the subjectivist focus of psychological research, calling instead for research on external aspects of culture amenable to direct measurement (Wuthnow 1987). In recent years, cognitivists have developed ingenious empirical techniques (reviewed in D'Andrade 1995) that permit strong inferences about mental structures, going far toward closing the observability gap between external and subjective aspects of culture.

Of course, the fit between the disciplines must not be exaggerated. Most of what psychologists do is irrelevant to sociologists of culture, and much of the culture sociologists' study is supra-individual. Common ground has increased but will remain limited by the different subject matters of the disciplines (Zerubavel 1997), which will remain complements rather than substitutes.

## COGNITIVE PRESUPPOSITIONS OF CULTURAL SOCIOLOGY

Sociologists who write about the ways that culture enters into everyday life necessarily make assumptions about cognitive processes. If we assume that a shared symbol evokes a sense of common identity (Warner 1959), that a certain frame provokes people to think about a social issue in a new way (Gamson 1992), that lessons about the structure of space and time learned in school are generalized to the workplace (Willis 1977), or that surveys can measure class consciousness (see Fantasia's critique 1995), we are then making powerful cognitive assumptions. Such assumptions, while metatheoretical to sociologists, are keenly empirical from the standpoint of cognitive psychology. It is crucial, then, to evaluate our assumptions (or adjudicate differences among them) by microtranslating presuppositions (Collins 1981) to the cognitive level and assessing their consistency with results of empirical research on cognition.

## *Coherence vs Fragmentation*

Many sociologists have come to reject the latent-variable view of culture as coherent, integrated, and ambiguous in favor of representations of culture as a "toolkit" (Swidler 1986) or "repertoire" (Tilly 1992): a collection of stuff that is heterogeneous in content and function. Yet much empirical work on culture still presumes that culture is organized around national societies or cohesive subnational groupings, is highly thematized, and is manifested in similar ways across many domains (Hofstede 1980, Bourdieu 1984).

Is culture a latent variable—a tight network of a few abstract central themes and their more concrete entailments, all instantiated to various degrees in a range of symbols, rituals, and practices? If so, then we would expect to find that group members share a limited number of consistent elements—beliefs, attitudes, typifications, strategies—and that the inclusion of any one element in the collective culture implies the exclusion of inconsistent elements.

Or is culture a grab-bag of odds and ends: a pastiche of mediated representations, a repertoire of techniques, or a toolkit of strategies? If so, then we might expect less clustering of cultural elements within social groups, less strong linkages among the elements, and weaker pressures for the exclusion of inconsistent elements.

Research in cognitive psychology strongly supports the toolkit over the latent-variable view and suggests that the typical toolkit is very large indeed. Particularly relevant here is research (summarized by Gilbert 1991) on how people attribute accuracy or plausibility to statements of fact and opinion. Consistent with Swidler's (1986) contention that "all people know more culture than they use," Gilbert reports that "The acceptance of an idea is a part of the automatic comprehension of that idea, and the rejection of the idea occurs subsequent to and more effortfully than its acceptance." In other words, our heads are full of images, opinions, and information, untagged as to truth value, to which we are inclined to attribute accuracy and plausibility.

Research on memory tells a similar story, revealing that information (including false information) passes into memory without being "tagged" as to source or credibility, and that active inference is required to identify the source of the information when it is recalled. Such inferences may be incorrect, yielding misattributions of source and credibility (Johnson et al 1991).

This work has several important implications for students of culture. First, it refutes the notion that people acquire a culture by imbibing it (and no other) through socialization. Instead, it directs the search for sources of stability and consistency in our beliefs and representations, first, to schematic organization, which makes some ideas or images more accessible than others; and, second, to cues embedded in the physical and social environment.

Second, learning that people retain (and store with a default value of "correct") almost every image or idea with which they have come into contact, renders intelligible otherwise anomalous research findings about inconsistency in expressions of attitudes across time, cultural volatility in periods of rapid change (e.g. the fall of the Soviet system), and the susceptibility of attitudes to framing effects (Sniderman & Piazza 1993).

Third, the research explains the capacity of individuals to participate in multiple cultural traditions, even when those traditions contain inconsistent elements. Fourth, it establishes the capacity of people to maintain distinctive and inconsistent action frames, which can be invoked in response to particular contextual cues. Fifth, this work raises the possibility that socialization may be less experientially based, and more dependent upon media images and hearsay, than many of our theories (for example, Bourdieu's habitus [1990] construct) imply.

Such inferences as these go beyond the scope of cognitive studies, to be sure, and much rides on the precise ways in which schematic organization imposes order upon stored knowledge and memory. Nonetheless, recent cognitive research strongly reinforces the "toolkit" as opposed to the "latent-variable" view of culture and, at the very least, places the burden of proof on those who depict culture as strongly constraining behavior or who would argue that people experience culture as highly integrated, that cultural meanings are strongly thematized, that culture is binding, and that cultural information acquired through experience is more powerful than that acquired through other means.

### *Institution and Agency*

Cognitive research can also enhance our appreciation of the view that culture both constrains and enables (Sewell 1992). Although this position has become virtually catechismic among sociologists of culture, we know little about the conditions under which one or the other is the case. Many sociologists believe, following Gramsci (1990), that culture, embedded in language and everyday practices, constrains people's capacity to imagine alternatives to existing arrangements. At the same time, we know that people act as if they use cultural elements strategically to pursue valued ends (Bourdieu 1990). Cognitive research cannot answer the essentially sociological question of when culture does each, but it can provide direction to the search.

The finding that culture is stored in memory as an indiscriminately assembled and relatively unorganized collection of odds and ends imposes a far stronger organizing burden on actors than did the earlier oversocialized view. The question, then, is how the actor organizes the information that she or he possesses. Psychological research points to two quite different mechanisms or modes of cognition.

AUTOMATIC COGNITION The first, and most important, which I refer to as automatic cognition is "implicit, unverbalized, rapid, and automatic" (D'Andrade 1995). This routine, everyday cognition relies heavily and uncritically upon culturally available schemata—knowledge structures that represent objects or events and provide default assumptions about their characteristics, relationships, and entailments under conditions of incomplete information.

Psychological research on schemata is central to the interests of sociologists both methodologically (due to advances in techniques that reveal taken-for-granted assumptions to which subjects may not have easy verbal access) and substantively, for what it tells us about how culture works. Indeed, for some purposes, it may be useful to treat the schema as a basic unit of analysis for the study of culture, and to focus on social patterns of schema acquisition, diffusion, and modification (Carley 1991 makes a related argument).

Schemata are both representations of knowledge and information-processing mechanisms. As representations, they entail images of objects and the relations among them. Psychologists use the term broadly [some would suggest too broadly (Fiske & Linville 1980)]. It can refer to simple, highly abstract concepts [for example, container (D'Andrade 1995)]; to concrete activities (buying chewing gum), or to complex social phenomena (group stereotypes or social roles). Event schemata or scripts (Abelson 1981, Garfinkel 1987) constitute an important class of schemata. Special attention has also been given to self schemata (Milburn 1987, Markus & Kitayama 1994, Markus et al 1997), culturally variable representations of the self that provide stability both to individual behavior across time and to social interactions within the group.

Schemata are also mechanisms that simplify cognition. Highly schematic cognition is the realm of institutionalized culture, of typification, of the habitus, of the cognitive shortcuts that promote efficiency at the expense of synoptic accuracy (Berger & Luckman 1967, Bourdieu 1990, Kahneman et al 1982). Much cognitive research demonstrates that "schematic material dominates other material in accurate recall, in intruded recall, in recognition confidence, in recall clustering and in resistance to disconfirmation.... Schemata also facilitate inaccurate recall when the information is schema consistent" (Fiske & Linville 1980: 545). In schematic cognition we find the mechanisms by which culture shapes and biases thought.

*People are more likely to perceive information that is germane to existing schemata* Von Hippel et al (1993) report that experimental subjects are more likely to perceive correctly terms that are schematically relevant than those that are not. Information embedded in existing schemata and information that is schema-dissonant are both more likely to be noticed than information orthogonal to existing structures (Schneider 1991). Such laboratory findings resonate with results in historical sociology and cultural studies: for example, the gradual and halting acceptance of information about the New World by early modern mapmakers (Zerubavel 1992); the ways in which archaic physical models constrained medical scientists' interpretation of new evidence about syphilis (Fleck 1979); and the penchant of male biologists for seeing dominance hierarchies when they watch apes and elephant seals (Haraway 1991).

*People recall schematically embedded information more quickly* Most psychological evidence is based on laboratory experiments, which reveal that subjects remember longer lists of words, or interpret ambiguous stimuli more accurately, and retrieve information about a story they have heard more effectively if it is relevant to preexisting mental structures that render the information interpretable (Sedikides & Skowronski 1991). But again, there are intriguing sociological parallels in studies that report cross-cultural differences in descriptions of the content of the same novel (Griswold 1987), television program (Liebes & Katz 1990), or movie (Shively 1992) that reflect collective preoccupations ("chronically activated mental structures" in psychological parlance).

*People recall schematically embedded information more accurately* When Freeman et al (1987) asked members of a faculty workshop to list the people who had attended the previous meeting, they found that long-term attenders correctly recalled participants who regularly attended, but forgot the infrequent attenders. Using a very different method (analysis of Watergate transcripts), Neisser (1981) reported that Nixon aide John Dean remembered schema-consistent events more accurately than events that were schema-inconsistent.

*People may falsely recall schematically embedded events that did not occur* Freeman et al's (1987) informants remembered regular attenders as present at the meeting in question even when they hadn't been there. When subjects are told to code small-group interactions and then given questionnaires about characteristics of group members shortly thereafter, the post-hoc evaluations yield much higher correlations of schematically related behaviors (e.g. criticizing or expressing hostility) than do the real-time codings (Shweder 1982). Similar confusion of schematic representations for real events may be observed in at least some reports of satanic child abuse (Hacking 1995) and in some of former President Reagan's speeches.

The parallel with sociological accounts of institutions is striking. Typifications (mental structures) influence perception, interpretation, planning, and action (Berger & Luckman 1967, DiMaggio & Powell 1991). Institutionalized structures and behaviors (i.e. those that are both highly schematic and widely shared) are taken for granted, reproduced in everyday action [Giddens' "structuration" (1984)] and treated as legitimate (Meyer & Rowan 1977). Indeed, an eminent psychologist (Bruner 1990:58) has written explicitly of the "schematizing power of institutions." Thus the psychology of mental structures provides a microfoundation to the sociology of institutions.

Research on social cognition enhances our understanding of how culture constrains but does not support theories that depict culture as overwhelmingly constraining. Instead, consistent with contemporary sociological theorizing, work in psychology provides microfoundational evidence for the efficacy of agency.

DELIBERATIVE COGNITION In contrast to automatic thought, psychologists note a quite different form of cognition, which is "explicit, verbalized, slow, and deliberate" (D'Andrade 1995). When sufficiently motivated, people can override programmed modes of thought to think critically and reflexively.

Such overrides are necessarily rare because deliberation is so inefficient in its rejection of the shortcuts that automatic cognition offers. Consequently, the key question is why people are ever deliberative. Psychologists have identified three facilitating conditions in studies that intriguingly parallel work in the sociology of culture.

*Attention* Psychological research suggests that people shift into deliberative modes of thought relatively easily when their attention is attracted to a problem. For example, experimenters can create false recollections of a videotape or story among laboratory "witnesses" by presenting inaccurate information or asking leading questions (Loftus et al 1989). But when the task is changed to ask subjects to think carefully about the source of particular bits of information, the experimental effect is diminished or eliminated (Johnson et al 1993). In experimental studies of attitude-behavior consistency, merely increasing self-awareness by placing a mirror in the face of the subject as he or she completes an attitude questionnaire significantly increases the attitude-behavior correlation (Abelson 1981:722). Such results parallel the insights of students of social movements, who have studied agenda-building and who have also noted the effectiveness as an organizing device of reframing issues in ways that call attention to problems salient to movement participants (Snow & Benford 1992).

*Motivation* People may also shift from automatic to deliberative cognition when they are strongly motivated to do so by dissatisfaction with the status quo or by the moral salience of a particular issue. For example, although racist schemata are accessible to most white Americans, whites can override such schemata to some extent through awareness and reflexivity (Devine 1989). Marx's theory of class consciousness—which contends that physically proximate workers facing immiseration will overcome false beliefs through interaction and reflection—is a classic sociological counterpart (and see Bourdieu 1974).

*Schema failure* Finally, people shift to more deliberative modes of processing when existing schemata fail to account adequately for new stimuli. Research on the psychology of intergroup relations suggests that people in task groups initially code others on the basis of stereotypes but shift to more deliberate evaluations when faced with very strong inconsistent evidence (Schneider 1991:536, Berger et al 1980). Moscovici, whose Durkheimian social psychology differs in many respects from other psychological accounts of mental structures (Farr & Moscovici 1984, Augoustinos & Innes 1990), argues that collectivities confronted with disjunctive social change construct new social representations (often anchored in analogies to pre-existing schemata, and often constructed deliberatively by experts in the social sciences and mass media) in order to interpret new stimuli. Such arguments are paralleled in Garfinkel's (1967) breaching experiments, which forcibly and painfully overrode automatic processing, and in Swidler's contention that ideologies and other consistent cultural forms are more influential during unsettled times (1986, Jepperson & Swidler 1994 on constitutive vs. strategic culture).

Psychologists may note that I have paid scant attention to active debates about the nature of mental structures and have drawn too sharp a contrast between automatic and deliberative processing. Research on culture, however, can already benefit from what research on cognition has resolved. The notion of schema is a fair approximation of phenomena identifiable in fuzzy outline, if not sharp relief, by experimental methods; research on schemata advances sociological understandings of culture, especially institutions; and research on automatic vs deliberative processing may help sociologists determine what to do with the widely believed but theoretically inert notion that both institution and agency are central to social life.

## *Culture as Supra-Individual*

It is no news to sociologists that culture exists, sui generis, at the collective level. (The position taken here—that culture is also manifest in people's heads—is probably more controversial.) Nonetheless, psychological research can help us appreciate several aspects of culture's supra-individual character that sociologists of culture sometimes neglect.

PLURALISTIC IGNORANCE A lively branch of social-psychological research derives from Robert K. Merton's notion of "pluralistic ignorance" (1957): the idea that people act with reference to shared representations of collective opinion that are empirically inaccurate. Such research directs us to distinguish between two senses in which culture is supra-individual: as an aggregate of individuals' beliefs or representations, or as shared representations of individuals' beliefs. Substantial evidence indicates that the latter deviates substantially from the former with significant behavioral consequences and that this process represents a basis for the relative autonomy of social norms (Miller & Prentice 1996, Noelle-Neumann 1993).

INTERGROUP CONTRAST AND POLARIZATION The existence of group-level cultures (shared understanding partly independent of individual beliefs) is also suggested by the tendency of groups to adopt public positions more extreme than the preferences of their members, especially when acting with reference to a contrasting group. What is striking is not polarization per se, but the cultural availability of polarized stances (representations of collective opinion) on which members of each group can converge (Tajfel 1981).

SCHEMATA AS CULTURE Not all schemata are cultural to the same degree. Some schemata reflect universal cognitive processes (for example, basic object categorization), whereas others may be quite idiosyncratic. Many schemata, however, and the schemata of greatest interest to sociologists of culture, enact widely held scripts that appear independent of individual experience. For example, the research, cited above, that found coherence in ratings of small group behavior emerging only after the fact, led the author (Shweder 1982) to speculate that much of what passes as clinical research on personality is really about cultural constructions of personhood (and see Meyer 1986).

COHERENT CULTURES AS EXTERNAL TO PERSONS Despite this chapter's focus on subjective representations of culture, we must not forget that relatively coherent cultural forms exist independently of persons in the broader environment. Indeed, one of the more notable characteristics of modern societies is the existence of a cultural division of labor in which intellectual producers intentionally create and diffuse myths, images, and idea systems (Douglas 1986, Farr & Moscovici 1984, Swidler 1997). Other relatively coherent representations exist less formally as narratives or stories repeatedly invoked in public discourse (Dobbin 1994, White 1992).

AN INITIAL SYNTHESIS Some would argue that whatever coherence exists flows from such externally available sources, i.e. that cultural coherence is entirely external to the person. As we have seen, however, such a position pushes the healthy shift from the latent-variable to the toolkit one step too far. Instead, the research reviewed here suggests that culture works through the interaction of three forms. First, we have information, distributed across persons (Carley 1991). Such distribution is patterned, but not highly differentiating, due to the indiscriminant manner in which bits of culture are accumulated and stored in memory (Gilbert 1991). Second, we have mental structures, especially schematic representations of complex social phenomena, which shape the way we attend to, interpret, remember, and respond emotionally to the information we encounter and possess. Such schemata are more clearly socially patterned than are memory traces. Finally, we have culture as symbol systems external to the person, including the content of talk, elements of the constructed environment, media messages, and meanings embedded in observable activity patterns.

Culture inheres not in the information, nor in the schemata, nor in the symbolic universe, but in the interactions among them. As we have seen, schemata structure our use of information. But people acquire many schemata throughout their lives, and some of these are inconsistent both in content and in implications for behavior. How is it that people invoke one among the many schemata available to them in a given situation?

To simplify greatly in order to focus upon the aspect of the process most relevant to the sociology of culture, selection is guided by cultural cues available in the environment. Although a few schemata may be chronically available, more often they are primed or activated by an external stimulus or frame (Sedikides & Skowronski 1991, Barsalou 1992, Gamson 1992:6–8, Schudson 1989). Framing effects in social surveys—e.g. the finding that whites are more likely to accept negative stereotypes of African-Americans if the question is preceded by a neutral reference to affirmative action (Sniderman & Piazza 1993:102–104)—are familiar examples. But schemata can also be activated through conversation, media use, or observation of the physical environment. Understanding the interaction between two distributions—of the schemata that constitute people's cultural toolkits, and of external cultural primers that act as frames to evoke (and, in evoking, exerting selection pressures upon) these schemata—is a central challenge for sociologists of culture.

## APPLICATIONS

This section reviews work on cognitive aspects of the sociology of culture in light of the perspective developed here. The topics are identity, collective memory, social classification, logics of action, and framing.

### *Identity*

Identity has become one of the most active research fields in the sociology of culture. It is useful to distinguish between two quite different kinds of collective identity: the identities of collectives, on the one hand, and collective aspects of the identities of individuals on the other.

IDENTITIES OF COLLECTIVES At the supra-individual level, collective identity is a shared representation of a collectivity. Research at this level portrays collective identities as highly constructed (Anderson 1983), through explicit messages and more subtle elements such as anthems and flags (Cerulo 1994). Collective identities are chronically contested, as groups vie to produce social representations capable of evoking schemata favorable to their ideal or material interests (Moscovici 1984, Zerubavel 1994, Friedland & Hecht 1996).

Another line of research, active in both psychology and sociology, views identities and selves as collective representations that vary cross-culturally and historically. Markus et al (1996) review research on differences in the cultural construction of identity in East Asian and Western societies. Meyer & Jepperson (1996) contend that the modern self (and its variations in different polities) is a constructed identity endowed with agency in relation to the collectivity.

COLLECTIVE ELEMENTS IN INDIVIDUAL IDENTITIES Much research on collective identity is actually about the more complex issue of the ways in which social identities enter into the constitution of individual selves. Social identity theory views individual identities as comprising prioritized identity-sets based on particularistic and role-based group affiliations (Stryker 1986). Self-categorization theories also portray collective identities as invoked by conditions that make particular identities especially salient (Tajfel & Turner 1986). In this view, individual identities reflect elaborated group-identity schemata in proportion to strength and recency of activation. Viewing identities as context-dependent in this way is consistent with observations of the volatility with which identities may gain and lose salience during periods of intergroup conflict.

### *Collective Memory*

Collective memory is the outcome of processes affecting, respectively, the information to which individuals have access, the schemata by which people understand the past, and the external symbols or messages that prime these schemata. Like collective identities, research on collective memory portrays the phenomenon in both supra-individual and individual terms.

Several scholars have studied institutional processes that maintain or suppress information as part of public culture, such as factors determining the reputation and popularity of particular persons or art works (Fine 1996, Griswold 1986, Lang & Lang 1988). Much research, however, focuses upon the schematic level, studying struggles to define the ways in which members of a society interpret widely shared information about their past, either tracking change in the ways in which a person or public figure is understood over time (Schudson 1992, Schwartz 1991) or analyzing conflict over alternative visions of a collective past (Maier 1988, Zerubavel 1994).

Little research has focused on the interaction between individual and collective memories. An exception is the work of Schuman & Scott (1989), who use survey methods to explore the possibility that the historical events that men and women of different generations remember most vividly structure their understanding of contemporary social issues.

## *Social Classification*

The study of social classification—the social construction and use of category schemes—has burgeoned in the last decade. Some work has analyzed processes of classification in historical time, describing the emergence of a strongly classified artistic high culture (DiMaggio 1982), or the use of social categorization in the formation and implementation of social policies (Starr 1992). Of particular interest is Mohr's (1994) analysis of "discourse roles," which uses structural equivalence analysis to identify the implicit classification of social problems and client groups embedded in self-descriptions of social-service and poverty-relief organizations in early twentieth-century New York City.

Other research has focused upon social differentiation in shorter time spans. Zelizer (1989) describes the process by which women find ways to differentiate even money, the universal medium of exchange, in order to imbue it with social meaning. Lamont (1992) analyzes the bases upon which men of different regional and national origins make social distinctions that reinforce their sense of social honor. Gieryn (1997) describes boundary work within scientific communities, examining how scientists respond when the strong classification science/nonscience is threatened.

Zerubavel, one of few sociologists to study classification from a cognitive perspective, points out that the drive to partition a continuous world appears to be a human universal, though the nature of the categories constructed may vary significantly among groups (Zerubavel 1991, 1997, Douglas 1966). Rosch (1978), whose work has dominated psychological thinking on the topic, proposes (with much experimental support) that cognition is most efficient when we chunk many separate features (bits of information) together by thinking with a prototype (complete mental image) of an object. Prototypical constructs emerge at the most efficient level of abstraction: i.e. where an increase in specificity provides the greatest marginal increase in information. Thus we have prototypes for "chair" but not "furniture" or "divan," and for "bird" but not for "animal" or "sparrow." Although the level at which object prototypes form appears to be relatively universal, the specific content of a prototype reflects a mix of typicality and availability in a given location (D'Andrade 1995).

Rosch applied her model of prototypes to relatively simple concepts. Self-categorization theory draws on the prototype model (Hogg & McGarty 1990), but it remains to be seen if complex social constructs are represented in such unambiguous terms. If so, application to role analysis may be useful, in light of an intriguing parallel between Rosch's characterization of a prototype as a core of essential features and Nadel's (1957) classic definition of social role as consisting of a core of entailments and a penumbra of optional features.

## *Logics of Action*

Many authors have used the expression "logics of action" to refer to an interdependent set of representations or constraints that influence action in a given domain. Sometimes, of course, the term is used as a synonym for "ideal type" (Orru 1991) or, in rational-actor approaches, to refer to situational constraints that induce parallel behaviors among players with similar resources given particular rules of the game (Block 1990, Offe 1985).

A richer, more cultural, sense of logics has emerged in recent work in political economy, a view that embeds them in the interaction between mental structures instantiated in practical reason (Bourdieu 1990), on the one hand, and institutional requirements on the other. Friedland & Alford (1991:248–49) provide the most thorough exposition and definition, describing "institutional logics" as sets "of material practices and symbolic constructions" that constitute an institutional order's "organizing principles" and are "available to organizations and individuals to elaborate." According to Friedland & Alford, these logics are "symbolically grounded, organizationally structured, politically defined and technically and materially constrained."

Similar imagery is apparent in Boltanski & Thévenot's notion of modes of justification (1991), institutionally linked discourses embodying specific orientations toward action and evaluation. Empirical development of similar ideas can be found in Fligstein's (1990) work on "conceptions of control" in corporate governance, and in Stark's (1990) analysis of shop floor politics in a Hungarian socialist factory.

Such work requires a taxonomy of institutions, each of which entails a distinctive logic. (For Friedland & Alford, the institutions are capitalism, the state, democracy, family, religion, and science, each of which has its own axial principle and linked routines and rituals.) Conflict erupts from the clash of institutional logics, as when a wife views her household labor through a marketplace logic of explicit exchange, whereas her husband imposes a family logic of selfless service upon the situation.

The notion of logics is immensely appealing. First, it proposes that external rituals and stimuli interact with internal mental structures to generate routine behavior. Second, it is consistent with the view that culture is fragmented among potentially inconsistent elements, without surrendering the notion of limited coherence, which thematization of clusters of rituals and schemata around institutions provides. Third, it provides a vocabulary for discussing cultural conflict as confrontation between inconsistent logics of action.

At the same time, the work remains frankly exploratory and calls attention to gaps in our current understanding of culture and cognition, which neither psychology nor sociology can address. These are the topics of the next section.

## KEY PROBLEMS IN THE STUDY OF CULTURE AND COGNITION

The notion of institutional logics can be reinterpreted as an effort to thematize schemata and link them to social structure. In order to exploit the insights this perspective offers, students of culture need three things that we now lack: an understanding of how schemata aggregate to more complex cultural structures, or "logics"; an understanding of cultural change, which, in turn, requires a clear understanding of the way in which actors switch among institutional logics; and a theory of analogy, which is necessary if we are to understand processes of schematic generalization that thematization and switching both require.

### *Models of Schematic Aggregation*

Perhaps the highest priority for students of culture and cognition is to develop models of thematization, by which I mean the ways in which diverse schemata aggregate to more general and sociologically interesting constructs like thought styles, stories, logics, paradigms, and ideologies. There are several candidates for such models.

ATOMISTIC DECOUPLING The null hypothesis is that everyday thought is populated by randomly invoked, loosely coupled schemata with little or no higher-level architecture. If so, thematization is simply imposed post hoc by cultural specialists or embedded in the environment and in everyday routines. Although this view is inconsistent with most work in the sociology of culture, and would seem ill-equipped to explain either experimental research on schemata or macro-cultural change, it cannot now be disconfirmed absolutely.

NESTED HIERARCHY At the opposite extreme is the view of cross-cultural psychologists that culture comprises a hierarchy of nested schemata, arrayed from abstract to concrete, with the latter entailed by the former. For example, Markus & Kitayama (1994) view a wide range of cognitive differences between Japanese and Americans as flowing from fundamental differences in self-schemata. Although they provide compelling evidence of significant intergroup differences, one need not assume as much coherence as they do.

DOMAIN-SPECIFICITY There is considerable evidence that information and schemata pertaining to different life domains is stored in distinct areas of memory, with schematic integration occurring within specific domains (Hirschfeld

& Gelman 1994). In this view, clusters of schemata are coherent only within limited boundaries; taken together, the domains are "more like the collected denizens of a tide pool than a single octopus" (D'Andrade 1995:249).

This view has considerable experimental support, though there is little consensus as to the size or character of the domains. It is tempting to equate "domain" with the institutional realms identified by Friedland & Alford (1991) or Boltanski & Thévenot (1990), and to posit that culturally specific "logics of action" are thus embedded in schematic organization, but there is at present little if any empirical warrant for doing so.

IDENTITY CENTRALITY Some evidence suggests that affectively hot schemata are more salient and have more extensive entailments than do emotionally neutral structures. Work on identity (Wiley & Alexander 1987, Hogg & McGarty 1990) suggests the possibility that "the self" may be an emotionally supersaturated cluster of schemata tending toward consistency and stability over time. Schemata that are embedded in the self-schemata, then, are more closely articulated with other schemata than those that are not incorporated into the self.

ROLE CENTRALITY By analogy, one can view roles as situationally evoked, emotionally activated, partial identities that provide integrated chunks of schematic organization and permit compartmentalization of different cultural contents. This perspective is appealing because it identifies a mechanism (i.e. role activation) connecting schematic triggering to contextual variation, and because it is consistent with evidence for domain-specificity of schematic organization. Moreover, because roles are embedded in distinctive role relations, this view points toward an integration of cultural and network analysis within a single framework (McCall 1987).

Which of these models of schematic thematization best describes the processes by which people integrate schemata is at present anybody's guess. Significant matters—the extent to which ideology enters into conscious experience, the patterning of cultural styles or orientations, and the stability of cognition across context—ride on its resolution.

## *Cultural Change*

A second priority for sociologists of culture is to create theories of cultural change that integrate ideas from research on culture and cognition with macrosociological perspectives. At least four different change processes are crucial to understand.

THEORY OF ENVIRONMENTAL TRIGGERING I have argued that culture enters into everyday life through the interaction of environmental cues and mental structures. I have further suggested, by combining logic-of-action theories in sociology and domain-specificity theories in psychology, that cultural understandings may be fragmented by domain, so that when persons or groups switch from one domain to another, their perspectives, attitudes, preferences, and dispositions may change radically. It follows that large-scale cultural changes may be caused by large-scale, more-or-less simultaneous frame switches by many interdependent actors.

At the micro level, we need a better understanding of how and why people switch among frames, logics, or domains (White 1995; from a rational choice perspective, Lindenberg & Frey 1993). The paradigmatic work on this comes from language, where research on code-switching has documented the circumstances (ordinarily changes in context, conversation partner, or topic) that trigger change in language or dialect (Gumperz 1982). At the macro level, the challenge is to create models that link environmental change to patterns of switching (White 1995).

THEORY OF SCHEMA ACQUISITION, DIFFUSION, AND EXTINCTION Psychologists have cast substantial light on the acquisition of schemata by individuals during development (Nelson & Gruendel 1981, Hirschfeld 1994). Sociologists of culture should turn their attention to factors leading to change in the distribution and level of activation of cultural representations or schemata in the population. Such change may occur if different cohorts acquire particular schemata at varying rates; or if changes in the distribution of environmental cues lead to enhanced activation or deactivation of particular schemata that have already been acquired.

Diffusion models of the sort that have been used to study the effects of media exposure on the adoption of new technologies or beliefs may be useful. Diffusion should be most effective where resonance exists between the new cultural element and existing schematic organization (Sperber 1985).

Work in the historical sociology of culture provides some guidance. Wuthnow's (1989) macro-theory of ideological change, which points to the importance of ecological effects on the life chances of new beliefs, may be usefully transposed to more micro levels. Tilly (1992) has developed and implemented a valuable approach to studying change over time in contentious movement repertoires. Buchmann & Eisner (1996) present evidence of accelerating change in the public presentation of selves during the second half of the twentieth century.

A particular challenge is to understand cognitive aspects of major collective events in which large numbers of persons rapidly adopt orientations that might have appeared culturally alien to the majority of them a short time before. Some religious revivals, the emergence of capitalism after the fall of the Soviet Union, and some spirals of ethnic antagonism are demanding cases of this kind.

THEORY OF DELIBERATIVE OVERRIDING It is important to understand not only how culture constrains, but how persons and groups can transcend the biasing effects of culture on thought. Work on this problem by psychologists (noted earlier) must be supplemented by research on the types of social interaction that lead large numbers of people to question and, ultimately, to revise their schematic representations of social phenomena.

## *Analogy and Generalization*

Related to the study of change, but so important that it warrants a section of its own, is the problem of analogy and generalization. Sociological theories that portray persons as actively incorporating culture into cognitive organization invariably rely on some notion like the habitus, which Bourdieu (1990) refers to as a "system of durable transposable dispositions." The key question for all of these theories is: Under what conditions are dispositions or schemata abstracted and transposed from one domain to another?

Almost all cultural change entails the transfer of some body of ideas or images from one content area to another on the basis of similarity judgments. Indeed, any attempt to characterize the culture of a group or a people in abstract terms—i.e., any analytic effort at thematization—takes for granted that actors have the capacity to draw analogies between classes of objects, actors, events, or actions, and thereby to understand them in similar ways.

Think of culture as a network of interrelated schemata, with analogies as the "ties" that create paths along which generalization and innovation occur. How are new "ties" created? The literature provides at least three alternatives.

FEATURE CORRESPONDENCE In the most straightforward models, two schemata or related structures lend themselves to analogy (and thus to generalization across domains) insofar as they share particular features (Lakoff & Johnson 1980) that create a correspondence between them. Thus Swinburne's line, "when the hounds of spring are on winter's traces," is meaningful because of the correspondence between temporal and spatial pursuit and between the destructive effects of hounds on hares and of spring on winter. Two problems with this view are that the correspondence itself is constructed rather than innate; and that analogical power would not seem to vary with the extent of overlap between tenor and vehicle.

STRUCTURE-MAPPING This view takes as its starting point the existence of some form of content-related domain-specificity. Analogies connect not simply schemata but whole domains (Tourganeau & Sternberg 1982), deriving their power from the network of entailed comparisons they trigger. The most powerful analogies connect domains that are structurally homologous. Put another way, generalizability across domains is a function not of the extent to which they share particular features in common, but of the extent to which relations among features are structurally similar (Gentner 1983).

EMOTIONAL RESONANCE Some research suggests that affectively hot schemata are more likely to be generalized across domains than affectively neutral schemata. For example, analogies are likely to be drawn between situations that elicit strong emotional reactions of a similar kind (Abelson 1981:725).

POLYSEMY AND SEMANTIC CONTAGION A final possibility is that polysemous expressions—those with distinct meanings that resonate with multiple schemata or domains—facilitate analogical transfer. Bakhtin's work (1986) on textual multivocality is suggestive in this regard, as is White's (1992) work on stories and rhetorics. Ross (1992) portrays meaning as emerging from the relations of words to one another in speech and to activities in real time. Because these constantly change, meanings are rarely fixed, but instead adapt, diverge, and spread across domains through semantic contagion. This perspective is particularly attractive because it acknowledges endemic change in language and other symbol systems and because it embeds generalization in social interaction.

## SYMBOLS, NETWORKS, AND COGNITION

Cognitive aspects of culture are only one—and not necessarily the largest—part of the sociology of culture's domain. But it is a part that we cannot avoid if we are interested in how culture enters into people's lives, for any explanation of culture's impact on practice rests on assumptions about the role of culture in cognition. I have argued that we are better off if we make such models explicit than if we smuggle them in through the back door and that work in cognitive psychology and social cognition, although animated by different questions, offers tools that we sociologists can use to pursue our own agendas.

Ultimately, the challenge is to integrate the micro perspectives on culture described here with analyses of cultural change in larger collectivities over longer stretches of time. I have argued for a perspective that privileges schemata and related constructs as units of analysis, and attends to mechanisms by which physical, social, and cultural environments differentially activate these schemata.

This argument has begged the question of which aspects of the environment are most worthy of study. Without denying the unquestionable importance of research on how media and activity structures interact with subjective cultural representations, I shall conclude by calling brief attention to new research on the relationship of cognitive and symbolic phenomena to social structures portrayed as social networks.

Some researchers have focused on cognitive representations of social structure. [Fiske & Linville (1980) claim that schema theory is especially relevant to the representation of social phenomena; and see Howard (1994).] The idea that social structures exist simultaneously through mental representations and in concrete social relations was central to Nadel's (1957) role theory. Both theorists (Emirbayer & Goodwin 1994, Orr 1995, White 1992) and researchers (Krackhardt 1987) are exploring the implications of this view.

Networks are crucial environments for the activation of schemata, logics, and frames. In a study of the Paris Commune, Gould (1995) argues that political protest networks did not create new collective identities, but rather activated identities that communards already possessed. Bernstein (1975) demonstrates the impact of network structures on individuals' tendency to employ cognitive abstraction. Erickson (1996), studying security guards, finds a correlation between the complexity of social networks and the diversity of conversational interests. Vaughan (1986) describes how people questioning marriage alter customary patterns of social relations in order to create new, independent identities as prologue to separation. Such studies point to a new, more complex understanding of the relationship between culture and social structure built upon careful integration of micro and macro, and of cognitive and material, perspectives.

ACKNOWLEDGMENTS

Thanks are due to the students in my Princeton graduate seminar on culture and cognition for insightful discussions of much of the work reviewed here; to my psychology colleagues Marcia Johnson, Dale Miller, and Deborah Prentice, who provided valuable guidance in my efforts to come to speedy terms with culture-relevant literature in cognitive and social psychology; and to Bob Wuthnow, Dale Miller, Eviatar Zerubavel, Roger Friedland, and John Mohr for opportunities to present these thoughts at meetings and workshops at Princeton, Rutgers, Santa Barbara, and the ASA meetings. For valuable readings of earlier drafts, I am indebted to Roger Friedland, Michèle Lamont, Diane Mackie, Calvin Morrill, Abigail Smith, Ann Swidler, and Eviatar Zerubavel.



*Literature Cited*

Abelson RP. 1981. Psychological status of the script concept. *Am. Psychol.* 36:715–29

Anderson B. 1983. *Imagined Communities: The Origin and Spread of Nationalism.* London: Verso

Bakhtin MM. 1986. Speech genres. In *Speech Genres and Other Late Essays,* ed. C Emerson, M Holquist, pp. 61–102. Austin: Univ. Texas Press

Barsalou LW. 1992. Frames, concepts, and conceptual fields. See Lehrer & Kittay 1992, pp. 21–74

Berger J, Rosenholtz SJ, Zelditch M. 1980. Status organizing processes. *Annu. Rev. Sociol.* 6:479–508

Berger PL, Luckman T. 1967. *The Social Construction of Reality.* Garden City, NY: Doubleday Anchor

Bernstein B. 1975. Social class, language and socialization. In *Class, Codes and Control: Theoretical Studies Towards a Sociology of Language,* pp. 170–189. New York: Schocken Books. 2nd ed.

Block F. 1990. Political choice and the multiple 'logics' of capital. In *Structures of Capital: The Social Organization of the Economy,* ed. S Zukin, P DiMaggio, pp. 293–310. New York: Cambridge Univ. Press

Boltanski L, Thévenot L. 1991. *De la Justification: Les Economies de la grandeur.* Paris: Gallimard

Bourdieu P. 1974. Avenier de classe et causalité du probable. *Revue Française de sociologie* 15:3–42

Bourdieu P. 1984. *Distinction: A Social Critique of the Judgement of Taste.* Transl. R Nice. Cambridge: Harvard Univ. Press

Bourdieu P. 1990 [1980]. Structures, habitus, practices. In *The Logic of Practice,* pp. 52–65. Stanford: Stanford Univ. Press

Bruner J. 1990. *Acts of Meaning.* Cambridge: Harvard Univ. Press

Buchmann M, Eisener M. 1996. *Images of the self: 1900–1992.* Pap. presented at Ann. Meet. Am. Sociol. Assoc., New York

Carley KM. 1989. The value of cognitive foundations for dynamic social theory. *J. Math. Sociol.* 14:171–208

Carley KM. 1991. A theory of group stability. *Am. Sociol. Rev.* 56:331–54

Cerulo K. 1995. *Identity Designs: The Sights and Sounds of a Nation.* New Brunswick, NJ: Rutgers Univ. Press

Cicourel AV. 1973. *Cognitive Sociology.* New York: Free Press

Collins R. 1981. On the microfoundations of macrosociology. *Am. J. Sociol.* 86:984–1014

D'Andrade R. 1995. *The Development of Cognitive Anthropology.* New York: Cambridge Univ. Press

Devine PG. 1989. Stereotypes and prejudice: their automatic and controlled components. *J. Pers. Soc. Psychol.* 56:5–18

DiMaggio P. 1982. Cultural entrepreneurship in nineteenth-century Boston. *Media Cult. Soc.* 4:33–50, 303–21

DiMaggio P, Powell WW. 1991. Introduction. In *The New Institutionalism in Organizational Analysis,* ed. WW Powell, P DiMaggio, pp. 1–38. Chicago: Univ. Chicago Press

Dobbin F. 1994. Cultural models of organization: the social construction of rational organizing principles. In *The Sociology of Culture: Emerging Theoretical Perspectives,* ed. D Crane, pp. 117–42. Cambridge: Blackwell

Douglas M. 1986. *How Institutions Think.* Syracuse, NY: Syracuse Univ. Press

Douglas M. 1966. *Purity and Danger.* London: Routledge & Kegan Paul

Emirbayer M, Goodwin J. 1994. Network analysis, culture, and the problem of agency. *Am. J. Sociol.* 99:1411–54

Erickson B. 1996. Culture, class and connections. *Am. J. Sociol.* 102:217–51

Fantasia R. 1995. Class consciousness in culture, action, and social organization. *Annu. Rev. Sociol.* 21:269–87

Farr RM, Moscovici S. 1984. *Social Representations.* Cambridge: Cambridge Univ. Press

Fine GA. 1996. Reputational entrepreneurs and the memory of incompetence: melting supporters, partisan warriors, and images of President Harding. *Am. J. Soc.* 101:1159–93

Fiske ST, Linville PW. 1980. What does the schema concept buy us? *Pers. Soc. Psychol. Bull.* 6:543–57

Fleck L. 1979 [1935]. *Genesis and Development of a Scientific Fact.* Chicago: Univ. Chicago Press

Fligstein N. 1990. *The Transformation of Corporate Control.* Cambridge, MA: Harvard Univ. Press

Freeman L, Romney AK, Freeman SC. 1987. Cognitive structure and informant accuracy. *Am. Anthropol.* 89:310–25

Friedland R, Alford R. 1991. Bringing society back in: symbols, practices, and institutional contradictions. In *The New Institutionalism in Organizational Analysis,* ed. WW Powell, P DiMaggio, pp. 223–62. Chicago: Univ. Chicago Press

Friedland R, Hecht R. 1996. *To Rule Jerusalem.* New York: Cambridge Univ. Press

Gamson WA. 1992. *Talking Politics.* New York: Cambridge Univ. Press

Garfinkel H. 1987 [1967]. Studies of the routine grounds of everyday activities. In *Studies in Ethnomethodology,* pp. 35–75. Oxford: Polity

Gentner, D. 1983. Structure-mapping: a theoretical framework for analogy. *Cogn. Sci.* 7:155–70

Giddens A. 1984. *The Constitution of Society: Outline of a Theory of Structuration.* Berkeley: Univ. Calif. Press

Gieryn TF. 1998. *Cultural Cartography of Science: Episodes of Boundary Work, Sociologically Rendered.* Chicago, IL: Univ. Chicago Press. In press

Gilbert DT. 1991. How mental systems believe. *Am. Psychol.* 46:107–19

Gould R. 1995. *Insurgent Identities: Class, Commmunity and Protest in Paris from 1848 to the Commune.* Chicago: Univ. Chicago Press

Gramsci A. 1990. Culture and ideological hegemony. In *Culture and Society: Contemporary Debates,* ed. J Alexander, S Seidman. New York: Cambridge Univ. Press

Griswold W. 1986. *Renaissance Revivals: City Comedy and Revenge Tragedy in the London Theatre, 1576–1980.* Chicago: Univ. Chicago Press

Griswold W. 1987. The fabrication of meaning: literary interpretation in the United States, Great Britain, and the West Indies. *Am. J. Sociol.* 92:1077–117

Gumperz JJ. 1982. *Discourse Strategies.* Cambridge: Cambridge Univ. Press

Hacking I. 1995. *Rewriting the Soul: Multiple Personality and the Sciences of Memory.* Princeton, NJ: Princeton Univ. Press

Haraway D. 1991. The past is the contested zone. In *Simians, Cyborgs, and Women: The Reinvention of Nature,* pp. 21–42. New York: Routledge

Hirschfeld LA. 1994. The child's representation of human groups. *Psychol. Learning & Motivation* 31:133–85

Hirschfeld, LA, Gelman, SA. 1994. Toward a topography of mind: an introduction to domain specificity. In *Mapping the Mind,* ed. LA Hirschfeld, SA Gelman, pp. 3–35. New York: Cambridge Univ. Press

Hofstede G. 1980. *Culture's Consequences: International Differences in Work-Related Values.* Beverly Hills: Sage

Hogg MA, McGarty C. 1990. Self-categorization and social identity. In *Social Identity Theory: Constructive and Critical Advances,* ed. D Abrams, MA Hogg, pp. 10–27. New York: Springer-Verlag

Howard JA. 1994. A social cognitive conception of social structure. *Soc. Psychol. Q.* 57:210–27

Jepperson R, Swidler A. 1994. What properties of culture should we measure? *Poetics* 22:359–71

Johnson MK, Hastroudi S, Lindsay, DS. 1993. Source monitoring. *Psychol. Bull.* 114:3–28

Kahnemann D, Slovic P, Tversky A. 1982. *Judgment Under Uncertainty: Heuristics and Biases.* New York: Cambridge Univ. Press

Kluegel J, Smith ER. 1986. *Beliefs about Inequality: Americans Views of What Is and What Ought To Be.* New York: DeGruyter

Krackhardt D. 1987. Cognitive social structures. *Soc. Networks* 9:109–34

Lakoff G, Johnson M. 1980. *Metaphors We Live By.* Chicago: Univ. Chicago Press

Lamont M. 1992. *Money, Morals, and Manners: The Culture of the French and American Upper-Middle Class.* Chicago, IL: Univ. Chicago Press

Lang GE, Lang K. 1988. Recognition and renown: the survival of artistic reputation. *Am. J. Sociol.* 94:79–109

Lehrer A, Kittay EF, eds. 1992. *Frames, Fields and Contrasts: New Essays in Semantic and Lexical Organization.* Hillsdale, NJ: Lawrence Erlbaum

Liebes T, Katz E. 1990. *The Export of Meaning: Cross-Cultural Readings of Dallas.* New York: Oxford Univ. Press

Lindenberg S, Frey BS. 1993. Alternatives, frames, and relative prices: a broader view of rational choice theory. *Acta Sociol.* 36:191–205

Loftus EF, Donders K, Hoffman HG, Schooler JW. 1989. Creating new memories that are quickly accessed and confidently held. *Memory Cognition* 17:607–16

Maier CS. 1988. *The Unmasterable Past: History, Holocaust, and German National Identity.* Cambridge: Harvard Univ. Press

Markus HR, Kitayama S. 1991. Culture and the self: implications for cognition, emotion and motivation. *Psychol. Rev.* 98:224–53

Markus HR. Kitayama S. 1994. The cultural construction of self and emotion: implications for social behavior. In *Emotion and Culture: Empirical Studies of Mutual Influence,* ed. S Kitayama, HR Markus, pp. 89–130. Washington, DC: Am. Psychol. Assoc.

Markus HR, Kitayama, S, Heiman, R. 1996. Culture and 'basic' psychological principles. In *Social Psychology: Handbook of Basic Principles,* ed. ET. Higgins, AW Kruglanski. New York: Guilford

Martin J. 1992. *Cultures in Organizations: Three Perspectives.* New York: Oxford Univ. Press

McCall GJ. 1987. The structure, content, and dynamics of self: continuities in the study of role-identities. See Yardley & Honess 1987, pp. 133–45

Merton RK. 1957. *Social Theory and Social Structure.* New York: Free Press

Meyer JW. 1986. Myths of socialization and of personality. In *Reconstructing Individualism,* ed. T Heller, S Morton, D Wellberry, pp. 212–25. Stanford, CA: Stanford Univ. Press

Meyer JW, Jepperson RL. 1996. The actor and the other: cultural rationalization and the ongoing evolution of modern agency. Ms., Stanford Univ. Dept. Sociol.

Meyer JW, Rowan B. 1977. Institutionalized organizations: formal structure as myth and ceremony. *Am. J. Sociol.* 83:340–63

Milburn MA. 1987. Ideological self-schemata and schematically induced attitude consistency. *J. Exp. Social Psychol.* 23:383–98

Miller DT, Prentice DA. 1994. Collective errors and errors about the collective. *Person. Soc. Psychol. Bull.* 20:541–50

Miller DT, Prentice DA. 1996. The construction of social norms and standards. *Handbook of Social Psychology,* ed. XX, pp. 799–829. XX: XX

Mohr JW. 1994. Soldiers, mothers, tramps and others: discourse roles in the 1907 Charity Directory. *Poetics* 22:327–58

Moscovici S. 1984. The phenomenon of social representations. In *Social Representations,* ed. RM Farr, S Moscovici, pp. 3–69. New York: Cambridge Univ. Press

Nadel SF. 1957. *A Theory of Social Structure.* London: Cohen & West

Neisser U. 1981. John Dean's memory: A case study. *Cognition* 9:1–22

Nelson K, Gruendel J. 1981. Generalized event representations: basic building blocks of cognitive development. In *Advances in Developmental Psychology,* ed. ME Lamb, AL Brown, pp. 131–58. Hillsdale, NJ: Lawrence Erlbaum

Noelle-Neumann E. 1993 [1980]. *The Spiral of Silence: Public Opinion—Our Social Skin.* Chicago: Univ. Chicago Press

Offe C. 1985. *Disorganized Capitalism.* Cambridge, MA: MIT Press

Orr SW. 1995. Language, values and social networks: on meaning and the micro-macro link in structural sociology. Ms., Center for the Social Sciences, Columbia Univ.

Orru M. 1991. The institutional logic of small-firm economies in Italy and Taiwan. *Stud. Compar. Int. Dev.* 26:3–28

Resnick LB, Levine JM, Teasley SD. 1991. *Perspectives on Socially Shared Cognition.* Washington, DC: Am. Psychol. Assoc.

Rogoff B, Chavajay P. 1995. What's become of research on the cultural basis of cognitive development? *Am. Psychol.* 50:859–77

Rosch E. 1978. Principles of categorization. In *Cognition and Categorization,* ed. E Rosch, B Lloyd, pp. 27–48. Hillsdale, NJ: Erlbaum

Ross J. 1992. Semantic contagion. See Lehrer & Kittay 1992, pp. 143–69

Salomon G, ed. 1993. *Distributed Cognition: Psychological and Educational Considerations.* New York: Cambridge Univ. Press

Schneider DJ. 1991. Social cognition. *Annu. Rev. Psychol.* 42:527–61

Schudson M. 1989. How culture works: perspectives from media studies on the efficacy of symbols. *Theory Soc.* 18:153–80

Schudson M. 1992. *Watergate in American Memory: How We Remember, Forget, and Reconstruct the Past.* New York: Basic

Schuman H, Scott J. 1989. Generations and collective memories. *Am. Sociol. Rev.* 54:359–81

Schwartz B. 1981. *Vertical Classification: A Study in Structuralism and the Sociology of Knowledge.* Chicago: Univ. Chicago Press

Schwartz B. 1991. Social change and collective memory: the democratization of George Washington. *Am. Sociol. Rev.* 56:221–36

Sedikides C, Skowronski JJ. 1991. The law of cognitive structure activation. *Psychol. Inquiry* 2:169–84

Sewell WH Jr. 1992. A theory of structure: duality, agency, and transformation. *Am. J. Sociol.* 98:1–29

Shively J. 1992. "Cowboys and Indians": perceptions of western films among American Indians and Anglos. *Am. Sociol. Rev.* 57:725–34

Shweder RA. 1982. Fact and artifact in trait perception: the systematic distortion hypothesis. *Progress in Exp. Personal. Res.* 2:65–100

Shweder RA, Bourne EJ. 1991. Does the concept of the person vary cross-culturally? In *Thinking Through Cultures: Explorations in Cultural Psychology,* ed. R. Shweder, pp. 113–56. Cambridge: Harvard Univ. Press

Sniderman PM, Piazza T. 1993. *The Scar of Race.* Cambridge, MA: Harvard Univ. Press

Snow DA, Benford, RD. 1992. Master frames and cycles of protest. In *Frontiers in Social Movement Theory,* ed. AD Morris, CM Mueller, pp. 133–55. New Haven, CT: Yale Univ. Press

Sorokin PA. 1957 [1927]. *Social and Cultural Mobility.* New York: Free Press

Sperber D. 1985. Anthropology and psychology: towards an epidemiology of representations. *Man* 20:73–89

Stark D. 1990. La valeur du travail et sa rétribution en Hongrie. *Actes de la Recherche en Sciences Sociales* 85:3–19

Starr P. 1992. Social categories and claims in the liberal state. *Soc. Res.* 59:263–95

Stryker S. 1987. Identity theory: developments and extensions. See Yardly & Honess 1987, pp. 89–104

Swidler A. 1986. Culture in action: symbols and strategies. *Am. Sociol. Rev.* 51:273–86

Swidler A. 1997. *Talk of Love: How Americans Use Their Culture.* Chicago: Univ. Chicago Press

Swidler A, Arditi J. 1994. The new sociology of knowledge. *Annu. Rev. Sociol.* 20:305–29

Tajfel H. 1981. *Human Groups and Social Categories: Studies in Social Psychology.* New York: Cambridge Univ. Press

Tajfel H, Turner JC. 1986. The social identity theory of intergroup behavior. In *Psychology of Intergroup Relations,* ed. S Worchel, WG Austin, pp. 7–24. Chicago: Nelson-Hall. 2nd ed.

Tilly C. 1992. *How to detect, describe, and explain repertoires of contention. Working Paper No. 150.* Cent. Stud. Soc. Change. New Sch. for Soc. Res.

Tourangeau R, Sternberg RJ. 1982. Understanding and appreciating metaphors. *Cognition* 11:203–44

Vaughan D. 1986. *Uncoupling: Turning Points in Intimate Relationships*. New York: Oxford Univ. Press

Von Hippel E, Jonides J, Hilton JL, Narayan S. 1993. The inhibitory effect of schematic processing on perceptual encoding. *J. Personal. Soc. Psych.* 64:921–35

Warner WL. 1959. *The Living and the Dead: A Study of the Symbolic Life of Americans.* New Haven: Yale Univ. Press

White HC. 1992. *Identity and Control: A Structural Theory of Social Action.* Princeton, NJ: Princeton Univ. Press

White HC. 1995. Network switchings and Bayesian forks: reconstructing the social and behavioral sciences. *Soc. Res.* 62:1–28

Wiley MG, Alexander, CN. 1987. From situated activity to self attribution: the impact of social structural schemata. See Yardley & Honess 1987, pp. 105–17

Willis P. 1977. *Learning to Labor.* New York: Columbia Univ. Press

Wrong DH. 1961. The oversocialized conception of man. *Am. Sociol. Rev.* 26:184–93

Wuthnow R. 1987. *Meaning and Moral Order: Explorations in Cultural Analysis.* Berkeley: Univ. Calif. Press

Wuthnow R. 1989. *Communities of Discourse: Ideology and Social Structure in the Reformation, the Enlightenment and European Socialism.* Cambridge: Harvard Univ. Press

Yardley K, Honess T, eds. 1987. *Self and Identity: Psychosocial Perspectives.* New York: John Wiley

Zelizer V. 1989. The social meaning of money: 'special monies.' *Am. J. Sociol.* 95:342–77

Zerubavel E. 1991. *The Fine Line.* New York: Free Press

Zerubavel E. 1992. *Terra Cognita: The Mental Discovery of America.* New Brunswick, NJ: Rutgers Univ. Press

Zerubavel E. 1997. *Social Mindscapes: An Invitation to Cognitive Sociology.* Cambridge: Harvard Univ. Press

Zerubavel Y. 1994. *Recovered Roots: Collective Memory and the Making of Israeli National Tradition.* Chicago: Univ. Chicago Press

Annu. Rev. Sociol. 1997. 23:289–313


# THE FAMILY RESPONSIVE WORKPLACE

*Jennifer L. Glass and Sarah Beth Estes*
Department of Sociology, W140 Seashore Hall, University of Iowa, Iowa City, Iowa 52442; e-mail: Jennifer-Glass@uiowa.edu

KEY WORDS: work/family conflict, organizations, employment benefits, family policy, child care

ABSTRACT

Women's entrance into the labor market in large numbers has exacerbated incompatibilities between employer and family interests. Research reveals that conflict between paid work and family responsibilities has been linked to decreased employee productivity as well as decreased family functioning. In this review, we explore the nature of job/family incompatibility, organizational interests in family responsive policies, and the current prevalence of various policies within work organizations. We then review what is known about the effectiveness of particular family-responsive policies on organizational and family functioning. Finally, we consider barriers to further institutionalization of family responsive policy and suggest future research and policy directions.

## INTRODUCTION

As the number of dual-earner and single-parent households raising children continues to grow, pressure on organizations to attend to the family responsibilities of employees has been increasing (Families and Work Institute 1991, Goodstein 1994). The sexual division of labor spawned by the development of industrial capitalism in the nineteenth century has given way to a new demographic reality—one in which the responsibilities of workers to provide primary physical care to their dependents are no longer segregated from their responsibilities to provide financially for their families. The US Census Bureau reported that 52% of mothers of infants under one year of age were in the labor force as of 1991 (US Bureau of the Census 1992), while projections indicate that over 85% of employed women can expect to become pregnant at some point during



0360-0572/97/0815-0289$08.00

their work life. Indeed, some demographers argue that 90% of women aged 18–49 should be considered active members of the labor force, since even those not currently employed will soon be again (Stipp 1988).

These high rates of female labor-force participation affect men as well, since men are increasingly partnered to women who are likely to be lifetime labor force participants. Without housewives at home to attend to the organization and provision of care to children, fathers are also experiencing tensions between their work and family obligations, although not necessarily the same kind nor to the same degree as mothers (Gerson 1993). Judging from the increased proportion of employed men reporting child-care problems in 1988 compared to 1984, a trend toward greater paternal involvement in family management may be emerging (Fernandez 1990).

## HISTORICAL SOLUTIONS

The problem of reconciling family caregiving with paid employment is not new in the history of industrial capitalism. In the nineteenth century, factories were sometimes filled with entire families working at the same location but at different tasks, justified in part by the need to adequately supervise and monitor children (Hareven 1982). But this pattern did not persist into the twentieth century as the supply of male labor increased and the effects of harsh working conditions on the health of mothers and children became a concern (Brenner & Ramas 1984). The family responsibilities of those women still compelled to work outside the home were addressed through protective labor legislation in the early twentieth century (Kessler-Harris 1982).

Throughout this period, men's roles as husbands and fathers were not ignored by unions and industrialists but were mostly redefined as only breadwinning responsibilities. Thus, some large companies in the early decades of the twentieth century competed for the loyalties of their predominantly male workers by offering a smorgasbord of benefits such as health, life, accident insurance, and pensions in a system that has become known as "welfare capitalism" (Edwards 1979). Because welfare capitalism proved to be expensive and failed to stop union activity, however, most programs did not survive the Great Depression (Edwards 1979).

World War II brought with it a resurgence of interest in work/family issues as the number of women workers in crucial defense industries dramatically increased. Federally funded child-care centers were opened near defense-related factories, temporarily setting aside the ideology of separate spheres for men and women. Although those child-care centers were closed soon after the war ended, some scholars have argued that the war nevertheless ushered in an era in which unions pushed for and corporations increasingly provided social welfare benefits (Cornfield 1990), mirroring many of the benefits offered under welfare capitalism—health and life insurance, pension plans, and disability protection. Importantly, however, this postwar expansion included federally mandated employer participation in such areas as workers' compensation and Social Security, institutionalizing the notion that employers had at least some obligation to provide for the security of the families of their employees.

Yet the degree to which employers rather than the state should be held responsible for the social welfare of families would continue to be contested. In the United States, to a far greater extent than in Western Europe's social democracies, employers have been allowed to vary in the degree of responsiveness they show to workers' family obligations. Strong welfare states in Western Europe assumed much greater responsibility for ensuring that employers contributed to the well-being of families, through legislative and tax policies that provide paid leaves and reduced work hours for parents of young children and that redistribute income to families with children. The early dependence of European economies on female labor after World War II resulted in explicitly fashioned "family policies" that were designed to protect birth rates while simultaneously incorporating mothers into the labor force (Haas 1991).

In the United States, by contrast, dependence on married women's labor has come relatively late, and employers have mostly avoided regulatory policies that assist parents. Instead, the US welfare state has been fashioned around direct provision of services to families with heads unable to secure employment, financed through general tax revenues. As of this writing, even that minimal guarantee of government assistance to families with children was being decisively limited by federal welfare reform legislation. Yet, legislation that would force employers to accommodate childbearing and family caregiving, or even to sponsor affordable high-quality substitute care while parents work has not been swiftly forthcoming. For instance, the Family and Medical Leave Act of 1993 was twice vetoed by Republican administrations. The version of federally mandated parental leave that ultimately was signed into law shortened the originally proposed leave and contained provisions that exempted small businesses and employees in any business whose job duties were considered essential to the organization's operation.

Some scholars believe nevertheless that the tide is slowly turning in favor of government intervention in the work/family relationship, pointing to the proliferation of bills in the US Congress dealing with work/family issues in recent years (Burstein et al 1995). Although few have yet been passed, the degree of interest certainly suggests possible expansion of the state's interest in regulating the employment of parents of minor children. And the state's abandonment of guaranteed support to parents of minor children might paradoxically increase pressure on lawmakers to legislate solutions to job/family conflict. At present, however, neither government nor employers in the free market have institutionalized policies or procedures for dealing with the influx of workers with caregiving responsibilities into the labor force. No new model has emerged of a relationship between labor, management, and the state that would loosen managerial control over the hours and scheduling of work, allow time for child-bearing, and guarantee adequate substitute care for young children.

Part of the problem stems from the fact that children need different types of parental care and supervision at different ages. This problem of heterogeneity in parents' needs is exacerbated by continued ideological debate over the appropriate approach to solving job/family conflicts—while some feel that employers should free workers' time and energy to care for their own children, others promote the transfer of caregiving functions from workers to other institutions such as schools, child-care providers, hospitals, and nursing homes, etc. These divergent perspectives suggest different policy alternatives—extended parental leave for newborns versus infant day care, paid sick days for family illness versus sick-child care, reduced or part-time work hours for parents versus extension of the school day and school year.

Another reason that employers and government have been slow to respond to the needs of parents has been the lack of information about the most efficacious and cost-effective policies to implement. Rigorous evaluation of various workplace policy initiatives designed to reduce job/family stress has, in our opinion, been conspicuously missing. The effects of family responsive policies on parental behavior and children's well-being have not yet received direct attention, although child development experts contributed heavily to the debate on mandated parental leave by summarizing the effects of mothers' early returns to work on the physical and emotional well-being of mothers and infants (Brazelton 1986, Hopper & Zigler 1989).

The remainder of this essay will (*a*) attempt to develop a conceptualization of "family responsiveness" that is rooted in an analysis of the problems employed parents face as well as the organizational problems that ensue from parents' caregiving responsibilities, (*b*) review the prevalence of policies designed to assist employed parents and the determinants of organizational adoption of workplace family policies, and (*c*) evaluate the extent to which various policy initiatives achieve their objectives, whether those relate to family well-being, worker satisfaction, or organizational productivity. We then conclude by discussing the disjuncture between policies that are most likely to solve the dilemmas faced by employed parents and the solutions that employers are likely to adopt strategically without legislative coercion.

## THE CHANGING AMERICAN WORKER

Ten years ago, in their review of literature in the then-burgeoning field of work/family conflict, Greenhaus & Beutell (1985) defined work/family conflict as "a form of interrole conflict in which the role pressures from the work and family domains are mutually incompatible in some respect" (p. 77). We look to the survey data on employed parents to determine the sources of job/family conflict as well as the working conditions and policies most desired by parents to ameliorate those conflicts.

## *What Do Parents Want*

It is difficult to state definitively what employees desire in terms of family accommodations. Some studies assessing employees' preferences for workplace initiatives toward reducing work/family conflict sample all employees, while others sample only those with current child-rearing responsibilities. Importantly, the family needs of employees are not homogenous or static. While childbearing employees need leave for childbirth and infant care, parents of preschoolers need high-quality affordable child care and reduced work hours to meet the emotional needs of young children. Parents of school-aged children need after-school, vacation, and summer care, while parents of teens and caregivers of elderly parents need schedule flexibility and leave for emergencies. In a study on the utility of child-care programs, Kossak (1990) showed that these different family and work factors mean that the policies that are optimal for one class of employees at one point in time may have little to no effect on reducing work/family conflict for another class, or even for the same employees at another point in time.

Keeping these methodological caveats in mind, we can draw a general picture of parents' preferences. In a *USA Today* poll (cited in Vanderkolk & Young 1991) in which employed parents were asked what job benefits they considered to be most important, 40% of mothers and 21% of fathers replied that family benefits were the most important job benefits. Another 10% of mothers replied that flexible hours were most important, while 5% of fathers responded in this way. Together, this means that 50% of mothers and 26% of fathers valued family responsive policies in their jobs more than they valued pay (64% of fathers and 42% of mothers considered pay to be most important).

*The National Study of the Changing Workforce*, utilizing a nationally representative sample of 2958 employees, revealed that close to one fourth of employees lacking flexible schedules or the ability to work at home would change jobs to gain these benefits. Additionally, 47% of those lacking leave time to tend to family illness said they would sacrifice pay or benefits to gain leave for sick family members. Finally, day-to-day family responsibilities were claimed by 87% not just of parents but of all surveyed. The study says this suggests that employee pressure on businesses to become more family-responsive is indicative not simply of special interests, but of widespread need in the labor force (*Social Science and the Citizen 1993/94*).

In another nationally representative study, respondents indicated that their quality of family life would be improved if, first, they were to receive merit raises, and second, they were provided with trained, family-accommodating supervisors (Galinsky & Stein 1990). In a sample of business and university employees, most indicated that some form of schedule flexibility or work reduction, such as flextime, part-time work, or parental leave, was their top choice toward improving the work/family balance. Rogers (1992) reported that his data from 20 Fortune 500 companies showed the work/family policy most consistently highly rated and desired by workers was full-time flexible scheduling; most employees with family responsibilities said they did not want to, or could not afford to, work less.

The types of family needs addressed through workplace initiatives fall into three general categories: (*a*) policies and benefits that reduce work hours to provide time for family caregiving through the provision of leave for vacation, illness, childbearing, and emergency child care or through reductions in average hours worked per week, (*b*) policies designed to give workers greater flexibility in the scheduling of work hours and the location of work hours while not decreasing average work hours, and (*c*) policies designed to provide workplace social support for parents, including forms of child-care assistance so that they work without concern for the care of dependents in their absence (for a similar categorization, see Silver & Goldscheider 1994). This categorization provides a useful heuristic for organizing the vast findings concerning individual-level and family outcomes of work/family conflict as well as for evaluating the effectiveness of organizational work/family policies.

Evidence of job/family conflict can be found both at the workplace and at home. Spillover from work to family affects the family by impairing both individual and family functioning. Spillover from the family to work often takes the form of lower productivity, higher absenteeism, and greater turnover. This family-to-work spillover can result in lowered career achievement for the employee. In the next section we investigate research on work-to-family spillover and its effects on family functioning and individual well-being. Then we review the available research on family-to-work spillover, focusing on the consequences for individual achievement and organizational functioning.

### *The Effects of Work/Family Spillover*

Research has demonstrated fairly consistent links between work/family conflict and physical and mental health as well as to some aspects of family functioning such as marital satisfaction and parenting behaviors. However, measures of work/family conflict often rely on parents' self-reports of conflict levels (Bohen & Viveros-Long 1981, Bedeian et al 1988, Voydanoff 1988, Frone et al 1992) and generally fail to distinguish among different sources of job/family conflict.

Because these measures combine conflict stemming from overwork, schedule inflexibility, and unsupportive work environments, it is hard to tell how particular sources of conflict affect various work and family outcomes. For example, Hughes and associates (1992) showed that nonspecific job/family incompatibility decreased marital companionship and increased marital tension. Studies using other measures, such as overtime hours or difficulties arranging child care (Kossak 1990), provide insight into the effects of specific types of work/family conflict. The individual and family outcomes we discuss are organized around the categorization of work/family issues outlined above—extended work hours, inflexibility, and unsupportive work environments.

WORK HOURS Extended work hours have been linked to work/family conflict (Piotrkowski et al 1987). Frone et al (1994) also demonstrated a link between lack of family time and compulsive drinking and smoking in employed mothers. While the relationship between lack of time and marital solidarity/satisfaction remains unclear (Piotrkowski et al 1987), some evidence suggests that parents' lack of time serves to diminish children's well-being. The increase in time spent in work results in a decrease in time spent with children (Nock & Kingston 1988) and an increase in the time children spend in substitute care, much of which is of relatively low quality in the United States (Cost, Quality & Child Outcomes Study Team 1995). Although decreased quantity of time spent with children does not necessarily indicate that the quality of interactions with children is decreased (Piotrkowski et al 1987), some scholars wonder whether there are upper limits to work hours above which even "quality time" suffers (Louv 1990, Hewlett 1991). Parents are aware of their sacrifice of time with their children to engage in paid employment. Schor (1996), for example, reported an increase in parents' interest in limiting their work time in recent surveys. Although we know that the lack of sensitive, responsive, and consistent care from overworked parents or substitute providers can lead to decreased cognitive and social skills (Parcel & Menaghan 1994) and can promote attachment insecurity in children (Belsky 1990), research is still unclear about the effects this time sacrifice may have on children.

FLEXIBILITY Lack of workplace flexibility has been linked to depression in both women and men (Googins 1991), and to increased physical distress such as difficulty in falling asleep and in staying asleep, changes in appetite, tension-related aches and pains, etc in men (Guelzow et al 1991). Ralston (1990) demonstrated that the proportion of employed women with rigid work schedules reporting difficulties in child-care arrangements and inadequacies in family time was much higher than the proportion of women with more flexible schedules who reported these problems, although significance levels were not reported.

WORKPLACE SOCIAL SUPPORT Finally, conflict arising from the lack of workplace social support, including child-care assistance, is manifested in the mental health of employees. Ross & Mirowsky (1988) demonstrated that employed mothers who had difficulty making child-care arrangements suffered increased depression. In a national survey, breakdowns in child-care arrangements served to decrease well-being for both mothers and fathers (Galinsky 1994). This study also revealed that workers in unsupportive work environments—those characterized by discrimination or favoritism—experienced more negative family consequences.

## *The Effects of Family/Work Spillover*

Family-to-work spillover also impairs organizational effectiveness, primarily by affecting absenteeism, productivity at work, and turnover. Child-care difficulties in particular commonly result in these problems. Parents report difficulty with several aspects of child care, such as "lack of time to deal with the very unpredictable nature of child care" (Fernandez 1990: 21), the availability of adequate care, and the affordability of such care (Fernandez 1990). Children who are barred when sick from attending their regular day care must have other arrangements made for them or stay home by themselves; breakdowns in regular child-care arrangements require unexpected time commitments to finding alternative care. Although parents may be able to find such care, their search often results in time lost from work or decreased productivity. Of the approximately 2300 employed mothers in the National Child Care Survey, 15% said they had either been late for work, left early from work, or missed a day of work in the month prior to being surveyed due to failure in their child-care arrangement (Hofferth et al 1991). Thirty-five percent of employed mothers reported that a child was sick on a work day during the past month, and 51% of these mothers stayed home to care for their child, resulting in an average of 2.2 days missed during the month for a sick child. Fernandez (1990) reported that in a 1987/88 survey of over 26,000 employees in diverse companies, 42% of women and 28% of men had missed work in the previous year due to personal/family problems.

Worker productivity is also impaired in other ways by family obligations. Fernandez (1986) reported that parents face work interruptions due to family responsibilities. These interruptions, like absenteeism, decrease as children grow older. Still, these interruptions were reported by 39% of mothers and 17% of fathers with children between ages 15 and 18 (Fernandez 1986). Fernandez (1990) intimated that interruptions probably occur more than parents report, but that parents make up for the infringement of family on work-time by working overtime or taking work home. Further, parental worry over sick children left alone at home, latchkey children who travel on their own from school to home to spend the afternoon alone, or the inadequacy of limited child-care choices has productivity consequences. One study showed that worry over children resulted in wasted time and mistakes in 53% of participants (Perry 1982). When asked if work/family stress affected their ability to concentrate at work, 28% of men and 53% of women sampled from 20 Fortune 500 companies replied positively (Rogers 1992). Evidence from experimental studies also supports the idea that the family affects worker productivity. In a sample of mothers, the incompatibility of family and work life decreased concentration and alertness, which resulted in the decreased effectiveness of task-oriented work (Barling & MacEwen 1991).

Another potential workplace outcome of family/work conflict is turnover. Felmlee (1995) found that among women, having preschool-age children was associated with greater rates of job changing and, in particular, job changing that resulted in downward mobility. Collins & Hofferth (1996) showed that the termination of child-care arrangements significantly increased the probability of employment exits among women with high per capita incomes. Other research reveals that women's disproportionate responsibility in the home results in significantly more turnover because of family illness, household duties, and changes in residence (Spilerman & Schrank 1991). Glass & Riley (1996) found that women in jobs requiring excessive time commitments were significantly more likely to change jobs or exit the labor force within one year of giving birth. The evidence supporting the link between family/work conflict and turnover is substantial, although Burke (1989) failed to find a link between work/family conflict and turnover.

The decreased productivity and increased absenteeism and turnover resulting from work/family conflict have serious consequences for the occupational attainment of workers and thus the financial stability of families. The experiences of women in the labor market are instructive. When family responsibilities expand, mothers are more likely than fathers to change jobs, to work part time, or exit the labor force for a spell because families cannot afford to lose father's wages. The result is often a decrease in mothers' financial and occupational attainment (Felmlee 1995, Corcoran et al 1984). Because the sex gap in wages is increasingly explained by differences in the effects of marriage and children on men's and women's wages, Waldfogel (forthcoming) has suggested that we view work/family conflict as the culprit, either through the mechanism of employer discrimination against mothers or employee behavioral adjustments that often result in curbed occupational attainment.

## ORGANIZATIONAL INTERESTS IN FAMILY RESPONSIVE POLICY

Organizations also suffer when employed parents experience absenteeism, turnover, and lower productivity (Spilerman & Schrank 1991, Goff et al 1990, Raabe 1990, Fernandez 1986). Capowski (1996) reported that over 35% of departing management associates at AT&T cited inability to balance work and family in their exit interviews; significant administrative and training costs were created when these employees had to be replaced. Increasingly, however, organizations are reporting difficulty recruiting employees, particularly managers and professionals, in the absence of family responsive policies (Scott 1992). Indeed, one report indicated that over two thirds of the Fortune 500 companies have instituted some type of family responsive program in order to remain competitive in the skilled labor market (Families and Work Institute 1991).

### *Prevalence of Family Responsive Policies in Work Organizations*

How prevalent are work/family programs at the present time? Organizational surveys differ in their sampling frames and definition of family responsive policy, but they generally agree on two points: (*a*) tremendous growth has occurred in the number of formal work/family programs in the past 15 years, and (*b*) most large companies have by now instituted some type of initiative designed to address the family needs of workers for greater schedule flexibility, child-care services, and/or work hours reduction (Families and Work Institute 1991, Friedman 1990, Hewitt Associates 1991). A distinction needs to be drawn, however, between those surveys conducted by the US Bureau of Labor Statistics on firms with over 100 employees and those conducted on very large organizations by private consulting firms, with the former finding far lower rates of family assistance than the latter. For example, in the hours reduction category, the Bureau of Labor Statistics 1989 Employee Benefits Survey shows that 40% of employees held jobs covered by paid or unpaid maternity leave, while the 1991 Hewitt Associates survey of large employers found 56% of employing establishments offering (paid or unpaid) parental leave. Similarly the BLS notes that 11% of workers had flexible schedules available to them, while the Hewitt Associates survey reports that 53% of establishments offered flexible schedules [a figure that rose to 71% in a 1995 Hewitt Associates survey of 681 large firms (Capowski 1996)]. Under the heading of social support, the BLS reported dependent-care reimbursement accounts (in which employees can set aside pre-tax earnings to pay for child or elder care) covered 23% of employees (Cooley 1990), while Hewitt Associates found 91% of firms offering dependent-care accounts.

Work/family policies are strongly associated with firm size, a finding confirmed by combined BLS statistics on benefit coverage from surveys of both large and small firms (small is defined as fewer than 100 employees). Grossman (1992) showed that maternity leave coverage dropped from 40% to 32% when small firms were included in the calculations; reimbursement accounts dropped from 23% to 18%. Using an earlier 1987 BLS special survey on child-care benefits, Hayghe (1988) reported a clear association between firm size and the proportion of establishments offering any type of direct child-care assistance (defined as financial assistance in paying for care, on-site child care, or information and referral services). Eleven percent of establishments provided some type of child-care assistance overall, but that figure ranged from 9% for firms with under 50 employees to 32% for firms with over 250 employees. Using a broader definition of flexible scheduling (flextime, flexible leave, and voluntary part-time schedules), the BLS survey on child care reported that 61% of establishments with over 10 employees provided some type of flexible work arrangement in 1987, but in contrast to other forms of assistance, there was no relationship between firm size and flexible scheduling (Hayghe 1988).

While these figures overall suggest impressive progress in the organizational adoption of work/family benefits, these benefits are far less institutionalized than others designed to protect traditionally male breadwinning responsibilities. For instance, while 40% of workers in the 1989 BLS survey received maternity leave in their jobs, 53% received leave for military service, 94% received life insurance, and 81% received some type of employer provided pension. Moreover, the extent and coverage of employer-reported family policies remain poorly understood. Survey questions on flextime, child-care assistance, and leave policies rarely explore the degree of employer commitment to the policy. Hyland (1990) showed, for example, wide variation in the duration of unpaid parental leaves for employees covered by leave policies in the 1989 BLS survey. Hayghe (1988) and Hewitt Associates (1991) both showed that flextime, which alters the start and end times of the workday while maintaining an eight hour day/40 hour week, was far more common than more innovative scheduling policies such as compressed work weeks, job-sharing, and work-at-home arrangements. Child-care assistance is similarly diverse, with the most common forms of assistance being the cheapest and least helpful—dependent-care spending accounts and information and referral services, rather than on- or near-site child care or a direct employer subsidy to pay for care. Even within categories, employer commitment can vary. Some information and referral services simply provide employees with lists of licensed care providers, while others utilize human resource staff to assist parents directly in screening caregivers and locating openings. Direct employer subsidies for child-care expenses vary in the amounts committed, sometimes requiring the sacrifice of other benefits in "cafeteria style" benefit plans.

Furthermore, the degree to which access to family responsive policies is formalized and extended to all employees in organizations remains suspect. In the BLS surveys, individual employees were not surveyed; instead, all employees were assumed to be covered if any employees were covered, an assumption that has been challenged by various researchers. Kush & Stroh (1994) report that in their survey of Chicago firms, most flextime programs were temporary ad hoc arrangements, often restricted to certain classes of employees and/or certain times of the year. Rather than having a permanent formal policy, many organizations implemented flextime in response to specific requests by individual employees. Capowski (1996) quotes one consultant as follows, "When companies say, 'Oh we have flextime, we have telecommuting,' what they mean is, 'We have an individual working here who does this.' They don't mean they have an integrated system.... The difference is that in a flexible company these options would be available to everyone, instead of employees having to cut deals." Miller (1992) reports that women in professional and managerial positions are much more likely to receive family friendly benefits such as funded maternity leave, schedule flexibility, and child-care assistance than are women in less skilled jobs. It may be that more highly skilled workers are concentrated in more responsive organizations or have access to formal benefits from which other classes of workers are excluded, but it is also possible that skilled workers are better able to individually negotiate special concessions from their employers because of their greater market power. Given the associations between fertility, education, and occupational status, this means that the mothers most in need of family accommodations (e.g. young single mothers with low earnings and little human capital) are least likely to receive them from their employers.

Even the most optimistic observers of corporate climate admit that very few employers have moved beyond token acknowledgment of the family needs of employees (Galinsky & Stein 1990, Raabe & Gessner 1988). Moreover, the policies and practices of small firms, which employ over one third of the total US labor force and represent the strongest sources of future employment growth, show far less cause for optimism. The available information suggests that small employers offer less generous leave policies and benefits, and poorer working conditions in general, although they compensate for these deficiencies somewhat by offering a broader array of work hours and work schedules than do larger employers (Miller 1992, Wiatrowski 1994).

Most human resource specialists agree that, to be effective, companies must combine various initiatives into comprehensive programs to meet the family needs of workers (Galinsky & Stein 1990, Smith 1992, Capowski 1996). Adoption of a single policy such as flextime is unlikely to yield great benefits to an organization in the absence of other types of organizational assistance. Raabe (1990) reports several studies that have shown earlier returns to work following childbirth among mothers when maternity leave is combined with some form of child-care assistance. In an effort to rate systematically the extent to which companies provided a comprehensive program of family responsive policies, Galinsky et al (Families and Work Institute 1991) developed a typology of stages, with stage 1 indicating no overall strategy and an emphasis on child care, stage 2 indicating an integrated approach with several experimental initiatives, and stage 3 representing integration of family responsive policy into overall business strategy and organizational culture. Using this typology with their survey of 188 large firms, they found that 79% of sampled firms had not moved beyond stage 1, with 33% falling below even stage 1 criteria. Using a comprehensive list of 22 possible types of family assistance among a regional sample of 178 companies with more than 50 employees, Seyler et al (1995) found that 80% had three or fewer types of assistance, with the modal category being only one type of assistance (30%).

Researchers also agree that policies must be combined with supervisor support and advocacy from upper management to close the gap between company policy and practice (Smith 1992, Galinsky 1988, Raabe & Gessner 1988, Capowski 1996). Qualitative evidence has repeatedly revealed that employees will not take advantage of family responsive policies, particularly leave, work reduction, and work schedule policies, if they feel that doing so will jeopardize their job security, work assignments, or promotional possibilities. In some reported cases, employees had to receive supervisor permission before altering work schedules or taking leave, giving managers room to subvert formal company policy. For these reasons, consultants now routinely recommend management training as part of the implementation of work/family programs (Smith 1992).

## *Determinants of Organizational Adoption of Family Responsive Policies*

Because the data on prevalence reveal great diversity in the extent to which employers have adopted family responsive policies, we turn now to the available literature on the organizational innovation and diffusion of work/family programs. Some scholars have used a rational choice perspective in which efficiency considerations either compel or retard organizational solutions to work/family conflict (Glass & Fujimoto 1995, Osterman 1995, Seyler et al 1995, Auerbach 1990). Others have explored the application of institutional theory to explain why employers implement work/family programs, focusing on isomorphism within organizational fields and the effects of professional personnel administration on employee benefits (Osterman 1995, Goodstein 1994, Glass & Fujimoto 1995, Auerbach 1990). Both perspectives suggest that organizations with predominantly female workforces and large firms in general should adopt policies earlier and more comprehensively than others, while institutional theory predicts quicker adoption of work/family policies in firms with formal personnel administration and among firms with frequent interactions with other organizations that have implemented work/family policies. Both perspectives also emphasize the importance of search and replacement costs in the instigation of efforts to reduce turnover—from an efficiency perspective this suggests that organizations with large training costs or greater reliance on skilled labor should more quickly implement family responsive programs, while an institutional perspective emphasizes the role of well-developed internal labor markets and high-commitment work systems (involving self-managed work teams and worker involvement in managerial decision-making) in the adoption of work/family programs.

The literature on this topic is just beginning to substantiate certain empirical regularities in the organizational characteristics of firms implementing family responsive policy. Using the total number of policies adopted by an organization (a rather crude measure given the variation in cost and employer commitment required by different policies), both Seyler et al (1995) and Osterman (1995) found that female concentration within firms and firm size were important determinants of the number of policies offered, although Osterman's results showed that the effect of female concentration disappeared after occupational controls were introduced. Using a categorization scheme that emphasized the comprehensiveness of coverage as well as the number of policies offered, Goodstein (1994) also showed dominant effects of female concentration and firm size. However, Glass & Fujimoto (1995), using a sample of employed women, found that firm size was positively related only to formal benefits, while informal leave policies and schedule policies that depended on supervisor cooperation (working at home or using sick leave for children's illnesses) were more likely to occur in small firms.

Regarding formal personnel management and the need to remain isomorphic with the organization's environment (key components of institutional theory), Osterman (1995) found that the presence of human resource departments increased the number of policies offered, while Goodstein (1994) found large effects of prior diffusion of work/family programs in the organization's industry group. But the conception of "institutional isomorphism" used to explore diffusion of family responsive policy may need to be broadened. Friedman (1990), Auerbach (1990), and others have noted that firms whose product markets target families or have family-sensitive constituents (government or nonprofit social welfare organizations) are often more likely to be committed to workplace family responsive policies in principle and to see the implementation of family responsive policy as good for improving their public image.

The results of studies designed to test the effects of search and replacement costs on the adoption of work/family policies have been mixed. Seyler et al (1995) did not find effects of training costs on the number of work/family policies offered, although they did find that larger recruiting budgets predicted greater financial aid policies for workers with dependent care responsibilities. Osterman (1995) found large effects of high-commitment work systems on the number of family responsive policies offered, as well as strong indications that firms relying on professional and technical workers were more likely to adopt policies, but did not find any effect of the presence of an internal labor market. Glass & Fujimoto (1995) also found that professional and managerial workers were more likely to be covered by formal leave policies and to be able to work regular hours at home.

The empirical work in this area, as in others, would be greatly improved by a more uniform and adequate conceptualization of family responsive policy, one that accounts for both the different types of assistance offered and the intensity of employer commitment to policies (including training of managers and organizational support for employees using these benefits). Another difficulty plaguing investigation of organizational responses to family needs of employees is the inadequate measurement of work/family policies—some studies look only at formally institutionalized policies while others include informal work arrangements negotiated by individual employees. Perhaps part of the strong empirical association between firm size and work/family policies comes from the failure of small firms to have formal personnel policies in general, although they may actually be more receptive to individually negotiated arrangements than are more bureaucratic workplaces. It is also possible that large firms by their size alone are more likely to have at least a few employees on informally negotiated work schedules, and hence they are more likely to report the existence of family responsive policies when in fact those policies are only weakly institutionalized.

## EVALUATION OF FAMILY RESPONSIVE POLICIES

### *Organizational Effects of Family Responsive Policies*

Evaluations of the effects of work/family initiatives focus primarily on employee recruitment, turnover, absenteeism, and productivity. While the literature suggests that organizations sometimes adopt family responsive policies in response to other concerns—the desire to avoid unionization, forestall government regulation, create a positive public image with important constituents, etc (Friedman 1990, Auerbach 1990)—the available literature centers on the cost effectiveness of various family responsive policies. Though some work/family policies are praised as productivity-enhancers and money-savers, the empirical evidence is rife with problems that impede firm conclusions.

The main impediments to good evaluation research on the productivity effects of family responsive policy have been summarized by Auerbach (1990: 395) as: "a) defining and measuring productivity, b) imputing causality between the [family responsive] benefit and outcomes, and c) determining whether impacts... are worth the program's cost to the employer." The few studies that exist often use perceptual measures of work/family policy outcomes rather than behavioral measures of these effects. The lack of longitudinal and comparative data poses another problem in assessing the organizational effectiveness of family responsive policies (Raabe 1990). Without such information, we really do not know how organizational outcomes differ given a different mix of work/family policies. Family responsive policies and their organizational effects will be evaluated in light of these methodological concerns.

WORK HOURS Policies that address employees' needs for reduced work hours have been linked to both increased organizational productivity and decreased turnover. In one study, 62% of permanent part-time employees attributed increased productivity to part-time employment. Further, for workers in experimental part-time programs who were doing their previously full-time jobs in part-time hours, productivity appears to have been increased (Rogers 1992). However, because these studies rely on soft data in the form of self-reports, the link between reduced work hours and individual productivity is not well established. Findings relating part-time work to turnover suffer from similar problems. Rogers (1992) reported that nearly all of the 30 respondents in a part-time employment program said that, in the absence of the ability to reduce their work hours, they would have left the labor force. However, the link between reduced work hours and turnover was not directly tested.

SCHEDULE FLEXIBILITY Flextime is the most widespread and time-tested of work/family policies. In their review of research on the organizational and individual-level effectiveness of flextime programs, Christensen & Staines (1990) found that these policies decreased tardiness, absenteeism, and turnover. Another study utilizing an experimental design demonstrated significant reductions in absenteeism with the implementation of flexible scheduling in the experimental group, although this study failed to find a link between flexible scheduling and turnover (Dalton & Mesch 1990). Further evidence of the efficacy of flexibility for organizations is offered by Rogers (1992). His research shows employees ranked the importance of the flexibility to balance work and family fourth out of sixteen factors in their decision to stay with the company. In the subsample of employees rated as high performers, flexibility ranked second only to compensation (Rogers 1992). Finally, other research has demonstrated a positive association between flextime policies and job satisfaction (Thomas & Ganster 1995, Christensen & Staines 1990). Given the documented link between job satisfaction and turnover (Mueller & Price 1990), policies that increase job satisfaction should be indirectly and negatively related to turnover.

WORKPLACE SOCIAL SUPPORT Formal social support policies, particularly onsite or employer assistance with child care, have shown limited organizational effects. In a study relying on supervisors' perceptions of job performance and child-care related absences, no link between on-site child care and absenteeism was found (Kossek & Nichol 1992). However, on-site child care positively affected employees' decisions to remain employed at the company and increased the extent to which they used the on-site child-care policy as a recruitment tool (Kossek & Nichol 1992). Youngblood & Chambers-Cook (1984) reported similar findings concerning on-site child care and turnover, and they also failed to find a link between on-site child care and absenteeism. Additionally, Goff et al (1990) failed to find support for the linkage between on-site child care and absenteeism. It appears that on-site child care may be more important for recruitment and retention than dealing with actual day-to-day productivity concerns such as absenteeism. If there is no provision for sick children at the on-site child-care center, parents still have few options for child care when their children are sick, and thus they may provide care themselves.

## *Effects of Family Responsive Policies on Families*

Individual workers and their families also benefit from the implementation of work/family policies, although few studies directly assess parenting behaviors or child outcomes. In this section, we evaluate the effects of flextime policies, reduced work hours, and both formal and informal social support on parents and their families.

REDUCED WORK HOURS Reduced work hours have been linked to increased mental health. Hyde et al (1995) showed that the combination of short maternity leave and marital concerns increased depression in women, while the combination of short maternity leave and low levels of job rewards resulted in increased anger in women. Longer time off work postpartum, in combination with other factors, served to decrease depression and anger. Similarly, full-time employment has been linked to increased anxiety levels in mothers. Homemakers and mothers working part-time displayed lower levels of anxiety than mothers who were employed full-time (Hyde et al 1995).

SCHEDULE FLEXIBILITY Some research has failed to find a link between formal flextime policies and reduced work/family conflict (Shinn et al 1989), while other research shows associations between flextime and many individual and family outcomes. In a study of nurses (99% of whom were mothers), flextime was linked to decreased work/family conflict, decreased depression, fewer somatic complaints, and lower blood cholesterol (Thomas & Ganster 1995). Other studies reveal that flextime policies can increase time spent with family (Winnet et al 1982) and time spent on family needs (Christensen & Staines 1990). Flextime has also been linked to decreases in employee perceptions of work/family conflict, although it appears to have the least beneficial effects for employed women with husband and children present. Decreases in work/family conflict due to flextime policies are most enhanced for those employees without primary child-care responsibilities (Christensen & Staines 1990).

SOCIAL SUPPORT Finally, workplace social support also serves to enhance families' well-being. Supportive supervisors have been linked to decreased symptoms of health problems in married men (Greenberger et al 1989), as well as decreased work/family conflict for parents of preschoolers (Warren & Johnson 1995, Goff et al 1990). However, in a sample of parents of preschoolers, on-site child care was unrelated to work/family conflict. On-site child care may not be as helpful to parents as diffuse policies such as flextime, reduced work hours, and supervisory support, which allow parents to take care of their family responsibilities on their own time.

### *Summary*

Although well-designed evaluative studies are still lacking in many areas, some general conclusions can be drawn about the effects of work/family policies on organizational and family functioning. Decreased work hours serve business by increasing employee productivity and decreasing turnover, and they serve families by decreasing depression in employees. Flextime policies increase employee productivity by decreasing absenteeism and turnover, and they positively influence family functioning by decreasing employee depression and work/family conflict while increasing the time families spend together. Importantly, most research conceptualizes schedule flexibility rather narrowly. This focus leaves unexamined policies that allow employees more autonomy in structuring their work hours.

The effects of workplace social support are mixed. On-site child care appears to have little effect on either family or organizational functioning, although a link between employer-provided child care and decreased turnover has been demonstrated. That employer-provided child care does not affect absenteeism, depression, or work/family conflict is somewhat surprising. The clearest advantage of on-site child care is the increase in the availability of child care; but the quality, hours of operation, and cost of on-site child care may not be substantially different than for off-site care. Further, even slots in on-site child-care centers may be limited, meaning spaces may not be available for all employees seeking care. These problems likely limit the effectiveness of on-site child care. However, evidence suggests that informal social support, in the form of sympathetic supervisors, does have positive effects on employees, decreasing symptoms of health problems and work/family conflict.

## BARRIERS TO FURTHER INSTITUTIONALIZATION OF FAMILY RESPONSIVE POLICY

Scholars are still debating whether organizational recruitment, retention, and productivity problems are sufficient in themselves to prompt widespread adoption of family responsive policies. Effective family responsive policies cost work organizations, particularly in the early stages of development and implementation. In general, the economic motivations to institute family responsive policies remain unclear at best. While work/family programs have generated enormous interest within professional human resource management and are the subject of numerous publications and books, solid research evidence showing economic benefits to corporations instituting work/family programs has been difficult to document. Several scholars doubt that work/family programs can ever be viewed as economically preferable to the simple exclusion of workers with dependent care responsibilities (Hunt & Hunt 1982, Kingston 1990). Tactically, employers may find that statistical discrimination against workers planning or having child-care responsibilities (mostly young women) may be economically rational, particularly for positions involving employer-provided training or entailing large search and replacement costs. For other positions, employers may be willing to hire those with actual or expected caregiving needs because they choose to tolerate greater turnover and ensuing search and replacement costs rather than expend resources on work/family policies.

While evidence suggests that employee demand for family responsive policy is increasing, it is nevertheless the case that most workers only need intensive employer accommodation to family needs for the short period in their life cycle when they have young children at home. Most employees may eventually need family responsive accommodations but not continuously over their life course, thus muting employee pressure on employers at any given time. Unions have expressed increased interest in negotiating family responsive policy as part of their interest in employment sectors predominantly employing women. However, whether unions will be successful in achieving family responsive benefits remains unknown, particularly in this era of declining union membership.

Given the current economic climate in the United States, workers may face even bigger obstacles to family responsive policy in the coming years. While both employers and employees want a "flexible workforce," that term means vastly different things to those two groups. Pressured by shareholders demanding strong economic performance and international competitors seeking to undermine domestic producers, many companies are downsizing their labor force, extracting longer work hours from those that remain, and encouraging the use of temporary and part-time workers paid lower wages and few if any benefits (Smith 1993, Schor 1992). To employers, this represents a new "flexible workforce." In contrast, employees use the term to indicate greater willingness to prorate benefits for part-time workers or job-sharing partners, allow work at home, and encourage creative scheduling such as fewer work days or staggered work hours to accommodate family schedules. Clearly, the forces of globalization and domestic economic restructuring are encouraging employers to increase productivity and exert more control over labor costs, goals that are often at odds with workers' attempts to increase their family time and preserve their families' well-being.

There may be cause for at least cautious optimism. Some human resource specialists are promoting the use of family responsive work options instead of the existing corporate tools of downsizing and subcontracting to deal with the ebb and flow of labor demand. Offering part-time work with prorated benefits instead of early retirement or layoffs, and using job-sharing, voluntarily reduced work hours, and work-at-home arrangements to cut payroll and physical plant costs are ways that companies can offer true flexibility while still maintaining profitability under intense competitive pressures (Scott 1992, Capowski 1996). Yet this win-win scenario assumes that the timing of workers' family needs will coincide with employers' needs to trim costs; moreover, it assumes that employers can cut costs and still meet caregivers' needs for adequate income (a questionable assumption given the costs of supporting dependents).

## FUTURE RESEARCH AND POLICY DIRECTIONS

This essay has focused on the needs of parents and organizations for accommodations to employees' family obligations, the prevalence and organizational diffusion of specific types of assistance, and the evaluation of those types of assistance on both organizational effectiveness and employee family functioning. However, the motivations of parents and employers are not the same, nor are employees and employers equally powerful in determining the initiatives that achieve widespread adoption. For example, some scholars have castigated the corporate consultants who promote work/family programs for their neglect of the most compelling needs expressed by employed parents—for higher wages and job security (Kingston 1990, Raabe 1990). A more radical view of family responsiveness would promote workplace policies that raise wages while avoiding both excessive work hours and frequent layoffs or downsizing.

In contrast, employers' motivation is to ensure an adequate, trained supply of labor to the firm at the lowest possible cost. That translates into policies that help employees cope with their childrearing or elder care responsibilities without actually increasing the time or money employees have to fulfill those responsibilities themselves. Family responsive policies that free workers to care for their own dependents cut into the unfettered supply of labor to the firm and thus are less likely to be institutionalized in the business community without considerable external pressure (Glass & Fujimoto 1995). While some classes of workers, particularly those with greater market power, may get concessions that limit their employer's ability to schedule work at will, such concessions are unlikely to be extended to the labor force as a whole.

Some examples of the most popular work/family initiatives succinctly illustrate this problem. Flextime has become a commonplace, low-cost policy among employers. Yet flextime typically requires work throughout the "core" hours of 10 am to 3 pm. Moreover, most employees must obtain supervisor consent before they change their specific start and end times of work. These restrictions prevent the kind of flexibility parents require to attend school events, consult with teachers or health care workers, and stagger work hours with a cooperating spouse to increase parental time with children. The really flexible scheduling options for parents—work at home, compressed work-weeks, freedom to schedule particular days or hours at work, freedom to leave work for emergencies, etc—are far more rare. Work reduction options, such as job-sharing, and reduced-hour work weeks are even more difficult to find (Russell 1988).

The most popular child-care initiatives, such as information and referral services and flexible spending accounts, are equally problematic. Information and referral services often only provide employees with lists of licensed or registered care providers in the local community. In themselves, these services do nothing to improve the supply, quality, or cost of child care in the community. Just as importantly, they provide no guarantees to parents that the listed child-care providers are adequately trained, have spaces available, or will stay in business. Flexible spending accounts permit employees to use pre-tax earnings to pay for dependent care, substantially lowering the cost of care for earners in higher earnings brackets. However, tax codes already enable most employed parents to save the same amount through the child and dependent care tax credit. Moreover, low-income workers who owe no federal income tax obtain no benefit at all from these spending accounts.

The available evidence suggests collective failure to provide policies to those most in need—low income workers, young and/or single parents at the early stages of their work careers. A more realistic assumption may be that federal intervention will be required to level the playing field for all employers and employees with caregiving responsibilities, in much the same way the minimum wage ensures that labor exploitation does not allow some employers to prosper at the expense of family and community well-being. This has been the path followed by the welfare states of Europe, with accompanying increases in taxation in return (Kamerman & Kahn 1987). However, the United States is moving toward decreased federal and increased state responsibility for social welfare. Without federal minimum safeguards, it seems unlikely that caregivers will be able to advance in the labor market as well as those without caregiving obligations, exacerbating existing problems with child welfare (Spilerman & Schrank 1991).

To develop any type of political consensus on how public policy should assist employed parents, more and better research is needed on the consequences of specific work/family initiatives. In particular, the lack of research directly linking employer policies to parental functioning and child well-being represents a formidable obstacle to policy-making. Moreover, the existing research on costs and benefits to employers needs to be supplemented with research using more rigorous and clearly defined measures of organizational outcomes, as well as more representative samples of employers (including small firms). Finally, we advocate closer attention to the measurement of family responsiveness itself, focusing on three central dimensions: the type of policy (hours reduction, schedule flexibility, or social support), the intensity of the policy (the degree of employer commitment to the policy objective), and the formalization of the policy (the extent to which the policy is available to all employees). With better measurement, the comparative impact of leaves and hours reduction, schedule flexibility, and social support on the functioning of families and organizations can be assessed, as well as the effects of different policy combinations. This remains the research agenda for the future.

## ACKNOWLEDGMENTS

Support for the research was provided by the University of Iowa Developmental Assignment Program and funding from the National Science Foundation (SES-90-23475) to the first author.



*Literature Cited*

Auerbach JD. 1990. Employer-supported child care as a woman-responsive policy. *J. Fam. Issues* 11:384–400

Barling J, MacEwen KE. 1991. Maternal employment experiences, attention problems and behavioral performance: a mediational model. *J. Org. Behav.* 12:495–505

Bedeian AG, Burke BG, Moffett RG. 1988. Outcomes of work-family conflict among married male and female professionals. *J. Mgmt.* 14:475–91

Belsky J. 1990. Parental and nonparental child care and children's socioemotional development: a decade in review. *J. Marriage Fam.* 52:885–903

Bohen H, Viveros-Long A. 1981. *Balancing Jobs and Family Life.* Philadelphia: Temple Univ. Press

Brazelton TB. 1986. Issues for working parents. *Am. J. Orthopsychiatry* 56:14–25

Brenner J, Ramas M. 1984. Rethinking women's oppression. *New Left Rev.* 144:33–71

Burke RJ. 1989. Some antecedents and consequences of work-family conflict. In *Work and Family: Theory, Research, and Applications,* ed. EB Goldsmith. pp. 287–302. Newbury Park, CA: Sage

Burstein P, Bricher MR, Einwohner R. 1995. Policy alternatives and political change: work, family and gender on the congressional agenda. *Am. J. Sociol.* 60:67–83

Capowski G. 1996. The joy of flex. *Mgmt. Rev.* March:14–18

Christensen KE, Staines GL. 1990. Flextime: a viable solution to work/family conflict? *J. Fam. Issues* 11:455–76

Collins N, Hofferth S. 1996. *Child care and employment turnover.* Presented at Annu. Meet. Pop. Assoc. Am., New Orleans

Cooley CA. 1990. 1989 employee benefits address family concerns. *Monthly Labor Rev.* June:60–63

Corcoran M, Duncan GJ, Ponza M. 1984. Work experience, job segregation, and wages. In *Sex Segregation in the Workplace,* ed. B Reskin, pp. 171–91. Washington, DC: Natl. Acad. Sci.

Cornfield D. 1990. Labor unions, corporations, and families: institutional isomorphism and collective rationality in organizationl fields. *Marriage Fam. Rev.* 15:37–57

Cost, Quality, and Child Outcomes Study Team. 1995. *Cost, Quality, and Child Outcomes in Child Care Centers, Public Report.* Denver: Dep. Econ., Univ. Colorado, Denver. 2nd ed.

Dalton DR, Mesch DJ. 1990. The impact of flexible scheduling on employee attendance and turnover. *Admin. Sci. Q.* 35:370–87

Edwards R. 1979. *Contested Terrain.* NY: Basic Books

Families and Work Institute. 1991. *Corporate Reference Guide to Work Family Programs.* New York

Felmlee DH. 1995. Causes and consequences of women's employment discontinuity, 1967–1973. *Work Occup.* 22:167–87

Fernandez JP. 1986. *Child Care and Corporate Productivity.* Lexington, MA: DC Heath

Fernandez JP. 1990. *The Politics and Reality of Family Care in Corporate America.* Lexington, MA: Lexington Books

Friedman DE. 1990. Corporate responses to family needs. *Marriage Fam Rev.* 15:77–98

Frone MR, Barnes GM, Farrell MP. 1994. Relationship of work-family conflict to substance use among employed mothers: the role of negative affect. *J. Marriage Fam.* 56:1019–30

Frone MR, Russell M, Cooper ML. 1992. Antecedents and outcomes of work-family conflict: testing a model of the work-family interface. *J. Appl. Psychol.* 77:65–78

Galinsky E. 1988. *The impact of supervisors' attitudes and company culture on work family adjustment.* Presented at Annu. Meet. Am. Psychol. Assoc., Atlanta

Galinsky E. 1994. Families and work: the importance of the quality of the work environment. In *Putting Families First,* ed. SL Kagan, B Weissbound, pp. 112–36. San Francisco: Jossey Bass

Galinsky E, Stein PJ. 1990. The impact of human resource policies on employees. *J. Fam. Issues* 11:368–83

Gerson K. 1993. *No Man's Land.* New York: Basic Books

Glass JL, Fujimoto T. 1995. Employer characteristics and the provision of family responsive policies. *Work Occup.* 22:380–411

Glass JL, Riley L. 1996. "Family friendly" policies and employee retention following childbirth. Unpublished manuscript, Univ. Iowa

Goff SJ, Mount MK, Jamison RL. 1990. Employer supported child care: work/family conflict and absenteesim: a field study. *Personnel Psychol.* 43:793–809

Goodstein JD. 1994. Institutional pressures and strategic responsiveness: employer involvement in work-family issues. *Acad. Mgmt. J.* 37:350–82

Googins BK. 1991. *Work/Family Conflicts: Private Lives—Public Responses.* New York: Auburn House

Greenberger E, Goldberg WA, Hamill S, O'Neil R, Payne CK. 1989. Contributions of a supportive work environment to parents' wellbeing and orientation to work. *Am. J. Community Psychol.* 17:755–83

Greenhaus JH, Beutell NJ. 1985. Sources of conflict between work and family roles. *Acad. Mgmt. J.* 10:76–88

Grossman GM. 1992. U.S. workers receive a wide range of employee benefits. *Monthly Labor Rev.* Sept:36–39

Guelzow MG, Bird GW, Koball EH. 1991. An exploratory path analysis of the stress process for dual-career men and women. *J. Marriage Fam.* 53:151–64

Haas L. 1991. Equal parenthood and social policy: lessons from a study of parental leave in Sweden. In *Parental Leave and Child Care,* ed. JS Hyde, MJ Essex, pp. 375–405. Philadelphia: Temple Univ. Press

Hareven TK. 1982. *Family Time and Industrial Time: The Relationship Between the Family and Work In a New England Industrial Community.* Cambridge: Cambridge Univ. Press

Hayghe HV. 1988. Employers and child care: What roles do they play? *Monthly Labor Rev.* Sept:38–44

Hewitt Associates. 1991. *Work and Family Benefits Provided by Major U.S. Employers in 1991*. Lincolnshire, IL: Hewitt Assoc.

Hewlett SA. 1991. *When the Bough Breaks*. New York: Basic Books

Hofferth SL, Brayfield A, Deich S, Holcomb P. 1991. *National Child Care Survey, 1990*. Washington, DC: Urban Inst.

Hopper P, Zigler E. 1989. The medical and social science basis for a national infant care leave policy. *Am. J. Orthopsychiatry*, 58:324–38

Hughes D, Galinsky E, Morris A. 1992. The effects of job characteristics on marital quality: specifying linking mechanisms. *J. Marriage Fam.* 54:31–42

Hunt JG, Hunt LL. 1982. Dual career families: vanguard of the future or residue of the past? In *Two Paychecks: Life in Dual-Earner Families*, ed. J Aldous, pp. 41–60. Beverly Hills: Sage

Hyde JS, Klein MH, Essex MJ, Clark R. 1995. Maternity leave and women's mental health. *Psychol. Women Q.* 19:257–85

Hyland SL. 1990. Helping employees with family care. *Monthly Labor Rev.* Sept:22–26

Kamerman SB, Kahn AJ. 1987. *The Responsive Workplace*. New York: Columbia Univ. Press

Kessler-Harris A. 1982. *Out to Work: A History of Wage-Earning Women in the United States*. New York: Oxford Univ. Press

Kingston P. 1990. Illusions and ignorance about the family responsive workplace. *J. Fam Issues* 11:438–54

Kossak N. 1990. Diversity in child care assistance needs: employee problems, preferences, and work-related outcomes. *Personnel Psychol.* 43:769–91

Kossek EE, Nichol V. 1992. The effects of on-site child care on employee attitudes and performance. *Personnel Psychol.* 45:485–509

Kush KS, Stroh LK. 1994. Flextime: myth or reality? *Business Horizons* Sept/Oct:51–55

Louv R. 1990. *Childhood's Future*. Boston, MA: Houghton Mifflin

Miller B. 1992. The distribution of family oriented benefits. *Issue Brief: Employee Benefits Res. Inst.* Oct:No. 130

Mueller CW, Price JL. 1990. Economic, psychological, and sociological determinants of voluntary turnover. *J. Behav. Econ.* 19:321–35

Nock SL, Kingston PW. 1988. Time with children: the impact of couples' work-time commitments. *Soc. Forces* 67:59–85

Osterman P. 1995. Work/family programs and the employment relationship. *Admin. Sci. Q.* 40:681–700

Parcel TL, Menaghan EG. 1994. *Parents' Jobs and Children's Lives*. New York: Aldine De Gruyter

Perry KS. 1982. *Employers and Childcare: Establishing Services Through the Workplace*. Washington, DC: US Dep. of Labor

Piotrkowski CS, Rapoport RN, Rapoport R. 1987. Families and work. In *Handbook of Marriage and the Family*, ed. MB Sussman, SK Steinmetz, pp. 251–79. New York: Plenum

Raabe P. 1990. The organizational effects of workplace family policies. *J. Fam. Issues*, 11:477–91

Raabe P, Gessner JC. 1988. Employer family-supportive policies: diverse variations on the theme. *Fam. Relations* 37:196–202

Ralston DA. 1990. How flexitime eases work/family tensions. *Personnel* August:45–8

Rogers CS. 1992. The flexible workplace: What have we learned? *Hum. Resources Mgmt.* 31:183–99

Ross CE, Mirowsky J. 1988. Child care and emotional adjustment to wives' employment. *J. Health Soc. Behav.* 29:127–38

Russell C. 1988. Who gives and who gets. *Am. Demographics* May:16–18

Schor J. 1992. *The Overworked American*. New York: Basic Books

Schor J. 1996. *Time, work, money: escaping the cycle of work and spend*. Paper presented at Our Time Famine Conference, Iowa City, IA. March 8

Scott M. 1992. Flexibility can be strategic in marketplace. *Employee Benefits Plan Rev.* March:16–20

Seyler DL, Monroe PA, Garan JC. 1995. Balancing work and family: the role of employer–supported child care benefits. *J. Fam. Issues* 16:170–93

Shinn M, Wong NW, Simko PA, Ortiz-Torres B. 1989. Promoting the well-being of working parents: coping, social support, and flexible job schedules. *Am. J. Community Psychol.* 17:31–55

Silver H, Goldscheider F. 1994. *Flexible work, family constraints, and women's earnings: a test of the theory of compensating differentials*. Presented at Annu. Meet. Am. Sociol. Assoc., Los Angeles

Smith DM. 1992. Company benefits and policies are only a start to becoming "family friendly". *Employee Benefits Plan Rev.* March:11–16

Smith V. 1993. Flexibility in work and employment: the impact on women. In *Research in the Sociology of Organizations*, ed. S Bacharach. pp. 195–217. Greewich CT: JAI Social Science and the Citizen. 1993–1994. Conflict in the workplace. *Society* 31:2–3

Spilerman S, Schrank H. 1991. Responses to the intrusion of family responsibilities in the workplace. In *Research In Social*

*Stratification and Mobility,* ed. R Althauser, M Wallace, 10:27–61. Greenwich, CT: JAI

Stipp HH. 1988. What is a working woman? *Am. Demographics* 10:24–27

Thomas LT, Ganster DC. 1995. Impact of family-supportive work variables on work-family conflict and strain: a control perspective. *J. Appl. Psychol.* 80:6–15

US Bureau of the Census. 1992. *Current Population Reports, Ser. P-20, No. 458. Household and Family Characteristics: 1991.* Washington, DC: US Govt. Printing Off.

Vanderkolk BS, Young AA. 1991. *The Work and Family Revolution: How Companies Can Keep Employees Happy and Business Profitable.* New York: Facts on File

Voydanoff P. 1988. Work role characteristics, family structure demands, and work/family conflict. *J. Marriage Fam.* 50:749–61

Waldfogel J. 1997. Working mothers then and now: a cross-cohort analysis of the effects of maternity leave on women's pay. In *Gender and Family Issues in the Workplace,* ed. F Blau, R Ehrenberg. New York: Russell Sage. In press

Warren JA, Johnson PJ. 1995. The impact of workplace support on work-family role strain. *Family Relations* 44:163–69

Wiatrowski WJ. 1994. Small businesses and their employees. *Monthly Labor Rev.* Oct:29–35

Winnet RA, Neale MS, Williams KR. 1982. The effects of flexible work schedules on urban families with young children: quasi-experimental, ecological studies. *Am. J. Community Psychol.* 10:49–64

Youngblood SA, Chambers-Cook K. 1984. Child care assistance can improve employee attitudes and behavior. *Personnel Admin.* 29:45–95

*Annu. Rev. Sociol. 1997. 23:315–39*


# NEW FORMS OF WORK ORGANIZATION

*Vicki Smith*
Department of Sociology, University of California, Davis, California 95616;
e-mail: vasmith@ucdavis.edu

KEY WORDS: flexible work, contingent employment, restructuring

ABSTRACT

A growing body of social science literature has examined the organizational innovations and staffing practices comprising new flexible forms of work. Researchers have investigated the depth and scope of these changes and questioned how they affect diverse groups of workers in the United States. Reviewing the research on this transformation reveals a model of combined and uneven flexibility, characterized by the opening of opportunities that are differentially distributed across different groups of American workers, emerging under conditions in which effort is intensified, control is decentered, and employment is destabilized. The essay concludes by suggesting additional areas of inquiry for sociologists concerned with new forms of work organization.

## INTRODUCTION

Simultaneous, mutually conditioning changes in global economic conditions and in organizational and employment innovations are dramatically reconfiguring a spectrum of work settings in the postindustrial United States (Aronowitz & DiFazio 1994, Block 1990, Harrison 1994, Reich 1991, Sabel 1991, Sayer & Walker 1992, Zuboff 1988). Recent social science literature on work, organizational change, technology, and industrial relations has focused on new flexible work systems (Osterman 1994) that have surfaced from the currents of those changes, and researchers have predictably debated their consequences. In the more idealized accounts of work flexibility, newly skilled, continually learning, empowered and engaged workers, aided by entrepreneurial managers, strive to relax and flatten rigid bureaucracies, trim excessive use of organizational resources (including time, space, and people), and use their experiential



0360-0572/97/0815-0315$08.00

knowledge to improve the way they produce goods or serve people (Heydebrand 1989, Kanter 1989). This revolution in work and organizational practice, it is argued, should align workers' interests with those of their managers, enhance productivity, innovativeness, and quality, and thereby enable American firms to regain the competitiveness and profitability that they took for granted in the postwar era (*Dep. of Labor Fact Finding Report* 1994, Nadler & Lawler 1983).

Critics of flexible systems, in contrast, see them as little more than a new permutation of work that disadvantages workers but offers employers significant dividends. Flexibility, in this view, may call for new production techniques or novel work group formations but doesn't entail a substantive break with traditional hierarchical modes of control and authority relations; rather, it embodies and even deepens them by obscuring power behind participatory language (Pollert 1988). Some have feared as well that flexible work systems, and the collaborative work relations on which such systems are based, will erode the power of the organized labor movement (Fantasia et al 1988), while others simply doubt that the corporate rhetoric about flexibility has materialized in real changes in the American workplace (Gordon 1996).

This essay strives to unpack and move beyond the polarized conceptions of flexibility by reviewing research on new forms of work organization and specifying their outcomes for different groups of workers. I first summarize the global context that has led many employers and managers to endorse the flexible model of work, normatively if not always in practice (Appelbaum & Batt 1994), and then I map out two interrelated, frequently overlapping elements of flexibility found in a variety of occupational and industrial settings.

The first element corresponds to what has been termed "functional" flexibility (Wood 1989) and includes organizational mechanisms and work flow innovations that "build in" employee involvement: new technologies, inventory methods, job enlargement schemes, self-managed teams, and quality circles. This set of innovations is premised on securing the deeper engagement of core workers, on continually training them, and on exploiting their accumulated knowledge and experience. While these innovations directly reshape the work of blue- and white-collar nonmanagerial workers, they indirectly reshape the function of supervision and management as well.

The second corresponds to what has been termed "numerical" flexibility (Wood 1989) and refers to the ascent of contingent jobs and workers and to the decline of the permanent employment model, with the latter directly affecting professionals and managers. Research on these two sets of changes points to a model of combined and uneven flexibility, characterized by the opening of opportunities that are differentially distributed across different groups of American workers, emerging under conditions in which effort is intensified, control is decentered, and employment is destabilized. The essay concludes by suggesting research directions for advancing the sociological understanding of changes in the contemporary workplace.

## THE GLOBAL CONTEXT: WHAT'S CHANGED?

The debate about flexible work systems has its origin in a series of deep-seated changes in manufacturing and production industries. In the postwar years, American mass-production-based industries dominated global product markets. Labor and management in core-sector firms forged an accord in this period that gave employers the right to make all decisions about production processes but in turn entitled blue- and white-collar workers, nearly all male, to a living wage and secure employment. Central to the postwar accord was a production infrastructure premised on hierarchy, standardization, and routinization that excluded workers from decision-making and authority but enabled productivity to rise and profits to soar (Womack et al 1990). This "Fordist" mass-production system (Harvey 1989), well-suited to an economic framework geared for stable, continuous output of huge product runs, was an "engine of growth" of the postwar period (Piore & Sabel 1984:183), and, in conjunction with favorable international conditions, enabled the United States to remain firmly in the lead for several decades.

Although ensuring financial success for American companies, this production system, requiring workers' labor power but formally sidelining their brain power and their initiative, incurred significant psychological and emotional costs to both blue- and white-collar workers: high dissatisfaction, boredom, alienation, and low self-esteem (Aronowitz 1973, *Work in America* 1973). Furthermore, the accord excluded a significant number of Americans who lacked access to the secure, "good" jobs of the postwar era. Instability, unpredictability, and low compensation were the hallmarks of employment for white women who worked in the labor force and for women and men of nonwhite racial and ethnic groups, who were confined largely to the secondary labor market (Gordon et al 1982) or who were otherwise underutilized (Sullivan 1978).

In the 1970s, American corporate profitability faced serious challenges, and the US economy began to lose its premier position in the international economy (Bluestone & Harrison 1982, Bowles et al 1984, Obey & Sarbanes 1986). Developing countries gained the capacity to mass produce goods more competitively. Thus, finding ways of changing product lines swiftly became imperative for US firms. Japan's economic success inspired widespread debate about the feasibility of and limitations to importing, into the American context, the Japanese lean production techniques (Abo 1994, Cole 1989, Kenney & Florida 1993, Milkman 1991, Wood 1989). As other economies began to compete with and overtake the United States in numerous markets, and as the United States struggled to maintain industrial competitiveness, researchers and management practitioners began to scapegoat the very business practices once considered to be the engine of growth, identifying them instead as accelerating America's decline.

In response to such national and international transformations, social scientists turned their attention to new forms of work that might undo the worst effects of the mass production orientation. Early on, theorists of flexible specialization (Piore & Sabel 1984) argued that work systems that tapped craft knowledge, increased participation, and provided continual training would enable workers on the shop floor to specialize flexibly and to vary their product lines rapidly and with high quality. Others focused on new manufacturing systems (Hirschhorn 1984) powered by advances in cybernetic technology that were driving, if not requiring, employers to adopt more flexible ways of organizing workers. Manufacturing work settings defined by standardization, hierarchy, constraint, and the curtailment of workers' input, would give way to new sociotechnical systems in which workers would be empowered to become pattern-finders and problem-solvers, to learn from their errors, and to deploy and redeploy machines for a multiplicity of purposes. Fluidity, a climate for ongoing learning, and meaningful participation could be imported into the corporate, white-collar world of work as well, providing a foundation for a more integrated, nonhierarchical, and innovative work environment (Kanter 1989).

The new emphasis on participation and flexibility was not without its detractors: Although American companies, throughout the 1980s, experimented extensively with small-group activities, work humanization, and job enrichment programs, critics of the quality and participative movement derided these as faddish, predicted early death, and doubted that the swell of interest in worker participation would be matched by a deep-seated commitment to genuinely empowering workers (see Cole 1989, Cole 1995).

Much of the research reviewed in this essay has explored and tested the expectations of this first wave of literature. A core expectation was that flexible work systems could be devised that not only would draw on workers' knowledge and judgment, but would privilege their knowledge above that of supervisors and managers by engaging them in design, planning, and identifying and solving problems. Combating the stultifying, alienating effects of mass production and scientific management, this innovation would create a basis for increasing the commitments of workers and lead to the convergence of their organizational interests with those of management.

To achieve this, flexible work arrangements would decentralize structurally, leaving production and service workers in comparatively autonomous positions. Flexible systems would institutionalize involvement, creating opportunities in which workers could interpret information, act on their experiential knowledge, make decisions in a timely way, spontaneously innovate in accordance with shifting product and service demands, and maximize their efforts by collaborating with others in offices and on shop floors. Specific organizational innovations most likely to enable workers to carry out these goals included quality circles, employee involvement programs, job enlargement and rotation, self-managing teams, continuous improvement processes, organizational decentralization, and the promulgation of a new ethos of participation. Just-in-time inventory procedures, outsourcing, and techniques for fine-tuning the size of the work force would institutionalize flexibility more firmly, enabling firms to move swiftly, to cut through excess and minimize waste.

As we near the end of the twentieth century, preoccupation with the possible benefits of flexibility has diffused throughout the American work and occupational system. Although the precise extent of the implementation of flexible practices is difficult to measure, there is little doubt that the new model is pervasive, even if unevenly developed across occupational, organizational, and industrial settings. Drawing on a survey of a random sample of US manufacturing establishments, Osterman (1994) estimated that about 35% of private sector firms with 50 or more employees had made substantial use of flexible work organization (that is, firms had implemented two or more flexible work innovations). Other studies (Appelbaum & Batt 1994:60) suggest that the proportion of Fortune 1000 firms with at least one employee-involvement practice stood at about 85% in 1990.

Unionized workers, although often reluctant participants, have helped craft a cooperative, high-trust industrial relations framework to enable American firms to adapt and change more rapidly (Bluestone & Bluestone 1992, Cornfield 1987, *Dep. of Labor Fact Finding Report* 1994, Heckscher 1988, Kochan et al 1986, Kochan & Osterman 1994). Assumptions about the benefits of participation have extended into nonunion manufacturing workplaces (Graham 1995) and service settings (Appelbaum & Batt 1994: Ch. 7, Smith 1990, Smith 1994), although research on flexibility in service work lags far behind research on manufacturing and production settings. And those writing popular management and organizational literature have circulated the faith in the new model of work by criticizing bureaucracy and by praising individual flexibility, empowerment, and organizational change (Davidow & Malone 1992, Peters & Waterman 1982). In other words, in response to the competitive turmoil of recent years, a new model of flexible work has seeped into corporate rhetoric and employer strategy. The social science literature on this seepage illuminates various, often contradictory, dimensions and consequences of the flexible model.

## INVOLVED WORKERS, FLEXIBLE PRODUCTION

Under the broader rubric of engaging production and service workers, organizing them to bring their hands-on knowledge and experientially-based judgment to bear on the way they do their work, enabling them to act in unpredictable and changing circumstances without having to seek formal authorization from managers, and giving them a stake in the outcomes of their actions, many work organizations have "built in" a number of interrelated organizational innovations. Researchers from the fields of management, organizational behavior, and economics have argued that these structural and processual innovations can lead to increased organizational productivity (Cooke 1989, Margulies & Black 1987, Rosenberg & Rosenstein 1980) and reduction of absenteeism, minor accidents, grievances, and quits (Havlovic 1991), but others caution against a simple causal relation between participation schemes and productivity increases (Levitan & Werneke 1985). The US Department of Labor's Dunlap Commission reports that efforts to establish positive correlations between participative innovations, on the one hand, and productivity, efficiency, and organizational effectiveness, on the other, have shown "mixed results" at best (*Dep. of Labor Fact Finding Report* 1994:45).

The studies reviewed in this section do not attempt to measure these particular administrative outcomes; they focus instead on issues such as control and consent, autonomy, hierarchy, and skills that are more central to the sociology of work, occupations, and organizations. This section reviews literature on two important aspects of organizational redesign: structural/labor process innovations and social relational change. Combined, they are constitutive of a new sociotechnical system predicated on limited flexibility and participation. Findings about organizational redesign do not support the claim for genuine decentralization and empowerment that has been so pervasive in the call for new ways of working, nor do they support the claim that there is nothing new about the flexible model. Flexible practices can amplify workers' responsibilities and degree of involvement, and in many cases provide openings to learn new skills and competencies. But these higher levels of participation are structured, constrained, and controlled in less visible although no less powerful ways, and workers can be held responsible for outcomes that were once the near-exclusive responsibility of supervisors and managers.

## *Structural, Organizational, and Technological Reorganization*

JUST-IN-TIME INVENTORY PRACTICES The goal of just-in-time inventory (JIT) systems in manufacturing is to achieve flexibility by minimizing parts, materials, and resources on hand, cutting back and eliminating waste, and improving product quality. In the "work-in-progress" (Adler 1992:135) or "just-in-case" (Kenney & Florida 1993:168) approaches to inventory accumulation typical of mass-production settings, companies maintain large stores of supplies, kept in accordance with predictions for long, stable product runs. JIT, modeled on the

Japanese kanban system, relies on outside suppliers to provide parts only and exactly when needed, in response to shifts in product demand or product specification (Piore & Sabel 1984). Production ideally is pared down to its bare bones so as to permit workers to shift quickly into new, specialized product batches and to identify defective parts or products before too many of them reach the end of the production line. JIT incorporates a participative model because it requires greater worker attentiveness to the timing of the production cycle, to planning and matching inventory to manufacturing need, and to the quality of their products. Factory workers often help develop new production lay-outs to facilitate the JIT system, learn the statistical control tools they need to track production, and become experts in problem- and defect-identification (Dawson & Webb 1989), potentially transferable skill sets of some value in a postindustrial economy.

Just-in-time systems also create a new set of pressures for workers, including intensified involvement, heightened accountability, and the need for vigilant watchfulness. JIT speeds up production processes, eliminates any idle time, yet makes the coordination of production more tenuous, with the sum effect of adding to workers' stress levels (Gottfried & Graham 1993, Kenney & Florida 1993, Sayer & Walker 1992). In the course of working on the line in a Subaru-Isuzu assembly plant in the midwest, Graham (1995) found that workers were often left waiting until the last minute for crucial inventory to be delivered by outside suppliers, an observation confirmed in Adler's (1992:136) study of the NUMMI auto plant. Workers both fell behind while waiting for critical components and ran to keep up when they had to install parts that either arrived late or required altering because they were of inferior quality or did not meet precise product specifications (Graham 1995:114).

JIT heightens workers' responsibility while heightening their visibility to management surveillance (Sewell & Wilkinson 1992, Shaiken et al 1986, Skorstad 1991). The system reduces and even eliminates temporal and spatial buffers that were once crucial for workers in maintaining some degree of autonomy from management. Workers have little opportunity to step back; they are also more tightly coupled to individuals on stations on either side of them, usually through mandatory collaboration.

The JIT system additionally can lead to a reduction of total labor requirements in the firm (Dawson & Webb 1989), a reduction of production workers' skills (Milkman & Pullman 1991), and increased difficulty and complexity in work scheduling (Brown & Mitchell 1991). Even ardent proponents of JIT acknowledge that it entails a "new, faster-paced, more intensive labor process" which fundamentally "pumps work out of workers" (Kenney & Florida 1993:264). Importantly, extra and intensified work may not be matched by additional compensation. In a service-delivery organization with a just-in-time production process, workers who were in the role of "team leaders" and were assigned the task of overseeing production in an organizationally decentralized work site, received no extra pay and were not considered to be formal supervisors (Smith 1994), a finding echoed in other studies.

JOB EXPANSION AND ROTATION At the heart of the flexible model is a criticism of a traditional division of labor characterized by numerous job classifications, narrowly defined and demarcated by rule, and highly fragmented. Narrowly classified jobs constrain managers' ability to redeploy labor in step with fluctuations in demand cycles and have been blamed for work organizations' inefficiency and for their inability to promote continual learning processes, to innovate and to adapt. The new model of work calls for the expansion and enrichment of jobs, for the blurring of occupational distinctions, and for job rotation. Illustrating the extent to which companies go to jettison cumbersome job pyramids in their search for flexibility, Adler (1992) found that an auto manufacturing plant in northern California reduced the number of skilled trades classifications from 18 to 2 and had only one classification for another category of personnel where previously there had been 80.

Reducing the number of job classifications and expanding remaining jobs can impart to workers new skill sets and new domains of responsibility. Yet many studies indicate that including a greater variety of tasks has often intensified the demands on individual workers, increasing the scope of their efforts and responsibilities without necessarily giving them new skills or upgrading their position in the work hierarchy. Job intensification is often confused with job enrichment and expansion: workers are asked to do more with fewer resources, although they do not necessarily acquire new skill areas, new decision-making powers, or higher organizational status or pay (O'Reilly 1994, Shaiken et al 1986). Job enrichment programs such as cross-training for different positions have been implemented in some cases only once the jobs themselves have been deskilled by technological innovation (Taplin 1995:430).

TECHNOLOGY JIT systems reorganize the work flow and inventory method while job expansion schemes reorganize the division of labor. Employers also implement new technologies that are designed to do both and to build in the capacity for participation and flexibility. "Stop-the-line" assembly production, a technological innovation frequently implemented in tandem with JIT, underscores job intensification. The assembly line system of mass production is well known for the way that it dictates to the worker the precise movements he or she will make and paces those movements, thereby removing all necessity for independent judgment or intervention. Under the stop-the-line principle, in contrast, workers use their discretion to pull a cord, push a button, or otherwise halt the flow of the line when an individual spots a defective part or evidence of shoddy assembly. The stop-the-line technique is often thought to democratize work (Womack et al 1990) because workers do not have to seek the approval of managers to halt the production flow, but in addition it speeds up the production process and compels workers to "work frantically to remedy production or quality problems" (Kenney & Florida 1993:265; see also Graham 1995:113).

Programmable technology poses a potential for genuinely decentralized shop-floor control for workers, if they are trained and empowered to change product design and to retool equipment. Organizational case study researchers have found that, while programmable technology can increase flexibility for the work organization, it may not necessarily increase the flexibility of workers' jobs. Although touted as facilitating decentralization, planning and design can remain in the hands of specialized programmers working under the direction of management rather than concentrated in workers' hands on the shop floor (Shaiken et al 1986).

Vallas & Beck's (1996) research on programmable control systems and continuous process technologies in manufacturing plants in the pulp and paper industry reinforces these findings. They found that in the absence of other innovations, technology introduced to bring plants into the new era of flexible production did not reconfigure and did indeed strengthen the traditional bureaucratic hierarchical relations of the plant. Furthermore, the ascendance of a technological paradigm in this manufacturing setting, which emphasized cutting-edge statistical knowledge and feedback but denigrated craft knowledge acquired over time and through hands-on experience, reinforced the supremacy of young, educated, cosmopolitan engineers over long-employed manual operators, generating new forms of inequality between the two groups. Formerly craft-based manual workers were trained to familiarize themselves with a wide range of data generated by computerized process controls, but they had little discretion in deploying those data.

Flexible technology such as computer-aided design and numerically controlled cutting systems is not inconsistent with and may even intensify the structure of "rigid jobs"—characterized by low trust, status, skill, and pay—typical of the traditional mass production system (Taplin 1995). Computerized systems can deskill jobs; they more subtly control their work force, as management uses it to monitor the location of products, provide detailed information about work performance, and build in quality control mechanisms (Taplin 1995:429).

### *Social Relational Change: Teams and Self-Managed Work Groups*

Integral to structural innovations has been the effort to reorganize interpersonal interactions, to structure personal involvement and collaboration between non-managerial workers. Introduced under the rubric of employee participation and empowerment, this reorientation of social relations cannot be extricated from the structural changes identified in the preceding section and indeed is woven throughout them. Workers come together to identify and solve problems, improve quality and efficiency, and innovate production processes in teams or self-managed work groups and consultative groups such as quality circles. Ideally, heightened engagement in work through greater engagement with coworkers can also give workers a greater stake in the profitability and competitiveness of the firm as a whole.

QUALITY CIRCLES Quality circles (QCs) are created on an intermittent basis to address immediate problems in the work process and to generate ideas for reducing costs, saving money, or improving other work outcomes. Often initiated by managers, they can include workers from different functional areas and hierarchical locations. Researchers find that, numerically, QCs are the most widespread [with some estimating that over 90% of Fortune 500 companies use them (Lawler & Mohrman 1985)], but organizationally they are the most shallow of the social-relational innovations. Many studies conclude that QCs are management-initiated practices that coopt or depoliticize workers (Grenier 1988), a panacea for a variety of organizational problems (Shea 1986), or a way to get employees more involved without conferring real power (Rafaeli 1985). Notably, however, QCs also are documented as increasing job satisfaction (Lincoln 1989).

TEAMS AND WORK GROUPS The spread of the team structure has had more limited application than QCs yet has greater potential for challenging traditional hierarchical modes of control and authority. Self-managed teams or work groups aren't simply organized ad hoc to discuss production processes; team organization is built into the labor process itself as small groups produce together, make decisions, rotate their positions, maintain machinery, and direct and pace their progress. Benefits to workers can include the opportunity to become multiskilled, the reduction of managerial supervision, increased autonomy and acquisition of new skills, and the growth of workers' pride in the goods and services they produce (Aquilano 1977, Safizadeh 1991). Theoretically the spread of teams suggests a deep-seated reworking of the division of labor, although the literature suggests a range of effects that fall short of that potential.

Individual team members can be cross-trained to perform different tasks within the team's domain, but the tasks can be repetitive and standardized (Taplin 1995:427), suggesting that team organization merely multiplies the number of deskilled areas for which any given worker is responsible. Remuneration schemes that are team- or group-based depart from fiercely protected, individualistic performance norms, leading workers to resist pooling their efforts with others (Kanter 1990, Taplin 1995). Managements' commitments to teams may be largely ceremonial, a nod paid to the normative model of flexibility, which obscures the reality that teams have little power (Graham 1995) or are organized top-down by managers (Vallas & Beck 1996). When a team-based, flattened organizational model of primary nursing was introduced in a large hospital, nurses experienced heightened job autonomy and reunification of tasks, but simultaneously they found that their jobs became greatly intensified and that they came under greater scrutiny by managers (Brannon 1994).

Studies of self-managed teams present one conclusion consistently: Team-based production methods represent a new, more decentered, and less visible tactic of control. Monitoring, evaluation, and disciplinary action moves down the hierarchy from the hands of supervisors and diffuses into the hands of teammates (Sewell & Wilkinson 1992, Shaiken et al 1986). Team-based systems of control have been termed a "tyranny" (Sinclair 1992), "concertive" (Barker 1993), "devolutionist" (Sewell & Wilkinson 1992), and "unobtrusive" (Prechel 1994)—multiple conceptualizations that have several common ingredients. Individual participation is held in line by intensified monitoring of the self, continual supervision and disciplining by work peers, shifting of responsibility for production goals and even for the company's survival onto the shoulders of workers, and the concealment of managerial power from team participants. In these ways, power potentially resides in all locations, emerging at different times and being exercised by different actors: supervisors, coworkers, and even customers.

Decentered control of this sort is reinforced by other strategies, off-center, off-site, and all pervasive. In sales and service settings in which employers and managers strive to maximize flexibility and competitiveness, architectural and spatial arrangements allow customers to watch every aspect of workers' movements and behavior, leaving nothing invisible (Walsh 1993). Customer surveys evaluate, monitor, and discipline workers, thus extending the nexus of control into all sets of interactions in the workplace; and "shoppers," individuals paid to use the firm's services anonymously, evaluate the performance of workers without the knowledge of the latter (Fuller & Smith 1991, Leidner 1993). Cultural strategies of control in professional, white-collar settings similarly decenter power by locating it in the fabric of everyday life. Cultural programs are deployed strategically to amplify normative commitments to constant change and pressure, to encourage self-monitoring and heightened involvement in shaping how corporate goals are achieved, and to position workers to continually self-reflect, improve, and innovate (Kunda 1992, Smith 1990).

Research on the structural and social-relational changes initiated with the goal of securing workers' involvement, to make workers, and thereby work organizations, more flexible and competitive, suggests that such changes institutionalize a basis both for the acquisition of new skills and competencies and for securing intensified effort within a context of decentered but hierarchical control. These outcomes are obviously ambiguous for US workers. The deeper personal and interpersonal engagement in the planning and execution of work, even when imposed from above, can afford numerous opportunities for individual and collective protection of interests and for greater self-determination on the shop and office floor.

## NONINVOLVED WORKERS, FLEXIBLE FIRMS

Employers have also achieved organizational flexibility by expanding and contracting the size of their work forces to accommodate fluctuations in production and service cycles. One of the most important employment trends in recent years has been the replacement of permanent by temporary and part-time jobs in American firms and an increase in the numbers of people who are hired and let go on a contingent (Callaghan & Hartmann 1991, Doeringer et al 1991) or externalized (Lozano 1989, Pfeffer & Baron 1988) basis. This side of the flexibility coin runs counter to the organizational redesign discussed in the previous section; indeed, participation and involvement is targeted for core, permanent workers, who are in turn buffered from market fluctuations by new hiring practices that "dispose of" (Geary 1992, Thomas 1994) or "throw away" (Graham 1995) marginalized workers. The peripheral or contingent work force consists of temporary, part-time, seasonal, and subcontracted workers (Belous 1989, Gottfried 1991, Henson 1996, Parker 1994, Uzzi & Barsness 1995). Precise measurement of its size is difficult because of definitional ambiguities and because researchers may count the number of jobs rather than the number of job holders in various categories (Tilly 1991), but researchers estimate that it includes from one quarter to one third of the American work force.

The research on flexible staffing practices reveals where men and women of diverse race and ethnic groups and white women fall in the flexibility equation. A little over one quarter of women (in contrast to a little over one tenth of men) who work for pay work part-time (Williams 1995), and two of three temporary workers are women; blacks are also overrepresented in the temporary work force at 20% of the total (Belous 1989, Callaghan & Hartmann 1991).

Researchers identify a number of factors governing the decision to use contingent workers to fine-tune staffing levels. Employers able to draw on a force of contingent workers avoid having workers on their payrolls when demand is slack; they reduce their wage and benefits costs when they have temporary or part-time workers on board and save by externalizing the administrative costs entailed with recruitment, hiring, and control of temporary workers [Pfeffer &

Baron 1988, Smith 1994; see also Harrison & Kelley (1993) on different dimensions of flexibility that corporations attempt to gain by outsourcing, Davis-Blake & Uzzi (1993) on organization-level, and Cassirer (1995) on occupational- and industrial-level variables that have positive effects on the use of temporary and part-time workers and independent contractors, and Hossfeld (1995) on employers' use of temporaries to forestall their permanent workers from joining unions].

The growth of the contingent labor force is associated with increased "downsizing" in American firms. Companies reduce the overall size of their permanent work forces and take on temporaries only as needed; and companies cut functional task areas from their business and subcontract the services of other firms to fill in this gap (Harrison 1994, Smith 1994). Of companies that reported job cuts between 1990 and 1995 [included in the American Management Association (1995:7) survey on downsizing, job elimination, and job creation], 59% reported the subsequent increased use of temporary workers to replace those terminated.

Employer rationale for using temporary workers has changed qualitatively in recent years. Whereas temporary workers have long been used to fill in for sick or vacationing workers, only recently have employers been hiring temporaries in massive numbers to fill formerly permanent positions. Temporary work now constitutes one of the fastest growing segments of the labor force (Plunkert & Hayghe 1995). The temporary help services industry has been a significant source of job growth in the 1990s (Gardner et al 1994) and will continue to lead job growth into the twenty-first century (Franklin 1995).

It is tempting but misleading to group together temporary, subcontracted, and part-time work into a homogeneous category of contingent workers. For example, part-timers are not externalized workers, as are temporaries and subcontracted workers (Reskin 1996). Further, there is only weak evidence for the claim that the staffing flexibility achieved by using part-time workers is new. Employers have long structured many part-time positions primarily as a solution to meeting fluctuating demand. Using part-timers allowed employers in retail sales firms and food service establishments, for example, to bring on extra staff, primarily women with children who desired flexible schedules, during peak periods of business. What does appear to be new is the degree to which employers are using part-timers explicitly to hold down or cut wage costs, reflected in the fact that the part-time work force has grown gradually, but that almost all of that growth has taken place in the ranks of involuntarily employed part-timers (Jacobs & Qian 1996, in press; Tilly 1991, Tilly 1992). Employers now create part-time jobs and convert full-time jobs to part-time, primarily as a strategy to cut labor and benefits costs. They use part-timers in jobs that aren't necessarily governed by daily ebbs and flows in the workload, such as data entry and claims processing positions in the insurance industry (Tilly 1991:16).

This trend has had implications for the gender composition of part-time work as well: As employers have structured more jobs on a part-time basis and fewer as full-time, the proportion of people working part-time involuntarily has risen, and the number of men working involuntarily in part-time positions has risen as well because they have been unable to obtain full-time employment (Tilly 1991). In large part because temporary work has held a clearer position as a strategic pillar of flexible staffing practices, researchers have disproportionately focused on temporary jobs and the temporary help service industry. More specifically, they have focused disproportionately on lower-paid, less-skilled temporary workers rather than highly paid independent contractors.

Early accounts, largely descriptive, of the growth of the contingent labor force and its role in creating flexibility for work organizations conveyed a sense that using contingent workers was a seamless process; workers were simply brought in when needed and let go when not. Employers benefited, in this picture, and permanent workers apparently were indifferent to, if not isolated from, the presence of new, tenuously positioned coworkers. The contingent work force was also portrayed in broad terms that didn't capture the range and complexity of temporary and part-time positions. The prevailing view was that the labor market was characterized by a two-tiered system of employment, divided into core workers receiving good pay, benefits, opportunities for training (and in fact were much more likely to encounter the flexible production practices discussed in the previous section), and some degree of job security, and peripheral, contingent workers who typically earned lower wages, received no benefits, worked in low skill jobs with few training opportunities, and faced significant job instability and insecurity (Callaghan & Hartmann 1991, Colclough & Tolbert 1992, Smith 1993). Core and peripheral workers also appeared to be hired for different jobs and in different locations. Recent studies have developed a more fine-grained analysis of the consequences of this employment trend: bifurcation of skill and status, and resistance and conflict that develop on shop floors and in offices between permanent and contingent employees.

### *Research Findings on the Contingent Work Force*

BIFURCATION AND VARIATION Temporary positions traverse occupational and labor market boundaries (Mangum et al 1985). Most temporary workers are concentrated in the lowest levels of the occupational hierarchy, are typically hired for the least skilled jobs, and earn, on average, only a percentage of what their permanent wage and salary counterparts earn (Callaghan & Hartmann 1991, Henson 1996, Thomas 1994). A smaller and growing number of individuals work in comparatively well-paid professional, technical, and managerial positions on a temporary basis (Christensen 1989, Meiksins & Whalley 1995, Parker 1994, Rogers 1994). These are more likely to be independent contractors than temporary help service employees, and thus they have higher, if not independent, status, earn higher wages, and work on an externalized (short-term but regular and predictable employment) and not necessarily contingent (short-term and irregularly and unpredictably employed) basis (Reskin 1996). Additionally, the temporary labor market cuts across peripheral and core firms (Cohen & Haberfeld 1993).

Researchers taking a close look at hiring arrangements have found significant variations in employment practices and job tenure of temporaries. The organizational boundaries between permanent and temporary workers and within the temporary work force itself are imprecise and often obfuscated. Some employees appear to be temporary workers from the viewpoint of one company's hiring practices—when their services are contracted by one firm on a delimited basis, when their wages are low and their work is routine—but in fact are permanent employees of another firm whose core business is to subcontract out the labor and service of their full-time and permanent workers (Smith 1994). Temporaries may be temporary in name only, often working for very long periods of time, receiving lower wages and no benefits, but performing the job and developing the skills and organizational experience that a permanent worker might (Henson 1996, Milkman 1992). Temporary status may, on the other hand, be of short duration but lead to long-term employment, when employers use the arrangement as a recruitment channel, screening temporaries and watching them on the job to decide if they are qualified and trustworthy enough to be hired on a permanent basis (Cohen & Haberfeld 1993, Henson 1996, O'Reilly 1994, Smith 1996).

Indeed, the boundaries between temporary and permanent workers can be ill-defined and multilayered, as both groups do the same tasks, hold the same positions (including informal supervisorial and coordinator positions), work the same hours, or wear the same uniforms. Companies can have multiple categories of temps, such as permanent and casual temporary workers (Project on Disney 1995). And the boundaries can be extended far afield, as firms, in their search for manufacturing flexibility, outsource production to small firms which, in turn, employ cadres of temporary workers.

HIDDEN COSTS, CONFLICTS, AND ACCOMMODATIONS The presence of temporary workers, posited to be cost-saving and flexible, can create hidden costs, rigidities, and tensions on the shop floor. A study of a white-collar service delivery site found that permanent workers collectively resisted management's effort to hire a batch of temps for an unexpected, large, and complex photocopy job (Smith 1994), on the grounds that temporary workers would not maintain the appropriate standards for producing quality documents. The literature contains numerous examples of permanent workers' animosity toward temporary workers when they work side by side, as they often do. Permanent assembly workers bore deep ill will toward temporary employees whom they considered to be unsuitable to carry out the job (Geary 1992); and permanent production workers felt that temps "just watched the clock" and ignored the quality of their work (Thomas 1994:123). Assembly workers in auto manufacturing felt that temporary assemblers performed "shoddy" work, yet their disapproval was complicated by their realization that their comparatively permanent, more privileged status was made possible by the exploitation of the temporary workers (Graham 1995:131–35).

Management and workers may have to dedicate additional, unanticipated time to managing the work efforts of temps (Geary 1992, Gottfried 1991, Smith 1994, Uzzi & Barsness 1995). In part, management policy toward temporaries often undercuts their own cost-cutting goals: Typically, temporary workers are not trained in the same fashion that permanent workers are (Geary 1992, Milkman 1992, Thomas 1994). Furthermore, temporaries typically are not invited to participate in company functions like picnics and holiday parties. In general, mixing permanent workers and temporaries yet not integrating temps into the culture of the shop or office floor can lead to tension and conflict, particularly if permanent workers view temporaries as a reserve army of labor, ready and willing to step into their full-time, permanent jobs (Geary 1992).

Dynamics surrounding the use of temporaries look somewhat different when examined from their perspective: Temporaries may overcompensate for their tenuous status in the workplace by striving to become "super" employees who do high-quality work (Henson 1996), and they may engage in multiple, albeit individualized, everyday acts of resistance against the degraded conditions of their jobs: restricting output and walking off the job before their contract expires under particularly stressful circumstances (Gottfried 1994, Parker 1994), and "looking busy" or "cruising" when they've been assigned very little work (Henson 1996:131, Rogers 1995). Temporaries also strive to control the conditions of their assignments by turning down jobs that they view as "emotion-intensive," in order to avoid being drawn too deeply into the politics and social relations of the firm (Rogers 1995).

### *Destabilized and Intensified Employment for Managers and Professionals*

Instability and insecurity once thought to be confined to workers in the lowest levels of the labor market have spread through the ranks of American managerial and professional workers. Researchers recently have focused on a broad, destabilizing set of changes touching the careers of salaried employees, professional and managerial alike. There is a growing body of literature on the "boundaryless" career, marked by continual mobility across and up through a number of work organizations (Baker & Aldrich 1996, Defillippi & Arthur 1994, Hirsch & Shanley 1996), although the evidence for the argument that people are changing careers and occupations at a greater rate is tentative. Swinnerton & Wial's (1995) data [which the authors note are "not conclusive evidence of a trend" (p. 303)] are cited widely: They found a slight but significant decrease in job stability for the years 1987–1991.

Despite the absence of definitive evidence, there is a widespread perception in the literature that career stability is on the decline (Brown 1995). Managerial and professional displacement and unemployment, and white-collar unemployment in general, has been unprecedented and the recreation of white-collar jobs slow (Mishel & Bernstein 1994). In-depth interview and observational studies of corporate restructuring and downsizing (Glassner 1994, Gould et al 1996, Heckscher 1995, Newman 1988, Smith 1990) and overviews of the erosion of internal labor markets and the subsequent transformation of managerial and professional employment (Brodsky 1994, Doeringer et al 1991, Hirsch 1993, Osterman 1988) have generated a picture of tremendous upheaval in the ranks of the middle-ranking employees of America's corporations. Reports abound, in both scholarly and popular literature, of the widespread elimination of managerial ranks, of the difficulty of finding comparably paid and secure positions, and of the downward mobility of professionals and managers. The American Management Association survey (1995) on downsizing and displaced workers bolsters this picture. Of the level-identified jobs that had been cut between 1988 and 1995, 18% were held by middle managers, who make up between 5% and 8% of the American work force. Strategic or structural cuts disproportionately affect management ranks (AMA 1995:4), suggesting that the middle ranks of large corporations are targets of cost-cutting strategies and that their work subsequently is being pushed into the lower levels of the firm.

Adding to the impression that intensification of work is permeating and reshaping managerial and professional employment, paralleling the intensification of nonmanagerial jobs, DiTomaso (1996) finds that even corporate workers employed on a permanent, secure basis are increasingly expected to act like subcontracted workers. Employers expect managers and professionals to think of themselves as entrepreneurs or as self-employed, to continually ask how they can add more value to their work organization, and to self-monitor, to deeply internalize the viewpoint that they "are likely to be retained by the organization only as long as their expertise serves the needs of the organization" (DiTomaso 1996:11). The strength of this normative system, in which "everyone is subcontracted," depends greatly on decentered organizational systems in which self-monitoring is essential (1996:10). Even those who dispute the argument that middle management has been decimated acknowledge the sea-change in the norms and expectations for professional careers (Gordon 1996).

## CONCLUSION: INTENSIFIED, DECENTERED, AND DESTABILIZED WORK

Social science research suggests that the transformation of production and the transformation of employment are reconfiguring the American workplace, in both practice and in rhetoric. Although specific outcomes of the flexible model are shaped by occupation and hierarchical position, its central features of employment instability, decentered control, and work intensification run across the occupational spectrum. I have suggested that the model can be characterized as combined and uneven, contradictory, and even flatly confusing. This ambiguity highlights the limitations to viewing the flexible model in polarized terms, as being either progressive, enabling, or a high-performance approach, or coercive, restrictive, or a low-performance approach (Appelbaum & Batt 1994, Gordon 1996). The new model combines elements of the two but in different configurations, playing different groups of workers off one another, eliciting participation from some by denying participative opportunities to others. Thus the two sets of changes discussed in this essay are integrally bound up with one another, although they paradoxically continually undermine one another as well.

A new participative basis for production has been institutionalized in many work settings, mostly production and manufacturing, mostly for a core group of employees. Individuals in the core are exposed to a context of opportunities: opportunities to learn new skills in technology, data gathering and processing, and self-management. New production methods raise responsibility levels and increase decision-making opportunities in many cases, albeit within a constrained and decentered system of control. Thus, while genuine autonomy and control remain beyond the grasp of most workers, workers are encountering genuinely new ways of producing and serving. Importantly, their gains in organizational responsibility and involvement are incurred at the expense of corporate workers in supervisorial and management positions, with the new culture of participation resting on the simultaneous downward transfer of managerial responsibilities and the elimination of layers of managers (Smith 1990:ch. 7).

The studies reviewed here strongly suggest that core workers benefit from the new approach because they are buffered by a peripheral work force brought in to absorb fluctuations in work cycles but specifically excluded from participating in these organizational innovations. Contingent workers are not trained in new production methods, nor are they authorized to participate in self-managed groups or quality circles. In contrast, by and large they are assigned to the least skilled, most easily filled jobs, and they are monitored by their permanent counterparts. They are typically excluded from the company events and rituals that are organized socially to glue together the new participative agenda.

It appears that the corporate agenda to secure workers' involvement and quality effort is bolstered by the presence of a large and growing contingent work force that signals to permanent workers what can happen if one should refuse or limit one's efforts. That significant numbers of people want full-time, permanent work but can't find it, and that "the character of unemployment has decidedly shifted: a much larger proportion of the work force is either underemployed, overemployed, low paid, or trapped in unfavorable job situations" (Mishel & Bernstein 1994), are important ingredients in understanding permanent workers' consent to new participative arrangements. In other words, the control embedded in organizational mechanisms intersects with the control exerted through employment practices. Cognizant of their dispensability, and aware of scores of contingent workers seeking full-time and permanent jobs, permanent workers may be more disposed to learning how to work, and working intensively, within the demands of the participative and flexible model.

An additional piece of evidence indirectly supports this. In a survey of companies that had downsized throughout the 1990s, 43% reported that they extended the working hours of remaining employees rather than hiring new ones (AMA Survey 1995:7). The question of whether US workers are working longer hours has been much debated (Schor 1991, Robinson & Bostrum 1994), yet the AMA figures, as well as data of economists (Gordon 1996, Mishel & Bernstein 1994), reinforces the claim that American workers are doing more, prompted by a context of downsizing, cutbacks, declining wages, and employment transformation.

Aside from the uneasy mix of permanent and temporary workers, another tension underlies the two approaches to achieving greater flexibility. When companies downsize they can erode the commitments of remaining employees to principles of quality, participation, and adaptability. As Cameron (1995) notes, downsizing is antithetical to improving the quality of individual efforts and of the work organization; and in the United States employers continue to deploy both strategies, often without regard to the way they run at cross-purposes (Appelbaum & Batt 1994).

Thus, unease and destabilization permeates work and employment in the late twentieth century. Involvement and empowerment are at the core of the new model of work, yet workers are compelled to engage in the organizational mechanisms by which they are achieved, by means of a multifaceted and decentered system of control. Decentered control systems incorporate and reproduce particular hierarchical features of traditional control systems, but their features have taken new forms. They insert mechanisms for monitoring and evaluating into all the pores of the organizational hierarchy: in new technological systems that keep track of workers' performances, in new ways of organizing the work flow that bring workers to the foreground of the attention of coworkers and supervisors, in work groups that heighten the degree to which individuals monitor themselves and each other, or in measures for incorporating the subjective interpretations of customers as a source of data for evaluating workers. Yet traditional control is coupled with a heightened job requirement to be more involved and responsible, often without added compensation or resources.

The current emphasis on involvement and intensification in the context of destabilized employment suggests a great irony, wherein sociologists of work and workers themselves may begin to romanticize earlier production arrangements in which secure nonmanagerial workers had the "privilege" of "leaving their brains at the door" of their hierarchical, centrally administered workplaces. While such nostalgia would simplify the historical record, the full and doubtless numerous implications of having to continually "own" and "manage" one's job to the maximum extent possible for the good of the firm, need to be considered in greater depth.

Finally, the changes documented in literature on new forms of work organization are most certainly redrawing the lines of gender and race hierarchy in the United States. Increased employment destabilization and contingent hiring practices likely will erode the stable, male career model characterizing large corporate bureaucracies of the postwar era (Acker 1990, Smith 1993). In tandem, these trends may increase some white men's "nonstandard" employment experiences, leading their employment patterns to converge with those marginalized and uncertain patterns of many white women and women and men of diverse racial and ethnic groups (Reskin 1996).

The terrain of work and employment in the era of flexibility is a relatively uncharted area of social science research. Recent studies have begun to illustrate the complexities and nuances of work organization, work relations, and hiring practices, but much remains to be understood. Four topics are of particular concern. First, more research is needed on service work settings and nonunionized workplaces. Service sector work far exceeds manufacturing work, on which the bulk of research on flexible models has been done. When workers produce services and even work on people, we would anticipate finding different organizational definitions of flexibility, as well as different outcomes related to team work, decision-making, skill, and autonomy than those found in production settings. Second, this field would benefit from having data on mobility processes and outcomes as they are shaped by the contradictory forces of production and staffing flexibility. A third research goal should be to analyze aspirations and identity at the crossroads of production and employment transformation, and corporate restructuring more broadly. We need a deeper understanding of personal experience, subjective interests, and of how aspirations are sustained or crushed as the opportunity structure undergoes changes that appear to be permanent and radical. These will be essential in our understanding of consent to new production arrangements and of corporate employees' participation in turmoil and instability. Finally, cross-cutting all these topics with a focus on the gendered and racialized dimensions of opportunity and outcome will integrally link the sociology of work and corporate transformation with the fields of stratification and inequality.

ACKNOWLEDGMENTS

I would like to thank Nicole Bennett for an outstanding job coordinating the reference section of this paper. I couldn't have finished it without her organization, patience, and eye for detail. I'd also like to thank Pam Forman, Ellen Scott, Suzanne Cole, and Raquel Kennedy Bergen for collecting many of the articles reviewed in this essay, and Steven Vallas and an anonymous reviewer for comments made on an earlier version of the paper. Finally, many thanks to Heidi Gottfried, with whom I have collaborated on the topic of flexible production and staffing practices and from whose work I have learned a great deal.



*Literature Cited*

Abo T. 1994. *Hybrid Factory: The Japanese Production System in the United States*. New York/Oxford: Oxford Univ. Press

Acker J. 1990. Hierarchies, jobs, bodies: a theory of gendered organizations. *Gender Soc.* 4(2):139–58

Adler PS. 1992. The 'learning bureaucracy': New United Motor Manufacturing, Inc. *Res. Org. Behav.* 15:111–94

American Management Association. 1995. *AMA Survey on Downsizing and Assistance to Displaced Workers*. New York: Am. Mgmt. Assoc.

Appelbaum E, Batt R. 1994. *The New American Workplace: Transforming Work Systems in the United States*. Ithaca, NY: ILR

Aquilano NJ. 1977. Multiskilled work teams: productivity benefits. *Calif. Mgmt. Rev.* 19(4):17–22

Aronowitz S. 1973. *False Promises: The Shaping of American Working Class Consciousness*. New York: McGraw-Hill

Aronowitz S, DiFazio W. 1994. *The Jobless Future: Sci-Tech and the Dogma of Work*. Minneapolis, MN: Univ. Minn. Press

Baker T, Aldrich HE. 1996. Prometheus stretches: building identity and cumulative knowledge in multi-employer careers. In *Boundaryless Careers: Employment in the New Organizational Era*, ed. M Arthur, D Rousseau, pp. 132–49. New York: Oxford Univ. Press.

Barker J. 1993. Tightening the iron cage: concertive control in self managing teams. *Admin. Sci. Q.* 38(3):408–37

Belous R. 1989. *The Contingent Economy: The Growth of the Temporary, Part-time, and Subcontracted Workforce*. Washington, DC: Natl. Planning Assoc.

Block FL. 1990. *Postindustrial Possibilities: A Critique of Economic Discourse*. Berkeley, CA: Univ. Calif. Press

Bluestone B, Bluestone I. 1992. *Negotiating the Future: A Labor Perspective on American Business*. New York: Basic Books

Bluestone B, Harrison B. 1982. *The Deindustrialization of America: Plant Closings, Community Abandonment, and the Dismantling of Basic Industry*. New York: Basic Books

Bowles S, Gordon DM, Weisskopf TE. 1984.

*Beyond the Waste Land: A Democratic Alternative to Economic Decline.* Garden City, NY: Anchor Books

Brannon RL. 1994. Professionalization and work intensification: nursing in the cost containment era. *Work Occup.* 21(2):157–78

Brodsky M. 1994. Labor market flexibility: a changing international perspective. *Monthly Labor Rev.* 117(11):53–60

Brown KA, Mitchell TR. 1991. A comparison of just-in-time and batch manufacturing: the role of performance obstacles. *Acad. Mgmt. J.* 34(4):906–17

Brown P. 1995. Cultural capital and social exclusion: some observations on recent trends in education, employment and the labour market. *Work, Employ. Soc.* 9(1):29–51

Callaghan P, Hartmann H. 1991. *Contingent Work: A Chart Book on Part-time and Temporary Employment.* Washington, DC: Inst. Women's Policy Res./Econ. Policy Inst.

Cameron K. 1995. Downsizing, quality, and performance. In *The Death and Life of the American Quality Movement,* ed. RE Cole, pp. 93–114. New York: Oxford Univ. Press

Cassirer N. 1995. *The restructuring of work in the United States: occupational and industrial determinants of contingent employment.* Presented Ann. Meet. Am. Sociol. Assoc., Washington, DC

Christensen K. 1989. *Flexible Staffing and Scheduling in U.S. Corporations. Research Bulletin No. 240.* New York: The Conference Board

Cohen Y, Haberfeld Y. 1993. Temporary help service workers: employment characteristics and wage determination. *Indust. Relat.* 32(2):272–87

Colclough G, Tolbert CM. 1992. *Work in the Fast Lane: Flexibility, Divisions of Labor, and Inequality in High-Tech Industries.* Albany, NY: State Univ. New York Press

Cole RE. 1989. *Strategies for Learning: Small-Group Activities in American, Japanese, and Swedish Industry.* Berkeley, CA: Univ. Calif. Press

Cole RE, ed. 1995. *The Death and Life of the American Quality Movement.* New York: Oxford Univ. Press

Cooke WN. 1989. Improving productivity and quality through collaboration. *Indust. Relat.* 28(2):299–319

Cornfield D. 1987. Labor/management cooperation or managerial control: emerging patterns of labor relations in the U.S. In *Workers, Managers, and Technological Change,* ed. D Cornfield, pp. 331–53. New York/London: Plenum

Davidow WH, Malone MS. 1992. *The Virtual Corporation: Structuring and Revitalizing the Corporation for the 21st Century.* New York: Harper Business

Davis-Blake A, Uzzi B. 1993. Determinants of employment externalization: a study of temporary workers and independent contractors. *Admin. Sci. Q.* 38(2):195–223

Dawson P, Webb J. 1989. New production arrangements: the totally flexible cage? *Work, Employ. Soc.* 3(2):221–38

Defillippi R, Arthur M. 1994. The boundaryless career: a competency-based perspective. *J. Org. Behavior* 15(4):307–24

Department of Labor, US Department of Commerce. 1994. *Fact Finding Report: Commission on the Future of Worker-Management Relations.* Washington, DC: US Dep. Labor, US Dep. Commerce

DiTomaso N. 1996. *The loose coupling of jobs: the subcontracting of everyone.* Presented Ann. Meet. Am. Sociol. Assoc., New York

Doeringer PB, Christensen K, Flynn PM, Hall DT, Katz HC, et al. 1991. *Turbulence in the American Workplace.* New York: Oxford Univ. Press

Fantasia R, Clawson D, Graham G. 1988. A critical view of worker participation in American industry. *Work Occup.* 15(4):468–88

Franklin JC. 1995. Industry output and employment projections to 2005. *Monthly Labor Rev.* 118(11):45–59

Fuller L, Smith V. 1991. Consumers' reports: management by customers in a changing economy. *Work, Employ. Soc.* 5(1):1–16

Gardner J, Hipple S, Nardone T. 1994. The labor market improves in 1993. *Monthly Labor Rev.* 117(2):3–13

Geary JF. 1992. Employment flexibility and human resource management: the case of three American electronics plants. *Work, Employ. Soc.* 6(2):251–70

Glassner B. 1994. *Career Crash: America's New Crisis and Who Survives.* New York: Simon & Schuster

Gordon DM. 1996. *Fat and Mean: The Corporate Squeeze of Working Americans and the Myth of Managerial 'Downsizing'.* New York: Martin Kessler Books/The Free Press

Gordon DM, Edwards R, Reich M. 1982. *Segmented Work, Divided Workers: The Historical Transformation of Labor in the United States.* New York: Cambridge Univ. Press

Gottfried H. 1991. Mechanisms of control in the temporary help service industry. *Sociol. Forum* 6(4):699–713

Gottfried H. 1994. Learning the score: the duality of control and everyday resistance in the temporary-help service industry. In *Resistance and Power in Organizations,* ed. JM Jermier, D Knights, WR Nord, pp. 102–27. New York: Routledge

Gottfried H, Graham L. 1993. Constructing difference: the making of gendered subcultures in a Japanese automobile assembly plant. *Sociology* 27(4):611–28

Gould M, Heckscher C, Domurad F. 1996. *Loyalty, professionalism, and rationality in corporate downsizing.* Presented Ann. Meet. Am. Sociol. Assoc., New York

Graham L. 1995. *On the Line at Subaru-Isuzu: The Japanese Model and the American Worker.* Ithaca, NY: Cornell Univ. Press

Grenier GJ. 1988. *Inhuman Relations: Quality Circles and Anti-Unionism in American Industry.* Philadelphia, PA: Temple Univ. Press

Harrison B. 1994. *Lean and Mean: The Changing Landscape of Corporate Power in the Age of Flexibility.* New York: Basic Books

Harrison B, Kelley MR. 1993. Outsourcing and the search for 'flexibility'. *Work, Employ. Soc.* 7(2):213–35

Harvey D. 1989. *The Condition of Postmodernity: An Enquiry into the Origins of Cultural Change.* Cambridge, MA: Basil Blackwell

Havlovic SJ. 1991. Quality of work life and human resource outcomes. *Indust. Relat.* 30(3):469–79

Heckscher CC. 1988. *The New Unionism: Employee Involvement in the Changing Corporation.* New York: Basic Books

Heckscher CC. 1995. *White-Collar Blues: Management Loyalties in an Age of Corporate Restructuring.* New York: Basic Books

Henson KD. 1996. *Just a Temp.* Philadelphia, PA: Temple Univ. Press

Heydebrand WV. 1989. New organizational forms. *Work Occup.* 16(3):323–57.

Hirsch PM. 1993. Undoing the managerial revolution?: Needed research on the decline of middle management and internal labor markets. In *Explorations in Economic Sociology,* ed. R Swedberg, pp. 145–57. New York: Russell Sage Found.

Hirsch PM, Shanley M. 1996. The rhetoric of 'boundaryless:' How the newly empowered and fully networked managerial class of professionals bought into and self-managed its own marginalization. In *Boundaryless Careers: Employment in the New Organizational Era,* ed. M Arthur, D Rousseau, pp. 218–33. New York: Oxford Univ. Press.

Hirschhorn L. 1984. *Beyond Mechanization: Work and Technology in a Postindustrial Age.* Cambridge, MA: MIT Press

Hossfeld K. 1995. Why aren't high-tech workers organized?: Lessons in gender, race and nationality from Silicon Valley. In *Working People of California,* ed. D Cornford, pp. 405–32. Berkeley, CA: Univ. Calif. Press

Jacobs JA, Qian Z. 1996. The career mobility of part-time workers. *Res. Soc. Strat. Mob.* 15: In press

Kanter RM. 1989. *When Giants Learn to Dance: Mastering the Challenge of Strategy, Management, and Careers in the 1990's.* New York: Simon & Schuster

Kanter RM. 1990. The new work force meets the changing workplace. In *The Nature of Work,* ed. K Erikson, SP Vallas, pp. 279–303. New Haven, CT: Am. Sociol. Assoc. Presidential Ser./Yale Univ. Press

Kenney M, Florida R. 1993. *Beyond Mass Production: The Japanese System and Its Transfer to the U.S.* New York: Oxford Univ. Press

Kochan TA, Katz HC, McKersie RB. 1986. *The Transformation of American Industrial Relations.* New York: Basic Books

Kochan TA, Osterman P. 1994. *The Mutual Gains Enterprise: Forging a Winning Partnership Among Labor, Management and Government.* Boston: Harvard Bus. Sch. Press

Kunda G. 1992. *Engineering Culture: Control and Commitment in a High-Tech Corporation.* Philadelphia, PA: Temple Univ. Press

Lawler E, Mohrman S. 1985. Quality circles after the fad. *Harvard Bus. Rev.* 63(1):64–71

Leidner R. 1993. *Fast Food, Fast Talk: Service Work and the Routinization of Everyday Life.* Berkeley, CA: Univ. Calif. Press

Levitan S, Werneke D. 1985. Worker participation and productivity change. *Monthly Labor Rev.* 107(9):28–33

Lincoln JR. 1989. Employee work attitudes and management practice in the U.S. and Japan: evidence from a large comparative survey. *Calif. Mgmt. Rev.* 32(1):89–106

Lozano B. 1989. *The Invisible Work Force: Transforming American Business with Outside and Home-Based Workers.* New York: The Free Press

Mangum G, Mayall D, Nelson K. 1985. The temporary help industry: a response to the dual internal labor market. *Indust. Labor Relat. Rev.* 38(4):599–611

Margulies N, Black S. 1987. Perspectives on the implementation of participative approaches. *Hum. Res. Mgmt.* 26(3):385–412

Meiksins P, Whalley P. 1995. *Technical workers and reduced work: limits and possibilities.* Presented Ann. Meet. Am. Sociol. Assoc., Washington, DC

Milkman R. 1991. *Japan's California Factories: Labor Relations and Economic Globalization.* Los Angeles: Inst. Indust. Relat., UCLA

Milkman R. 1992. The impact of foreign investment on U.S. industrial relations: the case of Calif.'s Japanese-owned plants. *Econ. Indust. Dem.* 13(2):151–82

Milkman R, Pullman C. 1991. Technological

change in an auto assembly plant: the impact on workers' tasks and skills. *Work Occup.* 18(2):123–47

Mishel L, Bernstein J. 1994. *The State of Working America 1994–1995.* Armonk, NY: ME Sharpe

Nadler D, Lawler E. 1983. Quality of work life: perspectives and directions. *Org. Dynamics* 11(3):20–30

Newman KS. 1988. *Falling From Grace: The Experience of Downward Mobility in the American Middle Class.* New York: Vintage

Obey DR, Sarbanes P, eds. 1986. *The Changing American Economy.* New York: Basil Blackwell

O'Reilly J. 1994. *Banking on Flexibility: A Comparison of Flexible Employment in Retail Banking in Britain and France.* Brookfield, VT: Avebury

Osterman P. 1988. *Employment Futures: Reorganization, Dislocation and Public Policy.* New York/Oxford: Oxford Univ. Press

Osterman P. 1994. How common is workplace transformation and who adopts it? *Indust. Labor Relat. Rev.* 47(2):173–88

Parker RE. 1994. *Flesh Peddlers and Warm Bodies: The Temporary Help Industry and Its Workers.* New Brunswick, NJ: Rutgers Univ. Press

Peters TJ, Waterman RH. 1982. *In Search of Excellence: Lessons from America's Best-Run Companies.* New York: Warner Books

Pfeffer J, Baron J. 1988. Taking the workers back out: recent trends in the structuring of employment. *Res. Org. Behav.* 10:257–303

Piore MJ, Sabel CF. 1984. *The Second Industrial Divide: Possibilities for Prosperity.* New York: Basic Books

Plunkert LM, Hayghe HV. 1995. Strong employment gains continue in 1994. *Monthly Labor Rev.* 118(2):3–17

Pollert A. 1988. The 'flexible firm': Fixation or fact? *Work, Employ. Soc.* 2(3):281–316

Prechel H. 1994. Economic crisis and the centralization of control over the managerial process: corporate restructuring and neo-Fordist decision-making. *Am. Sociol. Rev.* 59(5):723–45

Project on Disney. 1995. *Inside the Mouse: Work and Play at Disney World.* Durham: Duke Univ. Press

Rafaeli A. 1985. Quality circles and employee attitudes. *Personnel Psychol.* 38(3):603–15

Reich RB. 1991. *The Work of Nations: Preparing Ourselves for 21st-Century Capitalism.* New York: Knopf

Report of a Special Task Force to the Secretary of Health, Education, and Welfare. 1973. *Work in America: Report of a Special Task Force to the Secretary of Health, Education, and Welfare.* Cambridge, MA: The MIT Press

Reskin B. 1996. *A queueing perspective on nonstandard employee/employer relationships.* Presented Ann. Meet. Am. Sociol. Assoc., New York

Robinson JP, Bostrom A. 1994. The overestimated workweek?: What time diary measures suggest. *Monthly Labor Rev.* 117(8):11–23

Rogers JK. 1994. *Lawyers for rent: the gendering of temporary employment for lawyers.* Presented Ann. Meet. Am. Sociol. Assoc., Los Angeles

Rogers JK. 1995. Just a temp: experience and structure of alienation in temporary clerical employment. *Work Occup.* 22(2):137–66

Rosenberg R, Rosenstein E. 1980. Participation and productivity: an empirical study. *Indust. Labor Relat. Rev.* 33(3):355–67

Sabel CF. 1991. Moebius-strip organizations and open labor markets: some consequences of the reintegration of conception and execution in a volatile economy. In *Social Theory for a Changing Society,* ed. P Bourdieu, J Coleman, pp. 23–54. Boulder, CO: Westview

Safizadeh MH. 1991. The case of workgroups in manufacturing operations. *Calif. Mgmt. Rev.* 33(4):61–82

Sayer A, Walker R. 1992. *The New Social Economy: Reworking the Division of Labor.* Cambridge, MA: Blackwell

Schor JB. 1991. *The Overworked American: The Unexpected Decline of Leisure.* New York: Basic Books

Sewell G, Wilkinson B. 1992. 'Someone to watch over me': surveillance, discipline and the just-in-time labour process. *Sociology* 26(2):271–89

Shaiken H, Herzenberg S, Kuhn S. 1986. The work process under more flexible production. *Indust. Relat.* 25(2):167–83

Shea G. 1986. Quality circles: the danger of bottled change. *Sloan Mgmt. Rev.* 27(3):33–46

Sinclair A. 1992. The tyranny of a team ideology. *Org. Stud.* 13(4):611–26

Skorstad E. 1991. Mass production, flexible specialization and just-in-time: future development trends of industrial production and consequences on conditions of work. *Futures* 23(10):1075–84

Smith V. 1990. *Managing in the Corporate Interest: Control and Resistance in an American Bank.* Berkeley, CA: Univ. Calif. Press

Smith V. 1993. Flexibility in work and employment: the impact on women. *Res. Soc. Orgs.* 11:195–216

Smith V. 1994. Institutionalizing flexibility in a service firm: multiple contingencies and hidden hierarchies. *Work Occup.* 21(3):284–307

Smith V. 1996. Employee involvement, involved employees: participative work arrangements in a white-collar service occupation. *Soc. Prob.* 43(2):166–79

Sullivan TA. 1978. *Marginal Workers, Marginal Jobs: The Underutilization of American Workers.* Austin, TX: Univ. Texas Press

Swinnerton KA, Wial H. 1995. Is job stability declining in the U.S. economy? *Indust. Labor Relat. Rev.* 48(2):293–304

Taplin IM. 1995. Flexible production, rigid jobs: lessons from the clothing industry. *Work Occup.* 22(4):412–38

Thomas RJ. 1994. *What Machines Can't Do: Politics and Technology in the Industrial Enterprise.* Berkeley, CA: Univ. Calif. Press

Tilly C. 1991. Reasons for the continuing growth of part-time employment. *Monthly Labor Rev.* 114(3):10–18

Tilly C. 1992. Dualism in part-time employment. *Indust. Relat.* 31(2):330–47

Uzzi B, Barsness Z. 1995. *Moebius strip employment arrangements: the determinants of the use of externalized workers.* Presented at Annu. Meet. Am. Sociol. Assoc., Washington, DC

Vallas S, Beck J. 1996. The transformation of work revisited: the limits of flexibility in American manufacturing. *Soc. Prob.* 43(3):339–61

Walsh J. 1993. *Supermarkets Transformed: Understanding Organizational and Technological Innovations.* New Brunswick, NJ: Rutgers Univ. Press

Williams DR. 1995. Women's part-time employment: a gross flows analysis. *Monthly Labor Rev.* 118(4):36–44

Womack JP, Jones DT, Roos D. 1990. *The Machine That Changed the World: The Story of Lean Production.* New York: Harper Perennial

Wood SJ, ed. 1989. *The Transformation of Work?: Skill, Flexibility and the Labour Process.* Boston, MA: Unwin Hyman

Zuboff S. 1988. *In the Age of the Smart Machine: The Future of Work and Power.* New York: Basic Books

*Annu. Rev. Sociol. 1997. 23:341–60*


# SOCIOLOGY OF MARKETS

*John Lie*
Department of Sociology, University of Illinois at Urbana-Champaign,
702 South Wright Street, Urbana, Illinois 61801; e-mail: j-lie@uiuc.edu

KEY WORDS: exchange, trade, economic sociology, political economy

ABSTRACT

This paper surveys sociological approaches to the study of markets. After considering the economic approach, I delineate the wide range of theoretical schools, including alternative schools in economics, economic anthropology, cultural sociology, the embeddedness approach, and the new political economy. I also briefly discuss recent debates on the transition from planned economy to market and on globalization. I conclude by noting the difficulties of theorizing about the historical and institutional complexity of markets.

## *Introduction*

We live in the age of the market. The category of the market dominates everyday discourse and political reality. Jobs, spouses, and commodities are all said to be obtained in their respective markets. After the collapse of communism, the market appears as the desirable and perhaps even the only viable form of exchange or coordination in a complex economy.

The triumph of the market, in turn, elevates the standing of a science devoted to its explication. Neoclassical economics, in spite of persistent and powerful criticisms, emerges as the paradigmatic framework to analyze all spheres of social life, as evinced by the ascent of rational choice theory in political science and sociology. Nonetheless, the spread of the economic approach—orthodox microeconomic theory or neoclassical economics—to noneconomic spheres is problematic. More important, broadly sociological approaches challenge the economic approach even in the study of markets.

In this paper, I survey the major sociological approaches to the study of markets. Several caveats are in order. Excellent recent reviews describe the extensive and expanding literature on markets in particular (Friedland & Robertson 1990, Swedberg 1994) and economic sociology in general (Swedberg 1987,



0360-0572/97/0815-0341$08.00

1990, 1991; Smelser & Swedberg 1994). I am not vigilant in demarcating markets from economies *tout court*; the blurred boundaries are symptomatic of different conceptualizations of markets. Although I am not overly concerned about disciplinary distinctions, this paper has very little on labor markets or on the social psychology of market exchange.

### *The Neoclassical Market and the Economic Approach*

The market is a central category of economics. Mark Blaug (1985:6), the indefatigable chronicler of economic thought, writes: "The history of economic thought... is nothing but the history of our efforts to understand the workings of an economy based on market transactions." It is then curious that the market receives virtually no extended discussion in most works of economic theory or history. A promising title such as *Theory of Markets* (Allingham 1989) does not describe what constitutes a market or explain how it operates (cf Isachsen et al 1991). Similarly, three recent tomes on market and history offer but one sentence on the market itself (Anderson & Latham 1986, Galenson 1989, Haskell & Teichgraeber 1993). In point of fact, the absence or ambiguity of the market concept is as old as economics itself. JE Cairnes (1888:100), for example, criticized Adam Smith because "it is not quite clear... in what sense he [Smith] uses the word 'market'...." The market, it turns out, is the hollow core at the heart of economics.

What is the market in orthodox economics? Most economists follow Cournot (1897:51) in suggesting that price uniformity within a particular area signifies the existence of a market. The market clears—supplies are exhausted, while demands are satisfied at a given price. But what is the sociological description of the market? Milton Friedman (1962:14), for example, writes: "the central characteristic of the market technique of achieving co-ordination is fully displayed in the simple exchange economy that contains neither enterprises nor money." This accords with the usual dictionary definition: "Generally, any context in which the sale and purchase of goods and services take place. There need be no physical entity corresponding to a market" (Pearce 1986:263). In other words, the neoclassical market is shorn of social relations, institutions, or technology and is devoid of elementary sociological concerns such as power, norms, and networks.

The very abstraction of the market—its ontological indeterminacy—allows for its universal applicability (cf Rosenberg 1992). The analytical structure developed for the abstract market, in other words, can be used for nonmarket spheres precisely because there is nothing particular about the institution or the structure of the abstract market. According to the economic approach, the phenomenological diversity of markets—from the medieval marketplace to the modern placeless market—in fact reveals deep isomorphism, or market essentialism. For explanatory purposes, diverse relations and institutions of economic exchange can be analyzed as the singular market. Rather than analyzing markets, the market is used to explain different instances of market exchange.

The indisputable intellectual leader of the economic approach is Gary Becker. Ranging from racial discrimination to crime to marriage and the family, Becker has colonized literally all of the social sciences as grist for his analytical mill. The economic approach starts from the assumption that "all human behavior can be viewed as involving participants who maximize their utility from a stable set of preferences and accumulate an optimal amount of information and other inputs in a variety of markets" (Becker 1976:8). As he declares, the economic approach "is applicable to all human behavior" and to all types of human beings (Becker 1976:8). Pierre Bourdieu, in this regard, resembles Becker in applying the market or economic metaphor to other realms of social life (Bourdieu 1977). In a different vein, exchange theorists such as Blau and Homans sought to apply the essential exchange framework to disparate spheres of social life (Ekeh 1974). However, just as market theories are not the same as theories of markets, exchange theorists did not always theorize exchange. Rather than explaining markets or exchange, they employ markets or exchange to explain social and economic life.

The most concerted effort to apply microeconomic theory has occurred in the realm of politics. From the late 1950s, social scientists have used neoclassical economic analysis to make sense of governments and movements (e.g. Downs 1957). It is ironic that a presumed shortcoming of neoclassical economic analysis—the absence of power—turns out to be the sphere where it has had its most widely recognized success (e.g. Green & Shapiro 1994). In sociology, James Coleman (1990) has championed the use of the economic approach. Centered around the journal *Rationality and Society,* rational choice theory sustains a devoted, albeit still small, network of scholars. Its influence, owing in no small part to Coleman, is manifest in the diffusion of and the obeisance made to the choice-theoretic language in contemporary US sociology.

The economic approach has also been criticized in the very sphere—the market and the economy—from which it originated. Consider the US securities market, which is the paradigmatic instance of an actually existing market. To the extent that neoclassical economists consider the sociological grounding of the market, they usually envision a modern stock market as in Walras's (1954:83–84) classic account. The social organization of Wall Street, however, reveals little resemblance to the neoclassical imagery. The prevalence of network ties and the premium on inside information make market operations far from the ideal of individual utility maximization with perfect information. Indeed, stock markets across space and time are rife with political interventions, social networks, and power considerations. Hence, neoclassical economic analysis is problematic in making sense of either eighteenth-century London financiers or contemporary Wall Street moguls (Abolafia 1997, Baker 1984, Mirowski 1988:210–32, Carruthers 1996).

The social landscape of the economic approach is like a desert—far from the sociological concern with actual towns and cities. Externalities and institutions—the very areas of sociological research interests—are neglected (Hodgson 1988, Block 1990, Papandreou 1994). Thus, large corporations and the interventionist state are generally passed over (Chandler 1977, Sklar 1988, Fligstein 1990, Block 1994). It is not surprising, then, that corporate power remains a virtually untouched topic in the economic approach (cf Schwartz 1988, Granovetter 1994). Although the economic approach would apply economic logic to politics, it seems more appropriate to apply political logic to economics (cf Piore & Sabel 1984).

The economic approach is, moreover, antisociological. Consider Gary Becker's (1976:8) claim that the economic approach is applicable to all human beings: "rich or poor persons, men or women, adults or children, brilliant or stupid persons, patients or therapists, businessmen or politicians, teachers or students." In advancing this universalist claim, the economic approach elides social differences. Inequality—the backbone of contemporary sociology—does not play a significant role in the economic approach (Lie 1992). In other words, class, race and ethnicity, gender, or any other social attribute remains essentially outside the theoretical purview of the economic approach (e.g. Ferber & Nelson 1993, Folbre 1994, Nelson 1996). And what assumption would be more inimical for contemporary US sociology than the assertion of the abstract individual that renders social inequality and difference irrelevant?

In criticizing the economic approach, I do not mean to dismiss it altogether. The economic approach is, after all, not all of one piece (for latest developments, see *Journal of Economic Literature* and *Journal of Economic Perspectives*). Furthermore, the dialogic character of academic discussion ensures that once a criticism is raised against a particular view, it evolves to meet the criticism (and to deny that it had subscribed to one naive assumption or another).

## *Some Alternatives in Economics*

Many economists have opposed historically orthodox positions and challenged dominant paradigms (Heilbroner & Milberg 1995). Thorstein Veblen, Karl Polanyi, Piero Sraffa, Joan Robinson, Paul Sweezy, Gunnar Myrdal, and John Kenneth Galbraith are but some of the illustrious dissenters. Even in contemporary US economics, dominated as it is by the marginalist orthodoxy, there are evolutionary, institutionalist, Neo-Marxist, Post-Keynesian, Neo-Austrian, and other schools of thought (e.g. Bowles & Edwards 1990, Hodgson et al 1994). Journals, such as *Cambridge Journal of Economics, Economy and Society,*

*Journal of Economic Issues,* and *Review of Radical Political Economics*, feature information and insights unavailable in mainstream publications. Be that as it may, very few have made sustained efforts to analyze the market or to probe its theoretical foundations (cf Robinson 1980:146–167, Vickers 1995). Ironically, even some of the most vociferous dissenters often accept the orthodox position on the market. Let me, however, briefly survey some of the revisionist movements within the American economics profession.

Numerous theoretical leads have yet to be fully developed. It is unfortunate, for example, that so few economists have built on the early theories of monopoly competition, such as Chamberlin (1933) and Robinson (1933) (cf Blanchard & Kiyotaki 1987). A variety of post-Walrasian economics seeks to supersede the restrictive assumptions of orthodox microeconomic theory (Bowles et al 1993, Colander 1996). The innovative works of George Akerlof (1984) also articulate the consequences of considering assumptions different from those of orthodox theorizing. Some economists take conflict seriously (Garfinkel & Skaperdas 1996), while Telser (1987) argues that excessive competition undermines economic efficiency. John Hicks (1989) argues for the interdependence of methods of exchange, media of exchange, and market structures.

Industrial organization—a longstanding subfield of economics—is notable for its institutionalist orientation. Its primary task is to analyze the relationship between market structure and performance (Bain 1968, Scherer 1980, 1992). In analyzing barriers to entry, for example, students of industrial organization focus on issues ranging from advertising and product differentiation to monopoly power (Bain 1956, Schmalensee & Willig 1988). The leading scholars, however, analyze markets or industries that do not fit the condition of perfect competition, and hence they leave the orthodox economic theory intact. These exceptions are, however, probably more of a rule. In a relative vein, anti-trust economics analyzes institutions and the legal system (e.g. Williamson 1987). Another noteworthy development is the theory of contestable markets, which is, however, less concerned with institutions (Baumol et al 1982).

New institutional economics, inspired by Coase's theory of the firm, has also sought to overcome the limitations of orthodox economics (Williamson 1975, Coase 1988). In considering transaction costs, they incorporate the assumption of bounded rationality and regard the firm as a governance structure (cf Granovetter 1985). New institutional economics has inspired innovative works in economic history (e.g. North & Thomas 1973). In a relative vein, there are evolutionary economists who consider history and institutions in their analyses (Nelson & Winter 1982, Hodgson 1993).

Institutional economists also remain active (Hodgson 1988, Rutherford 1994). Inspired by the fundamentally sociological insights of John Commons and Thorstein Veblen, they analyze markets as patterned behavior following institutionalized rules. Their starting point is ownership; its transaction constitutes the ultimate unit of analysis. The old-style institutionalists criticize new institutional economics for failing to take seriously concrete institutions, historical variations, and power relations. In particular, radical institutionalists stress the role of corporate power in the US economy (Eichner 1976, 1991, Peterson 1988, Dugger 1989). Their marginality in the American economics profession stems from their putative focus on description (and lack of formalization) and their normative thrust (as opposed to the presumed neutrality of neoclassical analysis). The neglected works of John Kenneth Galbraith (1956) and Robert Brady (1943) on business power also deserve reconsideration.

Marxist economists have generally accepted the neoclassical conceptualization of the market, albeit usually dismissing it on political grounds (cf Moore 1993). Most notable theoretical developments—whether the revival of classical political economy via Piero Sraffa or the rise of analytical Marxism and the fusion of Marx and Walras—have also moved Marxists away from considering empirical markets (Sraffa 1960, Roemer 1981). A notable exception is Samuel Bowles and Herbert Gintis's (1990) effort to theorize contested exchange. In addition, William Lazonick (1991) challenges a number of cherished neoclassical economic assumptions, including the efficiency of competition.

Intellectual history has also provided powerful critiques of neoclassical economics (Tribe 1981, Hont & Ignatieff 1983; cf Winch 1996). Philip Mirowski's *More Heat Than Light* (1989) demonstrates the transposition of the mathematical formulae and thinking of classical mechanics and physics to marginalist economics, thereby questioning the foundations of neoclassical economics. Intellectual historians, however, do not propose an alternative framework (cf Fonseca 1991).

Finally, the popular writings of Greider (1992), Kuttner (1987, 1997), Heilbroner (1988), Silk & Silk (1996), and others have useful insights for understanding markets (see also Thurow 1983, Hirschman 1986). They should certainly not be dismissed as mere journalism.

### *The Moral Economy*

A persistent and powerful response to the market—whether the theory or the reality—is to reject it on moral or political grounds. An exemplary figure in this regard is John Ruskin, whose passionate and prophetic writings influenced generations of radical thinkers (Sherburne 1972). His criticism of greed and its negative consequences—such as the unraveling of the social fabric or the destruction of nature—have redounded throughout the twentieth century. Indeed, the development of markets is in many ways coeval with its critics (Thompson 1988).

The moral critique of the market has a long pedigree. Aristotle's economic thought is, for example, inextricable from his moral philosophy (Meikle 1995). The entwinement of markets and morals is not just a matter of intellectual history. The operations of the open market in seventeenth-century England cannot be told apart from extensive political regulations and the moral economy of the time (Thompson 1991, Lie 1993). Indeed, there are no self-sustaining markets without some form of rules and regulations—the Hobbesian problem of order remains a perennial predicament (cf Parry & Bloch 1989, Lie 1992).

Social economics and socioeconomics both take off from deep engagement with moral questions. Social economics, centered around the journal *Review of Social Economy*, is a variant of institutional economics. It seeks an interdisciplinary understanding of socioeconomic behavior with an explicit intent to enhance social welfare (Lutz 1990, O'Boyle 1996). Social economists therefore criticize the neoclassical market not only on scientific but on moral grounds as well. Similarly, Amitai Etzioni has called for socioeconomics, which is inspired in part by Talcott Parsons's insight that the economy should be analyzed as a subsystem of the larger social system, as well as by Kantian moral philosophy. He stresses the role of duties, trust, cooperation, and other integrative principles and mechanisms not only as descriptive tools but also as prescriptive principles (Etzioni 1988, Etzioni & Lawrence 1991). Etzioni's socioeconomics is thus far more notable for its humanistic impulse—as his advocacy of communitarianism suggests—than for its scientific accomplishments (cf Cantor et al 1992).

In addition, numerous writings combine scientific and moral impulses in the study of markets. This is explicit, for example, in the advocate of the market and laissez-faire economic and social policy (Waligorski 1990). Radical critics, in turn, denounce the market and its deleterious consequences. The market is blamed for social inequality, environmental destruction, and communal disintegration (Herman 1995, Baum 1996, Glasman 1996). In this vein, Robert Lane (1991) makes the most sustained case for changing the evaluation of market performance from purely economic to more political and moral standards (cf Scitovsky 1992).

Moral criticisms are an indispensable part of public discourse and play a significant role in shaping social-scientific theories of markets. The intersection of economic and moral theory has become an especially fertile field of intellectual inquiry (Farina et al 1996, Hausman & McPherson 1996). Nonetheless, moral critiques and concerns are inadequate in and of themselves to advance the effort to clarify our understanding and explanation of markets.

## *Economic Anthropology and Culture*

In surveying economic anthropology in the 1990s, the formalist-substantivist debate no longer offers a compelling starting point (cf Halperin 1994, Wilk 1996). The putatively sharp division between market and nonmarket (e.g. gift) exchange obscures the diversity of markets, just as the insistent distinction between the West and the rest exaggerates the difference between us and them

(Thomas 1992). The blurring of the boundaries between the industrial and nonindustrial economies leads some to anthropological analysis of the West (Carrier 1995). At the same time, others stress the motive of gain and the importance of market exchange in nonindustrial societies (Davis 1992, cf Gregory 1982:8–9).

Several lines of inquiry in economic anthropology are of interest. G. William Skinner's classical work (1964–1965) on the rural Chinese trading networks takes seriously the impulse to generalize and to consider geography and history. Developed as regional analysis, several formal models exist to make sense of local and regional trading networks (Smith 1976), although their applicability to different cultures and time periods remains contested (Wanmali 1981). Polly Hill's (1972) analysis of the Hausa economy (Nigeria) demonstrates sophisticated understanding of macrosociological and historical forces impinging on local markets (see also Hart 1982). Macfarlane (1987), Halperin (1988), and Gudeman (1986, Gudeman & Rivera 1990) stress the importance of culture in shaping economic categories and institutions. There are interesting works on gendering gift exchange (Strathern 1988) and on women traders (Clark 1994). Roy Dilley's edited collection (1992) deserves special mention (see also Plattner 1985, 1989).

Ethnographic observations yield descriptive richness missing in the economic approach (Gregory & Altman 1989), and ethnographies are veritable treasure troves of insights on markets (Firth 1939, Bohannan & Bohannan 1968, Strathern 1971, Beatty 1992). Paul Bohannan's (1955) discussion of distinct spheres of exchange and Mary Douglas's (1967) analysis of controlled exchange are redolent with implications for analyzing contemporary markets. There are also excellent studies of the relationship between inequality and markets (Hill 1982, Harriss 1984a) and that between states and markets (Bates 1981, Harriss 1984b). Nonetheless, in the age of globalization, fieldwork by itself may very well miss translocal and historical factors (cf Roseberry 1988, Thomas 1991, Carson & Harris 1995).

In addition to anthropologists, historians and sociologists have also investigated the interaction of culture and markets. Two contributions at the intersection of economic and cultural history are noteworthy. Jean-Christophe Agnew's (1986) *Worlds Apart* grounds its cultural history of England in the shift from an economy dominated by marketplaces to one dominated by placeless markets. The economic change underpins his analysis of the changing cultural tropes of early modern England. William Reddy's exploration of modern French society stresses the "mirage" of market society. According to Reddy, France became not so much a market society as a market culture—"when the language of the mirage insinuated its assumptions into the everyday practice" (Reddy 1984:1–2); the dominance of the market category contributed to the hegemony of capitalist order. Reddy argues that reformist and revolutionary efforts failed in part because they did not articulate a critique of market categories (see also Reddy 1987).

Sociologists have also explored the interrelationship between culture and markets (Chang 1991, DiMaggio 1994). Viviana Zelizer's books (1983, 1987) exemplify a cultural approach to the study of markets. Zelizer (1988:618) calls for a "multiple markets" model: "the market as the interaction of cultural, structural, and economic factors." In so doing, she seeks to avoid both the oversocialized and undersocialized conceptions of economic action and institutions (see also Blau 1993).

Inspired in part by the cultural turn in the social sciences, consumption has become a popular terrain of inquiry. Here there are several distinct threads. Economic, social, and cultural historians analyze the birth of modern consumer practice and society (Thirsk 1978, McKendrick et al 1983, Shammas 1990, Lebergott 1993, 1996). Several anthropological studies link the study of consumption with that of markets (Colson & Scudder 1988, Miller 1995). There are, furthermore, Marxist and Weberian theoretical frameworks for analyzing consumption (Campbell 1987, Fine & Leopold 1993, Fine et al 1996). In addition, a large literature on marketing research is at once diverse and informative (Brown 1995, Thomas 1995).

### *Embeddedness and Social Networks*

The revival of economic sociology in North America has catapulted Mark Granovetter's 1985 article into prominence as its programmatic text and the embeddedness approach as its primary framework (Swedberg 1991). Consciously departing from the old economic sociology of Talcott Parsons and his colleagues, the proximate theoretical inspiration of the embeddedness approach is Karl Polanyi's work, especially his collaborative book *Trade and Market in the Early Empires*: "The human economy... is embedded and enmeshed in institutions, economic and noneconomic" (Polanyi et al 1957:250).

The bedrock assumption of the embeddedness approach is that social networks—built on kinship or friendship, trust or goodwill—sustain economic relations and institutions. The basic idea is as old as sociology itself, such as in Durkheim's critique of Spencer—the existence and necessity of pre-contractual elements in contracts. To be sure, the insight is not unique to sociology. In *Industry and Trade*—one of the few texts where market is discussed by a prominent economist—Alfred Marshall (1920:182) wrote: "Everyone buys, and nearly everyone sells... in a 'general' market.... But nearly everyone has also some 'particular' markets; that is, some people or groups of people with whom he is in somewhat close touch: mutual knowledge and trust lead him to approach them... in preference to strangers." Although Marshall was responsible for widening the gulf between the study of economy and of politics, his work contains acute sociological insights (cf Collini et al 1983: Ch. 10). Goodwill, trust, and special tastes are but three of the many factors that sustain network ties that circumvent the simple calculus of utility maximization.

Most contemporary American economic sociologists work under the banner of the embeddedness approach. In particular, network analysis is central to the embeddedness approach (Powell & Smith-Doerr 1994, cf Axelsson & Easton 1992). The central motif of Granovetter's oeuvre is that "social relations are fundamental to 'market processes'" (Granovetter 1985:500). Granovetter (1994) himself expands on his programmatic article by considering a number of spheres ranging from the labor market to business groups.

Along with Granovetter, two sociologists exemplify the embeddedness approach. Harrison White's (1981) analysis of production markets as role structures was the first substantive work of the new economic sociology. He extends his analysis by stressing struggles for control and autonomy that generate the market as a social category (White 1992, 1993). Ronald Burt (1983, 1992) pursues a broadly network approach in his studies of contemporary US markets and competition. His conceptualization of structural hole—the agglomeration of ties with fewer relations among themselves—is not only a provocative idea but a fully operationalized empirical project.

Several scholars extend the work of Burt, Granovetter, and White. In addition to his study on corporate behavior (Baker 1990), Wayne Baker, in conjunction with Robert Faulker, incorporates structural, interactionist, and network considerations into White's analysis of markets as role structures (Baker & Faulkner 1991). Joel Podolny (1993) argues for the salience of status order and positions, rather than roles, in making sense of production markets (cf Han 1993). Brian Uzzi (1996) combines various threads in order to better operationalize the embeddedness approach. In another vein, Neil Fligstein (1996) advocates a political-cultural approach that combines the insights of the embeddedness approach with that of the cultural frame approach. He employs his framework to analyze the problem of the European Union (Fligstein & Mara-Drita 1996).

The embeddedness approach is salutary in stressing social relations and networks. In avoiding both the oversocialized (e.g. the substantivist school in economic anthropology) and undersocialized (e.g. the economic approach) approaches, it seeks to strike a correct balance in analyzing markets and other economic phenomena and institutions. In so doing, it registers the existence of disparate market relations and institutions. Harrison White (1992, 1993), in particular, emphasizes power and control struggles as a crucial constituent of markets. The embeddedness approach, in other words, avoids market essentialism and incorporates power.

Nonetheless, there are several grounds of criticism. The structuralist tenor of the embeddedness approach generally neglects nonsocial or nonstructural factors, such as culture, technology, and even macroeconomic forces. In spite of avoiding market essentialism, the embeddedness approach in practice largely eschews analyzing historical and cultural variations in markets. Power, especially in the noneconomic realm, remains elided—there is nary a mention of the state in many accounts. In addition, Marx's crucial insight—the structured inequality underlying the formal equality of the market—is well worth recovering. Social networks exist inevitably within the larger historical and structural context. The embeddedness approach must itself be embedded in larger, historically transient, social structures—not only state institutions and suprastate organizations, but also historically shifting transnational relations and structures.

### *Politics and Markets*

The classic question of power and wealth and the concern with big structures and large processes continue to be fundamental. But the economic approach, as I noted, disentangles markets from power considerations. As OH Taylor (1955:116) observed in 1934, "the real economist's utopia is now and forever laissez faire... of a scheme of policy eliminating all interference of all 'politics'... ." The disembedded economy—an idea traced to seventeenth-century England (Appleby 1978)—accompanies the belief in the separation of politics from markets as a desirable condition. Power is, however, a crucial fact of economic and social life, whether one seeks to understand corporate behavior or the interventionist state. Even in an ostensibly abstruse economic phenomenon, such as inflation, the politics of social classes is important (Goldthorpe 1978). Or, consider the fact of corporate downsizing in the 1990s. Although many economists would attribute massive lay-offs to market forces, David Gordon (1996) argues for the crucial importance of corporate decision-making. In other words, corporate or managerial power is important, and its neglect obscures the crucial forces at work in the economy.

The locus classicus of the new political economy approach that brings power and markets together is Charles Lindblom's *Politics and Markets* (1977) (see also Shonfield 1965). The relationship between states and markets has generated a large scholarly literature (Hall 1986, Freeman 1989, Przeworski 1991, Hollingsworth et al 1993, Schwartz 1988). Particularly noteworthy are comparative studies that explore the different parameters of state intervention and market structure (Sabel & Zeitlin 1985, Dobbin 1994, Herrigel 1996, Schmidt 1996). There are also interesting works on the role of regulation in shaping market structure and competition (Vietor 1994, Mercer 1995).

The new political economy approach demonstrates the extensive state intervention in the modern economy. Furthermore, political institutions and processes are viewed as constitutive of economic institutions and processes. This is especially true for East Asian economies such as Japan (Sheridan 1993, Vestal 1993, Uriu 1996). Similarly, studies of South Korean and Taiwanese development repeatedly find the preponderant role of the state in markets (Wade 1990, Fields 1995). Simon Reich (1990) argues that the post–World War II successes of Japan and West Germany are due in part to the institutional legacy of prewar state intervention. The debate over the decline of the British economy is an interesting case study (Alford 1993). Although some argue that state intervention in markets led to sluggish economic performance (Middleton 1996), others point out the deleterious consequences of Thatcher's market revolution (Gamble 1994).

Beyond the nation-state, there are studies on governance structures in the global economy (Michie & Smith 1995, Cox 1996). International trade and global markets remain areas of political intervention (Hirschman 1980, Milner 1988, Salvatore 1993). The interpenetration of interstate relations, state economic policies, and markets is a promising area of inquiry (Wurm 1993, Keohane & Milner 1996).

### *From Plan to Market*

In the early 1990s, perhaps the most salient market-related issue was the transition from planned economy to market, especially in Eastern Europe. Indeed, as *World Development Report 1996* noted in its subtitle, "From plan to market," privatization or market transition is a problematic for virtually all of the world (World Bank 1996).

The end of communism created an avalanche of proposals to privatize the formerly communist economies and to effect a transition from planned economy to market. There are several overarching overviews (Ramanadham 1993, Jeffries 1996; see also Centeno 1994). In general, economists advocate privatization and marketization (Blanchard et al 1991, Sachs 1993). To the extent that there are problems with privatization, they stem largely from the prevailing political power groups (Boycko et al 1995). What neoclassical economists prescribe is a wholesale transformation from plan to market. Empirical investigations, however, reveal the complexity of institutional legacies that differ across Eastern Europe. Just as pretransition economies were not simply centralized (Prout 1985, Szelényi 1989, Berend 1990, Åslund 1992; cf Kornai 1992), the posttransition strategies and outcomes are not all of one piece (Stark 1990, 1992, Burawoy & Lukács 1992, Bryant & Mokrzycki 1994, Kovács 1994). The same can be said about the market transition in China (Nee 1989, 1992, Shirk 1993, Wank 1993). In particular, comparative studies illuminate the diversity of the seemingly singular transition (Nee & Stark 1989, Walder 1995).

Globalization has also generated a great deal of hype and debate, leading some to proclaim the imminent arrival of a global market without national borders (cf Hirst & Thompson 1996). As with the transition in Eastern Europe, discussions of globalization are impoverished by the assumption of market essentialism. Historical or comparative variations are elided in favor of the quintessential market. In the economic approach, the expansion of the world market occurs across frontiers without prior structures of exchange relations, but such an image ignores the extensive commodity exchange networks in noncapitalist economies (Hill 1986).

Following Karl Polanyi's *The Great Transformation* (1957), scholars have sought to depict both globalization (market expansion) and its deleterious consequences (social responses) (Overbeek 1993, Stallings 1995, Walton & Seddon 1994, Mittelman 1996). The impact of globalization is especially interesting in Latin America, where many accounts depict far more negative portraits of privatization and market expansion than do their counterparts in Eastern Europe (Taylor 1990, Smith et al 1994, Collins & Lear 1995, cf Ryan 1995).

## *Conclusion*

As the empirical literature on market transitions suggests, the neoclassical market concept elides different types of market exchange. The most important and compelling evidence of market diversity is the work of Fernand Braudel (1982), especially the second volume of his magnum opus *Civilization and Capitalism.* Braudel synthesizes a staggering amount of information to present the sheer diversity of trade and markets across history and cultures. In spite of the rich array of materials he gathers, Braudel eschews formalistic or abstract presentations (see also Polanyi et al 1957, Hodges 1988). In the absence of a compelling theoretical alternative, however, we are left with descriptive diversity but theoretical monism.

The assumption of market essentialism forecloses considerations of alternative forms of exchange relations and structures. Given the historical and comparative diversity of market relations and institutions, there is at least a prima facie reason to consider alternative arrangements. If the only alternatives were plan and market, then market socialism, for example, would be an oxymoron. This claim has been made by both neoclassical economists and Marxists (cf Putterman 1990, McNally 1993, Arnold 1994, Stiglitz 1994). In fact, however, there are interesting studies on market socialism based both on empirical studies and on theoretical speculations (Brus 1975, Nove 1983, Le Grand & Estrin 1989, Miller 1989, Bardhan & Roemer 1993, Roemer 1994). In addition, alternative conceptualizations of exchange mechanisms include cooperatives and participatory economies (Clayre 1980, Elster & Moene 1989, Albert & Hahnel 1991, Ellerman 1992, Archer 1995).

In closing, I should stress that empirical eclecticism provides no panacea. Theoretical questions about the significance and role of power in social life or of macrosociological foundations provide contradictory answers. The economic approach is, in this view, incompatible with an elementary understanding of sociology (as much as there are sociologists who would wish to remedy this situation). In order to advance theoretical works on markets, the assumption of market essentialism should be jettisoned in favor of describing and analyzing the empirical diversity of actually existing markets. In addition, power and macrosociological foundations need to be better theorized. One possibility is to seek an integration of the embeddedness approach with the new political economy ("politics and markets") approach.

Many sociologists would regard sociology of markets or even economic sociology as outside the domain of sociology proper. I would argue that it is, in fact, quite crucial for sociologists to study markets. Consider only its valence in policy discussions. James Tobin (1980:46) notes: "The view that the market system possesses... strong self-adjusting mechanisms that assure the stability of its full employment equilibrium is supported neither by theory nor by capitalism's long history of economic fluctuations." But free market policies remain popular, whether in employment policy or macroeconomic policy. As we consider the intellectual and political significance of understanding markets, Wicksteed's (1950:784) conclusion remains relevant today: "the better we understand the true function of the 'market,' in its widest sense, the more fully shall we realise that it never has been left to itself, and the more deeply shall we feel that it never must be. Economics must be the handmaid of sociology." The study of markets is too important to be left to economists.



*Literature Cited*

Abolafia MY. 1997. *Making Markets.* Cambridge, MA: Harvard Univ. Press

Agnew JC. 1986. *Worlds Apart.* Cambridge, Eng.: Cambridge Univ. Press

Akerlof GA. 1984. *An Economic Theorist's Book of Tales.* Cambridge, Eng.: Cambridge Univ. Press

Albert M, Hahnel R. 1991. *The Political Economy of Participatory Economics.* Princeton, NJ: Princeton Univ. Press

Alford BWE. 1993. *British Economic Performance, 1945–1975.* Cambridge, Eng.: Cambridge Univ. Press

Allingham M. 1989. *Theory of Markets.* New York: St. Martin's Press

Anderson BL, Latham AJH, eds. 1986. *The Market in History.* London: Croom Helm

Appleby J. 1978. *Economic Thought and Ideology in Seventeenth-Century England.* Princeton, NJ: Princeton Univ. Press

Archer R. 1995. *Economic Democracy.* Oxford: Clarendon Press

Arnold NS. 1994. *The Philosophy and Economics of Market Socialism.* New York: Oxford Univ. Press

Åslund A, ed. 1992. *Market Socialism or the Restoration of Capitalism.* Cambridge, Eng.: Cambridge Univ. Press

Axelsson B, Easton G, eds. 1992. *Industrial Networks.* London: Routledge

Bain JS. 1956. *Barriers to New Competition.* Cambridge, MA: Harvard Univ. Press

Bain JS. 1968. *Industrial Organization.* New York: John Wiley. Rev. ed.

Baker WE. 1984. The social structure of a national securities market. *Am. J. Sociol.* 89:775–811

Baker WE. 1990. Market networks and corporate behavior. *Am. J. Sociol.* 96:589–625

Baker WE, Faulkner RR. 1991. Role as resource in the Hollywood film industry. *Am. J. Sociol.* 97:279–309

Bardhan PK, Roemer JE, eds. 1993. *Market Socialism.* New York: Oxford Univ. Press

Bates RH. 1981. *Markets and States in Tropical Africa.* Berkeley: Univ. Calif. Press

Baum G. 1996. *Karl Polanyi on Ethics and Economics.* Montreal: McGill-Queen's Univ. Press

Baumol WJ, Panzar JC, Willig RD. 1982. *Contestable Markets and the Theory of Industry Structure.* New York: Harcourt Brace Jovanovich

Beatty A. 1992. *Society and Exchange in Nias.* Oxford: Clarendon Press

Becker GS. 1976. *The Economic Approach to Human Behavior.* Chicago: Univ. Chicago Press

Berend IT. 1990. *The Hungarian Economic Reforms 1953–1988.* Cambridge, Eng: Cambridge Univ. Press

Blanchard O, Dornbusch R, Krugman P, Layard R, Summers L. 1991. *Reform in Eastern Europe.* Cambridge, MA: MIT Press

Blanchard O, Kiyotaki N. 1987. Monopolistic competition and the effects of aggregate demand. *Am. Econ. Rev.* 77:647–66

Blau JR. 1993. *Social Contracts and Economic Markets.* New York: Plenum

Blaug M. 1985. *Economic Theory in Retrospect.* Cambridge, Eng: Cambridge Univ. Press. 4th ed.

Block F. 1990. *Postindustrial Possibilities.* Berkeley: Univ. Calif. Press

Block F. 1994. The role of the state in the economy. See Smelser & Swedberg 1994, pp. 691–710

Bohannan P. 1955. Some principles of exchange and investment among the Tiv. *Am. Anthropol.* 57:60–70

Bohannan P, Bohannan L. 1968. *Tiv Economy.* London: Longmans Green

Bourdieu P. 1977. *Outline of a Theory of Practice.* Transl. R Nice. Cambridge, Eng: Cambridge Univ. Press

Bowles S, Edwards R, eds. 1990. *Radical Political Economy.* 2 vols. Aldershot, UK: Edward Elgar

Bowles S, Gintis H. 1990. Contested exchange: new microfoundations of the political economy of capitalism. *Polit. Soc.* 18:165–222

Bowles S, Gintis H, Gustafsson B, eds. 1993. *Markets and Democracy.* Cambridge, Eng.: Cambridge Univ. Press

Boycko M, Shleifer A, Vishny R. 1995. *Privatizing Russia.* Cambridge, MA: MIT Press

Brady RA. 1943. *Business as a System of Power.* New York: Columbia Univ. Press

Braudel F. 1982. *Civilization and Capitalism, 15th-18th Century.* Vol. 2. Transl. S Reynolds. New York: Harper & Row

Brown S. 1995. *Postmodern Marketing.* London: Routledge

Brus W. 1975. *Socialist Ownership and Political Systems.* London: Routledge & Kegan Paul

Bryant CGA, Mokrzycki E, eds. 1994. *The New Great Transformation?* London: Routledge

Burawoy M, Lukács J. 1992. *The Radiant Past.* Chicago: Univ. Chicago Press

Burt R. 1983. *Corporate Profits and Cooptation.* New York: Academic

Burt R. 1992. *Structural Holes.* Cambridge, MA: Harvard Univ. Press

Cairnes JE. 1888. *Some Leading Principles of Political Economy Newly Expounded.* London: Macmillan

Campbell C. 1987. *The Romantic Ethic and the Spirit of Modern Consumerism.* Oxford: Blackwell

Cantor R, Henry S, Rayner S. 1992. *Making Markets.* Westport, CT: Greenwood

Carrier JG. 1995. *Gifts and Commodities.* London: Routledge

Carruthers BG. 1996. *City of Capital.* Princeton, NJ: Princeton Univ. Press

Carson B, Harris O, eds. 1995. *Ethnicity, Markets, and Migration in the Andes.* Durham, NC: Duke Univ. Press

Centeno MA. 1994. Between rocky democracies and hard markets: dilemmas of the double transition. *Annu. Rev. Sociol.* 20:125–47

Chamberlin EH. 1933. *The Theory of Monopolistic Competition.* Cambridge, MA: Harvard Univ. Press

Chandler AD. 1977. *The Visible Hand.* Cambridge, MA: Harvard Univ. Press

Chang Y. 1991. The personalist ethic and the market in Korea. *Compar. Stud. Soc. Hist.* 33:106–29

Clark G. 1994. *Onions Are My Husband.* Chicago: Univ. Chicago Press

Clayre A, ed. 1980. *The Political Economy of Co-operation and Participation.* Oxford: Oxford Univ. Press

Coase RH. 1988. *The Firm, the Market, and the Law.* Chicago: Univ. Chicago Press

Colander D, ed. 1996. *Beyond Microfoundation.* Cambridge, Eng: Cambridge Univ. Press

Coleman JS. 1990. *Foundations of Social Theory.* Cambridge, MA: Harvard Univ. Press

Collini S, Winch D, Burrow J. 1983. *That Noble*

*Science of Politics*. Cambridge, Eng: Cambridge Univ. Press
Collins J, Lear J. 1995. *Chile's Free-Market Miracle*. San Francisco: Inst. for Food Dev. Policy
Colson E, Scudder T. 1988. *For Prayer and Profit*. Stanford, CA: Stanford Univ. Press
Cournot A. 1897. *Research into the Mathematical Principles of the Theory of Wealth*. Transl. N Bacon. London: Macmillan
Cox RW. 1996. *Approaches to World Order*. Cambridge, Eng.: Cambridge Univ. Press
Davis J. 1992. *Exchange*. Buckingham, UK: Open Univ. Press
Dilley R, ed. 1992. *Contesting Markets*. Edinburgh: Edinburgh Univ. Press
DiMaggio P. 1994. Culture and economy. See Smelser & Swedberg 1994, pp. 27–57
Dobbin F. 1994. *Forging Industrial Policy*. Cambridge, Eng.: Cambridge Univ. Press
Douglas M. 1967. Primitive rationing: a study in controlled exchange. In *Themes in Economic Anthropology*, ed. R Firth, pp. 119–47. London: Tavistock
Downs A. 1957. *An Economic Theory of Democracy*. New Haven, CT: Yale Univ. Press
Dugger WM. 1989. *Corporate Hegemony*. New York: Greenwood
Eichner AS. 1976. *The Megacorp and Oligopoly*. Cambridge, Eng.: Cambridge Univ. Press
Eichner AS. 1991. *The Macrodynamics of Advanced Market Economies*. Armonk, NY: ME Sharpe
Ekeh P. 1974. *Social Exchange Theory*. Cambridge, MA: Harvard Univ. Press
Ellerman D. 1992. *Property and Contract in Economics*. Oxford: Blackwell
Elster J, Moene KO, eds. 1989. *Alternatives to Capitalism*. Cambridge, Eng.: Cambridge Univ. Press
Etzioni A. 1988. *The Moral Dimension*. New York: Free Press
Etzioni A, Lawrence PR, eds. 1991. *Socio-Economics*. Armonk, NY: ME Sharpe
Farina F, Hahn F, Vannucci S, eds. 1996. *Ethics, Rationality, and Economic Behaviour*. Oxford: Clarendon Press
Ferber M, Nelson J, eds. 1993. *Beyond Economic Man*. Chicago: Univ. Chicago Press
Fields KJ. 1995. *Enterprise and the State in Korea and Taiwan*. Ithaca, NY: Cornell Univ. Press
Fine B, Heasman M, Wright J. 1996. *Consumption in the Age of Affluence*. London: Routledge
Fine B, Leopold E. 1993. *The World of Consumption*. London: Routledge
Firth R. 1939. *Primitive Polynesian Economy*. London: Routledge & Kegan Paul
Fligstein N. 1990. *The Transformation of Corporate Control*. Cambridge, MA: Harvard Univ. Press
Fligstein N. 1996. A political-cultural approach to market institutions. *Am. Sociol. Rev.* 61:656–73
Fligstein N, Mara-Drita I. 1996. How to make a market: reflections on the attempt to create a single market in the European Union. *Am. J. Sociol.* 102:1–33
Folbre N. 1994. *Who Pays for the Kids?* London: Routledge
Fonseca EG da. 1991. *Beliefs in Action*. Cambridge, Eng.: Cambridge Univ. Press
Freeman JR. 1989. *Democracy and Markets*. Ithaca, NY: Cornell Univ. Press
Friedland R, Robertson AF. 1990. Beyond the marketplace. In *Beyond the Marketplace*, ed. R Friedland, AF Robertson, pp. 3–49. New York: Aldine de Gruyter
Friedman M. 1962. *Capitalism and Freedom*. Chicago: Univ. Chicago Press
Galbraith JK. 1956. *American Capitalism*. Boston: Houghton Mifflin. Rev. ed.
Galenson DW, ed. 1989. *Markets in History*. Cambridge, Eng.: Cambridge Univ. Press
Gamble A. 1994. *Britain in Decline*. New York: St. Martin's Press. 4th ed.
Garfinkel MR, Skaperdas S, eds. 1996. *The Political Economy of Conflict and Appropriation*. Cambridge, Eng.: Cambridge Univ. Press
Glasman M. 1996. *Unnecessary Suffering*. London: Verso
Goldthorpe JH. 1978. The current inflation: towards a sociological account. In *The Political Economy of Inflation*, ed. F Hirsch, JH Goldthorpe, pp. 186–214. Cambridge, MA: Harvard Univ. Press
Gordon D. 1996. *Fat and Mean*. New York: Free Press
Granovetter M. 1985. Economic action and social structure: the problem of embeddedness. *Am. J. Sociol.* 91:481–510
Granovetter M. 1994. Business groups. See Smelser & Swedberg 1994, pp. 453–75
Green DP, Shapiro I. 1994. *Pathologies of Rational Choice Theory*. New Haven, CT: Yale Univ. Press
Gregory CA. 1982. *Gifts and Commodities*. London: Academic
Gregory CA, Altman JC. 1989. *Observing the Economy*. London: Routledge
Greider W. 1992. *One World, Ready or Not*. New York: Simon & Schuster
Gudeman S. 1986. *Economics as Culture*. London: Routledge & Kegan Paul
Gudeman S, Rivera A. 1990. *Conversations in Colombia*. Cambridge, Eng: Cambridge Univ. Press

Hall PA. 1986. *Governing the Economy.* New York: Oxford Univ. Press
Halperin RH. 1988. *Economies across Cultures.* London: Macmillan
Halperin RH. 1994. *Cultural Economies Past and Present.* Austin: Univ. Texas Press
Han SK. 1993. *Claiming Status.* PhD thesis. Columbia Univ., New York
Harriss B. 1984a. *Exchange Relations and Poverty in Dryland Agriculture.* New Delhi: Concept
Harriss B. 1984b. *State and Market.* New Delhi: Concept
Hart K. 1982. *Political Economy of West African Agriculture.* Cambridge, Eng.: Cambridge Univ. Press
Haskell TL, Teichgraeber RF, eds. 1993. *The Culture of the Market.* Cambridge, UK: Cambridge Univ. Press
Hausman DM, McPherson MS. 1996. *Economic Analysis and Moral Philosophy.* Cambridge, Eng: Cambridge Univ. Press
Heilbroner R. 1988. *Behind the Veil of Economics.* New York: Norton
Heilbroner R, Milberg W. 1995. *The Crisis of Vision in Modern Economic Thought.* Cambridge, Eng: Cambridge Univ. Press
Herman ES. 1995. *Triumph of the Market.* Boston: South End Press
Herrigel G. 1996. *Industrial Constructions.* Cambridge, Eng.: Cambridge Univ. Press
Hicks J. 1989. *A Market Theory of Money.* Oxford: Clarendon Press
Hill P. 1972. *Rural Hausa.* Cambridge, Eng: Cambridge Univ. Press
Hill P. 1982. *Dry Grain Farming Families.* Cambridge, Eng.: Cambridge Univ. Press
Hill P. 1986. *Development Economics on Trial.* Cambridge, Eng: Cambridge Univ. Press
Hirschman AO. 1980. *National Power and the Structure of Foreign Trade.* Berkeley: Univ. Calif. Press. Expanded ed.
Hirschman AO. 1986. *Rival Views of Market Society and Other Recent Essays.* New York: Viking
Hirst P, Thompson G. 1996. *Globalization in Question.* London: Polity
Hodges R. 1988. *Primitive and Peasant Markets.* Oxford: Basil Blackwell
Hodgson GM. 1988. *Economics and Institutions.* Philadelphia, PA: Univ. Penn. Press
Hodgson GM. 1993. *Economics and Evolution.* Cambridge, Eng.: Polity
Hodgson GM, Samuels WJ, Tool MR, eds. 1994. *The Elgar Companion to Institutional and Evolutionary Economics.* 2 vols. Aldershot, UK: Edward Elgar
Hollingsworth JR, Schmitter PC, Streeck W, eds. 1993. *Governing Capitalist Economies.* Cambridge, Eng: Cambridge Univ. Press
Hont I, Ignatieff M, eds. 1983. *Wealth and Virtue.* Cambridge, Eng: Cambridge Univ. Press
Isachsen AJ, Hamilton CB, Gylfason T. 1991. *Understanding the Market Economy.* Oxford: Oxford Univ. Press
Jeffries I. 1996. *A Guide to the Economies in Transition.* London: Routledge
Keohane RO, Milner HV, eds. 1996. *Internationalization and Domestic Politics.* Cambridge, Eng.: Cambridge Univ. Press
Kornai J. 1992. *The Socialist System.* Princeton, NJ: Princeton Univ. Press
Kovács JM, ed. 1994. *Transition to Capitalism?* New Brunswick, NJ: Transaction
Kuttner R. 1987. *The End of Laissez-Faire.* New York: Knopf
Kuttner R. 1997. *Everything for Sale.* New York: Knopf
Lane RE. 1991. *The Market Experience.* Cambridge, Eng.: Cambridge Univ. Press
Lazonick W. 1991. *Business Organization and the Myth of the Market Economy.* Cambridge, MA: Harvard Univ. Press
Lebergott S. 1993. *Pursuing Happiness.* Princeton, NJ: Princeton Univ. Press
Lebergott S. 1996. *Consumer Expenditures.* Princeton: Princeton Univ. Press
Le Grand J, Estrin S, eds. 1989. *Market Socialism.* Oxford: Clarendon Press
Lie J. 1992. The concept of mode of exchange. *Am. Sociol. Rev.* 57:508–23
Lie J. 1993. Visualizing the invisible hand: the social origins of "market society" in England, 1550–1750. *Polit. Soc.* 21:275–305
Lindblom CE. 1977. *Politics and Markets.* New York: Basic
Lutz MA, ed. 1990. *Social Economics.* Boston: Kluwer Academic
Macfarlane A. 1987. *The Culture of Capitalism.* Oxford: Blackwell
Marshall A. 1920. *Industry and Trade.* London: Macmillan. 3rd ed.
McKendrick N, Brewer J, Plumb JH. 1983. *The Birth of a Consumer Society.* Bloomington: Indiana Univ. Press
McNally D. 1993. *Against the Market.* London: Verso
Meikle S. 1995. *Aristotle's Economic Thought.* Oxford: Clarendon Press
Mercer H. 1995. *Constructing a Competitive Order.* Cambridge, Eng: Cambridge Univ. Press
Michie J, Smith JG, eds. 1995. *Managing the Global Economy.* Oxford: Oxford Univ. Press
Middleton R. 1996. *Government Versus the Market.* Cheltenham: Edward Elgar
Miller D. 1989. *Market, State and Community.* Oxford: Clarendon Press
Miller D. 1995. Consumption and commodities. *Annu. Rev. Anthropol.* 24:141–61

Milner HV. 1988. *Resisting Protectionism.* Princeton, NJ: Princeton Univ. Press

Mirowski P. 1988. *Against Mechanism.* Totowa, NJ: Rowman & Littlefield

Mirowski P. 1989. *More Heat than Light.* Cambridge, Eng: Cambridge Univ. Press

Mittelman JH, ed. 1996. *Globalization.* Boulder, CO: Lynne Rienner

Moore S. 1993. *Marx Versus Markets.* University Park: Penn. State Univ. Press

Nee V. 1989. A theory of market transition: from redistribution to markets in state socialism. *Am. Sociol. Rev.* 54:663–81

Nee V. 1992. Organizational dynamics of market transition: hybrid forms, property rights, and mixed economy in China. *Adm. Sci. Q.* 37:1–27.

Nee V, Stark D, eds. 1989. *Remaking the Economic Institutions of Socialism.* Stanford, CA: Stanford Univ. Press

Nelson J. 1996. *Feminism, Objectivity and Economics.* London: Routledge

Nelson RR, Winter SG. 1982. *An Evolutionary Theory of Economic Change.* Cambridge, MA: Harvard Univ. Press

North DC, Thomas RP. 1973. *The Rise of the Western World.* Cambridge, Eng.: Cambridge Univ. Press

Nove A. 1983. *The Economics of Feasible Socialism.* London: George Allen & Unwin

O'Boyle EJ, ed. 1996. *Social Economics.* London: Routledge

Overbeek H, ed. 1993. *Restructuring Hegemony in the Global Political Economy.* London: Routledge

Papandreou, AA. 1994. *Externality and Institutions.* Oxford: Clarendon Press

Parry J, Block M, eds. 1989. *Money and the Morality of Exchange.* Cambridge, Eng.: Cambridge Univ. Press

Pearce DW. 1986. *The MIT Dictionary of Modern Economics.* Cambridge, MA: MIT Press. 3rd ed.

Peterson WC. 1988. *Market Power and the Economy.* Boston: Kluwer Academic

Piore, M, Sabel C. 1984. *The Second Industrial Divide.* New York: Basic Books

Plattner S, ed. 1985. *Markets and Marketing.* Lanham, MD: Univ. Press of America

Plattner S, ed. 1989. *Economic Anthropology.* Stanford, CA: Stanford Univ. Press

Podolny J. 1993. A status-based model of market competition. *Am. J. Sociol.* 98:829–72

Polanyi K. 1957. *The Great Transformation.* Boston: Beacon

Polanyi K, Arensberg CM, Pearson HW, eds. 1957. *Trade and Market in the Early Empires.* Glencoe, IL: Free Press

Powell WW, Smith-Doerr L. 1994. Networks and economic life. See Smelser & Swedberg 1994, pp. 368–402

Prout C. 1985. *Market Socialism in Yugoslavia.* Oxford: Oxford Univ. Press

Przeworski A. 1991. *Democracy and the Market.* Cambridge, Eng.: Cambridge Univ. Press

Putterman L. 1990. *Division of Labor and Welfare.* Oxford: Oxford Univ. Press

Ramanadham VV, ed. 1993. *Privatization.* London: Routledge

Reddy WM. 1984. *The Rise of Market Culture.* Cambridge, Eng: Cambridge Univ. Press

Reddy WM. 1987. *Money and Liberty in Modern Europe.* Cambridge, Eng.: Cambridge Univ. Press

Reich S. 1990. *The Fruits of Fascism.* Ithaca, NY: Cornell Univ. Press

Robinson J. 1933. *The Economics of Imperfect Competition.* London: Macmillan

Robinson J. 1980. *Collected Economic Papers.* Vol. V. Cambridge, MA: MIT Press

Roemer JE. 1981. *Analytical Foundations of Marxian Economic Theory.* Cambridge, Eng.: Cambridge Univ. Press

Roemer JE. 1994. *A Future for Socialism.* Cambridge, MA: Harvard Univ. Press

Roseberry W. 1988. Political economy. *Annu. Rev. Anthropol.* 17:161–85

Rosenberg A. 1992. *Economics—Mathematical Politics or Science of Diminishing Returns?* Chicago: Univ. Chicago Press

Rutherford M. 1994. *Institutions in Economics.* Cambridge, Eng.: Cambridge Univ. Press

Ryan P. 1995. *The Fall and Rise of the Market in Sandinista Nicaragua.* Montreal: McGill-Queen's Univ. Press

Sabel C, Zeitlin J. 1985. Historical alternatives to mass production: politics, markets and technology in nineteenth century industrialization. *Past Present* 108:134–76

Sachs, J. 1993. *Poland's Jump to the Market Economy.* Cambridge, MA: MIT Press

Salvatore D, ed. 1993. *Protectionism and World Welfare.* Cambridge, Eng: Cambridge Univ. Press

Scherer FM. 1980. *Industrial Market Structure and Economic Performance.* Chicago: Rand-McNally. 2nd ed.

Scherer FM. 1992. *International High Technology Competition.* Cambridge, MA: Harvard Univ. Press

Schmalensee R, Willig RD, eds. 1988. *Handbook of Industrial Organization.* Amsterdam: North-Holland

Schmidt VA. 1996. *From State to Market.* Cambridge, Eng.: Cambridge Univ. Press

Schwartz M, ed. 1988. *The Structure of Power in American Business.* New York: Holmes & Meier

Scitovsky T. 1992. *The Joyless Economy.* New York: Oxford Univ. Press. Rev. ed.

Shammas C. 1990. *The Pre-Industrial*

*Consumer in England and America.* Oxford: Clarendon Press
Sherburne JC. 1972. *John Ruskin or the Ambiguities of Abundance.* Cambridge, MA: Harvard Univ. Press
Sheridan K. 1993. *Governing the Japanese Economy.* Cambridge: Polity Press
Shirk SL. 1993. *The Political Logic of Economic Reform in China.* Berkeley: Univ. Calif. Press
Shonfield A. 1965. *Modern Capitalism.* London: Oxford Univ. Press
Silk L, Silk M. 1996. *Making Capitalism Work.* New York: New York Univ. Press
Skinner GW. 1964–65. Marketing and social structure in rural China, 3 parts. *J. Asian Stud.* 24:3–43, 195–228, 363–99
Sklar MJ. 1988. *The Corporate Reconstruction of American Capitalism, 1890–1916.* Cambridge, Eng: Cambridge Univ. Press
Smelser N, Swedberg R, eds. 1994. *The Handbook of Economic Sociology.* Princeton, NJ: Princeton Univ. Press
Smith C. 1976. *Regional Analysis.* 2 vols. New York: Academic
Smith WC, Acuña CH, Gamarra EA, eds. 1994. *Latin American Political Economy in the Age of Neoliberal Reform.* New Brunswick, NJ: Transaction
Sraffa P. 1960. *Production of Commodities by Means of Commodities.* Cambridge, Eng.: Cambridge Univ. Press
Stallings B. 1995. *Global Change, Regional Response.* Cambridge, Eng.: Cambridge Univ. Press
Stark D. 1990. Privatization in Hungary: from plan to market or from plan to clan. *E. Eur. Polit. Soc.* 4:351–92
Stark D. 1992. Path dependence and privatization strategies in East Central Europe. *E. Eur. Polit. Soc.* 6:17–54
Stiglitz JE. 1994. *Whither Socialism?* Cambridge, MA: MIT Press
Strathern A. 1971. *The Rope of Moka.* Cambridge, Eng.: Cambridge Univ. Press
Strathern M. 1988. *The Gender of the Gift.* Berkeley: Univ. Calif. Press
Swedberg R. 1987. Economic sociology: past and present. *Curr. Sociol.* 35:1–221
Swedberg R. 1990. *Economics and Sociology.* Princeton, NJ: Princeton Univ. Press
Swedberg R. 1991. Major traditions of economic sociology. *Annu. Rev. Sociol.* 17:251–76
Swedberg R. 1994. Markets as social structures. See Smelser & Swedberg 1994, pp. 255–82
Szelényi I. 1989. East Europe in an epoch of transition: toward a socialist mixed economy? See Nee & Stark, pp. 208–32
Taylor I, ed. 1990. *Effects of Free Market Policy.* New York: St. Martin's Press
Taylor OH. 1955. *Economics and Liberalism.* Cambridge, MA: Harvard Univ. Press
Telser L. 1987. *A Theory of Efficient Cooperation and Competition.* Cambridge, Eng.: Cambridge Univ. Press
Thirsk J. 1978. *Economic Policy and Projects.* Oxford: Clarendon Press
Thomas MJ, ed. 1995. *Gower Handbook of Marketing.* Aldershot, UK: Gower. 4th ed.
Thomas N. 1991. *Entangled Objects.* Cambridge, MA: Harvard Univ. Press
Thomas N. 1992. The inversion of tradition. *Am. Ethnol.* 19:213–32
Thompson EP. 1991. *Customs in Commons.* New York: New Press
Thompson N. 1988. *The Market and Its Critics.* London: Routledge
Thurow LC. 1983. *Dangerous Currents.* New York: Random House
Tobin J. 1980. *Asset Accumulation and Economic Activity.* Chicago: Univ. Chicago Press
Tribe K. 1981. *Genealogies of Capitalism.* London: Macmillan
Uriu RM. 1996. *Troubled Industries.* Ithaca, NY: Cornell Univ. Press
Uzzi B. 1996. Embeddedness and Economic Performance: The Network Effect. *Am. Sociol. Rev.* 61:674–98
Vestal JE. 1993. *Planning for Change.* Oxford: Clarendon Press
Vickers D. 1995. *The Tyranny of the Market.* Ann Arbor: Univ. Mich. Press
Vietor RHK. 1994. *Contrived Competition.* Cambridge, MA: Harvard Univ. Press
Wade R. 1990. *Governing the Market.* Princeton, NJ: Princeton Univ. Press
Walder AG, ed. 1995. *The Waning of the Communist State.* Berkeley: Univ. Calif. Press
Waligorski CP. 1990. *The Political Theory of Conservative Economists.* Lawrence: Univ. Press of Kansas
Walras L. 1954. *Elements of Pure Economics.* Transl. W Jaffé. Homewood, IL: Richard D. Irwin
Walton J, Seddon D. 1994. *Free Markets and Foot Riots.* Oxford: Blackwell
Wank DL. 1993. *From State Socialism to Community Capitalism.* PhD diss. Harvard Univ., Cambridge, MA
Wanmali SV. 1981. *Periodic Markets and Rural Development.* Delhi: BR Publishing
White HC. 1981. Where do markets come from? *Am. J. Sociol.* 87:517–47
White HC. 1992. *Identity and Control.* Princeton, NJ: Princeton Univ. Press
White HC. 1993. Markets in production networks. In *Explorations in Economic Sociology,* ed. R Swedberg, pp. 161–75. New York: Russell Sage Found.
Wicksteed P. [1914] 1950. The scope and method of political economy in the light of

the "marginal" theory of value and distribution. In *The Common Sense of Political Economy and Selected Papers and Reviews in Economic Theory,* Vol. 2, pp. 772–92. New York: Kelley

Wilk RR. 1996. *Economies and Cultures.* Boulder, CO: Westview

Williamson OE. 1975. *Markets and Hierarchies.* New York: Free Press

Williamson OE. 1987. *Antitrust Economics.* Oxford: Blackwell

Winch D. 1996. *Riches and Poverty.* Cambridge, Eng.: Cambridge Univ. Press

World Bank. 1996. *World Development Report 1996.* New York: Oxford Univ. Press

Wurm CA. 1993. *Business, Politics, and International Relations.* Cambridge, UK: Cambridge Univ. Press

Zelizer VA. 1983. *Morals and Markets.* New Brunswick, NJ: Transaction

Zelizer VA. 1987. *Pricing the Priceless Child.* New York: Basic Books

Zelizer VA. 1988. Beyond the polemics on the markets: establishing a theoretical and empirical agenda. *Sociol. Forum* 3:614–34

*Annu. Rev. Sociol. 1997. 23:361–83*


# POLITICS AND CULTURE: A Less Fissured Terrain

*Mabel Berezin*
Department of Sociology, University of California at Los Angeles, Los Angeles, California 90095-1551

KEY WORDS: political culture, civil society, political communication, symbols, rituals

ABSTRACT

In the past few years, the area of politics and culture has moved from the margins of cultural inquiry to its center as evidenced by the number of persons who identify themselves as working within the area and by its growing institutionalization within sociology. "Politics and culture" suggests that each term constitutes an autonomous social realm; whereas "political culture" suggests the boundaries of cultural action within which ordinary politics occurs. Bourdieu's emphasis on boundary making, Foucault's disciplinary mechanisms, and Habermas's conception of the public are setting the research agenda of scholars who focus on macro-level social change. Interdisciplinary dialogues are emerging, conducted on a landscape of historical and contemporary empirical research. Four sub-areas have crystallized: first, political culture, which focuses on problems of democratization and civil society; second, institutions, which includes law, religion, the state, and citizenship; third, political communication and meaning; and fourth, cultural approaches to collective action. Promising directions for future work are historical ethnographies, participant observation and interview studies of political communication, and studies of political mobilization that examine how emotion operates in politics. Paradigms are not yet firm within this area, suggesting that politics and culture is a disciplinary site of theoretical, methodological, and empirical innovation.

## MAPPING THE FIELD

Three years ago I wrote a preliminary review of current research on politics and culture (Berezin 1994a). I oriented my first review toward methodology



0360-0572/97/0815-0361$08.00

and asked how sociologists might pose relevant questions that wed culture to political analysis. My premise was that academic discourse was beginning to link the words "politics" and "culture" with more frequency than analytic precision. I argued that sociologists should guard against the seductions of the linguistic turn and be wary of the idea (influenced more by literary than social theory) that representations of power equal realities of power (Freedberg 1989, Friedlander 1992).

Sociology's strongest potential contribution to this emerging and hybrid field lay in empirically grounded studies that built on the traditional areas of political analysis such as states, social movements, and even voting behavior. In 1993, much of the empirical work was located in history (Hunt 1989), anthropology (Cohen 1974, Kertzer 1988, Ortner 1984), and to a lesser extent in political science (Laitin 1986). While sociologists studied problems that fell under the rubric of politics and culture (for example, Goldfarb 1991, Bellah et al 1985, 1991, Hunter 1991), very few labeled their work as such.[1] Much sociological discussion of politics and culture consisted of theoretical debates about postmodernism (Alexander 1992, Giddens 1990), history (Calhoun 1992, Hall 1990), and power (Lamont 1989, Mitchell 1990).

In the three short years that have elapsed since the writing of that first review, a sea change has occurred in the perception of politics and culture within sociology, and steps have been taken toward institutionalizing it as a disciplinary subfield. First, the number of persons who identify their work as falling within the field has increased. For example, the American Sociological Association's (ASA) section on Sociology of Culture now contains a working network devoted exclusively to issues of Politics and Culture. A brief perusal of the ASA annual meeting program for the last two years reveals whole panels devoted to politics and culture, national identity and political symbolism. Second, a number of major university presses now have book series devoted to issues of culture and politics.[2] Third, dialogues are emerging within sociology conducted on a landscape of historical and contemporary empirical research. For this review, I have identified four sub-areas that have crystallized within the last three years: first, political culture, which focuses on problems of democratization and civil society; second, institutions, which includes law, religion, the

[1]The broad sweep of Hunter's (1991) and Goldfarb's (1991) analyses of contemporary American cultural dilemmas follows in the tradition of Bell's (1976) *The Cultural Contradictions of Capitalism.*

[2]The most prominent among these are: Craig Calhoun's "The Contradictions of Modernity" at Minnesota; Jeffrey C. Alexander's and Steven Seidman's "Cambridge Cultural Social Studies" at Cambridge; David Laitin's and George Steinmetz's "Wilder House Series in Culture, Politics and History" at Cornell; and Lynn Hunt's and Victoria Bonnell's "Studies in the History of Society and Culture" at Berkeley.

state, and citizenship; third, political communication and meaning; and fourth, collective action.[3]

## POLITICAL CULTURE VERSUS POLITICS AND CULTURE

The terms "political culture" and "politics and culture" are not reducible to each other. Failure to draw a distinction between them leads to analytic imprecision and linguistic confusion. As this distinction is implicit in much of the literature I review, it is important to flag at the outset. I distinguish between the two terms as follows. "Politics and culture" suggests that each term constitutes an autonomous social realm. It suggests that there are broad cultural themes that are sometimes mobilized in the service of politics and sometimes not. These themes would exist independently of their political uses. The task of the social analyst is to understand how the two intersect.

Sewell's (1992) discussion of the play of schema and resources in social transformation as well as Swidler's (1986) analysis of culture as "tool kit" are useful analytic frames for specifying the distinction and testing the interaction between politics and culture. Sewell argues that schemas are deep rules of behavior that can be used as resources by those who know and wish to change the rules of the cultural game. Language is the vehicle that enables agents to act upon structures, as well as the cultural form that activates transformation. Agents may dip into Swidler's cultural "tool-kit" when the available repertoire of social and political practices requires reinforcement, when it changes or collapses completely. Sewell and Swidler ascribe a relative autonomy to culture. Cultural rules, symbols, and practices may serve to create a new political culture, or they may simply contribute to the political culture that is already in place.

Luker's (1984) study of abortion activists and Merelman's (1991) comparative study of political culture in Canada, Britain, and the United States convey the spirit of my distinction even if they do not rely on either Swidler's or Sewell's definitions. Luker discovered that the cultural meanings that women attached to the role of motherhood made possible prediction not only of their stance on abortion but also their level of activism. Feelings and meanings about motherhood are latent and cultural and exist independently of political exigencies; however, certain types of political issues, such as abortion, have the capacity to

[3]While I have tried to be as inclusive as possible in citations, space constraints have forced me to focus on trends, published as opposed to unpublished work, and frequently books rather than articles. Many of the citations could be in multiple categories but for the purposes of simplicity I have grouped them in the area where they have had the most impact. Needless to say, the four sub-areas which I have identified merit their own *Annual Review* articles.

force those meanings to the surface where they may become the foci of political mobilization. Merelman studied cultural artifacts such as television sitcoms, magazine advertisements, school textbooks, and corporate publications to determine what types of popular narrative shaped democratic ideas and practices. He discovered that representations of the family revealed national differences in perceptions of collectivity and individualism that link these underlying cultural ideals to the types of democracy present in Britain, the United States, and Canada. In Merelman's study, culture shaped political practice.

In contrast to "politics and culture," "political culture" I view as the matrix of meanings embodied in expressive symbols, practices, and beliefs that constitute ordinary politics in a bounded collectivity. The debate between Laitin and Wildavsky (1988), Inglehart's call for a "renaissance" in political culture (1988), and Eckstein's discussion of political development and culture (1988), as well as numerous review articles (Chilton 1988, Davis 1989, Brint 1994a), suggest that political scientists rediscovered political culture in the late 1980s. In the "old" literature (Almond & Verba 1989 is the classic reference here), political culture meant political attitudes studied quantitatively [with rare exceptions such as Banfield's (1967) ethnographic account of political stagnation in a southern Italian village]. The assumption was that attitudes directly determined political practices. Laitin and Eckstein present the clearest challenge to that approach. Laitin calls for historical and ethnographic accounts of politics that view culture as "points of concern" where symbols and language are appropriated instrumentally to achieve cultural and political ends. Eckstein, invoking Talcott Parson's action theory, argues that culture affects political transformation by determining the context in which social actors make collective and individual political decisions. Wilson (1992) develops an institutional theory of political culture.

Social scientists have not completely abandoned the study of political attitudes. For example, Inglehart (1990) contends that since the mid-1970s, what he terms "post-materialist" values have shaped political attitudes in Europe. Inglehart uses attitudinal data taken from the Eurobarometer survey to explain what others have called New Social Movements (Cohen 1985), that is, movements that focus on identities and values, e.g. women's movements, anti-nuclear movements, and ecology movements. Brint (1994b) uses American survey data to explore the political behavior of middle class professionals. Szelenyi et al (1996) use results derived from demographic and public opinion survey data to explain the unexpected 1994 Hungarian election results in terms of the "strength of social democratic sentiment."

The new attitude studies, while more theoretically sophisticated and historically embedded than their predecessors, exist more as methodological residues than as harbingers of new directions. The new literature on political culture is theoretical in that it challenges the concept itself, and it is historical in its careful attention to context and decided focused upon ethnographic and historical methods. Much of the focus of this literature has been on issues of civil society and democratization—at the level of both theory and empirical analysis.

## *Theories of Civil Society*

Before 1989, civil society theorists were primarily concerned with the revivification of democratic socialist political practice (Mouffe & LaClau 1985, Keane 1988, Barber 1984). Political events and the resurgence of ethnic nationalism in the former Eastern Europe have forced a shift in focus. While there is a clear historical reason for sociological interest in civil society, the question remains as to why civil society is important and how this is linked to questions of democratization.

Civil society is generally conceptualized as the social space in which a democratic polity is enacted. What constitutes "social" ranges from every institution that is not market- or state-based to relatively restrictive conceptions that focus on family and what Alexis de Tocqueville called mediating social institutions. While the term originates with Hegel, Jurgen Habermas's *Structural Transformation of the Public Sphere* (1989), particularly after its English translation in 1989, has established (whether it is acknowledged or not) the terms of much of the debate. According to Habermas, what separates democratic practices from what has gone before is the existence of a separate sphere that is neither state nor church, where individuals form publics and debate political ideas and practices. Habermas's ideal of the public sphere is the eighteenth century coffee house, the salon, and the rise of a free press. His contribution is inherently cultural because, in contrast to other theories of democratization that simply link it to markets and the development of nation-states, Habermas argues for a communicative space in which democratic practices and values evolve.

The academic discussion of civil society begins with elaborations of Habermas's idea (Cohen & Arato 1992). Kumar & Weintraub's anthology (1996) underscores the importance of the division between public and private. Challenges to the idea of civil society include the charge that it is historically specific and lacks analytic power in view of contemporary realities (Kumar 1993, Bryant 1993, Taylor 1990, Calhoun 1993a). Seligman (1992) argues that the "idea" of civil society is a moral concept that originates in the Scottish enlightenment. According to Seligman, a vibrant civil society such as that in the United States depends upon a political culture is which the boundaries between public and private are firmly held. For this reason, he is dubious about applying the concept to political developments in the former Eastern Europe.

Somers (1995a,b) criticizes current discussions of politics and culture because they do not take into account the historical specificity of the terms of debate. Focusing on the "old" political culture literature and Habermas' discussion of a public, she argues for a historical sociology of concept formation and locates the idea of Anglo-American citizenship theory in its cultural and historical milieu. Somers' principal contribution lies in the argument that even the most taken-for-granted building block of modern democracy is highly contextual and that we must be cautious about simply taking these terms up in toto and applying them to other temporal and spatial locales. In a series of articles (Alexander & Smith 1993, Alexander 1994, Alexander 1996), Alexander offers an innovative approach to civil society that introduces the conception of solidarity. He argues that members of the polity experience belonging in a series of binary discourses in which they articulate issues of good and evil. Those discourses generate an important, but unstated, dimension of civil society—a feeling of membership and community.

Empirical work on the public sphere is just beginning to emerge. The essays in Calhoun's (1993d) anthology take up the issue of gender and cross-national variation of public sphere development. Somers (1993) examines divergent conceptions of citizenship in different parts of Britain in the prerevolutionary period. Her argument is that, rather than being an attribute of persons based upon rights (the Marshall distinction), citizenship is relational and is reflective of a diverse set of local institutional arrangements that give rise to different notions of a public sphere and political cultures. Building on earlier work (Zaret 1989), Zaret (1996) argues that much discussion of the public sphere has failed to look closely at the available forms of political communication. By examining the evolution of "petitions" in sixteenth century England, he is able to locate the origins of the public sphere not in the development of the bourgeoisie and Enlightenment ideology but in the effect that printing had on the medieval practice of petitioning local authorities. This practice of political communication was open to all social classes, and Zaret argues that it reveals the populist roots of the public sphere and allows it a greater democratic potential than critics of modernity would suggest. Variations on this theme include studies of the socialist public sphere (Tucker 1996) and the cultural dimensions of democracy (Creppell 1989, Edles 1995).

### *Democracy and Culture*

The debate about civil society and democracy has not remained at the purely theoretical level. Bellah and his colleagues, who would probably not label themselves civil society theorists, have provided a prominent empirical contribution to the debate about democracy in the American context. Bellah's (1980) comparative study of "civil religion," which evokes Rousseau's conception of "republican virtue," calls for an active political community with citizen participation. Bellah's collaborative works, *Habits of the Heart* (Bellah et al 1985) and *The Good Society* (Bellah et al 1991), placed the idea of political culture and democratic practice firmly on the American research agenda. Turning to Alexis de Tocqueville rather than contemporary continental social theory, Bellah and his colleagues interviewed Americans about their participation in the polity and how they viewed themselves as political actors and members of a political community. Both books call for a new public spiritedness based upon the revivification of community and public commitment, and both see a retreat to individualism as one of the features that has weakened contemporary American democracy.

Lichterman (1995, 1996) conducted a field study on the local level of two American environmental protection groups, and he challenges Bellah's conclusions. Rejecting what he terms the "seesaw model" (i.e. one is either a liberal or a communitarian), he argues that the retreat to "personalism" and self-fulfillment does not have to lead to a lack of public spiritedness. His study suggests that an ethic of personal fulfillment in some circumstance may contribute to a renewed sense of political commitment and a reinvigorated democratic community.

If Bellah's work has been the linchpin of discussion of American political culture, Robert Putnam's *Making Democracy Work* (1994) and the debate around it (for example, Laitin 1995, Tarrow 1996) has become a focal point for research on international political culture. It has also had a surprising influence on public debate in the United States, as evidenced by the three-page article that Putnam had in no less a venue than *People Magazine*! Putnam, a political scientist, studied regional government in Italy over a 20-year period. Despite the apparently limited empirical focus of his work, its influence has extended well beyond the exigencies of Italian political development. Putnam argues that the practices of democracy are based on the trust that a high degree of social capital bestows. He argues that the success or failure of self-governance in Italy was linked to the patterns of cooperation and trust that were established in early renaissance city states. He argues that a vital civic culture is linked to the experience of cooperation learned in voluntary organizations that range from mutual credit associations to choral societies.

Calhoun's *Neither Gods Nor Emperors* (1994b), which focuses upon the Chinese student movement and the events that led to the massacres in Tiananmen Square, discusses how informal student networks were able to mobilize dissent even in a controlled society such as China. Calhoun argues that the value of mobilization in creating new identities and the idea of democracy and public participation are important dimensions of civil society and transformative politics even if the movements themselves fail. Calhoun's owes his emphasis on identity and democratic practice to Taylor's (1989) discussion of the relation between "ordinary life" and political practice (Calhoun 1991).

Another strand of the debate on civil society is the emerging literature on multiculturalism, which scholars usually discuss in terms of group rights. In the United States, the focus is on difference and social equality (Taylor 1994, Gitlin

1993, Spencer 1994); whereas in the non-American context, multiculturalism tends to be associated with ethnic conflict (Joppke 1996, Kymlicka 1995). Multiculturalism relates to civil society in that it takes up the issue of who shall participate in the polity based upon cultural identity.

Within the literature I have reviewed under the rubric of "political culture," there is an underlying, although unstated, anthropological view of culture as shared mental grids or meanings that is part of the process of a political practice such as democracy.

## STATES AND INSTITUTIONS

Civil society and democratization discussions assume a political culture but do not explicitly theorize it. In contrast, the literature that I group under states and institutions begins with problems traditionally falling within the purview of political sociology and organizations. Lying closer to my discussion of politics and culture, this literature views culture as a variable that enters into the process of institution formation and action.

State theory traditionally looks to finance, military structure, and bureaucracy to define the state. Analysts with an interest in culture have begun to question the adequacy of these variables in defining state formation. Jasper (1987) attributes the divergent outcomes in nuclear energy policy in France, Sweden, and the United States to the policy styles of government planners. The study by Berezin (1991) of artistic production and censorship in Fascist Italy argues that theories of state action apply in nominatively totalitarian as well as democratic states. Using game theory and focusing on language policy in Catalonia and Africa, Laitin (1989, 1992, Laitin & Sole 1994) attributes the political and social cohesion of the modern state to its ability to establish language repertoires. Ikegami (1995) studies Japan in the Tokagowa period and argues that "honorific individualism," carried by permutations in Samarai culture, was integral to the formation of the Japanese variant of the nation-state. Burke (1992) identifies the "fabrication" of Louis XIV as an example of a person becoming a symbol to consolidate central state power.

Foucault's (1977a,b) conception of discipline and the social has influenced new directions in state theory. In a theoretical exegesis on the concept of the state, Mitchell (1991b) argues that the state is merely a vector of structural forces. He elaborates this argument in his study of the Egyptian colonial state (Mitchell 1991a), where he argues that the "power to colonize" is the power to impose meanings in the form of British hegemonic discourse. Steinmetz (1993) turns to Foucault's conception of the "social" to explain the particular iterations of the German welfare state on the local level. Gorski (1993) argues that theories of state formation have failed to adequately theorize the relation between Protestantism and Calvinism and the form of the modern state. Drawing on both Foucault's notion of public discipline and Elias's conception of personal discipline, Gorski argues that Protestantism extended the notion of self discipline to the obligation to discipline the entire community. The wedding of Protestantism's disciplinary imperative to collective organization was as important as war and bureaucratic rationality for the formation of the modern state. Lustick (1993) in his comparative study of territorial dispute in the Gaza Strip, Algeria, and Northern Ireland uses a Gramscian notion of hegemony and position to argue for a culturalist theory of colonial warfare.

An emerging strand of state and culture literature is one that incorporates the idea of gender. Verdery (1994) summarizes this most succinctly when she talks of the nation state as being a gendered concept, with nation representing the soft feminine side of the equation and state representing the hard bureaucratic masculine side. Scholars are beginning to recognize the gendered nature of the state in a range of areas. Prominent examples of this approach include Hunt's (1992) discussion of the "family romance," Connell's discussion of state and masculinity (1995), Borneman's (1992) equation of state and kinship, as well as works on the gendered nature of citizenship (Orloff 1993) and patriarchy (Adams 1994).[4]

The growing appeal of the "new" institutionalism within sociology has propelled culture to the forefront of the study of policy, law, and even markets. The work of Thomas, Meyer and collaborators (1987) and the influential Powell & DiMaggio anthology (1991) have set the research agenda in this area. Friedland & Alford's (1991) injunction to "bring society back in" summarizes much of the cultural dimension of institutionalism as it underscores the importance of rules and repertoires of practices and symbols in social behavior and organizational action. For example, Skrentny's (1996) analysis of the cultural contradictions of affirmative action pays attention to the institutional context within which this policy emerged, while arguing that the notion of context has to be broadened to include multiplicity of rules, shifting rhetorics, and audience expectations. Fligstein (1996) argues that the political dimension of markets cannot be adequately understood if we do not understand the deeper cultural structures that give rise to them. Dobbin (1994) challenges the received wisdom that economic efficiency determines industrial policy choices. In a study of railway policy in Britain, France, and the United States, Dobbin argues that the diverse political cultures of these states contributed to the choices they made regarding railroad development. He thus shows that institutions themselves are as cultural as more typically studied cultural objects such as symbols.

[4]For an explicit discussion of the relation between state and culture, see Steinmetz's 1997 anthology, *State/Culture*.

In a novel vein, Soysal (1994) uses institutional theory to explore the issue of citizenship. Focusing upon the incorporation of immigrants into post-World War II European national labor markets, she argues that a conception and practice of citizenship that had been theorized in the language of national rights has been replaced in the contemporary era by post-national citizenship. She argues that the discourse of citizenship is now a discourse of human rights and that this is carried by diverse international agencies, particularly the United Nations. This language of humanity and personhood institutionally buttressed by fluid national labor markets and international governing agencies decouples citizenship from territory.

Most theorizing on citizenship does not go so far as Soysal to make a cultural argument for its transformation from its nineteenth century form into something arguably postmodern. Brubaker (1992) focuses upon immigration policy in France and Germany and asks why two countries facing similar influxes of immigrants have not changed their policies to accommodate changing realities. He argues, borrowing from Pierre Bourdieu, that citizenship is a boundary setting device that limits who is and who is not a member of the polity and that divergent notions of incorporation in France and Germany reflect the different political cultures in which the idea of nation was conceived during the nineteenth-century period of state formation.

Scholars who label themselves as institutionalists tend to focus on law and markets—standard political and economic institutions; students of religion, a potent cultural institution, are also contributing to these debates (Williams & Demerath 1992). The intersection of religion and organization figures prominently in several studies of culture and politics. David Laitin (1986) studies how Muslim and Christian culture and religious practices contributed to different political outcomes in different parts of Nigeria. Casanova (1994) links religion to politics by identifying what he terms public and private religions. Wuthnow (1989) studies the discourse and diffusion of Protestantism and its relation to other forms of political ideology. Zaret (1985) in his study of covenant theology rewrites Walzer (1965) by pointing to the role of organization in the diffusion of Protestant ideology. A somewhat related study is Kertzer's *Comrades and Christians* (1980), which analyzes how the Italian communist party appropriated Roman Catholic symbols and institutions to broaden its constituency in the 1970s.

A renewed focus on nationalism has developed in parallel to the interest in institutions, states, and culture. Anderson's (1991) *Imagined Communities*, which points to the constructed nature of nation/state coupled with the contemporary reemergence of nationalist movements, has fueled this research agenda (see for example, Calhoun 1995b). The literature on nationalism is voluminous and growing (Calhoun 1993c). The central debates in this literature concern whether nationalism represents a retreat to primordial sentiments fueled by class resentment (Greenfeld 1992), an instance of nation/state building (Sahlins 1989, Medrano 1995, Smith 1995), or a form of ideological imperialism (Chatterjee 1993, Bhabha 1990). National identity, and identity in general, had been the focus of much theorizing (AD Smith 1991, 1996, Gellner 1987, Somers 1994, Somers & Gibson 1994, Calhoun 1994a, 1995a, Handler 1994) with emerging empirical contributions (McDonaugh 1995, Meadwell 1990, Eyal 1996, Phillips 1996). Verdery's (1991) study of Rumania, using a framework borrowed from Foucault and Bourdieu, explores identity formation under conditions of totalitarianism. Ringmar (1996) is one of the first social analysts to offer a "cultural explanation" of a historical event, Sweden's entry into the Thirty Years War, that draws on theories of identity and nationhood. Brubaker (1996) offers an innovative approach to the study of nationalism, which ties together the culturalist and institutionalist versions of national problematizing. Focusing on the former Soviet Union, Brubaker argues that nationalist projects are best understood as sets of practices that get institutionalized under certain conditions.

## POLITICAL COMMUNICATION AND MEANING

Culture functions as an exogenous variable in institutional and state-oriented studies whose principal purpose is to explain some organizational or policy outcome. Political communication and meaning is the largest and growing sub-area within politics and culture. Cultural practices such as rituals and symbols, broadly defined to include national constitutions and histories as well as more standard aesthetic objects such as art and literature, provide the empirical focus for analysis of the dissemination of knowledge about politics. Sociological contributions attempt to theorize the autonomous, or sometimes relatively autonomous, status of culture.

Political communication and meaning is the most theoretically and empirically eclectic sub-area of politics and culture at the moment. The range of work and the objects of study vary as well as the literature cited. In focusing on the political meaning of cultural symbols, objects, and practices, the focus shifts from the production of meaning to the reception of meaning (Brown 1993, Cohen 1989, Goldberg 1991, Breckenridge 1989, Gambetta 1991). Production analyses, such as institutionalism, tell plausible stories about how culture constrains and enhances the actions of political actors and organizations. The studies that I now consider focus on how political audiences—ordinary citizens—respond to cultural politics. Although response is the key issue in this body of work, that does not suggest that practitioners have solved the problem of impact. One way to obtain this information is to ask citizens what they think and feel about politics, as did Lane (1962) in his study of lower-middle-class men in New Haven, and Gamson (1992) in his focus group study of contemporary American politics. Eliasoph (1990, 1996) uses a snowball sample and asks men and women "on the street" what they thought of the Iran-Contra hearings; in later work she explored the issue of political apathy by listening to the language of ordinary citizens. In both studies, Eliasoph finds that people interpret politics in ways that are counterintuitive to the manner in which we study politics and to the way politicians act out politics. However, despite these exceptions, much of the literature that I now review has to deal with what anthropologist Verdery (1991) in her study of Ceausescu's Romania calls the "Is anyone listening problem?"

## *Politics and Cultural Objects*

Griswold's (1987) definition of "cultural object" as "significance embodied in form" is a useful label for the range of entities that this section addresses. With politics lagging behind sociology and history, Edelman (1995) has written a monograph signaling the importance of art to politics. Within sociology, Goldfarb (1980, 1982) was one of the earliest contributors to this literature when, before 1989, he studied Polish student theater as a vehicle of dissent and the different enactments of cultural freedom in the United States and Poland. Haraszti (1987) studied how Hungarian writers under state socialism managed to produce in spite of state censorship. Corse (1995, 1997) has asked how literary canons are created in the service of national identities by comparing novel production in the United States and Canada. Beisel (1993) shows that art censorship is more a product of the class position of the patrons than of any objective qualities of pure and impure art.

The relationship between form, content, and meaning is an emerging theme in studies of cultural politics. Burns's (1992) study of the ideological pronouncements of Catholic bishops and the Comaroffs' (1991) study of religious conversion in South Africa argue that it was the rhetorical strategies, rather than content, that were mobilized in the service of ideological persuasion. Berezin (1994b) asks how fascist theater conveyed fascist meaning if theatrical content appeared not to contain fascist ideology. She argues that it was the formal properties of theater, staging and style, that communicated fascist meaning. Mukerji (1994) argues that the design of seventeenth-century French formal gardens was the aesthetic parallel of the geopolitical maneuvering of a state bent on territorial aggrandizement. In a similar vein, Cerulo's (1995) study of anthems and flags as national symbols argues that it is the syntax or the symbolic structure, rather than explicit content, that conveys meaning.

A more textualized approach to the study of art and politics is found in Bowler's (1991) and Falasca-Zamponi's (1995) studies of Italian futurism and fascism. Both articles use texts to explore the relation between an aesthetic and political movement. Wagner-Pacifici's (1986) study of the kidnapping and murder of Italian prime minister Aldo Moro borrows Victor Turner's notion of liminality to discuss this event as a dramatic genre. Her study of an urban bombing in Philadelphia (1994) continues this type of analysis by focusing on strategic discourse.

Cultural objects are more than simply aesthetic. Scholars are beginning to look to constitutions as national narratives (Arjomand 1992, Hart & Stimson 1993, Norton 1992). Spillman (1996) examines constitutions as vehicles of national identity by comparing debate at constitutional conventions in the United States and Australia. History as cultural object is the subject of work on memory and politics (Halbwachs 1980, Connerton 1989). Beginning with the influential anthology by Hobsbawm & Ranger (1983) on the "invention of tradition," the constructed past has become a fertile subfield of political and cultural analysis. Much of this work has been on material objects of memory such as monuments and museums (Gillis 1994), with exceptions (Golden 1988). Schwartz (1991, 1996) and Fine (1996) have contributed a range of studies on the historic reconstruction of American Presidents. Schudson's (1994) study of Watergate and the study by Schwartz and Wagner-Pacifici (1991) of the Vietnam War Memorial in Washington, DC, have discussed how a political event of dubious significance shaped American political commitment and confidence. The study of past events that nation-states would prefer to forget has been the object of much analysis that focuses upon Europe. Studies of the Nazi Holocaust (Maier 1988, Friedlander 1992), French collaboration (Rousso 1991), and the fall of Italian fascism (Berezin 1996) have focused upon how the memory of a morally questionable past affects current political practices.

### *Ritual and Symbolic Processes*

Students of ritual, broadly conceived to include repeated expressive and symbolic actions in public spaces, have contributed much to the study of politics. Here, as in the study of political culture, we can identify an older and a newer approach. Edelman (1985, 1988) was among the first in social science to argue that there was an important symbolic dimension to political action. Within anthropology, Geertz's work (1980) on the Negara as theater state and the anthropology of power (1983) lent this mode of analysis legitimacy and elegance. Geertz's work is seamless—its virtue and its limitation (for example, Cannadine 1987, Ozouf 1989, Von Geldern 1993, Davis 1975, Lane 1981).

The new studies of ritual divide in two ways. Those that treat it as a process of the production of belief, ideology, or identity (Kertzer 1988) and those that look at it as a narrative of domination (Scott 1990). Kertzer's (1996) study of the reinvention of the Italian Communist party looks to party history and national politics to explain shifts in the meaning of the naming of the party. Berezin (1997a) examines Italian fascist ritual and reveals that the fascist identity project was an attempt to rewrite the rules of cultural game through the appropriation of the Italian cultural values of family and the popular practices of Roman Catholicism. Fascist ritual was a vehicle of subversion and solidarity, and sometimes both simultaneously, but never a narrative of identity. Laba's (1991) discussion of the "sacred politics" of the Polish Solidarity movement, Burawoy & Luckacs's (1992) description of "painting socialism," Gal's (1991) discussion of the reburying of Bartok's body in Hungary, and Gilmore's (1993) study of Andalusian carnival pursue a similar line of analysis. These works start with a historical problem, fascism, communism, or socialism, and look to ritual to link cultural conditions to ideology and political practice. They pay careful attention to historical context, and context is as important as any single event that they seek to describe.

In contrast to this productivist approach to ritual, there is an evolving and important Durkheimian strand of analysis (Alexander 1988a,b, Rothenbuhler 1988, Tiryakian 1988). Lukes (1975) has criticized the unreconstructed Durkheimian position that sees ritual as purely a dramatization of the social order. Moore & Meyerhoff (1977) attacked the codification of politics into sacred and profane. The new Durkheimianism emphasizes the complexity of ritual analysis and in some instances incorporates Foucault. This approach starts with the ritual events themselves and works backward from that point (P Smith 1991, 1996, Ben-Amos & Ben-Ari 1995). This work combines a Durkheimian idea of ritual with Foucauldian notion of power and domination. Ritual becomes an expressive vehicle of the power to discipline and punish or to describe or inscribe historical events and meanings.

## COLLECTIVE ACTION

The study of collective action, which had been dominated by structural approaches, is taking a decidedly culturalist turn. New work on the study of revolutions and social movements attempts to understand the role that culture plays in political actions. As in the institutions literature, culture is a new preoccupation for many students of social movements.

Within both history and sociology, Hunt's *Politics, Culture and Class in the French Revolution* (1984) and Sewell's *Work and Revolution in France* (1980) legitimated the importance of culture for the study of revolutions and momentous political events. However, for the past 18 years, Skocpol's *States and Social Revolutions* (1979) has set the research agenda within sociology. Skocpol (1985) and Sewell (1985) had a frequently cited debate on the role of ideology in social revolutions. Sewell called for an integrative approach to the study of culture and politics; and Skocpol replied that "cultural idioms" invoked at particular points in time were "probably" useful in enhancing the study of political outcomes. Given Skocpol's leading role in the study of revolutions for the past 18 years, it is not surprising that two of the spokespersons for a more cultural account of revolution are her students, Goldstone (1991a,b) and Goodwin (1994). Goldstone and Goodwin began as structuralists, so they argue that culture must be incorporated as a form of structural variable into cultural analysis. Other persons working in this area began with a primary interest in culture, and they tend to focus upon the role of ideological discourse in revolutions (Moaddel 1992b, Sewell 1994, Burns 1996).

Social movements have always attracted scholars who were attentive to the role of culture and collective mobilization (Gusfield 1963, Klatch 1987). For example, Rieder (1985) found that ethnicity and the cultural visions it generated contributed to the different mobilization patterns among members of the Jewish and Italian lower middle class community that he studied. An influential volume of *Social Research* (Volume 52, 1985) devoted to new social movements (Cohen 1985) and an article by Snow et al (1986) that introduced the concept of "framing" initiated the cultural turn in social movement theory and research. The term "new social movements" was coined to label the movements that emerged in the post–student movement period in Europe (roughly 1969 to 1977); these were about issues of identity (women's and gay rights) and values (peace, environment). Although Calhoun (1993b) has claimed that these movements did have historical precedents, the label stuck as a way to deal with movements that were not based on claims for material advantage (such as labor movements, or even voting rights movements). The interest in new social movements introduced culture or cultural claims to the study of social movements (Beisel 1990, Jasper & Nelkin 1992, Eder 1993, Eyerman & Jamison 1991, Moaddel 1992a, Melucci 1996).

Snow's work (Snow et al 1986, 1988, 1992) as well as that of his associates (Benford & Hunt 1992, Guthrie 1995) captured the imagination of scholars who had traditionally worked in the field of social movements from a decidedly nonculturalist perspective (Tarrow 1992, 1994, Gamson 1988, 1991, Gamson & Modigliani 1989, Gamson & Stuart 1992). In Snow's original formulation, a frame was a bounded and easily recognizable narrative package that activists could impose on events. The more successful a movement was, the more likely it was able to tap into these deeply resonant preset frameworks (Zald 1996, Johnston et al 1994, McAdam 1994, 1996). The problem with frame analysis is that while its boundedness appeals to those who started out as structuralists, it is overly rigid to persons who have a more fine-grained sense of cultural and historical analysis. An interest in rhetorical strategies or language (Blain 1994, Ellingson 1995) and political mobilization is beginning to emerge and will be a major competitive paradigm to frame analysis. The critique by Emirbayer & Goodwin (1994) of network theory introduced a new pathway linking culture to social movements that has yet to be fully explored.

## THE ROAD AHEAD

In general, the terms, "politics" and "culture" are somewhat underspecified and have different meanings for persons who label themselves as working in the field. Swidler (1986), who wrote possibly the most cited article in this entire area, and Sewell (1992) have exercised a distinct theoretical influence on recent work—particularly work with a historical orientation. Bourdieu's emphasis on boundary making (Lamont 1992, Lamont & Fournier 1993), Foucault's disciplinary mechanisms, and Habermas' conception of the public are setting the research agenda of scholars who focus on macro-level social change. The interest in politics and culture is driven as much by current history as by theory. The events of the last eight years in the former Eastern Europe and Soviet Union, as well as the concern with the weakening of political engagement and growing social inequality in the United States, together are fueling research in this area.

Politics and culture has always been an interdisciplinary area. Promising directions for future work derive from theory, history, and anthropology, and these are already to some extent visible in the works that I have discussed. First, historical work with an ethnographic bent offers a promising method for mining the past to understand the present. Second, political communication—how citizens actually view themselves as political subjects coupled with a closer scrutiny of the public vehicles that disseminate political ideas—needs more attention. We know very little of how people think about politics and the language in which they express "ordinary" political beliefs. We also know very little about how the "public sphere" operates to shape ideas and practices. "Talking" about politics is an important focus of future work. Third, the field of social movements as it moves away from interest models and extends frame analysis offers a promising area to recast political mobilization in cultural terms. The rethinking of this area points us in the direction of emotion and politics (Goodwin 1997, Berezin 1997b)—to date, a neglected area that promises to bring social psychology and gender into the sociological study of politics and to refine and extend current discussion of identity.

The terrain that I have mapped in this review is somewhat less fissured than the one I described three years ago. While it is easier to identify sub-areas of interest, paradigms have not yet crystalized, and there is still, as evidenced by the variety of works cited, a great deal of empirical eclecticism. The field is open to new ideas, new theoretical approaches, and new research methods.

Politics and culture is still a frontier, and frontiers by their nature are sites of innovation. The increasing numbers of researchers working in this area suggest that the next review of this area will reveal clear paths—most likely forged through the trends that I have identified.

## ACKNOWLEDGMENTS

I began this review while I was a Fellow in the Department of Social and Political Sciences at the European University Institute in Florence, Italy. I thank Professor Christian Joppke for making my study at the Institute possible. Craig Calhoun and Paul Lichterman made suggestions on the early planning of the manuscript. John Choi provided superb research assistance.



*Literature Cited*

Adams J. 1994. The familial state: elite family practices and state-making in the early modern Netherlands. *Theory Soc.* 23:505–39

Alexander JC. 1988a. Introduction: Durkheimian sociology and cultural studies today. In *Durkheimian Sociology: Cultural Studies,* ed. JC Alexander, pp. 1–21. New York: Cambridge

Alexander JC. 1988b. Culture and political crisis: 'Watergate' and Durkheimian sociology. In *Durkheimian Sociology and Cultural Studies,* ed. JC Alexander, pp. 187–224. New York: Cambridge Univ. Press

Alexander JC. 1992. General theory in the postpositivist mode: the 'epistemological dilemma' and the search for present reason. In *Postmodernism and Social Theory: The Debate over General Theory,* ed. S Seidman, DG Wagner, pp. 322–68. Oxford: Blackwell

Alexander JC. 1994. The paradoxes of civil society. *Occas. Pap. #16.* Univ. Hong Kong: Soc. Sci. Res. Cent.

Alexander JC. 1996. Collective action, culture and civil society: secularizing, updating, inverting, revising and displacing the classical model of social movements. In *Alain Touraine,* ed. M Diani, J Clarke, pp. 205–34 New York: Falmer

Alexander JC, Smith P. 1993. The discourse of American civil society: a new proposal for cultural studies. *Theory Soc.* 22:151–207

Almond G, Verba S. 1989. *The Civic Culture: Political Attitudes and Democracy in Five Nations.* Beverly Hills, CA: Sage

Anderson B. 1991. *Imagined Communities: Reflections on the Origin and Spread of Nationalism.* London: Verso

Arjomand SA. 1992. Constitutions and the struggle for political order. *Arch. Eur. de Sociol.* 33(1):39–82

Banfield E. 1967. *The Moral Basis of a Backward Society.* New York: Free Press

Barber B. 1984. *Strong Democracy.* Berkeley: Univ. Calif. Press

Beisel N. 1990. Class, culture, and campaigns against vice in three American cities, 1872–1892. *Am. Sociol. Rev.* 55(Feb):44–62

Beisel N. 1993. Morals vs. art: censorship, the politics of interpretation and the Victorian nude. *Am. Sociol. Rev.* 58(Dec):753–67

Bell D. 1976. *The Cultural Contradictions of Capitalism.* New York: Basic

Bellah RN, Hammond, PE. 1980. *Varieties of Civil Religion.* New York: Harper & Row

Bellah RN, Madsen R, Sullivan WM, Swidler A, Tipton SM. 1985. *Habits of the Heart: Individualism and Commitment in American Life.* Berkeley: Univ. Calif. Press

Bellah RN, Madsen R, Sullivan WM, Swidler A, Tipton SM. 1991. *The Good Society.* New York: Knopf

Ben-Amos A, Ben-Ari E. 1995. Resonance and reverberation: ritual and bureaucracy in the state funerals of the French Third Republic. *Theory Soc.* 24(2)(Apr):163–91

Benford RD, Hunt SA. 1992. Dramaturgy and social movements: the social construction and communication of power. *Sociol. Inq.* 62(1)(Feb):36–55

Berezin M. 1991. The organization of political ideology: culture, state and theater in Fascist Italy. *Am. Sociol. Rev.* 56(Oct):639–51

Berezin M. 1994a. Fissured terrain: methodological approaches and research styles in culture and politics. In *The Sociology of Culture,* ed. D Crane, pp. 91–116. London: Basil Blackwell

Berezin M. 1994b. Cultural form and political meaning: state subsidized theater, ideology and the language of style in Fascist Italy. *Am. J. Sociol.* 99(Mar):1237–86

Berezin M. 1996. 'The dead are equal': history making, moral relativism and the rise of the new Italian right. *Univ. Mich: CSST Working Paper 109; CRSO Work. Pap. 534.* Ann Arbor, MI

Berezin M. 1997a. *Making the Fascist Self: The Political Culture of Inter-war Italy.* Ithaca, NY: Cornell Univ. Press

Berezin M. 1997b. Making political love: state, nation and identity in Fascist Italy. In *State/Culture,* ed. G Steinmetz. Ithaca, NY: Cornell Univ. Press

Bhabha HK. 1990. *Nation and Narration.* London: Routledge

Blain M. 1994. Power, war and melodrama in the discourse of political movements. *Theory Soc.* 23(6):805–37

Borneman J. 1992. *Belonging in the Two Berlins: Kin, State and Nation.* New York: Cambridge Univ. Press

Bowler A. 1991. Italian futurism and fascism. *Theory Soc.* 20(6)(Dec):763–94

Breckenridge CA. 1989. The aesthetics and politics of colonial collecting: India at world fairs. *Comp. Stud. Soc. Hist.* 31:195–216

Brint S. 1994a. Sociological analysis of political culture: an introduction and assessment. *Res. Democracy Soc.* 2:3–41

Brint S. 1994b. *In an Age of Experts.* Princeton, NJ: Princeton Univ. Press

Brown RH. 1993. Cultural representation and ideological domination. *Soc. Forc.* 71(3)(Mar):657–76

Brubaker R. 1992. *Citizenship and Nationhood in France and Germany.* Cambridge, MA: Harvard Univ. Press.

Brubaker R. 1996. *Nationalism Reframed: Nationhood and the National Question in the New Europe.* Cambridge, Eng.: Cambridge Univ. Press

Bryant CGA. 1993. Social self-organisation, civility and sociology: a comment on Kumar's 'Civil Society.' *Br. J. Sociol.* 44(3)(Sept): 397–401

Burawoy M, Luckacs J. 1992. *The Radiant Past.* Chicago, IL: Univ. Chicago Press

Burke P. 1992. *The Fabrication of Louis XIV.* New Haven, CT: Yale Univ. Press

Burns G. 1992. Commitments and noncommitments: the social radicalism of U. S. Catholic bishops. *Theory Soc.* 21:703–33

Burns G. 1996. Ideology, culture, and ambiguity: the revolutionary process in Iran. *Theory Soc.* 25:349–88

Calhoun C. 1991. Morality, identity, and historical explanation: Charles Taylor on the sources of the self. *Sociol. Theory* 9(2)(Fall): 232–263

Calhoun C. 1992. Culture, history, and the problem of specificity in social theory. In *Postmodernism and Social Theory: The Debate over General Theory,* ed. S Seidman, DG Wagner, pp. 244–88. Oxford: Basil Blackwell

Calhoun C. 1993a. Civil society and the public sphere. *Public Cult.* 5:267–80

Calhoun C. 1993b. 'New social movements' of the early nineteenth century. *Soc. Sci. Hist.* 17(Fall):385–427

Calhoun C. 1993c. Nationalism and ethnicity. *Annu. Rev. Sociol.* 19:211–39

Calhoun C, ed. 1993d. *Habermas and the Public Sphere.* Cambridge, MA: MIT Press

Calhoun C. 1994a. Social theory and the politics of identity. In *Social Theory and the Politics of Identity,* ed. C Calhoun, pp. 9–36. Cambridge, Eng.: Blackwell

Calhoun C. 1994b. *Neither Gods Nor Emperors: Students and the Struggle for Democracy in China.* Berkeley: Univ. Calif. Press

Calhoun C. 1995a. *Critical Social Theory: Culture, History and the Challenge of Difference.* Cambridge, Eng.: Blackwell.

Calhoun C. 1995b. *Civil society, nation-building and democracy: The importance of the public sphere to the constitutional process.* Int. Symp. on Making of the Eritrean Constitution. 1st, Asmara, Eritrea

Cannadine D. 1987. Introduction: Divine Rites of Kings. In *Rituals of Royalty: Power and Ceremonial in Traditional Societies,* ed. D Cannadine, S Price, pp. 1–19. Cambridge, Eng.: Cambridge Univ. Press

Casanova J. 1994. *Public Religions in the Modern World.* Chicago, IL: Univ. Chicago Press

Cerulo K. A. 1995. *Identity Designs: The Sights and Sounds of a Nation.* New Brunswick, NJ: Rutgers Univ. Press

Chatterjee P. 1993. *The Nation and Its Fragments: Colonial and Postcolonial Histories.* Princeton, NJ: Princeton Univ. Press

Chilton S. 1988. Defining political culture. *Western Polit. Q.* 41(3):419–45

Cohen A. 1974. *Two Dimensional Man: An Essay on the Anthropology of Power and Symbolism in Complex Society.* Berkeley: Univ. Calif. Press

Cohen JL. 1985. Strategy or identity: new theoretical paradigms and contemporary social movements. *Soc. Res.* 52:663–716

Cohen JL, Arato A. 1992. *Civil Society and Political Theory*. Cambridge, MA: MIT Press
Cohen W. 1989. Symbols of power: statues in nineteenth-century provincial France. *Comp. Stud. Soc. Hist.* 31(3):491–513
Comaroff J, Comaroff J. 1991. *Of Revelation and Revolution: Christianity, Colonialism and Consciousness in South Africa*. Chicago, IL: Univ. Chicago Press
Connell RW. 1995. *Masculinities*. Berkeley: Univ. Calif. Press
Connerton P. 1989. *How Societies Remember.* Cambridge, Eng.: Cambridge Univ. Press
Corse SM. 1995. Nations and novels: cultural politics and literary use. *Soc. Forc.* 73(4)(June):1279–1308
Corse SM. 1997. *Nationalism and Literature: The Politics of Culture in Canada and the United States*. Cambridge, Eng.: Cambridge Univ. Press
Creppell I. 1989. Democracy and literacy: the role of culture in political life. *Arch. Eur. de Sociol.* 30(1):22–47
Davis G. 1989. Culture as a variable in comparative politics: a review of some recent literature. *Politics* 24(2)(Nov):116–24
Davis NZ. 1975. The reasons of misrule. In *Society and Culture in Early Modern France*, pp. 97–123. Stanford, CA: Stanford Univ. Press
Dobbin F. 1994. *Forging Industrial Policy: The United States, Britain, and France in the Railway Age*. New York: Cambridge Univ. Press
Eckstein H. 1988. A culturalist theory of political change. *Am. Polit. Sci. Rev.* 82(3)(Sept):789–804
Edelman M. 1985. *The Symbolic Uses of Politics*. New afterword by M Edelman. Urbana and Chicago, IL: Univ. Ill. Press
Edelman M. 1988. *Constructing the Political Spectacle*. Chicago, IL: Univ. Chicago Press
Edelman M. 1995. *From Art to Politics: How Artistic Creations Shape Political Conceptions*. Chicago, IL: Univ. Chicago Press
Eder K. 1993. *The New Politics of Class: Social Movements and Cultural Dynamics in Advanced Societies*. London: Sage
Edles LD. 1995. Rethinking democratic transition: a culturalist critique and the Spanish case. *Theory Soc.* 24(3)(June):355–84
Eliasoph N. 1990. Political culture and the presentation of a political self: a study of the public sphere in the spirit of Erving Goffman. *Theory Soc.* 19:465–94
Eliasoph N. 1996. Making a fragile public: a talk-centered study of citizenship and power. *Sociol. Theory* 14(3):262–89
Ellingson S. 1995. Understanding the dialectic of discourse and collective action: public debate and rioting in antebellum Cincinnati. *Am. J. Sociol.* 101(1)(July):100–44
Emirbayer M, Goodwin J. 1994. Network analysis, culture and the problem of agency. *Am. J. Sociol.* 99:1411–54
Eyal G. 1996. The discursive origins of Israeli separatism: the case of the Arab village. *Theory Soc.* 25(3):389–429
Eyerman R, Jamison A. 1991. *Social Movements: A Cognitive Approach*. Cambridge, Eng.: Polity
Falasca-Zamponi S. 1995. The artist to power? *Theory, Culture Soc.* 13(2):39–58
Fine GA. 1996. Reputational entrepreneurs and the memory of incompetence: melting supporters, partisan warriors, and images of President Harding. *Am. J. Sociol.* 101(5)(March):1159–93
Fligstein N. 1996. Markets as politics: a political-cultural approach to market institutions. *Am. Sociol. Rev.* 61(Aug):656–73
Foucault M. 1977a. *Discipline and Punish: The Birth of the Prison*. Transl. A. Sheridan. New York: Pantheon
Foucault M. 1977b. Two lectures. In *Power/ Knowledge: Selected Interviews and Other Writings 1972–1977*, ed. C Gordon, pp. 78–108. New York: Pantheon
Freedberg D. 1989. *The Power of Images*. Chicago, IL: Univ. Chicago Press
Friedland R, Alford RR. 1991. Bringing society back in: symbols, practices, and institutional contradictions. In *The New Institutionalism in Organizational Analysis*, ed. WW Powell, PJ DiMaggio, pp. 232–63. Chicago, IL: Univ. Chicago Press
Friedlander S, ed. 1992. *Probing the Limits of Representation: Nazism and the 'Final Solution'*. Cambridge, MA: Harvard Univ. Press
Gal S. 1991. Bartok's funeral: representations of Europe in Hungarian political rhetoric. *Am. Ethnol.* 18(1991):440–58
Gambetta D. 1991. 'In the beginning was the Word...' The symbols of the Mafia. *Arch. Eur. Sociol.* 32(1):53–77
Gamson WA. 1988. Political discourse and collective action. *Int. Soc. Movements Res.* 1:219–44
Gamson WA 1991. Commitment and agency in social movements. *Sociol. Forum* 6(1):27–50
Gamson WA. 1992. *Talking Politics*. New York: Cambridge Univ. Press
Gamson WA, Modigliani A. 1989. Media discourse and public opinion on nuclear power: a constructionist approach. *Am. J. Sociol.* 95(1):1–37
Gamson WA, Stuart D. 1992. Media discourse as a symbolic contest: the bomb in political cartoons. *Sociol. Forum* 7(1):55–86
Geertz C. 1980. *Negara*. Princeton, NJ: Princeton Univ. Press
Geertz C. 1983. Centers, kings and charisma:

reflections on the symbolics of power. In *Local Knowledge: Further Essays in Interpretive Anthropology,* pp. 121–146. New York: Basic Books
Gellner E. 1987. *Culture, Identity and Politics.* Cambridge, Eng.: Cambridge Univ. Press
Gillis JR. 1994. Memory and identity: the history of a relationship. In *Commemorations: The Politics of National Identity,* ed. JR Gillis, pp. 3–24. Princeton, NJ: Princeton Univ. Press
Gilmore DD. 1993. The democratization of ritual: Andalusian carnival after Franco. *Anthropol. Q.* 66(Jan):37–47
Gitlin T. 1993. *The Twilight of Common Dreams.* New York: Metropolitan
Goldberg E. 1991. Smashing idols and the state: the Protestant ethic and Egyptian Sunni radicalism. *Comp. Stud. Soc. Hist.* 33:3–35
Golden MA. 1988. Historical memory and ideological orientations in the Italian Workers' movement. *Polit. Soc.* 16(1)(March):1–34
Goldfarb JC. 1980. *The Persistance of Freedom: The Sociological Implications of Polish Student Theater.* Boulder, CO: Westview
Goldfarb JC. 1982. *On Cultural Freedom: An Exploration of Public Life in Poland and America.* Chicago, IL: Univ. Chicago Press
Goldfarb JC. 1991. *The Cynical Society: The Culture of Politics and the Politics of Culture in American Life.* Chicago, IL: Univ. Chicago Press
Goldstone J. 1991a. Ideology, cultural frameworks, and the process of revolution . *Theory Soc.* 20(4)(Aug):405–53
Goldstone J. 1991b. *Revolution and Rebellion in the Early Modern World.* Berkeley: Univ. Calif. Press
Goodwin J. 1994. Toward a new sociology of revolutions. *Theory Soc.* 23(6)(Dec):731–69
Goodwin J. 1997. The libidinal constitution of a high-risk social movement: affectual ties and solidarity in the Huk rebellion. *Am. Sociol. Rev.* 62(1):53–69
Gorski PS. 1993. The protestant ethic revisited: disciplinary revolution and state formation in Holland and Prussia. *Am. J. Sociol.* 99(2)(Sept):265–316
Greenfeld L. 1992. *Nationalism: Five Roads to Modernity.* MA: Harvard Univ. Press
Griswold W. 1987. A methodological framework for the sociology of culture. *Sociol. Methodol.* 14:1–35
Gusfield JR. 1970. *Symbolic Crusade: Status Politics and The American Temperance Movement.* Urbana, IL: Univ. Ill. Press
Guthrie DJ. 1995. Political theater and student organizations in the 1989 Chinese movement: a multivariate analysis of Tiananmen. *Sociol. Forum* 10(3):419–54
Habermas J. 1989. *The Structural Transformation of the Public Sphere.* Transl. T Burger. Cambridge, MA: MIT Press
Halbwachs M. 1980. *Collective Memory.* New York: Harper & Row
Hall JR. 1990. Epistemology and sociohistorical inquiry. *Annu. Rev. Sociol.* 16:329–52
Handler R. 1994. Is 'Identity' a useful cross-cultural concept? In *Commemorations: The Politics of National Identity,* ed. JR Gillis, pp. 27–40. Princeton, NJ: Princeton Univ. Press
Haraszti M. 1987. *The Velvet Prison: Artists under State Socialism.* New York: Basic
Hart V, Stimson SC, eds. 1993. *Writing a National Identity: Political, Economic, and Cultural Perspectives on the Written Constitution.* Manchester, Eng.: Mancester Univ. Press
Hobsbawm E, Ranger T, eds. 1983. *The Invention of the Tradition.* Cambridge, UK: Cambridge Univ. Press
Hunt L. 1984. *Politics, Culture and Class in the French Revolution.* Berkeley: Univ. Calif. Press
Hunt L, ed. 1989. *The New Cultural History.* Berkeley: Univ. Calif. Press
Hunt L. 1992. *The Family Romance of the French Revolution.* Berkeley: Univ. Calif. Press
Hunter JD. 1991. *Culture Wars: The Struggel to Define America.* New York: Basic
Ikegami E. 1995. *The Taming of the Samurai: Honorific Individualism and the Making of Modern Japan.* Cambridge, MA: Harvard Univ. Press
Inglehart R. 1988. The renaissance of political culture. *Am. Polit. Sci. Rev.* 82(4)(Dec):1203–30
Inglehart R. 1990. *Culture Shift in Advanced Industrial Society.* Princeton, NJ: Princeton Univ. Press
Jasper JM. 1987. *Nuclear Politics: Energy and the State in the United States, Sweden, and France.* Princeton, NJ: Princeton Univ. Press
Jasper JM, Nelkin D. 1992. *The Animal Rights Crusade: The Growth of a Moral Protest.* New York: Free Press
Johnston H, Larana E, Gusfield JR. 1994. Identities, grievances and new social movements. In *New Social Movements: From Ideology to Identity,* ed. JR Gusfield, E Larana, pp. 3–35. Philadelphia, PA: Temple Univ. Press
Joppke C. 1996. Multiculturalism and immigration: a comparison of the United States, Germany and Great Britain. *Theory Soc.* 25(4):449–500
Keane J. 1988. *Civil Society and the State.* London: Verso
Kertzer DI. 1980. *Comrades and Christians: Religion and Political Struggle in Communist Italy.* Cambridge, Eng.: Cambridge Univ. Press

Kertzer DI. 1988. *Ritual, Politics, and Power.* New Haven, CT: Yale Univ. Press

Kertzer DI. 1996. *Politics And Symbols: The Italian Communist Party and the Fall of Communism.* New Haven, CT: Yale Univ. Press

Klatch, RE. 1987. *Women of the New Right.* Philadelphia, PA: Temple Univ. Press

Kumar K. 1993. Civil society: an inquiry into the usefulness of an historical term. *Br. J. Sociol.* 44(3)(Sept):375–95

Kumar K, Weintraub J. 1996. *Public and Private Thought and Practice: Perspectives on a Grand Dichotomy.* Chicago, IL: Univ. Chicago Press

Kymlicka W. 1995. *Multicultural Citizenship.* New York: Oxford Univ. Press

Laba R. 1991. *The Roots of Solidarity: A Political Sociology of Poland's Working Class Democratization.* Princeton, NJ: Princeton Univ. Press

Laitin DD. 1986. *Hegemony and Culture: Politics and Religious Change Among the Yoruba.* Chicago, IL: Univ. Chicago Press

Laitin DD. 1989. Linguistic revival: politics and culture in Catalonia. *Comp. Stud. Soc. Hist.* 31(2):297–317

Laitin DD. 1992. *Language Repertoires and State Construction in Africa.* New York: Cambridge Univ. Press

Laitin DD. 1995. The civic culture at 30. *Am. Polit. Sci. Rev.* 89(1)(March):168–73

Laitin DD, Sole C. 1994. Language and the construction of states: the case of Catalonia in Spain. *Polit. Soc.* 22(1)(March):5–29

Laitin DD, Wildavsky A. 1988. Political culture and political preferences. *Am. Polit. Sci. Rev.* 82(2)(June):589–97

Lamont M. 1989. The power-culture link in comparative perspective. *Comp. Soc. Res. Cult.* 11:131–50

Lamont, M. 1992. *Money, Morals and Manners.* Chicago, IL: Univ. Chicago Press

Lamont M, Fournier M. 1992. *Cultivating Differences: Symbolic Boundaries and the Making of Inequality.* Chicago, IL: Univ. Chicago Press

Lane C. 1981. *The Rites of Rulers: Ritual in Industrial Society—the Soviet Case.* Cambridge: Cambridge Univ. Press

Lane R. 1962. *Political Ideology.* New York: Free Press

Lichterman P. 1995. Beyond the seesaw model: public commitment in a culture of self-fulfillment. *Sociol. Theory* 13(3)(November):275–300

Lichterman P. 1996. *The Search for Political Community: American Activists Reinventing Commitment.* Cambridge: Cambridge Univ. Press

Luker K. 1984. *Abortion and the Politics of Motherhood.* Berkeley: Univ. Calif. Press

Lukes S. 1975. Political ritual and social integration. *Sociology* 9:289–308

Lustick IS. 1993. *Unsettled States, Disputed Lands: Britain and Ireland, France and Algeria, Israel and the West Bank-Gaza.* Ithaca, NY: Cornell Univ. Press

McAdam D. 1994. Culture and social movements. In *New Social Movements: From Ideology to Identity,* ed. JR Gusfield, E Larana, pp. 36–57. Philadelphia, PA: Temple Univ. Press

McAdam D, ed. 1996. *Comparative Perspective on Social Movements: Political Opportunities, Mobilizing Structures, and Cultural Framings.* New York: Cambridge Univ. Press

McDonough P. 1995. Identities, ideologies, and interests: democratization and the culture of mass politics in Spain and Eastern Europe. *J. Polit.* 57(3)(Aug):649–76

Maier CS. 1988. *The Unmasterable Past: History, Holocaust and National Identity.* Cambridge, MA: Harvard Univ. Press

Meadwell H. 1990. The politics of language: Republican values and Breton identity. *Arch. Eur. Sociol.* 31(2):263–83

Medrano JD. 1995. *Divided Nations: Class, Politics, and Nationalism in the Basque Country and Catalonia.* Ithaca, NY: Cornell Univ. Press

Melucci A. 1985. The symbolic challenge of contemporary movements. *Soc. Res.* 52(4)(Winter):789–816

Melucci A. 1996. *Challenging Codes: Collective Action in the Information Age.* Cambridge, Eng.: Cambridge Univ. Press

Merelman RM. 1991. *Partial Visions: Culture and Politics in Britian, Canada, and the United States.* Madison, WI: Univ. Wisc. Press

Mitchell T. 1990. Everyday metaphors of power. *Theory Soc.* 19:545–77

Mitchell T. 1991a. *Colonizing Egypt.* Berkeley: Univ. Calif. Press

Mitchell T. 1991b. The limits of the state: beyond statist approaches and their critics. *Am. Polit. Sci. Rev.* 85(1)(March):77–96

Moaddel M. 1992a. Shi'i political discourse and class mobilization in the tobacco movement of 1890–1892. *Sociol. Forum* 7(3):447–68

Moaddel M. 1992b. Ideology as episodic discourse: the case of the Iranian revolution. *Am. Sociol. Rev.* (June):57:353–79

Moore SF, Meyerhoff BG. 1977. Secular ritual: forms and meanings. In *Secular Ritual,* ed. SF Moore, BG Meyerhoff, pp. 3–24. Amsterdam: Van Gorcum

Morris A, Mueller CM, eds. 1992. *Frontiers in Social Movement Theory.* New Haven, CT: Yale Univ. Press

Mouffe C, Laclau E. 1985. *Hegemony and Socialist Strategy.* London: Verso

Mukerji C. 1994. The political mobilization of nature in seventeenth-century French formal gardens. *Theory Soc.* 23:651–77
Norton A. 1993. *Republic of Signs: Liberal Theory and American Popular Culture.* Chicago, IL: Univ. Chicago Press
Orloff AS. 1993. Gender and the social rights of citizenship. *Am. Sociol. Rev.* 58:303–28
Ortner SB. 1984. Theory in anthropology since the sixties. *Comp. Stud. Hist. Soc.* 26:126–66
Ozouf M. 1988. *Festivals and the French Revolution.* Transl. A Sheridan. Harvard Univ. Press
Phillips TL. 1996. Symbolic boundaries and national identity in Australia. *Br. J. Sociol.* 47(1)(March):113–34
Powell W, DiMaggio PJ, eds. 1991. *The New Institutionalism in Organizational Analysis.* Chicago, IL: Univ. Chicago Press
Putnam RD. 1993. *Making Democracy Work.* Princeton, NJ: Princeton Univ. Press
Rieder J. 1985. *Canarsie: The Jews and Italians of Brooklyn Against Liberalism.* Cambridge, MA: Harvard Univ. Press
Ringmar E. 1996. *Identity, Interests and Action: A Cultural Explanation of Sweden's Intervention in the Thirty Years War.* New York: Cambridge Univ. Press
Rothenbuhler EW. 1988. The liminal fight: mass strikes as ritual and interpretation. In *Durkheimian Sociology and Cultural Studies,* ed. JC. Alexander, pp. 66–89. Cambridge: Cambridge Univ. Press
Rousso H. 1991. *The Vichy Syndrome: Historical Memory in France since 1944.* Cambridge: Harvard
Sahlins P. 1989. *Boundaries: The Making of France and Spain in the Pyrenees.* Berkeley: Univ. Calif. Press
Schudson M. 1994. *Watergate in American Memory.* New York: Basic
Schwartz B. 1991. Social change and collective memory: the democratization of George Washington. *Am. Sociol. Rev.* 56:221–36
Schwartz B. 1996. Memory as a cultural system: Abraham Lincoln in World War II. *Am. Sociol. Rev.* 61:908–27
Scott JC. 1990. *Domination and the Arts of Resistance: Hidden Transcripts.* New Haven: Yale Univ. Press
Seligman AB. 1992. *The Idea of Civil Society.* New York: Free Press
Sewell WH. 1980. *Work and Revolution in France.* New York: Cambridge Univ. Press
Sewell WH. 1985. Ideologies and Social Revolutions: Reflections on the French Case. *J. Mod. Hist.* 57:57–85
Sewell WH. 1992. A theory of structure: duality, agency, and transformation. *Am. J. Sociol.* 98(1)(July):1–29
Sewell WH. 1994. *A Rhetoric of Bourgeois Revolution: The Abbe Sieyes and What is the Third Estate?* Durham, NC: Duke Univ. Press
Skocpol T. 1979. *States and Social Revolutions: A Comparative Analysis of France, Russia, and China.* Cambridge: Cambridge Univ. Press
Skocpol T. 1985. Cultural idioms and political ideologies in the revolutionary reconstruction of state power: a rejoinder to Sewell. *J. Mod. Hist.* 57:86–96
Skrentny, JD. 1996. *The Ironies of Affirmative Action: Politics, Culture and Justice in America.* Chicago: Univ. Chicago Press
Smith AD. 1991. *National Identity.* Reno, NV: Univ. Nev. Press
Smith AD. 1996. Culture, community and territory: the politics of ethnicity and nationalism. *Int. Affairs* 72(3):445–58
Smith HW. 1995. *German Nationalism and Religious Conflict: Culture, Ideology, Politics 1870–1914.* Princeton, NJ: Princeton Univ. Press
Smith P. 1991. Codes and conflict: toward a theory of war as ritual. *Theory Soc.* 20:103–38
Smith P. 1996. Executing executions: aesthetics, identity, and the problematic narratives of capital punishment ritual. *Theory Soc.* 25(2)(April):235–61
Snow DA, Benford RD. 1988. Ideology frame resonance and participant mobilization. *Int. Soc. Movement Res.* 1:197–217
Snow DA, Benford RD. 1992. Master frames and cycles of protest. In *Frontiers in Social Movement Theory,* ed. AD Morris, CM Mueller, pp. 133–55 New Haven, CT: Yale Univ. Press
Snow DA, Rochford EB, Worden SK, Benford RD. 1986. Frame alignment processes, micromobilization, and movement participation. *Am. Sociol. Rev.* 51(August):464–81
Somers MR. 1993. Law, community, and political culture in the transition to democracy. *Am. Sociol. Rev.* 58(5)(Oct):587–620
Somers MR. 1994. The narrative constitution of identity: a relational and network approach. *Theory Soc.* 23:605–49
Somers MR. 1995a. What's political or cultural about political culture and the public sphere? Toward an historical sociology of concept formation. *Sociol. Theory* 13(2):115–143
Somers MR. 1995b. Narrating and naturalizing civil society and citizenship theory: the place of political culture and the public sphere. *Sociol. Theory* 13(3):229–273
Somers MR, Gibson GD. 1994. Reclaiming the epistemological 'other': narrative and the social constitution of identity. In *Social Theory*

*and the Politics of Identity,* ed. C Calhoun, pp. 37–99. London: Blackwell
Soysal YN. 1994. *Limits of Citizenship.* Chicago, IL: Univ. Chicago Press
Spencer ME. 1994. Multiculturalism, 'political correctness,' and the politics of identity. *Sociol. Forum* 9(4):547–67
Spillman L. 1996. 'Neither the same nation nor different nations': constitutional conventions in the United States and Australia. *Comp. Stud. Soc. Hist.* 38(1)(Jan):149–81
Steinmetz G. 1993. *Regulating the Social: The Welfare State and Local Politics in Imperial Germany.* Princeton, NJ: Princeton Univ. Press
Steinmetz G, ed. 1997. *State/Culture.* Ithaca, NY: Cornell Univ. Press
Swidler A. 1986. Culture in action. *Am. Sociol. Rev.* 51:273–86
Szelenyi S, Szelenyi I, Poster W. 1996. Interests and symbols in post-communist political culture: the case of Hungary. *Am. Sociol. Rev.* 61(June):466–77
Tarrow S. 1992. Mentalities, political cultures, and collective action frames: constructing meanings through action. In *Frontiers in Social Movement Theory,* ed. AD Morris, CM Mueller, pp. 174–202. New Haven, CT: Yale Univ. Press
Tarrow S. 1994. *Power in Movement: Social Movements, Collective Action and Politics.* New York: Cambridge Univ. Press
Tarrow S. 1996. Making social science work across space and time: a critical reflection on Robert Putnam's *Making Democracy Work. Am. Polit. Sci. Rev.* 90(2)(June):389–97
Taylor C. 1989. *Sources of the Self.* Cambridge, MA: Harvard Univ. Press
Taylor C. 1990. Modes of civil society. *Public Culture* 3:95–118
Taylor C. 1994. The politics of recognition. In *Multiculturalism,* ed. A Gutmann, pp. 25–73. Princeton, NJ: Princeton Univ. Press
Thomas GM, Meyer JW, Ramirez F, Boli J, eds. 1987. *Institutional Structure: Constituting State, Society, and the Individual.* Beverly Hills, CA: Russell Sage
Tiryakian EA. 1988. From Durkheim to Managua: revolutions as religious revivals In *Durkheimian Sociology and Cultural Studies,* ed. JC Alexander, pp. 44–65. Cambridge, Eng.: Cambridge Univ. Press
Tucker KH. 1996. *French Revolutionary Syndicalism and the Public Sphere.* New York: Cambridge
Verdery, K. 1991. *National Ideology Under Socialism: Identity and Cultural Politics in Ceausescu's Rumania.* Berkeley: Univ. Calif. Press
Verdery, K. 1994. From parent-state to family patriarchs: gender and nation in contemporary Eastern Europe. *East Eur. Polit. Soc.* 8(2)(Spring):225–56
Von Geldern J. 1993. *Bolshevik Festivals 1917–1920.* Berkeley: Univ. Calif. Press
Wagner-Pacifici R. 1986. *The Moro Morality Play: Terrorism as Social Drama.* Chicago, IL: Univ. Chicago Press
Wagner-Pacifici R. 1994. *Discourse and Destruction: The City of Philadelphia versus MOVE.* Chicago, IL: Univ. Chicago Press
Wagner-Pacifici R, Schwartz B. 1991. The Vietnam Veterans Memorial: commemorating a difficult past. *Am. J. Sociol.* 97(2)(Sept):376–420
Walzer M. 1965. *The Revolution of the Saints: Studies in the Origins of Radical Ideology.* Cambridge, MA: Harvard Univ. Press
Williams RH, Demerath NJ. 1992. *A Bridging of Faiths: Religions and Politics in a New England City.* Princeton, NJ: Princeton Univ. Press
Wilson RW. 1992. *Compliance Ideologies: Rethinking Political Culture.* New York: Cambridge Univ. Press
Wuthnow R. 1989. *Communities of Discourse: Ideology and Social Structure in the Reformation the Enlightenment and European Socialism.* Cambridge, MA: Harvard Univ. Press
Zald MN. 1996. Culture, ideology, and strategic framing. In *Comparative Perspectives on Social Movements: Political Opportunities, Mobilizing Structures and Cultural Framings,* ed. MN Zald, D McAdam, pp. 261–74 New York: Cambridge Univ. Press
Zaret D. 1985. *The Heavenly Contract.* Chicago, IL: Univ. Chicago Press
Zaret D. 1989. Religion and the rise of liberal-democratic ideology in 17th-century England. *Am. Sociol. Rev.* 54(April):163–79
Zaret D. 1996. Petitions and the ínvention' of public opinion in the English Revolution. *Am. J. Sociol.* 101:1497–1555

*Annu. Rev. Sociol. 1997. 23:385–409*


# IDENTITY CONSTRUCTION: New Issues, New Directions

*Karen A. Cerulo*
Department of Sociology, Rutgers University, New Brunswick, New Jersey 08903-5073; e-mail: cerulo@rci.rutgers.edu

KEY WORDS: identity construction, collective identity, identification processes, social movements, virtual identity

ABSTRACT

The study of identity forms a critical cornerstone within modern sociological thought. Introduced by the works of Cooley and Mead, identity studies have evolved and grown central to current sociological discourse. Microsociological perspectives dominated work published through the 1970s. Sociologists focused primarily on the formation of the "me," exploring the ways in which interpersonal interactions mold an individual's sense of self. Recent literature constitutes an antithesis to such concerns. Many works refocus attention from the individual to the collective; others prioritize discourse over the systematic scrutiny of behavior; some researchers approach identity as a source of mobilization rather than a product of it; and the analysis of virtual identities now competes with research on identities established in the copresent world. This essay explores all such agenda as raised in key works published since 1980. I close with a look toward the future, suggesting trajectories aimed at synthesizing traditional and current concerns.

## INTRODUCTION

The study of identity forms a critical cornerstone within modern sociological thought. Introduced by the works of Cooley and Mead, identity studies have evolved and grown central to current sociological discourse. Microsociological perspectives (social psychology, symbolic interactionism), perspectives focused primarily on the individual, dominated work published through the



0360-0572/97/0815-0385$08.00

1970s.[1] Sociologists focused primarily on the formation of the "me," exploring the ways in which interpersonal interactions mold an individual's sense of self. But identity research of the past two decades proves antithetical to traditional concerns, a shift largely fueled by three important trends.

1. Social and nationalist movements of the past three decades have shifted scholarly attention to issues of group agency and political action. As a result, identity studies have been relocated to the site of the collective, with gender/sexuality, race/ethnicity, and class forming the "holy trinity" of the discursive field (Appiah & Gates 1995:1). Writings attend, in particular, to that which constitutes a collective and the political implications that result from collective definitions.

2. Intellectual concerns with agency and self-direction have re-energized the study of identification processes. At the level of the collective, scholars are examining the mechanics by which distinctions are created, maintained, and changed.

3. New communication technologies have freed interaction from the requirements of physical copresence; these technologies have expanded the array of generalized others contributing to the construction of the self. Several research foci emerge from this development: the substance of "I," "me," and the generalized other in a milieu void of place, the establishment of "communities of the mind," and the negotiation of copresent and cyberspace identities.

This essay explores each of these research agenda. Because of the literature's expanse, I limit discussion to key works published since 1980. My review includes several nonsociological works, a strategy demanded by the makeup of this field. (I revisit this issue in the conclusion.) The essay closes with a look toward the future, as I suggest trajectories aimed at synthesizing traditional and current concerns.

## THE "NATURE" OF COLLECTIVE IDENTITY

Collective identity is a concept grounded in classic sociological constructs: Durkheim's "collective conscience," Marx's "class consciousness," Weber's Verstehen, and Tonnies' Gemeinschaft. So rooted, the notion addresses the "we-ness" of a group, stressing the similarities or shared attributes around which group members coalesce. Early literature approached these attributes as "natural" or "essential" characteristics—qualities emerging from physiological traits, psychological predispositions, regional features, or the properties

[1] For recent directions in this literature, see Stryker (1992).

of structural locations. A collective's members were believed to internalize these qualities, suggesting a unified, singular social experience, a single canvas against which social actors constructed a sense of self.

Recent treatments of collective identity question the essentialism of collective attributes and images. Anti-essentialist inquiries promote the social construction of identity as a more viable basis of the collective self. Other works stress the problems inherent in collective categorization, presenting a postmodern challenge to arguments of unified group experiences.[2]

## *Social Constructionism: The Anti-Essentialist View*

In concert with theories of WI Thomas, Peter Berger, Erving Goffman, Howard Becker, and others, the social constructionist approach to identity rejects any category that sets forward essential or core features as the unique property of a collective's members. From this perspective, every collective becomes a social artifact—an entity molded, refabricated, and mobilized in accord with reigning cultural scripts and centers of power.

Social constructionism informs much of the work on gender identity. Such studies challenge essentialist dichotomies of gender and dismiss notions of gender's primordial roots. Constructionists conceptualize gender as an interactional accomplishment, an identity continually renegotiated via linguistic exchange and social performance. From this stance, researchers also explore subjective definitions of femininity and masculinity, attending to the symbols and norms that initiate and sustain either/or classifications (e.g. Bem 1993, Connell 1995, Coser 1986, C Epstein 1988, Fausto-Sterling 1985, Gailey 1987, Gerson & Peiss 1985, Hearn 1992, Kupers 1993, Margolis 1985, Marshall 1991, Probyn 1993, Richardson 1989, D Smith 1987, 1990, West & Zimmerman 1987, Wittenstrom 1995, Wittig 1981, 1986). Constructionist works often scrutinize agents of socialization, delineating their role in gender identity acquisition: the family (e.g. Caldera et al 1989, MacDonald & Parke 1986, Ross & Taylor 1989, Whiting & Edwards 1988), the schools (e.g. Best 1983, Cookson & Persell 1985, AJ Davis 1984, Eder 1995, Gilligan 1990, Hyde & Linn 1988, Hyde et al 1990, Raissiguier 1994, Sadker & Sadker 1994, Thorne 1995, Trepanier & Romatowski 1985), popular culture and media (e.g. Atkin 1982, Eilberg-Schwartz & Doniger 1995, Gaines 1991, Kalisch & Kalisch 1984, Kaplan 1983, CL Miller 1987, Sidel 1991, Signorielli 1990, Signorielli & Morgan 1988). While such studies reflect numerous intellectual traditions, all are concerned with the ways in which socialization agents organize and project the affective, cognitive, and behavioral data individuals use to form a gendered self.

An important outgrowth of gender constructionism rests with works that problematize the gender-sex link. Researchers dissect the differences in male

[2]I employ these broad labels for ease of presentation and fully acknowledge the variety of perspectives subsumed in each category.

and female biology—the body and reproductive system in particular. By questioning the meaning of biological distinctions, scholars expose the social rituals, symbols, and practices that transform such differences into social facts. In so doing, this literature demonstrates the inscription of gender on the body, simultaneously dismantling notions of gender as emergent from the body (e.g. Acker 1989, Arditi et al 1985, Bartky 1988, Bordo 1993, Corea 1985, Martin 1987, Medicine 1983, Nanda 1990, Oakley 1984, Papanek 1990, Sault 1994, Shilling 1993, Spallone & Steinberg 1987, Stacey & Thorne 1985). In highlighting the subjective nature of gender, constructionists do not deemphasize the effects of gender categories. Rather, they argue that socially defined maleness and femaleness severely constrict human behavior. Subjective definitions imprison individuals in spheres of prescribed action and expectation. Dorothy Smith writes of this effect within scholarship, dubbing it "the alienation of utterance . . . models of speaking, writing, and thinking that took (women's) powers of expression away from us even as we used them" (1990:199–201). Gender scripting attitudes, behaviors, emotions, and language, and treating these scripts as natural signals, ensures that social members both succumb to and recreate the "armor" of gender identity stereotypes.

Constructionist approaches to sexual identity complement the gender literature. Important entries include the work of Verta Taylor and Nancy Whittier (1992) on lesbian identity and lesbian social movements. Taylor & Whittier map a three-step process, itemizing (*a*) the construction of boundaries that both insulate and differentiate nonmainstream groups from the dominant sexual collective, (*b*) the emergence of shared consciousness and goals among nonmainstream sexual groups, and (*c*) processes of politicization that valorize a group's minority status. Janice Irving (1994) takes a similar approach to adolescent sexual identity. Irvine identifies nine "axes of constructed domains" (p. 11) that contribute to identity building and identity-based experience: gender relations, sexual identities, reproductive strategies and behavior, sexual language and public discourse, the role of the family, nonreproductive sexuality, the purpose of sex and the role of pleasure, knowledge and meaning of the body, and sexual violence. Irving also explores the cultural differences that can color sexual identification as it occurs in varying social locations. These works exemplify a much broader literature exploring the origins, meaning, and renegotiation of sexual communities (e.g. D'Emilio 1983, Faderman 1981, Faraday 1981, Plummer 1981, Raymond 1994, E Stein 1992b, Troiden 1988, Whatley 1994).

Race and ethnic studies represent another stronghold of constructionism. F. James Davis (1991), for example, provides a fascinating historical excursion that charts definitions of blackness in America. Davis documents the history of the "one drop rule," a vehicle for racial classification. He unpacks the rule's development and highlights its triumph over competing alternatives. Davis follows the one drop rule in action, itemizing its role in the struggle to maintain the slave system. He also contrasts the US classification experience with racial categorization in other nations. Davis concludes with thoughtful speculation regarding the one drop rule's impact on the future of US race relations—particularly in light of developing demographic shifts. In another arena, Balibar & Wallerstein (1991) view racial identity within a broad analytical landscape, considering race in conjunction with nation and class. Blending constructionist premises with the socioeconomic lenses for which the authors are renowned, Balibar & Wallerstein thoughtfully analyze both imposed racialization and self-racialization, variantly considering racial identity and collective repression, the struggle for collective autonomy, and the search for collective shelter.

Several works on racial and ethnic identity incorporate the subject's voice into their inquiries. Examples include Richard Alba's (1990) work on European-descended Americans. In keeping with constructionist premises, Alba argues that ethnic identity is no longer anchored in strongly ethnic social structures. Rather, he presents ethnicity as a symbolic entity "concerned with the symbols of ethnic cultures rather than with the cultures themselves" (1990:306). Alba argues that symbolic ethnicities are easily reshaped in response to varying situational contexts and growing social needs. His data suggest one such reconstruction—a renegotiation that unites European descendents under the broad umbrella of a European-American identity. Alba argues that this identity shift bears significant social benefits for those it encompasses; the shift provides white-Euro descendents with a larger, more comfortable base as they face a rapid influx of non-Euro, nonwhite immigrants.

Identity shifts and their implications are also central to Mary Waters's (1990) research. Like Alba, Waters brings forward a constructed, symbolic ethnicity. However, her work problematizes the relentlessness with which individuals cling to ethnicity. Waters scrutinizes ethnic identification in light of its social payoff—rewards, she argues, that prove negligible for white, Euro-descendents and potentially negative for Americans of nonwhite, non-Euro lineage. Ultimately, Waters comes to understand ethnic identity as the product of personal choice—a social category individuals actively decide to adopt or stress. Her research documents the ways in which those of mixed ancestry switch and amend their primary ethnic affiliations. In this way, Waters locates the attraction of ethnicity within a double-edged American value. Commitment to ethnic identity stems from a culturally based need for community—community lacking individual cost.

In another arena, Joann Nagel (1995) examines ethnic identity shifts as a sociopolitical phenomenon. Using US Census figures (1960–1990), Nagel documents changing patterns of Native American identification. She explains identity shifts with reference to three sociopolitical factors: changing federal

Indian policy, increased American ethnic politics, and growing American Indian political activism. Nagel argues that these factors raised Native American ethnic consciousness, and she traces the ways in which policy and politics encouraged an ethnic renewal. (Also see Blakely 1993, Conzen et al 1992, DeVos 1992, Dyson 1993, Farley 1991, Frankenberg 1993, Hout & Goldstein 1994, Ignatiev 1995, Jewell 1993, Shively 1992, Smedley 1993, Wade 1993, Williams 1990.)

Social constructionism drives a multifaceted literature on national identity. A rich collection of sociohistorical works on commemoration, narrative, and symbolization chart the ways in which actors, particularly elites, create, manipulate, or dismantle the identities of nations, citizenships, allies, and enemies (e.g. Agulhon 1981, Beaune 1991, Berezin 1997, Brubaker 1992, Corse 1996, Fine 1996, Gillis 1994, Griswold 1992, Hobsbaum 1992, Hobsbaum & Ranger 1983, Kubik 1994, Lane 1981, Schudson 1992, Schwartz 1987, 1991, Spillman 1997, Wagner-Pacifici & Schwartz 1991, Y Zerubavel 1995). In related work, several studies grapple with constructionist issues as they consider the constitution of the American self (e.g. Bellah et al 1985, 1991, Hewitt 1989, Meyer 1987). One also finds innovative elaborations of constructionism, such as Benedict Anderson's (1991) work on imagined community. Anderson approaches national identity as a sociocognitive construct—one both spatially and temporally inclusive, both enabled and shaped by broader social forces. He documents key moments of identity construction, times during which cultural (language) and social factors (capitalism, print technology) convene in a particular historical moment, effectively remaking collective images of the national self (also see Bloom 1990).

Yet, more than any arena before the identity scholar's eye, national identity work presents a multivoiced excursion. Works probing nationalism with reference to the state and world markets continue to thrive (e.g. Armstrong 1982, Gellner 1983, Giddens 1984, Tilly 1990). "New institutionalism" brings middle-range questions to bear, examining political structures and organizational principles and their influence on policy, political agenda, and ultimately collective self-definition (e.g. Birnbaum 1988, Boli 1987, 1989, Jepperson & Meyer 1991, Skocpol 1985). Newer trends include Yasemin Soysal's (1994) "postnational model," which addresses changing definitions of national membership. Soysal examines the different strategies by which Western European nations incorporate guestworkers into the national citizenry. She argues that citizen collectives increasingly are defined not by their primordial ties to a territory, but according to entitlements emerging from both a transnational discourse and a set of structures celebrating human rights (also see Shapiro & Alker 1995).

Anthony D Smith (1991) poses perhaps the greatest challenge to constructionism. Smith adopts a middle-ground approach to national identity, linking social constructionism to more essentialist views. He defines national identity as a product of both "natural" continuity and conscious manipulation. Natural continuity emerges from pre-existing ethnic identity and community; conscious manipulation is achieved via commemoration, ideology, and symbolism. Smith compliments this duality with a social psychological dimension, citing a "need for community" as integral to identity work. In Smith's view, this tri-part combination distinguishes national identity, making it the most fundamental and inclusive of collective identities. (Complimentary positions include Connor 1990, Greenfield 1992, Hutchinson 1987. Calhoun 1993 and Hutchinson & Smith 1994 offer extensive literature reviews.)

### *Postmodernism: Deconstructing Categories*

While supporting the antiessentialism that drives constructionist inquiries on identity, postmodernists cite serious flaws in the school's approach. Some find constructionism's agenda insufficient, suggesting that it simply catalogues the identity construction process. Further, many contend that the constructionist approach implies identity categories built through interactive effort. Such a stance underemphasizes the role of power in the classification process (e.g. Connell 1987, Gilman 1985), mistakenly suggesting "a multidirectional flow of influence and agency" (Calhoun 1995:199). These weaknesses leave postmodern identity theorists skeptical of social constructionism's trajectory, fearing that the paradigm ultimately approximates the very essentialism it fights against. Diane Fuss elaborates in evaluating the constructionist approach to gender: "specifying more precisely these subcategories of 'woman' does not necessarily preclude essentialism. 'French bourgeois woman' or 'Anglo-American lesbian,' while crucially emphasizing in their very specificity that 'woman' is by no means a monolithic category, nonetheless reinscribe an essentialist logic at the very level of historicism" (Fuss 1989:20).

In an effort to broaden the social constructionist agenda, postmodernists examine the "real, present day political and other reasons why essentialist identities continue to be invoked and often deeply felt" (Calhoun 1995:199). Further, in the study of identity, they view the variation within identity categories—i.e. women, African-Americans, working class—as important as the variation between identity categories. Finally, postmodernists advocate a shift in analytic focus, deemphasizing observation and deduction and elevating concerns with public discourse. In the spirit of Jean Baudrillard, Jacques Derrida, Michel Foucault, and Jean-Francois Lyotard, the postmodern-identity scholar deconstructs established identity categories and their accompanying rhetoric in an effort to explore the full range of "being." Works in this tradition call into question models that equate discourse with truth; they expose the ways in which discourse objectified as truth both forms and sustains collective definitions, social arrangements, and hierarchies of power.

For students of identity, postmodern works on gender and sexuality prove richest. Judith Butler (1990), Patricia Hill Collins (1991), Jane Flax (1990),

Marjorie Garber (1992), Donna Haraway (1991), bell hooks (1984), and Trinh T Minh-Ha (1989) reconsider gender identity, giving voice to women of color, those of various social classes, and lesbian and bisexual women. They expose the dangers in approaching gender collectives as homogeneous entities and urge careful consideration of the complex, often contradictory, nature of collective existence. In contrast to the social constructionist, postmodern gender theorists challenge the dualistic, oppositional nature by which gender is traditionally framed. Patricia Hill Collins (1991), for example, notes that elements such as race and social class produce multiple variations of "women" and "men," distinctions that many societies use to build complex hierarchical stratification systems. The existence of these multiple categories alerts us to the flaws of binary gender conceptualizations, focusing us instead on the ways in which multiple identity affiliations qualitatively change the nature of human experience (see also Agger 1993, Baca Zinn & Thornton Dill 1994, Fraser 1989, Leps 1992, Nicholson 1990, Nicholson & Seidman 1995, Raissiguier 1994, Riley 1988).

Core postmodern works on sexual identity follow a similar thrust, problematizing sexual categories and contesting sexual hierarchies (Butler 1993, Connell 1987, Sedgwick 1990, Seidman 1992). In contrast to prior treatments of sexual identity (i.e. studies exploring the construction of a particular sexual identity or community—e.g. homosexual, lesbian, etc), current "queer theories" advocate an inclusive approach. They suggest, first, simultaneous considerations of heterosexual and homosexual identity construction, and second, serious focus on identities excluded by the hetero/homo duality—e.g. bisexual or transgender identities (also see De Lauretis 1984, S. Epstein 1992, Stein 1992, Warner 1991). These basic tenets carry a provocative methodology. Queer theorists advocate a new "reading" of materials using an "inside/outside" opposition. In such an analysis, the reader must assume the connotation of homosexuality in the denotation of heterosexuality; the reader must reinterpret a product in terms of a homosexual presence. Further, the explication of a cultural product's hetero/homo opposition must direct readers to all excluded forms of sexuality as well. Any work under analysis must be read with an eye for that which it itemizes and thus simultaneously implies. When queer theorists read television sitcom *Laverne and Shirley* (Doty 1993) or Alfred Hitchcock's film *Rope* (DA Miller 1991) from a homosexual "subject-position," they contest current hierarchical structures of sexuality. Constructing alternative readings of a work's sexual implications deconstructs the taken-for-grantedness of the dominant sexual model. Reminiscent of Garfinkel's approach to identifying "invisible" normative structures, queer theory's subject-positioned readings jolt the very process of classification. (Agger 1991 and Fuchs & Ward 1994 offer recent, comprehensive reviews of postmodernism.)

Despite their differences, the issues raised by social constructionists and postmodernists alike direct scholarly attention to a collective's struggle to self-name, self-characterize, and claim social prerogative. Such concerns underscore the politics of identity.

## *Identity Politics and Collective Mobilization*

Collective identity and the political movements it spurs constitute an important concern for identity scholars. Issues of politics are raised in previously cited works on gender/sexuality and race. Identity politics also provides the focus for many works on the formation and experiencing of social class (e.g. Blumin 1989, Burawoy 1985, Carter 1985, Davidoff & Hall 1987, Dudley 1994, Eichar 1989, Farrell 1993, Form 1985, 1995, Gallie 1983, Gans 1995, Garcia 1991, Halle 1984, 1993, Katz 1993, Katznelson & Weir 1985, Katznelson & Zolberg 1986, McNall et al 1991, Vanneman & Cannon 1987, Wright 1989). However, concerns with identity politics move scholars beyond this "holy trinity" of the discursive field. Animal protectionists, environmentalists, the health conscious, the homeless, members of the 1960s student counterculture—in current literature, these groups too exemplify collectives moved by issues of collective definition, signification, and power.

When moved by identity, collectives take on distinct properties. Spurred not by ideology or resource mobilization, identity-based movements act rather than react; they fight to expand freedom, not to achieve it; they mobilize for choice rather than emancipation. Alberto Melucci, central in this area, notes:

> The freedom to have which characterized ... industrial society has been replaced by the freedom to be. The right to property has been, and remains, the basis of both industrial capitalism and its competitor model, 'real socialism'. In post-material society, there emerges a further type of right, the right to existence, or rather, to a more meaningful existence (1989:177–78; also see Calhoun 1991a:51, Giddens 1991:207–17).

In this way, identity politics creates "new social movements," collective initiatives that are self-reflexive and sharply focused on the expressive actions of collective members (Melucci 1989:60, 1997).

Identity politics and new social movements suggest a special form of agency—a self-conscious "collective agency." Identities emerge and movements ensue because collectives consciously coordinate action; group members consciously develop offenses and defenses, consciously insulate, differentiate, and mark, cooperate and compete, persuade and coerce. In such a context, agency encompasses more than the control and transformation of one's social environment. Rather, borrowing from Charles Taylor's discussion of agency and the self (1985:287), I suggest that collective agency includes a conscious sense of group as agent. Further, collective agency is enacted in a moral space. A collective pursues the freedom to be because that which frames the collective's identity defines their existence as right and good (Taylor 1989).

In connection with issues of identity politics and collective agency, David Snow, Robert Benford, William Gamson, Doug McAdam, and others address the framing and schematization of identity as it occurs within social movements. Studies in this area delineate the frame alignment processes that bring both group focus and shared identity to particular collectives at specific historical moments. Further, these works itemize the ways in which resulting collective identities then direct movement participants by defining the parameters and appropriate arenas of collective action. Such analyses remain fully mindful of the ways in which movement participants' perceptions of history, social structures, and cultural arrangements constrain or enhance the interpretive processes. This work's appeal rests in its multifaceted theoretical base. By merging sociocognitive construction processes with concerns for structural and organization factors, this literature creates an exciting conceptual bridge, linking micro and macro analyses, linking cultural and social concerns. Such works provide a model that forces the simultaneous consideration of thought, articulation, and action (see e.g. Benford 1993, Benford & Hunt 1992, Cohen 1985, Fantasia 1988, Gamson 1992, Gamson et al 1982, Gerhards & Rucht 1992, Hunt et al 1994, Jasper & Nelkin 1992, Johnston 1991, Johnston et al 1994, Larana et al 1994, Lichterman 1996, McAdam 1982, 1988, 1994, Morris & Muellar 1992, Snow et al 1986, Snow & Benford 1992, Tarrow 1992, Taylor & Whittier 1992).

Recent literature raises concerns regarding the long-term social consequences of identity politics. Michael J Piore (1995), for example, writes of identity-based movements as isolated, cohesive "communities of meaning." Because such groups are narrowly focused and formed relative to distinctions, Piore argues that they find themselves incapable of cross-boundary exchange. Further, he believes such groups often remain unaware of the economic conditions that may constrain their collective goals. Based on these observations, Piore locates identity movements in America's ideological roots of individualism. He suggests that current socioeconomic conditions beckon a change in this stance. Using cognitive theories derived from sociology and anthropology, Piore presents a five-step plan aimed at replacing identity politics with a shared commitment to a unified national structure.

## IDENTIFICATION PROCESSES

Attention to collectives and the establishment of their identities has re-energized scholarly interests in the identification process itself. A growing literature explores the mechanics by which collectives create distinctions, establish hierarchies, and renegotiate rules of inclusion. Such works are closely linked to important knowledge theories, including Bourdieu's theories of distinction, Derrida's focus on difference, Foucault's genealogy of epistomes, the semiotic models of Saussure and Pierce, and Zerubavel's work on sociomental classification. This section elaborates on a variety of identification processes currently under study.

Michele Lamont (1992) documents the role of *symbolic boundaries* in the construction of valued identities. Using rich data drawn from interviews with upper-middleclass men in France and the United States, Lamont specifies the conditions under which moral, socioeconomic, and cultural boundaries successfully create objective conditions of socioeconomic inequality. In contrast to Bourdieu, Lamont maintains a tri-part focus, demonstrating that the importance of boundary types varies across space and time. Her work also emphasizes boundary strength; her findings indicate that only those boundaries firmly grounded in widely shared meaning prove sufficiently strong to generate hierarchy and confer relative value to collective identities (Lamont 1995, 1997; also see Cohen 1986, Lamont & Fournier 1992, Sahlins 1989). In related work, Jill Quadagno & Catherine Forbes (1995) use cultural and social lenses to explore identification and distinction among US Job Corps participants. The authors examine the workings of both symbolic boundaries and structural barriers as these factors contribute to gender reproduction and gender inequality. Concerns with symbolic boundaries characterize recent inquiries in life course research as well. Works by Gaines (1991), Jeffreys (1989), Modell (1989), Postman (1982), Waksler (1991), Winn (1983), and Zelizer (1985) help to refocus sociologists on the cultural contexts within which age categories are constructed, age identities are built, and age transitions occur.

Margaret Somers (1994) and Harrison White (1992) approach issues of identification by specifying the *cultural repertoires* or systems of meaning that characterize various symbolic communities. These authors are especially concerned with the ways in which social context and social location enable the invoking of such repertoires. In this regard, Paul DiMaggio's (1982, 1987, 1992) landmark research on the arts also proves important. DiMaggio demonstrates the ways in which art acquisition and classification solidify status categories and distinguish the elite from the ordinary.

In a different arena, Jane Bachnik & Charles Quinn (1994) focus on *indexicality* and its role in the construction of Japanese identity. Building on the Japanese concepts "uchi" (inside) and "soto" (outside), various authors explore the ways in which these boundary distinctions direct collective orientation and pattern behavior. In probing identity, all authors consider both linguistic communication and social practice through their linkage to context. Elsewhere, Eviatar Zerubavel (1997a) offers a special edition that brings his concepts of *lumping and splitting* to life. Authors chart these complementary sociomental processes as they explore identification and distinction in monetary exchange, fetal classification, the construction of sexual identities, and other interesting areas (also see E Zerubavel 1991, 1997b). Among social psychologists, John C Turner presents *depersonalization* as a process enabling collective identities. His work maps the ways in which depersonalization permits social stereotyping, group cohesiveness, ethnocentrism, cooperation and altruism, emotional contagion and empathy, collective action, and other processes (Turner et al 1987, 1994). Finally, James Aho (1994) invokes Berger & Luckman's five steps of *reification* to elaborate both the construction and deconstruction of political enemies. Aho situates his analysis in a variety of recent incidents, including the Ruby Ridge affair, the dissolution of the Soviet Union, and a case study of a KKK defection. Using media reports, government documents, and interviews, Aho carefully explores the development of collective moral righteousness. He notes the processes by which such sentiments legitimate the destruction of the "other." Grappling with the question "Can one struggle effectively against evil without become tainted by it?", Aho builds an interesting case for an enemy that is both "them" and "us."

The study of objects also proves key to recent research on identification. Several works note the ways in which individuals and groups use art objects (Martorella 1989), commodities and commodity signs (Appadurai 1986, Goldman 1992, Hennion & Meadel 1993, O'Barr 1994), or clothing (Rubenstein 1995) to articulate and project identities. Complimenting this agenda, Dauber's (1992) work on Pueblo pottery, Mukerji's (1994, 1997) studies of formal French gardens, and Zukin's (1991) exploration of city structures use objects to better understand the political, cultural, social, and economic contexts in which the objects are produced. Finally, Nippert-Eng (1996) and Silver (1996) offer especially interesting excursions on the role of personal possessions in bridging identity transitions.

Several works, anchored in the study of discourse and symbolization, provide a multitiered analysis of collective identification and the ideologies that support it. In contrast to deterministic theories, such studies approach identification as a process that unfolds in relation to economic, historical, and political contexts. As such, multitiered investigations view identification at critical junctures in a collective's history, including periods of identity production, its institutionalization, and periods of identity interpretation. Further, these works cast identity discourse and symbols as mediators of structure and action. Robert Wuthnow's (1989) work on communities of discourse exemplifies the approach. Wuthnow explores the general cultural, political, and economic conditions that enabled three specific ideologies: the Protestant Reformation, the Enlightenment, and Marxist socialism. After charting the historical sources of these agendas, Wuthnow traces the modes by which each ideology was institutionalized, taking readers through the schools, religious and scientific groups, and the governments and media that modeled and disseminated each perspective. Finally, Wuthnow examines audience reception and reaction, analyzing the collective application and experience of the three ideologies through the decades. Wuthnow's rich inquiry demonstrates the complex chain by which movement ideologies and resulting identities are both born and sustained.

Following Wuthnow's example, Valentine Moghadam (1994) adopts the multitiered approach, analyzing fundamentalist discourse and its relationship to gender and national identities. Other multitiered works include Michele Dillon's (1993, 1996) studies of discourse on divorce and abortion. Her works explore the ways in which political climate and the institutional status of discourse producers relates to both the nature and the effect of discursive strategies. In a similar vein, David Campbell (1992) examines the American "discourse of danger," exploring the ways in which such a discourse shapes visions of the American "us," the enemy "them," and ultimately, the form of American foreign policy. Cerulo (1995), too, applies a multitiered perspective in her study of national identity symbolization. Probing the various contexts of anthem and flag adoption, she identifies a set of social structural variables that appear to delimit general rules of symbolic expression. Cerulo also explores the institutionalization of identity symbols, suggesting a new theoretical model for predicting symbol change. Finally, her inquiries on symbol reception and interpretation elucidate faulty identity symbolization, thus specifying the conditions under which symbols can fail to capture the fervency of those they portray.

## TECHNOLOGY AND IDENTITY

In the present environment, one cannot consider identity without reference to new communication technologies (NCTs). NCTs have changed the backdrop against which identity is constructed; they have reframed the generalized others and the "generalized elsewheres" (Meyrowitz 1989) from which the self takes its cues.

Joshua Meyrowitz (1985, 1989, 1997) was among the first to fully explore the NCT/identity link. His works examine the ways in which electronic media reorganize the sites of social interaction. According to Meyrowitz, NCTs weaken or sever the connections between physical and social "place." In this way, NCTs locate the self in new hybrid arenas of action; they mesh public and private, beckon new types of performances, and form new collective configurations:

> Television has fostered the rise of hundreds of "minorities"—people who in perceiving a wider world, begin to see themselves as unfairly isolated in some pocket of it. Television has empowered the disabled and the disenfranchised by giving them access to social information

> in spite of their physical isolation. Television has given women an outside view of their incarceration in the home. Television has weakened visible authorities by destroying the distance and mystery that once enhanced their aura and prestige. And television has been able to do this without requiring the disabled to leave their wheelchairs, without asking the housewife to stop cooking dinner, and without demanding that the average citizen leave his or her easy chair (1986:309).

According to Meyrowitz, the places enabled by NCTs reconfigure the boundaries that distinguish collectives. Thus at the present social moment, the differences dividing children from adults may be less stark than those that distinguish the computer literate from the nonliterate. The line that separates home from work may now pale in comparison to online/offline borders.

David Altheide (1995) poses complementary positions in his work on NCTs and the self. He argues that NCTs enable new communication formats—new modes of selecting, organizing, and presenting information. In turn, these new formats reshape social activity; they modify or dismantle current practices, and spur or shape new ones. In this way, NCTs create new environments for self-development and identification; they present new opportunities for collective affiliation and mobilization. Altheide's writings on keyboard technology illustrate these ideas. In considering human experience with telephones, ATMs, computers, video games, calculators, and television controls, the author casts the keyboard as a new door to interaction. He argues that keyboard technology initiates a large majority of modern exchange. But while keyboards may transport us to places not easily accessed in the past, Altheide argues that the technology limits and directs the form and substance of the social interaction it enables. For example, keyboard technology reduces the distance between children and adults, often promoting a type of reverse socialization. Similarly, keyboard technology homogenizes work and play sites; keyboards merge adult work and play worlds, link adult workspaces and children's play spaces, and reconfigure children's play via the world of adult tools (1995: chaps. 2, 3). Beyond specific communication tools, Altheide also explores the intersection of communication, power, and social control. He considers the ways in which technology and its resulting communication formats provide some with the power to define a social situation while leaving others vulnerable to the reality of crafted images. In these and similar discussions, Altheide outlines the ways in which communication formats can "block" the social stage, scripting emergent action even in realms thought to possess an internal logic.

In the spirit of Meyrowitz and Altheide, many explore the impact of NCTs on community formation and resulting collective identity. Beniger (1987) initiated this agenda, suggesting specific ways in which media-generated communities provide a "pseudo-gemeinschaft" experience. Subsequent works describe technologically generated communities as more tangible and real. Several authors document the processes by which NCT's build "we-ness," demonstrating the concrete effects of techno-links and charting emergent cultures of reference that can unify once disparate social actors (Cerulo et al 1992, Cerulo & Ruane 1997, Dayan 1992, Liebes 1990, Purcell 1997, Steuer 1992, Tichi 1991). But others are less enthusiastic regarding the impact of NCTs on community and identity. Schlesinger (1993), for example, notes both the potential and the surprising failure of electronic media in constructing a unified European identity among the nations that comprise the Euro-community (also see Morley & Robins 1995). Similarly, Fisher's (1992) sociohistorical research on the telephone suggests that community structure can be remarkably resilient to technological change. Overall, Fisher (1997) remains skeptical of NCT's ability to reconfigure social bonds (also see Postman 1992). These contradictory positions have led some to initiate multidimensional models, models designed to address and distinguish varying forms of NCT-generated bonds (see Calhoun 1991b, Cerulo 1997).

Related works magnify identification processes within specific NCT domains. Sherry Turkle (1995), for example, explores online communities and their impact on personal identity construction. She follows members of a virtual community as they interact in "multi-user domains" (MUDS). Testimony of MUD members, along with Turkle's keen insights, provide a unique picture detailing the building and experiencing of online persona. Further, Turkle documents the ways in which individuals negotiate online identities relative to other facets of the self. By probing the balance between "virtual" selves and "real" selves, Turkle's work forces us to question any perspective that places virtual experience second to the concrete. In another arena, Byron Reeves & Clifford Nass (1996) approach communication media as objects relevant to identity-building interactions. In essence, the authors find that media objects become a viable "other" in the building of self, and they outline the ways in which human-to-machine relationships mirror purely human relationships. Reeves & Nass discover, for instance, that people treat computers with female voices differently than those with male voices; people are polite to computers even though they don't need to be; the size and movement of TV screen images affects physical responses and perceptions of personal bodyspace in ways identical to real-life motion. These patterns hold implications for identity studies and beyond. Indeed, relevant to communication efficacy, the authors suggest that the human brain has not sufficiently evolved relative to technology's rapid advancement. Reeves & Nass suggest ways in which this knowledge can improve future technological products.

## CONCLUSION

The literature here reviewed constitutes an antithesis to traditional identity studies, an antithesis built upon several research fronts. The works cited here refocus scholarly attentions from the individual to the collective. These works often prioritize discourse over the systematic scrutiny of behavior. Many studies approach identity as a source of mobilization rather than a product of it. Finally, the analysis of virtual identities now competes with research on identities established in the copresent world. In considering the old and the new of identity, one finds a field ripe for synthesis. This section suggests potential avenues for synthesis, noting works that exemplify such efforts. The works chosen here are not "ideal types," but rather suggestive models—models that illustrate what can be gained when the future is mined from careful reflection on past and present.

Some have achieved a productive synthesis of identity work through the reconciliation of theory. In recent work on gender identity, for example, Judith Lorber (1994) synthesizes constructionist and postmodern concerns of the day with issues raised by sex role theorists and Marxist feminists of past decades. Her efforts result in an interesting theory that frames gender as a social institution—a free-standing entity that establishes patterns of expectations, orders social processes, and drives social organizations. In another arena, Norbert Wiley (1995) merges Peircian and Meadian paradigms to form a neo-pragmatist view of the self—the self as a three-dimensional dialogue between "I," "you," and "me." Wiley then works with pragmatist notions of reflexivity and Durkheimian solidarity concepts to create a model of "a semiotic self," a sui generis self resistant to social determination. In a historical era spurred by identity politics, Wiley argues that conceptions of a sui generis self may prove vital to the defense of democratic principles.

Others attend to macro-micro linkages in promoting the cause of synthesis.[3] Indeed, several recent theoretical advances relevant to identity studies rest on successful macro-micro linkages: Bourdieu's work on habitus, Giddens's structuration theory, or Habermas's theories of communicative action. Further, a number of the works heretofore discussed have successfully established the links of which I speak. Research on social movements or several of the multitiered identity projects represent prime illustrations. Other macro-micro initiatives are underway. For example, determined to eradicate the micro-macro divide, Deidre Boden (1994) innovatively combines elements of each arena, thus building a unique analytic approach to organizational identity, form, and function. Boden maps conversational exchanges across varied organizational settings, using these data to configure the structure of talk in organizations. She then examines talk structures as vehicles that constitute organizations, analyzing organizations as they emerge within daily interaction. Boden argues that "the ways in which organizational actors realize both the

[3]Within sociology at large many advocate this path (Collins 1986, Huber 1991, Ritzer 1990), in particular, with reference to issues addressing the intersection of the social and the cultural (Schudson 1989, Sewell 1992, Swidler 1986).

constraints and opportunities in their working environments is critical to what actually constitutes an 'environment' " (p. 32). For Boden, the micro-processes of talk become the macro-structure of the organization. (Snow 1987 offers a similarly interesting project on talk and identity.) In another arena, Cerulo (1997b) pursues macro-micro linkages in analyzing narratives of violence. She explores the institutionalization of storytelling formats in this area and documents the impact such formats can have on audience evaluations of violent acts. In essence, her study elucidates the conditions under which macro-social norms of communication can direct complex micro-patterns of cognition and identification. Among social psychologists, Peggy Thoits & Lauren Virshup (1997) propose a macro-micro merger that hinges on social theories of the mind. Specifically, they suggest ways in which self-schema theory might unify inquiries on individual and collective identity.

In the cause of synthesis, scholars of collective identity also might revisit traditional micro-level studies in the area. Much common ground exists between traditional and new approaches to the topic. For example, I noted earlier that collective identity scholars are currently exploring the ways in which multiple identity affiliations qualitatively change the nature of human experience. During the 1980s, social psychologists' addressed similar themes, focusing on multiple roles, their resulting identities, and the impact of both on human experience (see e.g. Burke & Franzoi 1988, Stryker 1980, Thoits 1986). To be sure, collective and micro-level inquiries pursue different elements of "human experience." Yet, knowledge of the cognitive processes, social practices, and symbolic tools with which identity is constructed, enacted, and projected is integral to each school of thought. Knowing this, focused efforts to translate certain findings from the social psychological realm to the macro level could hold rich rewards for collective identity studies.

At the broadest level, an important site of synthesis rests in the careful blending of intellectual perspectives. Within the past two decades, the humanist or cultural studies approach to identity has dominated the field. To be sure, sociologists of identity cannot afford to ignore these works, for they provide a rich and thorough treatment of the symbols, rituals, and world views that constitute identity. At the same time, the sociologist must consider this literature with some care. At present, the cultural studies position appears somewhat trapped in a singular conclusion that locates the constructed nature of culture in the sole service of power. Further, such works frequently frame social action as a process that is fully culturally constituted. In tapping identity materials garnered from the cultural studies approach, sociologists must diligently maintain the critical analytic distinction between the social and the cultural (see Schudson 1997). Via careful consideration of actors, collectives, and broader social institutions, via thoughtful attention to lived experience and the cultural products and rituals associated with such experience, the sociology of identity can fully elucidate the intricate links between the social and cultural domains.

## ACKNOWLEDGMENTS

Thanks to Paul DiMaggio and Michele Lamont for helpful comments on an earlier version of this manuscript.



*Literature Cited*

Acker J. 1989. Making gender visible. In *Feminism and Sociological Theory,* ed. RA Wallace, pp. 65–81. Newbury Park, CA: Sage

Agger B. 1991. Critical theory, poststructuralism and postmodernism: their sociological relevance. *Annu. Rev. Sociol.* 17:105–31

Agger B. 1993. *Gender, Culture and Power: Toward a Feminist Postmodern Critical Theory.* Greenwich, CT: Praeger

Agulhon M. 1981. *Marianne Into Battle: Republican Imagery and Symbolism in France, 1789–1880.* Cambridge, Engl: Cambridge Univ. Press

Aho JA. 1994. *This Thing of Darkness: A Sociology of the Enemy.* Seattle: Univ. Wash. Press

Alba RD. 1990. *Ethnic Identity: The Transformation of White America.* New Haven, CT: Yale Univ. Press

Altheide DL. 1995. *An Ecology of Communication: Cultural Formats of Control.* Hawthorne: Aldine de Gruyter

Anderson B. 1991. *Imagined Communities.* London: Verso. 2nd ed.

Appadurai A. 1986. *The Social Life of Things: Commodities in Cultural Perspective.* Cambridge, Engl: Cambridge Univ. Press

Appiah KA, Gates HL Jr. 1995. Editors introduction: multiplying identities. In *Identities,* ed. KA Appiah, HL Gates Jr, pp. 1–6. Chicago, IL: Univ. Chicago Press

Arditi R, Klein RD, Minden S. 1985. *Test Tube Women.* Boston: Pandora

Armstrong JA. 1982. *Nations Before Nationalism.* Chapel Hill: Univ. N. Carolina Press

Atkin C. 1982. Changing male and female roles. In *TV and Teens: Experts Look At The Issues,* ed. M Schwartz, pp. 66–70. Reading: Addison-Wesley

Bachnik J, Quinn CJ Jr. 1994. *Situated Memory.* Princeton, NJ: Princeton Univ. Press

Balibar E, Wallerstein I. 1991. *Race, Nation, and Class: Ambiguous Identities.* London: Verso

Bartky S. 1988. Foucault, feminism, and patriarchal power. In *Feminism and Foucault: Reflections On Resistance,* ed. I Diamond, L Quinby, pp. 61–86. Boston, MA: Northeastern Univ. Press

Beaune C. 1991. *The Birth of an Ideology: Myths and Symbols of Nation in Late-Medieval France.* Transl. SR Huston. Berkeley: Univ. Calif. Press

Bellah RN. 1991. *The Good Society.* New York: Knopf

Bellah RN, Madsen R, Sullivan WM, Swidler A, Tipton SM. 1985. *Habits of the Heart.* New York: Harper & Row

Bem SL. 1993. *The Lenses of Gender: Transforming the Debate on Sexual Inequality.* New Haven, CT: Yale Univ. Press

Benford RD. 1993. You could be the hundredth monkey: collective action frames and vocabularies of motive within the nuclear disarmament movement. *Sociol. Q.* 34(2):195–216

Benford RD, Hunt SA. 1992. Dramaturgy and social movements: the social construction and communication of power. *Sociol. Inq.* 62(1):36–55

Beniger JR. 1987. The personalization of mass media and the growth of pseudo-community. *Commun. Res.* 14(3):352–71

Berezin M. 1997. *Communities of Feeling: Culture, Politics, and Identity in Fascist Italy.* Ithaca, NY: Cornell Univ. Press. In press

Best R. 1983. *We've All Got Scars: What Boys and Girls Learn in Elementary School.* Bloomington: Indiana Univ. Press

Birnbaum P. 1988. *States and Collective Action: The European Experience.* Cambridge, Engl: Cambridge Univ. Press

Blakely A. 1993. *Blacks In The Dutch World:*

*The Evolution Of Racial Imagery In Modern Society.* Bloomington: Indiana Univ. Press
Bloom W. 1990. *Personal Identity, National Identity and International Relations.* Cambridge, Engl: Cambridge Univ. Press
Blumin SM. 1989. *The Emergence of the Middle Class: Social Experience in the American City, 1760–1900.* Cambridge, Engl: Cambridge Univ. Press
Boden D. 1994. *The Business of Talk: Organizations in Action.* Cambridge, Engl: Polity Press
Boli J. 1987. World polity sources of expanding state authority and organization, 1870–1970. In *Institutional Structure: Constituting State, Society, and the Individual,* ed. GM Thomas, JW Meyer, FO Ramirez, J Boli, pp. 71–91. Newbury Park, CA: Sage
Boli J. 1989. *New Citizens for a New Society: The Institutional Origins of Mass Schooling in Sweden.* New York: Pergamon
Bordo S. 1993. *Unbearable Weight: Feminism, Western Culture, and the Body.* Berkeley: Univ. Calif. Press
Brubaker R. 1992. *Citizenship and Nationhood in France and Germany.* New York: Cambridge Univ. Press
Burawoy M. 1985. *The Politics of Production.* London: Verso
Burke P, Franzoi SL. 1988. Studying situations and identities: using experiential sampling methodology. *Am. Sociol. Rev.* 53(4):559–68
Butler J. 1990. *Gender Trouble: Feminism and the Subversion of Identity.* New York: Routledge
Butler J. 1993. *Bodies That Matter: On the Discursive Limits of "Sex".* New York: Routledge
Caldera YM, Aletha CH, O'Brien M. 1989. Social interactions and play patterns of parents and toddlers with feminine, masculine, and neutral toys. *Child Dev.* 60(1):70–76
Calhoun C. 1991a. The problem of identity in collective action. In *Macro-Micro Linkages in Sociology,* ed. J Huber, pp. 51–75. Newbury Park, CA: Sage
Calhoun C. 1991b. Indirect relationships and imagined communities: large-scale social integration and the transformation of everyday life. In *Social Theory for a Changing Society,* ed. P Bourdieu, JS Coleman, pp. 95–121. New York: Russell Sage Found.
Calhoun C. 1993. Nationalism and identity. *Annu. Rev. Sociol.* 19:211–39
Calhoun C. 1995. *Critical Social Theory: Culture, History, and the Challenge of Difference.* Oxford, UK: Blackwell
Campbell D. 1992. *Writing Security.* Minneapolis: Univ. Minn. Press
Carter R. 1985. *Capitalism, Class Conflict, and the New Middle Class.* London: Routledge
Cerulo KA. 1995. *Identity Designs: the Sights and Sounds of a Nation.* New Brunswick, NJ: Rutgers Univ. Press
Cerulo KA. 1997a. Re-framing sociological concepts for a brave new (virtual?) world. *Sociol. Inq.* 67(1):48–58
Cerulo KA. 1997b. *Deciphering Violence: The Cognitive Order of Right And Wrong.* New York: Routledge. In press
Cerulo KA, Ruane JM. 1997. Death comes alive: technology and the reconception of death. *Sci. Cult.*
Cerulo KA, Ruane JM, Chayko M. 1992. Technological ties that bind: media generated primary groups. *Commun. Res.* 19(1):109–29
Cohen AP. 1986. *Symbolizing Boundaries: Identity and Diversity in British Cultures.* Manchester:
Cohen J. 1985. Strategy or identity: new theoretical paradigms and contemporary social movements. *Soc. Res.* 52(4):663–716
Collins PH. 1991. *Black Feminist Thought.* New York: Routledge
Collins R. 1986. Is 1980s sociology in the doldrums? *Am. J. Soc.* 86(5):1336–55
Connell RW. 1987. *Gender and Power: Society, the Person, and Gender Politics.* Cambridge: Polity Press
Connell RW. 1995. *Masculinities.* Berkeley: Univ. Calif. Press
Connor W. 1990. When is a nation? *Ethn. Racial Stud.* 13(1):92–100
Conzen KN, Gerber DA, Morawska E, Pozetta GE, Vecoli RJ. 1992. The invention of ethnicity: a perspective from the USA. *J. Am. Ethn. Hist.* 12(1):3–41
Cookson PW Jr, Persell CH. 1985. *Preparing for Power: America's Elite Boarding Schools.* New York: Basic Books
Corea G. 1985. *The Mother Machine.* New York: Harper & Row
Corse S. 1996. *Nationalism and Literature: The Politics of Culture in Canada and the United States.* New York: Cambridge Univ. Press
Coser RL. 1986. Cognitive structure and the use of social space. *Sociol. Forum* 1(1):1–26
Dauber K. 1992. Object, genre, and Buddhist sculpture. *Theory Soc.* 21(4):561–92
Davidoff L, Hall C. 1987. *Family Fortunes: Men and Women of the English Middle Class.* Chicago, IL: Univ. Chicago Press
Davis AJ. 1984. Sex differentiated pictures in non-sexist picture books. *Sex Roles* 11(1):1–16
Davis FJ. 1991. *Who Is Black? One Nation's Definition.* Univ. Park: Penn. State Univ. Press
Dayan D. 1992. *Media Events: The Live Broadcast of History.* Cambridge, MA: Harvard Univ. Press

De Lauretis T. 1984. *Alice Doesn't: Feminism, Semiotics, Cinema*. Bloomington: Indiana Univ. Press

D'Emilio J. 1983. *Sexual Politics, Sexual Communities*. Chicago, IL: Univ. Chicago Press

De Vos GA. 1992. *Social Cohesion and Alienation: Minorities in the U.S. and Japan*. Boulder, CO: Westview

Dillon M. 1993. *Debating Divorce: Moral Conflict In Ireland*. Lexington: Univ. Press Kentucky

Dillon M. 1996. Cultural differences in the abortion discourse of the Catholic Church: evidence from four countries. *Sociol. Relig.* 57(1):25–36

DiMaggio P. 1982. Cultural entrepreneurship in nineteenth-century Boston. Parts 1, 2. *Media Cult. Soc.* 4:33–50, 303–22

DiMaggio P. 1987. Classification in art. *Am. Sociol. Rev.* 52(4):440–55

DiMaggio P. 1992. Cultural boundaries and structural change: the extension of the high culture model to theatre, opera, and the dance, 1900–1940. In *Cultivating Differences*, ed. M Lamont, M Fournier, pp. 21–57. Chicago. IL: Univ. Chicago Press

Doty A. 1993. *Making Things Perfectly Queer: Interpreting Mass Culture*. Minneapolis: Univ. Minn. Press

Dudley KM. 1994. *The End of the Line: Lost Jobs, New Lives in Postindustrial America*. Chicago, IL: Univ. Chicago Press

Dyson M. 1993. *Reflecting Black: African American Cultural Criticism*. Minneapolis: Univ. Minn. Press

Eder D. 1995. *School Talk: Gender and Adolescent Culture*. New Brunswick: Rutgers Univ. Press

Eichar DM. 1989. *Occupation and Class Consciousness in America*. New York: Greenwood

Eilberg-Schwartz H, Doniger W. 1995. *Off With Her Head!: The Denial of Women's Identity in Myth, Religion, and Culture*. Berkeley: Univ. Calif. Press

Epstein CF. 1988. *Deceptive Distinctions: Sex, Gender, and the Social Order.* New Haven, CT: Yale Univ. Press

Epstein S. 1992. Gay politics, ethnic identity: the limits of social constructionism. In *Forms of Desire*, ed. E Stein, pp. 239–93. New York: Routledge

Faderman L. 1981. *Surpassing the Love of Men*. New York: Morrow

Fantasia R. 1988. *Cultures of Solidarity*. Berkeley: Univ. Calif. Press

Faraday A. 1981. Liberating lesbian research. In *The Making of the Modern Homosexual*, ed. K Plummer, pp. 112–29. London: Hutchinson

Farley R. 1991. The new census question about ancestry: What did it tell us? *Demography* 28:411–29

Farrell BG. 1993. *Elite Families: Class and Power in Nineteenth-Century Boston*. Albany: State Univ. NY Press

Fausto-Sterling A. 1985. *Myths of Gender: Biological Theories About Women and Men*. New York: Basic Books

Fine GA. 1996. Reputational entrepreneurs and the memory of incompetence: melting supporters, partisan warriors, and images of President Harding. *Am. J. Sociol.* 101(5):1159–93

Fisher C. 1992. *America Calling: A Social History of the Telephone To 1940*. Berkeley: Univ. Calif. Press

Fisher C. 1997. Technology and community: historical complexities. *Sociol. Inq.* 67:(1):113–18

Flax J. 1990. Postmodernism and gender relations in feminist theory. In *Feminism and Postmodernism*, ed. LJ Nicholson, pp. 39–62. New York: Routledge

Form W. 1985. *Divided We Stand: Working Class Stratification in America*. Urbana: Univ. Ill. Press

Form W. 1995. *Segmented Labor, Fractured Politics: Labor Politics in American Life*. New York: Plenum

Frankenberg R. 1993. *White Women, Race Matters: The Social Construction of Whiteness*. Minneapolis: Univ. Minn. Press

Fraser N. 1989. *Unruly Practices: Power, Discourse and Gender in Contemporary Social Theory*. Minneapolis: Univ. Minn. Press

Fuchs S, Ward S. 1994. What is deconstruction and where and when does it take place? Making facts in science, building cases in law. *Am. Sociol. Rev.* 59(4):484–500

Fuss D. 1989. *Essentially Speaking: Feminism, Nature, and Difference*. New York: Routledge

Gailey CW. 1987. Evolutionary perspectives on gender hierarchy. In *Analyzing Gender: A Handbook of Social Science Research*, ed. B Hess, MM Ferree, pp. 32–67. Newbury Park, CA: Sage

Gaines D. 1991. *Teenage Wasteland: Suburbia's Dead End Kids*. New York: Pantheon

Gallie D. 1983. *Social Inequality and Class Radicalism in France and Britain*. Cambridge, Engl: Cambridge Univ. Press

Gamson WA. 1992. *Talking Politics*. New York: Cambridge Univ. Press

Gamson WA, Fireman B, Rytina S. 1982. *Encounters With Unjust Authority*. Homewood: Dorsey

Gans H. 1995. *The War Against The Poor: The Underclass and Antipoverty Policy*. New York: Basic Books

Garber M. 1992. *Vested Interests. Cross-Dressing and Cultural Anxiety.* New York: Routledge
Garcia RA. 1991. *The Rise of the Mexican-American Middle Class: San Antonio, 1929–1941.* College Station: Texas A & M Univ. Press
Gellner E. 1983. *Nations and Nationalism.* Ithaca, NY: Cornell Univ. Press
Gerhards J, Rucht D. 1992. Mesomobilization: organizing and framing in two protest campaigns in West Germany. *Am. J. Sociol.* 98(2):555–95
Gerson JM, Peiss K. 1985. Boundaries, negotiation, consciousness: reconceptualizing gender relations. *Soc. Probl.* 32(4):317–31
Giddens A. 1984. *The Nation State and Violence.* Berkeley: Univ. Calif. Press
Giddens A. 1991. *Modernity and Self-Identity.* Stanford, CA: Stanford Univ. Press
Gilligan C. 1990. Teaching Shakespeare's sister: notes from the underground of female adolescence. *Women's Stud. Q.* 19(1/2):31–44
Gillis J. 1994. *Commemorations: The Politics of National Identity.* Princeton, NJ: Princeton Univ. Press
Gilman SL. 1985. *Difference and Pathology: Stereotypes of Sexuality, Race, and Madness.* Ithaca, NY: Cornell Univ. Press
Goldman R. 1992. *Reading Ads Socially.* New York: Routledge
Greenfield L. 1992. *Nationalism: Five Roads To Modernity.* Cambridge, MA: Harvard Univ. Press
Griswold W. 1992. The writing on the mud wall: Nigerian novels and the imaginary village. *Am. Sociol. Rev.* 57(5):709–24
Halle D. 1984. *America's Working Man: Work, Home, and Politics Among Blue-Collar Property Owners.* Chicago, IL: Univ. Chicago Press
Halle D. 1993. *Inside Culture: Art and Class in the American Home.* Chicago, IL: Univ. Chicago Press
Haraway D. 1991. *Simians, Cyborgs, and Women: The Reinvention of Nature.* New York: Routledge
Hearn J. 1992. *Men in the Public Eye: The Construction and Deconstruction of Public Men and Public Patriarchies.* London: Routledge
Hennion A, Meadel C. 1993. The artisans of desire: the mediators of advertising between product and consumer. *Soc. Theory* 11(1):191–209
Hewitt JP. 1989. *Dilemmas of the American Self.* Philadephia, PA: Temple Univ. Press
Hobsbaum E. 1992. *Nations and Nationalisms Since 1780: Programme, Myth, Reality.* New York: Cambridge Univ. Press. 2nd ed.
Hobsbawm E, Ranger T. 1983. *The Invention of Tradition.* Cambridge, Engl: Cambridge Univ. Press
hooks b. 1984. *Feminist Theory From Margin to Center.* Boston: South End Press
Hout M, Goldstein JR. 1994. How 4.5 million Irish immigrants became 40 million Irish Americans: demography and subjective aspects of the ethnic composition of white Americans. *Am. Sociol. Rev.* 59(1):64–82
Huber J. 1991. *Macro-Micro Linkages in Sociology.* Newbury Park, CA: Sage
Hunt SA, Benford RD, Snow DA. 1994. Identity fields: framing processes and the social construction of movement identities. See Laraña et al 1994, pp. 185–208
Hutchinson J. 1987. *The Dynamics of Cultural Nationalism.* London: Allen & Unwin
Hutchinson J, Smith AD. 1994. *Nationalism.* New York: Oxford
Hyde JS, Fennema E, Lamon SJ. 1990. Gender differences in mathematics performance. *Psychol. Bull.* 107(2):139–55
Hyde JS, Linn MC. 1988. Gender differences in verbal ability. *Psychol. Bull.* 104(1):53–69
Ignatiev N. 1995. *How the Irish Became White.* New York: Routledge
Irving JM. 1994. Cultural differences and adolescent sexualities. In *Sexual Cultures and the Construction of Adolescent Identities,* ed. JM Irving, pp. 3–28. Philadelphia, PA: Temple Univ. Press
Jasper J, Nelkin D. 1992. *The Animal Rights Crusade: The Growth of a Moral Protest.* New York: Free Press
Jeffreys M. 1989. *Growing Old in the Twentieth Century.* London/New York: Routledge
Jepperson RL, Meyer JW. 1991. The public order and the construction of formal organizations. In *The New Institutionalism in Organizational Analysis,* ed. WW Powell, PJ DiMaggio, pp. 204–31. Chicago, IL: Univ. Chicago Press
Jewell KS. 1993. *From Mammy to Miss America and Beyond: Cultural Images and the Shaping of US Social Policy.* New York: Routledge
Johnston H. 1991. *Tales of Nationalism: Catelonia, 1939–1979.* New Brunswick: Rutgers Univ. Press
Johnston H, Laraña E, Gusfield JR. 1994. Identities, grievances, and the new social movements. See Laraña et al 1994, pp. 3–35
Kalisch PA, Kalisch BJ. 1984. Sex role stereotypes of nurses and physicians on TV: a dichotomy of occupational portrayals. *Sex Roles* 10(11/12):533–53
Kaplan EA. 1983. Is the gaze male? In *Powers of Desire: The Politics of Sexuality,* ed. A Snitow, C Stansell, S Thompson, pp. 309–27. New York: Monthly Rev.
Katz M. 1993. *The "Underclass" Debate:*

*Views from History.* Princeton, NJ: Princeton Univ. Press

Katznelson I, Weir M. 1985. *Schooling for All: Class, Race, and the Decline of the Democratic Ideal.* New York: Basic Books

Katznelson I, Zolberg A. 1986. *Working Class Formation: Nineteenth-Century Patterns in Western Europe and the United States.* Princeton, NJ: Princeton Univ. Press

Kubik J. 1994. *The Power of Symbols Against the Symbols of Power: The Rise of Solidarity and the Fall of State Socialism in Poland.* University Park, PA: Penn. State Univ. Press

Kupers TA. 1993. *Revisioning Men's Lives: Gender, Intimacy, and Power.* New York: Guilford

Lamont M. 1992. *Money, Morals, and Manners: The Culture of the French and the American Upper Middle Class.* Chicago, IL: Univ. Chicago Press

Lamont M. 1995. National identity and national boundary patterns in France and the US. *French Hist. Stud.* 19(2):349–65

Lamont M. 1997. Colliding moralities between black and white workers. In *Sociology and Cultural Studies,* ed. E Long. New York: Basil Blackwell. In press

Lamont M, Fournier M. 1992. *Cultivating Differences.* Chicago, IL: Univ. Chicago Press

Lane C. 1981. *The Rites of Rulers.* Cambridge, Engl: Cambridge Univ. Press

Laraña E, Johnston H, Gusfield JR, eds. 1994. *New Social Movements.* Philadelphia, PA: Temple Univ. Press

Leps M. 1992. *Apprehending the Criminal: The Production of Deviance in Nineteenth-Century Discourse.* Durham, NC: Duke Univ. Press

Lichterman P. 1996. *The Search for Political Community: American Activists Reinventing Commitment.* New York: Cambridge Univ. Press

Liebes T. 1990. *The Export of Meaning: Cross Cultural Readings of Dallas.* New York: Oxford Univ. Press

Lorber J. 1994. *Paradoxes of Gender.* New Haven: Yale Univ. Press

MacDonald K, Parke RD. 1986. Parent-child physical play: the effects of sex and age on children and parents. *Sex Roles* 15(7/8):367–78

Margolis DR. 1985. Re-defining the situation: negotiations on the meaning of "woman." *Soc. Probl.* 32(4):332–34

Marshall BL. 1991. Reproducing the gendered subject. In *Current Perspectives in Social Theory,* Vol. 11. Greenwich, CT: JAI

Martin E. 1987. *The Woman in the Body: A Cultural Analysis of Reproduction.* Boston: Beacon

Martorella R. 1989. *Corporate Art.* New Brunswick, NJ: Rutgers Univ. Press

McAdam D. 1982. *Political Process And The Development of Black Insurgency, 1930–1970.* Chicago, IL: Univ. Chicago Press

McAdam D. 1988. *Freedom Summer.* New York: Oxford Univ. Press

McAdam D. 1994. Culture and social movements. See Laraña et al 1994, pp. 36–57

McNall SG, Levine RF, Fantasia R. 1991. *Bringing Class Back In Contemporary and Historical Perspectives.* Boulder, CO: Westview

Medicine B. 1983. Warrior women: sex role alternatives for plains Indian women. In *The Hidden Half: Studies of Plains Indian Women,* ed. P Albers, B Medicine, pp. 267–80. New York: Univ. Press Am.

Melucci A. 1989. *Nomads of the Present: Social Movements and Individual Needs in Contemporary Society.* Philadelphia, PA: Temple Univ. Press

Melucci A. 1997. *Challenging Codes: Collective Action in the Information Age.* New York: Cambridge Univ. Press

Meyer J. 1987. Self and life course: institutionalization and its effects. In *Institutional Structure: Constituting State, Society, and the Individual,* ed. GM Thomas, JW Meyer, FO Ramirez, J Boli, pp. 242–60. Newbury Park, CA: Sage

Meyrowitz J. 1985. *No Sense of Place.* New York: Oxford Univ. Press

Meyrowitz J. 1989. The generalized elsewhere. *Crit. Stud. Mass Commun.* 6(3):323–34

Meyrowitz J. 1997. Shifting worlds of strangers: medium theory and changes in "them" versus "us." *Soc. Inq.* 67(1):59–71

Miller CL. 1987. Qualitative differences among gender-stereotyped toys: implications for cognitive social development. *Sex Roles* 16(9/10):473–88

Miller DA. 1991. Anal rope. In *Inside/Out: Lesbian Theories, Gay Theories,* ed. D Fuss, pp. 119–41. New York: Routledge

Modell J. 1989. *Into One's Own: From Youth To Adulthood in the United States.* Berkeley: Univ. Calif. Press

Moghadam VM. 1994. *Gender and National Identities: Women and Politics in Muslim Societies.* London: Zed Books

Morley D, Robins K. 1995. *Spaces of Identity: Global Media, Electronic Landscapes, and Cultural Boundaries.* London: Routledge

Morris AD, Mueller CM. 1992. *Frontiers in Social Movement Theory.* New Haven, CT: Yale Univ. Press

Mukerji C. 1994. The political mobilization of nature in seventeenth century formal French gardens. *Theory Soc.* 23:651–77

Mukerji C. 1997. *Territorial Ambitions and the*

*Gardens of Versailles*. New York: Cambridge Univ. Press
Nagel J. 1995. American Indian ethnic renewal: politics and the resurgence of identity. *Am. Sociol. Rev.* 60(6):947–65
Nanda S. 1990. *Neither Man Nor Woman: The Hijaras of India*. Belmont: Wadsworth
Nicholson LJ, ed. 1990. *Feminism/Postmodernism*. New York: Routledge
Nicholson LJ, Seidman S, eds. 1995. *Social Postmodernism: Beyond Identity Politics*. New York: Cambridge Univ. Press
Nippert-Eng CE. 1996. *Home and Work: Negotiating Boundaries Through Everyday Life*. Chicago, IL: Univ. Chicago Press
Oakley A. 1984. *The Captured Womb: A History of the Medical Care of Pregnant Women*. London: Basil Black
O'Barr W. 1994. *Culture and the Ad*. Boulder, CO: Westview
Papanek H. 1990. To teach less than she needs, from each more than she can do; allocations, entitlements, and value. In *Persistent Inequalities: Women and World Development*, ed. I Tinker, pp. 162–81. New York: Oxford Univ. Press
Piore MJ. 1995. *Beyond Individualism*. Cambridge, MA: Harvard Univ. Press
Plummer K. 1981. *The Making of the Modern Homosexual*. London: Hutchinson
Postman N. 1982. *The Disappearance of Childhood*. New York: Delacorte
Postman N. 1992. *Technopoly: The Surrender of Culture to Technology*. New York: Knopf
Probyn E. 1993. *Sexing the Self: Gendered Positions In Cultural Studies*. London: Routledge
Purcell K. 1997. Towards a communication dialectic: embedded technology and the enhancement of place. *Soc. Inq.* 67(1):101–12
Quadagno J, Forbes C. 1995. The welfare state and the cultural reproduction of gender: making good girls and boys in the Job Corps. *Soc. Probl.* 42(2):171–90
Raissiguier C. 1994. *Becoming Women Becoming Workers: Identity Formation in a French Vocational School*. Albany: State Univ. NY Press
Raymond D. 1994. Homophobia, identity, and the meaning of desire: reflections on the cultural construction of gay and lesbian adolescent sexuality. See Irving 1994, pp. 115–50
Reeves B, Nass C. 1996. *The Media Equation: How People Treat Computers, Television, and New Media Like Real People and Places*. Cambridge, Engl: Cambridge Univ. Press
Richardson L. 1989. Gender stereotyping in the English language. In *Feminist Frontiers. II: Rethinking Sex, Gender, and Society*, ed. L Richardson, V Taylor, pp. 5–9. New York: Random House
Riley D. 1988. *Am I That Name?* Minneapolis: Univ. Minn. Press
Ritzer G. 1990. Micro-macro linkage in sociological theory: applying a metatheoretical tool. In *Frontiers of Social Theory: The New Synthesis*, ed. G Ritzer, pp. 347–70. New York: Columbia Univ. Press
Ross H, Taylor H. 1989. Do boys prefer daddy or his physical style of play? *Sex Roles* 20(1):23–33
Rubenstein RP. 1995. *Dress Codes: Meanings And Messages In American Culture*. Boulder, CO: Westview
Sadker M, Sadker D. 1994. *Failing At Fairness: How American Schools Cheat Girls*. New York: Scribner's
Sahlins P. 1989. *Boundaries: The Making of France and Spain in the Pyrénnées*. Berkeley: Univ. Calif. Press
Sault N. 1994. *Many Mirrors: Body Image and Social Relations*. New Brunswick: Rutgers Univ. Press
Schlesinger P. 1993. Wishful thinking: cultural politics, media, and collective identities in Europe. *J. Commun.* 43(2):6–17
Schudson M. 1989. How culture works: perspectives from media studies on the efficacy of symbols. *Theory Soc.* 18:153–80
Schudson M. 1992. *Watergate In American Memory: How We Remember, Forget, and Reconstruct The Past*. New York: Basic Books
Schudson M. 1997. Cultural studies and the social construction of "social construction": notes on 'Teddy Bear Patriarchy'. In *Engaging Sociology and Cultural Studies*, ed. E Long. New York: Basil Blackwell. In press
Schwartz B. 1987. *George Washington: The Making of an American Symbol*. Ithaca, NY: Cornell Univ. Press
Schwartz B. 1991. Mourning and the making of a sacred symbol: Durkheim and the Lincoln assassination. *Soc. Forces* 70(2):343–64
Schwartz M. 1987. *The Structure of Power in America: The Corporate Elite as a Ruling Class*. New York: Holmes & Meier
Sedgwick E. 1990. *The Epistemology of the Closet*. Berkeley: Univ. Calif. Press
Seidman S. 1992. *Embattled Eros*. New York: Routledge
Sewell WH Jr. 1992. A theory of structure: duality, agency, and transformation. *Am. J. Sociol.* 98(1):1–29
Shapiro MJ, Alker H. 1995. *Challenging Boundaries: Global Flows, Territorial Identities*. Minneapolis: Univ. Minn. Press
Shilling C. 1993. *The Body and Social Theory*. London: Sage

Shively J. 1992. Cowboys and Indians: perceptions of western films among American Indians and Anglos. *Am. Sociol. Rev.* 57(6):725–34

Sidel R. 1991. *On Her Own: Growing Up In The Shadow Of The American Dream.* New York: Viking

Signorielli N. 1990. Children, television, and gender roles. *J. Adolesc. Health Care* 11(1):50–58

Signorielli N, Morgan M. 1988. *Cultivation Analysis.* Newbury Park, CA: Sage

Silver I. 1996. Role transitions, objects, and identity. *Symb. Interact.* 19(1):1–20

Skocpol T. 1985. Bringing the state back in: strategies of analysis in current research. In *Bringing The State Back In,* ed. PB Evans, D Rueschemeyer, T Skocpol, pp. 3–43. Cambridge, Engl: Cambridge Univ. Press

Smedley A. 1993. *Race in North America: Origin and Evolution of a World View.* Boulder, CO: Westview

Smith AD. 1991. *National Identity.* Reno: Univ. Nevada Press

Smith DE. 1987. *The Everyday World As Problematic: A Feminist Sociology.* Boston, MA: Northeastern Univ. Press

Smith DE. 1990. *The Conceptual Practices of Power.* Boston, MA: Northeastern Univ. Press

Snow DA. 1987. Identity work among the homeless: the verbal construction and avowal of personal identities. *Am. J. Sociol.* 92(6):1336–71

Snow DA, Benford R. 1992. Master frames and cycles of protest. In *Frontiers in Social Movement Theory,* ed. AD Morris, CM Mueller, pp. 133–55. New Haven, CT: Yale Univ. Press

Snow DA, Rochford E, Burke W Jr, Steven K, Benford RD. 1986. Frame alignment processes, micromobilization, and movement participation. *Am. Sociol. Rev.* 51(3):464–81

Somers MR. 1994. The narrative constitution of identity: a relational and network approach. *Theory Soc.* 23:605–49

Soysal YN. 1994. *Limits of Citizenship: Migrants and Postnational Membership in Europe.* Chicago, IL: Univ. Chicago Press

Spallone P, Steinberg DL. 1987. *Made To Order: The Myth of Reproductive And Genetic Progress.* Oxford: Pergamon

Spillman L. 1997. *Nation and Commemoration: Creating National Identities in the United States and Australia.* New York: Cambridge Univ. Press

Stacey J, Thorne B. 1985. The missing feminist revolution in sociology. *Soc. Probl.* 32(4):301–16

Stein A. 1992a. Sisters and queers: the decentering of lesbian feminism. *Social. Rev.* 22(1):33–55

Stein E. 1992b. *Forms of Desire.* New York: Routledge

Steuer J. 1992. Defining virtual reality: dimensions determining telepresence. *J. Commun.* 42(4):73–93

Stryker S. 1980. *Symbolic Interactionism: A Social Structural Version.* Menlo Park, CA: Benjamin/Cummings

Stryker S. 1992. Identity theory. In *Encyclopedia of Sociology,* ed. EF Borgatta, ML Borgatta, pp. 871–76. New York: Macmillan

Swidler A. 1986. Culture in action: symbols and strategies. *Am. Sociol. Rev.* 51(2):273–86

Tarrow S. 1992. Mentalities, political cultures, and collective action frames: constructing meaning through action. See Morris & Mueller 1992, pp. 174–202

Taylor C. 1985. The Person. In *The Category of the Person: Anthropology, Philosophy, History,* ed. M Carrithers, S Collins, S Lukes, pp. 256–81. Cambridge, Engl: Cambridge Univ. Press

Taylor C. 1989. *Sources of the Self: The Making of the Modern Identity.* Cambridge, MA: Harvard Univ. Press

Taylor V, Whittier NE. 1992. Collective identity in social movement communities: lesbian feminist mobilization. See Morris & Mueller 1992, pp. 104–29

Thoits P. 1986. Multiple identities: examining gender and marital status differences in distress. *Am. Sociol. Rev.* 51(2):259–72

Thoits P, Virshup L. 1997. Me's and we's: forms and functions of social identities. In *Self and Identity: Fundamental Issues,* ed. RD Ashmore, L Jussim, Vol. 1. New York: Oxford Univ. Press. In press

Thorne B. 1995. Girls and boys together . . . but mostly apart: gender arrangements in elementary school. In *Sociology: Exploring the Architecture of Everyday Life,* ed. DM Newman, pp. 93–102. Thousand Oaks, CA Pine Forge

Tichi C. 1991. *Electronic Hearth: Creating an American Television Culture.* New York: Oxford Univ. Press

Tilly C. 1990. *Coercion, Capital, and European States AD 990–1990.* Oxford: Blackwell

Trepanier ML, Romatowski JA. 1985. Attributes and roles assigned to characters in children's writing: sex differences and sex role perceptions. *Sex Roles* 13(5/6):263–72

Trinh TM. 1989. *Native, Other: Writing Postcoloniality and Feminism.* Bloomington: Indiana Univ. Press

Troiden RR. 1988. *Gay And Lesbian Identity: A Sociological Analysis.* Dix Hills, NY: General Hall

Turkle S. 1995. *Life On The Screen.* New York: Simon & Schuster

Turner JC, Hogg MA, Oakes PJ, Reicher SD,

Blackwell MS. 1987. *Rediscovering the Social Group: A Self-Categorization Theory.* Oxford: Basil Blackwell

Turner JC, Oakes PJ, Haslam SA, McGarty C. 1994. Self and collective: cognition and social context. *Pers. Soc. Psychol. Bull.* 20(5):454–63

Vanneman R, Cannon LW. 1987. *The American Perception of Class.* Philadelphia, PA: Temple Univ. Press

Wade P. 1993. *Blackness And Race Mixture: The Dynamics of Racial Identity In Colombia.* Baltimore: John Hopkins Univ. Press

Wagner-Pacifici R, Schwartz B. 1991. The Vietnam veterans memorial: commemorating a difficult past. *Am. J. Sociol.* 97(2):376–420

Waksler FC. 1991. *Studying the Social Worlds of Children: Sociological Readings.* New York: Falmer

Warner M. 1991. Fear of a queer planet. *Social Text* 9(14):3–17

Waters MC. 1990. *Ethnic Options: Choosing Identities in America.* Berkeley: Univ. Calif. Press

West C, Zimmerman D. 1987. Doing gender. *Gender Soc.* 1:125–51

Whatley MH. 1994. Keeping adolescence in the picture: construction of adolescent sexuality in textbook images and popular fiction. See Irving 1994, pp. 183–205

White H. 1992. *Identity and Control.* Princeton, NJ: Princeton Univ. Press

Whiting BB, Edwards CP. 1988. *Children of Different Worlds: The Formation of Social Behavior.* Cambridge, MA: Harvard Univ. Press

Wiley N. 1995. *The Semiotic Self.* Chicago, IL: Univ. Chicago Press

Williams R. 1990. *Hierarchical Structures and Social Value: The Creation of Black and Irish Identities in the United States.* Cambridge, Engl: Cambridge Univ. Press

Winn M. 1983. *Children Without Childhood.* New York: Random House

Wittenstrom K. 1995. Work and/or caring: processes ofidentifying women's activities. *Inf. Behav.* 5:396–409

Wittig M. 1981. One is not born a woman. *Fem. Issues* Fall:47–54

Wittig M. 1986. The mark of gender. In *The Poetics of Gender,* ed. NK Miller, pp. 63–73. New York: Columbia Univ. Press

Wright EO. 1989. *The Debate on Classes.* London/New York: Verso

Wuthnow R. 1989. *Communities of Discourse: Ideology and Social Structure in the Reformation, the Enlightenment, and European Socialism.* Cambridge, MA: Harvard Univ. Press

Zelizer V. 1985. *Pricing the Priceless Child.* New York: Basic Books

Zerubavel E. 1991. *The Fine Line: Making Distinctions in Everyday Life.* New York: Free Press

Zerubavel E. 1997a. Special Issue: lumping and splitting. *Sociol. Forum* 11:3

Zerubavel E. 1997b. *Social Mindscapes: An Invitation To Cognitive Sociology.* Cambridge, MA: Harvard Univ. Press

Zerubavel Y. 1995. *Recovered Roots: Collective Memory and the Remaking of Israeli National Tradition.* Chicago, IL: Univ. Chicago Press

Zinn MB, Dill BT. 1994. *Women of Color in US Society.* Philadelphia, PA: Temple Univ. Press

Zukin S. 1991. *Landscapes of Power: From Detroit to Disneyland.* Berkeley: Univ. Calif. Press

*Annu. Rev. Sociol. 1997. 23:411–30*


# NEW SOCIAL MOVEMENTS: A Critical Review

*Nelson A. Pichardo*
Department of Sociology, State University of New York, Albany, New York 12222; e-mail: NP662@louise.csbs.albany.edu

KEY WORDS: identity, culture, postindustrial, new middle class

ABSTRACT

Discussions of New Social Movements have sought to explain the apparent shift in the forms of contemporary social movements in Western nations by linking it to the rise of a postmodern world. However, the central propositions of the NSM paradigm have not been critically analyzed in terms of its concepts or the evidence. This review provides a critical analysis of the NSM thesis, finding that the central propositions are not defensible as a theory or a paradigm.

## INTRODUCTION

The "New" Social Movement (NSM) paradigm is a recent addition to social theory that stresses both the macrohistorical and microhistorical elements of social movements. On the macro level, the NSM paradigm concentrates on the relationship between the rise of contemporary social movements and the larger economic structure, and on the role of culture in such movements. On the micro level, the paradigm is concerned with how issues of identity and personal behavior are bound up in social movements. The NSM paradigm offers a historically specific vision of social movements as associated with new forms of middle-class radicalism. It presents a distinctive view of social movements and of the larger sociopolitical environment, of how individuals fit into, respond to, and change the system. However, whether this nascent view qualifies as a cogent and empirically grounded paradigm has not been seriously examined. This review provides a critique of the central propositions of the NSM paradigm, assessing the evidence supporting its claims.



0360-0572/97/0815-0411$08.00

The NSM paradigm argues for a temporal, structurally linked understanding of social movements. Social movements are seen as being shaped and largely determined by social structure. In the industrial era, following a Marxist logic, social movements were believed to be centered in the working class. Working class movements were seen as instrumentally based actions concerned with matters of economic redistribution. Regardless of whether social movements of the industrial era can be characterized in such categorical terms, it was the standard by which contemporary movements were compared. Contemporary movements (post-1965) were, however, not well explained by social theories that saw the working class as the site of revolutionary protest (Eyerman 1984, Olofsson 1988). In Europe, the defining events were the wide-scale student protests that took place in France and Berlin in 1968 and in Italy in 1969. In the United States, the rise of the student antiwar movement of the mid-1960s was seen as marking a similar radical departure from the past. In Europe, where Marxist theories of social movements dominated, Marxist theorists were unable to provide a convincing explanation for why students had become the vanguard of protest and why movement demands centered around quality of life rather than redistributive issues (Touraine 1971). With the predicted Marxist revolution not in sight, the shift of protest away from the working class, and the changing shape and form of protest in contemporary times, Marxist theorists saw the need to reformulate their ideas. While not all Marxist went in the same direction (see Boggs 1986), some of them postulated the NSM paradigm as an alternative (see Cohen 1985, Melucci 1980, 1985, Touraine 1977, 1981). In fact, much of the NSM discourse can be said to be a direct reaction to the perceived deficiencies of Marxism (Epstein 1990, Laclau & Mouffe 1985, Plotke 1990).

## NSM PARADIGM

Although there are differing perspectives on NSMs (see Buechler 1995 for an overview), a set of core concepts and beliefs can be said to comprise the NSM paradigm. The central claims of the NSM paradigm are, first, that NSMs are a product of the shift to a postindustrial economy and, second, that NSMs are unique and, as such, different from social movements of the industrial age. NSMs are said to be a product of the postmaterial age (some refer to it as mature capitalism or postindustrialism) and are seen as fundamentally different from the working class movements of the industrial period (Olofsson 1988). NSM demands are believed to have moved away from the instrumental issues of industrialism to the quality of life issues of postmaterialism (Buechier 1995, Burklin 1984, Inglehart 1990, Parkin 1968). NSMs are, in short, qualitatively different (Melucci 1981).

However, when broadly related to contemporary movements, these observations are essentially flawed. Just as the Marxist theories tended to marginalize protest that did not stem from the working class, so too have NSM theorists marginalized social movements that do not originate from the left. Contemporary right-wing movements are not the subject of their focus. Thus, the NSM paradigm describes (at best) only a portion of the social movement universe. But there is no a priori reason for eliminating conservative and counter movements from consideration. One might excuse the omission of countermovements because they are believed to be reactions to insurgent movements, largely determined by the goals, ideology, tactics, and participants (in a negative way) of these (see Mottl 1980, Pichardo 1995, Zald & Useem 1987). However, this is not the case for movements, many of which over the last 20 years seem to be unique reactions (of a conservative character) to the alienating effects of postindustrial society. Some examples include the Christian Right and militia movements. However, the NSM paradigm is based solely on observations of left-wing movements and reflects this ideological bias undergirding the NSM paradigm. Yet, movements of both the left and the right are linked to changes in social structure. Understanding how other social groups perceive and react to these changes can only broaden our knowledge of social change.

The NSM paradigm can only claim to explain left-wing movements of the modern age.[1] Among the movements typically studied by NSM researchers are the "urban social struggles, the environmental or ecology movements, women's and gay liberation, the peace movement, and cultural revolt linked primarily to student and youth activism" (Boggs 1986:39–40). Is there any reason to believe that the populations supporting these movements, which are said to be a product of a fundamental change in the economic structure, should be affected while those populations supporting the militia, right-to-life, wise use, and Christian right movements should not be similarly affected? Although a possible rationale for this distinction could be constructed, the NSM perspective offers none, and its failure to do so marks a serious flaw in its reasoning.[2] It is not the purpose of this review to extend the NSM thesis to right-wing movements, although I shall offer some tentative suggestions in the conclusion.

Putting this aside for now, let's review the NSM paradigm in terms of what it claims. As is typical of new paradigms in the process of establishing themselves, their propositions are strongly stated (or perhaps overstated) to firmly

[1]In all fairness, most social movement theories are based on observations of left-wing movements; this is a broad failing of social movement research in general. Nonetheless, with the current growth of right-wing conservative movements in the modern era, it is perhaps especially pertinent to NSM theory to account for them as well.

[2]This refers specifically to why other social groups (especially conservative groups) do not engage in activism.

distinguish them from other theories. Subsequently, these strong propositions are reevaluated, and weaker propositions may be substituted. Strong statements may be hard to defend. This is especially the case for the NSM paradigm. Many of its original strong propositions have been found wanting. Therefore, I focus here primarily on the weaker versions.

## *Are Contemporary Movements Unique?*

The first claim of the NSM paradigm is that contemporary movements are fundamentally different in character than movements of the past. These differences are said to appear in the ideology and goals, tactics, structure, and participants of contemporary movements.

IDEOLOGY AND GOALS The central factor characteristic of NSMs is their distinct ideological outlook (Dalton et al 1990). It is from this difference that all others flow. The NSM paradigm states that contemporary social movements represent a fundamental break from industrial era movements. Rather than focusing on economic redistribution (as do working-class movements), NSMs emphasize quality of life and life-style concerns. Thus, NSMs question the wealth-oriented materialistic goals of industrial societies. They also call into question the structures of representative democracies that limit citizen input and participation in governance, instead advocating direct democracy, self-help groups, and cooperative styles of social organization. "The theme of the self-defense and democratization, raised implicitly (and sometimes explicitly) by the movements, . . . [is] the most significant element in the contemporary struggle for democratization" (Cohen 1983:102). Taken together, the values of NSMs center on autonomy and identity (Offe 1985).

In many ways, identity claims are the most distinctive feature of NSMs (Kauffman 1990), although all previous movements can also be described as expressing identity claims (see e.g. Aronowitz 1992). The focus on identity is considered unique in modern movements because "identity politics also express the belief that identity itself—its elaboration, expression, or affirmation—is and should be a fundamental focus of political work. In this way, the politics of identity have led to an unprecedented politicization of previously nonpolitical terrains . . ." (Kauffman 1990:67). This is expressed in the notion that "the personal is political." However, whether the politics of identity represents a liberation or stagnation of modern politics is a point of contention. The liberation of joining the personal with the political may represent a radical challenge to the hegemony of state domination, but it may also result in an "anti-politics of identity"—an apolitical withdrawal from politics (Kauffman 1990).

However, little empirical work has examined the impact of identity claims on social movement participation, with two notable exceptions: Klandermans

(1994) has examined, in the Dutch peace movement, how the varying collective identities, as represented by the different organizational memberships, predicted the defection of participants from the movement. NA Pichardo, H Sullivan-Catlin, & G Deane (unpublished manuscript) have examined the role of personal identity in relation to participation in the environmental movement. Their findings show a significant, though not strong, association between self-reported environmental identity and participation both in conventional social movement activities (event participation, organizational membership, movement contributions) and in everyday behaviors (conserving energy and water, using alternative transportation, and purchasing products made from recycled materials). Clearly, more empirical work on the connection between identity, at all its levels, and movement participation needs to be done.

The other, supposedly unique, ideological feature of NSMs is its self-reflexive character. This means that participants are constantly questioning the meaning of what is being done (Cohen 1985, Gusfield 1994, Melucci 1994). This has led to conscious choices of structure and action—choices said to typify NSMs. The best example of this is the consciousness-raising groups characteristic of the feminist movement (Van der Gaag 1985; see also the volume edited by Katzenstein & Muller 1987). The decision to organize in a decentralized fashion, to operate under democratic principles with rotating leadership, is seen by some as consistent with Michel's Iron Law of Oligarchy, whereby the goals of organizations become displaced (Kitschelt 1990). The unique ideological orientation and self-reflexive character largely dictate the kinds of tactics, structures, and participants evidenced in NSMs.

TACTICS The tactics of NSMs mirror their ideological orientation. The belief in the unrepresentative character of modern democracies is consistent with its anti-institutional tactical orientation. NSMs prefer to remain outside of normal political channels, employing disruptive tactics and mobilizing public opinion to gain political leverage. They also tend to use highly dramatic and preplanned forms of demonstrations replete with costumes and symbolic representations (Tarrow 1994).

This, however, does not mean that NSMs do not involve themselves in politics, nor avoid becoming institutionalized themselves. As noted by Eder (1985), "NSMs manifest a form of middle-class protest which oscillates from moral crusade to political pressure group to social movement" (p. 881). Some NSMs have become integrated into the party system and gained regular access to regulatory, implementation, and decision-making bodies, while others have formed political parties that regularly contest for electoral representation (Berry 1993, Hager 1993, Kitschelt 1990, Gelb & Paley 1982, Rochon 1990, Rochon & Mazmanian 1993, Tarrow 1990). A number of Green parties are prominent in

Europe, with several having local manifestations in the United States (Bahro 1986, Burklin 1982, 1985, Capra & Spretnak 1984, Hershey 1993, Kolinsky 1989, Muller-Rommel 1985, 1990, Poguntke 1993). However, no direct correspondence appears between supporters of NSMs and those who vote for Green parties (Chandler & Siaroff 1986, Muller-Rommel 1985). So, the NSM paradigm recognizes that there is no truly distinctive tactical style of NSMs; rather, public opinion and anti-institutional politics have been recent and more prominent additions to the repertoire of social movements.

STRUCTURE The anti-institutional posture of NSMs also extends to the way they organize. NSMs attempt to replicate in their own structures the type of representative government they desire. That is, they organize themselves in a fluid nonrigid style that avoids the dangers of oligarchization. They tend to rotate leadership, vote communally on all issues, and to have impermanent ad hoc organizations (Offe 1985). They also espouse an anti-bureaucratic posture, arguing against what they perceive as the dehumanizing character of modern bureaucracy.

> [NSMs] oppose the bureaucratization of society in economics and politics that allegedly suffocates the ability of individual citizens to participate in the definition of collective goods and identities. Instead they call for a culturally libertarian transformation of social institutions that gives more leeway to individual choice and collective self-organization outside the economic commodity cycle or bureaucratic political organization (Kitschelt 1993:15).

Thus, they call for and create structures that are more responsive to the needs of the individuals—open, decentralized, nonhierarchical (Zimmerman 1987). Motivated by the lessons of the past, they hope to avoid becoming coopted or deradicalized. This is to claim, not that all NSMs are so organized, but that this form of organizing is more prevalent than in past times. The ideal-typical organizational style of NSMs should not be seen as reflecting the organizational styles of every NSM. Groups such as the National Organization of Women, and various environmental groups employ more traditional centralized, hierarchical forms of organization (Paley & Leif 1982, Shaiko 1993).

PARTICIPANTS There are two views on who the participants of NSMs are and why they join. The first places the base of support within the "new" middle class: a recently emerged social stratum employed in the nonproductive sectors of the economy (Cotgrove & Duff 1981, Lowe & Goyder 1983, Rudig 1988). Research on the rise of the new middle class within postindustrial society seems to establish the credibility of this social phenomenon (Brint 1994). But NSM theorists go a step beyond, by arguing that this stratum produces the chief participants of NSMs because they are not bound to the corporate profit motive nor dependent on the corporate world for their sustenance. Instead, they tend to work in areas that are highly dependent upon state expenditures such as academia, the arts, and human service agencies, and they tend to be highly educated (Offe 1985). Another explanation posits that NSMs are the result of conflict over the control of work.

> In this conflict, the professionals whose control is based on expertise and skills are defending themselves against the encroachments on their work autonomy by colleagues who are primarily involved in the administration of the large private and public employers for whom the former work. Tending to lose out in this conflict, the skills and service-oriented professionals constitute a crucial structural potential for the new social movements, all of which attack in one way or another the unrestricted reign of technocracy (Kriesi et al 1995:xix).

However, there is recognition that within this overall descriptive categorization differences exist.

The other view of the participants of NSMs is that they are not defined by class boundaries but are marked by a common concern over social issues. It is an ideological, rather than ethnic, religious, or class-based community. In this light Arato & Cohen (1984) refer to the West German Greens as a "catch-all" party. They are defined by common values rather than a common structural location. Offe (1985) offers a slightly different view of who the NSM participants are. He argues that they are drawn from three sectors: the new middle class, elements of the old middle class (farmers, shop owners, and artisan-producers), and a "peripheral" population consisting of persons not heavily engaged in the labor market (students, housewives, and retired persons). A number of studies of the peace movement in various countries have demonstrated an equally diverse set of participants (Parkin 1968; see also the volume edited by Kaltefleiter & Pfaltzgraff 1985). Diani & Lodi (1988) show that within the Milan ecology movement, several different currents attract somewhat different sets of participants.

However, neither view, in its narrowly defined sense, is supported by the evidence. Studies of environmental movements reveal that NSM participants are drawn primarily from two populations: The "new" middle class is one; the other is geographically bound communities that are being directly affected by the negative externalities of industrial growth. Participants are the more ideologically committed middle class as well as communities that protest the siting of hazardous waste sites, landfills, and waste incinerators, or chemical and/or radiation poisoning of the local environment (see Apter & Sawa 1984, 1970, Opp 1988, Szasz 1994, Walsh 1981). The old middle class typically is also involved in regional issues (Touraine 1981). In short, the participants of environmental movements do not draw significantly from outside the white middle class unless there is some motivating, geographically based, grievance. For example, minority communities have rarely participated in the environmental movement, except in protest over the placement of unwanted waste facilities (Bullard 1990).[3] The lack of minority participation is equally true of most other NSMs, including the animal rights, feminist, peace, and gay and lesbian movements.

Whether middle-class participants engaged significantly in protest in the past is a critical question for the NSM paradigm. Such activity has been severely underestimated. Waves of middle-class protest have occurred since the early 1800s in both Europe and the United States. These include the abolition, prohibition, suffrage, and progressive (as well as a number of nativist) movements. Thus, whether the middle class is only newly involved in social movements is indeed open to question.

Are these proposed characteristics unique? If such differences exist, then it would mark a significant break from the past. The problem is that too many exceptions are cited. NSMs espouse open, democratic, nonhierarchical structures, yet there are many NSM organizations that are not so characterized. They disdain institutional politics, yet many NSMs are regularly consulted by governmental bodies, and others have formed political parties. NSMs tend to draw from the new middle class, yet many community-based mobilizations (primarily environmental) have developed. Furthermore, the middle class is not a new site of social protest. NSMs tend to employ nontraditional tactics but also use those commonly employed by social movements of the past (lobbying, getting out the vote, court cases, etc).

> One cannot evade the fact that the striking feature of the contemporary... situation of the movements is its heterogeneity. The old patterns of collective action certainly continue to exist. In some movements they may even be statistically preponderant (Cohen 1985:665).

Not only are the individual characteristics of movements in question, so too are those of the new social movements in general. D'Anieri et al (1990) argue that there is no difference between utopian movements of the 1800s and present-day movements. In a similar vein, Calhoun (1991) sees no stark differences between movements of the nineteenth and twentieth centuries, arguing that social movements of the nineteenth century were not dominated by economistic organizations.

The notion of movement "newness" has also been criticized in terms of whether contemporary movements represent a distinct break from movements of the past. For Touraine (1982), this radical departure is a function of their level of reflexivity and the changed locuses and stakes of the struggles. For Evers (1985), what is new about NSMs is that the "transformatory potential within new social movements is not political, but socio-cultural" (p. 49). That is, they aim to reappropriate society from the state. However, a host of other

[3]This kind of placement has been referred to as environmental racism, a term grounded in the belief that decisions about locating hazardous waste sites ignore the interests of minority groups.

authors have stressed the continuity of NSMs with previous movements (Cohen 1985, Crighton & Mason 1986, Eder 1985). Perhaps Melucci (1994) put the nature and importance of this controversy in the best light when he said it was futile. It is not a question of deciding whether the empirical data observed are equivalent and comparable; instead, the question is whether their meaning and the place they occupy in the system of social relations can be considered to be the same (1994:105).

Apart from whether NSMs represent breaks from previous movements, a related question is whether NSMs are new at all. As noted above, NSMs often contain elements of the old and new. Eder (1985) sees NSMs as embracing two types of phenomena: Cultural movements that "oppose present social life . . . [and] political movements [that] challenge modern state domination" (p. 5). Mouffe (1984) sees the novelty of NSMs not in the new antagonisms but in the "diffusion of social conflict into other areas and the politicization of more and more relations" (p. 141).

However, some have been especially critical of the claims to originality of new social movements. Rather than arguing continuity or discontinuity with previous movements, Plotke (1990) criticizes the impact of NSM theory on the direction of social movements. He argues that accounts of a widespread "new social movement discourse" are wrong in crucial ways. Dubious claims about the movements, about what they are and should be, are politically significant because they are taken seriously both by analysts and by some participants within the movements" (p. 81). These "dubious claims" are an outgrowth of the theoretical conflict with Marxism, which has left NSM theorists "unprepared to engage in the theoretical and political debate in the United States, where neoconservative interpretations became dominant in the late 1970s and 1980s" (p. 82). In other words, the debate over what's new is not just an academic polemic; it has real consequences for movements that may leave them vulnerable to counterattacks.

### *Are Contemporary Movements a Product of the Postindustrial Era?*

Related to the question of "what's new" is a second issue—whether NSMs are a product of the shift to a postindustrial economy. There is disagreement over the exact nature of this relationship. Two schools of thought exist—one stresses an objective and the other, a subjective class position (see Eder 1985). The objective school stresses social structural factors that formed "new" social classes as oppositional groups, while the subjective school of thought stresses attitudinal changes that have formed like-minded groups. Within the objective school, the first variation, what I call the "state intrusion" hypothesis, is a post-Marxist view that links the rise of NSMs to the changing requirements of capital accumulation in the postmodern age. With the advent of a service/technical economy with its emphasis on growth and information management, capital accumulation necessitates social as well as economic domination. Social domination involves controlling dissent and knowledge (ensuring conformity) and therefore requires an expansion of the state's coercive mechanisms into the civic sphere (Habermas 1987, Melucci 1984, Sassoon 1984, Touraine 1971). NSMs are concerned with the "self-defense of 'society' against the state ... and the market economy ..." (Cohen 1985:664). Habermas (1981) refers to the process by which the state and market economy substitute strategic action for the symbolic processes of communication as "inner colonization."

Mouffe (1984) offers a different version. She sees a similar process except that she links it to the commodification of social life (where social needs depend on the market for satisfaction), bureaucratization (resulting from the intervention of the state into all areas of social reproduction), and cultural massification (resulting from the pervasive influence of the mass media that destroys or modifies existing collective identities). These new forms of subordination are responsible for the rise of NSMs, which represent novel forms of resistance.

The unique nature of conflict in modern societies is said to be partly a function of three characteristics of domination and deprivation. First, the impact of the state and economy on society is said to no longer be class specific but "dispersed in time, space, and kind so as to affect virtually every member of society in a broad variety of ways" (Offe 1985:844). Second, there has been a deepening of domination and social control, making its effects more comprehensive and inescapable. Third, the political and economic institutions have lost the ability to correct their own defects (irreversibility) requiring action from outside the official political institutions to correct its flaws (Offe 1985).

NSMs are believed to be a reaction to the state's attempts to control the civic sphere.[4] For some, what is unique about NSMs is that they "emerge primarily outside the bourgeois public sphere ... as extra-institutional phenomena rooted in civil society ... [that] point to a recovery of civil society" (Boggs 1986:47). Thus, we see movements that are concerned with cultural questions (involving matters of sexual identification, role definitions, and community). NSMs are also reactions to the expansive (growth oriented) nature of postindustrialism, which needs to neglect the social costs of growth to maintain profitability. This growth orientation has two principal consequences. First, it produces a mass consumer culture marked by mega-malls, strip malls, mass advertising, and planned obsolescence. Many NSMs reject this form of cultural manipulation. Second, the requirements of a mass consumer culture have negative environmental manifestations that are largely unwelcome and unwanted. These include garbage dumps, incinerators, and toxic pollution as well as the exploitation of

[4]This should not be confused with the tactical choices of movements, such as the animal rights movement, that often attempt to mobilize the state to enter into the civic sphere to attain their goals.

the environment for the raw materials of industrial production. Thus, NSMs also represent quality of life concerns. Ultimately, the aim of participants in NSMs is "not to seize power in order to build a new world, but to regain power over their own lives by disengaging from the market rationality of productivism" (Gorz 1982:75).

Some theorists have used the writings of Gramsci to illuminate the processes of cultural domination that the state employs to maintain power (see Carroll 1992 for an overview). This "cultural Marxism" is a critique of "Marx's concepts of the relations and forces of production for inadequate attention to the conscious experience of institutions and creative practical reasoning" (Weiner 1982:13). This emphasis on the cultural basis of conflict in the modern era is imputed to be one of the defining characteristics of NSMs (Cohen 1983, Eder 1985, Feher & Heller 1983, Gorz 1982, Melucci 1980, Scott 1990). The ideological hegemony of the state requires counter-hegemonic actions by social movements to dismantle the dominant social views that reinforce the legitimacy of the capitalist system (Cohen 1983). Current notions, such as that "the personal is political," that is, that everyday behavior has political ramifications and, by implication, supports the hegemony of the ruling classes, reflect the emphasis of NSMs on doing battle not only on an economic level but also on a cultural level (Mooers & Sears 1992). This "culture conflict" is manifested in the life-style emphasis of NSMs and is fought on symbolic and identity levels (Kauffman 1990, Weiner 1982).

The second school of thought concerning the origins of NSMs places their cause in the subjective consciousness of the actors. There are two principal variants. The first is the "value shift" hypothesis that centers around the larger economic, political, and social context of Western nations.[5] This view states that the people of Western nations have reached a point of economic and political security in the modern age (where their basic needs for sustenance and survival are relatively assured). This confidence led to a shift in public opinion (culture) away from issues relating to economic or political security to issues of personal growth and self-actualization. The underlying mechanism is based on a Maslowian psychological scheme where an individual is first and foremost concerned with issues of survival and security; once these basic needs are satisfied, one is able to move up the ladder to higher-order concerns (Falik 1983, Inglehart 1977, 1981). This scheme implies that the socialization experiences of various age cohorts, and the conditions of scarcity present during their formative years, result in a fixed materialistic or postmaterialistic orientation. Thus, NSMs represent the shift to postmaterial values that stress issues of identity, participation, and quality of life rather than economic matters. But the value

[5]This is referred to by Poguntke (1993) as a *structural change* approach. See also Kitschelt (1988) and Markovits & Meyer (1985).

changes are not the only attitudinal changes that result in NSMs. For Inglehart (1977), postmaterial values combine with increases in political efficacy and political distrust to result in increased political activism. This view says nothing about actions of the state except in so much as it provides for the economic and political security of its populace.

The second value change variant concerning the origins of NSMs is the "cycle of protests" argument. It states that NSMs are simply recent manifestations of a cyclical pattern of social movements (see Tarrow 1983). Some link the cycles to "anti-modern or romantic-ideological reactions to functional principles, contradictions, and alienating effects of modern societies" (Brand 1990:24; see also Eder 1982), others to recurring waves of cultural criticisms linked to changes in the cultural climate (Brand 1990) or to political and social events. These periods are said to act as fertile ground for the proliferation of social movements sensitizing the population to the problems of modern societies (Brand 1990, Rudig 1988).

However, the evidence supporting these views is not conclusive. The "state intrusion" hypothesis suffers because of the difficulty in empirically establishing a link between the actions of the state and incidence of NSMs. Such connections can only be drawn by inference, by establishing the meaning and intent of actions of the state and hypothesizing about their consequences. "The work of interpretation is inevitably risky and less totalizing" (Cohen 1985:665). Specifically, the hypothesized changes in the state are vague and difficult to operationalize, and the mechanism by which actions of the state are linked to social movements is not specified.

The "value shift" hypothesis, on the other hand, is based on empirical observations of changes in public opinion over the last 30 years. The evidence of a value shift seems compelling. Opinion studies in both Europe and North America have chronicled a change in the values of the public that moved from economic to non-economic concerns, as is suggested by the hypothesis (Inglehart 1977, 1981, 1990, Kaase 1990). However, there are several problems with this thesis.

First, the hypothesis locates the value change in a specific class segment: the so-called "new" middle class (Inglehart 1990). However, the "new" middle class is defined in widely divergent ways that contribute to inconsistent results from various investigations. This is also true of the indicators employed to mark the differences between the "new" middle class and other social classes. Several formulations of the "new" middle class (Ehrenreich & Ehrenreich 1977, Gouldner 1979, Kristol 1972, Ladd 1978, 1979) employed differing definitions of the new middle class and produced inconsistent results. Brint (1984) tested the four variations by looking at the presence of "antibusiness" and "egalitarian" sentiment among the groups as defined by each of the above researchers. He found that the four groups defined as composing the "new" middle class did not possess dissenting attitudes. He concluded that "the theorists were simply incorrect in [that they] ... exaggerated the levels of dissent and even the levels of liberalism found in the new class" (p. 60). Brint's review shows that NSM scholars have failed to provide empirical evidence that would allow them to conclude with confidence that such a new and militant class, linked to NSMs, has arisen in the United States or Europe.

The second problem with the value shift hypothesis is that the cause for the value change is imputed to be a function of the increasing security and prosperity of modern Western countries. This connection is less amenable to direct empirical verification. Other possible explanations for the rise in postmodern values could be offered including the growing bureaucratization of society, or that the values are cyclical rather than rooted in the ability of the economic structure to provide for the material benefit of the population.[6]

Third, relying strictly on economic affluence as indicating postmaterialism may miss more important determinants of social values. As stated by Cotgrove & Duff (1981), "perhaps Inglehart and later researchers have been looking at the wrong kind of variables to explain support for postmaterialism. By concentrating on the level of affluence of an individual as determinant, they have neglected ideals [that is, personal values] as a possible cause" (p. 98). The point is that there may be a difference between public and private values and that one's public values may be more central to predicting support for postmaterial values.

Fourth, the two elements of Inglehart's model, the arguments concerning scarcity and socialization, lead to contradictory expectations. As stated by Boltken & Jagodzinski (1985),

> If the responses to the value index reflect internalized value orientations, they should be fairly stable in adulthood. If, on the other hand, respondent behavior is affected to a larger extent by economic changes, usually no stability can be expected. But the same sequence of actions cannot be both stable and unstable (p. 444).

The "cycle of protests" argument that ties changes in the cultural climate to waves of movements differs from the "value shift" hypothesis in that it adds a time dimension to the shift in social mood and makes no assertions about the structural source of social movements. There is no significant body of literature testing the historical dimension of the argument, although such shifts have been noted by other authors (Hirschman 1981, Huntington 1981, Namenwirth & Weber 1987, Schlesinger 1986). Brand (1990) has done a comparative study of Germany, England, and the United States that shows a linkage between phases of

[6]A discussion of new social movements in Latin America, by Slater (1985) also indirectly refutes the belief that economic prosperity and the concomitant value changes it begets underlie the rise of NSMs. Latin American nations can hardly be described as capable of satisfying the basic needs for economic and physical security of their people. However, without ascertaining whether the model provided by NSMs is in some manner being diffused, the existence of NSMs in Latin America cannot be used as definitive refutation of the value change hypothesis.

cultural criticisms and the manifestation of new middle-class radicalism (social movements) from 1800–1990. Pichardo (1993) presents a similar argument for the Populist/Progressive era movements in the United States, which demonstrate striking similarities to the rise of NSMs. The middle-class radicalism of that period is linked to the advancing restrictions on community space brought about by industrialism. But these data are too preliminary to be convincing.

However, in terms of whether NSMs are a product of the postindustrial age, the cycles-of-protest argument implicitly responds in the negative. For if the values are tied to the rise of postindustrial society or linked to the rise of the new middle class, then they could not have been present before. Brand's formulation may be a way to reconcile the two views, but that would require the NSM thesis to be substantially altered.

Yet another strain of critique casts doubt on the connection between the larger macro-historical societal changes associated with postindustrialism and NSMs. Olofsson (1988) argues that the "cultural revolutionary activities . . . [of NSMs] can be articulated with very different politico-ideological formations, social groups, and classes" (p. 31). In other words, there is no necessary connection between postindustrialism and the project of NSMs.

Similarly, the "cycles of protest" argument has an alternative explanation.[7] Rather than seeing them as a consequence of changing values associated with modernization, which in turn dictate tactical options that are in concert with the values, another point of view suggests that changes in the tactical repertoire of movements are independent of the values and goals expressed by the movement. Rather than linking changes in tactics to new values and goals, they are to be seen more in terms of an evolving interaction between the agents of repression and movement actors where new tactics are an outcome of the ability of agents of repression to accommodate to the old tactics, thereby rendering them ineffective (Koopmans 1983). New tactics are a response to the need to find new forms of effective tactics. Another explanation for the waves of protest argues that they are the outcome of competition between movement organizations (Tarrow 1989, 1991). In this view, the competition for resources and membership between movement organizations leads to innovation, militancy, then decline. Tarrow (1991) further argues that those who argue for the "newness" of contemporary movements have simply mistaken an early phase of movement development for a new historical stage of collective action.

Finally, the NSM thesis limits the phenomenon to Western nations, yet some authors have attempted to extend the thesis to underdeveloped countries. Slater (1985), in an interesting turn on the NSM thesis, relates Latin American contemporary movements to excessive centralization of decision-making power, the state's incapacity to deliver adequate social services, and the eroding legitimacy

[7]This idea was suggested by Bert Klandermans.

of the state.[8] But the mere presence of NSMs in non-Western nations argues against both hypotheses—of state intrusion (because NSMs are triggered by the change to a postindustrial economy, a change not occurring in Latin American nations) or of value change (because the value changes are a product of the economic and physical security of a country's population, which also cannot be said to be characteristic of Latin American nations).

What remains is of questionable value as a paradigm or theory. The relationship between structure and the rise of contemporary movements is at best uncertain, and most of the so-called unique characteristics and features are not unique. What seems to be unique is their ideological (identity) orientation—the one hypothesized characteristic that seems truly to mark a break from the past.

## SUMMARY

So what have we? There is significant doubt in terms of whether contemporary movements are specifically a product of postindustrial society. The mechanisms cited within the NSM literature disagree significantly, depending on the variation. In turn, each of these variations has significant weaknesses—inconclusive empirical support, questionable operationalization of variables, ambiguous or abstract concepts, and feasible alternative explanations. The same could be said for whether contemporary movements represent anything unique. Except for the issue of identity, the so-called unique characteristics of contemporary movements are not unique at all. At best, it can be argued that they are recent additions to the repertoire of social movements. But changes in repertoires have been noted by other authors (most notably Tilly 1979) without employing explanations that call for new theories.

The principal contributions of the NSM perspective are its emphases on identity, culture, and the role of the civic sphere—aspects of social movements that had been largely overlooked. The failure to attend to identity issues was rooted in the belief that social movement participation was instrumentally based. In fact, Parkin (1968) believes that the expressive dimension of participation may be a feature of social movements dominated by the middle class. The expressive nature of participation is linked to the cultural aspects of movements as the goal of expressive action is guided by a particular moral outlook concerning the appropriate normative order. The civic sphere, where culture resides, which had traditionally been seen as being dominated or determined by the economic sphere, is now seen as a locus of social protest. This "liberation" of the civic sphere has brought to focus the realization that the civic sphere is an area of contention just as are the economic and political spheres.

[8]Slater employed Mouffe's commodification variation of the state-intrusion hypothesis, which is not linked to the capacity of governments to provide for the physical and economic security of its populace.

However, the need for a new theory of social movements to account for these differences is uncertain. Not that social movement theory (in particular the resource mobilization theory) presented a complete account of movement dynamics (see Canel 1992, Klandermans 1986, Klandermans & Tarrow 1986). But a modification of theory that attended to the "why" of movements in addition to the "how" would seem to be a better direction to proceed.

## CONCLUSION

The inability of the NSM school to adequately defend its most central propositions argues against labeling or referring to the NSM thesis as a paradigm or theory about contemporary movements. Nor can simply arguing that the NSM thesis applies only to left-wing movements of the contemporary era salvage its image as a theory. Even limiting the thesis to oppositional movements (which traditionally come from the left) is insufficient as many conservative movements can also be so characterized. The added inability to argue convincingly for a typology of contemporary movements or a link to changes in socioeconomic structures leaves the NSM thesis untenable as a theory.

Does that mean that there is nothing behind this school of thought? Is it, as Tarrow (1991) believes, that researchers mistook an early phase of movement development for a new historical stage of collective action, or did something genuinely unique take place? The principal question is not whether contemporary movements display unique characteristics, for the tactics and styles of movements are often a function of expediency rather than principle and thus are guided by the utilitarian logic of achieving goals. It is more a matter of whether contemporary movements are reacting to the changing nature of domination in the postindustrial world. Put another way, are contemporary movements unique because of the unique character of domination necessitated by the emergence of the postindustrial era?

In my opinion, any rescue of the NSM thesis must begin with an inclusion of contemporary conservative movements both presently and historically. With such an inclusion the process of government intrusion into the civic sphere would be more clearly highlighted as conservative mobilizations are also reacting to the actions of governments to control the civic sphere. The religious values that underpin the ideological structure of many conservative movements must be seen as an additional source of friction that has always resided in and traditionally dominated the civic sphere. With the separation of church and state that took place in the eighteenth century, religious groups lost their state-sanctioned privileged position within the civic sphere.[9] Many conservative

[9]This was because the coercive mechanisms of the state were no longer available to religious groups to sanction wayward believers. Thus, the cultural behavioral codes preferred by religious groups could no longer be guaranteed to dominate the civic sphere.

mobilizations in the United States of the eighteenth and nineteenth centuries can be understood as attempts by religious groups to coerce the state to enforce behavioral and moral codes consistent with their beliefs. Thus, the evolving history of the civic sphere and the social and political conflicts involving the civic sphere need to be detailed. In this way, we can better understand the nature of modern conflict and the role of the civic sphere in generating and maintaining that conflict. It is the observation concerning the role of the civic sphere (where culture and identity reside) in modern conflict that is perhaps the most provocative and informative aspect of the NSM thesis and the element around which a reformulation of the NSM thesis should be constructed.

ACKNOWLEDGMENTS

Thanks to Bert Klandermans, Richard Lachmann, John Logan, and Steve Seidman for comments on earlier drafts.



*Literature Cited*

Apter DE, Sawa N. 1984. *Against the State: Politics and Social Protest in Japan*. Cambridge, MA: Harvard Univ. Press

Arato A, Cohen J. 1984. The German Green Party: a movement between fundamentalism and modernism. *Dissent* 31:327–32

Aronowitz S. 1992. *The Politics of Identity*. New York: Routledge

Bahro R. 1986. *Building the Green Movement*. Philadelphia: New Soc. Publ.

Berry JM. 1993. Citizen groups and the changing nature of interest group politics in America. *Ann. Am. Acad. Polit. Soc. Sci.* 528:30–41

Boggs C. 1986. *Social Movements and Political Power*. Philadelphia, PA: Temple Univ. Press

Boltken F, Brand K. 1990. Cyclical aspects of new social movements: waves of cultural criticism and mobilization cycles of new middle-class. In *Challenging the Political Order*, ed. RJ Dalton, DM Kuechier, pp. 23–42. New York: Oxford Univ. Press

Boltken F, Jagodzinski W. 1985. In an environment of insecurity: postmaterialism in the European Community, 1970–1980. *Comp. Polit. Stud.* 4:453–84

Brint S. 1984. New class and cumulative trend explanations of the liberal attitudes of professionals. *Am. J. Sociol.* 90:30–71

Brint S. 1994. *In an Age of Experts: The Changing Role of Professionals in Politics and Public Life*. Princeton, NJ: Princeton Univ. Press

Bullard RD. 1990. *Dumping in Dixie: Race, Class and Environmental Quality*. Boulder, CO: Westview

Burklin WP. 1984. *Grune Politik*. Opladen: Westdeutscher Verlag

Burklin WP. 1985. The German Greens: the post industrial non-established and the political system. *Int. Polit. Sci. Rev.* 6(4)463–81

Calhoun C. 1993. What's new about new social movements? The early 19th century reconsidered. *Soc. Sci. Hist.* 17:385–427

Canel E. 1992. New social movement theory and resource mobilization: the need for integration. In *Organizing Dissent: Contemporary Social Movements in Theory and Practice,* ed. WK Carroll, pp. 22–51. Toronto: Garamond

Capra F, Spretnak C. 1984. *Green Politics*. New York: EP Dutton

Carroll WK, ed. 1992. *Organizing Dissent: Contemporary Social Movements in Theory and Practice*. Toronto: Garamond

Chandler WM, Siaroff A. 1986. Postindustrial politics in Germany and the origins of the Greens. *Comp. Polit.* 18:303–25

Cohen J. 1983. Rethinking social movements. *Berkeley J. Sociol.* 28:97–114

Cohen J. 1985. Strategy or identity: new theoretical paradigms and contemporary social movements. *Soc. Res.* 52:663–716

Cotgrove S, Duff A. 1981. Environmentalism, values, and social change. *Br. J. Sociol.* 32:92–110

Crighton E, Mason DS. 1986. Solidarity and the Greens: the rise of new social movements in East and West Europe. *Res. in Soc. Movements: Conflict and Change* 9:155–75

Dalton RJ, Kuechler M, Burklin W. 1990. The challenge of new social movements. In *Challenging the Political Order,* ed. RJ Dalton, M Kuechler, pp. 3–20. New York: Oxford Univ. Press

D'Anieri P, Ernst C, Kier E. 1990. New social movements in historical perspective. *Comp. Polit.* 22:445–58

Diani M, Lodi G. 1988. Three in one: currents in the Milan ecology movement. In *International Social Movement Research,* ed. B Klandermans, E Kriesi, S Tarrow, 1:103–24. Greenwich, CT: JAI

Eder K. 1982. A new social movement? *Telos* 52:5–20

Eder K. 1985. The 'new' social movements: moral crusades, political pressure groups, or social movements? *Sociol. Res.* 52:869–901

Ehrenreich J, Ehrenreich B. 1977. The professional-managerial class. *Radical Am.* 11:7–31

Epstein B. 1990. Rethinking social movement theory. *Socialist Rev.* 21:35–65

Evers T. 1985. Identity: the hidden side of social movements in Latin America. In *New Social Movements and the State in Latin America,* ed. D Slater, pp. 43–71. Amsterdam: CEDLA

Eyerman R. 1984. Social movements and social theory. *Sociology* 18:71–82

Falik M. 1983. *Ideology and Abortion Policy Politics.* New York: Praeger

Feher F, Heller A. 1983. From Red to Green. *Telos* 59:35–44

Gelb J, Palley ML. 1982. *Women and Public Policies.* Princeton: Princeton Univ. Press

Gorz A. 1982. *Farewell to the Working Class.* London: Pluto

Gouldner AW. 1979. *The Future of Intellectuals and the Rise of the New Class.* New York: Seabury

Gusfield JR. 1994. The reflexivity of social movements: collective behavior and mass society theory revisited. In *New Social Movements: From Ideology to Identity,* ed. E Laraña, H Johnston, JR Gusfield, pp. 58–78. Philadelphia:Temple Univ. Press

Habermas J. 1981. New social movements. *Telos* 49:33–37

Habermas J. 1987. *The Theory of Communicative Action.* Vol 2. Cambridge, Eng.: Polity

Hager C. 1993. Citizen movements and technological policymaking in Germany. *Ann. Am. Acad. Polit. Soc. Sci.* 528:42–55

Hershey MR. 1993. Citizens' groups and political parties in the United States. *Ann. Am. Acad. Polit. Soc. Sci.* 528:142–56

Hirschman AO. 1981. *Shifting Involvements.* Princeton, NJ: Princeton Univ. Press

Huntington S. 1981. *American Politics: The Promise of Disharmony.* Cambridge, MA: Harvard Univ. Press

Inglehart R. 1977. *The Silent Revolution: Changing Values and Political Styles Among Western Publics.* Princeton, NJ: Princeton Univ. Press

Inglehart R. 1981. Post-materialism in an environment of insecurity. *Am. Polit. Sci. Rev.* 75:880–900

Inglehart R. 1990. Values, ideology, and cognitive mobilization in new social movements. In *Challenging the Political Order,* ed. RJ Dalton, M Kuechler, pp. 23–42. New York: Oxford Univ. Press

Kaase M. 1990. Social movements and political innovation. In *Challenging the Political Order,* ed. RJ Dalton, M Kuechler, pp. 84–101. New York: Oxford Univ. Press

Kaltefleiter W, Pfaltzgraff RL, eds. 1985. *The Peace Movements in Europe and the United States.* London: Croom Helm

Katzenstein MF, Muller CM, eds. 1987. *The Women's Movements of the United States and Western Europe.* Philadelphia: Temple Univ. Press

Kauffman LA. 1990. The anti-politics of identity. *Socialist Rev.* 20:69–80

Kitschelt H. 1990. New social movements and "New Politics" parties in Western Europe. In *Challenging the Political Order,* ed. RJ Dalton, M Kuechler, pp. 179–208. New York: Oxford Univ. Press

Kitschelt H. 1993. Social movements, political parties, and democratic theory. *Ann. Am. Acad. Polit. Soc. Sci.* 528:13–29

Klandermans B. 1986. New social movements and resource mobilization: the European and the American approach. *Int. J. Mass Emergencies & Disasters* 4:13–37

Klandermans B. 1994. Transient identities? Membership patterns in the Dutch peace movement. See Laraña et al, pp. 168–84

Klandermans B, Tarrow S. 1986. Mobilization into social movements: synthesizing European and American approaches. In *From Structure to Action: Comparing Social Movement Research Across Cultures,* Vol. 1, Int. Soc. Movement Res., ed. B Klandermans, H Kriesi, S Tarrow, pp. 1–38. Greenwich, CT: JAI

Kolinsky E. 1989. *The Greens in West Germany,* New York: Berg

Koopmans R. 1983. The dynamics of protest waves: West Germany, 1965 to 1989. *Am. Sociol. Rev.* 58:637–58

Kriesi H, Koopmans R, Dyvendak JW, Guigni MG. 1995. *New Social Movements in Western*

*Europe*. Minneapolis, MN: Univ. Minn. Press

Kristol I. 1972. About equality. *Commentary* 54:41–47

Laclau E, Mouffe C. 1985. *Hegemony and Socialist Strategy: Towards a Radical Democratic Politics*. London: Verso

Ladd EC Jr. 1978. The new lines are drawn: class and ideology in America. Part I. *Public Opin.* 3:48–53

Ladd EC Jr. 1979. Pursuing the new class: social theory and survey data. In *The New Class?* ed. B Bruce-Briggs, pp. 101–22. New Brunswick, NJ: Transaction Books

Laraña E, Johnston H, Gusfield JR, eds. 1994. *New Social Movements: From Ideology to Identity.* Philadelphia: Temple Univ. Press

Lowe PD, Goyder JM. 1983. *Environmental Groups in Politics*. London: Allen & Unwin

Melucci A. 1980. The new social movements: a theoretical approach. *Soc. Sci. Info.* 19:199–226

Melucci A. 1981. Ten hypotheses for the analysis of social movements. In *Contemporary Italian Sociology,* ed. D Pinto, pp. 173–94. New York: Cambridge Univ. Press

Melucci A. 1984. An end to social movements? *Soc. Sci. Info.* 23:819–35

Melucci A. 1985. The symbolic challenge of contemporary movements. *Sociol. Res.* 52:789–815

Melucci A. 1994. A strange kind of newness: what's new in new social movements. See Laraña et al, pp. 101–30

Molotch H. 1970. Oil in Santa Barbara and power in America. *Sociol. Inquiry* 40:131–44

Mooers C, Sears A. 1992. The "New Social Movements" and the withering away of state theory. In *Organizing Dissent: Contemporary Social Movements in Theory and Practice,* ed. WK Carroll, pp. 52–68. Toronto: Garamond

Mottl TL. 1980. The analysis of countermovements. *Soc. Probl.* 27:620–35

Mouffe C. 1984. Towards a theoretical interpretation of new social movements. In *Rethinking Marx.* New York: Int. Gen./IMMRC

Muller-Rommel F. 1985. Social movements and the Greens: the new internal politics in Germany. *Eur. J. Polit. Res.* 13:53–67

Muller-Rommel F. 1990. New political movements and the decline of party organization. In *Challenging the Political Order,* ed. RJ Dalton, M Kuechler, pp. 209–31. New York: Oxford Univ. Press

Namenwirth ZJ, Weber RP. 1987. *Dynamics of Culture.* Boston: Allen & Unwin

Offe C. 1985. New social movements: challenging the boundaries of institutional politics. *Sociol. Res.* 52:817–68

Olofsson G. 1988. After the working-class movement? An essay on what's 'new' and what's 'social' in the new social movements. *Acta* 31:15–34

Opp K. 1988. Grievances and participation in social movements. *Am. Sociol. Rev.* 53:853–64

Parkin F. 1968. *Middle Class Radicalism.* New York: Praeger

Pichardo NA. 1993. *Social movements and social structure: the onset of industrialization and the changing shape of social movements in the United States.* Am. Sociol. Assoc. Conf.

Pichardo NA. 1995. The power elite and elite-driven countermovements: the associated farmers of California during the 1930s. *Sociol. Forum* 10:21–50

Pichardo NA, Sullivan-Catlin H, Deane G. 1995. *Is the personal political: everyday behavioral correlates of environmental identity.* Am. Social Assoc. Conf., Washington, DC

Plotke D. 1990. What's so new about new social movements? *Socialist Rev.* 20:81–102

Poguntke T. 1993. *Alternative Politics*. Edinburgh: Edinburgh Univ. Press

Rochon TR. 1990. The West European peace movement and the theory of new social movements. In *Challenging the Political Order,* ed. RJ Dalton, M Kuechler, pp. 105–21. New York: Oxford Univ. Press

Rochon TR, Mazmanian DA. 1993. Social movements and the policy process. *Ann. Am. Acad. Polit. Soc. Sci.* 528:75–87

Rudig W. 1988. Peace and ecology movements in Western Europe. *Western Europe Polit.* 11:26–39

Sassoon J. 1984. Ideology, symbolic action and rituality in social movements: the effects on organizational forms. *Soc. Sci. Info.* 23:861–73

Schlesinger AM Jr. 1986. *The Cycles of American History*. Boston: Houghton Mifflin

Scott A. 1990. *Ideology and the New Social Movements*. London: Unwin Hyman

Shaiko RG. 1993. Greenpeace U.S.A.: something old, new, borrowed. *Ann. Am. Acad. Polit. Soc. Sci.* 528:88–100

Slater D, ed. 1985. *New Social Movements and the State in Latin America*. Amsterdam: CEDLA

Szasz A. 1994. *Ecopopulism: Toxic Waste and the Movement for Environmental Justice*. Minneapolis, MN: Univ. Minn. Press

Tarrow S. 1983. *Struggling to Reform: Social Movements and Policy Change During Cycles of Protest*. Ithaca, NY: Cornell Univ. (Western Societies Pap. No. 15)

Tarrow S. 1989. *Democracv and Disorder: Protest and Politics in Italy 1965–1975*. Oxford, England: Clarendon

Tarrow S. 1990. The Phantom of the Opera: political parties and social movements of the 1960s and 1970s in Italy. In *Challenging the Political Order,* ed. RJ Dalton, M Kuechler, pp. 251–73. New York: Oxford Univ. Press

Tarrow S. 1991. *Struggle, Politics, and Reform: Collective Action, Social Movements, and Cycles of Protest.* Ithaca, NY: Cornell Univ. (Western Societies Pap. No. 21)

Tarrow S. 1994. *Power in Movement.* New York: Cambridge Univ. Press

Tilly, C. 1979. Repertoires of contention in America and Britain, 1750–1830. In *The Dynamics of Social Movements*, ed. MN Zald, J McCarthy, pp. 126–55. Cambridge, MA: Winthrop

Touraine A. 1971. *The May Movement: Revolt and Reform.* New York: Random House

Touraine A. 1977. *The Self-Production of Society*. Chicago: Univ. Chicago Press

Touraine A. 1981. *The Voice and the Eye: An Analysis of Social Movements.* Cambridge, MA: Cambridge Univ. Press

Touraine A. 1982. Triumph or downfall of civil society? In *Humanities in Review,* ed. D Reiss, pp. 218–34. New York: Cambridge Univ. Press

Van der Gaag M. 1985. Women organizing. In *The Invisible Decade*, ed. G Ashworth, L Bonnerjea, pp. 133–40. London: Gower

Walsh EJ. 1981. Resource mobilization and citizen protest in communities around Three Mile Island. *Soc. Probl.* 29:1–21

Weiner R. 1982. Collective identity formation and social movements. *Psychol. Soc. Theory* 3:13–23

Zald MN, Useem B. 1987. Movement and countermovement interaction: mobilization, tactics, and state involvement. In *Social Movements in an Organizational Society*, ed. MN Zald, JD McCarthy, pp. 319–36. New Brunswick, NJ: Transaction Books

Zimmerman MK. 1987. The women's health movement: a critique of medical enterprise and the position of women. In *Analyzing Gender,* ed. BB Hess, MM Ferree, pp. 442–72. Newbury Park, CA: Sage

*Annu. Rev. Sociol. 1997. 23:431–53*


# WOMEN'S EMPLOYMENT AND THE GAIN TO MARRIAGE: The Specialization and Trading Model

*Valerie Kincade Oppenheimer*
10345 Strathmore Drive, Los Angeles, California 90024; e-mail: valko@ucla.edu

KEY WORDS: women's independence effect, delayed marriage, marital instability, theory of marriage

ABSTRACT

This chapter critically examines the hypothesis that women's rising employment levels have increased their economic independence and hence have greatly reduced the desirability of marriage. Little firm empirical support for this hypothesis is found. The apparent congruence in time-series data of women's rising employment with declining marriage rates and increasing marital instability is partly a result of using the historically atypical early postwar behavior of the baby boom era as the benchmark for comparisons and partly due to confounding trends in delayed marriage with those of nonmarriage. Support for the hypothesis in multivariate analyses is found only in cross-sectional aggregate-level studies, which are poor tests of an individual-level behavioral hypothesis and which also present difficulty in establishing the appropriate causal direction. Individual-level analyses of marriage formation using longitudinal data and hazard modeling uniformly fail to support the hypothesis, while analyses of marital dissolution yield mixed results. Theoretically, the hypothesis also has severe limitations. The frequent tendency to equate income equality between spouses with women's economic independence and a lowered gain to marriage fails to distinguish between situations where high gains to marriage may be the result of income equality from situations where the result is a very low gain to marriage. Focusing on income ratios alone also tends to distract attention from the underlying causes of these ratios and their structural determinants. Finally, the independence hypothesis is based on a model of marriage that views the gain to marriage as a result of gender-role specialization and exchange. Historical evidence on the family indicates that this is a high risk and inflexible family strategy for independent nuclear families and one that is in strong contrast to contemporary family patterns.



0360-0572/97/0815-0431$08.00

## INTRODUCTION

The economic role of American women, especially married women, has been undergoing a major transformation since World War II. These changes have inspired a large and varied literature, some of it focusing primarily on women's labor-market status and some on the familial implications of women's expanded work roles. This chapter emphasizes one facet of the latter body of work: the hypothesis that women's rising employment has led to a decrease in the desirability of marriage and hence is responsible for what is increasingly being called the "retreat from marriage" or, alternatively, the "decline of marriage." In the pages below I critically examine both the theoretical basis of this hypothesis and the empirical research it has inspired.

A long-standing and influential tradition in the social science literature is the importance of differentiated sex roles for a stable marriage system. In the early postwar period this idea was emphasized by Talcott Parsons (1949), who argued that sex-role segregation was a functional necessity for marital stability and even for the viability of society itself. More recently, this same theme has been elaborated somewhat differently in the economic theory of marriage by Gary Becker (1981). In an argument very similar to one Durkheim (1960) made over a century ago, Becker maintains that the major gain to marriage lies in the mutual dependence of spouses, arising out of their specialized functions—the woman in domestic production (and reproduction), the man in market work. Marriage then involves trading the fruits of these different skills. In response to economic growth and the rising wages it produces, however, women's market work also rises. The result is that women become less specialized and more economically independent, leading, in turn, to a decline in the desirability of marrying or of staying married.

Not all scholars necessarily agree with Becker's argument in its entirety. Nevertheless, an economic independence argument of one sort or another has had wide appeal among sociologists as well as economists and is currently one of the major contenders among attempts to explain recent marriage and family trends in the United States (Ross & Sawhill 1975, Cherlin 1979, 1992, Preston & Richards 1975, Waite & Spitze 1981, Fuchs 1983, Espenshade 1985, Goldscheider & Waite 1986, Farley 1988, Schoen & Wooldredge 1989, McLanahan & Casper 1995). One reason is that the model seems to have tremendous face validity. The notion of specialized sex roles fits in well with our views of how the traditional family historically functioned, and the rapid changes in marital behavior appear to have followed very closely upon the rapid rise in married women's employment, especially that of young women. Moreover, the theory has the elegance of simplicity; yet it can apparently explain a wide variety of complex changes and differentials in marriage and family behavior—from delayed marriage to nonmarriage, marital instability, nonmarital cohabitation, female-headed households, declining fertility, and so forth.

This review examines several aspects of the research on the hypothesis that women's increasing market work has discouraged marriage formation and encouraged marital instability, hereafter referred to as the "independence hypothesis." The discussion deals first with the work relevant to the empirical status of the hypothesis and then critically examines the underlying theory—the specialization and trading model of marriage.

## EMPIRICAL ISSUES

The following discussion investigates four major aspects of the empirical analysis of the independence hypothesis. The first examines how well simple time series data match the patterns predicted by the theory. The second investigates whether the marital behavior predicted by the theory is what is actually being observed. Next we consider the result of multivariate tests of the theory, distinguishing between aggregate- and individual-level analyses.

### *Evidence from Time Series*

WORK AND MARITAL BEHAVIOR The apparently close correlation between the trends in married women's work and marriage behavior is cited by many scholars as providing general support for the independence hypothesis (Becker 1981, Davis 1985, Espenshade 1985, Farley 1988, Cherlin 1992, McClanahan & Casper 1995). And the changes are very impressive. On the one hand, although married women's employment had been slowly rising throughout the twentieth century, this shift was greatly accelerated in the postwar period. Most importantly, starting in the 1960s, the rise in the labor force participation of young married women really accelerated, and since then the age pattern of their employment has increasingly resembled men's, with proportions approaching 70% for women into their mid-fifties (Oppenheimer 1994). On the other hand, dating from the late 1960s, very substantial changes have occurred in marriage and family behavior. As a consequence, by the 1990s, age at marriage was much later than in the 1960s, and the proportions of those never marrying may be rising as well. For example, the proportions of women who were never married by age 25 rose from 14% in 1960 to 42% in 1990 (US Bureau of the Census 1991). All this is especially true for African Americans. For all, marital instability has also become much more prevalent, and although remarriage rates may be high, they are lower than in the past; female-headed families have been on the rise, again especially for African Americans. All these changes in marital and family behavior, on the one hand, and married women's employment behavior, on the other, tend to create the presumption that there must be a major causal connection between the two, and the economic independence argument seems to provide one important possible explanation.

Impressive as the time-series data are, however, their support of the independence hypothesis may be more apparent than real. The problem is that if one follows the historical series back in time—before the 1950s—marriage and family behavior are no longer so nicely correlated with trends in women's employment. Central to the hypothesis is the idea that when the traditional family prevails, characterized as it is by marital sex-role specialization, and the gain to marriage is presumably high, age at marriage will be young, marriage will be universal, and marital instability low. However, age at marriage was by no means historically low in American society, any more than it was in Western European societies (Cherlin 1992, Oppenheimer 1994, Hajnal 1965, Goldstone 1986, Banks 1954). Age at marriage seems to have been quite young for American women around 1800 but subsequently rose and was relatively high and quite variable for late nineteenth century cohorts (Sanderson 1979, Thornton & Rodgers 1983). Age at marriage, as well as its variability, then declined, reaching a low for the cohorts marrying in the early post-World War II period. Since then, it has risen again to the levels exhibited by early twentieth century cohorts; in fact, as Cherlin (1992) points out, it appears that women's age at marriage has now risen even above that of late nineteenth century cohorts. However, this is probably not too significant since, compared to the present day, the delayed marriages of late nineteenth century cohorts existed despite much higher proportions of rural dwellers whose age at marriage was relatively young (Taeuber & Taeuber 1958).

In short, the early postwar period did not represent "typical" traditional marriage timing patterns. On the contrary it was most atypical in its young age at marriage and low variability in marriage timing. Nevertheless, that period has become the benchmark against which all subsequent behavior has been compared. More historically typical was a tendency for age at marriage to fluctuate, probably in response to changing circumstances, and long before one could establish a major causal role for women's economic independence (Thornton & Rodgers 1983, Oppenheimer 1994). In fact, age at marriage was dropping in the first half of the twentieth century at the same time that single women's market employment was rising (Goldin 1990).

With regard to marital instability, although the proportion of all marriages ending in divorce has risen substantially since the 1950s and 1960s, the trend toward increased marital instability is of long-standing in American society and greatly predates the postwar rise in married women's labor force participation (Preston & McDonald 1979). There is also some evidence that part of the rise in marital instability may be more apparent than real—at least for African Americans. Thus, in an analysis of the 1910 census public use sample, Preston and his colleagues (1992) found evidence that, high though mortality was, there was also a considerable over-reporting of widowhood among African-American women with children, indicating that there was much more marital or union instability in this period than was directly reported in the census or than is commonly believed to be the case. Some evidence also suggests that the long-term increase in marital instability has leveled off and could possibly be reversing itself (Martin & Bumpass 1989, Schoen & Weinick 1993), but it is too soon to determine this conclusively, especially given the possible role of business-cycle fluctuations and shifts in the proportion of separations ending in divorces. However, the divorce rate peaked in 1979 at 22.8 per 1000 married women aged 15 years and over and has declined gradually since then, reaching 19.8 in 1995, the lowest rate since 1974 (National Center for Health Statistics 1990, 1995). Given the well-documented tendency of marriages formed at a young age to be unstable, the rise in delayed marriage may be contributing to the declines in marital instability.

One marriage-related trend that is of fairly recent origin is the rapid rise in cohabitation in the United States. Even descriptive data on cohabitation was very poor until the 1987–1988 National Survey of Family and Households provided valuable retrospective data on cohort shifts in cohabitation behavior (Bumpass & Sweet 1989). That study revealed that although only 3% of the 1940–1944 cohort of women had cohabited before age 25, 37% of the 1960–1964 cohorts had done so. However, the extent to which this enormous growth in cohabitation represents a "retreat" from marriage greatly depends on the extent to which cohabitation is a substitute for marriage or a stage in the courtship process. In this respect, cohabitation appears to be a heterogeneous phenomenon. An increasing proportion of first marriages start as cohabitations—rising from 9% for the first marriages formed in 1965–1974 to 39% for the 1980–1984 cohorts. Moreover, of first cohabitations started in the 1975–1984 period, 56% turned into marriages by the end of the fifth year. Hence, the rapid rise in cohabitation should be contributing to marriage delays, but for a substantial proportion of cohabitators it does not signify a rejection of marriage. In fact, Bumpass and his colleagues (1991) found that most of those currently cohabiting expected to marry their partners. Moreover, in his event-history analysis of young women's marriage formation from the NLSY (National Longitudinal Survey of Youth), Lichter (1992) found that the odds a woman married in a year were 66% higher if she was cohabiting at the previous interview. Hence, here cohabiting seemed to be operating as a proxy for being engaged.

In sum, trends in marital instability had their inception long before the rapid rise in married women's employment started. In the case of marriage formation, the historical record is characterized by considerable fluctuations, indicating a responsiveness to changing circumstances rather than the pattern of early and universal marriage supposed to be characteristic of the specialization model of marriage. And while cohabitation is a relatively recent phenomenon, for a substantial segment of those who cohabit it obviously represents a stage in the courtship process rather than a retreat from marriage. In short, these patterns raise serious doubts about putting too much reliance on a truncated time series' apparent support of the independence hypothesis.

DELAYED MARRIAGE OR NONMARRIAGE? The independence hypothesis is essentially a theory of nonmarriage, for it is arguing that if, by their own endeavors, women can achieve approximately the same income as a prospective spouse, there is not much to gain by marrying and specializing in home production. However, to date, there has been little effort to articulate how this argument could lead to delayed instead of nonmarriage. If most of the changes we are observing are shifts in marriage timing rather than in nonmarriage, then the independence hypothesis is not really highly relevant. It will, in fact, be garnering far more empirical support than it analytically deserves if there is a serious confounding of delayed marriage with nonmarriage in the statistics. Moreover, a considerable delay in marriage may, even on its own, promote some nonmarriage, especially for women whose marriage-market position appears to deteriorate with age (Goldman et al 1984, Watkins 1984).

Aside from the confounding problem, nonmarriage and delayed marriage are two rather different phenomena. There are many reasons why varying numbers of people may want to or feel compelled to delay marriage but still wish to marry eventually—i.e. they still see a major gain from marriage. For example, economic factors, school enrollment, service in the military, getting established in a career, and so on, may all signify the necessity or advantage of delaying marriage without affecting the desirability of marriage per se. Hence, theories designed to explain nonmarriage may not be very pertinent if much of what is really happening is delayed marriage. Moreover, the particularly late age at which late marriers marry in a period of delayed marriages greatly increases the difficulty of interpreting whether or not currently observed trends signify a considerable rise in nonmarriage. This is especially the case for men, who usually marry later than women.

So far, the evidence indicates that, while there is considerable evidence of delayed marriage, nonmarriage will not rise markedly for white women and will remain at or below the proportions for late nineteenth century cohorts. For example, various estimates made in the 1980s suggest that about 9% of white women born in the early 1950s would never marry, up from the low of 5% for the cohorts born during the 1920s but below the 12% for the 1880 cohort. Marriage is so delayed among African Americans that predictions of the proportion never marrying are much riskier; however, these estimates have ranged from about 25% to 30% (Rodgers & Thornton 1985, Bennett et al 1989). In sum, the independence argument may still be potentially useful in explaining the apparently sharp rise in nonmarriage among African Americans. However, unless the hypothesis can be made more explicitly relevant to the question of *delayed* marriage, it can explain little of the observed trends in marriage formation for white women despite the enormous postwar changes in their labor-market behavior and, more recently, in their marriage behavior as well.

## *Multivariate Analyses*

The use of time series data in the investigation of the role of women's rising employment in changing marital behavior has been largely limited to illustrating the similarity among the two trends. A more rigorous approach involves the use of multivariate techniques to try to establish the causal connection between women's labor-market behavior and marital behavior. Basically two types of multivariate approaches have been used to test the independence hypothesis, each of which is usually applied with a different type of data. One is aggregate-level analyses, which typically use census data; the unit of analysis is a geographic area such as a metropolitan area or a labor market area. The second and larger group of studies consists of micro-level analyses of longitudinal data, where the individual is the unit of analysis. Micro-level analyses generally use samples that have longitudinal individual-level data, either of a retrospective nature or because they are panel studies, or they may include a combination of both sources of life-history data. A recent development is also to supplement the micro-level data with aggregate-level information in the form of contextual variables in order to provide information on the characteristics of the respondent's marriage market (Lichter et al 1992, Lloyd & South 1996).

AGGREGATE-LEVEL ANALYSES The major support for the independence hypothesis in the regression analyses of marriage formation has come from aggregate level analyses using census data (Preston & Richards 1975, Lichter et al 1991, Fossett & Kiecolt 1993, and McLanahan & Casper 1995). The dependent variables in these studies are all prevalence measures—for example, the proportion of women who are currently or recently married. The explanatory variables relevant to the independence hypothesis are usually measures of employment and of economic status—typically, earnings. Some also have educational attainment data, useful as an indicator of long-term labor-market position. In general, all these studies have found that earnings (or an SES indicator in the case of the Fossett & Kiecolt study on African Americans), employment, and schooling (where included) had a negative impact on the marital status composition of an area.

While these results appear to support the independence hypothesis, aggregate-level analyses of marriage timing have several serious drawbacks. One is that the hypothesis itself refers to individual-level behavior, and testing it with aggregate-level data can lead to misleading results because the same factors that produce area-level differences in the prevalence of married people do not necessarily produce the same kind and level of individual differences in the incidence of marriage. Moreover, it is not at all unusual to get opposite-sign results from macro- and micro-level analyses of approximately the same phenomenon, leading to what has been called the "ecological fallacy" (Robinson 1950, Achen & Shively 1995).

One reason why aggregate-level tests of the independence hypothesis may be misleading comes from the difficulty of establishing causal ordering between marital status and economic behavior by using cross-sectional census-type data. One cannot assume that the economic behavior and characteristics of women are necessarily the *determinants* of marriage characteristics because, in many circumstances, they may be the *consequences*. One of the usual "solutions" to the causal ordering problem in social research is to try to establish the appropriate time order of the variables. However, with census data, most of the variables are measured at the time of the census or, at best, during the previous year. Moreover, the dependent variable is a prevalence rather than an incidence variable. The proportion who are currently married in any particular area is a residual of those who were married at some unspecified time prior to the census and who did not separate, divorce, or become widowed before the census or, if they did, had remarried. And for an unknown number of women, none or only a few of these events may even have occurred in the area in which they were living at the time of the census.[1] In short, the proportion married in an area at the date of a census is a complex variable, resulting from a number of processes that have occurred over an unspecified length of time and in unspecified locations, making it very difficult to determine time order or the spatial connections essential to establishing causal connections.

One recent analysis well illustrates some of these problems. Using metropolitan areas in the 1970–1990 censuses as the unit of analysis, McLanahan & Casper (1995) regressed the percentage of women aged 25–29 who were married on, among other variables, the percentage of women, also aged 25–29, who were working full-time year-round. They found that employment experience had an apparently large negative effect on marital status and interpreted this as support for the independence hypothesis. However, the true causal direction is very likely to be from marital-status composition to employment composition,

[1]Thus in their analysis of labor market areas (LMA) in the 1980 census, Lichter and his colleagues (1991) found that, on average, 33% of currently married women, aged 20–29, had in-migrated into the LMA in the previous five years.

rather than the reverse. Married women in the 25–29 age group are in the midst of their reproductive period and likely to have young children; we also know from individual-level data that such women are less likely to work year-round full-time than other women in that age group. For example, in 1990, for the United States as a whole, although 68% of mothers of children under six had some work experience during the previous year, only 28% worked year-round full-time (Bianchi 1995, p. 125). Moreover, married women, especially those with young children, were even less likely to be so employed in previous censuses. Hence, if there is a higher proportion of women aged 25–29 who are married in some areas rather than others or married with young children, the proportions working year-round will be greatly depressed in those areas. Similarly, metropolitan areas with a higher proportion of single or separated/divorced women are likely to have considerably higher proportions working year-round full-time because these women usually have to work to support themselves. In sum, given the difficulty of unambiguously establishing causal ordering in such analyses, combined with a frequently strong argument for a causal direction that is the reverse of that hypothesized, aggregate-level analyses of this nature offer a poor empirical test of the independence hypothesis.

However, an entirely different approach from the regression analyses discussed above has been developed by Schoen (1988), and it comes up with rather different conclusions. Schoen's approach is basically a marriage market analysis and has the advantage of including both sexes and hence can distinguish between the effect of changes in the availability of partners with certain characteristics and the desirability of these partners—what Schoen has called the "force of attraction." Using *Current Population Survey* data, Qian & Preston (1993) applied this model to changes in white marriage behavior from 1972–1979–1987 by age and educational attainment. Among other things, they found that marriage propensities rose among college educated women over age 25 in the 1979–1987 period, despite a decline in the availability of college educated men in the appropriate age groups, indicating that women in the presumably most favorable labor-market position were not using their economic independence to avoid marriage and were sufficiently attractive marriage prospects that they were able to overcome a marriage squeeze situation.[2] In addition, Qian & Preston observed a sharp rise in the "force of attraction" for older women compared to younger between 1979 and 1987, suggesting that delayed rather than nonmarriage was occurring.

[2]These findings were in strong contrast to a study by Bennett & Bloom that was widely reported in the popular press but never published in a peer-reviewed journal. They estimated that college-educated white women who were still single at age 30 would have only a 20% chance of ever marrying. For a discussion of the popular and scientific controversy surrounding these estimates, see Cherlin 1990.

MICRO-LEVEL ANALYSES In contradistinction to the results from aggregate level analyses, multivariate studies of the marriage formation behavior of individuals have rarely provided any support for the independence hypothesis. Most of these studies utilize longitudinal data and were thus able to establish time order between the explanatory and dependent variables; hence they can make a better case for causal ordering, although time order is not always a reliable criterion. Most also are event-history analyses of one sort or another and hence are able to avoid the inherent selectivity biases that used to characterize analyses of the age at marriage of samples of relatively young ever-married people (Yamaguchi 1991).

While the independence argument would lead to the prediction that, net of school enrollment, more educated women should be more economically independent of marriage, these micro-level regression analyses show that they have a higher rather than a lower propensity to marry (Cherlin 1980, Goldscheider & Waite 1986, Mare & Winship 1991, Lichter et al 1992, Oppenheimer & Lew 1995, Oppenheimer et al 1995). Moreover, there is some evidence that the positive effect of schooling on marriage formation has even been increasing over time (Oppenheimer et al 1995). Educational attainment can also be an important factor in remarriage. Using the National Survey of Family and Households (NSFH), Smock (1990) found that although, compared to white women, African Americans generally had a much lower likelihood of remarriage, schooling had a very strong positive effect on remarriage probabilities for African American women whereas it had little impact for whites.

With regard to the effects of employment, the findings also do not support the independence hypothesis (Cherlin 1980, Goldscheider & Waite 1986, Bennett et al 1989, Lichter et al 1992, Oppenheimer & Lew 1995). One exception was Mare & Winship's 1991 micro-level analysis of 1940–1980 census public use sample data, which found a generally negative effect of employment on marriage formation (for white women). However, the employment variable used was constructed rather than observed and hence may not be an entirely unbiased indicator.[3] Women's earnings are also almost always found to have a positive effect on the likelihood of marriage, again the reverse of what is predicted by the independence hypothesis (Goldscheider & Waite 1986, Mare & Winship 1991, Lichter et al 1992, and Oppenheimer & Lew 1995). Moreover, the Oppenheimer & Lew study found that the positive effect of earnings only showed up for women in their mid-to-late twenties rather than among younger women, for whom no effect was observed—a pattern that is the opposite of what would be true if greater economic independence increased the

[3]Because it is generally impossible to determine the time order of variables in the census, Mare & Winship estimated "expected" employment but the variables used to develop these predictions were also measured in the same year as the marriage occurred.

likelihood of never marrying. Oppenheimer & Lew also looked at the effect of occupational level to see whether women in professional and managerial occupations would be any less likely to marry than those in lower-level white-collar occupations—traditionally more typical women's occupations that might be more easily combined with marriage. They found no significant effect except for a negative one for unskilled workers. One micro-level panel study found no effect of weekly earnings (Teachman et al 1987); however, only weekly earnings in the first week in October of each year were available to use, and this may have distorted the results.

A characteristic of virtually all these micro-level analyses of marriage formation is that they use employment and earnings data of the recent past—typically referring to the time of the interview or the year just before each year at risk. This raises several conceptual and measurement problems. First, employment has been both the statistical and social norm for single out-of-school women for over 50 years (Goldin 1990). Aside from the nonemployment that can be attributed to business cycles, those who are not employed should therefore be a highly select group. Hence, it is unclear what the employment status of single women is really measuring; it certainly is not distinguishing between "traditional" and "nontraditional" women. Second, if what we want to get at is the likely long-term labor-market position of women to assess their "independence" of the marriage state, the recent earnings or employment patterns of respondents may be very poor indicators of this, especially given the low earnings and employment instability characteristics of young people, males as well as females. Hence, it is not too surprising that these variables have no negative impact on marriage formation. Probably the best indicator of long-run labor-market position used to date is educational attainment; however, this too has not exhibited a negative effect on women's marriage formation.

In sum, several aggregate-level studies found that women's education, employment, and earnings were negatively related to the proportions married in an area. However, studies of this type generally have serious methodological drawbacks as a vehicle for the analysis of individual-level phenomena and are usually incapable of establishing causal ordering. Moreover, life-history analyses at the more appropriate micro-level, and which typically employ more sophisticated methodologies, have found that similar indicators of labor market position have either little effect or a positive one on marriage formation. These results may reflect offsetting factors at work and hence do not necessarily mean there is no such thing as an independence effect. However, they do indicate that it is unlikely that the independence effect is the driving force behind recent trends in marriage formation.

The analysis of marital instability also provides an opportunity for testing the independence hypothesis. Moreover, if one has information on both partners, it is possible to study not only whether couples with higher-income wives are more likely to separate but, in addition, whether women's relative earnings are an important factor in marital stability. Given the availability of data on husbands, therefore, most panel studies during the past 25 years have included both husbands' and wives' economic behavior in their analyses of the effect of wives' employment on marital instability. Generally, the problem has been formulated in terms of "income" and "independence" effects (Ross & Sawhill 1975, Cherlin 1979). The idea is that a higher income (whatever the source) improves the quality of family life, thereby contributing to family stability. Since the husband has typically been the source of most of the family's income, his labor-market position should have an important effect on marital stability. Husband's economic position has usually been conceptualized in terms of both employment characteristics and earnings in recognition of the possibility that it is the stability of a man's income as well as its size that may affect marital outcomes. A wife's earnings can also have an income effect, but offsetting this is the hypothesized independence effect of her earnings as well as of other sources of income such as AFDC.

By and large, the results of investigations of the independence and income effects on marital stability have been mixed. Some studies have found evidence of an independence effect (Ross & Sawhill 1975, Hannan & Tuma 1978, Cherlin 1979, Moore & Waite 1981, Tzeng 1992), whereas others have come up with negative results (Bumpass, Martin & Sweet 1991, Hoffman & Duncan 1995,[4] Greenstein 1990, 1995, South & Lloyd 1995, and Tzeng & Mare 1995).[5] There are a number of possible reasons for these conflicting findings, including differences in the data sets analyzed, variations in the conceptualization of the problem and in the variables included in the model. A few issues are important to mention, however.

Analyses of marital dissolution are best conducted by taking the marriage at its start and studying the factors affecting it over several years' duration. Otherwise, the sample is increasingly biased across marital durations due to the selective withdrawal of the more divorce prone and those who may have dissolved their marriages for the very reasons the investigator is studying. However, studies using many of the earlier data sets were hampered by serious left-censoring:

[4]The generalizability of this study is somewhat limited, however. The major interest of the researchers was to measure the influence of welfare benefits on marital disruptions; hence they limited the sample to couples with children. The analysis may therefore underestimate an independence effect, should it exist.

[5]Tzeng & Mare's results were actually somewhat mixed. They found that the combined income of the couple had no effect on the odds of a marital disruption and neither did the difference between the earnings of the partners—all of which failed to support the independence argument. However, an increase in the wife's earnings over the marriage did have a small positive effect on the likelihood of a marital disruption.

i.e. marriages of varying durations were picked up in the sample and, although followed from that point on, it was not possible to reconstruct the entire history of a marriage and most particularly the history of the explanatory variables before the panel started. This was the case with the PSID (Panel Study of Income Dynamics) used by Ross & Sawhill (1975) and the NLS panel of women aged 30–44 at the first interview (Cherlin 1979). Hence, there is bound to be a certain amount of selectivity bias in these samples, and it is difficult to determine how this affected the results although it probably biases coefficients downward. Moreover, the methodology of analyzing longitudinal data has greatly improved in recent years and now usually involves hazard modeling of one sort or another. Except for the pioneering methodological work of Hannan & Tuma (1978), these methods were not yet generally available for the earlier studies, and it is these studies that have tended to show that women's market position is likely to lead to marital disruption.

Two additional factors may produce different results among studies, and these refer more to how the independence effect is conceptualized and measured. Some studies use absolute income while others use some measure of relative income. While the hypothesis implies that the relative earnings of wives might be an important factor in the gain to marriage and hence should be directly modeled, using the ratio of wives' to husbands' income alone can lead to ambiguous results. Thus, one study found that the higher the ratio of wife's/husband's income, the greater the likelihood of a separation (Cherlin 1979). But there are two very different explanations of why relative income might be higher for some families than others. One is that the wife's earnings in some families are higher compared to others, reflecting a better labor-market position and, consequently, indicating a greater financial independence of her husband. However, the ratio could also be high because the husband's earnings are low compared to other men, while the wife herself may be also in a very weak labor-market position. This latter situation does not really seem to fit the original conceptualization of the independence effect. Furthermore, given the sex differentials in earnings, husband's earnings are likely to be quite low when the ratio is high indicating that the "independence" and "income" effects may be confounded. Hence, the income of the husband also needs to be controlled in some fashion.

A second problem, characteristic of almost all studies of women's economic role in marital instability, is the difficulty of establishing causal direction. This is one case where time order is not really a reliable indicator of causal ordering. Finding out that the likelihood of a separation in any given year increases when a woman's earnings or employment position were more favorable in the previous year does not necessarily support the independence hypothesis; this is because women who believe their marriage is in trouble may increase their work effort, and hence their earnings, in anticipation of a breakup. A number of researchers have suggested this possibility, and at least two empirical analyses have found some evidence that this is the case (Johnson & Skinner 1986, Peterson 1989). This possibility of a reverse causal direction suggests that the general practice of limiting regression models to information on the behavior and characteristics of respondents in the immediate past may not provide enough data for an adequate evaluation of the independence hypothesis (Spitze 1988). In fact, studies of marriage formation are also generally weak in building in information on the individual's life course and tend to limit themselves to data on the very recent past. Furthermore, few studies follow young people long enough to capture life-cycle changes in explanatory variables or long enough for a relatively large proportion to have made the transition to marriage. Hence right-censoring may be a particular problem in this period of delayed marriage.

## THEORETICAL ISSUES

### *Income Equality and the Gain To Marriage*

Although much used, "economic independence" is really a rather vague concept whose ambiguities need to be more clearly recognized in assessing the effect of women's market work on marriage behavior. A relatively small amount of earnings may actually provide a married woman with the ability to act independently in the sense of making a variety of consumption decisions on her own and increasing her influence in joint consumption decisions. And many women could, with much less income than a prospective spouse, live at a level comparable to families with only the husband-father working. Whether this would also be true for mothers heading their own households is somewhat less clear and partly depends on how much the cost of childcare offsets the greater expense of a two-adult household. In any event, a lot of independence can be bought with earnings that are well below those of similar males who are supporting a family on their earnings alone. This, of course, has always provided the rationale for labor market discrimination against women. Multivariate analyses that use women's absolute earnings may implicitly be getting at this sort of independence.

However, a recurrent theme in sociological discussions of the independence hypothesis is the notion that a woman's economic independence is defined in terms of income equality with her husband and that, furthermore, the gain to marriage is much less with economic independence defined in this manner (Cherlin 1979, Espenshade 1985, Farley 1988, McLanahan & Casper 1995, Sørensen 1995). While this might be considered the logical conclusion of Becker's theory, it is an approach that may often confuse rather than help clarify the nature of the social processes we are trying to study. Neither economic independence nor low gains to marriage necessarily follow from income equality; moreover, income equality may lead to low gains to certain marriages but not because economic independence has been achieved. Basically, the issue revolves around the question: What is economic independence, and what does it have to do with income equality and the gain to marriage? I briefly consider some of these issues below.

Using 1940–1980 census data, Sørensen & McLanahan (1987) addressed the problem of how to measure the extent of married women's dependency (on their husbands) and how this has changed over time. The measure they developed assumed that husbands and wives pool all their economic resources and share them equally; economic dependency is then defined as the difference between the husband's and wife's relative contribution to their combined income. If the wife's income is equal to the husband's then there is no dependence. As expected, given women's rising employment, they found that their indicator of married women's dependency decreased over time. However, it seems very likely that the measure does not just reflect degrees of dependency but also taps differences in the nature of the dependency involved. Two-earner families where the couple pool their resources are families whose level of living is based on their combined income. When the income contribution of each spouse is equal, given economies of scale, neither partner could live as well on his/her own or save and invest as much. Hence if, under the pooling assumption, each is dependent on their joint income, what is really being measured is how symmetrical the economic dependency is. A wife (or husband) who has little or no income exhibits a very asymmetrical as well as a large income dependency and presumably must make other important types of contributions to the marriage for there to be a gain to both partners. This is the classical picture of the specialization and trading model of marriage.

Couples with equal earnings also exhibit dependence, however—a symmetrical dependency in this case. Although increasing symmetrical dependency should improve women's status and bargaining position in the family, marriage still involves important economic interdependencies, and there should still be a substantial economic gain to marriage for this reason alone.[6] What this may also indicate is that the combined income of the two-earner family has come to form the social standard, rather than the husband's income alone. To the extent this is the case, it becomes increasingly difficult for single earners and married couples with a more traditional division of labor to achieve the same level of living as the two-earner family. Hence, the mutual dependence of the two-earner family may not only contribute to their own gain to marriage but

[6]However, even if women achieved economic equality with men in the labor market, this would not necessarily translate to income equality in a marriage. That depends on assortative mating patterns as well as family decisions on how much the woman works over the family life cycle.

may also reduce the relative gain to being single and to marriages characterized by a specialized division of labor (Oppenheimer 1982).

An unfortunate concomitant of defining economic independence in terms of earnings equality is that the significance of the absolute amount of earnings involved and of earnings adequacy almost drops out of the picture. Take, for example, the argument that

> the hypothesis about the decline in marriageable males is really an extension of the women's independence argument, since women's independence is a function of women's earning power relative to men's earning power. Women's independence can increase either because women's earning power goes up faster than men's or because it goes down more slowly than men's ... In principal, the independence argument can account for declines in marriage among men and women at all points in the income distribution (McLanahan & Casper 1995, pp. 34–35).

Following this logic, it is sometimes suggested that the main reason that African Americans are married in much smaller proportions than whites is not their generally poorer and more unstable economic position compared to whites. Rather, the relative earnings of African American women are much higher than those of white women (Farley 1988).[7] Similarly, measuring independence in the analysis of marital instability with earnings ratios alone, without also including some measure of absolute income, tends to equate earnings equality with women's economic independence, no matter how low the income of each partner is. Moreover, emphasizing income ratios per se obscures the underlying determinants of these ratios and discourages research into them and hence impedes the achievement of a greater understanding of the dynamics of social change and socioeconomic differentials. This emphasis also goes against the original rationale of the independence hypothesis, which was that women's increasing earning power increased their economic independence of men thereby reducing the gain to marriage (Becker 1981). It was not that the deteriorating labor-market position of men somehow increased women's economic independence, even if the women involved were themselves in an extremely weak labor-market position. If not dependent on their husbands or another partner, many women with very poor labor market prospects will still be partly or wholly financially dependent on other sources of income—family support or welfare transfers, for example. This seems to be a situation where

[7]This perspective also promotes such rhetorical questions as: "If the earnings of white women rise, compared with those of white men, will we find that white families increasingly resemble current black families? Two decades from now, will the majority of white children be born to unmarried women and raised in families headed by their mothers? Will 30% or 40% of white children live below the poverty line?" (Farley 1988, p. 491). This seems like an exceedingly strange outcome to posit for a rational choice model.

equality at a very low level reduces the gain to marriage but not because it signifies a woman's independence—certainly not in the sense of indicating economic self-sufficiency. In addition, the argument attributes far more power to women in the decision to marry than they actually possess. Many women in a poor labor-market position will not be very attractive marriage prospects themselves—either to men in a better labor-market position or to those in an equally poor position.

## *Coping with Risk and Change*

Most theories, and perhaps economic theories most of all, make certain simplifying assumptions in order to facilitate the process of theory construction and empirical testing. These assumptions, however, can often provide the Achilles heel of a theory. In the case of the specialization model of marriage, the family's environment generally seems to be considered unvaryingly benign, and a family's needs and goals are assumed to be relatively constant over its developmental cycle. Questioning these assumptions, however, raises major doubts about some of the presumed "efficiency" of the specialization model of marriage. For example, although rarely considered in explications of the theory, historical research on the family indicates that extreme sex-role specialization in marriage is essentially a high-risk and inflexible family strategy unless accompanied by supplementary support mechanisms. Even with such supports, specialization often entailed considerable individual and social costs. An inherent problem is that the temporary or permanent loss of one specialist in a family can mean that functions vital to the well-being of the complementary specialist and children are not being performed. Husbands/fathers can die or become ill or disabled; they can lose their jobs and have difficulty finding another one; they could desert the family for a variety of reasons or become an alcoholic; and so on. The result is that the family is left without its major source of income. Except for employment-related shifts, there are similar problems involving the wife-mother specialist. In that case, there could be no one to take care of the children or the home. Specialization may be a feasible strategy in a large extended family household where no particular individual is indispensable because of the redundancy in personnel that can characterize such a system. However, for independent nuclear families and their individual members, specialization entails considerable risks.

Extreme sex-role specialization is also not a very flexible way to deal with the varying needs of nuclear families over their developmental cycle. Since individuals' consumption needs and productive capabilities vary markedly by age, a basic feature of nuclear families is that the ratio of consumers to producers, and hence the family's level of living, can vary substantially over the family's developmental cycle (Berkner 1972, Oppenheimer 1982, Lee 1983). Hence, specialization involves a potentially serious inflexibility in dealing both with changes in a family's internal composition and with the stresses posed by its environment.

The large literature on family history in Western societies indicates that a variety of strategies were developed to maintain economic stability over the family's developmental cycle and in the event of the temporary or permanent loss of specializing parents (Oppenheimer 1982, Ch. 9, Lee 1983). In the past, many of these strategies involved utilizing the productive labor of children, daughters as well as sons (Rowntree 1922, Anderson 1971, Haines 1979, Goldin 1981, Tilly & Scott 1978). The evidence also indicates that utilizing the labor of one's children could exact substantial costs. A sufficient number of children old enough to make an economic difference was generally not available until the middle or later stages of the family cycle. Families who temporarily or permanently lost the contribution of the father early in the family cycle were not greatly helped by such a strategy. And if the mother was lost when the children were young, the family might break up, with children being parcelled out among relatives or even going to orphanages. In general, this economic reliance on one's offspring often led to a pattern of "life cycle poverty" where periods of poverty and comparative plenty alternated over the life cycle of workers (Rowntree 1922). Another well-known disadvantage to the extensive employment of children to supplement their family's income was that it tended to discourage schooling and hence had a negative effect on children's adult socioeconomic status (Perlmann 1988, Goldin 1981, Parsons & Goldin 1989).

Even aside from the drawbacks of using children's work, the economic advantages of this strategy were eventually bound to decline during industrialization. As the structure of demand shifted to a much more skilled labor force and adult male earnings correspondingly rose, the potential relative contribution of the unskilled labor of the family's children declined, particularly in middle class families. This suggests that other equilibrating mechanisms were likely to develop. Hence, from an historical perspective, the rise in married women's employment might be viewed as a functional substitute for the work of their children, facilitating the more extensive schooling of the next generation and thereby fostering intergenerational upward social mobility. In addition, wives' employment is not limited to the later stages of the family's developmental cycle, and wives, as adults, usually have educational attainments roughly similar to those of their husbands, and hence can command much higher wages than can their unskilled children. Moreover, recent research indicates that wives' employment currently plays an important role in offsetting a less favorable earnings position of their husbands (Cancian et al 1993, Levy 1996).

## CONCLUSION

Although the popularity of the women's economic independence explanation of marriage behavior remains strong in the 1990s, this review of the literature found little real empirical support for the hypothesis. Micro-level event-history analyses that follow cohorts throughout their young adulthood generally show that women's educational attainment, employment, and earnings either have little or no effect on marriage formation or, where they do have an effect, find it to be positive, the opposite effect of that hypothesized. The only support for the hypothesis from multivariate analyses is found in aggregate-level studies. However, aggregate-level analyses have serious drawbacks for investigating this micro-level hypothesis, not the least of which is establishing a convincing causal ordering.

The juxtaposition of time series data of marriage behavior with women's employment appears to provide convincing evidence for the hypothesis, but upon closer examination this evidence becomes much less persuasive. In the case of marriage formation, a large part of the support for the hypothesis results from the confounding of delayed marriage with nonmarriage. The independence hypothesis is basically an argument about nonmarriage but, for white women at least, the major trend has been an increase in delayed marriage. The hypothesis could presumably be modified to say that the gain to marriage increases with age, but it is bound to lose a lot of its punch if, instead of making predictions about the gain to marriage in general, it is reduced to making predictions about the gain to marrying at age 22 versus age 20. But, in any event, that case has never even been made.

An additional major problem is that the apparently high correlation of the various time-series trends is largely a function of the starting point chosen. This is almost invariably sometime in the 1950s or early 1960s—i.e. the era that produced the baby-boom, early and universal marriage, lowered divorce rates, and so on. However, when one pushes the time series farther back, it is obvious that the divorce rate had been rising for many decades before married women's employment started its rapid rise. And as far as marriage timing is concerned, the period before World War II exhibited long-term fluctuations in age at marriage and in its variability, all within the era when sex-role specialization in marriage was typical. Hence, the decision to use the benchmark of the 1950s and early 1960s was critical for how the linked time series have been evaluated.

While it is widely recognized that the marriage behavior of the early postwar period is statistically atypical of American historical patterns, it has nevertheless achieved a moral stature that seems to justify its use as the model against which more recent family behavior is evaluated, often in a pejorative light. For example, the desirability of an early marriage is implicit when delayed marriages are described as a "retreat" from marriage or a "decline" in marriage. However, during the period when age at marriage actually was early, there was no such universal approval of it,[8] and it is well known that marriages of the young are much more unstable than marriages formed at older ages.

At the same time that the empirical support for the hypothesis is weak, its theoretical underpinnings are by no means immune from questioning. First, the notion of the efficiency of specialization and exchange as a basis of the marital relationship largely depends on certain assumptions regarding the stability and benevolence of the environment. However, real-world conditions indicate that specialization can be a risky and inflexible strategy for maintaining a family's economic well-being over time; achieving this has often been a result of having more than one earner in the household. What has changed is the identity of the additional earner(s)—now it is the wife, whereas historically it was more likely to be the family's children. Another major problem lies in the tendency to equate independence with equality of earnings. However, this approach fails to appreciate the economic gains to marriage where earnings are approximately equal, and the low gains that may result from a weak labor-market position, whether or not earnings are equal. Moreover, the underlying causes of low gains to marriage may be obscured when earnings ratios become the major focus rather than the conditions producing these ratios.

In sum, this review of the economic independence argument provides little support for the extensive explanatory claims made for the hypothesis. The idea that specialization creates the gain to marriage, and hence that the desirability of marriage tends to disappear once women can earn a living wage, reflects a rather simplistic view of the basis of the marital relationship. Married women's employment undoubtedly has an effect on marriage, but we are more likely to understand that effect if a model of marriage is developed that is more multidimensional and flexible in its view of social roles. Certainly the fact that almost 70% of married women now work and thus play an important part in their family's economic welfare suggests that a model of marriage needs to be developed to reflect observed behavior rather than the marital role behavior of the nineteenth century.

## ACKNOWLEDGMENTS

Research support for this paper was provided by NICHD Grant R01HD27955.

[8]For example, the rationale that Preston & Richards provide for their 1975 article investigating the relationship of women's employment and marriage timing is to understand factors that might raise the age at marriage because of the "deleterious effects of its [the population's] early marrying" at that time (p. 209).

*Literature Cited*

Achen CH, Shively WP. 1995. *Cross-Level Inference*. Chicago: Univ. Chicago Press

Anderson M. 1971. *Family Structure in Nineteenth Century Lancashire*. Cambridge, Eng: Cambridge

Banks JA. 1954. *Prosperity and Parenthood*. London: Routledge & Kegan Paul

Becker GS. 1981. *A Treatise on the Family*. Cambridge: Harvard Univ. Press

Bennett NG, Bloom DE, Craig PH. 1989. The divergence of black and white marriage patterns. *Am. J. Sociol.* 95:692–722

Berkner L. 1972. The stem family and the developmental cycle of the peasant household: an 18th century Austrian example. In *The American Family in Social-Historical Perspective*, ed. M Gordon, pp. 34–58. New York: St. Martins

Bianchi SM. 1995. Changing economic roles of women and men. In *State of the Union*, ed. R Farley, 1:107–54. New York: Russell Sage Found.

Bumpass LL, Martin TC, Sweet JA. 1991. The impact of family background and early marital factors on marital disruption. *J. Fam. Issues* 12:22–42

Bumpass LL, Sweet JA. 1989. National estimates of cohabitation. *Demography* 26:615–25

Bumpass LL, Sweet JA, Cherlin A. 1991. The role of cohabitation in declining rates of marriage. *J. Marriage Fam.* 53:913–27

Cancian M, Danziger S, Gottschalk, P. 1993. Working wives and family income inequality among married couples. In *Uneven Tides: Rising Inequality in America*, ed. S Dansiger, P Gottschalk, pp. 195–221. New York: Russell Sage Found.

Cherlin AJ. 1979. Work life and marital dissolution. In *Divorce and Separation*, ed. G Levinger, O Moles, pp. 151–66. New York: Basic Books

Cherlin AJ. 1980. Postponing marriage: the influence of young women's work expectations. *J. Marriage Fam.* 42:355–65

Cherlin AJ. 1990. The strange career of the "Harvard-Yale" study. *Public Opinion Q.* 64:117–24

Cherlin AJ. 1992. *Marriage, Divorce, and Remarriage*. Cambridge: Harvard Univ. Press

Davis K. 1985. The future of marriage. In *Contemporary Marriage*, ed. K Davis, pp. 25–52. New York: Russell Sage Found.

Durkheim E. 1960 [1893]. *The Division of Labor in Society*. Glencoe, IL: Free Press

England P, Farkas G. 1986. *Household, Employment, and Gender*. New York: Aldine

Espenshade TJ. 1985. Marriage trends in America: estimates, implications, and underlying causes. *Pop. Dev. Rev.* 11:193–245

Farley R. 1988. After the starting line: blacks and women in an uphill race. *Demography* 25:477–95

Fossett MA, Kiecolt KJ. 1993. Mate availability and family structure among African Americans in U.S. metropolitan areas. *J. Marriage Fam.* 55:288–302

Fuchs V 1983. *How We Live: An Economic Perspective on Americans from Birth to Death*. Cambridge: Harvard Univ. Press

Goldin C. 1980. Family strategies and the family economy in the late nineteenth-century: the role of secondary workers. In *Philadelphia: Work, Space, Family, and Group Experience in the Nineteenth Century*, ed. T Hershberg, pp. 277–310. New York: Oxford Univ. Press

Goldin C. 1990. *Understanding the Gender Gap: An Economic History of American Women*. New York: Oxford Univ. Press

Goldman N, Westoff CF, Hammerslough C. 1984. Demography of the marriage market in the United States. *Pop. Index* 50:5–26

Goldscheider FK, Waite LJ. 1986. Sex differences in the entry into marriage. *Am. J. Sociol.* 92:91–109

Goldstone JA. 1986. The demographic revolution in England: a re-examination. *Pop. Stud.* 49:5–33

Greenstein TN. 1990. Marital disruption and the employment of married women. *J. Marriage Fam.* 52:657–76

Haines M. 1979. Industrial work and the family life cycle, 1889–1890. *Res. Econ. Hist.* 4:449–95

Hajnal J. 1965. European marriage patterns in perspective. In *Population in History*, ed. DV Glass, DEC Eversley, pp. 101–38. Chicago: Aldine

Hannan MT, Tuma NB. 1978. Income and independence effects on marital dissolution: results from the Seattle and Denver income-maintenance experiments. *Am. J. Sociol.* 84:611–33

Hoffman SD, Duncan GJ. 1995. The effect of incomes, wages, and AFDC benefits on

marital disruptions. *J. Hum. Resourc.* 30:19–41
Johnson WR, Skinner J. 1986. Labor supply and marital separation. *Am. Econ. Rev.* 76:455–69
Lee RD. 1983. Economic consequences of population size, structure and growth. *Int. Union for Sci. Stud. Pop. Newsletter* 17:43–59
Levy F. 1996. *Where did all the money go? A layman's guide to recent trends in U.S. living standards.* Presented at Annu. Meet. Pop. Assoc. Am., New Orleans
Lichter DT, Le Clere FB, McLaughlin DK. 1991. Local marriage markets and the marital behavior of black and white women. *Am. J. Sociol.* 96:843–67
Lichter DT, McLaughlin DK, Kephart G, Landry DJ. 1992. Race and the retreat from marriage: a shortage of marriageable men? *Am. Sociol. Rev.* 57:781–99
Lloyd KM, South SJ. 1996. Contextual Influences on young men's transition to first marriage. *Soc. Forc.* 74:1096–1119
Mare RD, Winship C. 1991. Socioeconomic change and the decline of marriage for blacks and whites. In *The Urban Underclass,* ed. C Jencks, PE Peterson, pp. 175–202. Washington, DC: Brookings Inst.
Martin, TC, Bumpass LL. 1989. Recent trends in marital disruption. *Demography* 26:37–51
McLanahan S, Casper L. 1995. Growing diversity and inequality in the American family. In *State of the Union: America in the 1990s*, ed. Reynolds Farley, 2:1–45. New York: Russell Sage Found.
Moore K, Waite L. 1981. Marital dissolution, early motherhood, and early marriage. *Soc. Forc.* 60:20–40
National Center for Health Statistics. 1990. Advance report of final divorce statistcs, 1987. *Monthly Vital Statist. Rep.* 38(12)
National Center for Health Statistics. 1995. Births, marriages, divorces, and deaths for 1995. *Monthly Vital Statist. Rep.* 44(12)
Oppenheimer VK. 1982. *Work and the Family: A Study in Social Demography*. New York: Academic
Oppenheimer VK. 1994. Women's rising employment and the future of the family in industrial societies. *Pop. Devel. R.* 20:293–342
Oppenheimer VK, Blossfeld HP, Wackerow A. 1995. New developments in family formation and women's improvement in educational attainment in the United States. In *Family Formation in Modern Societies and the New Role of Women,* ed. HP Blossfeld, pp. 150–73. Boulder, Col.: Westview
Oppenheimer VK, Lew V. 1995. American marriage formation in the eighties: How important was women's economic independence? In *Gender and Family Change in Industrialized Countries*, ed. KO Mason, AM Jensen, pp. 105–38. Oxford: Clarendon
Parsons DO, Goldin C. 1989. Parental altruism and self-interest: child labor among late nineteenth-century American families. *Econ. Inquiry* 27:637–59
Parsons T. 1949. The social structure of the family. In *The Family: Its Function and Destiny,* ed. R Anshen, pp. 173–201. New York: Harper & Brothers
Perlmann J. 1988. *Ethnic Differences: Schooling and Social Structure among the Irish, Italians, Jews, and Blacks in an American City, 1880–1935.* New York: Columbia Univ. Press
Peterson RR. 1989. *Women, Work, and Divorce.* Albany, NY: State Univ. of New York Press
Preston SH, Lim S, Morgan SP. 1992. African-American marriage in 1910: beneath the surface of census data. *Demography* 29:1–15
Preston SH, McDonald J. 1979. The incidence of divorce within cohorts of American marriages contracted since the Civil War. *Demography* 16:1–25
Preston SH, Richards AT. 1975. The influence of women's work opportunities on marriage rates. *Demography* 12:209–22
Qian Z, Preston SH 1993. Changes in American marriage, 1972 to 1987: availability and forces of attraction by age and education. *Am. Sociol. Rev.* 58:482–95
Robinson WS. 1950. Ecological correlations and the behavior of individuals. *Am. Sociol. Rev.* 15:351–57
Rodgers W, Thornton A. 1985. Changing patterns of first marriage in the United States. *Demography* 22:265–79
Ross HL, Sawhill IV. 1975. *Time of Transition: The Growth of Families Headed by Women.* Washington, DC: Urban Inst.
Rowntree BS. 1922. *Poverty: A Study of Town Life*. London: Longmans, Green
Sanderson WC. 1979. Quantitative aspects of marriage, fertility and family limitation in nineteenth century America: another implication of the Coale specifications. *Demography* 6:339–58
Schoen R. 1988. *Modeling Multigroup Populations*. New York: Plenum
Schoen R, Weinick RM. 1993. The slowing metabolism of marriage: figures from 1988 U.S. marital status life tables. *Demography* 30:737–46
Schoen R, Wooldredge J. 1989. Marriage choices in North Carolina and Virginia, 1969–71 and 1979–81. *J. Marriage Fam.* 51: 465–81
Smock PJ. 1990. Remarriage patterns of black and white women: Reassessing the role of educational attainment. *Demography* 27:467–73

Sørensen A. 1995. Women's education and the costs and benefits of marriage. In *Family Formation in Modern Societies and the New Role of Women,* ed. HP Blossfeld, pp. 229–35. Boulder, CO: Westview

Sørensen A, McLanahan S. 1987. Married women's economic dependency, 1940–1980. *Am. J. Sociol.* 93:659–87

South SJ, Lloyd K. 1995. Spousal alternatives and marital dissolution. *Am. Sociol. Rev.* VOL:21–35

Spitze G. 1988. Women's employment and family relations. *J. Marriage Fam.* 50:595–668

Taeuber CA, Taeuber IB. 1958. *The Changing Population of the United States*. New York: Wiley

Teachman JD, Polonko KA, Leigh GK. 1987. Marital timing: race and sex comparisons. *Soc. Forc.* 66:239–68

Thornton A, Rodgers WL. 1983. *Changing patterns of marriage and divorce in the United States. Final Report, Contract No. N01-HD-02850.* Bethesda, MD: Natl. Inst. Child Health Hum. Dev.

Tilly LA, Scott JW. 1978. *Work and the Family*. New York: Holt, Rinehart & Winston

Tzeng JM, Mare RD. 1995. Labor market and socioeconomic effects on marital stability. *Soc. Sci. Res.* 24:329–51

Tzeng MS. 1992. The effects of socioeconomic heterogamy and changes on marital dissolution for first marriages. *J. Marriage Fam.* 54:609–19

US Bureau of the Census. 1991. Marital status and living arrangements: March 1990. *Current Population Reports. Series P-20, No. 450.* Washington, DC: USGPO

Waite L, Spitze GD. 1981. Young women's transition to marriage. *Demography* 18:681–94

Watkins SC. 1984. Spinsters. *J. Fam. Hist.* 9:310–25

Yamaguchi K. 1991. *Event History Analysis*. Newberry Park, CA: Sage

*Annu. Rev. Sociol. 1997. 23:455–78*


# PEOPLE'S ACCOUNTS COUNT: The Sociology of Accounts

*Terri L. Orbuch*
Department of Sociology, University of Michigan, Ann Arbor, MI 48109;
e-mail: Orbuch@Umich.edu

KEY WORDS: accounts, narratives, stories, meaning, account-making

ABSTRACT

Humans are inexorably driven to search for order and meaning in their own and others' lives; accounts are a major avenue for sociologists to depict and understand the ways in which individuals experience and identify with that meaning and their social world. The accounts concept has a solid foundation and history in early sociological analysis and research. The current work on accounts focuses on "story-like" interpretations or explanations and their functions and consequences to a social actor's life. The concept is useful for gaining insight into the human experience and arriving at meanings or culturally embedded normative explanations. This concept deserves greater explicit attention in sociology and is in need of further theoretical development and stimulation. I argue that sociologists should embrace the concept of accounts; the foundation is set for a resurgence of work on accounts in sociology.

## INTRODUCTION

Recently in the social sciences, scholars have been encouraged to collect and interpret stories that people tell about their lives (Bochner 1994, Bruner 1986, 1990, Coles 1989, Gergen & Gergen 1987, 1988, Harvey et al 1990a, Howard 1991, Maines 1993, Mishler 1986, Orbuch et al 1993, Polkinghorne 1988, Sarbin 1986). Robert Coles (1989), in *The Call of Stories*, suggests that stories are everyone's rock-bottom capacity—a universal gift to be shared with others. Accounts and other related concepts, such as stories and narratives, represent ways in which people organize views of themselves, of others, and of their social world.



0360-0572/97/0815-0455$08.00

Sociologists first advanced the concept of accounts over two decades ago (Lyman & Scott 1970, Scott & Lyman 1968). According to Scott and Lyman, accounts are verbal statements made by one social actor to another to explain behaviors that are unanticipated or deviant. This early work was influenced by Goffman's (1959) arguments about how people present themselves to others, often in a self-protective manner, and by Garfinkel's (1956) analysis of the conditions necessary for successful status degradation. The concept also developed along parallel and sometimes overlapping lines with classical attribution theory and symbolic interactionism.

The more recent work on accounts still recognizes these verbal and written statements as social explanations of events, but it places far less emphasis on the construction of accounts to justify unexpected or disrupted social interaction. Current scholars broaden the focus to consider "story-like" interpretations or explanations (Bruner 1990, Harvey et al 1990a, Maines 1993, McAdams et al 1996, Surra et al 1995, Veroff et al 1993b). In many of these programs of research, respondents are asked to explain and interpret a stressful event (e.g. divorce, sexual assault) or the development of a relationship (e.g. courtship, then marriage). Recent theoretical developments also emphasize the process by which individuals develop an account (account-making), while continuing to focus on the specific contents of accounts, the major theme in the earlier work. For example, Harvey et al (1990a,b) focus on the motivations and reasons behind the presentation of accounts and the influence of others (audience) in the account-making process.

Although early sociological analysis and research were important in defining and conceptualizing the term account, the phenomenon has received only modest attention in mainstream sociology since the 1970s.[1] Whether under the heading of account-making, storytelling, or narration, the development of theory and empirical research has flourished largely in other disciplines (e.g. psychology, literature, communications, anthropology, history) and has increased rapidly in the last two decades. A major premise of this chapter is that the work on accounts has a prominent history in the discipline of sociology. This legacy, along with current theoretical and empirical work on accounts, can make a valuable contribution to contemporary sociology.

[1] After an extensive review of four mainstream sociology journals (*Social Psychology Quarterly, American Sociological Review, American Journal of Sociology,* and *Social Forces*) from 1990 to 1996, I found only four articles that focused on accounts, personal narratives, or story-telling: Connell (1992), Ellingson (1995), Griffin (1993), and Jacobs (1996). Other journals that are highly relevant to sociology and consistently publish articles on these topics include *Journal of Narrative and Life History, Symbolic Interaction,* and *Journal of Contemporary Ethnography. Social Science History* also published a series of five articles on the subject of narrative and the formation of social identities (Sewell 1992).

## THE EMERGENCE OF THE ACCOUNT CONCEPT IN SOCIOLOGY

The writings of sociologists such as Garfinkel (1956, 1967), Goffman (1959, 1971), and Scott & Lyman (1968, Lyman & Scott 1970) led the theoretical development on accounts. In general these scholars were interested in three questions: (*a*) What is the content of accounts? (*b*) Under what conditions do people present accounts?, and (*c*) Under what conditions do people "honor" or accept the accounts of others? The norms of a situation, the actor, and the audience all determine the content of an account and whether it is accepted in a given social situation. As to when individuals give accounts, sociologists held two distinct viewpoints; they regarded accounts (i) as justifications or excuses for socially undesirable or problematic occurrences, and (ii) as a means of weaving together disparate social events.

Goffman's (1959, 1971) seminal work, *The Presentation of Self in Everyday Life*, exemplifies the conceptual foundation for contemporary research on how people tactically present themselves to others when social acts have potentially negative implications. When an individual commits an offense, a powerful script for account-making is set in motion:

> Regardless of the particular objective which the individual has in mind and of his motivation for having this objective, it will be in his interests to control the conduct of others, especially their responsive treatment of him (Goffman 1971, p. 3).

This control is accomplished by providing accounts to nullify any negative implications flowing from appearance and demeanor. Goffman also argued that self-presentations or "performances" are socially constructed for the existing public audience to maintain social identities.

Whereas Goffman was concerned with the use of accounts to counteract socially undesirable or problematic experiences, Garfinkel (1956, 1967) argued that accounts were a more general aspect of social life. Garfinkel acknowledges that such explanations or interpretations are more salient to others when the circumstances become problematic, but he also stresses that individuals organize and manage their everyday affairs so as "to be accountable" to others for all actions and behaviors. Although Garfinkel considered accounts a regular day-to-day experience, he wrote most prominently (1956) during the McCarthy hearings of the 1950s about how people's self-worth may be degraded in societal or institutional rituals.

Scott & Lyman (1968, Lyman & Scott 1970) were the most explicit in delineating account strategies for different social situations and in discussing how others might react differentially to the accounts. Like Goffman, they argued that accounts are presented to others to explain potentially problematic events or behaviors. They defined an account as "a linguistic device employed whenever an action is subjected to valuative inquiry" (1968, p. 46). Their writing focused on the notion that at the microsociological level, daily interactions and the use of talk are the significant mechanisms by which individuals neutralize negative acts or their consequences. They discussed two general types of accounts that contain socially approved vocabularies: justifications (whereby one accepts responsibility for the act in question, but denies the pejorative quality associated with it) and excuses (whereby one admits that the act in question is bad or wrong, but denies full responsibility). Both types are presented to others to protect self-esteem, social status, or social order.

Many of the substantive concerns formulated by sociologists such as Scott & Lyman, Goffman, and Garfinkel have been extended or refined in other programs of research. For example, Semin & Manstead (1983) refined the notion of accounts to examine specific practices, which they call collectively "the accountability of conduct" (p. x). These involve the repair of disrupted social interaction in a variety of social situations. Like Scott & Lyman, Semin & Manstead rely on talk as the medium for these accounting practices. Also employing the Scott & Lyman (1968) framework, Blumstein (1974) examined the conditions under which other social actors would or would not honor accounts. On the basis of experimental data, Blumstein found that the content of an account predicted more strongly than the negative act itself whether individuals could neutralize negative actions and their consequences. Similarly, the work of communication studies scholars McLaughlin, Cody, and colleagues (1990, 1992) builds directly on the ideas of Scott & Lyman (1968) and Blumstein (1974). Their research continues to elaborate on the various types of justifications that people communicate to others following failures or social predicaments and the consequences of specific justifications to the maintenance of social interaction and identities.

## CURRENT VIEWPOINTS ON ACCOUNTS

The current literature on accounts differs in several ways from the literature in which the concept of accounts initially emerged. The early work on accounts was intrigued with the notion that individuals present impressions of themselves to others to maintain social interaction as well as personal status and esteem. This work was clearly oriented toward understanding deviance or disruptions in social interaction and the consequences of accounts for the nature and maintenance of that interaction.

The current work on accounts and narratives is more social psychological in nature and focus; the functions and consequences of accounts to a social actor's life have become more prominent (Bochner et al 1997b, Harvey et al 1990b,

McAdams et al 1996, Surra et al 1995, Weber et al 1987). In this work, accounts are viewed as story-like constructions that contain individuals' recollections of events, including plot, story line, affect, and attributions. Individuals continually update and reflect on these accounts, on the basis of feedback from others and the collective stories within which individuals reside (Harvey et al 1990a, Heath 1983, Maines 1993, Orbuch et al 1993, 1994).

An example of the foregoing argument is provided by Harvey et al (1990); they contrast current viewpoints of accounts with that of an interesting study by McLaughlin et al (1983), concerning students' retrospective reproaches for potentially blameworthy actions. McLaughlin et al (1983) describe a reproach as a projected account, meaning that the questioner offers it as a possible a priori justification to the person who must answer for some problematic behavior. An example of a reproach that was reported by a wife who was late to meet her husband is "My husband said to me 'Where the hell have you been? Did you forget to wind your watch again?'" Current scholars interested in story-like accounts (Harvey et al 1990b) would examine the reproach, but would also emphasize the rest of the story that likely exists in the relationship between the husband and the wife and the consequences and functions of that fuller story. He may, for instance, have developed a strong belief and accompanying story that his wife is engaging in extramartial relationships. This story may include denial, anger, sadness, and confusion along with reports of his efforts to cope with the situation given this meaning. On the other hand, she may believe that her husband is jealous and unreasonable in his expectations and inferences; she too may have stories to go with that theme which focus on why he is so jealous (perhaps going back to alienated relations with parents or to betrayal in a past relationship).

Current theoretical viewpoints also emphasize that accounts are not merely social constructions to protect the self; they also (*a*) give individuals a greater sense of control and understanding of their environment, (*b*) allow individuals to cope with emotionally charged and stressful events, (*c*) produce some degree of closure, (*d*) provide a greater sense of hope and will for the future, and (*e*) establish order in daily relational experiences. McAdams et al (1996) state that "beginning in late adolescence and young adulthood, men and women living in modern societies seek to construct more-or-less integrative narratives of the self to provide their lives with a semblance of unity and purpose."

An explanation of the consequences of account-making for individuals was first inspired by Weiss's (1975) powerful analysis of individuals' accounts following marital separation. In his book, Weiss proposed that newly separated individuals develop accounts to explain and understand what happened and why. More importantly, these accounts were psychologically effective in dealing with the stress and distress accompanying separation. The development of the account was vital to the chain of events in which a person achieved closure about the loss of a relationship and motivation to move on in life (Weiss 1975).

The current work on accounts also acknowledges that accounts may reflect culturally embedded normative explanations. Although the original content of accounts, including reports of plans and intentions, style of presentation, and context of presentation is of primary importance to most scholars working with accounts, these explanations are seen as serving as much a communicative-persuasive mission as they do a function of explanation and self-insight. For example, Harre et al (1985) argue that in producing their accounts, actors are displaying knowledge of the ideal ways of acting and ideal reasons for doing what they have done. These investigators collect accounts from various populations or cultures, such as football fans, and then search through the accounts for descriptions of what should happen. They then represent this material as a system of rules representing a system of knowledge or beliefs. A similar position is adopted by Shotter (1984) who focuses on how people make their behavior accountable in a moral world. He stresses how people must talk about themselves in terms of the social order and socially constructed morality in which they exist. People must account for their experiences in ways that are intelligible and legitimate in their current social context.

In contrast to the early literature on accounts, the current literature also emphasizes the value of communicating accounts to others as a mechanism for coping with major life events (Harber & Pennebaker 1992, Harvey et al 1990a, 1992, Pennebaker & Harber 1993, Silver et al 1983, Weiss 1975). Failure to engage in this account-making process can lead to chronic problems, including psychosomatic illness (Orbuch et al 1994). In his book, *Opening Up*, James Pennebaker (1990) documents many of the negative psychological and physical effects (e.g. long-term physical problems such as high blood pressure, depression, prolonged grief) associated with not confiding in others about traumatic experiences and losses. More recently, research has examined the activities of account-making and confiding across a wide array of stressful events (e.g. transition to a nursing home, sexual assault, Vietnam War). Evidence suggests that the interaction/social process of confiding accounts to others has positive consequences for individuals' psychological and physical well-being (Harvey et al 1991, Harvey et al 1995, Lichtman & Taylor 1986, Orbuch et al 1994, Pennebaker 1990, Weber et al 1987).

This broad and more recent conceptualization of accounts has also been applied extensively to research and theory in interpersonal relationships (Berscheid 1994, Burnett & McGhee 1987, Fincham 1992, Harvey et al 1990a, 1992, Matthews 1986, Murray & Holmes 1994, Orbuch et al 1993, Surra et al 1995, Veroff et al 1993a,b). Accounts of close relationships contain rich and detailed information about various sources of relational and self knowledge, such as the nature and dynamics of a present relationship and preexisting normative beliefs and rules about what makes a relationship and how to behave appropriately in that relationship (Surra & Bohman 1991, Surra et al 1995).

It is likely that the concept of accounts was broadened for both conceptual and methodological reasons. The accounts-as-stories framework is better able than standardized survey instruments to represent the rich, complex, interwoven reports that investigators are currently collecting, often with populations who are facing major life stressors. Accounts may also give a fuller understanding than a checkmark on a questionnaire regarding the ambivalences, uncertainties, and angsts that are a day-to-day reality. "If we wish to learn the realities of personal relationships, we would do well to pay attention to such natural forms these realities take on" (Weber 1992). It also makes sense to complement, rather than supplant, the structured questionnaire with a story format because respondents may be comfortable in "telling their stories" or describing the meaning they make of their experiences as naturally unfolding events, rather than as structured responses (Baumeister & Stillwell 1992).

Veroff et al (1993a) argue that "direct questions can elicit historical truth to some extent, but they often engage much more of the person's social self-presentation and hence are primarily useful in understanding situations where self-presentations are particularly salient" (p. 439). Further, direct questions often fail to examine how individuals perceive their experiences to be related to social, cultural, and personal circumstances (Mishler 1986). In contrast, accounts are more likely to reveal nonconscious motives and meanings and to illuminate individuals' interpretations in a social, cultural, and personal context.

Weber (1992) gives a poignant example of the importance of personal context in the following account of a 67-year old woman describing her painful divorce and its aftermath.

> I can honestly say that today I am a resourceful person, a warm and caring person, without any bitterness. I am retired, living alone in my little house and very involved with family and a few friends. Oddly, I am not into church activities. I do help individuals when I can . . . but I can't say I'm a "do-gooder."
>
> I am a happy person, truly, at this stage of my life. I do remember good things about our marriage—some of the funny things, the sweet, thoughtful gestures. I also remember the very bad times, but I don't dwell on them. I remember being carried over the threshold of each new apartment or house with each new move. I remember a Christmas stocking tied to the foot of my hospital bed after the birth of our first child on Christmas eve. My feelings now are, weren't we lucky to have had so much once. Perhaps now at 67 I'm remembering more often (Weber 1992, p. 186).

The self-descriptions of herself (warm, caring, self-confident, resourceful) and the current meaning of her divorce (e.g. she does not want to dwell on the bad times, weren't they lucky to have so much once) are better understood only after we consider the context of the larger story of her loss.

These written or verbal accounts can be left in the form of a story and reported as such. Alternatively, the material can be coded and treated within quantifiable categories (Antaki 1988, Fletcher 1983, Harvey et al 1988, Orbuch et al 1993, Veroff et al 1993b). Berscheid (1994) suggests that this latter task can be interpretive and must be planned and executed carefully. Mishler (1986), Riessman (1993), Veroff et al (1993b), Surra (1988), and Weiss (1994) have written extensively on various stages of the gathering, coding, and analysis of accounts. Nonetheless, future research will require greater emphasis on and discussion of strategies for coding and analyzing accounts. The coding and analyzing of accounts can be an arduous and time-consuming task.

## RELATED THEORETICAL CONCEPTS AND DEVELOPMENTS

A number of related theoretical concepts and developments have been instrumental in expanding current knowledge of accounts and their utility in sociological analysis. A concern with subjective interpretations of social reality and the construction of meaning through social interaction has a long, varied history in sociology. Even the early ethnographic research (Cressey 1932, Park & Burgess 1921) from the Chicago School of sociology was motivated by questions about process and interaction that are dominant themes in much of the work on accounts and narratives (Abbott 1992).

### *Communicated Language*

The foundations of accounts are similar to the classic concepts of "vocabularies of motive" postulated by C Wright Mills (1940) and the "grammar of motives" proposed by Burke (1945). Both Mills and Burke examined language as a vehicle by which individuals communicate explanations of their actions. Burke (1945) was concerned with the grammar that is presented and its persuasive tendency rather than with the historical reality of the action and what motivated it. Burke's logic is similar to that emphasized in current frameworks of accounts; the focus shifts from individuals' reasons for events or actions, to account-making as a persuasive endeavor designed to convince self and other of the credence of one's reality. In an experimental study, Orbuch et al (1992) found that respondents assigned trait inferences to others (e.g. respectable, selfish, mature, trustworthy) and formed impressions of others as people (likability) based on their presented accounts. Respondents were also persuaded to interact or not interact with others based on their presented accounts.

In contrast to Burke and in a way similar to Goffman (1959) and Mead (1934), Mills (1963) emphasized that motives originate not within the individual but from the social setting and audience at hand. "Motives are accepted justifications for present, future or past programs or acts" (p. 443). Appropriate motives and vocabularies also differ with culture or group context. According to Stokes & Hewitt (1976), Mills's "motive talk" and Scott & Lyman's "accounts" are significant constructs because they provide a link between culture (collective understandings) and individual behavior. Accounts and motive talk can be seen as "aligning actions;" in the face of negative behavior, individuals align their behavior with culturally acceptable language to restore order and interaction.

## *Deviance*

The vast literature on the sociology of delinquency or deviance is also germane to much of the early work on accounts as explanations for potentially blameworthy actions (Sutherland 1955, Sykes & Matza 1957). A main theme in this literature is that individuals give justifications or rationalizations for their deviant behavior to deflect blame and protect self-esteem. Sykes & Matza (1957) report four techniques for neutralizing self-blame: (*a*) denial of responsibility, (*b*) denial of injury, (*c*) denial of the victim, and (*d*) condemnation of the condemners. These techniques of neutralization follow deviant behavior and protect the individual from self-blame and the blame of others after the act.

Many of these theoretical ideas run parallel to the concerns expressed in the early work on accounts, especially the writings of Scott & Lyman (1968). Like the scholars who were trying to explain the causes of deviant behavior, according to Scott & Lyman, accounts are presented in response to the violation of social norms and are "voiced" after a behavior to avoid detrimental consequences to self.

## *Attributions*

The early work on accounts developed in close association with theory and research on attributional processes (Crittenden 1983, Felson 1981, Harvey et al 1978, Heider 1958, Jones & Davis 1965, Weary et al 1989). Classical attribution theory focuses on the process by which individuals arrive at subjective explanations for actions and events. These explanations allow social actors to integrate and explain the events and occurrences around them. Fritz Heider's (1958) writing is significant for much of the past and present work on accounts. Heider viewed people as possessing, using, and often articulating a commonsense psychology of their understanding of interpersonal and other events. For example, people often explain their achievement of a task as a function of their own ability (internal cause), their own efforts (internal cause), conditions associated with the performance situation (external cause), or luck (external cause).

In the late 1970s, many attribution theorists began to broaden their focus and to formulate account-like concepts (Crittenden 1983, Felson 1981, Harvey et al 1978, Wiley & Eskilson 1981). Some years passed, however, before scholars (Harvey et al 1986, 1990a) began to appreciate more fully the value of examining attributions within the context of natural stories that people tell about their lives and linked attributions explicitly to the earlier work by Lyman & Scott (1970) and to Weiss's (1975) account work on marital separation. These scholars were also influenced by a number of British social psychologists who had already embraced the concept of accounts and were analyzing the stages of account-making and the strategies by which individuals choose to perform or not perform specific accounts (Antaki 1987, Harre 1977, Schonbach 1980, 1990, Shotter 1987).

Currently, accounts are viewed as more than collections of disparate attributions. Accounts are packages of attributions (including attributions of causality, responsibility, and blame, and trait ascriptions both to other and to self), tied together by descriptive and emotive material (Harvey et al 1992). Attributions concentrate more strongly on the cognitive aspects of judgments and responsibility than on the social processing of these statements; accounts emphasize the cognitive, emotional, and social aspects of these explanations. Further, accounts contain much more elaborate and more complex general information than do attributions, including but not confined to statements about affect-laden memories.

Berscheid (1994) states that "the current use of account narratives appears to derive from two sometimes incompatible perspectives: the information-processing and the ethnographic perspectives" (pg. 99).[2] She maintains that the former tradition represents theory and research focused solely on social cognition (attribution theory). In contrast, the ethnographic approach focuses on the construction of meaning to make sense of one's self and social world (Bruner 1990, Gergen & Gergen 1988). This distinction between meaning-making and information-processing is not clear and may be an unwarranted characterization of the literature on accounts. Certainly the area of social cognition (including classical attribution work in social psychology) has influenced the formulation of accounts as narratives, but the major part of recent work on accounts (Harvey et al 1990a,b, McAdams et al 1996, Orbuch et al 1993, Surra et al 1995) embodies principles from both perspectives. The current viewpoint on accounts as story-like constructions describes them as cognitive processes by which individuals create and organize meaning from their social world (account-making).

[2]Berscheid labels accounts that are story-like in nature as account narratives. This is contrasted with the more traditional use of the word "account" (e.g. Scott & Lyman 1968).

### *Symbolic Interactionism*

As implied in the previous discussion of Goffman and Garfinkel, the work on accounts also has intellectual ties to symbolic interactionism (Blumer 1969, Cooley 1902, Fine 1993, Mead 1934, Stryker 1981, 1983). A common goal of these frameworks is to understand the role of subjective experience to human behavior, in the context of personal and social interaction. Further, the link between individual and society through the construction of meaning is a powerful theme in both perspectives.

In 1981, Stryker & Gottlieb wrote a chapter that compared symbolic interactionism and attribution theory. They argued that both theories share an interest in individuals' subjective interpretations of their social world. However, symbolic interactionism is the broader of the two frameworks, because it addresses the interactional bases of such subjective interpretations and the sociocultural aspects of social behavior (Stryker & Gottlieb 1981). This distinction is legitimate but does not generalize to a comparison of accounts theory and symbolic interactionism. Recent work on accounts examines the social interactional processes by which individuals develop accounts and their meaning in the context of individuals' personal, social, and cultural histories.

Concepts such as self, identity, taking the role of the other, self-presentation, and generalized other, which were central to the early development and writings of symbolic interactionism (Blumer 1969, Cooley 1902, Mead 1934), are salient processes and topics in the work on accounts and narratives. Many argue that identity is generated or maintained through the process of storytelling (Crites 1986, McAdams et al 1996, Polkinghorne 1988, Somers 1994, Surra et al 1995). LaRossa (1995) theorizes that although stories may be recordings of the past, they also function to create and shape the definitions that individuals create of themselves and of others. Hopper (1993) found that individuals' accounts of divorce were not motivated by the actual events, feelings, and intentions of their experiences, but instead were driven by the individuals' identities in the divorce process (initiator, noninitiator).

Currently, although symbolic interactionism includes many different approaches (Burke & Reitzes 1991, Couch 1992, Denzin 1985, Simon 1995, Thoits 1991), the perspective as a whole has made some progress in bridging the gap between macro and micro sociologies (Fine 1992). As an example, current frameworks incorporate the influence of structured roles and identities as constraints in interpersonal interaction and in the process of meaning construction (Stryker & Stratham 1985).[3] This elaboration has led to fragmentation but

[3]Stryker and his colleagues (1983, Stryker & Stratham 1985) argue that a structural symbolic interactionism is more appropriate for sociological social psychologists interested in how interactions are constructed and become meaningful according to the roles and structured identities that we possess.

also to a general acceptance and integration of symbolic interactionist doctrines into mainstream sociology (Fine 1993). Accounts scholars may want to pay attention to the efforts of symbolic interactionists; a future goal for scholars studying accounts is to increase their efforts at synthesizing and integrating macrosociological concerns into their frameworks and analyses.

## *Narratives*

At present, there are numerous approaches to the study of narratives; the literature cuts across various theoretical and disciplinary boundaries. Riessman (1993) states that "the study of narrative does not fit neatly within the boundaries of any single scholarly field" (p. 1). Further, while the concept of accounts can be linked to developments in mainstream sociology and social psychology, narrative analysis was largely inspired by the "crisis of confidence" in social science promoted by poststructuralism, postmodernism, and deconstruction (Bochner et al 1997a). Among social science historians, the use of narratives "marks a global change in the relationship of the social sciences to the humanities" (Sewell 1992, p. 480). "Over the past two decades, historically minded social scientists have gone from a general disdain for the humanities toward curiosity about, respect for and increasing intellectual collaboration with them. Narrative is one of the emerging points of intersection" (p. 481).

In general, the narrative perspective moves away from describing language as a means to discover or mirror reality to the view that language and meaning are an ongoing and constitutive part of reality. Narratives play a "dual role"; they represent or reconstruct the past and they are a "sort of 'independent variable' active in shaping the past" (Hart 1992, p. 634). For narrative scholars, there is no "real" event, such as a relationship break-up, whose objective nature exists and can be learned or inferred through various sources. Instead, narratives are "real" events as presented, and narrative analysis pays special attention to the form, coherence, and structure of these stories (Steinmetz 1992).

Theory and research on accounts and on narratives are quite similar, even though these two concepts have been analyzed in quite different ways. First, both concepts emphasize that these story-like conceptions are first-person interpretations or explanations. Systematic research within each framework has focused on the process by which individuals construct these stories and on the recognition that stories formulate, control, and represent self, other, and relationships (Harvey et al 1990a, LaRossa 1995, Orbuch et al 1994, Surra et al 1997, Sternberg 1995, Veroff et al 1993b,c). "People construct identities (however multiple and changing) by locating themselves or being located within a repertoire of emplotted stories" (Somers 1994, p. 614). Sternberg (1995) claims that people organize their views of relationships in story schemas; future relationships are then shaped and controlled through the process of storytelling.

Both concepts also highlight the idea that these subjective explanations develop and evolve in the context of cultural and social factors. Whether the story is constructed to fit the social audience or whether it is constructed privately and influenced by an imagined audience or cultural script (Harvey et al 1990a), the social nature of these stories is explicit and dominant in writings on both narratives and accounts. Further, individuals' positions or statuses (e.g. class, gender, race) socially influence the appropriate stories to tell and the reasons for telling them (Barbre et al 1989, Veroff et al 1993a). Rosenwald & Ochberg (1992) stress the importance of cultural discourse in understanding the narratives that individuals present; cultural conditions may constrain individuals' behaviors as well as the language and stories they produce.

Finally, there is widespread consensus about the necessary components of both narratives and accounts. Despite some variation, narrative scholars argue that the retelling of events follows a temporal sequence and that plot, character, theme, and emotion are evident in these stories. The temporal sequence of events is also addressed in the work on accounts. A dominant theme throughout both literatures is that narrative order allows an individual to make sense of events, situations, or identities. For example, in a study of the communication dynamics found in epilepsy self-help groups, Arnston & Droge (1987) suggest that narrative order (A happened, then B) makes the events portrayed seem more understandable and predictable. From the standpoint of the other social actor, the story is more likely to be comprehended and accepted if a sequential plot exists and if order is evident.

Although the two perspectives have much overlap in concerns and basic assumptions, there are issues that differentiate the two approaches. An account and a narrative differ: The standard meaning of narrative is that of an individual telling his or her story, usually orally (Gergen & Gergen 1983); account-making includes both the telling of a story in public and those activities that occur in private such as diary keeping, rumination, and other intrapersonal processes. These private activities are defined as social acts in light of Mead's (1934) view of the imagined reactions of others and their influence on all actions (Harvey et al 1992), but they are not necessarily literally told to others. Antaki (1987) distinguishes between performable accounts (those which we present to others) and unperformable accounts (those which we do not present to others perhaps because of secrets or embarrassing information). In contrast, narratives are public and involve overt social behavior or an audience.

Another difference between these two story-like concepts is the degree to which each develops in response to a stressful or imposing event. Current views of accounts embrace a wider array of situations than in the past (positive and negative events); however, a major assumption is that people tend to engage in account-making when they are troubled by imposing problems or stressful life events (Harvey et al 1990b, Huston et al 1981, Orbuch et al 1993). A stressful or difficult situation is not required for the telling of a narrative, especially in the context of a life narrative. Further, since individuals may be more likely to assess and explain causality in the face of a stressful event, attributions become an important component of the conceptualization of accounts. In contrast, narrative perspectives do not emphasize attributional statements.

### *Summary*

In general, the fundamental questions in the literature on communicated language and on deviance are strikingly similar to those in the early accounts work. Individuals present impressions of themselves to others in the face of potentially blameworthy actions to maintain social interaction and personal status and esteem. An analysis of attribution theory, symbolic interactionism, and more current viewpoints of accounts also yields a shared premise—"that individual behavior is guided by the subjective contruction of reality rather than by objective properties of external stimuli" (Strker & Gottlieb 1981, p. 427). It is important to note however, that underlying differences also emerge in this comparison. It is also the case that the terms "narrative" and "account as a story-like construction" are often used to signify the same phenomenon or process. Although substantively unique, the distinct meanings of these two concepts are often difficult to disentangle.

## ACCOUNTS AND THE GOALS OF SOCIOLOGY

Accounts as story-like conceptions have much to offer and contribute to sociological inquiry. For sociologists, especially sociological social psychologists, accounts can be an important means and product of inquiry because these stories treat the human being and his/her mind as invaluable to understanding and explaining social behavior.

Ewick & Silbey (1995) discuss three mechanisms by which narratives enter scholarly research: "Narrative can be the object of inquiry, the method of inquiry or the product of inquiry" (p. 201). I employ this classification as a heuristic device to illustrate the potential value of accounts for sociological inquiry. Further, challenging questions for future sociological work are addressed within each section.

### *The Object of Inquiry*

A vast literature examines accounts as the object of inquiry. This work focuses on the nature of accounts (Fincham 1992, Harvey et al 1992, Mishler 1995, Schonbach 1990), how they are formed (McLaughlin et al 1990), and their function in individuals' lives (Gergen & Gergen 1987, Harvey et al 1990a,

Weber et al 1987). The study of accounts as the object of inquiry also allows sociologists to observe how individuals impose order and subjective meaning on the experiences around them (Riessman 1993). Sociologists, especially social psychologists, have always been interested in the processes by which individuals establish balance in their interactions with others. Whether that balance is necessary as a result of "disrupted or fractured" social interaction (Goffman; Scott & Lyman), because of a stressful event (Harvey et al 1990a, Orbuch et al 1993, Pennebaker & Harber 1993), or as part of everyday living, the process of imposing order by developing an account conveys important information about this process to sociologists.

It has sometimes been argued that accounts are reported by people only when investigators ask them explicitly to do so. Others contend that individuals develop accounts for anything that is called on by self or other to explain, whether that be researcher driven or not (Harvey et al 1990a,b). The former argument has also been strongly challenged in work on spontaneous or unsolicited interpretation (Fletcher 1983, Harvey et al 1988, Holtzworth-Munroe & Jacobson, 1985). This empirical work suggests that it is possible to code people's free response reactions to events in such a way as to reveal meaning-making and various types of attributions. Nonetheless, whether individuals develop accounts (private or public accounts) without being prompted is a much debated topic that needs to be further examined.

One of the most challenging issues for future work on accounts as objects of inquiry, yet central to all sociological inquiry, is a detailed focus on the context in which individuals make and present accounts. Are there certain periods of life or stages of the life course (e.g. major transitions such as mid-life crisis, change in profession, retirement) when account-making is intensified or when a fuller account is presented to others (perhaps because individuals received feedback and refined the account over time). A related topic that needs further discussion is the importance of status (e.g. gender, ethnicity) or personality (e.g. extroversion, empathy) characteristics in understanding the narratives that individuals present.

Relevant to this later concern is work on social memory which suggests that women may be more likely than their male significant others to take on the role of "relationship historian" and to maintain a continuing effort to observe, document, and analyze major relationship events (Holtzworth-Munroe & Jacobson 1985, Ross 1988). Further, Veroff, Orbuch, and their colleagues (Veroff et al 1993a,b,c, Orbuch et al 1993) have examined the relationship stories of black and white newlyweds in a longitudinal study of marriage. Results from the study suggest that by and large the couple narratives are quite similar in both groups, but important differences do emerge. It is their contention that these differences yield especially meaningful information about how race/ethnicity influences the means and product of storytelling. I select two examples from this study for illustration. First, among black couples, there was greater mention of affects for which the husband was the source than in white couples, whether the affect was mentioned by the wife or the husband (e.g. "My husband didn't want to have a large wedding"). Veroff et al (1993a) state that these findings may suggest that husbands have more influence in forming the meaning of marriage for black couples than they do for white couples. Second, in a study by Orbuch et al (1993), white husbands and wives were significantly less dramatic in storytelling than black husbands and wives. These results support Heath's work (1983), which indicates that blacks may have more experience with the storytelling discourse.

There are also only a few clues available in the literature on account-making about the various themes per types of events that people may emphasize (Harvey et al 1990b, Veroff et al 1993a,b). A categorization of various themes would be extremely useful when coding and analyzing individuals' accounts, and a lack of such is one of the major weaknesses of the current accounts literature. While justification and exoneration of self are common themes in the marital separation literature, these themes may not resonate with accounts of satisfying relationships or illnesses that are life-threatening. Gergen & Gergen (1987, 1988) have also discussed the ways that account themes differ with social context. They contend that accounts change over time and presentation; the presentation of an account is analogous to other social behaviors; it is influenced by the current circumstances, audience, and social setting.

Thus, another important direction still largely ignored in the literature is the persuasive nature of these constructions. I have discussed the self-presentational motivation for account-making; however, the accounts literature gives us little insight into the dynamics of the influence process. Many argue that stories are not based on historical truth but instead are used to manipulate or persuade some preferred self-presentation to others. LaRossa (1995) suggests that "more attention should be paid to how people socially create stories about what really happened back then, to suit their own political interests" (p. 553). The reasons for these myths and manipulations, rather than the accounts themselves, have promise for investigation of the persuasion processes as they are influenced by account-making. The audience and cultural understandings for our account-making activities are important in this persuasion process.

## *The Means of Inquiry*

Sociologists also can use respondents' accounts as a means of assessing (or illuminating) other aspects of the social world (Ewick & Silbey 1995). An emerging literature demonstrates how widely accounts are used to study other social processes or phenomena that interest sociologists. Respondents' explanations in story-like form have been found to reveal distinctive information about interpersonal relationships (Huston et al 1981, Orbuch et al 1993, Surra et al 1995, Veroff et al 1993b), adjustment and coping with stress or loss (Ellis 1995, Harvey 1996, Harvey et al 1990b, Pennebaker 1989, 1990, Silver et al 1983, Vaughn 1986), the construction of gender (Barbre et al 1989, Etter-Lewis 1993, Stanley 1993), and the development or generativity of the self (Baumeister 1986, 1989, McAdams et al 1996).

The following excerpt is from an account that was provided by a 47-year old male who experienced sexual assault between the ages of 3 and 12 by his father, cousin, and men who worked at his family home. It provides insight into how accounts can be used as a means to understand or assess the severity of sexual assault and its aftermath.

> It has affected every portion of my external and internal life for the last 44 years. Close relationships? I don't have any, and never have had... And I've been married for 25 years now! But it is not a close, personal or intimate relationship. If anything, it is abusive to me. I don't trust anyone... " (Orbuch et al 1994, p. 260).

Further, we do not, as yet, have evidence about how the more subtle and complete types of accounts that probably predominate in most people's lives are related to behavioral expectations or actual lines of behavior (Harvey et al 1990b). For example, a type of explanation for a past break-up that emphasized a too rapid movement to intimacy might be related to future expectations of "going slower" in developing the next relationship or "getting to know someone" before getting involved in another relationship.

As significant is the challenge of trying to establish causality in the link between accounts and social psychological phenomena (e.g. social behavior, identity formation, adjustment to stressor). Most of the research conducted to date has been nonexperimental in design and cross-sectional in nature. It is crucial, however, to explore whether the relationship between accounts and social psychological phenomena holds up longitudinally and across different domains of social life.

As part of a longitudinal study of the early years of marriage (Veroff et al 1995), joint accounts by couples were "used to understand the meaning that newlyweds in modern urban society make of their relationship and how this emerging meaning may relate to present and future well-being" (Orbuch et al 1993, p. 815). These joint accounts provided researchers with new information about marital processes, beyond anything that can be assessed with standard survey measures (Veroff et al 1993c). A good illustration of this contribution is provided in an analysis of collaboration in these joint accounts. For all but the black husbands, the fact that the couple had some conflict in telling their courtship story in Year 1 (of their marriage) was indicative of less marital happiness in Year 3 than if the couple did not have this kind of conflict. Apparently, not being able to agree on the story of the relationship has long-term implications for the well-being of the marriage. These findings support a causal link between collaboration in couples' joint accounts and future marital well-being.

A number of sociologists have utilized storytelling methods or accounts-like concepts in their research (Connell 1995, Hochschild 1989, Leidner 1993, Martin 1997, Stacey 1990), but they do not refer to or think of these concepts as accounts. I argue that in these programs of work, story-like constructions are used to illuminate the processes by which individuals impose order to their lives. For instance, in the book *The Second Shift,* Hochschild (1989) discusses what could be called the "Holts' account" of their division of home labor based on the upstairs/downstairs division. This "sharing" arrangement functions to make their marriage work and allows each of them to hold onto their gender ideologies. Hochschild conceptualizes this arrangement as a gender strategy or a family myth, but it could also be conceptualized and analyzed as an account, if greater attention were paid to the temporal sequencing of events, attributional statements, and the affective qualities of the story.

Further, if we assume that people learn accounts primarily in the same ways as they learn other social behaviors—from parents, peers, and other institutions such as the media and religion—then the examination of accounts and the process of account-making can contribute to theory and the understanding of socialization, norms, conformity, and other interactive learning processes. Future accounts work might also explore which institutions or agents of socialization are most important for the development of accounts and their presentation to others and why some stories are kept private, while others are confided in public.

### *The Product of Inquiry*

Ewick & Silbey (1995) believe that narratives enter scholarship when social researchers themselves function as storytellers in producing accounts of social life. Accounts can enter sociology by similar means. This form of representation can include a researcher's description of the data, the interpretation of the results, or the telling of his or her own account of a personal experience (Bochner et al 1997b, Ellis 1995, Stanley 1993). In addition, when qualitative researchers such as Stacey (1990) and Hochschild (1989) describe their own role in the research process and in the gathering of data, then the researcher also becomes a part of the storytelling process.

## *The Use of Accounts in Sociology*

The discipline of sociology has a history of theory and research focused on accounts as justifications of events, beginning with the early work of Scott

& Lyman, Goffman, and Garfinkel. Despite this prominent history and the "current enthusiasm for viewing storytelling as a way to make sense out of personal or relational experience" (Veroff et al 1993b, p. 440), few sociologists have explicitly used accounts as sources of data in their present empirical work and analysis.

For several alternative but complementary reasons, a greater number of sociologists have not been much involved in recent research and theory on accounts. Some argue that sociology is embedded in theoretical paradigms and methodologies characterized by a positivist and empiricist orientation, which thus prevent the acceptance and use of narratives or accounts (Maines 1993). Others (Abbott 1992) maintain that current sociological analyses ignore a more general sense of process or story because sociology emphasizes causality and the principles of logical positivism. According to Abbott (1992), "Our normal methods parse social reality into fixed entities with variable qualities. They attribute causality to the variables—hypostatized social characteristics—rather than to agents; variables do things, not social actors. Stories disappear" (p. 428).

Bruner (1986) distinguishes between narrative and logico-scientific modes of cognitive reasoning. These two means of constructing reality are quite distinct from one another in terms of ordering social experience, principles of thought, procedure, and verification. It is argued that sociology and other social sciences generally have promoted and supported the logico-scientific mode and have suppressed the narrative mode in mainstream publication outlets. (For a broader discussion of the two modes of reasoning and this viewpoint, see Bochner et al 1997b, Maines 1993, Richardson 1990).

In addition, the accounts concept has been tied to the foundations of symbolic interactionism, a perspective that has developed and changed greatly over time (Fine 1993). This theoretical framework lost popularity in sociology in the 1970s and was severely criticized for being nonempirical and lacking a structural emphasis; the work on accounts provoked a similar response. It may also be the case that since the initial developers of accounts (Burke, Goffman, Garfinkel, Mills, and Scott & Lyman) hardly mentioned how the concept should be operationalized and empirically tested, the narrower but closely related concept of attribution (see Crittenden 1983), rather than accounts, received far more empirical attention in the 1970s and into the 1980s. More recently, however, accounts and other related concepts have been tested usefully via different methods, both in sociology and in related fields (e.g. Baumeister & Newman 1994, McAdams et al 1996, Orbuch et al 1993, Veroff et al 1993c). Finally, and quite significant to whether greater numbers of sociologists embrace the concept of accounts, is the currently wider recognition and acceptance by sociologists and other social scientists of postpositivist, poststructuralist perspectives, which have reopened the door to more interpretive, qualitative, and meaning-centered research.

## CONCLUSION

The foundation is set for a resurgence of work on accounts in sociology. I have reviewed early sociological writing that played an important role in defining and conceptualizing the term account. In the early analyses, the phenomenon of accounts generally was conceptualized as verbal explanations, presented in interaction, for potentially blameworthy or unanticipated behavior. Sociologists embraced this concept; it played a central role in the development of theory and research on individuals' search for and presentation of justifications and explanations of their social behavior.

More recent work envelops a broader concept of accounts-as-stories to encompass both private and public explanations for a wider array of social actions (which include but are not limited to potentially negative acts). This work also highlights the social process of account-making, the interactive nature of confiding the account to others, and the functions of accounts and account-making for individuals' lives. A variety of theoretical frameworks and related concepts in communicated language, deviance, attributions, symbolic interactionism, and narratives have also motivated and influenced theory and research on accounts.

Many social scientists believe that narration or account-making is at the heart of all social behavior (Bruner 1990, Coles 1989, Polkinghorne 1988). Yet despite the wide enthusiasm for the use of stories in scientific inquiry, few sociologists have addressed or employed this broad concept in their empirical research. It has flourished in other disciplines including psychology, anthropology, and communication studies. On the other hand, I propose that there are perhaps "hidden" accounts in the work of many sociologists. The implicit nature of accounts is apparent in much of sociology. Many of the qualitative approaches to interviewing, especially in-depth interviewing techniques (e.g. Mishler 1985, Weiss 1994), as well as ethnographies, autobiographies, artful science, and ethnomethodology, could be considered methods of collecting accounts (Alder & Alder 1987, Barbre et al 1989, Bochner et al 1997, Denzin 1990, Ellis & Bochner 1997).

The accounts concept, which has a solid foundation in early sociological work is quite valuable and relevant to sociologists' interests and goals. The concept is useful for gaining insight into the human experience and arriving at meanings or collective understandings of other cultural, gender, or ethnic groups. This concept deserves greater explicit attention in mainstream sociology. Broadly construed, the ideas of accounts and account-making may be viewed as central to the enterprise and endeavors of contemporary sociology. "From time to time sociologists might well pause from their ongoing pursuits to inquire whether their research interests contribute in any way to the fundamental questions of sociology" (Scott & Lyman 1968, p. 46).

ACKNOWLEDGMENTS

The author is grateful for continued research collaboration on the topic of accounts with John Harvey, Joseph Veroff, Ann Weber, and Sandra Eyster. I would also like to thank John Harvey, Carolyn Ellis, Andy Modigliani, Karin Martin, James House, and an anonymous reviewer for their comments and suggestions on this chapter.

**Visit the *Annual Reviews home page* at http://www.annurev.org.**

*Literature Cited*

Abbott A. 1992. From causes to events: notes on narrative positivism. *Sociol. Meth. Res.* 2(4):428–55

Alder PA, Alder P. 1987. *Membership Roles in Field Research.* Newbury Park, CA: Sage

Antaki C. 1987. Performed and unperformable: a guide to accounts of relationships. In *Accounting for Relationships,* ed. R Burnett, D Clark, P McGhee, pp. 97–113. London: Methuen

Antaki C. 1988. *Analyzing Everyday Explanation.* Beverly Hills, CA: Sage

Arnston P, Droge D. 1987. Social support in self-help groups: the role of communication in enabling perceptions of control. In *Communicating Social Support,* ed. TL Albrecht, MB Adelman, pp. 148–71. Newbury Park, CA: Sage

Barbre JW, Farrell A, Garner SN, Geiger S, Joeres REB, et al. 1989. *Interpreting Women's Lives: Feminist Theory and Personal Narratives.* Bloomington: Indiana Univ. Press

Baumeister RF. 1986. *Identity: Cultural Change and the Struggle for Self.* New York: Oxford Univ. Press

Baumeister RF. 1989. *Masochism and the Self.* Hillsdale, NJ: Erlbaum

Baumeister RF, Newman LS. 1994. How stories make sense of personal experiences: motives that shape autobiographical narratives. *Pers. Soc. Psychol. Bull.* 20(6):676–90

Baumeister RF, Stillwell AM 1992. Autobiographical accounts, situational roles, and motivated biases: when stories don't match up. In *Attributions, Accounts and Close Relationships,* ed. J Harvey, TL Orbuch, AL Weber, pp. 52–70. New York: Springer

Berscheid E. 1994. Interpersonal relationships. *Annu. Rev. Psychol.* 45:79–129

Blumer, H. 1969. *Symbolic Interactionism.* Englewood Cliffs, NJ: Prentice-Hall

Blumstein PW. 1974. The honoring of accounts. *Am. Sociol. Rev.* 39:551–66

Bochner AP. 1994. Perspectives on inquiry. II: theories and stories. In *Interpersonal Communication,* ed. M Knapp G Miller, pp. 21–41. Newbury Park, CA: Sage. 2nd ed.

Bochner AP, Ellis C, Tillman LM. 1997a. Relationships as stories. In *Handbook of Personal Relationships,* ed. S Duck, pp. 307–24. Sussex, Eng: Wiley & Son

Bochner AP, Ellis C, Tillman-Healy LM. 1997b. Mucking around looking for truth. In *Dialectical Approaches to Studying Personal Relationships,* ed. B Montogomery, L Baxter. Mahwah, NJ: Erlbaum. In press

Bruner JS. 1986. *Actual Minds, Possible Worlds.* Cambridge, MA: Harvard Univ. Press

Bruner JS. 1990. *Acts of Meaning.* Cambridge, MA: Harvard Univ. Press

Burke K. 1945. *A Grammar of Motives.* New York: Prentice Hall

Burke P, Reitzes D. 1991. The link between identity and role performance. *Soc. Psychol. Q.* 44(2):83–92

Burnett R, Clark D, McGhee P. 1987. *Accounting for Relationships.* London: Methuen

Coles R. 1989. *The Call of Stories: Teaching and Moral Imagination.* Boston, MA: Houghton Mifflin

Connell RW. 1992. A very straight gay: masculinity, homosexual experience, and the dynamics of gender. *Am. Sociol. Res.* 57(2):735–51

Connell RW. 1995. *Masculinities.* Berkeley: Univ. California Press

Cooley CH. 1902. *Human Nature and the Social Order.* New York: Scribner's

Couch C. 1992. Toward a formal theory of social processes. *Symbolic Interact.* 15(2):117–34

Cressey PG. 1932. *The Taxi-Dance Hall.* Chicago: Univ. Chicago Press

Crites S. 1986. Storytime: recollecting the past

and projecting the future. In *Narrative Psychology: The Stories Nature of Human Conduct,* ed. T Sarbin, pp. 152–73. New York: Praeger
Crittenden KS. 1983. Sociological aspects of attribution. *Annu. Rev. Sociol.* 9:425–46
Denzin N. 1985. Emotion as lived experience. *Symbolic Interact.* 8(2):223–40
Denzin N. 1990. Harold and Agnes: a feminist narrative undoing. *Sociol. Theory* 8(2):198–216
Ellingson S. 1995. Understanding the dialectic discourse and collective action: public debate and rioting in antebellum Cincinnati. *Am. J. Sociol.* 101:100–44
Ellis C. 1995. *Final Negotiations: A Story of Love, Loss, and Chronic Illness.* Philadelphia: Temple Univ. Press
Ellis C, Bochner AP. 1997. Writing from sociology's periphery. In *What's Wrong With Sociology?* ed. S Cole. Princeton, NJ: Princeton Univ. Press. In press
Etter-Lewis G. 1993. *My Soul Is My Own: Oral Narratives of African-American Women in the Professions.* New York: Routledge
Ewick P, Silbey S. 1995. Subversive stories and hegemonic tales: toward a sociology of narrative. *Law Soc. Rev.* 29(2):197–226
Felson RB. 1981. The attributions of actors and observers concerning performance in a football game. *J. Soc. Psychol.* 115(1):15–23
Fincham FD. 1992. The account episode in close relationships. In *Explaining One's Self to Others: Reason Giving in a Social Context,* ed. ML McLaughlin, MJ Cody, SF Read, pp. 167–82. Hillsdale, NJ: Erlbaum
Fine G. 1992. Agency, structure, and comparitive contexts toward a synthetic interactionism. *Symbolic Interact.* 15:87–102
Fine G. 1993. The sad demise, mysterious disappearance, and glorious triumph of symbolic interactionism. *Annu. Rev. Sociol.* 19:61–87
Fletcher GJO. 1983. The analysis of verbal explanations for marital separation: implications for attribution theory. *J. Appl. Soc. Psychol.* 13:245–58
Garfinkel H. 1956. Conditions of successful degradation ceremonies. *Am. J. Sociol.* 61:420–24
Garfinkel H. 1967. *Studies in Ethnomethodology.* Engelwood Cliffs, NJ: Prentice Hall
Gergen KJ, Gergen MN. 1983. Narratives of the self. In *Studies of Social Identity,* ed. TR Sarbin, KE Scheibe, pp. 254–72. New York: Praeger
Gergen KJ, Gergen MM. 1987. Narratives of relationship. In *Accounting for Relationships,* eds. R Burnett, D Clark, P McGhee, pp. 269–88. London: Methuen
Gergen KJ, Gergen MM. 1988. Narrative and the self as relationship. In *Advances in Experimental Social Psychology,* ed. L Berkowitz, 22:211–44. New York: Academic
Goffman E. 1959. *The Presentation of Self in Everyday Life.* Garden City, NY: Doubleday-Anchor
Goffman E. 1971. *Relations in Public.* New York: Basic Books
Griffin LJ. 1993. Narrative, event-structure analysis, and causal interpretation in historical sociology. *Am. J. Sociol.* 98(5):1094–1133
Harber KD, Pennebaker JW. 1992. Overcoming traumatic memories. In *The Handbook of Emotion and Memory,* ed. SA Christiason, pp. 359–87. Hillsdale, NJ: Erlbaum
Harre R. 1977. The ethogenic approach: theory and practice. In *Advances in Experimental Social Psychology,* ed. L Berkowitz, 10:284–314. New York: Academic
Harre R., Clark D, DeCarlo N, 1985. *Motives and Mechanisms.* New York: Methuen
Hart J. 1992. Cracking the code: narrative and political mobilization in the Greek Resistance. *Soc. Sci. His.* 16(4):631–67
Harvey JH. 1996. *Embracing Their Memory: Loss and the Social Psychology of Storytelling.* Needham Heights, MA: Allyn & Bacon
Harvey JH, Orbuch TL, Weber AL. 1990a. *Interpersonal Accounts.* Oxford: Blackwell
Harvey JH, Orbuch TL, Weber AL. 1990b. A social psychological model of account-making in response to severe stress. *J. Lang. Soc. Psychol.* 9(3):191–207
Harvey JH, Orbuch TL, Chwalisz KD, Garwood G. 1991. Coping with sexual assault: the roles of account-making and confiding. *J. Traumatic Stress* 4(4):515–31
Harvey JH, Orbuch TL, Weber AL. 1992. *Attributions, Accounts, and Close Relationships.* New York: Springer-Verlag
Harvey JH, Turnquist DC, Agostinelli G. 1988. Identifying attributions in oral and written explanations. In *Analysing Everyday Explanation: A Casebook of Methods,* ed. C Antaki, pp. 32–42. London: Sage
Harvey JH, Weber, AL, Galvin, KS, Huszati HC, Garnick, NN. 1986. Attribution and the termination of close relationships: a special focus on the account. In *The Emerging Field of Close Relationships,* ed. R. Gilmour, S. Duck, pp. 189–201. Hillsdale, NJ: Erlbaum.
Harvey JH, Wells GL, Alvarez MD. 1978. Attribution in the context of conflict and separation in close relationship. In *New Directions in Attribution Research,* ed. JH Harvey, W Ickes, RF Kidd, pp. 235–59. Hillsdale, NJ: Erlbaum
Heath, SB. 1983. *Ways With Words: Language,*

*Life and Work in Communities and Classrooms*. Cambridge, Eng: Cambridge Univ. Press.

Heider F. 1958. *The Psychology of Interpersonal Relations*. New York: John Wiley

Hochschild A. 1989. *Second Shift*. New York: Avon

Hopper J. 1993. The rhetoric of motives in divorce. *J. Marriage Fam.* 55:801–13

Howard GS. 1991. Cultural tales: a narrative approach to thinking, cross-cultural psychology, and psychotherapy. *Am. Psychol.* 46:187–97

Huston TL, Surra CA, Fitzgerald NM, Cate RM. 1981. From courtship to marriage: mate selection as an interpersonal process. In *Personal Relationships*, Vol. 2, *Developing Personal Relationships*, ed. S Duck, R Gilmour, pp. 53–88. London: Academic

Jacobs RN. 1966. Civil society and crisis: culture, discourse, and the Rodney King beating. *Am. J. Sociol.* 101(5):1238–72

Jones EE, Davis KE. 1965. From acts to dispositions: the attribution process in personal perception. In *Advances in Experimental Social Psychology*, ed. L Berkowitz, 2:220–66. New York: Academic

LaRossa R. 1995. Stories and relationships. *J. Soc. Pers. Relat.* 12(4):553–58

Leidner, R. 1993. *Fast Food, Fast Talk: Service Work and the Routinization of Everyday Life*. Berkeley: Univ. Calif. Press

Lichtman RR, Taylor SE. 1986. Close relationships of female cancer patients. In *Women with Cancer*, ed. BL Andersen, pp. 233–56. New York: Springer-Verlag

Lyman SM, Scott MB. 1970. *A Sociology of the Absurd*. New York: Appleton-Century Crofts

Maines D. 1993. Narrative's moment and sociology's phenomena: toward a narrative sociology. *Sociol. Q.* 34(1):17–38

Martin K. 1997. *Puberty, Sexuality and the Self*. New York: Routledge. In press

Matthews SH. 1986. *Friendship Through the Life Course: Oral Biographies in Old Age*. Beverly Hills, CA: Sage

McAdams DP, Diamond A, de St. Aubin E, Mansfield E. 1996. Stories of commitment: the psychosocial construction of generative lives. *J. Pers. Soc. Psychol.*

McLaughlin ML, Cody MJ, O'Hair HD. 1983. The management of failure events: some contextual determinants of accounting behavior. *Hum. Commun. Res.* 9:209–24

McLaughlin ML, Cody MJ, Read SJ. 1992. *Explaining Oneself to Others: Reason-Giving in a Social Context*. Hillsdale, NJ: Erlbaum

McLaughlin ML, Cody MJ, French, K. 1990. Account-giving and the attribution of responsibility: impressions of traffic offenders. In *The Psychology of Tactical Communication*, ed. MJ Cody, ML McLaughlin, pp. 244–67. Clevedon, Eng: Multilingual

Mead GH. 1934. *Mind, Self, and Society*. Chicago: Univ. Chicago Press

Mills CW. 1940. Situated actions and vocabularies of motive. *Am. Sociol. Rev.* 5:904–13

Mills CW. 1963. *Power, Politics and People*. New York: Oxford Univ. Press

Mishler EG. 1986. *Research Interviewing: Context and Narrative*. Cambridge, MA: Harvard Univ. Press

Mishler EG. 1995. Models of narrative analysis: a typology. *J. Narr. Life Hist.* 5(2):87–123

Murray SL, Holmes JG. 1994. Storytelling in close relationships: the construction of confidence. *Pers. Soc. Psychol. Bull.* 20(6):650–63

Orbuch TL, Harvey J, Russell SM, Sorenson K. 1992. Account-making through accounts: three studies. *J. Soc. Behav. Pers.* 7(1):79–94

Orbuch TL, Harvey J, Davis S, Merbach N. 1994. Account-making and confiding as acts of meaning in response to sexual assault. *J. Fam. Viol.* 9(3):249–64

Orbuch TL, Veroff J, Holmberg D. 1993. Becoming a married couple: the emergence of meaning in the first years of marriage. *J. Marriage Fam.* 55:815–26

Park RE, Burgess EW. 1921. *An Introduction to the Science of Sociology*. Chicago: Univ. Chicago Press

Pennebaker JW. 1989. Confession, inhibition, and disease. In *Advances in Experimental Social Psychology*, ed. L Berkowitz, 22:211–45. New York: Academic

Pennebaker JW. 1990. *Opening Up: The Healing Powers of Confiding in Others*. New York: William Morrow

Pennebaker JW, Harber KD. 1993. A social stage model of collective coping: the Loma Prieta earthquake and the Persian Gulf war. *J. Soc. Iss.* 49(4):125–45

Polkinghorne D. 1988. *Narrative Knowing and the Human Sciences*. Albany, NY: State Univ. NY Press

Richardson L. 1990. Narrative and sociology. *J. Contemp. Ethnol.* 19(1):116–35

Riessman CK. 1993. *Narrative Analysis*. Newbury Park: Sage

Rosenwald GC, Ochberg RL, eds. 1992. *Storied Lives: The Cultural Politics of Self-Understanding*. New Haven, CT: Yale Univ. Press

Sarbin TR. 1986. *Narrative Psychology*. New York: Praeger

Schonbach P. 1980. A category system for account phases. *Eur. J. Soc. Psychol.* 10:195–200

Schonbach P. 1990. *Account Episodes: The Management or Escalation of Conflict*.

Cambridge, Eng./New York: Cambridge Univ. Press
Scott MB, Lyman S. 1968. Accounts. *Am. Sociol. Rev.* 33:46–62
Semin GR, Manstead ASR. 1983. *The Accountability of Conduct: A Social Psychological Analysis.* London: Academic
Sewell, WH 1992. Introduction: narratives and social identities. *Soc. S. His.* 16(3):479–87
Shotter J. 1984. *Social Accountability and Selfhood.* Oxford: Blackwell
Shotter J. 1987. The social construction of an "us." In *Accounting for Relationships,* ed. R Burnett, P McGhee, D Clark, pp. 225–47. London: Methuen
Silver RL, Boon C, Stones MH. 1983. Searching for meaning in misfortune: making sense of incest. *J. Soc. Issues* 39:81–101
Simon R. 1995. Gender, multiple roles, role meaning, and mental health. *J. Health Soc. Behav.* 35:182–94
Simon W, Gagnon, J. 1986. Sexual scripts: permanence and change. *Arch. Sex. Behav.* 15(2):97–120
Somers MR. 1994. The narrative constitution of identity: a relational network approach. *Theory Soc.* 23(5):605–49
Stacey J. 1990. *Brave New Families.* New York: Basic
Stanley L. 1993. The knowing because experiencing subject: narratives, lives, and autobiography. *Women's Stud. Int. Forum.* 16(3):205–15
Steinmetz G. 1992. Reflections on the role of social narratives in working-class formation: narrative theory in the social sciences. *Soc. S. His.* 16(3):489–515
Sternberg RJ. 1995. Love as a story. *J. Soc. Pers. Relat.* 12(4):541–46
Stokes R, Hewitt JP. 1976. Aligning actions. *Am. Sociol. Rev.* 41(5):838–49
Stryker S. 1981. Symbolic interactionism: themes and variations. In *Sociological Perspectives on Social Psychology,* ed. M Rosenberg, RH Turner, pp. 3–29. New York: Basic Books
Stryker S. 1983. Social psychology from the standpoint of a structural symbolic interactionism. In *Advances in Experimental Social Psychology,* 16:181–219. New York: Academic
Stryker S, Gottlieb A. 1981. Attribution theory and symbolic interactionism: a comparison. In *New Directions in Attribution Research,* ed. JH Harvey, W Ickes, RF Kidd, 3:425–59. New Jersey: Erlbaum
Stryker S, Stratham A. 1985. Symbolic interaction and role theory. In *The Handbook of Social Psychology,* ed. G. Lindzey, E Aronson, pp. 311–78. New York: Random House. 3rd ed.
Surra CA. 1988. *Turning point coding manual. III.* Unpublished manuscript, Univ. Texas, Austin
Surra CA, Batchelder ML, Hughes DK. 1995. Accounts and the demystification of courtship. In *Explaining Family Interactions,* ed. MA Fitzpatrick, AL Vangelisti, pp. 112–41. Thousand Oaks, CA: Sage
Surra CA, Bohman T. 1991. The development of close relationships: a cognitive perspective, In *Cognition in Close Relationships,* ed. GJO Fletcher, FD Fincham, pp. 281–305. Hillsdale, NJ: Erlbaum
Sutherland, EH. 1955. *Principles of Criminology.* Rev. by DR Cressey. Chicago, IL: Univ. Chicago Press
Sykes GM, Matza D. 1957. Techniques of neutralization: a theory of delinquency. *Am. Sociol. Rev.* 22:664–70
Thoits P. 1991. On merging identity theory and stress research. *Soc. Psychol. Q.* 54(2):101–12
Vaughn D. 1986. *Uncoupling: Turning Points in Intimate Relationships.* New York: Oxford Univ. Press
Veroff J, Douvan E, Hatchett S. 1995. *Marital Instability.* Westport, CT: Praeger
Veroff J, Chadiha L, Leber D, Sutherland L. 1993a. Affects and interactions in newlyweds narratives: black and white couples compared. *J. Narr. Life Hist.* 3(4):361–90
Veroff J, Sutherland L, Chadiha L, Ortega RM. 1993b. Newlyweds tell their stories: a narrative method for assessing marital experiences. *J. Soc. Pers. Relat.* 10(3):437–57
Veroff, J, Sutherland L, Chadiha LA, Ortega RM. 1993c. Predicting marital quality with narrative assessments of marital experience. *J. Marriage Fam.* 55:326–37
Weary G, Stanley MA, Harvey JH. 1989. *Attribution.* New York: Springer-Verlag
Weber AL. 1992. The account-making process: a phenomenological approach. In *Close Relationship Loss,* ed. T. Orbuch, pp. 174–91. New York: Springer
Weber AL, Harvey JH, Stanley MA. 1987. The nature and motivations of accounts for failed relationships. In *Accounting for Relationships,* ed. R Burnett, P McGhee, DC Clark, pp. 114–33. London: Methuen
Weiss RS. 1975. *Marital Separation.* New York: Basic Books
Weiss RS. 1994. *Learning From Strangers.* New York: Free Press
Wiley MG, Eskilson A. 1981. Repairing a spoiled identity: an application of attribution theory. *Soc. Forc.* 14(4):321–30

*Annu. Rev. Sociol. 1997. 23:479–515*


# THE LEGAL ENVIRONMENTS OF ORGANIZATIONS

*Lauren B. Edelman*
Center for the Study of Law and Society, University of California, Berkeley, California 94720; e-mail: ledelman@uclink4.berkeley.edu

*Mark C. Suchman*
Department of Sociology and School of Law, University of Wisconsin, Madison, Wisconsin 53706; e-mail: suchman@ssc.wisc.edu

KEY WORDS: law, organizations, institutional theory, professions, environments

ABSTRACT

Sociology has recently witnessed a rapprochement between research on organizations and research on law. This essay reviews a number of central developments and tendencies in this emerging literature, with a particular emphasis on the characteristics of law as an element of the organizational environment. We begin by distinguishing two metatheoretical perspectives on law and organizations: the materialist perspective, which portrays organizations as rational wealth-maximizers and sees the law as a system of substantive incentives and penalties; and the cultural perspective, which portrays organizations as cultural rule-followers and sees the law as a system of moral principles, scripted roles, and sacred symbols. Within each of these traditions, we examine three distinct facets of organizations' legal environments: the facilitative environment, in which law passively provides an arena for organizational action; the regulatory environment, in which law actively seeks to control organizational behavior; and the constitutive environment, in which law defines the basic building blocks of organizational forms and interorganizational relations. Finally, we distinguish between literature that sees law as an independent variable, determining organizational behavior; literature that sees law as a dependent variable, determined by organizational behavior; and a growing literature that discusses the endogeneity between law and organizations. Although any taxonomy tends to depict clear lines where they are in fact murky, we think that this approach not only provides a means of categorizing the literature on law and organizations, it also calls attention to the many different ways in which law and organizations are dynamically intertwined.



0360-0572/97/0815-0479$08.00

## *Introduction*

Classical social theorists saw the sociology of law and the sociology of organizations as intimately intertwined. To Marx, each historical epoch generated distinctive legal forms that simultaneously reflected and reproduced that epoch's fundamental organization of production (Marx & Engels 1977, Cain & Hunt 1979). To Durkheim (1964), the division of labor in society established the functional imperatives underlying prevailing legal institutions. To Weber (1947), legal-rational organizational structures and rationally organized legal structures embodied kindred tensions between efficacy, predictability, and domination. Yet, despite these early linkages, subsequent scholarship in the sociology of organizations and in the sociology of law developed for the most part independently. A few key theorists (e.g. Selznick 1969, Hurst 1964, Stone 1975) attempted to bridge the gap between these subfields, but most research in each tradition remained largely oblivious of the other.

In recent years, however, the conceptual separation between organizational and legal sociology has become increasingly difficult to maintain. Modern organizations are immersed in a sea of law. They are born through the legal act of incorporation, and they die through the legal act of bankruptcy. In between, they raise capital under securities law, hire employees under labor and antidiscrimination law, exchange goods and services under contract law, develop public identities under trademark law, innovate under patent and copyright law, and engage in production under environmental, and health and safety law. Specific bodies of legal rules define, protect, and regulate many industries and most professions. Even the basic distinctions between "private," "public," and "nonprofit" are in part legal constructs. Moreover, the legal environment seems to have become more pervasive (or at least more visible) with the passage of time, as organizations face increased levels of litigation, regulation, and certification in many areas of activity.[1]

Modern law, for its part, is awash in a flood of organizations. Law often emerges from the importunings of social movement organizations, charitable foundations, and corporations, and it is erased at the behest of such organized interests as well. In between, it develops meaning through its interpretation by organized professions, and it develops substance through its application by organizational compliance officers. It finds force in organizations' litigation decisions, and it realizes limits in organizations' buffering and decoupling

[1]This observation should not be read as a critique. Research suggests that organizations themselves have generated—and benefited from—a great deal of the recent rise in litigation, regulation, and certification. Managerial grumbling notwithstanding, the law is an invited guest, not an intruder, in most precincts of organizational life.

strategies. Moreover, just as organizational life seems to have become more legalized, legal life also seems to have become more bureaucratized, with organizational actors assuming increasingly pivotal roles in turning the wheels of justice.

In light of these trends, it is hardly surprising that sociology has begun to experience a quiet reconvergence of research on law and research on organizations. This rapprochement is still in its early stages, and much important conceptual work remains to be done. Nonetheless, the broad outlines of the endeavor are beginning to emerge. In the hope of accelerating these intellectual developments, this essay reviews and synthesizes some of the most significant strands in the still-disparate literature on the legal environments of organizations.

Before beginning this exploration, it is important to note a number of topics that we do not cover here, despite their relevance to the general subject of law and organizations. First and perhaps most notably, although many of our observations may apply to criminal as well as civil matters, we review neither the large criminological literature on white collar crime (e.g. Coleman 1989, Wheeler et al 1982; see Braithwaite 1985 for a review) nor the smaller (but growing) literature on "organizational crime" (e.g. Cullen et al 1987). Further, we focus primarily on the relationship between the law and nonlegal organizations, and we do not address the large literature on the organizational characteristics of legal institutions such as legislatures, regulatory agencies, courts, law firms, police departments, and prisons. We also focus primarily on those legal policies that operate through judicial and quasi-judicial enforcement mechanisms, and we therefore intentionally exclude spending, taxation, and the direct provision of goods and services by nonjudicial state agencies. Finally, due to space limitations, we largely confine our attention to the sociological literature, and we therefore do not systematically cover the sizable parallel literatures in political science and "law and economics." The following pages, then, examine sociological accounts of how organizations that are formally outside the legal realm relate to the civil laws and regulations that they encounter in their social environments. While this scope does not encompass every possible body of relevant thought, it nonetheless covers quite a wide range of material.

## *Dimensions in the Analysis of Law and Organizations*

Our review divides the literature into two metatheoretical perspectives on law and organizations. The first might be labeled a *rational materialist* perspective. Prominent in both classical studies of organizations and the newer law and economics tradition, this perspective sees organizations as rational wealth maximizers and sees the law as a system of substantive incentives and penalties (for a recent survey of law and economics, see Cooter & Ulen 1996).[2] Thus, organizations instrumentally invoke or evade the law, in a strategic effort to "engineer" legal activities that bring the largest possible payoff at the least possible cost. In opposition to this materialist perspective, a somewhat smaller camp (primarily composed of neoinstitutional sociologists) offers what could be called a *normative cultural alternative* (for reviews of neoinstitutional theory, see Powell & DiMaggio 1991, Scott 1987, Scott & Meyer 1994, Scott 1995, Suchman & Edelman 1996). Here, material costs and benefits are, at best, a secondary concern. Instead, this perspective sees organizations as cultural rule-followers and sees the law as a system of moral principles, scripted roles, and sacred symbols.[3] Thus, organizations look to the law for normative and cognitive guidance, as they seek their place in a socially constructed cultural reality. Law provides a model of and for organizational life, defining roles for organizational actors and meanings for organizational events—and imbuing those roles and meanings with positive or negative moral valence (cf Geertz 1983). If materialist accounts speak in the language of game theory, deterrence theory, and transaction cost analysis, culturalist accounts invoke labeling theory, symbolic management theory, and institutional analysis.

The material-cultural dichotomy is not the only noteworthy split in the literature on law and organizations. A second set of divisions arise because the legal environment is multifaceted, and different research traditions emphasize different aspects. Specifically, organizations encounter law in at least three distinct guises, which we here call the facilitative, regulatory, and constitutive legal environments, respectively (cf Suchman 1993a, Scott 1993).[4]

As a *facilitative environment*, law provides an exogenously generated, but fundamentally passive set of tools and forums, which managers actively employ to accomplish various organizational goals. This is the world of the lawsuit, the public hearing, and the Freedom of Information request, as well as of the

[2]Some models relax this claim by positing that organizations are merely bundles of quasi-contractual relations between rational wealth-maximizing individuals (Alchian & Demsetz 1972, Jensen & Meckling 1976). Others add the possibility that when information is costly, rational maximizing may give way to boundedly rational satisficing (March & Simon 1958, Arrow 1974, Williamson 1975). Nonetheless, the general emphasis on materially driven, instrumental action remains at the core of all such accounts.

[3]Many culturalist models emphasize that legitimation processes can give organizations a material interest in at least superficial conformity (Meyer & Rowan 1977, Dowling & Pfeffer 1975, for a review, see Suchman 1995b). While such accounts clearly allow some room for rational decision-making dynamics, they nevertheless continue to accord a central place to culturally driven symbolic action.

[4]Broadly, the facilitative, regulatory, and constitutive environments in our analysis correspond to procedural law, substantive law, and definitional law, respectively, in Suchman (1993a) and Scott (1993).

numerous informal maneuvers that arise "in the shadow of the law" (Mnookin & Kornhauser 1979). Here, law appears as a system of procedural rules, furnishing legal vehicles for organizational initiatives that might otherwise occur through market tactics, media campaigns, industrial espionage, violent self-help, etc. In facilitative law, organizations are the players, and the legal system is merely an arena—albeit an arena whose shape may dramatically affect the course of the game.[5]

The *regulatory environment*, in contrast, places law in a far more active posture. This is the world of antidiscrimination laws, health and safety laws, antitrust laws, environmental protection laws, and the like.[6] Here, law appears as a system of substantive edicts, invoking societal authority over various aspects of organizational life. The rhetoric, if not the reality, of regulation is one of top-down sovereign control: The legal system (presumably on society's behalf) is taking the initiative directly to modify organizational behavior.

The third facet of law—the role of law as a *constitutive environment*—is at once more subtle and more profound than the other two. Here, the legal system constructs and empowers various classes of organizational actors and delineates the relationships between them. Thus, if the facilitative legal environment is comprised primarily of procedural rules, and the regulatory legal environment is comprised primarily of substantive edicts, the constitutive legal environment is comprised primarily of definitional categories—those basic typologies that identify the legally cognizable components of the social world and that explain the natures and attributes of each. Constitutive law generally functions almost invisibly, providing taken-for-granted labels, categories, and "default rules" for organizational behavior; however, by establishing the background understandings that frame social discourse, constitutive law helps to determine what types of organizations come into existence and what types of organizational activity gain formal recognition. Thus, for example, the constitutive legal environment describes how various classes of organizations are born and how they die; it

[5]We use the term "facilitative" not only because this facet of law "facilitates" certain organizational strategies, but also (and primarily) because the word hints at law's ability to provide "facilities" for organizational action. Patent infringement suits, for example, may not facilitate organizational activity on the part of the defendant corporations, but they do offer a forum in which the parties can build competitive advantages over—or cooperative relations among—one another.

[6]It is perhaps worth noting that the regulatory legal environment, as we define it here, is not precisely coterminous with either lay or legal conceptions of "regulation." Seen as the invocation of societal authority over organizational life, the regulatory legal environment includes common law as well as statutes, but it largely excludes laws (or parts of laws) that establish operating procedures for administrative agencies or that define categories of regulated activity. (In our typology, these legal elements would be classified as facilitative and constitutive, respectively.) Further, although we do not specifically address general criminal law in this essay, most such material would fall within our definition of the regulatory environment, broadly understood.

defines whether particular interorganizational relationships are to be understood as transitory or open-ended; and it establishes which organizations can act as corporate "persons" and which can act only as collections of separable interests. In short, although constitutive law often seems more placid and routine than facilitative and regulatory law, this aspect of the legal environment provides the fundamental definitional building blocks that undergird the other two.

As well as being separated by metatheoretical orientation (material/cultural) and by focal environment (facilitative/regulatory/constitutive), writings on law and organizations also vary in the nature of the causal questions that they ask. Most investigations, especially within the sociology of organizations, treat law as an independent variable, and examine how exogenously established legal conditions affect the practices and outcomes of various organizational entities. Other analyses, particularly within the sociology of law, treat law as a dependent variable, and ask how exogenously determined organizational activities contribute to the formulation and implementation of various legal initiatives. Most recently, a third causal imagery has begun to emerge, primarily among scholars working at the border between law and organizations. Rather than treating either legal or organizational events as purely exogenous, this approach highlights the endogeneity of both organizations and their legal environments, arguing that organizations construct and configure legal regimes even as they respond to them.

The divisions in the literature are not entirely independent. Materialist accounts, for example, tend to focus on the facilitative and regulatory legal environment, whereas culturalist accounts tend to focus on the regulatory and constitutive environment. In addition, materialists are somewhat more likely to treat law as purely dependent or purely independent, whereas culturalists are beginning to attend more closely to endogeneity. The following pages review first materialist and then culturalist writings, in both cases exploring how metatheory directs attention toward particular facets of the legal environment and toward particular types of causal argument. As becomes clear, however, the literature on law and organizations encompasses a wide range of issues and perspectives, and it often defies easy categorization.

## *Materialist Approaches*

Materialist approaches to the relationship between law and organizations trace their intellectual ancestry back to Beccaria (1988), Marx (Marx & Engels 1964), Holmes (1897, 1881), and Weber (1978). In keeping with this heritage, recent contributors come not only from sociology but also from economics, political science, and law, and many of their writings conjoin abstract theory and empirical description with substantial doses of prescriptive policy analysis. In broad outline, materialists see the law as a system of concrete penalties and rewards, designed to deter some lines of action and to encourage others. Organizations, for their part, respond as self-interested rational actors, making calculated decisions about when and how to influence, invoke, obey, and evade the legal system in order to avoid law's costs and exploit law's benefits. Because of its emphasis on material sanctions, this approach tends to assume that legal rules will be most efficacious (and therefore most worthy of study) when they are substantive and unambiguous; because of its emphasis on organization-level rational action, this approach tends to assume that organizational identities, interests, and capacities exist independent of the law. Consequently, materialists generally downplay endogenous and constitutive processes. Instead, they focus primarily on how facilitative and regulatory legal apparatuses emerge from and subsequently determine organizational activity.

### *Materialist Perspectives on the Facilitative Environment*

The legal system provides tools and forums for a wide range of organizational activities, from dispute resolution (Westin & Feliu 1988, Ewing 1989) to information gathering (Casey et al 1983, Farrell 1984) to coalition building (McCann 1991, 1994); however, perhaps the most frequently studied aspect of the facilitative legal environment is litigation.[7] Business litigation rates have risen dramatically since the early 1970s, in part due to increased litigation by individuals against firms, but largely due to an increased willingness of corporations to sue one another (Cheit 1990, 1991, Dungworth et al 1990, Galanter & Rogers 1991, cf Wanner 1974). This change has brought with it both an expansion of in-house counsel offices (Chayes & Chayes 1985, Galanter & Rogers 1991) and a burgeoning of independent corporate law firms (Galanter & Palay 1991, Nelson 1988). Thus, litigation is becoming an increasingly salient aspect of day-to-day organizational operations.

Significantly, although research on individual-level litigation often highlights symbolic and expressive factors (see, e.g., Felstiner et al 1980–1981, Danet 1980, Lind & Tyler 1988, Mather & Yngvesson 1980–1981), organizational research almost invariably adopts a more materialist stance, emphasizing the strategic choices that organizations make in using lawsuits as tools of direct (nonmarket) competition (e.g. Priest & Klein 1984, Cheit 1991:129–30). Much of this literature emerges out of policy debates surrounding litigation reform. Such studies generally treat procedural rules as exogenous variables affecting the costs and benefits (and hence the form and frequency) of organizational disputing. Standing-to-sue doctrines (Snyder 1985, Alpert 1988, Rabkin 1989), class-action requirements (Scott 1975, Yeazell 1987), contingency fee

[7]This having been said, it is also worth noting that litigation involving businesses appears radically understudied when compared to litigation involving individuals (Cheit 1991, Hayden 1989).

arrangements (Olson 1991, Donohue 1991, Gravelle & Waterson 1993), and jurisdictional rules (Bumiller 1980–1981) have all attracted attention as determinants of litigation behavior—both litigation by organizations and litigation against them (see, generally, Cotterrell 1992:250–57, Cappelletti 1989). Further, several observers have posited that aggregate changes in litigation may produce a wide array of systemic side-effects, including increased insurance use (Cheit 1991:127), elevated bankruptcy rates (Delaney 1989), and a societal undersupply of high-risk innovation (Cheit 1991:130; see generally, Huber 1988). In short, as independent variables, procedural rules determine how attractive court-oriented disputing will be, and this in turn determines whether or not the facilitative legal environment will absorb organizational energies that, for better or worse, might otherwise be directed elsewhere.

Alongside such analyses of facilitative law as a determinant of organizational behavior, other materialist researchers have reversed the causal arrow, to explore the ways in which organizational behavior may shape this legal environment in return. Formally, at least, courts are passive institutions, and although procedural rules may encourage or discourage the filing of court papers, most litigated disputes originate outside the judicial arena. As Galanter & Rogers (1991) observe, lawsuits are only one of several ways that organizations can govern their interactions. Others include: markets (Williamson 1975, 1981), state regulation (see below), community norms (Macaulay 1963, Ellickson 1986), labor organizations (Vittoz 1987, Rogers 1990), and trade associations (Streeck & Schmitter 1985, Aldrich et al 1994). If litigation arises, in part, from the failure of these alternative mechanisms, then extra-legal organizational conditions—such as competition, product specialization, relational duration, deal complexity, economic globalization, and economic instability—may play a crucial role in shaping the work of the courts (Galanter & Rogers 1991:41 ff).

This influence may extend beyond the rate of litigation to include the nature of litigation as well. Strategic decisions about when and how to mobilize the facilitative legal environment can, in the aggregate, produce lasting shifts in underlying legal rules (Priest & Klein 1984). Moreover, as well-endowed "repeat players," organizations are often uniquely capable of using litigation to conform the law to their needs (Galanter 1974, Wanner 1975, Wheeler et al 1987, but cf McIntosh 1985). This is perhaps clearest with regard to substantive principles of liability and remedy; however, it applies with equal force to procedural principles of access, initiative, and proof as well. Thus, over time, accumulated pressures from new forms (or new levels) of litigation may alter the very practices that define the disputing arena in the first place (Galanter 1990, Yeazell 1987).[8] In the long run, both the docket and the structure of the

[8]The impact of strategic action on disputing procedures may not always be so gradual and inadvertent. More critical analyses tend to argue that procedural law, like substantive law, often responds quite directly to the interests of powerful elites in civil society (e.g. Chambliss & Seidman 1982).

court system are likely to reflect material conditions and economic concerns in the larger organizational world.

### *Materialist Perspectives on the Regulatory Environment*

Perhaps the largest branch of the materialist literature addresses not the use of facilitative law by organizations, but rather the imposition of regulatory law on organizations. From this perspective, the legal environment consists of a system of incentives and penalties, designed largely to compensate for market imperfections such as monopolies and externalities (Friendly 1962, Burk 1985). Law, in this view, is justified by the need for collective societal intervention into certain areas of organizational life, but it is constantly in danger of being captured by its targets and turned against the common good that it supposedly defends.

Within a materialist perspective, analyses of regulatory law as an independent variable generally seek to determine how specific legal sanctions impinge on the strategic choices of rational organizational decision-makers (e.g. Peltzman 1976, Diver 1980, Scholz 1984, Paternoster & Simpson 1993, 1996, Braithewaite & Makkai 1991, Genn 1993). The regulatory regime, in this view, is simply one element among many in the larger managerial cost-benefit picture. Significantly, however, regulatory costs differ somewhat from market costs, particularly in the degree to which organizations can escape or influence them. As a result, materialist accounts of regulation often argue that self-interested organizations respond not only to the incentives and penalties enunciated by law "on the books," but also to the real-world gaps provided by ambiguous statutes and manipulable regulatory agencies. Thus, while some theoretical treatments assume that regulation is explicit, authoritative, and coercive (for a review, see Suchman & Edelman 1996), empirical analyses generally suggest that this "legal formalist" imagery is at best an abstract ideal (e.g. Macaulay 1963) and that, in reality, the regulatory environment is often ambiguous, contested, and riddled with loopholes. Although few materialists would rule out the possibility of successful deterrence (see e.g. McCaffrey 1982, Scott 1989, Paternoster & Simpson 1993), the overall picture is one of noncompliance, subversion, and evasion (e.g. Kagan & Scholz 1983).

Truly rational organizations are difficult to regulate in part because they lack the moral sentiments that promote individual-level obedience to law (cf Tyler 1990), and in part because their structures often insulate the managers who engineer lucrative transgressions. Christopher Stone's *Where the Law Ends* (1975) points out that since corporations cannot be imprisoned, and since individual employees are rarely held responsible for corporate wrongdoing, the corporate pocketbook often becomes the primary target of efforts at social control. Legal sanctions, however, are usually too small and too slow to affect rational organizational planning. Stone also suggests that common organizational characteristics such as task specialization, decentralized decision-making, and interdepartmental competition often marginalize legal requirements and encourage noncompliance (see also Jowell 1975). Similarly, Katz (1977) shows how corporate officers can effectively mask regulatory violations from outside review (see also Ekland-Olson & Martin 1988). Perhaps for these reasons, recent research suggests that conventional deterrence theory does a relatively poor job of predicting managerial responses to regulatory law (Braithewaite & Makkai 1991, Makkai & Braithewaite 1994, Simpson & Koper 1992, Paternoster & Simpson 1996; but see Block et al 1981).[9]

In the materialist view, the regulatory legal environment not only confronts recalcitrant self-interested organizations, it also often suffers from internal complexities and contradictions. While law creates sanctions for certain behaviors, it also creates defenses and loopholes that rational organizations may exploit to escape those sanctions (Mashaw 1979). As a result, the history of regulation is replete with unintended consequences. Examples from the literature include: the use of vertical integration as a means of evading sales tax (Stigler 1968); the spread of poison-pill takeover defenses as a buffer against the market for corporate control (Davis 1991, Powell 1993); the proliferation of uninformative disclaimers as an alternative to meaningful securities disclosure (Samuels 1996); the creation of wholly owned subsidiaries as a "liability firewall" (Barney et al 1992); and utilities meeting local pollution standards not by reducing effluents but by building tall smokestacks, thereby transporting their emissions to distant regions (Ackerman & Hassler 1981). The common theme behind all of this research is that the regulatory legal environment may exert its largest effects not by motivating compliance, but rather by motivating evasion.[10]

To a substantial extent, the complexity of real-world regulation stems from the fact that few (if any) regulatory regimes actually emerge independently of the organizational actors whom they ostensibly govern. This insight forms the basis for a large body of work on the regulatory environment as a dependent variable. In particular, several streams of research have explored the

[9]As we discuss below, regulatory deterrence theory may also perform poorly because it exaggerates the extent to which organizations behave as fully rational actors, free from normative and cognitive cultural constraints. Stone (1975) hints at such considerations when he advocates creating internal monitoring roles to bring the voice of conscience into corporate decision-making.

[10]While this literature raises doubts about the ability of regulation to deter organizational wrongdoing, a handful of studies also question whether organization-level rationality is necessarily the best metaphor for understanding the material effects of the regulatory environment. In some settings, regulation's primary consequence may be to empower intraorganizational interest groups (Pfeffer 1981, Edelman et al 1992) or to influence founding and failure rates in super-organizational populations (Wholey & Sanchez 1991). If so, then organization-level evasions may prove largely epiphenomenal.

autonomous impact of "regulated" organizations on both the legislative and the administrative process.

With respect to legislation, research suggests that most legal initiatives emerge out of complex networks of power, in which organizations are central to all sides of the debate (Laumann & Knoke 1987, Perrucci & Potter 1990). Recent studies of social movements, for example, clearly document the extent to which formal organization has become a key determinant of political success (McCarthy & Zald 1977, Zald & McCarthy 1980, Wolfson 1995). At the same time, other investigations equally clearly document the extent to which target organizations, themselves, band together into countermovements or "action sets," often under the aegis of trade associations, industry working groups, and the like (Aldrich & Whetten 1981). Both individually and in collaboration, such organizations make substantial investments in electoral politics and in backstage agenda-setting (Lukes 1974, Domhoff 1983).[11] In a study of energy and health care policy, for example, Laumann & Knoke (1988) find that large organizations dominate the national decision-making process, often playing a greater role than do elected representatives. Even the frequently noted pervasiveness of lawyers in national policy debates is less a source of autonomy for the legal system than a source of influence for those lawyers' corporate clients (Nelson et al 1988).

Although popular accounts often assume that organizations enter the political process primarily to minimize government "interference," empirical evidence argues to the contrary. In many cases, organizations actively seek regulation as a means of controlling their environments or obtaining advantages over their competitors. Historically, for example, the railroad industry has lobbied for weight and size limitations on interstate trucking (Stigler 1971); the National Association of Manufacturers has lobbied for restrictive labor legislation (Gable 1953); and the medical, dental, and legal professions have lobbied for licensure statutes that artificially depress the supply of practitioners (Holen 1965, Pfeffer 1974, Zhou 1993). In light of this evidence, Posner (1974) goes so far as to suggest that regulation, like other commodities, may be supplied at a price and may face a demand distribution. Certainly, a great deal of lawmaking seems to respond primarily to the parochial interests of targeted firms, industries, and sectors (Downs 1957, Kolko 1963, Fiorina & Noll 1976, Sabatier 1975, McCormick 1979).

Moreover, the ability of organizations to shape the legal environment does not end with the passage of legislation but rather continues on into the implementation phase as well. In a significant departure from the "explicit, authoritative

[11]Organizations also make substantial investments in litigation strategies designed to yield favorable rulings on points of statutory ambiguity (Galanter 1974).

and coercive" ideal, legislative compromises often yield statutes that either provide little regulatory guidance, or demand impossible regulatory results, or both (Clune 1983, Hawkins 1984, Baier et al 1988, Blumrosen 1993).[12] Consequently, administrative agencies enjoy a great deal of discretion in rule-making and enforcement, and regulators can become politicized both on the basis of personal preferences and on the basis of bureaucratic agendas (Luchansky & Gerber 1993, Newman & Attewell 1985, Jowell 1975). To avoid alienating powerful constituencies, regulatory agencies generally avoid full use of their statutory powers ("hard enforcement") and instead favor informal enforcement methods such as education, persuasion, negotiation, and publicity (Hawkins 1984, Bardach & Kagan 1982, Cranston 1979, cf Vogel 1986).

In addition, owing to poor funding, public agencies often rely on industry for information, personnel, and technical expertise, further heightening the influence of ostensibly subordinate organizations on the regulatory process (Leiserson 1942, Bardach 1989, Breyer 1982, Makkai & Braithewaite 1992). Materialist models often refer to such bottom-up dynamics as "regulatory capture" (Bernstein 1955), highlighting the ability of regulated industries to ensure supportive policies through power-dependence relations with key agencies and key agency personnel (cf Pfeffer & Salancik 1978, but see Levine 1981, McCaffrey 1982, Freitag 1983). Thus, far from imposing external social control on organizational deviance, the regulatory legal environment often merely institutionalizes the indigenous practices of the regulated population itself (Blumrosen 1965, 1993, Wirt 1970, Ackerman et al 1974, Katz 1977, Conklin 1977, Cranston 1979, Diver 1980, Clune 1983, Vaughan 1983, Hawkins 1984; but see Levine 1981, Horwitz 1986, Luchansky & Gerber 1993).

The materialist perspective on regulatory law, then, suggests that state-imposed penalties and incentives may do less to deter wrongdoing than to motivate circumvention and manipulation. In this sense, the regulatory environment merges somewhat with the facilitative environment, as organizations employ regulatory tools to reconfigure their markets and to divert attacks on their autonomy.

### *Materialist Perspectives on the Constitutive Environment*

As suggested above, because of its emphasis on concrete sanctions and rational choice, the materialist perspective tends to downplay law's more constitutive aspects. Nonetheless, at least one strand of this literature does address the

[12]Indeed, one plausible way to understand ambiguous statutes is as devices for overcoming legislative contention by implicitly allowing each side to "make a bet" on the outcome of subsequent interpretation. This technique has the political appeal of permitting the ultimate loser to plead good intentions and to decry the sorry perversion of "legislative intent."

role of legal categories, capacities, and "default rules" in organizational life—albeit in a way that owes more to information economics (Stigler 1961) than to social phenomenology (Berger & Luckmann 1967, see below). This is the "transaction cost analysis" tradition, most often associated with institutional economists such as Coase (1937, 1960), Williamson (1975, 1981, 1985), and North (1981), but also reflected in more sociological work on industrial structure and governance (e.g. Campbell & Lindberg 1990, Campbell et al 1991).

Building on the path-breaking work of Ronald Coase (1937, 1960), transaction cost analysis argues that organizations are best understood as devices for efficiently governing economic relations when markets fail due to uncertainty, bounded rationality, monopoly, and opportunism (Williamson 1975, 1981, 1985). Significantly, the incidence of market failures—and, hence, the need for organizations—reflects not only technical factors and human frailties (cf Williamson 1975:40), but also the nature and clarity of the prevailing legal regime (Coase 1960, North 1981). Law-and-economics research, for example, has traditionally emphasized the ability of "efficient" rules to minimize transaction costs in the market and, by implication, to maximize the scope of markets versus organizational and regulatory hierarchies (e.g. Posner 1972). More recently, researchers have also noted that legal rules may operate on the other side of the ledger as well, providing rights and immunities that enhance or impede the efficiency of hierarchical governance mechanisms—and hence, that affect their desirability relative to markets (Masten 1990, Williamson 1991).

All of this suggests that law can exert a substantial influence on organizations by creating an encompassing framework of basic property rights.[13] Campbell & Lindberg (1990), in particular, have argued that by failing to recognize the legal system's capacity to establish such rights, prior research may have grossly underestimated the role of the state (especially the American state) in the economy. In reality, these authors suggest, both the state's direct actions and its overall institutional structure "define and enforce property rights [that determine] social relations, and, therefore, the balance of power among a wide variety of economic actors" (1990:636). The legal system, in this view, both creates and responds to pressures for governance change by modifying the rights regime. Further, once a range of new governance mechanisms has begun to emerge, property rights (both pre-existing and newly created) channel the social processes that select among competing alternatives. In particular, by ratifying (or refusing to ratify) certain arrangements, rights rulings effectively delimit the search for new solutions. Thus, law shapes the transaction costs to which organizations respond, and it determines the viability of various organizational responses.

[13]This literature tends to define "property rights" broadly, to include enforceable legal claims that practicing lawyers would identify as being grounded in principles of contract, tort, antitrust, etc, as well as those grounded in the law of property, per se (see, e.g., Campbell & Lindberg 1990:635).

Of course, as Campbell and Lindberg acknowledge (1990:643), changes in legal rights may be a consequence, as well as a cause, of organizational governance decisions. Within organizations theory, it is fairly well established that the strategies of firms and the structures of industries can exert lasting impacts on the distribution of transaction costs (e.g. Chandler 1962, 1977, 1990, Bernstein 1992, Suchman & Cahill 1996). This implies that such organizational phenomena can also influence the efficiency of various legal regimes. Moreover, organizations may occasionally seek new "legal devices" to address specific governance problems (Powell 1993, cf Roy 1990). In Gilson's (1984) memorable phrase, corporate lawyers then act as "transaction cost engineers," assembling basic legal building blocks into novel social arrangements.[14] Over time, these hand-tailored organizational creations may diffuse and become prototypes for the more standardized "off the rack" objects of the constitutive legal environment (Powell 1993, Suchman 1994a, Klausner 1995).[15]

In sum, materialist perspectives tend to focus on organizations' strategic efforts to maneuver around and within the world of law. Motivated by interests in profits and efficiency, organizations seek, embrace, and exploit laws that promise economic rewards—and they oppose, evade, or ignore laws that impose economic burdens. In the materialist view, then, law is largely exogenous to organizations but greatly relevant to the rational choices that organizations make. Law may be a tool, it may be a commodity, it may be a system of costs and incentives, or it may be a set of coordinating ground rules; but it is virtually always an environment that organizations encounter concretely and contemplate rationally. This imagery changes considerably in cultural renditions.

### *Cultural Perspectives*

Cultural perspectives on law and organizations are relatively recent arrivals on the intellectual scene, tracing their ancestry largely to the theoretical work of Philip Selznick (1948, 1949, 1957, 1969) and Peter Berger & Thomas Luckmann (1967). From Selznick's early work (1948, 1949, 1957) this literature

[14]This is not always a desirable development. The literature features several "innovations"—such as strategic bankruptcy (Delaney 1989) and legal tax evasion (McBarnet 1992)—that arguably enrich individual adopters at the expense of the larger economy.

[15]Whether or not these phenomena properly fall under the "constitutive" label represents a debatable point. If states intentionally adjust legal rights to accomplish policy goals, one might argue that such actions are regulatory in character; and if organizations strategically employ legal routines to resolve business problems, one might claim that the law's role is merely facilitative. Alternatively, however, one might also note (as do Campbell & Lindberg, 1990:635, 38) that rights regimes often change without a calculated policy impetus, and that new governance mechanisms often spread without deliberate foresight. To the extent that these processes arise from the law's ability to lay the ground rules of an entire field of organizational activity—including defining the boundaries, capacities, endowments, and relationships of the key participants—the claim that law is constitutive of that field seems well justified.

inherits an interest in how the normative and political commitments of organizational participants (often stimulated by pressures from the external sociopolitical environment) can lead certain ostensibly rational bureaucratic structures and practices to become "institutionalized"—or "infused with value beyond the technical requirements of the task at hand" (Selznick 1957:17). From Selznick's later work (1969, Nonet & Selznick 1978), the literature inherits a parallel interest in the ways in which societal principles of "legality" get reproduced (both reflected and perpetuated) through the enunciation of "citizenship rights" by the "private governments" of firms. Finally, from Berger & Luckmann (1967), the culturalist literature inherits an attentiveness to the importance of societal rule systems in constructing organizational forms—not only in establishing normative guidelines for good and bad organizational behavior, but also in establishing cognitive frameworks for meaningful and meaningless organizational behavior.

As this heritage suggests, recent culturally oriented writings on the interface between law and organizations derive primarily from the "new institutionalism" in organizational analysis, a tradition that stresses the impact of cultural rules, models, and mythologies on organizational structures and practices (Meyer & Rowan 1977, DiMaggio & Powell 1983, Meyer & Scott 1983, Powell & DiMaggio 1991, Scott & Meyer 1994, Scott 1995). At the same time, however, many culturalist "law and organizations" studies also reflect the persistent influence of the "law and society" movement, with its emphasis on the filtering of legal doctrines through concrete social institutions (e.g. Macaulay 1963, 1966, Hurst 1964, Galanter 1974, Mnookin & Kornhauser 1979, Friedman 1985; see Suchman & Edelman 1996 for an analysis of the relationship between organizational institutionalism and the law-and-society tradition).

In contrast to the materialist view of law as a clearly delineated incentive structure that realigns organizational cost-benefit analysis, cultural perspectives see law as a pervasive belief system that permeates the most fundamental morals and meanings of organizational life: Law constructs and legitimates organizational forms, inspires and shapes organizational norms and ideals, and even helps to constitute the identities and capacities of organizational "actors." Thus, whereas the materialist literature focuses on organizations' strategic efforts to evade and manipulate legal sanctions, culturalist approaches emphasize organizations' subtle but profound responsiveness to legal ideals, norms, forms, and categories. And whereas the materialist perspective sees law as shaping organizational behavior by creating incentives and penalties, the cultural perspective suggests that organizations adopt certain structures and practices because the socio-legal environment constructs those structures and practices as proper, responsible, legitimate, and natural. Moreover, in recent years, cultural theorists have begun to argue for a reverse causal dynamic, as well: At times, the legal system may bless certain organizational structures and practices, in part, because extra-legal organizational communities have already endogenously constructed those structures and practices as sensible, efficient, feasible, or modern. Moreover, in many settings, legal and organizational understandings of rationality, propriety, and meaning coalesce simultaneously and endogenously, through an ongoing exchange of symbols and enactments, gestures and interpretations.

### *Cultural Perspectives on the Facilitative Environment*

Because cultural accounts generally minimize the strategic motives of organizations, they are significantly less likely than materialist perspectives to focus on the legal tools and facilities available for instrumental use. One major exception is the study of how organizations strategically deploy legal symbols in pursuit of sociopolitical legitimacy (Edelman 1990, 1992, Friedland & Alford 1991). Because such strategies generally emerge in response to regulatory laws or societal normative pressures, however, we discuss this phenomenon in the section on the regulatory environment, below.

Cultural perspectives on law as a facilitative environment do come into play, though, in literatures that address the cultural components of disputing. Whereas materialist perspectives focus on organizations' use of legal procedures as tools of competition, cultural perspectives emphasize the relationship between styles of dispute resolution and "softer" organizational phenomena such as inter-organizational cooperation, community-building, public relations, and reputation. The focus here is often on alternative dispute resolution (ADR)—methods of conflict handling that have developed in response to the problems of litigation, such as its cost in money and time, its inflexibility, and its tendency to destroy relationships.

The literature on ADR by organizations primarily addresses law as an independent variable, in the sense that the costs of litigation—both financial and relational—are seen as the primary motivation for employing various ADR techniques. Thus, ADR has enjoyed growing legitimacy in the business community as a means of smoothing over workplace conflict, cooling out grievances, and avoiding lawsuits (Edelman et al 1993, Morrill 1995, Lande 1995, Edelman et al 1996, Edelman & Cahill 1998).[16] In addition to the academic literature on this topic, there is also a large (and largely atheoretical) practitioner literature, advocating ADR as preferable to litigation, primarily because it ostensibly avoids the costs of litigation and gives firms greater control over the disputing process by relaxing formal due process protections (e.g. Westin & Feliu 1988, Ewing 1989).

[16]The critical view, which sees ADR as a means by which employers seek to control employees, is based on a literature in the sociology of law that critiques ADR in the context of disputes between individuals (e.g. Silbey & Sarat 1989, Delgado et al 1985, Cobb & Rifkin 1991, Fiss 1984, Hofrichter 1987).

The ADR literature also points to law as a dependent variable by suggesting ways in which the organizational embracing of ADR injects new values and principles into the legal system. Professional ideologies within organizations play a large role in determining the extent to which organizations use ADR as opposed to litigation (Lande 1995). And the internal legal culture of organizations, in turn, affects the extent to which employees mobilize both formal legal rights and internal dispute resolution procedures in resolving grievances against their employers (Fuller et al 1997). Further, in the process of using ADR, organizational grievance handlers tend to infuse legal norms with managerial values, such as the importance of smooth relations, the therapeutic underpinnings of most disputes, and the importance of building relationships and preserving community. Over time, these values tend to influence the resolution of analogous disputes in the formal legal system, and even to be incorporated into the official construction of the law (Edelman et al 1993, Edelman & Cahill 1998). Many new employment laws, such as the 1991 Civil Rights Act and the 1990 Americans With Disabilities Act, in fact explicitly encourage the use of ADR to resolve legal claims.

### *Cultural Perspectives on the Regulatory Environment*

In contrast to the materialist approach, culturalist theories of the regulatory environment place less emphasis on the role of legal sanctions in deterring undesirable behavior, and more emphasis on the role of legal symbols in evoking desirable normative commitments. Regulatory law, in this view, is less a threat than a sermon. One of the most salient consequences of this shift appears with respect to the issue of compliance: Unlike materialist accounts, which often focus on organizations' strategic attempts to evade external control, culturalist perspectives stress that even as firms maneuver around particular legal rules, they cannot escape the law's larger normative influence. Further, because culturalists focus on law as a source of symbol and meaning, rather than as a source of coercive constraint, these researchers tend to emphasize the diffuse and indirect consequences of the legal environment as much as its targeted and direct effects. In this rendition, law serves less as a restraining deterrent for organizational malfeasance than as a supporting framework for all organizational activity. Consequently, organizations often come to embody the underlying logic of the regulatory legal environment even as they try to evade its most burdensome provisions; and, conversely, organizations often come to shape the law through their collective sense-making activities (Weick 1993) even when they fail to control it through their self-interested lobbying efforts.

In discussing regulatory law as an independent variable, culturalist research draws heavily on more general "neoinstitutional" accounts of how organizations respond to societal rule systems, broadly defined (e.g. Meyer & Rowan 1977, DiMaggio & Powell 1983, Scott 1995). Legal compliance is, in essence, simply a special case of "institutional isomorphism"—the process by which organizations facing the same cultural rules and understandings become both increasingly similar to one another and increasingly congruent with the myths of their shared environment. The central argument is that attributes of the institutional environment—such as proximity to the public sphere, unionization, and the presence of various professional groups—explain organizational responses to law better than do traditional technical considerations (e.g. Edelman 1992, Sutton et al 1994, Konrad & Linnehan 1995).

Within this general orientation, however, one can identify important divergences in how particular researchers characterize the mechanisms of legal influence. Different accounts emphasize, to varying degrees, three distinct sources of organizational conformity with law: In *coercive* models (e.g. Fligstein 1991), organizations conform because law commands them to do so and imposes sanctions for noncompliance. This is essentially the same dynamic as that emphasized by materialist perspectives—although perhaps with an added skepticism about whether the underlying legal rules reflect material needs or cultural myths. In *normative* models (e.g. Edelman et al 1991, Edelman et al 1992), organizations conform because law enunciates social values, ethics, and role expectations, which organizations (and their members) then elaborate and, to various extents, internalize. And in *cognitive* models (e.g. Dobbin et al 1993), organizations conform because law makes certain forms of action seem more natural, plausible, and fitting than others.[17]

Moreover, within each of these perspectives, accounts differ in the extent to which they depict organizational responses as deeply transformative versus superficially ceremonial. As Edelman (1990, 1992) suggests, organizations may adopt outwardly compliant structures as a visible demonstration of attentiveness to legal mandates, norms, and schemas—while at the same time preserving traditional managerial prerogatives by decoupling structural symbols from substantive practices (for similar observations, see Oliver 1991, Kaplan & Harrison 1993). While some studies portray such activities as cynical window-dressing, ceremonialism may also arise out of either hypocritical self-righteousness or agnostic acquiescence to established conventions. Regardless of the underlying motivation, the decoupling of ceremony from substance arguably undercuts and marginalizes the role of law in organizational life. Nonetheless, several

[17]Readers familiar with the sociology of organizations will recognize that this depiction parallels DiMaggio & Powell's (1983) influential trichotomy of institutional isomorphisms: "Coercive isomorphism," occurs when organizations submit to the demands of powerful external actors, such as the regulatory agencies of the state; "normative isomorphism" occurs when organizations import the outlooks and ethics of professionals and other organized value-carriers; and "mimetic isomorphism" occurs when organizations resolve cognitive uncertainty by copying the practices of other, similar organizations.

analysts have pointed out that, if the primary impact of law is a diffuse cultural one, widespread ceremonialism may not be equivalent to outright illegality, since the former re-presents and thereby reifies the law's cultural claims in a way that the latter does not (see e.g. Friedland & Alford 1991:250, Edelman 1992:1569, Suchman 1995b:588).

Although culturalist writings widely acknowledge the theoretical distinction among these various sources of conformity/isomorphism, the literature increasingly suggests that multiple isomorphic pressures may operate together in any particular historical instance. While early neo-institutional writings generally paralleled the materialist literature in viewing the regulatory legal environment as primarily coercive (see, e.g., DiMaggio & Powell 1983, Scott 1991, Fligstein 1991; for a more extensive review, see Suchman & Edelman 1996), recent studies have been somewhat more eclectic. Even authors who focus on the impact of ostensibly coercive legal sanctions occasionally inject cognitive or normative elements into their accounts—for example by highlighting the ability of coerced isomorphism to foster taken-for-grantedness (Tolbert & Zucker 1983),[18] or by exploring how the (mis)perception of a coercive threat can affect the intra-organizational influence of certain professional groups (Edelman et al 1992). Other analyses have moved still farther away from a primarily coercive view, emphasizing that coercive, cognitive and normative sources of conformity often operate co-equally (e.g. Baron, Dobbin & Jennings 1986).

Indeed, a number of recent studies of the spread of bureaucratized personnel practices go so far as to suggest that coercive conformity may, if anything, play only a subsidiary role. Edelman (1990) depicts the extension of due process protections to non-union employees primarily as a normative spillover from the civil rights movement, which legitimated employees' claims to fair treatment. Since personnel practices changed even in firms that did not formally fall under equal employment opportunity (EEO) law, such legal enactments presumably served not so much to mandate the new organizational structures as to symbolize their sociocultural importance. Similarly, Edelman (1992) and Dobbin et al (1993) argue that the numerous ambiguities of US employment law often render it toothless as a source of coercion, even for firms falling within its official purview. At the same time, however, this statutory indeterminacy (coupled with substantial rhetorical posturing) creates a climate of legal uncertainty, in which the cognitive dynamics of inter-organizational mimesis and the normative dynamics of professional proselytizing can flourish. In this view, coercive effects may actually follow normative and cognitive effects, rather than preceding them: Initially ambiguous laws acquire sufficient specificity for

[18]Interestingly, Zucker (1988:33) offers a dissenting voice on this point, arguing that overt coercion tends to undercut exteriority and objectivity, two key components of taken-for-grantedness (see also Suchman 1995b).

judicial enforcement only after professional and organizational communities have socially constructed a taken-for-granted definition of compliant behavior (Edelman et al 1996, Suchman & Cahill 1996, Suchman & Edelman 1996).

One important implication of such noncoercive models is that the effects of legal change should not appear instantaneously with the enactment of new sanctions, but rather should build gradually over time, as normative and cognitive beliefs become increasingly institutionalized. Consistent with this prediction, a substantial body of empirical evidence suggests that organizations adopt the structural trappings of legal compliance at a rate that is directly proportionate to the number of prior adopters: Tolbert & Zucker (1983) report essentially this pattern in the diffusion of civil service reforms, and several researchers find analogous trends in the diffusion of workplace due-process protections (Dobbin et al 1988, Edelman 1990, Sutton et al 1994) and in the spread of organizational responses to EEO law (Edelman 1992, Dobbin et al 1993).[19] Similarly, Mezias (1990) discusses the accelerated diffusion of a novel financial reporting strategy, once the new formulation had received the professional imprimatur of the Accounting Principles Board; and Suchman (1995a) describes the decade-long spread of standardized venture capital financing contracts from Silicon Valley to more socio-geographically remote locales. In each of these analyses, the authors attribute observed diffusion patterns primarily to the gradual institutionalization of supportive professional norms and to the mimetic routinization of plausible cognitive models.[20]

As illustrated by the significance of proactive professional proselytizing in many institutionalist accounts, the characteristics of the regulatory legal environment may be a consequence, as well as a cause, of extralegal cultural dynamics. Although to date the culturalist literature on law and organizations has devoted relatively little attention to the role of organizational beliefs in generating new statutory enactments (but see Dobbin 1994, Suchman & Cahill 1996), it has built on a long history of law and society research that depicts extralegal organizations as "filtering agents" (Kidder 1983) between "law on

[19]Interestingly, Abzug & Mezias (1993) suggest that institutionalization has followed a different, and much slower, path in the case of comparable worth policies, where the courts have generally rejected employee claims, than in other EEO contexts, where the courts have been more favorably disposed (but see McCann 1994). While this finding does not necessarily require a purely coercive explanation, it does suggest that extra-legal normative and cognitive dynamics are not entirely autonomous from the influence of formal legal institutions.

[20]It is perhaps worth noting that the stickiness of enforcement mechanisms might produce some lag in legal impact, even if only coercive dynamics were involved. Given this, an S-shaped diffusion curve provides, at best, ambiguous evidence for normative and mimetic hypotheses. Nonetheless, the leisureliness of the adoption patterns reported in the literature—coupled with the pervasive impact of professionalization—strongly suggests that coercive perspectives capture only part of the picture.

the books" and "law in action." Culturalist research has focused, particularly, on three such filters: professional groups, organizational bureaucracies, and inter-organizational communities.

Beyond simply serving as "conduits" for the diffusion of pre-existing legal norms (DiMaggio & Powell 1983, Kagan & Rosen 1985), professional groups also extensively filter and transform those norms, in the process. Drawing on the pioneering work of Selznick (1949, 1957, 1969), as well as on influential comments by DiMaggio & Powell (1983), many culturalist accounts of law and organizations call attention to the important role of professional discourses in constructing the meaning of initially ambiguous laws, in determining the situations to which legal reasoning applies, and more generally, in advocating for the legality and legitimacy of particular worldviews. Significantly, these "law-making" activities are undertaken not only by attorneys, but also by nonlegal professionals, such as personnel officers, doctors, teachers, and accountants.

Thus, for example, Edelman and her colleagues (Edelman 1992, Edelman et al 1996, Edelman et al 1991) draw on Selznick's work to posit not only that professionals within organizations play an active role in promoting particular structural responses to law (here, EEO offices and bureaucratized personnel procedures), but also that they bring their own political and normative commitments to bear in defining the role of the resulting structures (particularly, the extent to which managers are challenged to make compliance substantive as well as symbolic). Similarly, in an analysis of neo-natal intensive care, Heimer (1993) shows that law has a much greater impact when it conforms with the authority claims of key organizational professionals (in this case, doctors). Further, Heimer suggests that different groups of professionals may be responsive to different elements of the normative environment, and that these groups may enjoy substantial leeway to choose among competing institutional models embodied in divergent bodies of law (cf Friedland & Alford 1991). In this sense, legal regulation is often "enacted" (Weick 1979) at a fairly local level, with intraorganizational professional constituencies playing a significant part in determining which institutional norms and scripts get reflected in organizational structures and practices (Scheid-Cook 1992).

Empirical evidence on the filtering role of the professions suggests that professional activities can either dampen or amplify the impact of law, depending on the circumstances. At times, professional staffs will reframe reform-minded legal ideals so as to minimize the law's impact on established bureaucratic routines. Edelman et al (1993) report, for example, that organizational complaint-handlers tend to construe EEO law as merely requiring the same sorts of fair and consistent employment practices as are implied by preexisting norms of good management. In recasting discrimination complaints as personality conflicts or issues of "management style," grievance officers enact a therapeutic understanding of civil rights law that emphasizes the restoration of harmony to the workplace, rather than the vindication of formal legal rights. Discrimination is thus depoliticized and individualized, and legal influences tend to be undermined.

Conversely, at other times professionals can act as a kind of Greek chorus, amplifying and reifying legal threats in ways that may have little to do with reality (Edelman et al 1993, Galanter 1983, Givelber et al 1984, Edelman et al 1996). Givelber et al (1984), for example, discuss the media's role in (mis)educating therapists about the *Tarasoff* decision, which held that psychotherapists owe a duty of care to third parties who may be in danger from the therapists' patients. Similarly, Edelman et al (1992) show that the personnel and legal professions greatly inflated the risk of wrongful discharge lawsuits, encouraging employers to revise employment policies to address a largely nonexistant legal hazard. Following Pfeffer (1981) and Larson (1977), these authors suggest that professionals sought to increase their power and prestige within organizations—as well as the market demand for their services—by constructing the legal environment as a major threat and then claiming the unique expertise to craft an effective response. In such cases, managers' professionally filtered perceptions of the legal environment may be substantially more constraining than the law itself.

Professions, of course, are not alone in their ability to filter (and thereby transform) the law. Individual organizations, too, participate in the social construction of the regulatory environment, primarily through their bureaucratic practices and internal legal cultures. Indeed, organizational constructions of law often provide the chief conduits between formal law and everyday legal consciousness. For most people, the legal system is both remote and arcane, and popular understandings of law and legality come largely from day-to-day experiences in concrete bureaucratic settings, not from exposure to abstract doctrine (Macaulay 1987, Sarat 1990, Ewick & Silbey 1992, Fuller et al 1997). In these mundane organizational encounters, formal structures symbolize commitment to legal objectives, while informal norms give content to legal principles. Consequently, organizational responses to law play a key role in reifying legal mandates in daily life.

Once again, such filtering agents can act either to amplify or to dampen law's impact. Selznick's (1969) account of the spread of legalism in the workplace illustrates the organizational reinforcement and extension of official legal doctrines, and this theme reappears in more recent work on "organizational citizenship" (e.g. Scott & Meyer 1991, Monahan et al 1994) and "psychological contracts" (Rousseau & Parks 1992) as well. Not all organizational responses to the legal environment involve rights-enhancing rules, however. Thus, for instance, Edelman et al (1992) and Sutton & Dobbin (1996) both describe how employers have inserted disclaimers into personnel manuals and application forms, in an apparent attempt to preserve employment-at-will in the face of more pro-employee doctrinal developments. Interestingly, Sutton & Dobbin (1996) point out that organizational characteristics associated with the creation of rights-enhancing structures are also associated with the creation of rights-negating structures; both are responses to the institutional environment.

Finally, law is often also mediated by entire communities of organizations acting in concert. At this level of analysis, the influence of extra-legal organizational actors may go beyond merely filtering the interpretation and application of preexisting laws to include the active construction of new regulatory regimes. Along these lines, the cultural perspective offers an alternative view of what materialists see as the organizational "capture" of state enforcement agencies, stressing shared belief systems rather than quid-pro-quo power dependence. Where materialists emphasize the ability of regulated industries to "buy off" their putative overseers, a cultural analysis would suggest that legal institutions often adopt industry-friendly measures because both regulators and regulatees operate within the same institutional fields. Thus, continuous flows of information, participation by the same professional groups, extensive personnel exchanges, and exposure to a common set of rational myths lead state agencies and the organizations under their jurisdiction to adopt a common ideological outlook and mutually compatible practices (Edelman 1996, Suchman & Edelman 1996, Suchman & Cahill 1996). Further, even when agencies manage to avoid cultural co-optation, constrained budgets and weakly conceptualized statutory objectives often lead law enforcers to prefer culturally constructed symbols of compliance over less certain tests of material results (Hawkins 1984, Blumrosen 1993)—and regulated organizations are quite willing to collaborate in constructing symbolic criteria that meet the needs of regulators without fundamentally disrupting the established routines of the targeted sector (Edelman 1992, Suchman & Edelman 1996).

As the preceding pages demonstrate, culturalist discussions of the regulatory legal environment routinely invoke a large number of explanations in which law is either explicitly the independent variable or explicitly the dependent variable. Nonetheless, the overarching assumption that legal meanings are socially constructed, and that this construction process often takes place at the level of entire organizational fields, implies that the relationship between law and organizations is not so much reciprocally causal as endogenously coevolutionary (Suchman 1993b).

If all legal doctrine were substantive and unequivocal and if all legal implementation were coercive and undeviating, then one could imagine a simple feedback loop, in which organizations would adjust their behaviors exclusively in response to existing laws and would exercise their influence exclusively in pursuit of future laws. In the culturalist account, however, the plot-line is much messier than this. Because the ambiguity of law-on-the-books is not an occasional aberration but rather a political fact of life (Baer et al 1988), the practical meaning of any given law-in-action can only emerge through a highly interactive process of social construction. Perhaps not surprisingly, this sense-making exercise is likely to involve not only the official agents of the legal system (regulators, judges, litigators, and the like), but also the members of the focal organizational field (including individual firms, professional groups, trade associations, media observers, and legal advisors). Together—through dialogue, litigation, and mimesis—these entities collaborate to enact simultaneously the meaning of the law, the nature of the enforcement threat, and the options for compliance. Eventually these efforts may produce a working agreement on what the law "is" and what it "requires," and that agreement may gradually become reified and institutionalized in formal structures and rational myths; nonetheless, to say that the legal rules "cause" the organizational practices (or vice versa) is, at best, a gross simplification. The two emerge in tandem, and as the underlying belief system permeates both the legal and the organizational worlds, the boundaries between these realms become increasingly ambiguous.

Applied to the regulatory legal environment, this endogenous imagery suggests that justifications for social control, professional commitments, organizational structures, state enforcement mechanisms, and judicial reasoning all flow from interlinked contemporaneous discourses. To explicate the endogeneity of law, Edelman (1996) suggests that the organizations of the legal system, like other organizations, operate within organizational fields. The socio-legal field overlaps with the fields of regulated organizations, so that ideas of rationality, morality, and legality flow freely between the legal system and extra-legal organizational realms. Practices in one field help to constitute ideas of legitimacy in the other, and the dynamic interplay between these fields gives rise to socially constructed legalities in both arenas. Thus, for example, Edelman et al (1996) illustrate how the rationality of grievance procedures is jointly constructed across organizational and legal realms, and in particular, how courts incorporate emergent organizational practices into the legal definition of reasonable compliance with civil rights law.[21]

[21]It is perhaps worth noting that this image of unimpeded communication between legal and organizational fields contrasts sharply with European "autopoietic" theories of law, which stress the incomensurability of legal and economic discourses (see, e.g., Luhmann 1985, Teubner 1988). In the autopoietic view, law (like other discursive realms) is a self-referential system, in which external phenomena appear only as legal representations, constructed in terms of legal orientations and legal imperatives. Efforts to communicate across the boundaries of such systems are at best hazardous, and at worst impossible. While autopoiesis theory serves as a useful reminder that similar signifiers may have quite different meanings and consequences in different social spheres, it has yet to exert a substantial impact on empirical investigations into the relationship between law and organizations—at least within the intellectual traditions reviewed here.

## *Cultural Perspectives on the Constitutive Environment*

Like materialists, culturalists see constitutive law as providing the basic definitional building blocks of organizational life. However, where materialists see these building blocks as simply being default starting points for rational engineering and negotiation, culturalists see them as being largely pre-conscious frameworks for making sense of the social world.[22] In this view, law plays a central role in the "social construction of reality" (Berger & Luckmann 1967), with legal definitions often becoming reified and institutionalized as taken-for-granted components of "the way the world works." The central task, then, becomes understanding how these consciousness-framing legal schemas construct—and are constructed by—organizational activity.[23]

As an independent cultural variable, constitutive law establishes a structure of categories and definitions for understanding social relations—and provides a set of accepted routines for manipulating that structure. Law generates understandings, for example, of what is and is not a corporation and who is or is not an employee; moreover, law offers taken-for-granted scripts for forming corporations and for hiring and firing employees (Suchman & Edelman 1996). Such constitutive dynamics can be seen in several central aspects of organizational life, including inter-organizational relations, organizational structures, and the cultural mindset of "legal-rationality" (Weber 1947).

Law constructs inter-organizational relations in part by providing a "cultural toolkit" (Swidler 1976) that organizations draw on when they interact with one another. This is most obviously true of contract law, which delineates appropriate symbols and rituals for forming binding commitments (Suchman 1994a; cf Macaulay 1963, Gabel & Feinman 1982). However, it applies to other branches of law, as well: Property law outlines means by which organizations claim control over resources and ideas (Campbell & Lindberg 1990); tort law helps to construct the scope of organizations' spontaneous responsibilities to their social surroundings; and bankruptcy law defines the priority of organizations' competing obligations to their various stakeholders (Delaney 1989).

[22]Rational decision-making holds, at best, a subordinate position in most culturalist accounts of constitutive law. While self-interested actors may tinker instrumentally at the margins, fundamental legal forms go mostly unquestioned. After all, if law shapes our understanding of reality, organizations have no truly extra-legal vantage point from which to strategize; indeed, as "artificial persons" even their capacity to engage in instrumental activity is, itself, largely a legal construct.

[23]It is perhaps worth re-emphasizing that we use the term "constitutive legal environment" to refer to law's impact in constituting organizations, rather than to organizations' impact in constituting law. As we argue in the text, organizations and professions do play a constitutive role in the social construction of law; however, such effects are at least as likely to arise in the contexts that we, here, label "regulatory" as in those that we label "constitutive." Indeed, one might argue that the taken-for-grantedness of constitutive legal definitions actually renders them less susceptible to "bottom-up" influences than are more openly contested regulatory legal mandates.

Beyond providing a "vocabulary of significant gestures" (Mead 1934) that pre-existing organizations employ in their interactions, law also helps to construct organizational structure, itself. In a limited way, this occurs whenever law defines the characteristics of a particular organizational feature, such as an affirmative action policy (Edelman 1990), or a "poison pill" takeover defense (Powell 1993, Davis 1991). More broadly, law also codifies ground-rules for entire organizational forms, suggesting alternative models for collective action and imbuing each with certain chartered attributes and capacities (cf Meyer, Boli & Thomas 1987, Krasner 1988). To paraphrase Scott (1993), organizations are not "real" primordial creatures, but are social constructions, defined and given meaning in large part by legal institutions. Historical and comparative work, for example, reveals the central role of law in constructing the modern limited-liability corporation (Coleman 1974, 1990, Seavoy 1982, Roy 1990, Creighton 1990, Klein & Majewski 1992) and in shaping the boundaries between private firms, public agencies, collective enterprises, and nonprofit organizations (Nee 1992, Hansman 1996, Campbell & Lindberg 1990). Moreover, the available evidence suggests that such issues of legal form are often significant determinants of organizational behavior and performance (Haveman 1993, Rao & Neilsen 1992, but cf Macaulay 1963).

Finally, the legal system sometimes constructs organizational practices less directly, simply by contributing to the elaboration of an underlying cultural logic of "legal-rationality." As Weber (1947) observed, modern organizations and modern law both embrace a legal-rational orientation, and consequently the two realms share a great deal of their justificatory rhetoric. Although it would be wrong to see legal-rationality as entirely a product of the formal law, it is clear that legal definitions often generate sympathetic vibrations in other legal-rational social structures, including organizations (cf Sitkin & Bies 1993). Thus, organizational embodiments of "fairness" (Edelman 1990); "citizenship" (Selznick 1969, Monahan et al 1994); "negligence" (Ellickson 1986, 1990), and the like tend to mimic their legal counterparts.[24]

To the extent that laws construct organizations rather than merely regulating them, the ability of organizations to exert a truly exogenous impact on law would seem to be quite limited—particularly when legal definitions are stable, uniform, and fully institutionalized. Legal definitions, however, are rarely fully

[24]Early hints of this analogical outlook can be found in Selznick's (1969) foundational work on the evolution of legality: Although organizations occasionally adopt procedural safegaurds in response to regulatory mandates, on the whole these procedures spread simply because they become the definition of fair treatment. In this sense, by creating and publicizing forms of legal procedure, the law establishes models that constitute the meaning of legality even in extra-legal settings. Further, the reconstruction of these procedural elements within organizations more or less parallels the bottom-up reconstruction of other legal devices within organizational communities, as described below.

institutionalized, and this opens the door for a number of investigations into constitutive law as a dependent variable.

First, to the extent that organizations enjoy sufficient cognitive latitude to create genuine innovations, these novel devices may eventually serve as the basis for new legal categories and definitions (e.g. Powell 1993, Edelman 1992, 1996, Suchman 1994a, 1995a, Suchman & Cahill 1996). Second, even without engaging in intentional innovation, organizations may inadvertently destabilize the constitutive legal environment by implementing established forms imperfectly (see e.g. Westney 1987, Lewis & Siebold 1993) or by elaborating established forms unsuitably (see, e.g., McBarnett 1992, Delaney 1989, Barney, Edwards & Ringleb 1992). In this way, organizations often generate legal pluralism (Merry 1988) and legal contradiction (Tushnet 1984) as an unintended consequence of everyday activity. Third, given a modicum of pre-existing pluralism and contradiction, organizations may skew the development of constitutive law by favoring some legal alternatives over others: Assuming that legal definitions operate like other institutional models, specific formulations will tend to gain cognitive legitimacy as the number of visible organizational examplars rises (cf Tolbert & Zucker 1983, Hannan & Carroll 1992, Aldrich & Fiol 1994, Edelman 1990, Suchman 1995b).

Finally, and perhaps most importantly, organizations (and organized professions) participate actively in the social construction processes that give new laws their meanings. This applies not only to the regulatory laws described in the previous section, but to constitutive laws as well. Initially, new statutory definitions often provide an abstract vocabulary without concrete referents. When called upon to apply this vocabulary, judges look to the extra-legal world for "data points" that might give substance to the law's abstract labels. In several fields, for example, courts openly employ "trade practices" and "industry standards" as key interpretive guideposts (Suchman & Cahill 1996). The same inductive process occurs within organizations, too, as employees and managers come to understand the categories of the legal system in terms of the examples that they see in their own workplaces (Scheid-Cook 1992, Fuller et al 1997). Consequently, the prevailing routines of organizational communities frequently define the content of legal categories.

Suchman's work on the role of lawyers in Silicon Valley (Suchman 1994a,b, 1995a, Suchman & Cahill 1996) illustrates a number of these dynamics. Because the formation of high-technology start-up companies was only weakly institutionalized within the larger socio-legal environment, Silicon Valley's legal, financial, and industrial sectors enjoyed substantial leeway to experiment during the community's early years. Such freedom, however, came at the price of profound cognitive uncertainty, and from 1975 to 1990, the region's leading law firms and venture capital funds worked to moderate this uncertainty by fostering community-level normative and cognitive structures, and by introducing Silicon Valley customs into the rules of the larger legal system. In particular, due to their distinctive structural position, local law firms were able to play a central role as inter-organizational pollinators, compiling case-by-case innovations into standardized constitutive formulae. Over time, the resulting "Silicon Valley model" of routinized venture capital financing gradually achieved codification both in legal form-books and in national securities law, ultimately becoming a virtually taken-for-granted element of the constitutive legal environment.[25]

Beyond the emergence and institutionalization of particular legal devices, the systemic impact of organizations on constitutive law is perhaps clearest in the case of the legal-rational "sympathetic vibrations" described above. While the legal system enjoys cultural primacy with regard to the "legal" components of legal-rationality, the organizational world often enjoys a similar position of leadership with regard to the "rational" components. Bureaucratic notions of planning, efficiency, and economic necessity exert a substantial impact on judicial doctrines regarding reasonable responses to law as well as on legislative understandings of wise policy-making. Moreover, just as organizations mimic legal models of justice, legal institutions often mimic organizational models of efficiency (Heydebrand & Seron 1990, Savelsberg 1992). The debate over the legalization of organizational life has its parallel in the debate over the bureaucratization of legal life.

In reality, of course, both legal and organizational actors collaborate in the elaboration of a single, endogenous regime that encompasses (and transcends) both sectors. Endogeneity may be a bit harder to see in the case of the constitutive legal environment—which often operates as a set of background assumptions—than in the case of the more openly contested regulatory environment; nonetheless, the juxtaposition of legally constituted organizations and organizationally embodied laws creates a substantial potential for coevolution between the two. Even as organizations are passively constructed by highly institutionalized elements of the constitutive legal environment, those same organizations may actively participate in the discursive elaboration of other, less well-institutionalized elements. In this regard, organizations are no different from other social actors, whose ability to change their culture is predicated on their constitution and empowerment by that culture.

[25] Suchman's findings can be contrasted, to some extent, with Macaulay's (1963) classic study of "non-contractual relations" in business. In the terms of the present discussion, Macaulay's research highlights the ability of local community norms to buffer organizational interactions from the impact of legal categories and definitions—a finding replicated in a number of other studies in the law and society tradition as well (e.g. Ross 1980, Ellickson 1986).

## *Toward an Integrative Model*

The sociology of law and organizations has experienced something of a renaissance recently as it has become clear that organizations interact with their legal environments in multiple contexts. Law and, more broadly, legal environments create, constrain, shape, enable, define, and empower organizations. Law and legal environments, moreover, provide forums and templates for interactions among organizations. At the same time, organizations, for their part, provide an important terrain for the interpretation of legal rules and for the structuration of legal environments.

We have identified three facets of organizations' legal environments—facilitative, regulatory, and constitutive—and we have argued that on each of these dimensions, causation may flow in both directions (albeit to varying extents). Facilitative environments provide the tools for legal interaction and dispute resolution but those tools are constantly transformed in the organizational context. Regulatory environments place law in the posture of seeking to control organizations, but much regulation grows out of organizations' actions and agendas, and organizational responses to regulation often define the meaning of compliance. Constitutive environments come into play as legal forms, and categories help to define the very nature of organizations and their environments; but the rules, principles, and values that comprise legal forms and categories often arise out of organizational practices and norms.

We have also pointed to two metatheoretical perspectives on organizations and law: the materialist approach, which views law as a set of economic incentives and organizations as rational-actors; and the cultural approach, which sees both law and organizations as socially constructed phenomena. Literature in the materialist camp emphasizes the facilitative and regulatory facets of the legal environment, whereas literature in the cultural camp emphasizes the regulatory and constitutive.

In short, we have constructed a typology of three facets of the legal environments of organizations, crossed by two metatheoretical perspectives. Future work on law and organizations should expand this typology from a static set of categories into a comprehensive understanding of the dynamics linking the three facets of the legal environment, and of the interplay between materialist and culturalist concerns. In our view, such a dynamic model should pursue three objectives.

First, scholars should study interactions among all three types of legal environments. Regulatory law, for example, may often achieve its effects through the facilitative environment, as when organizations accuse each other of antitrust violations, civil rights violations, labor law violations, or false advertising. The constitutive environment, for its part, defines the legally cognizable actors and actions that can enter into the arenas of facilitative law. And outcomes of facilitative law often need to be enforced by regulatory agents of the state. Perhaps most strikingly, essentially regulatory statutes often generate substantial constitutive spillovers, as the social construction of compliance yields new legal and bureaucratic devices (such as bureaucratized personnel reviews or financial "due diligence" investigations), which then become reified as taken-for-granted building blocks of organizational structure.

Second, scholars in the materialist and cultural camps, respectively, must each address the findings and concerns of the other. In particular, research should consider the relative import of rationality on the one hand, and normative and cognitive beliefs on the other—and should devote special attention to the social conditions or locations that lead each mode of explanation to become most valid. For example, under what conditions do organizations behave rationally in response to law, and under what conditions do ideas about rationality, itself, change in response to legal and social norms? To what extent do legislatures, courts, and administrative agencies incorporate organizational constructions of rationality, and vice versa? To a large degree, of course, the debate between material and cultural perspectives reflects an analogous debate in organization theory generally, and the same questions ought to be asked in other contexts. But it may be that legal environments provide an especially interesting context in which to examine these issues, because laws are intended both to set forth general normative principles and to impose costs and benefits for particular organizational behaviors.

Third, in order to address the connections between the three facets of the legal environment and to mediate between the materialist and cultural perspectives, researchers should develop more specific models of the endogeneity that exists between law and organizations. With luck, in explaining the processes by which organizations incorporate legal ideals and the processes by which the law incorporates organizational models, we will better discern the relationship among rational, normative and cognitive factors or better understand the interaction between facilitative, regulatory, and constitutive environments.

ACKNOWLEDGMENTS

Authorship of this paper was fully collaborative. We would like to express our appreciation to thank Dan Steward for his invaluable research assistance, and to Andrew Creighton for generously sharing his insights into several of the topics we discuss.

*Literature Cited*


Abzug R, Mezias SJ. 1993. The fragmented state and due process protections in organizations: the case of comparable worth. *Organ. Sci.* 4:433–53

Ackerman BA, Ackerman SR, Sawyer JW Jr, Henderson DW. 1974. *The Uncertain Search for Environmental Quality.* New York: Free Press

Ackerman BA, Hassler WT. 1981. *Clean Coal and Dirty Air: Or How the Clean Air Act Became a Multibillion Dollar Bail-out for High-Sulfur Coal Producers and What Should Be Done About It.* New Haven, CT: Yale Univ. Press

Alchian AA, Demsetz H. 1972. Production, information cost, and economic organization. *Am. Econ. Rev.* 62:777–95

Aldrich HE, Fiol CM. 1994. Fools rush in? The institutional context of industry creation. *Acad. Manage. Rev.* 19:645–70

Aldrich HE, Whetten DA. 1981. Organization-sets, action-sets, and networks: making the most of simplicity. In *Handbook of Organizational Design,* ed. PC Nystrom, WH Starbuck, 1:385–408. New York: Oxford Univ. Press

Aldrich HE, Zimmer CR, Staber UH, Beggs JJ. 1994. Minimalism, mutualism, and maturity: the evolution of the American trade association population in the 20th century. In *Evolutionary Dynamics of Organizations,* ed. JAC Baum, JV Singh, pp. 223–39. New York: Oxford Univ. Press

Alpert PA. 1988. Citizen suits under the Clean Air Act: universal standing for the uninjured private attorney general? *Boston Coll. Environ. Affairs Law Rev.* 16:283–328

Arrow KJ. 1974. *Limits of Organization.* New York: Norton

Bardach E. 1989. Social regulation as a generic policy instrument. In *Beyond Privatization: The Tools of Government Action,* ed. LM Salamon, pp. 197–230. Washington, DC: Urban Inst.

Bardach E, Kagan R. 1982. *Going by the Book: The Problem of Regulatory Unreasonableness.* Philadelphia, PA: Temple Univ. Press

Baer X, March JG, Saetren X. 1988. Implementation and ambiguity. In *Decisions and Organizations,* ed. J March, pp. 150–64. Oxford: Blackwell

Barney JB, Edwards FL, Ringleb AH. 1992. Organizational responses to legal liability: employee exposure to hazardous materials, vertical integration, and small firm production. *Acad. Manage. J.* 35:328–49

Baron JN, Dobbin FR, Jennings PD. 1986. War and peace: the evolution of modern personnel administration in U.S. industry. *Am. J. Sociol.* 92:350–83

Beccaria C. 1988. *On Crimes and Punishments.* New York: Macmillan

Berger PL, Luckmann T. 1967. *The Social Construction of Reality.* New York: Doubleday

Bernstein L. 1992. Opting out of the legal system: extralegal contractual relations in the diamond industry. *J. Legal Stud.* 21:115–57

Bernstein MH. 1955. *Regulating Business by Independent Commission.* Princeton, NJ: Princeton Univ. Press

Blumrosen A. 1965. Anti-discrimination laws in action in New Jersey: a law-sociology study. *Rutgers Law Rev.* 19:187–287

Blumrosen A. 1993. *Modern Law: The Law Transmission System and Equal Employment Opportunity.* Madison, WI: Univ. Wis. Press

Block MK, Nold FC, Sidak JG. 1981. The deterrent effect of antitrust enforcement. *J. Polit. Econ.* 89:429

Braithwaite J. 1985. White collar crime. *Annu. Rev. Sociol.* 11:1–25

Braithewaite J, Makkai T. 1991. Testing an expected utility model of corporate deterrence. *Law Soc. Rev.* 25:7

Breyer S. 1982. *Regulation and Its Reform.* Cambridge, MA: Harvard Univ. Press

Bumiller K. 1980–1981. Choice of forum in diversity cases: analysis of a survey and implications for reform. *Law Soc. Rev.* 15:749

Burk J. 1985. The origins of federal securities regulation: a case study in the social control of finance. *Soc. Forces* 63:1010–29

Cain M, Hunt A. 1979. *Marx and Engels on Law.* New York: Academic Press

Campbell JL, Lindberg LN. 1990. Property rights and the organization of economic activity by the state. *Am. Sociol. Rev.* 55:634–47

Campbell JL, Lindberg LN, Hollingsworth JR, eds. 1991. *Governance of the American Economy.* New York: Cambridge Univ. Press

Cappelletti M. 1989. *The Judicial Process in Comparative Perspective.* Oxford: Oxford Univ. Press

Casey WL, Marthinsen JE, Moss LS. 1983. *Entrepreneurship, Productivity, and the Freedom of Information Act: Protecting Circumstantially Relevant Business Information.* Lexington, MA: Lexington Books

Chambliss WJ, Seidman R. 1982. *Law, Order and Power.* Reading PA: Addison-Wesley. 2nd ed.

Chandler AE. 1962. *Strategy and Structure: Chapters in the History of the American Industrial Enterprise.* Cambridge, MA: MIT Press

Chandler AE. 1977. *The Visible Hand: The*

*Managerial Revolution in American Business.* Cambridge, MA: Harvard Univ. Press

Chandler AE. 1990. *Scale and Scope: The Dynamics of Industrial Capitalism.* Cambridge, MA: Harvard Univ. Press

Chayes A, Chayes A. 1985. Corporate counsel and the elite law firm. *Stanford Law Rev.* 32:277–300

Cheit RE. 1990. *Patterns of contemporary business litigation in Rhode Island.* Paper presented to the Law & Soc. Assoc., Berkeley, CA

Cheit RE. 1991. Corporate ambulance chasers: the charmed life of business litigation. *Stud. Law, Polit. Soc.* 11:119–40

Clune WH. 1983. A political model of implementation and the implications of the model for public policy, research, and the changing role of lawyers. *Iowa Law Rev.* 69:47–125

Coase RH. 1937. The nature of the firm. *Economica* (ns)4:386–405

Coase RH. 1960. The problem of social cost. *J. Law Econ.* 3:1–44

Cobb S, Rifkin J. 1991. Practice and paradox: deconstructing neutrality in mediation. *Law Soc. Inquiry* 16:35

Coleman J. 1974. *Power and the Structure of Society.* New York: Norton

Coleman J. 1989. *The Criminal Elite.* New York: St. Martin's

Coleman J. 1990. *Foundations of Social Theory.* Cambridge, MA: Belknap

Conklin JE. 1977. *Illegal But Not Criminal: Business Crime in America.* Englewood Cliffs, NJ: Prentice-Hall

Cooter R, Ulen T. 1996. *Law and Economics.* New York: Harper Collins. 2nd ed.

Cotterrell R. 1992. *The Sociology of Law: An Introduction.* London: Butterworths. 2nd ed.

Cranston R. 1979. *Regulating Business: Law and Consumer Agencies.* London: Macmillan

Creighton AL. 1990. *The emergence of incorporation as a legal form of organizations.* PhD diss. Dept. Sociol., Stanford Univ.

Cullen F, Maakestad WJ, Cavender G. 1987. *Corporate Crime Under Attack: The Ford Pinto Case.* Cincinatti: Anderson

Danet B. 1980. Language in the legal process. *Law Soc. Rev.* 14:445–64

Davis GF. 1991. Agents without principles? the spread of the poison pill through the intercorporate network. *Admin. Sci. Q.* 36:583–613

Delaney KJ. 1989. Power, intercorporate networks, and "strategic bankruptcy." *Law Soc. Rev.* 23:643–66

Delgado R, Dunn C, Brown P, Lee H, Hubbert D. 1985. Fairness and formality: minimizing the risk of prejudice in alternative dispute resolution". *Wisc. Law Review* 1985:585

DiMaggio PJ, Powell WW. 1983. The iron cage revisited: institutional isomorphism and collective rationality in organizational fields. *Am. Sociol. Rev.* 48:147–60

Diver C. 1980. A theory of regulatory enforcement. *Public Policy* 28:257

Dobbin FR. 1994. *Forging Industrial Policy: the United States, Britain, and France in the Railway Age.* New York: NY: Cambridge Univ. Press

Dobbin FR, Edelman LB, Meyer JW, Scott WR, Swidler A. 1988. The expansion of due process in organizations. In *Institutional Patterns in Organizations,* ed. LG Zucker, pp. 71–100. Cambridge, MA: Ballinger

Dobbin FR, Sutton JR, Meyer JW, Scott WR. 1993. Equal opportunity law and the construction of internal labor markets. *Am. J. Sociol.* 99:396–427

Domhoff JW. 1983. *Who Rules America Now?* Englewood Cliffs, NJ: Prentice-Hall

Donohue JJ. 1991. The effects of fee shifting on the settlement rate: theoretical observations on costs, conflicts, and contingency fees. *Law Contemp. Probl.* 54:195–222

Dowling J, Pfeffer J. 1975. Organizational legitimacy: social values and organizational behavior. *Pacific Sociol. Rev.* 18:122–36

Downs A. 1957. *An Economic Theory of Democracy.* New Yorki: harper & Row

Dungworth T, Galanter M, Rogers J. 1990. *Corporations in court: recent trends in American business litigation.* Pap. presented to Law & Soc. Assoc. Berkeley, CA

Durkheim E. 1964. *The Division of Labor in Society.* New York: Free Press

Edelman LB. 1990. Legal environments and organizational governance: the expansion of due process in the American workplace. *Am. J. Sociol.* 95:1401–40

Edelman LB. 1992. Legal ambiguity and symbolic structures: organizational mediation of law. *Am. J. Sociol.* 97:1531–76

Edelman LB. 1996. Constructed legalities: organizational fields as sources of endogeneity. Unpubl. ms

Edelman LB, Abraham SE, Erlanger HS. 1992. Professional construction of the legal environment: the inflated threat of wrongful discharge doctrine. *Law Soc. Rev.* 26:47–83

Edelman LB, Cahill ML. 1998. How law matters in disputing and dispute resolution (or, the contingency of legal matter in alternative dispute resolution). Evanston, IL: Northwestern Univ. Press. In press

Edelman LB, Erlanger HS, Lande J. 1993. Employers' handling of discrimination complaints: the transformation of rights in the workplace. *Law Soc. Rev.* 27:497–534

Edelman LB, Petterson SE, Chambliss E, Erlanger HS. 1991. Legal ambiguity and the politics of compliance: affirmative action

officers' dilemma. *Law Policy* 13:73–97
Edelman LB, Uggen C, Erlanger HS. 1996. *The endogeneity of law: grievance procedures as rational myth.* Unpubl. ms.
Ekland-Olson S, Martin SJ. 1988. Organizational compliance with court-ordered reform. *Law Soc. Rev.* 22:359–83
Ellickson RC. 1986. *Order Without Law: How Neighbors Settle Disputes.* Cambridge, MA: Harvard Univ. Press
Ewick P, Silbey SS. 1992. Conformity, contestation, and resistance: an account of legal consciousness. *New England Law Rev.* 26:731–49
Ewing DW. 1989. *Justice on the Job: Resolving Grievances in the Nonunion Workplace.* Boston: Harvard Univ. Press
Farrell K. 1984. Competition: using Freedom of Information. *Venture* 6:39–40
Felstiner WLF, Abel RL, Sarat A. 1980. The emergence and transformation of disputes: naming, blaming, claiming.... *Law & Soc. Rev.* 15:631–54
Fiorina M, Noll R. 1976. Majority rule models and legislative elections. *J. Polit.* 41:1031
Fiss OM. 1984. Against settlement. *Yale Law J.* 93:1073
Fligstein N. 1990. *The Transformation of Corporate Control.* Cambridge, MA: Harvard Univ. Press
Fligstein N. 1991. The structural transformation of American industry: an institutional account of the causes of diversification in the largest firms, 1919–1979. In *The New Institutionalism in Organizational Analysis,* ed. WW Powell, PJ DiMaggio, pp. 331–336. Chicago: Univ. Chicago Press
Freitag PJ. 1983. The myth of corporate capture: regulatory commissions in the United States. *Soc. Probl.* 30:480–91
Friedland R, Alford RR. 1991. Bringing society back in: symbols, practices, and institutional contradictions. In *The New Institutionalism in Organizational Analysis,* ed. WW Powell, PJ DiMaggio, pp. 204–31. Chicago, IL: Univ. Chicago Press
Friedman LM. 1985. *American Law: An Introduction.* New York: Norton
Friendly FHJ. 1962. *The Federal Administrative Agencies: The Need for Better Definition of Standards.*
Fuller SR, Edelman LB, Matusik S. 1997. *The internal legal culture of organizations.* Unpubl. ms.
Gabel P, Feinman JM. 1982. Contract law as ideology. In *The Politics of Law: A Progressive Critique,* ed. ZD Kairys, pp. 172–84. New York: Pantheon
Gable RW. 1953. NAM: Influential lobby or kiss of death? *J. Polit.* 15:254–73
Galanter M. 1974. Why the 'haves' come out ahead: speculations on the limits of legal change. *Law Soc. Rev.* 9:95–160
Galanter M. 1983. Reading the landscape of disputes: What we know and don't know (and think we know) about our allegedly contentious and litigious society. *UCLA Law Rev.* 31:4–84
Galanter M. 1984. *Competing Equalities: Law and the Backward Classes in India.* Berkeley: Univ. Calif. Press
Galanter M. 1990. Case congregations and their careers. *Law Soc. Rev.* 24:371–95
Galanter M, Palay T. 1991. *Tournament of Lawyers: The Growth and Transformation of the Big Law Firm.* Chicago: Univ. Chicago Press
Galanter M, Rogers J. 1991. *A transformation of American business disputing? Some preliminary observations.* Work. Pap. Madison: Inst. Legal Stud.
Geertz C. 1983. *Local Knowledge.* New York: Basic Books
Genn H. 1993. Business responses to the regulation of health and safety in England. *Law Policy* 15:219–33
Gilson, RJ. 1984. Value creation by business lawyers: legal skills and asset pricing. *Yale Law J.* 94:239
Givelber DJ, Bowers WJ, Blitch CL. 1984. Tarasoff, myth and reality: an empirical study of private law in action. *Wisconsin L. Rev.* 2:443–97
Gravelle H, Waterson M. 1993. No win, no fee: some economics of contingent legal fees. *Econ. J.* 103:1205–20
Hannan MT, Carroll GR. 1992. *Dynamics of Organizational Populations: Density, Legitimation, and Competition.* New York: Oxford Univ. Press
Hansmann H. 1996. *The Ownership of Enterprise.* Cambridge, MA: Belknap
Haveman H. 1993. Organizational size and change: diversification in the savings and loan industry after deregulation. *Admin. Sci. Q.* 38:20–50
Hawkins K. 1984. *Environment and Enforcement: Regulation and the Social Definition of Pollution.* Oxford: Clarendon
Hayden R. 1989. *The cultural logic of a political crisis: common sense, hegemony, and the great American liability famine of 1986.* Working paper. Madison, WI: Inst. Legal Stud.
Heimer C. 1993. Competing institutions: law medicine, and family in neonatal intensive care. *Am. Bar Found. Wor. Pap. #9308*
Heimer C. 1995. Explaining variation in the import of law: organizations, institutions, and professions. *Stud. Law, Polit., Soc.* 15:29–60
Heydebrand W, Seron C. 1990. *Rationalizing Justice: The Political Economy of Federal*

*District Courts*. Albany, NY: State Univ. of NY Press

Hofrichter R. 1987. *Neighborhood Justice in Capitalist Society: The Expansion of the Informal State*. New York: Greenwood

Holen AS. 1965. Effects of professional licensing arrangements on interstate labor mobility and resource allocation. *J. Polit. Econ.* 73:492–98

Holmes OW. 1897. The path of the law. *Harvard Law Rev.* 10:457–78

Holmes OW. 1981. *The Common Law*. Cambridge, MA: Harvard Univ. Press

Horwitz RB. 1986. Understanding deregulation. *Theory Soc.* 15:139–74

Huber PW. 1988. *Liability: The Legal Revolution and Its Consequences*. New York: Basic Books

Hurst WJ. 1964. *Law and Economic Growth: The Legal History of the Lumber Industry in Wisconsin 1836–1915*. Cambridge, MA: Harvard Univ. Press

Jensen MC, Meckling WH. 1976. Theory of the firm: managerial behavior, agency costs, and ownership structure. *J. Financial Econ.* 3:305–60

Jepperson RL. 1991. Institutions, institutional effects, and institutionalization. In *The New Institutionalism in Organizational Analysis,* ed. WW Powell, PJ DiMaggio, pp. 143–163. Chicago: Univ. Chicago Press

Jowell JL. 1975. *Law and Bureaucracy: Administrative Discretion and the Limits of Legal Action*. Port Washington, NY: Kennikat

Kagan RA, Rosen RE. 1985. On the social significance of large law firm practice. *Stanford Law Rev.* 37:399–443

Kagan RA, Scholz JT. 1983. The "criminology" of the corporation and regulatory enforcement strategies. In *Enforcing Regulation,* ed. K Hawkins, JM Thomas. Boston: Kluwer-Nijhoff

Kaplan MR, Harrison RJ. 1993. Defusing the director liability crisis: the strategic management of legal threats. *Organ. Sci.* 4:412–32

Katz J. 1977. Cover-up and collective integrity: on the natural antagonism of authority internal and external to organizations. *Soc. Probl.* 25:3–xx

Kidder RL. 1983. *Connecting Law and Society*. Englewood Cliffs, NJ: Prentice-Hall

Klausner, M. 1995. Corporations, corporate law, and networks of contracts. *Virginia Law Rev.* 81:757–852

Klein DB, Majewski J. 1992. Economy, community, and law: The turnpike movement in New York, 1797–1852. *Law & Soc. Rev.* 26:469–512

Kolko G. 1963. *The Triumph of Conservatism: A Reinterpretation of American History 1900–1916*. New York: Free Press

Konrad AM, Linnehan F. 1995. Formalized HRM structures: coordinating equal employment opportunity or concealing organizational practices? *Acad. Manage. J.* 38:787–820

Krasner SD. 1988. Sovereignity: an institutional erspective. *Compar. Polit. Stud.* 21:66–94

Lande J. *The diffusion of a process pluralist ideology of disputing: factors affecting opinions of business lawyers and executives*. PhD diss. Univ. Wisc., Madison

Larson MS. 1977. *The Rise of Professionalism: A Sociological Analysis*. Berkeley: Univ. Calif. Press

Laumann EO, Knoke D. 1987. *The Organizational State: Social Choice in National Policy Domains*. Madison: Univ. of Wisc. Press

Laumann EO, Knoke D. 1988. The increasingly organizational state. *Society* 25:21–28

Leiserson A. 1942. *Administrative Regulation: A Study in Representation of Interests*. Chicago, IL: Univ. Chicago Press

Levine M. 1981. Revisionism revised? Airline deregulation and the public interest. *Law Contemp. Probl.* 44:179–95

Lewis LK, Siebold DR. 1993. Innovation modification during intraorganizational adoption. *Acad. Manage. Rev.* 18:322–354

Lind EA, Typer TR. 1988. *The Social Psychology of Procedural Justice*. New York: Plenum

Luchansky B, Gerber J. 1993. Constructing state autonomy: the federal trade commission and the Celler-Kefauver Act. *Sociol. Perspect.* 36:217–40

Luhmann N. 1985. *A Sociological Theory of Law*. London: Routledge & Kegan Paul

Lukes S. 1974. *Power: A Radical View*. New York: Macmillan

Macaulay S. 1963. Non-contractual relations in business. *Am. Sociol. Rev.* 28:55–70

Macaulay S. 1966. *Law and the Balance of Power: The Automobile Manufacturers and their Dealers*. New York: Russell Sage Found.

Makkai T, Braithewaite J. 1992. In and out of the revolving door: making sense of regulatory capture. *J. Public Policy* 12:61–78

Makkai T, Braithewaite J. 1994. The dialectics of corporate deterrence. *J. Res. Crime Delinquency* 31:347

March JG, Simon HA. 1958. *Organizations*. New York: Wiley

Marx K, Engels F. 1977. [Orig. trans. 1947] *The German Ideology*. New York: Int. Publ.

Mashaw G. 1979. Regulation, logic and ideology. *Regulation* Nov-Dec:44

Masten SE. 1990. A legal basis for the firm. In *The Nature of The Firm: Origins, Evolution, and Development,* ed. OE Williamson,

SG Winter, pp. 196–212. New York: Oxford Univ. Press

Mather L, Yngvesson B. 1980–1981. Language, audience and the transformation of disputes. *Law Soc. Rev.* 15:775–822

McBarnet D. 1992. It's not what you do but the way you do it: tax evasion, tax avoidance, and the boundaries of deviance. In *Unraveling Criminal Justice: Eleven British Studies,* ed. D Downes, pp. 257–75. London: Macmillan

McCaffrey DP. 1982. Corporate resources and regulatory pressures: toward explaining a discrepancy. *Admin. Sci. Q.* 27:398–419

McCann MW. 1991. Legal mobilization and social reform movements: notes on theory and its application. *Stud. Law, Polit. Soc.* 11:225–54

McCann MW. 1994. *Rights at Work: Pay Equity and the Politics of Legal Mobilization.* Chicago, IL: Univ. Chicago Press

McCarthy JD, Zald MN. 1977. Resource mobilization and social movements: a partial theory. *Am. J. Sociol.* 82:1212–41

McCormick AE. 1979. Dominant class interests and the emergence of anti-trust legislation. *Contemp. Crises* 3:399–417

McIntosh WV. 1985. A state court's clientele: exploring the strategy of trial litigation. *Law Soc. Rev.* 19:421–47

Mead GH. 1934. *Mind, Self, Society.* New York:

Merton RK. 1936. The unanticipated consequences of purposive social action. *Am. Sociol. Rev.* 1:894–904

Merton RK. 1957. *Social Theory and Social Structure.* Glencoe, IL: Free Press (first published in 1940)

Meyer JW, Boli J, Thomas GM. 1987. Ontology and rationalization in the western cultural account. In *Institutional Structure: Constituting State, Society, and the Individual,* ed. GM Thomas, J Meyer, X Ramirez, pp. 12–37. Newbury Park, CA: Sage

Meyer JW, Rowan B. 1977. Institutionalized organizations: formal structure as myth and ceremony. *Am. J. Sociol.* 83:340–63

Meyer JW, Scott WR, assisted by B Rowan, T Deal. 1983. *Organizational Environments: Ritual and Rationality.* Beverly Hills, CA: Sage

Mezias SJ. 1990. An institutional model of organizational practice: financial reporting at the Fortune 200. *Admin. Sci. Q.* 35(3):431–57

Mnookin RH, Kornhauser L. 1979. Bargaining in the shadow of the law: the case of divorce. *Yale Law Rev.* 88:950–97

Monahan SC, Meyer, Scott WR. 1994. Employee training: the expansion of organizational citizenship. In *Institutional Environments and Organizations,* ed. WR Scott, JW Meyer. Thousand Oaks, CA: Sage

Nee V. 1992. Organizational dynamics of market transition: hybrid forms, property rights, and mixed economy in China. *Admin. Sci. Q.* 37:1–27

Nelson RL. 1988. *Partners with Power: Social Transformation of the Large Law Firm.* Berkeley, CA: Univ. Calif. Press

Nelson RL, Heinz JP, Laumann EO, Salisbury RH. 1988. Lawyers and the structure of influence in Washington. *Law Soc. Rev.* 22:237–300

Nelson WE. 1990. Contract litigation and the elite bar in New York City, 1960–1980. *Emory Law Rev.* 39:413–

Newman KS, Attewell P. 1985. A compliance-resource theory of regulatory failure: the case of O.S.H.A. *Int. J. Sociol. Soc. Policy* 5:29–53

Nonet P, Selznick P. 1978. *Law and Society in Transition: Toward Responsive Law.* New York: H Jarper & Row

North D. 1981. *Structure and Change in Economic History.* New York: Norton

Olson W. 1991. Sue City: the case against the contingency fee. *Policy Review* 55:46–51

Paternoster R, Simpson S. 1993. A rational choice theory of corporate crime. In *Advances in Criminological Theory: Routine Activity and Rational Choice,* ed. RV Clarke, M Felson. New Brunswick, NJ: Transaction

Paternoster R, Simpson S. 1996. Sanction threats and appeals to morality: testing a rational choice model of corporate crime. *Law Soc. Rev.* 30:549–83

Peltzman S. 1976. Toward a more general theory of regulation. *J. Law Econ.* 19:211–40

Perrucci R, Potter HR, ed. 1990. *Networks of Power: Organizational Actors at the National, Corporate, and Community Levels.* Hawthorne, NY: Aldine de Gruyter

Pfeffer J. 1974. Administrative regulation and licensing: social problem or solution? *Soc. Probl.* 21:468–79

Pfeffer J. 1981. *Power in Organizations.* Marshfield, MA: Pitman

Pfeffer J, Salancik G. 1978. *The External Control of Organizations: A Resource Dependence Perspective.* New York: Harper & Row

Posner RA. 1972. *Economic Analysis of Law.* Boston: Little, Brown

Posner RA. 1974. Theories of economic regulation. *Bell J. Econ.* 5:335–58

Powell MJ. 1993. Professional innovation: corporate lawyers and private lawmaking. *Law Soc. Inquiry* 18:423

Powell WW, DiMaggio PJ, eds. 1991. *The New Institutionalism in Organizational Analysis.* Chicago: Univ. Chicago Press

Priest GL, Klein B. 1984. The selection of disputes for litigation. *J. Legal Stud.* 13:1

Rabkin J. 1989. *Judicial Compulsions: How Public Law Distorts Public Policy.* New York: Basic Books

Rao H, Neilsen EH. 1992. An ecology of agency arrangements: moralilty of savings and loan associations 1960–1987. *Admin. Sci. Q.* 37:448–70

Rogers J. 1990. Divide and conquer: further reflections on the distinctive character of American labor laws. *Wisc. Law Rev.* 1990:1

Ross HL. 1980. *Settled Out of Court: The Social Process of Insurance Claims Adjustment.* New York: Aldine. 2nd ed.

Rousseau DM, Parks JM. 1992. The contracts of individuals and organizations. *Res. in Organ. Behav.* 15:1–43

Roy W. 1990. Functional and historical logics in explaining the rise of the American industrial corporation. *Compar. Soc. Res.* 12:19–44

Sabatier P. 1975. Social movements and regulatory agencies: toward a more adequate—and less pessimistic—theory of "clientele capture." *Policy Sci.* 6:301–42

Samuels PD. 1996. Litigation law creates work for disclaimer writers. *New York Times* April 14, pp. 3 (Sec 3)

Sarat A. 1990. The law is all over: power, resistance and the legal consciousness of the welfare poor. *Yale J. Law Humanities* 2:343–79

Scheid-Cook TL. 1992. Organizational enactments and conformity to environmental prescriptions. *Hum. Relat.* 45:537–54

Scholz JT. 1984. Cooperation, deterrence, and the ecology of regulatory enforcement. *Law Soc. Rev.* 18:179–224

Scott DW. 1989. Policing corporate collusion. *Criminology* 27:559

Scott KE. 1975. Two models of the civil process. *Stanford Law Rev.* 27:937–50

Scott WR. 1987. The adolescence of institutional theory. *Admin. Sci. Q.* 32:493–511

Scott WR. 1991. Unpacking institutional arguments. In *The New Institutionalism in Organizational Analysis.* ed. WJ Powell, PJ DiMaggio. Chicago, IL: Univ. Chicago Press

Scott WR. 1993. Law and organizations. In *The Legalistic Organization,* ed. SB Sitkin, RJ Bies. Newbury Park: Sage

Scott WR. 1995. *Institutions and Organizations.* Thousand Oaks, CA: Sage

Scott WR, Meyer J. 1991. The rise of training programs in firms and agencies: an institutional perspective. In *Research in Organization Behavior,* ed. BM Staw, LL Cummings, 13:297–326. Greenwich, CT: JAL

Scott WR, Meyer JW. 1994. *Institutional Environments and Organizations: Structural Complexity and Individualism.* Thousand Oaks, CA: Sage

Seavoy RE. 1982. *The Origins of the American Business Corporation, 1784–1855.* Westport, CT: Greenwood

Selznick P. 1948. Foundations of the theory of organization. *Am. Sociol. Rev.* 13:25–35

Selznick P. 1949. *TVA and the Grass Roots.* Berkeley: Univ. Calif. Press

Selznick P. 1957. *Leadership in Administration.* New York: Harper & Row

Selznick P. 1969. *Law, Society, and Industrial Justice.* New York: Russell Sage Found.

Silbey S, Sarat A. 1989. Dispute processing in law and legal scholarship: from institutional critique to the reconstruction of the juridical subject. *Denver Univ. Law Rev.* 66:437

Simpson S, Koper CS. 1992. Deterring corporate crime. *Criminology* 30:347

Sitkin SB, Bies RJ, eds. 1993. *The Legalistic Organization.* Newbury Park, CA: Sage

Snyder EA. 1985. Efficient assignment of rights to sue for antitrust damages. *J. Law Econ.* 28:469–82

Stigler GJ. 1961. The economics of information. *J. Polit. Econ.* 69:213–25

Stigler GJ. 1968. *The Organization of Industry.* Homewood, IL: RD Irwin

Stigler GJ. 1971. The theory of economic regulation. *Bell J. Econ.*:2(Spring):3–21

Stone C. 1975. *Where the Law Ends: The Social Control of Corporate Behavior.* New York: Harper & Row

Streeck W, Schmitter PC. 1985. Community, market, state—and associations?: the prospective contributions of interest governance in social order. In *Private Interest Government: Beyond Market and State,* ed. W Streeck, PC Schmitter, pp. 1–29. Beverly Hills, CA: Sage

Suchman MC. 1993a. *Conceptualizing the legal environments of organizational activity.* Paper presented to the Stanford Conf. on Organizations. Asilomar, CA

Suchman MC. 1993b. *On the coevolution of law, finance, and industry in Silicon Valley.* Pap. pres. Annu. Meet. Acad. Manage., Atlanta, GA

Suchman MC. 1994a. *On advice of counsel: legal and financial firms as information intermediaries in the structuration of Silicon Valley.* PhD thesis. Stanford Univ., Stanford, CA

Suchman MC. 1994b. *On the role of law firms on the structuration of Silicon Valley.* Work. pap. Madison, WI: Inst. for Legal Stud.

Suchman MC. 1995a. Localism and globalism in institutional analysis: the emergence of contractual norms in venture finance. In *The Institutional Construction of Organizations: International and Longitudinal Studies,* ed. WR Scott, S Christensen, pp. 39–63, Thousand Oaks, CA: Sage

Suchman MC. 1995nb. Managing legitimacy:

strategic and institutional approaches. *Acad. Manage. Rev.* 20:571–610

Suchman MC, Cahill ML. 1996. The hired-gun as facilitator: the case of lawyers in Silicon Valley. *Law Soc. Inquiry.* 21:679–712

Suchman MC, Edelman LB. 1996. Legal rational myths: the new institutionalism and the law and society tradition. *Law Soc. Inquiry.* Forthcoming

Sutton JR, Dobbin FR, Meyer JW, Scott WR. 1994. The legalization of the workplace. *Am. J. Sociol.* 99:944–71

Swidler A. 1986. Culture in action: symbols and strategies. *Am. Sociol. Rev.* 51:273–86

Teubner G, ed. 1988. *Autopoietic Law: A New Approach to Law and Society.* Berlin: de Gruyter

Tolbert PS, Zucker LG. 1983. Institutional Sources of Change in the formal struction of organizations: the diffusion of civil service reform, 1888–1935. *Admin. Sci. Q.* 30:22–39

Tushnet M. 1984. An essay on rights. *Texas Law Rev.* 62:1363–1403

Tyler T. 1990. *Why People Obey the Law.* New Haven, CT: Yale Univ. Press

Vaughan D. 1983. *Controlling Unlawful Organizational Behavior: Social Structure and Corporate Misconduct.* Chicago, IL: Univ. Chicago Press

Vittoz S. 1987. *New Deal Labor Policy and the American Industrial Economy.* Chapel Hill: Univ. N. Carolina Press

Vogel D. 1986. *National Styles of Regulation: Environmental Policy in Great Britain and the United States.* Ithaca, NY: Cornell Univ. Press

Wanner C. 1974. The public ordering of private relations: initiating civil cases in urban trial courts (Part one). *Law Soc. Rev.* 8:421–40

Wanner C. 1975. The public ordering of private relations (Part two): winning civil court cases. *Law Soc. Rev.* 9:293–306

Weber M. 1947. *The Theory of Social and Economic Organization.* New York: Oxford Univ. Press

Weber M. 1978. *Economy and Society.* Berkeley, CA: Univ. Calif. Press

Weick KE. 1976. Educational organizations as loosely coupled systems. *Admin. Sci. Q.* 21:1–19

Weick KE. 1979. *The Social Psychology of Organizing.* Reading, MA: Addison-Wesley. 2nd ed.

Weick KE. 1993. Sensemaking in organizations: small structures with large consequences. In *Social Psychology in Organizations: Advances in Theory and Research,* ed. JK Murninghan, pp. 10–37. Englewood Cliffs, NJ: Prentice-Hall

Westin AF, Feliu AG. 1988. *Resolving Employment Disputes Without Litigation.* Washington, DC: Bur. Natl. Affairs

Westney DE. 1987. *Imitation and Innovation: The Transfer of Western Organizational Patterns to Meiji Japan.* Cambridge, MA: Harvard Univ. Press

Wheeler S, Cartwright B, Kagan RA, Friedman LM. 1987. Do the "haves" come out ahead? Winning and losing in state supreme courts, 1870–1970. *Law Soc. Rev.* 21:403–45

Wheeler S, Weisburd D, Bode D. 1982. Sentencing the white collar offender: rhetoric and reality. *Am. Sociol. Rev.* 47:641–59

Wholey DB, Sanchez SM. 1991. The effects of regulatory tools on organizational populations. *Acad. Manage. Rev.* 16:743–67

Williamson OE. 1975. *Markets and Hierarchies.* New York: Free Press

Williamson OE. 1981. The economics of organization: the transaction cost approach. *Am. J. Sociol.* 87:548–77

Williamson OE. 1985. *The Economic Institutions of Capitalism.* New York: Free Press

Williamson OE. 1991. Comparative economic organization: the analysis of discrete structural alternatives. *Admin. Sci. Q.* 36:269–96

Wirt F. 1970. *The Politics of Southern Equality: Law and Social Change in a Mississippi County.* Chicago: Aldine

Wolfson M. 1995. The legislative impact of social movement organizations: the anti-drunken-driving movement and the 21-year-old drinking age. *Soc. Sci. Q.* 76:311–27

Yeazell SC. 1987. *From Medieval Group Litigation to the Modern Class Action.* New Haven, CT; Yale Univ. Press

Zald MN, McCarthy JD. 1980. Social movement industries: competition and cooperation among social movement organizations. *Res. Soc. Movements, Conflicts Change* 3:1–20

Zhou X. 1993. Occupational power, state capacities and the diffusion of licensing in the American states, 1890–1950. *Am. Sociol. Rev.* 58:536–52

Zucker LG. 1983. Organizations as institutions. In *Research in the Sociology of Organizations* 1–42. Greewich, CT: JAI

Zucker LG, ed. 1988. *Institutional Patterns and Organizations: Culture and Environment.* Cambridge, MA: Ballinger

# SUBJECT INDEX

## A

# B



# C

# D

# H

# I

# N

# Q



# R

# T



# U

# Z

# CUMULATIVE INDEXES

## CONTRIBUTING AUTHORS, VOLUMES 1–23

# CHAPTER TITLES, VOLUMES 1–23

INDIVIDUAL AND SOCIETY